**SUNDAY, JANUARY 28, 1945**

Boys At Front Want To Know:

# Why Don't We Have Big Tanks To Combat Nazis'

**By VICTOR O. JONES**
North American Newspaper Alliance

ADVANCED HEADQUARTERS, 7TH ARMY, Jan. 25—(Delayed)—The story as we got it back here, was that two Sherman medium tanks, lying in ambush in the woods just outside a village the Germans

"You can tell they're going instead of coming because you can hear the echo," he said with a grin. "Or, there's another saying in the army. If they rattle the windows they're ours; if they break the windows they ain't."

Then we rode into a village where every back yard seemed to house a tank, and groups of infantrymen leaned against every crossroad building, rifles cradled in their arms. The battalion command post was down at the railroad station and at a table flanked by two captains sat a young but old-looking

lieutenant colonel, map in front of him. The colonel's eyes were about to sink entirely through his face but he rose to shake hands with us as we told him we were looking for the two tanks with which he had knocked out 10 German panzers.

"You'll have a hell of a time

# Tank Critics Hit by Blast Of Gen. Patton

WASHINGTON —(A)— Lieutenant-General George S. Patton Jr. has fired a high-velocity volley of words and figures at "certain misguided or perhaps deliberately mendacious individuals" who criticize American tanks.

The War Department made public today a letter from the Third Army Commander to Lieutenant General Thomas T. Handy, deputy chief of staff, in which Patton attacked criticism that American tanks are not comparable with the German Panther or Tiger tanks. This, said Patton, "is wholly incorrect for several reasons."

One he cited is that since the Third Army started fighting the Germans last August German tank losses have been virtually double those of the Third—2,287 to 1,136.

"These figures of themselves refute any inferiority of our tanks."

For Want of a Gun

History would not be what it is, the record of man's crimes and follies, if logic and decency governed its events and great decisions.[3]
—Ladislas Farago, *Patton: Ordeal and Triumph*

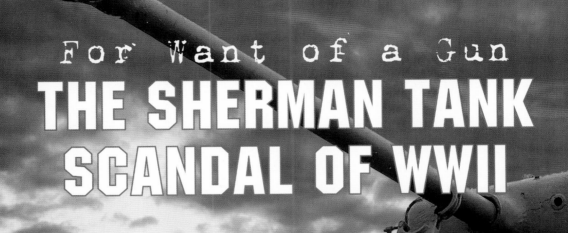

For Want of a Gun
# THE SHERMAN TANK
# SCANDAL OF WWII

By Christian Mark DeJohn
Photos by Robert Coldwell Sr.

Schiffer Publishing Ltd.
4880 Lower Valley Road • Atglen, PA 19310

# ABOUT THE TITLE

I recalled from my student days at the Cavalry School at Fort Riley, Kansas, the large wooden sign inside the riding hall that reminded me: "For want of a nail, the shoe was lost...[6]
—Maj. Albyn Irzyk, 4th Armored Division

"For Want of a Gun" recalls an old English nursery rhyme based on John Gower's *Confesio Amantis*, dated c. 1390:

> For want of a nail, the shoe was lost
> For want of a shoe, the horse was lost
> For want of a horse, the rider was lost
> For want of a rider, the battle was lost
> ...and all for the want of a nail.[7]

The sad irony is the US cranked out nearly 50,008 Sherman tanks with inferior guns and inadequate armor protection, but did not lose the ground war, thanks in part to the sacrifice—as reported to Congress by Gen. George Marshall—of at least 62,417 armored division soldiers[9] who depended on the M4—some killed and wounded by more powerful German tanks.

# DEDICATION

Why write of them at this hour? Why open the door of a room sealed off in my mind for many years?
I chose to walk among these buddies of the past so that they may be remembered.[4]
—Lawrence Stallings, *The Doughboys*

We were never able to build a tank as good as the German tank. But we made so many of them, it really didn't matter.[5]
—General Lucius D. Clay

Christian respectfully dedicates this work to the United States Army tankers of WWII, including his great-uncle Sergeant Albert Diodato, 709th Tank Battalion. Lions led by goats, they deserved better from the "Arsenal of Democracy." Still they drove on in the face of lies from their leadership to win a hard and bitter victory.

To the thousands of American armored division soldiers killed and wounded 1942–1945, and to the loved ones at home that mourned their loss. In spite of Gen. Clay's claim, I submit that their deaths mattered to parents, wives, fatherless war orphans, and unborn generations that never were. May we never forget the sacrifices of these men and apply the hard lessons they learned then to today's GI in other wars and in other places.

As a United States Cavalry tank gunner of a later generation I was honored to follow in their footsteps. "To us, and those like us—damn few left!"

And to Col. George Jarrett, Ordnance Corps US Army, who told the truth about the Sherman tank scandal in his "Little Green Book."

Bob respectfully dedicates this work to his father, Electrician's Mate First Class Ferdinand K. Coldwell, USNR (Yard Minesweeper [YMS] -76, New York Harbor, WWII)

To his uncle, US Army Pvt. Atlee G. Cullison, 190th Field Artillery Battalion (Omaha Beach, St. Lo, Hurtgen Forest, and Battle of the Bulge)

And to their friend, Sgt. Edwin N. Yagle, 702nd Tank Battalion, Killed In Action 20 August 1944, Normandy.

The truth is, the years have glossed it all over, and given
World War II a polish and a glow that it did not have at the time.
The process of history makes me think of the way the Navajos polish their turquoise. They
put the raw chunks in a barrel half filled with birdshot, and then turn the barrel, and keep
turning until the rough edges are all taken off, and the nuggets come out smooth and shining.
Time, I think, does the same thing with history, and especially with wars.[2]
—Sgt. James Jones, 24th Infantry Division, author of *From Here To Eternity*


But if the cause be not good, the King himself hath a heavy reckoning to make, when all those
legs and arms and heads chopped off in a battle shall join tighter at the latter day, and cry all,
"We died at such a place," some swearing, some crying for a surgeon, some upon the wives left
poor behind them, some upon the debts they owe, some upon their children rawly left.... Now if
these men do not die well, it will be a black matter for the king that led them to it...[1]
—William Shakespeare, *The Life of Henry the Fifth*, Act IV, Scene 1

The human cost of the Sherman tank scandal. As Pentagon generals and Roosevelt administration officials denied problems with the M4, insisting American soldiers were equipped with the finest tanks on the battlefield, the burden of their folly was borne by young tankers such as Sgt. John Parks of Mill Creek, Indiana. He was photographed December 10, 1944, days before German tanks spearheaded the Ardennes offensive, the US Army's worst defeat in the European theater. The picture shows the toll armored combat took on American tankers facing Tigers and Panthers with under-gunned Shermans. Sgt. Parks—just twenty-four years old— was killed in a tank battle in Germany soon after.

Type set in Machine & ITC Franklin Gothic Std

ISBN: 978-0-7643-5250-8

Printed in China

Published by Schiffer Publishing, Ltd.
4880 Lower Valley Road
Atglen, PA 19310
Phone: (610) 593-1777; Fax: (610) 593-2002
E-mail: Info@schifferbooks.com
Web: www.schifferbooks.com

For our complete selection of fine books on this and related subjects, please visit our website at www.schifferbooks.com. You may also write for a free catalog.

Schiffer Publishing's titles are available at special discounts for bulk purchases for sales promotions or premiums. Special editions, including personalized covers, corporate imprints, and excerpts, can be created in large quantities for special needs. For more information, contact the publisher.

We are always looking for people to write books on new and related subjects. If you have an idea for a book, please contact us at proposals@schifferbooks.com.

# CONTENTS

Howard Brodie,
*Squadron Leader*

# Foreword

## Col. David Johnson, US Army (ret.)

This is an angry book—and rightly so, based on the evidence author Christian DeJohn has uncovered in his exhaustive research. Sgt. DeJohn brings the voice of the American enlisted soldier into the discussion about the failure of one of the key US fighting vehicles of WWII— the M4 Sherman tank. This is the story the author tells: the horror of knowing you're in a battle of attrition against an enemy with better weapons, but without sufficient resources to win the war. At the same time, your higher-ups are extolling the prowess of a tank that you know can get you and your crew killed in any engagement with a German *Panzer*. In these lopsided fights, it was common to lose five Shermans for every panzer kill, even with the assistance of Allied air strikes and artillery. Shermans had to get up close and on the flanks or rear of Panthers and Tigers (where the armor was thinner) to have a chance at a killing shot—and many Shermans were lost trying to do this.

*For Want of a Gun* reminds me of my own anger when I wrote my dissertation at Duke University in 1990, on how the US Army dealt with the key technologies that emerged from WWI: the tank and the airplane. My dissertation—*Fast Tanks and Heavy Bombers: Innovation in the U.S. Army, 1917 to 1945*—was published in 1998, after my retirement from the Army as a colonel.

My focus in the book was principally on how the ground Army shaped tank doctrine and technology to fit traditional missions supposedly validated in WWI, while a group of air power insurgents sought freedom from that Army to realize the potential of what they saw as a new, war-winning weapon—the strategic bomber. In short, I wrote from an Army officer's and academic's perspective about what lessons could be learned for the future from this experience. In this book the author's slant is much different. Again, DeJohn brings the pragmatic views of the Cavalry sergeant to the issue.

How did the Sherman scandal happen? Briefly, after WWI, the Army made decisions about what to do in the future. Under the provisions of the National Defense Act of 1920, the WWI US Tank Corps was disbanded. Future development of tanks was assigned to the Infantry, who not surprisingly believed the purpose of the tank was to support advancing Infantry.

When Gen. Douglas MacArthur was the Army's Chief of Staff in the 1930s, he allowed experimentation with mechanization. The Cavalry branch began experimenting with tanks, euphemistically called "combat cars" to avoid the restrictions of the National Defense Act. Aviation enjoyed a happier fate with the creation of the Army Air Service as a branch of the Army.

Not surprisingly, the development of tanks and airplanes in the interwar period was significantly affected by the culture of both the branches and the Army itself. The last "Infantry tank" designed for WWII, the M2 medium, had eight machine guns and a small 37mm cannon to deal with trenches and bunkers—the WWI problem. The Cavalry essentially viewed tanks as "iron horses" to execute traditional Cavalry missions, but were loath to give up horses for more combat cars.

Neither branch believed American tanks would have to fight other tanks, and tank destroyers became the approved solution to the enemy tank problem. In short, the Sherman was exactly the tank the United States wanted. Unfortunately, tanks did have to fight other tanks—and the M4 was woefully outgunned by German panzers. As DeJohn eloquently points out, Allied tankers paid a heavy price for the US Army's prewar institutional failures.

So the question remains: when the Sherman's problems became known, why didn't the Army field a better tank that was available—the T26? The author and I have discussed this key issue on several occasions. I believe the M4 Sherman's deficiencies never rose to the crisis level until after the Battle of the Bulge. Only then—in the last weeks of the war in Europe—was the T26 rushed to the ETO. In the aftermath of WWII, Army after-action reviews recommended future American tanks be capable of defeating enemy tanks and surviving, and that the Army get rid of tank destroyers. Ironically, the M1A1 that the author crewed as an Abrams tank gunner looks more like a German Tiger II in profile than it does a Sherman.

The story of strategic bombing was equally tragic. Members of the by-then renamed Army Air Forces argued that daylight, high-altitude, precision bombing by large, self-protecting bomber formations—unescorted by fighter aircraft—could destroy the key industrial sites of an enemy state and knock it out of the war, all with "acceptable" losses. The Air War Plans Division even went so far as to tell President Roosevelt that if they received the resources they needed, a land invasion of Europe might be unnecessary. They had largely disregarded improvements in air defenses and fighter aircraft that became embedded assumptions in emerging strategic bombing doctrine in the 1930s.

In October 1943, the 8th Air Force lost 164 bombers during operations over Germany—nearly 25% of the bombers dispatched on each mission were lost. By late 1943, casualties among heavy bomber crews (those not completing twenty-five missions) were nearly 70%. Unlike the failures of the Sherman tank in combat, this created a crisis in the Army Air Forces that had to be addressed for strategic bombing to continue—and the response was rapid. Fuel drop tanks extended the range of Allied fighters, providing bomber formations protection against Luftwaffe aircraft firing from beyond the reach of US .50-caliber machine guns. That said, flak still took a heavy toll among bomber formations flying at a constant airspeed and altitude to enable bombing accuracy. Consequently, the Army Air Forces suffered almost as many dead during WWII as the Marine Corps and Navy combined.

For the Allied tanker who ran into a German Tiger or Panther in his Sherman and watched his main gun rounds bounce off his opponent's armor (or the B-24 or B-17 bomber crewman who saw his machine gun tracers fall short of German aircraft, with no friendly escort fighters to keep them at bay), these institutional failures were deadly and horrifying. Explanations by higher-ups about production schedules, shipping demands, or proving new theories of warfare rang hollow to frontline GIs.

When WWII ended, the Army quickly demobilized from a 1945 high of over eight million soldiers to less than one million in 1947. Tankers and air crewmen who survived the war went home and tried to put the war behind them, although many relived their terrifying experiences in their nightmares for the rest of their days.

DeJohn's book is also a cautionary tale. Peacetime professionals must understand the environments in which they may put the young citizen soldiers of our country in future wars—something they missed with tanks and heavy bombers in WWII. The recent history of unarmored trucks being destroyed in Afghanistan and Iraq by insurgents with homemade improvised explosive devices—with no demand initially from the services for lifesaving Mine Resistant Ambush Protected vehicles (MRAPs)—shows the enduring nature and the cost in blood and treasure of this challenge.

**David Johnson is a principal researcher at the RAND Corporation and the author of *Fast Tanks and Heavy Bombers: Innovation in the U.S. Army, 1917 to 1945.* He is a retired US Army colonel with twenty-four years of service in the Infantry, Quartermaster, and Field Artillery branches. His work has been on the professional reading lists of the US Army and US Air Force Chiefs of Staff, the US Army Training and Doctrine Commander, the Chief of Staff of the Royal Air Force (United Kingdom), the Royal Australian Air Force Chief of Staff, and the US Army Maneuver Center of Excellence. From 2012–2014, he was on loan to the Army to establish and direct the Chief of Staff of the Army's Strategic Studies Group for Gen. Raymond Odierno. His latest RAND books are *Hard Fighting: Israel in Lebanon and Gaza* and *The 2008 Battle of Sadr City: Reimagining Urban Combat.* Johnson received a PhD in history from Duke University, is an adjunct scholar at the Modern War Institute at the United States Military Academy, West Point, and an adjunct professor at Georgetown University.**

# Foreword

## Dr. Richard Hallion

This is a remarkable study on a controversial topic. The M4 Sherman tank was one of America's iconic mechanized weapons in WWII, together with the C-47 transport, B-17 bomber, the Jeep, and the Liberty ship. Produced in the thousands, it became ubiquitous, serving with Allied armies on every front and around the world. Today, surviving Shermans are found in military museums and as monuments around the world, and it has figured prominently in popular culture and cinema, most recently in the motion picture *Fury* starring Brad Pitt as Sgt. Don "Wardaddy" Collier, a hard-bitten tank commander fighting through Germany in the war's last weeks.

Age tends to endow individuals and artifacts with a respectability and amiable aura they neither possessed nor deserved in their youth. For all their success, each of the vehicles above had various deficiencies that limited their effectiveness and, in some cases, endangered their crews and others aboard them. But the Sherman was a special case: a design so vulnerable it earned the grim (and unfortunately all-too-appropriate) nickname "Ronson" because of its propensity to burn when hit. Reasonably fast and maneuverable, it had a high and distinctive profile that made it an especially easy target for enemy gunners. Worse, it had inadequate armor protection and a poorly thought out internal design that often made it a death trap for its crews. To some degree, if it had possessed a powerful, long-range cannon this might have been acceptable. Instead, it had a 75mm cannon that had limited punch and required the tank commander to place his tank and crew as close as possible to their foes, deep within the lethal footprint of enemy weapons.

Those weapons included two German threats that constituted a particular nemesis for the Sherman: the 88mm cannon and the *Panzerfaust*. The 88mm, designed originally as an antiaircraft cannon, had demonstrated its antiaircraft/anti-tank abilities during the Spanish Civil War. The Panzerfaust, a bulbous shaped charge grenade fired from a hand-held launch tube, gave the ordinary German soldier a weapon at least as effective (though not as safe to use) as the American Bazooka. Both were devastatingly effective against the M4: the hardened 88mm shell moving at high supersonic speed sliced through the Sherman's thin armor almost without resistance, while the Panzerfaust, bursting upon contact, formed a hot jet of liquid metal that burst into the tank with horrifying effect. But even smaller cannon carried by other German armored vehicles could wreak havoc on Sherman tanks and their crews.

As author Christian De John shows, the defects of the Sherman should not have surprised. Indeed, like other flawed American weapons—for example, the Navy's aerial and submarine torpedoes at the war's outset, or early models of the B-17 bomber—the flaws it possessed were readily discernible even before it entered combat service. Deficient doctrine, inadequate

comprehension of future trends in tank (and cannon) development, poor design, inadequate review by acquisition authorities, and overly optimistic expectations of commanders all contributed to introducing a tank that lacked even a marginal advantage over any of its principal opponents: the *Pz.Kpfw IV*, Panther, Tiger, and *Königstiger*. Instead, it triumphed by sheer numbers that were in service on the fighting front: in tactical engagements, ant-like Shermans would be steadily attrited until the survivors were close enough to overwhelm their foes. In an engagement against even small numbers of opponents, the price of victory could be dozens of Sherman crewmen killed or wounded.

The tragedy is compounded by—admittedly in retrospect—the astonishing unwillingness of senior commanders (including such revered figures as Gens. Dwight Eisenhower, Leslie McNair, and even George Patton) to acknowledge the Sherman's deficiencies and work forthrightly to replace it with a better tank. Such a vehicle—the T-26 (later M-26) Pershing, with a 90mm cannon—was already in development, and could have entered service in Europe far earlier than it did (a few made their way to Europe in the last months of the war, only serving in combat in an operational test and evaluation role).

WWII is replete with numerous examples where commanders persisted in following discredited prewar doctrine or remained loyal to impractical or deficient weapons, but even by the standards of the worst of these, the sad saga of the Sherman tank occupies a place of special infamy.

The author is to be congratulated for going beyond conventional narratives and simplistic accounts. He examines how the M4 reflected long-standing deficiencies and flawed assumptions in American armored vehicle development, placing it within the context of what the late Dr. Russell Weigley (one of the author's mentors) called "The American Way of War." But more than this, he examines the complex human story—how key decisions, attitudes, and values of commanders led to the Sherman, minimized its deficiencies, and thus tragically made possible a victory in Europe bought at the price of numerous killed, maimed, and crippled crewmen.

The story of the Sherman tank scandal is a cautionary tale, one to be read and considered by any concerned with acquisition of combat systems for land, sea, or air warfare. It is also a sobering case, forcing the reexamination of decision making and the ethical responsibilities of acquisition authorities and combatant commanders.

The author has undertaken a responsible historical reexamination, forcing military historians to look beyond the easy rationalizations and forgiving narratives of the past. It is a welcome book, a tanker's book, and fittingly written by one who is a tanker of distinction.

**Dr. Richard Hallion has served as a senior advisor to the Pentagon, a visiting professor at the US Army War College, a Smithsonian Institution curator, and as the official historian of the US Air Force. A military historian, author, and graduate history professor, his many books include *Air Power Confronts an Unstable World*, *Storm Over Iraq*, and *The Rise of the Fighter Aircraft*.**

# THE WEAPONS OF YESTERDAY

"MANY OF OUR TANKERS are angry," read the *New York Times* for Friday, March 9, 1945. "Angry because of the inferiority of the equipment with which they are expected to defeat the Germans," wrote respected military columnist Hanson Baldwin, and "angry because of the official "whitewash" that has been applied to that inferiority."[4]

A cover-up at the highest civilian and military levels—in 1945? Resentful American soldiers back then? If one accepts the sanitized version of America in WWII so prevalent in popular culture, surely this must be a page from the Vietnam War, or the Iraq War? Wasn't our hallowed "Good War" all sweetness and light, the righteous crusade of a "Greatest Generation?"

In recent decades, the sugarcoating surrounding America's participation in that war has reached new heights. The year 2015 featured seventieth-anniversary ceremonies for the Battle of the Bulge and Victory in Europe Day, coverage of which honored aging veterans likely observing their last commemorations of the war's pivotal events. From dedications attended by presidents to highly influential films like *Saving Private Ryan*, *Band of Brothers*, *Flags of Our Fathers*, and *The Pacific*, the war and those who fought and led it have been wrapped in a

We cannot afford to fight the war of today or tomorrow with the weapons of yesterday.... If we do not keep constantly ahead of our enemies in the development of new weapons, we pay for our backwardness with the life's blood of our sons.... Everything we are and have will be given.[1]
—President Franklin Roosevelt, 1945, State of the Union Address

mantle of reverential glory that is a disservice not only to the historical truth, but to the men involved.

Author and WWII Army Infantry Officer Paul Fussell, who lamented "a return, especially in popular culture, to military romanticism,"[5] observed "the difficulty of piercing the barrier of romantic optimism about human nature implicit in the Allied victory, and the resounding Allied extirpation of flagrant evil."[6] According to Thomas Childers, who wrote a book on the problems of returning WWII servicemen, veterans' pain has "been muffled under a blanket of nostalgic adulation...a reassuring, uncomplicated portrait repeated so often in public commemorations and memorial addresses that it has become almost an incantation, more liturgical than historical...a view that seems increasingly intent on sentimentalizing and sanitizing a conflict that killed fifty-five million people around the world and left millions more broken, either physically or emotionally."[7]

With all this fawning, wrote author David Colley, an Army veteran of a later generation, "We have lost touch with the immense pain and suffering caused by the war, and the ripples of sorrow that still flow across America from that devastating conflict."[8] British historian Sir Max Hastings quoted an American colleague's crack that some have "taken to raising monuments,

Tank assembly line.

rather than writing history."[9] The late distinguished historian Russell F. Weigley, who taught the author, observed "a certain tendency to romanticize World War II, to make all our soldiers brave and gallant and all our generals more than competent, if not mostly brilliant." Dr. Weigley condemned such "nonsense" because it "sugarcoats the realities of battle, the deficiencies of American training and equipment, and the shortcomings of preparation and leadership in World War II."[10]

One wartime myth is that of the "Arsenal of Democracy's" supposedly superior weapons. "We won because the United States smothered the enemy in an avalanche of production, the likes of which he had never seen or dreamed of," said Gen. William S. Knudsen, Director of Production in the Office of the Undersecretary for War.[11] "It is a thrilling thing," exulted the *New York Times*'s Sidney Shallett in late 1942, "to see American industry in action":

> In a way, it's a shame that military reasons make it impossible for everyone in the land to have a look inside a few factories, for all the words and pictures and movies in the world can't quite capture and convey the feeling that huge war plants in action can give you.
>
> The clackety-clack of acres of machines, the rat-a-tat-tat of endless rivets being driven home, the fearsomeness of giant cranes swooping overhead carrying cranes, tanks, and mammoth cauldrons of molten steel as if they were so many carpet tacks under a magnet; then the sight of the sleek, strong planes, the elephantine tanks with their deadly cannon trunks, the millions of machine gun bullets jumping from the machines like a plague of locusts…well, they make you feel better![12]

> As things go now, every man has resigned himself to dying sooner or later, because we don't have a chance against the German tanks. All of this stuff we read about their tanks knocked out by ours makes us sick, because we know what price we have to pay in men and equipment to accomplish this…. Our tanks are no match for the Panther and Tiger, and it is just suicide to tackle them.[2]
>
> —A tank crew quoted in the secret White-Rose Reports to General Eisenhower, March 1945

Newsreels show long lines of tanks and planes pumped out by the American industrial colossus, seemingly effortlessly. "The nation was encouraged to believe," wrote journalist Eric Sevareid, "that it could produce its way to victory."[13] While the sheer quantities are impressive, an honest assessment must ask were these weapons effective? Were they what our soldiers needed to match and beat the arms of our enemies?

Decades later, instead of unsentimental depictions of the American leadership in WWII, the cult of Franklin Roosevelt worship prevails. An exhaustive 2013 history of American wartime production carefully skates over President Roosevelt's involvement in the Sherman tank scandal. Instead, we get a shell game, the exaltation of quantity over quality:

> For ground warfare, American factories produced 88,410 tanks, Germany only 46,857, and Japan a meager 2,515. Of artillery, including anti-tank and anti-aircraft weapons, the United States turned out 257,390 to 159,147 for Germany and 13,350 for Japan. Some 2.38 million military trucks rolled off American assembly lines compared to 345,914 for Germany and 165,945 for Japan. The United States also manufactured 6.5 million rifles and 40 billion bullets.[14]

Author Maury Klein does refer to FDR making his 1945 State of the Union Address, but neglects to mention that within it, Roosevelt was forced to address the uproar over American tanks in the national media. Considering the book's length—897 pages—it seems unlikely such a glaring omission was for lack of space. Instead of a more honest look at FDR and the tank scandal, decades-old fawning is rehashed: "No mere politician… could put into (his speeches) the same degree of conviction and the deep spiritual quality that Roosevelt conveyed."[15] We are also assured that upon Roosevelt's death, even mass murderer Joseph Stalin "appeared to be deeply moved."[16]

At the other extreme from worshipful "Arsenal of Democracy" celebrations, some books and films have begun to tear down the veil of wartime propaganda. The year 2014 saw the release of the refreshingly unsentimental film *Fury*, concerning Sherman tank combat in Germany during the European war's last days. The film depicts the M4 as a virtual death trap, in stark contrast to the wartime boasts of politicians, manufacturers, and generals.

Author Steve Zaloga wrote:

> When I was growing up in the 1950s, the Sherman tank was regularly portrayed in the press as one of the great war-winning weapons of World War II. [Over] a half-century later, this image has been completely reversed. A popular book about American tanks in World War II is grimly entitled *Death Traps*. Television documentaries enthusiastically embellish this gruesome theme. *Suicide Missions* was the title of one popular TV show about Sherman tank crews. So which is it: death trap or war winner?[17]

If one does not look too closely, there is much truth to the newsreel legends of American technological superiority. Consider the situation facing the Japanese in the last months of the war. Fleets of hundreds of warships, including dozens of aircraft carriers, closed in on Japan. Above, huge B-29 Superfortress bombers (an industrial marvel for its day, with pressurized cabins and fire control computer guided guns) obliterated what remained of Japan's cities. Had the war gone on, those advanced bombers might have been escorted by the new P-80 Shooting Star jet fighter, ushering in the jet age of American military aviation.

To oppose all this might, the Japanese planned to repulse Operation OLYMPIC-CORONET (the invasion of mainland Japan) with kamikaze aircraft and boats, and by throwing women and children with pikes and satchel charges against Allied tanks.

Surely, the Allies enjoyed numerical superiority. During the Anzio campaign German paratrooper Joachim Liebschner survived an American Artillery bombardment, only to find "the whole fore field was full of Americans and tanks and jeeps and lorries [trucks]—above all, tanks."[18] After being taken prisoner and given a ride—not marched on foot—by his GI captors to a POW compound, Liebschner realized:

> This was the first time that I thought we could not win the war because of all the war materiel I could see the Americans moving forward—the roads were simply full of tanks, lorries, jeeps—and moving during daytime. We Germans couldn't move a bicycle in the daytime without being shot at. The roads were jammed with traffic; they were moving this huge mass of war materiel, guns, and tanks.[19]

Decades after the war Allied victors' pride is understandable, but the emphasis on romanticized tales and quantity of equipment alone—without examining the quality of those weapons—does an injustice to the young men killed and wounded.

Today, thanks to dramatic examples that have entered our popular culture, America's technological superiority over its WWII enemies is an entrenched cliché. To the general public, the wartime propagandists' insistence that the US soldier had the finest weapons and equipment is a given.

*Fury* exhibit at the Tank Museum, Bovington, Dorset, UK. *Massimo Foti*

Panzer IV Ausf. D at the Tank Museum, Bovington, Dorset, UK. *Massimo Foti*

*US Army Signal Corps*

Until 2014's groundbreaking *Fury*, many movies highlighted gratuitous displays of American industrial might. In the epic *The Longest Day* (1962), the camera lingers on huge formations of warships disgorging troops and vehicles onto the Normandy coast. There, long lines of Allied tanks, trucks, jeeps, and fresh, well-equipped men advance up hills while overhead American fighters and bombers fill the sky.

Decades later *Saving Private Ryan* (1998), while made by a more cynical generation, retains the same sense of an unstoppable flood of American technology; an endless supply of weapons and equipment overwhelming the Nazis. Ultimate victory seems inevitable once Detroit's tank factories and sunny California's aircraft plants began to hum. True, many American in-

ventions, from jeeps to C-47s, were among the best of the war. Her factories produced huge numbers of planes, tanks, ships, small arms, and ammunition. Equally impressive and necessary to fight a global war, the US military created and maintained a worldwide logistical and repair network to support all those men, weapons, and equipment. But the wartime boasts repeated today are often one-dimensional. The truth, while troubling, is more interesting than the prevailing mythology.

In land warfare, one would expect the country that perfected mass automobile production to succeed at fielding something so essential as a decent, powerful tank. "To stay alive," observed Col. William Triplett, with decades of armor experience, "a tank gunner had to make first-round hits, like a gunfighter in a barroom brawl."[20] Yet US tank gunners fired again and again impotently, only to be swatted down by German tanks with better firepower and armor protection.

"The Allies' most serious problem [in the Normandy campaign]," wrote British historian Sir Max Hastings in *Inferno: The World At War, 1939–1945*, "was the inferiority of their tanks: numerical advantage counted for little when British and American shells often bounced off well-armoured German Panthers and Tigers, while a hit on a Sherman, Churchill or Cromwell was almost invariably fatal."[21] While Allied propaganda rhapsodized about the free people of aroused democracies churning out huge numbers of superior weapons to smite the evil dictators, qualitatively, it was the dictatorships who built better tanks. "One Tiger II [a.k.a. the King or Royal Tiger tank]," claimed Albert Speer in 1944, "has…the same effect as 25 to 30 Shermans."[22]

The German Panther and Soviet T-34 were among the best tank designs of the war, ahead of the third-place American M4. Up to the last days of fighting, GIs were piling sandbags, logs, and cement on obsolete tanks, hoping to increase their odds of survival against foes like the Tiger, King Tiger, and Panther. "When the US Third Armored Division captured a cement factory at Stolberg," wrote Hastings in *Armageddon: The Battle for Germany, 1944–45*, "crews ignored warnings that overloading hulls could wreck suspensions, and mixed concrete to lay on the front of their Shermans." As Lt. Belton Cooper remembered, "They would grab at any straws; they were desperate to survive."[23]

German tankers dubbed the Sherman tank the "Ronson," after the cigarette lighter guaranteed to light up the first time. "Ronsons, you know…" elaborated a German prisoner of war:

> Ronsons, yes, like for a cigarette. Our gunners see your tanks coming…and they say to each other, "Here comes another Ronson." Why do the Americans do this for us? Bang!…it burns like twenty haystacks. All the people inside—my God.
>
> Those funny tanks with the little guns…so tall, we can see them coming from a long way in our gun sights… those square sides [the Sherman's flat sides were more vulnerable than tanks with curved or sloped armor] and thin armor.
>
> We know if we hit one, it goes up.

Why does the country of Detroit send their men out to die in these things?[24]

While Germany and Russia steadily and dramatically improved their tank designs, American armor remained relatively stagnant. Yet in the air from 1941 to 1945, the US Army's pilots progressed from fabric-covered biplanes to jet fighters and hemispheric heavy bombers toting atomic bombs. "In 1941," Gen. "Hap" Arnold boasted to Gen. George Marshall in 1945,

our propeller-driven fighters were limited to speeds of 300 miles an hour, a range of 200 to 300 miles, and effective ceilings of 20,000 feet. Today our conventional fighters have speeds of 500 miles an hour, combat ranges of 1,300 miles, and effective ceilings of 35,000 feet. Improvements of our jet fighters may well produce within the next five years an aircraft capable of the speed of sound and of reaching targets 2,000 miles away at altitudes of above 50,000 feet. When the barrier of compressibility has been hurdled, as it surely will be, there is no practicable limit to the speed of piloted aircraft.[25]

While the sky was the limit for American airmen, the tanker on the ground was saddled with under-gunned, poorly armored tanks by his leadership, designs that were years behind those of his enemies.

Official histories by government bureaucracies rarely feature dramatic mea culpas, but even the Army Ordnance Department's account of its performance in WWII conceded in 1960, "The tank was the source of more trouble and more criticism than any other item of American equipment":

All during the war, tanks were the objects of sharp verbal attacks. Army spokesmen, eager to build up public confidence, asserted time after time that US tanks were superior to anything the enemy could produce. Army Ordnance officials strongly defended them against all criticism, and cited laudatory letters from combat commanders to prove the point.

But the secret reports on tank performance submitted by overseas commanders and the Armored Force Board told a somewhat different story...the inferiority of US tank guns and armor to the German guns and armor pitted against them. Why, it was asked, could not the United States, with its unrivaled industrial capacity for making cars and trucks of all kinds, produce better tanks than Germany? In particular, why did the US Army have no heavy tank to match the German Tiger? By 1945, the chorus of criticism reached a point where leading American newspapers were calling for a congressional investigation of "a situation that does no credit to the War Department."[26]

Gen. George C. Marshall, 1947.

The popular impression persists that the WWII American soldier had the finest equipment, which historian Gerald Linderman called "the assumption of American material superiority."[27] Nothing, it would seem, was too good for the GI, who wore dashing, well-made uniforms that wowed local girls from England to Australia. He was issued cigarettes in his daily rations. He enjoyed fresh ice cream, Coca-Cola, and beer, even while stationed on remote Pacific islands. And he got the highest pay. Surely this was the best-cared-for soldier in history?

His political and military leaders are often depicted as kindly and indulgent. Wartime "human interest stories" tell of servicemen or their families granted favors by a humane leadership after writing to the president or his wife, or to Gens. Marshall or Eisenhower. Gen. George Marshall responded to GI complaints about the lack of recreational facilities, the quality of Army food, and the shortage of warm GI socks in an Army Post Exchange (PX). As he boasted to his biographer Forrest Pogue in 1956:

I would check [on such things] myself. I remember my great pleasure when I went into Italy and got right up behind the firing line, and they brought a battalion out from a front-line position to go into a support position as a picket. And before the men had gotten their pup tents up, one sergeant opened up the post exchange from two barrels that had been delivered to him, and here was tobacco and here was Coca-Cola and here was the various things you want right away, and they sold them right there over the barrel.[28]

In his 1945 "Report On The Winning of the War" to Congress and the public, Marshall praised the Army's "By Request" films: "A group of men in New Guinea wanted to see pictures of a

snowstorm…. One enlisted man wanted to hear a quartet sing 'Down By The Old Mill Stream.' These and similar requests were met."[29]

If such esoteric creature comforts could be provided, why couldn't Army Chief of Staff Marshall, after years of warnings—including from Gen. Eisenhower in early 1943—supply his tankers with a medium tank with decent armor and a powerful main gun able to take on Germany's best?

When Gen. George S. Patton humiliated two sick GIs in Army hospitals in Sicily, public outrage resulted; he was nearly relieved and sent home in disgrace. In contrast to Patton's bullying, the public held up Dwight D. Eisenhower as the ideal American general, a down-to-earth, likable man from Abilene, Kansas. Favorable stories of "General Ike," his grin, and his easy manner with the troops are legion. We read of him visiting his "boys" before the Normandy invasion, standing on an English airfield in near tears, full of pride and compassion. While a cloud hung over Patton, "Ike" emerged as the most popular Allied general of the war, riding a reputation for humane leadership all the way to the White House.

When we think of contempt for human life on the part of WWII military and political leaders, the Red Army's generals clearing mine fields by ordering their men into them may come to mind. As well as German guns to his front, the Soviet soldier faced those of his own officers at his back; political commissars shot those who hesitated to advance. One might also recall Hitler ordering besieged soldiers to fight to the last man at Stalingrad, or his desire to die in the rubble of Berlin, bringing Germany down with him.

In the Pacific war, Japanese recruits were taught to admire the chrysanthemum, which falls in its prime, and were assured, "Duty is as heavy as a mountain, but death is as light as a feather." The American public recalls *Banzai* charges where Japanese officers armed only with swords led their men, well fortified with sake, in human wave attacks on Allied machine guns. The Japanese glorification of the kamikaze handcuffed to the controls of his bomb-laden aircraft, with just enough fuel for a one-way trip into an Allied warship, has become an icon of contempt for human life.

The popular perception of callous Russian, German, and Japanese wartime leadership—in contrast, we are told, to American leaders' decency—is well established. In April 1944, soon before many of their sons participated in the Normandy invasion, *Liberty* magazine assured civilian readers at home that to Gen. Marshall, "soldiers should live, and avoiding losses to personnel is a most important rule of combat." *Liberty* predicted:

There will be no needless loss of life in the American Army in World War II if the orders and plans of our High Command are carried out. No postwar poet will sing a new "Charge of the Light Brigade," paying tribute to some sentimentally heroic but foolishly sacrificial exploit. No "noble six hundred" will charge unprotected to the guns.[30]

A Panther in rare running condition at the *Musée des Blindés*, Saumur, France. *Massimo Foti*

But little known then and now is that American political and military leaders also held, and acted on, callous attitudes toward their troops. Dismissing warnings from men in the field actually using mediocre American tanks against German *Panzers*, they denied problems with them. They stubbornly adhered to obsolete armor doctrine, and this failure to take decisive action in time sacrificed many young men.

A fresh look behind some of the myths of "The Good War" and peeling back the veneer of unquestioning reverence reveals a troubling story that explodes wartime propaganda. "What has been celebrated as the Greatest Generation," cautioned Paul Fussell, "included among the troops and their officers plenty of criminals, psychopaths, cowards, and dolts."[31]

American leaders handicapped soldiers with inadequate weapons that prolonged the tank war in Europe and contributed to thousands of casualties. Yet undeniably, the Sherman tank had a great redeeming feature: assembly lines could crank it out by the tens of thousands to overwhelm more powerful German tanks through weight of numbers. Using decoy tactics to draw fire, two or four mediocre Shermans had a chance against one Tiger or Panther. But behind the impressive production statistics Roosevelt spouted on the radio, what of the four or five GIs inside those Shermans, some of whom burned to death after just a few blows, even as their leadership insisted on the superiority of the M4?

America's WWII production effort is justifiably celebrated as an industrial triumph, but one of the war's greatest scandals has never had a reckoning: the persistent inferiority of the armament and armor protection of US tanks. Our tank designs were so far behind Germany's, they contributed to some of the US Army's greatest routs of the war: humiliating debacles in North Africa and Tunisia; the near-failure of the Sicilian invasion (almost thrown off the beaches by a few Tigers); and the stunning initial German success in the Ardennes, where GIs fled in terror at the sound or sight of any Panzer, assuming them to be the rare, monstrous Konig (King, or Royal) Tiger. Under-gunned, weakly armored American tanks and tank destroyers—and the high-level flawed decisions that created and perpetuated them—led to severe shortages of vehicles and crews, and to the avoidable death and maiming of thousands of untrained young men. "Wait and see," an Infantry officer told Sgt. Nat Frankel, 4th Armored Division. "After the war we'll be talking about how savage the Germans were for using unqualified men as cannon fodder. Nobody will remember that we sent our cooks out to fight."[32]

"Most military historians," says the controversial memoir *Death Traps*, featuring Ordnance Lt. Belton Cooper, US Third Armored Division,

> have failed completely to understand the enormous impact on American tankers of having to fight superior German tanks.... In all the key capabilities of a main battle tank—firepower, armor, and mobility—the M4 Sherman was decidedly inferior to the superior German tanks it encountered in battle. This major disadvantage not only resulted in tremendous pain and suffering and losses in personnel and armor, but also delayed the successful conclusion of the War in Europe.[33]

To many, the Sherman tank scandal is little known today. The triumphs of our American industry are glorified: the jeep, Liberty Ship, and P-51 Mustang fighter. Atomic bombs and B-29s are impressive, but for the duration of the war, the industrial giant that debuted the automobile assembly line failed to deliver an updated, adequate tank for fighting Germany's best armor. To Dr. Russell Weigley, "Perhaps the most questionable element in American ground fighting power was the American tank...[the Sherman] was inferior to the German Panther as well as to the heavier Tiger in almost every respect save endurance, including armament and defensive armor." The US, Dr. Weigley noted, went all through WWII refusing "to develop, until too late to do much good, heavier tanks comparable to the German Tigers and Panthers, let alone the Royal Tiger or the Russian Stalin."[34] To Max Hastings, "No single Allied failure had more important consequences on the European battlefield than the lack of tanks with adequate punch and protection."[35]

But critics will respond if the Sherman tank was so bad, how did the Allies win the ground war? Instead of the usual cheery recitation of FDR's bold production figures, a more honest expla-

Chief of Ordnance Gen. Levin H. Campbell. *US Army Signal Corps*

nation might lie in the words of a German officer captured in Italy whose GI guard admitted to "riding" his prisoner:

I said, "Well, if you're so tough, if you're all supermen, how come you're here captured, and I'm guarding you?"

And he looked at me and said, "I was on this hill as a battery commander with six 88mm anti-tank guns, and the Americans kept sending tanks down the road. We kept knocking them out. Every time they sent a tank, we knocked it out. Finally we ran out of ammunition, and the Americans didn't run out of tanks."[36]

"We won the [tank] war," remembered US Army tanker Lawrence Butler, "by losing more tanks and cluttering up the battlefield... the Sherman was a deathtrap. At one time, I was on fire thirteen times in one day."[37]

In wartime propaganda photos and newsreels, columns of imposing new tanks roll out of American factories, but some were obsolete while still on the drawing board. America was successful at mass production of under-gunned, poorly armored tanks. Seventy years later, there has never been a reckoning for "The Allied inability to build a main battle tank, despite extensive experience and a wealth of technical data from two theatres, which resulted in horrendous casualties to both its Armored Forces and the accompanying Infantry. Capitalist industry's failure to forge what the Soviets and Nazis had accomplished by 1942 has been called by some 'The Great Tank Scandal.'"[38]

From 1942 onward, tankers on the battlefields recognized shortcomings in American armor, warned of the Tiger and Panther threat, and called for better mounts. But even after they met with setbacks in North Africa, Tunisia, Sicily, and Italy, Gen. Lesley McNair (commanding Army Ground Forces and a key figure in the tank scandal) continued to insist in late 1943, "I see no reason to alter our previous stand...that we should defeat Germany by use of the M4 series of medium tanks. There have been no factual developments overseas, so far as I know, to challenge the superiority of the M4 Sherman."[39]

In early 1945, after the shock of the Ardennes campaign, the tank scandal erupted in stateside press. "We need not only have no apology for any item of American ordnance in comparison with that of the enemy," Army Ordnance Chief Gen. Lewin Campbell claimed; furthermore, "we're leading them all the way."[40] Along with politicians and stateside generals, Eisenhower, Bradley, and Patton in Europe issued denials and misleading statistics that contradicted not only the opinions of the men using the M4 in the field, but their own knowledge and observations.

When Patton (an avid photographer) came across destroyed American tanks, he would take shots of the damage and mark the photos with a grease pencil, showing the holes where German rounds had entered and exited with grisly effect on the crew inside. In his own diary, he wrote of personally counting hundreds of burned-out hulks near Bastogne.

But when questioned by the press at the height of the Sherman tank controversy, Gen. Patton contemptuously dismissed the concerns of frontline GIs with years of combat experience. In statements for public consumption he chose bluster over candor: "We've got the finest tanks in the world," he told incredulous reporters. "We just love to see the German King Tiger come up on the field." The same article also reported that according to Ordnance Chief Gen. Campbell, "Every United States Army commander in Europe, from Gen. Dwight D. Eisenhower down, is completely satisfied with American tanks, and none of them want any heavier tanks on the order of the German Royal Tiger..."[41]

GIs of all ranks saw through their leaders' dishonesty. "You know," said Cpt. James Burt, 66th Armored Regiment, to the Army newspaper *Stars and Stripes* in February 1945,

our morale would be a lot better if there weren't so many cock-and-bull stories in the papers about how our

**Restored Konig (King or Royal) Tiger at the Musée des Blindés, Saumur, France.** *Massimo Foti*

A Direct Drive (DD) Sherman tank intended to be a "swimming tank."

tanks are world-beaters…when the layman reads that we've knocked out twice as many Jerry tanks as they have of ours, he doesn't realize that it's not our tanks alone that did the job. It's tanks plus artillery plus planes—plus guts."[42]

In hindsight, Patton's remarks look particularly ridiculous. Not only was he well aware of the M4's weaknesses, having personally photographed their burned-out hulks, but when offered a more powerful new tank (the T26, later known as the Pershing), he turned it down.

To their credit, honest generals affirmed the GIs' warnings, but privately. "It is my opinion," Brig. Gen. J. H. Collier, who led Combat Command A, Second Armored Division, wrote confidentially to Eisenhower in March 1945, "that press reports of statements by high-ranking officers [Campbell and Patton] to the effect that we have the best equipment in the world do much to discourage the soldier who is using equipment that he knows to be inferior to that of the enemy."[43]

Where was the press as the tank scandal steadily worsened, especially from Normandy onward? Author James Tobin, a reporter and Pulitzer Prize nominee who wrote a biography of war correspondent Ernie Pyle, has condemned the "sanitized and superficial portrait of the war" that we read in our "history" books:

Seen from the perspective of the post-Vietnam consensus that governments are as a rule unreliable if not downright venal, the correspondents of World War II appear as little more than cheerleaders—hardworking and talented, perhaps, but essentially and irresponsibly uncritical of the things they covered. Caught up in the national cause, they allowed themselves to be coopted by military officialdom, and thus ignored errors and excesses that should have been brought to public attention. They were patriots first, observers second.

The result was a half-reported war, with the nastiest truths neglected, censored, downplayed, or discreetly screened from public view…. John Steinbeck and other correspondents and critics charged themselves with a host of untruths…that "we had no cruel or ambitious or ignorant commanders…that officers were universally admired by their men"; that "the war was won without a single mistake, by a command consisting exclusively

of geniuses"; and that "everyone on the Allied side was sort of nice."

"It was crap—and I don't exclude the Ernie Pyles," a Canadian reporter for the Reuters news agency reflected long after the war. "We were a propaganda arm of our governments."[44]

Before 1945, censorship helped suppress the growing tank controversy until the Battle of the Bulge exposed deficiencies in weapons and doctrine so glaring that Army and Roosevelt administration leaders could no longer deny them. The resulting furor in the press led up to the White House, as newspapers that had been parroting propaganda boasts for years reversed themselves to call for a congressional investigation. Forced to address the scandal in his 1945 State of the Union Address, President Roosevelt spoke of "thousands" of powerful, advanced new T26 heavy tanks on the way—tanks that would never arrive.

After the war Gen. Marshall acknowledged the problem, but his "explanations" were patronizing and insulting. In a case of shooting the messenger, the Army's Chief of Staff faulted officers for not silencing tankers' warnings that (rather inconveniently for politicians and brass hats) had been all too true. While assuring Congress and the public that "Excuses and explanations are not acceptable to the soldier, and would not be tolerated by the political leaders," Marshall offered a litany of just such "excuses and explanations" for the tank scandal, while damning "a succession of criticisms, largely unjustified in my opinion, since the critics seldom are aware of the salient facts and basic requirements."[45]

In his best-selling 1949 memoir *Crusade in Europe*, Gen. Eisenhower—who had written to Marshall after the 1943 Kasserine Pass disaster, "I refuse to indulge in alibis,"[46]—omits the Sherman tank scandal. Instead, while ignoring problems with the thousands of standard model M4 Shermans, one of the most prominent figures involved in the tank controversy raves about obscure tanks built in small numbers, like the amphibious

Maj. Gen. Dwight Eisenhower, 1942. *US National Archives*

Sherman "DD" tanks. Yet to recent biographer Jean Edward Smith, Eisenhower's memoir is "a remarkably complete record of the war in Europe," in which Eisenhower "did not avoid subjects that were embarrassing, and did not hesitate to accept responsibility for matters that went wrong."[47]

Ironically, instead of a technological breakthrough that hastened the Allied victory, the rare DD (Donald Duck) tanks praised by Eisenhower were a conspicuous failure on Omaha Beach. There, American tankers were killed not by German fire, but by drowning before even reaching the Normandy shore, because the flotation devices on their "swimming" Sherman tanks failed almost from the moment they were launched into the surf. But to Eisenhower, "There was no sight in the war that so impressed me with the industrial might of America as the wreckage on the landing beaches. To any other nation the disaster would have been almost decisive. But so great was America's productive capacity that the [losses] occasioned little more than a ripple in the development of our build-up."[48]

Recognizing the political dimensions of the controversy, GIs were bitter toward leaders who placed protecting careers over addressing a problem that enlarged casualty lists and prolonged the fighting. "Generals can face the wrath of the enemy," an anonymous but perceptive "second lieutenant of Cavalry" noted in one of Pulitzer-Prize winning *New York Times* reporter Hanson Baldwin's 1945 articles on the scandal, "but never that of the people. The only reason our foremost exponent of armor [Patton] does not champion the tanker's cause is…because the blame belongs to a fraternity of which he is a member, and would result in professional suicide for an ambitious man to do so."[49]

The official explanations for American armor's shortcomings amount to excuses: Army leaders were unaware of the problem until it was too late (although the Ordnance Department had been warned of German tank designs since the mid-1930s), or that for most of the war tankers had not wanted more powerful tanks, so Ordnance merely built the tanks it was asked to build, never mind if they were inadequate for the task.

While the first excuse was easily disproved, the second contains some truth. Until 1945, influential generals persisted in supporting prewar armor doctrine that favored small, lightly armored and armed (but mobile) tanks at the expense of firepower and armor protection. But the Germans and Soviets showed such

Sgt. James Jones, Pearl Harbor and Guadalcanal veteran and author of *From Here to Eternity*, perhaps the most accurate depiction of US Army life.

thinking to be out of date; throughout the war, their vehicles grew steadily more powerful and larger, and gained thicker armor. In the T-34 medium tank (which owed much to cantankerous American inventor J. Walter Christie, who sold his designs to the Russians after being rebuffed by Congress), the Soviets had perhaps the war's best tank design: an effective balance of firepower, mobility, and armor protection.

Although each successive generation of German and Soviet tanks evidenced a trend towards more firepower and armor, US Army leaders opposed matching or surpassing them. When stubborn Col. Blimp types insisted the ideal tank design should emphasize speed and mobility, firepower and crew protection suffered. Confronted with German behemoths, tankers in outclassed American vehicles were ordered to somehow avoid combat. Due to high-level obstructionism, although design work on the T26 heavy tank began in 1942, Army leaders prevented its adoption as a Sherman replacement until 1945, when it was too late.

Until the last months of the war, the perspective of the frontline enlisted and non-commissioned tanker overseas was frequently censored while the politically motivated boasts and denials of stateside generals and politicians dominated headlines.

Today, reviewing yellowed newspapers printed on fragile, rationed wartime pulp, one notices articles praising the M4 have a conspicuous omission: the opinions of the men actually using it in combat, derived from years of firsthand experience. Instead, the carefully worded statements often feature assurances of stateside "experts": technicians, desk-bound generals, and Roosevelt administration officials who rarely left their comfortable offices.

Usually generals write history, not privates and sergeants. To Army Sgt. James Jones (a veteran of Pearl Harbor and Guadalcanal who championed the Army enlisted man in novels like *From Here to Eternity*), "History is always written from the viewpoints of the leaders":

And increasingly, in our age, war leaders do not get shot at with any serious consistency…. As in most wars, in the United States in World War II, most of the commanding was done by the upper classes, and most of the fighting was done by the lower…. Thus, when an official Army historian (almost always an educated member of

Restored Tiger I used in the movie *Fury* at the Tank Museum, Bovington, Dorset, UK. *Massimo Foti*

the upper classes himself) came onto the field after a fight, it was usually the commanders and higher officers (themselves members of the upper classes) to whom he talked. He might talk to a few truck-driver privates for textural material (How muddy it was. How scary the enemy charge was.) But when he wrote it, it was always filtered through the ideals system he and the other members of his class, the commanders, shared and adhered to.

And thus it is possible—it is even probable—that you can read the history of a campaign in which you served, and find the history doesn't at all tally with the campaign you remember. The private remembers it from the viewpoint of his lower class ideals, or lack of them, while the historian has written it from the viewpoint of the upper class commanders and their totally different ideals. That is why there can be such a glaring discrepancy between the history of a battle, and the way it was played out in reality on the field. And yet both views are (or believe they are) totally honest.[50]

The existing literature on the Sherman tank scandal is fragmentary; one sees tantalizing hints here and there, but little comprehensive coverage. Richard Hunnicutt, who wrote extensive volumes on the developmental history of the main American tanks of WWII, noted that while there are many books on German armor, in comparison, a much smaller amount of information has been published regarding the Allied tank development effort. This has been true partly because of continuing security restrictions, and partly due to the difficulty in sorting the necessary material from the mountains of documents and test reports prepared during this period. Wholesale destruction of many such documents before declassification also contributes to the research problem.[51]

The Sherman's greatest deficiency lies in its firepower, which is most conspicuous by its absence. Lack of a principal gun with sufficient penetrating ability to knock out the German opponent has cost us more tanks, and skilled men to man more tanks, than any failure of our crews—not to mention the heartbreak and sense of defeat I and other men have felt when we see twenty-five or even many more of our rounds fired, and they ricochet off the enemy attackers. To be finally hit, once, and we climb from and leave a burning, blackened, and now useless pile of scrap iron. It would yet have been a tank, had it mounted a gun.[3]

—Cpl. Francis Vierling, US Second Armored Division

While the video game *World of Tanks* has brought general knowledge of tank history to a larger audience, as an old US Cavalry tanker, I can't help but be disturbed that the (simulated) gruesome death the Army trained me to avoid has become a source of amusement for teenagers worldwide—don't they realize there would be four or five GIs in that burning tank? I regret so much of the available literature on American tanks in WWII is coldly impersonal, leaning towards the technical, engineering, and trivial side; columns of statistics about nuts and bolts, armor thickness, and muzzle velocity of tanks, rather than the stories of the men inside them.

Readers can easily find obscure details about multiple versions of air filters on the Sherman tank and production charts full of cold statistics, but rarely the answers to such questions as "How did it feel to be lied to by your leaders when Patton/ Bradley/ Eisenhower denied the tank scandal?" This book is an old tanker's attempt to redress this, to remind readers that beyond the impersonal facts about tanks that appear in most books, there were men inside them.

Until now, there has never been a major work exploring all of the complicated aspects of the Sherman tank scandal: the influence of domestic politics; the Army's bitter, decades-long, unresolved internal dispute over the tank's role on the battlefield; the failure of Allied intelligence; bureaucratic infighting among tank design agencies; the rapidly changing state of tank technology and doctrine; and the generals' refusal to reconsider obsolete armor doctrine.

A pioneering work is Col. Charles Baily's 1983 *Faint Praise: American Tanks and Tank Destroyers during World War II*, a brief introduction that emphasizes the military bureaucracy side of the problem, rather than the equally vital influence of civilian politics. Though many books are available on the engineering details of Shermans, Tigers, and Panthers, they often list specifications out of historical context, without detailing the complicated reasons why US tanks were designed differently from Germany's. *Arms of Destruction: Ranking the World's Best Land Weapons of WWII* (2004) contains a few chapters on the Sherman versus the T-34, Tiger, and Panther. A brief introduction to the controversy, it is a casual look rather than an exhaustive, extensively documented work.

Coverage of the troubling performance of American tanks in North Africa and Sicily is particularly weak. The general reader browsing a public library can find shelves full of books on Omaha Beach, but is hard pressed to find more than passing references to the humiliating routs at Kasserine Pass and El Guettar, or what a close-run thing the Sicilian invasion was, when a few Tigers nearly threw American Infantry back into the sea. Historians and Hollywood enamored of the Normandy epic (a tidy story with easily defined heroes and villains and a happy ending) have overlooked the more troubling campaigns, as well as the long, bitter tank war in the hills and mountains of Italy, a virtually forgotten theater today.

Judging from seventieth anniversary coverage of the war's major 1945 events that typically glossed over failures and foul-ups to focus on victories, one would think that for the United States, the war began on June 6, 1944. Then—according to this simplistic but pervasive story line—Roosevelt's invincible "Arsenal of Democracy" disgorged a horn of plenty full of advanced technology on the French coast, beginning an inevitable march to Berlin that rolled on Ford engines and Goodyear tires.

Today, the Omaha Beach cliché occupies an honored place in the war's mythology and how it is remembered in our pop culture, while the two years of embarrassing defeats that preceded Operation Overlord, from Bataan to Kasserine Pass, are little known and virtually ignored; who in 2017 cries for the men of Corregidor? The Normandy campaign has been glorified, wrapped in a halo of "Greatest Generation" heroics, but few are aware of the brutal tank fighting in Normandy that a German Korps commander called "a monstrous bloodbath."[52] To an American tank officer in the Second Armored Division, fighting SS Panzers was "the most Godless sight I have ever witnessed on any battlefield."[53]

There are a few books that discuss the Army's high-level doctrinal climate of the era, but they overlook the complicity of civilian politicians and the point of view of the enlisted tanker. British Army Col. G. Macleod Ross, who served in the US during the war as Chief British Technical Liaison to the Ordnance Department, was involved in the design and production of American armor. His memoir *The Business of Tanks* is a Washington insider's perspective on Sherman tank production and mentions Roosevelt's role in the tank controversy. But while it has a few succinct chapters on the tank scandal, this excellent book is from an exclusively British and high-ranking view, focusing on British use of American Lend-Lease tanks.

*Tank Tactics from Normandy to Lorraine,* by Roman Jarymowycz, a former Canadian Army tank officer, includes a brief discussion of the scandal and relates methods Allied tankers were forced to use because their tanks were so inferior to Germany's. But it discusses detailed battlefield tactics almost in a vacuum, without explaining the complicated political, doctrinal, technological, and intelligence factors that forced desperate Allied tankers to resort to them.

As to personal accounts of the war, there are volumes on glamorous American "fly boys" in leather jackets and silk scarves, and about elite units such as the Airborne, Rangers, and OSS. And judging from the overabundance of books celebrating scrappy US Marines in the Pacific, one would think the US Army was AWOL from that theater.

But personal accounts of the Sherman tank scandal's main victims—the enlisted or non-commissioned Army combat tanker—are rare. The Army Ordnance Department's official histories[54] are surprisingly candid in some ways, but they reflect the perspective of stateside generals and civilian politicians seeking to preserve careers and reputations by attempting to explain away the M4's shortcomings. There are a few memoirs by individual tankers[55] recounting personal stories (including the notorious *Death Traps*, which, along with heated opposition to some of its controversial claims, raised questions about the extent of a ghost writer's assistance to Lt. Cooper in compiling "his" firsthand recollections), but until now no comprehensive, big picture history of GI tankers' struggle to defeat superior German tanks with the mediocre M4.

Historian Arthur Schlesinger, looking back almost six decades later, recalled "It was, I suppose, a Good War. But like all wars, our war was accompanied by atrocity and sadism, by stupidity and lies, pomposity and chickenshit."[56] A fresh, unsentimental

Lt. Gen. Leslie J. McNair. *US Army Signal Corps*

France 1945: Wrecked Sherman tanks at an Army Ordnance depot.

who had "given his life for his country." But an unsentimental look reveals an arrogant politician who cold-bloodedly ordered the Army to build thousands of inferior tanks so he could respond to the *blitzkrieg* of 1940 with dramatic political gestures, reciting large figures of future tank production in his radio "fireside chats."

Five years later, notwithstanding his 1945 State of the Union Address promises to the troops and the nation that "Everything we are and have will be given,"[57] Roosevelt failed to get the new T26 heavy tank to the front when it was desperately needed. Yet reverential books still claim it arrived in the nick of time. Or, as a dual biography of Roosevelt and Marshall claims, we read categorical assertions such as by the summer of 1944, "at this point in the war, though the armament might be improved, a new tank could hardly appear in time to save the situation."[58] Never mind that design work on more powerful tank guns and on the up-gunned, up-armored T26 heavy tank had been

look at the Sherman tank scandal from the GI tankers' perspective reveals his leaders' negligence and their continued failure to supply him with tanks at least as good as Germany's, if not better. Not only did stateside leaders downplay combat soldiers' warnings and reject solutions that might have been implemented before 1945, they decreased tank production and tanker training for 1944, hoping to muddle through with the under-gunned, poorly armored M4, and with the exhausted tank crews on hand.

Misguided high-level decisions led to a shortage of tanks, spare parts, and tankers, forcing the use of decoy tactics that sacrificed GIs as literal "Tiger bait." When newspapers at home cheered a Tiger tank's destruction, they may have had no idea it might have required the loss of multiple Shermans and the death or wounding of some of the poorly trained (or untrained) crewmen inside them.

After Victory in Europe (VE) Day, the tank controversy was whitewashed. Roosevelt, Patton, and Gen. Lesley McNair died during or shortly after the war, conveniently shielding them and their wartime decisions from criticism. Like other presidents who have died in office, Roosevelt was canonized as a virtual martyr

proceeding since 1942, or that Eisenhower and Patton had been offered—but refused—more powerful tanks since before the Normandy landings.

The high-ranking culprits closed ranks. Blame has fallen on Gen. Lesley McNair (who, killed during the war by "friendly fire," was unable to defend himself) as a scapegoat—as if one man could be solely responsible for such a multifaceted problem. Generals eager to advance to high command after the war gave "explanations" that went unchallenged. While McNair has been excoriated, few works examine the roles of Roosevelt, Marshall, Eisenhower, and Patton, although all share responsibility in failing to address and then denying the problem.

Benefiting from his reputation as a caring leader, Eisenhower became the first general since Ulysses S. Grant to win the White House. At that time, being totally forthcoming about wartime failures of tank design and armor doctrine—failures in which he bore some responsibility as the Supreme Commander in Europe—would not have enhanced his kindly grandfather image. And as the Cold War heated up other reasons arose to overlook the wartime tank scandal. With outnumbered US and NATO forces facing the monolithic, tank-heavy Red Army in Europe, the 1950s was not the time to challenge upbeat wartime propaganda and expose problems with American weapons in a conflict just ended, nor to demand a reckoning from wartime leaders. Rather, the reassuring myth of the "Arsenal of Democracy" was sustained and perpetuated.

In postwar Germany, an idea took hold: that the Third Reich's soldiers had lost not through lack of ability or will, but were overwhelmed by Detroit's assembly lines. Resentful German veterans spoke of massive Allied advantages in aircraft, artillery, and vehicles. They argued the American and British conscript soldier was inferior to Germany's finest, who had not fallen to a better opponent, but to greater numbers of machinery. It was an echo of the "stab-in-the-back" myth of 1918: instead of being fairly defeated in WWI, the German army had been betrayed by its political leaders. This idea was barely contested by the Allies during the Cold War because West Germany was needed as an ally against the Soviet Union.

Along with encouraging the perception of superior American weapons in the 1950s went the desire to conserve friendly lives (and take more enemy lives) through technological superiority—"more bang for the buck." Why lead human waves of men in suicide attacks as the Red Army had done and the Chinese and North Koreans in the Korean War when the US Army had tactical nuclear artillery, as well as the ultimate manifestation of the "Arsenal of Democracy," the atomic bomb?

To set the stage for a fresh look at the Sherman tank scandal, recall that with the 1960s and '70s came widespread public distrust in government and military leaders and an ever-widening "credibility gap." After Vietnam, Watergate, and revelations of CIA covert activities, popular culture imagined government conspiracies and cover-ups everywhere, yet unsentimental criticism of the conduct of America's leaders in "The Good War" seemed to be off limits. Certainly there were films and novels that showed American military incompetence in WWII (such as *Catch-22* and *Slaughterhouse Five*), but unlike the Vietnam War, the older conflict and the men who led and fought it were often portrayed through a sentimental haze, an aura of glory and honor.

Even disillusioned 1960s anti-military types pointed with pride to their fathers and uncles of the GI generation, the soldier heroes of their youth. To draft dodgers of the Woodstock generation, perhaps attempting to compensate for their own shame, the American soldier in Vietnam was epitomized by the drug-addled hooch burners of the My Lai Massacre. Yet their relatives who had served in "The Good War" were often depicted as larger than life, like Sergeant Rock in the comic books or Vic Morrow as Sergeant Saunders on TV's *Combat*. On the big screen, John Wayne, Robert Mitchum, and Henry Fonda rallied the troops to victory on Omaha Beach in *The Longest Day*. In this distorted version of popular history, how could Lt. Calley compete with Audie Murphy?

As a graduate student in military history after the September 11, 2001, terrorist attacks, and as a Cavalry trooper recently returned from service in Bosnia-Herzegovina in 2002–2003, I became very aware of this dichotomy in how the two wars are portrayed today. I had a socialist history professor at Temple University who took fierce pride in his opposition to the Vietnam War and in his draft dodging. An educated, intelligent man with a PhD, he once assured me—a soldier just home from Bosnia—that my fellow GIs in Vietnam often threw innocent civilians out of helicopters for entertainment, and regularly committed unspeakable atrocities as a matter of formal policy. He assumed the worst of the American soldier in Vietnam and of his leadership.

But without skipping a beat, the same professor who denigrated the Vietnam grunts' service (after he had avoided serving himself) could get misty-eyed speaking of his admiration for a soldier: an uncle of his that had been killed in Normandy. Clearly he was deeply affected by his uncle's service. He would talk bitterly about the American leadership that (he claimed) sent over 58,000 men to senseless deaths in Vietnam, yet at the same time, he held the actions of FDR and other leaders who sent his young uncle to his death in Normandy seemingly above reproach.

As Vietnam receded somewhat into the past—though always lurking in the American cultural background—a curious phenomenon arose among media and Hollywood: some who had opposed America's political and military establishment during the Vietnam era began to romanticize WWII, now sanctified as "the good war." With starry-eyed reverence, draft dodgers of 1969 referred to the men who served in the earlier war not as baby killers or lowly, dehumanized "grunts," but as "The Greatest Generation"—in capital letters no less.

So why does the otherwise disillusioned Woodstock generation, in popular works on World War II, show such a romanticized view of America's political and military leadership in the 1940s? Might their fawning reflect guilt over their *own* misconduct during the Vietnam War? After all, honoring your uncles who survived the Kasserine Pass in Tunisia, braved flak "so thick you could walk on it" to bomb Berlin in '43, or who helped liberate Manila with the First Cavalry Division in '45 diverts attention from what members of this generation were doing in 1969. Spitting on returning wounded GIs can't compare to storming Omaha Beach in what Ike sanctified as "The Great Crusade," or what FDR described as "a mighty endeavor to preserve…our civilization, and to set free a suffering humanity."[59]

The 1960s generation spoke of never trusting anyone over thirty. When its members were young, it was easy for draft dodgers to protest and dehumanize the Vietnam GI, because few college-age, upper middle class student protestors had a personal connection to the drafted, ethnic, often working class "grunts" mostly fighting the war.

While politicians in the Vietnam era were mistrusted and the worst was assumed of them, WWII leadership was often portrayed with a romantic gloss: noble, true, and honest. But Franklin Roosevelt was happy to engage in deception toward the American people; to Harold Lasswell, involved with Roosevelt's Orwellian Office of Facts and Figures (OFF), propaganda needed "a large element of fake in it…. That only truthful statements should be used…seems an impractical maxim." To the University of Chicago's Sherman Dryer, who wrote *Radio In Wartime* in 1942, "The strategy of truth…is a handicap. It might enhance the integrity of our officialdom, but it is a moot question whether it will enhance the efficiency or the effectiveness of our efforts to elicit concerned action from the public."[60]

If the same distrust of Vietnam-era leaders was extended back to WWII, it might open to question the heretical idea that

President Roosevelt might not have been a martyr. If those who accused the Vietnam grunt of atrocities (while avoiding service beside him) put the GI and his leaders under the same microscope, they might have to call into question a dad who sweated out the "88s" on the beaches of Anzio, or a beloved uncle who rolled to glory across France with Patton, or perhaps a Marine relative who held the line on Guadalcanal in the dark days of 1942.

To Paul Fussell, cultural critic and WWII Army Infantry officer, "There has been so much talk about 'The Good War,' the Justified War, the Necessary War, and the like, that the young and the innocent could get the impression that it was really not such a bad thing after all."[61] The mantle of sappy reverence wrapped around the American leadership in the war cheapens the sacrifice and suffering of the common enlisted GI who fought on in spite of his leaders' callousness and incompetence.

The time has come for a reappraisal through the prism of the Sherman tank scandal.

This work is a loving tribute to the WWII tanker from a fellow tanker of a later generation. It is not presented in a spirit of malice towards the officer class; some of the key Army leaders involved in the controversy suffered as well. Gen. Lesley McNair (defender of the ill-fated tank destroyer concept) was one of the highest ranking American officers to be killed during the war—by "friendly fire" from American bombers over Normandy during Operation Cobra in July 1944. And while Gen. George Marshall failed to decisively address the shortcomings of American tanks and armor doctrine from the Pentagon, his beloved stepson, a Sherman tank commander, was killed in his M4 outside of Rome. Gen. Maurice Rose, who led the Fourth Armored Division, spoke up for the GIs, warning Eisenhower of problems with American tanks. Shortly afterward he was killed in action in Germany in the last weeks of the war after surrendering to a Tiger tank crew.

Do I have a bias here? Certainly, one of compassion toward the victims of the scandal: my fellow tankers, the Army enlisted man and non-commissioned officer whose sacrifices have remained largely unknown to the general public. If I show anger or a cynicism toward the powers-that-be or a hard edge towards the GIs' leadership, it comes from hands-on, real world experience as an enlisted soldier, a tanker, and an old US Cavalry sergeant.

Sgt. James Jones wrote in *From Here to Eternity* of the great distance between the GI and his leadership that affects written history—mostly by and for the officer class. This gap is particularly noticeable between the desk-bound, stateside brass and the enlisted soldiers serving in the field overseas, and it has helped to perpetuate wartime myths about the tank scandal for decades.

The distance between the common soldier and his leadership was driven home to me while serving as a dismounted Cavalry scout with the historic First Troop Philadelphia City Cavalry, part of the 1/104th Cavalry Regiment, 28th Infantry Division, in rural Bosnia-Herzegovina in 2002–2003. In between missions, my squad would stop for chow at Eagle Base, near Tuzla, a major US Army base in Bosnia. A few hours there was a treat, because compared to our tiny Forward Observation Base Morgan (a frontier outpost not much larger than a football field), Eagle Base had a full range of impressive amenities, from a bigger PX to the latest *Sopranos* and *Band of Brothers* DVDs from the States.

The author serving as a member of the First Troop Philadelphia City Cavalry, NATO Stabilization Force (SFOR) 12, Bosnia-Herzegovina, 2002–2003.

While focused on things like avoiding land mines, drunk Serbian snipers, driving near and through mine fields, Al Queda cells shadowing us, rumors of booby traps with trip wires set at the height of a man's groin, and even plots to mortar our base using a pickup truck, or to drop chemical agents using a small, light plane—here, at Camp McGovern, a rear-area base, I looked on in amazement at clean-shaven officers in starched, creased uniforms and shiny boots; quite a contrast to us "field" Cavalry troopers. I listened in disbelief as pampered colonels and majors pondered what were to them the weightier decisions of the day: while my mind was preoccupied with mine fields, snipers, IEDs, and Al Queda plots, the brass debated in loud voices whether to enjoy steak or lobster tail for dinner that night.

Is it any wonder that much military history reflects the views of the officer class to the detriment of the enlisted GI? I can only nod in agreement when reading James Jones's dead-on comments about this rank bias in many accounts. Concerning the dishonesty of the WWII GIs' political leaders, who substituted denials for meaningful action, I can relate completely; I see the months after September 11, 2001, as a replay of the politicians' reaction to the blitzkrieg of 1940–41.

As a soldier who finished Basic Combat Training in the late 1990s, I witnessed the results of cuts to the Army's training budget. We were unable to receive full instruction and practice in such basic skills as rifle marksmanship and hand grenades. Shortages were so bad soldiers were getting stomach viruses because, after training in the field, crawling through mud and sand, they could not wash their hands before eating dinner; often, there were no bars of soap or paper towels in the chow hall latrine, and we were told no funding for them. Yet our civilian leaders, unwilling to fund bullets, found the money for "diversity and

Operation Bright Star, Egypt 2005: 1/104th Cavalry Abrams tanks in the Sahara desert. The author served as an M1A1 tank gunner in this multinational wargame.

attacks in rapid succession, were symbols of American freedom like Philadelphia's Independence Hall or the Liberty Bell next?

Concerned but eager, I dutifully climbed to the roof. With the radio I was in touch with other Troopers on the ground, who inquired along the lines of "Why is that U-Haul truck driving the wrong way down a one-way street, toward

sensitivity training" in topics peripheral to being a United States Army soldier.

This "instruction" had more to do with attempting to force feed current social and political agendas to a captive audience of impressionable young adults. Some of these soldiers may have been killed a few years later in Afghanistan, Iraq, and other places, because instead of banging away at the rifle range learning basic marksmanship skills they were forced to attend mandatory "classes" foisted on the Army by politicians who viewed the United States Army not as the bedrock of America's defense, but rather as a petri dish for radical social change. Here, in a social scientists' dream come true, a captive audience of young recruits could be indoctrinated in the latest trendy ideas on "cultural diversity" and "multiculturism" dreamed up by a far away, pampered academic elite.

While it is easy today to mock the US Army's unpreparedness in WWII, history has a funny way of repeating itself; I grew up reading of clerks at Pearl Harbor who refused to unlock gun vaults and issue weapons even as the attack was going on without written orders from an officer. I also chuckled at the naiveté of West Coast civilians, including well-meaning teenage boys who took it upon themselves to patrol lonely beaches at night, presuming their trusty Daisy "Red Ryder" BB guns would be enough to repulse the Japanese hordes in the expected invasion of California.

On September 11, 2001, my gut reaction to the attacks was to get into Army uniform, pack a duffel bag with a few days' worth of clothes and supplies, and in the finest National Guard citizen soldier tradition show up without being ordered at the historic armory of my First Troop Philadelphia City Cavalry, in Center City Philadelphia.

There I was met by my platoon sergeant, SFC Logan Fenstermacher, a long-serving, wise old soldier and pillar of the unit who praised me for showing up on my own, handed me a backpack radio and binoculars, and sent me up to the roof of the armory to scout for suspicious vehicles, aircraft, and individuals. Meanwhile, confusing reports of the attacks were flooding in and being passed on: Manhattan, Arlington, and Pennsylvania. With three

the armory?" I also watched Philadelphia Police helicopters fly close to me, understandably curious (given the ongoing attacks) as to why a man in full camouflage uniform was scoping them out with binoculars, then giving them a friendly wave, as if I had "okayed" their presence.

With my adrenaline and patriotism at a peak, it took a minute to laugh at the fact that until Sgt. Fenstermacher downstairs was able to cut through the red tape surrounding the SOP to open our arms vault to issue weapons and ammunition if needed (shades of December 7, 1941), none of us well-meaning citizen soldiers was (officially) armed. Had we received orders to repel an attack on Philadelphia, my contribution as then equipped might have amounted to throwing a radio or pair of binoculars at the enemy, or climbing down off the roof to retrieve an original 1861 lance or "War Between the States" Cavalry saber from our museum, the better to wield them once again.

So while it is easy decades later to laugh at American soldiers in 1940 forced to train with broomsticks for rifles and sacks of flour as hand grenades during a national emergency, I can relate to their unpreparedness in a highly personal way.

In the finest Minuteman tradition, those of us who had reported for duty without orders were ready to move out if needed, well ahead of the official calls to duty from our state officials, who had to follow a large "phone chain" of calls and authorizations—not very efficient under the chaotic circumstances. In an era of political correctness, our kinder, gentler Army hands out "awards" for things like completing basic, or for showing up somewhat sober at the airport for the flight home from a deployment. But those few of us who were at the First City Troop Armory on that dramatic September 11 will always treasure the Army Achievement Medals we were awarded a year later (while the 1/104th Cavalry was serving in Bosnia) for "ensuring the unit was ready to perform all tasks…during the National crisis," actions which "reflect great credit upon himself, his unit, and the Pennsylvania Army National Guard."

After the September 11 attacks, I watched politicians who had short-changed GIs in the late 1990s stand on the steps of the US Capitol. Waving little American flags for the cameras, they

assured us they were all "behind our troops." Though they sent soldiers to places like Afghanistan, Iraq, Bosnia, and Kosovo with the barest of supplies and training, for their nightly on-camera "sound bites" on the national TV news these non-veterans were sure to wear the seemingly obligatory US flag pin on their lapels.

I deployed to Bosnia in 2002 with obsolete body armor, twenty-year-old broken radios, and 1942-manufactured and -dated .50-caliber machine gun ammunition. But the politicians were sure to slap "Support Our Troops" yellow ribbon bumper stickers on their chauffeured limousines on their way to a three-martini lunch in Georgetown as my fellow GIs and I in Yugoslavia ate cold MREs.

Later, as an M1A1 Abrams tank gunner during Operation Bright Star in 2005—a massive, multinational war game in Egypt—I watched hard working young soldiers without showers, hot food, laundry, e-mail, phones, or mail. While they toiled on without complaining in the 115-degree Sahara Desert heat, rear-echelon officers helped themselves to the finest supplies and equipment (supposed to be issued to all), forcing us "Combat Arms" types to equip ourselves at our own expense.

A cynical old Cavalry sergeant, I was proud to work beside young privates in oil-stained, sweaty uniforms, lying on their backs under Abrams tanks surrounded by tools for removing engine packs. Later, I watched incredulously as clean-shaven, clean-smelling generals and colonels in starched uniforms approached us. They were on their way to happy hour and an elegant dinner at the Cairo Hilton (whisked there in their own private helicopters), while we Cavalry troopers could only look forward to more hours of backbreaking work. After that, a hasty MRE, a towel bath from a canteen, and a few hours restless sleep in an Egyptian army tent surrounded by snakes, spiders, scorpions, and packs of wild jackals and thieving Bedouins.

But on the way to their Cairo cocktail party, the generals assured us lowly grunts, "Son, I know just how you feel."

After such experiences, I can identify with the enlisted Army tanker of 1941–1945. I understand his anger towards desk-bound generals and Roosevelt administration officials who depicted the M4 as the best tank on the battlefield. Having seen (or personally experienced) Sherman tanks burst into flame after taking one or two hits from more powerful German Panzers and lost friends in tank battles, the GI took a dim view of articles in the *Stars and Stripes* in which generals safe at home implied that he did not know what he was talking about.

Thanks to the propaganda, we have a sugarcoated image of the American soldier as virginal, dewy-cheeked, and wide-eyed. But to Sgt. James Jones, "There was a lot more bitterness in World War II than historians allow.... Basically, the men were bitter at getting their asses shot off."[62] To Jones, the GI "was about the foulest-mouthed individual who ever existed on earth.

The Sahara desert: Author with an M1A1 Abrams tank of his 1/104th Cavalry in Egypt during Operation Bright Star multinational wargame.

Every other word was fucking this or fucking that. And internally, his soul was about as foul and as cynical as his mouth. He trusted nobody but his immediate outfit, and often not them.... He had pared his dreams and ambitions down to no more than relief and a few days away from the line, and a bottle of booze, a woman, and a bath."[63]

If by 1944, GI tankers were far removed from the happy-go-lucky, trusting innocents in the 1942 newsreels, it was because of things like the tank scandal. The GI's political and military leadership failed him, singing Rooseveltian hymns to democracy even as they sent them to their deaths in inadequate tanks. Yet this tragedy that killed and wounded thousands of men remains little known. New works continue to repeat cheery, sanitized views of "the good war."

As a disabled Army veteran and old Abrams tank gunner, I identify more with James Jones's cynical GIs than with the one-dimensional characters of wartime myth: naïve, virginal youth dreaming of mom and apple pie, singing "Don't Sit Under the Apple Tree" as they cheerfully march into the fray. After fifteen years of research into the obstacles these men faced, the fact they repeatedly climbed back into their under-gunned, inadequately armored M4s to fight more powerful enemy tanks—in the face of lies and denials from their leaders—only increases my admiration of them.

The tank scandal resembles the 1920s air power debate, which culminated in the court martial of Gen. Billy Mitchell: a new weapon arises to challenge the dominance of the older branches of a stuffy, hidebound Army. Its leaders, jealous of their bureaucratic turf, oppose the upstarts. The innovators are shunned, but though impudent and controversial, they are ultimately proven right—in Mitchell's case vindicated in December 1941, on a quiet Sunday morning in Hawaii.

But the tankers lacked a champion as forceful as Gen. Mitchell to make the case for better tanks and doctrine, which may partly explain why today the controversy is not as well known as the Billy Mitchell fight. As will be seen, Col. George Jarrett at Aberdeen Proving Ground (one of the Army's most knowledgeable experts on captured enemy ordnance) tried to warn generals of problems with US tank guns, and to speak truthfully to civilian audiences in wartime, but he was censored and ostracized when he refused to "toe the line" coming down from his Ordnance Department superiors.

Thankfully, Col. Jarrett wrote his expert opinions on the unfolding Sherman tank scandal in pungent comments in a wartime scrapbook ("My Little Green Book") filled with hand-annotated newspaper clippings. Finding it in 2005 among his personal papers at the Army's Military History Institute while researching this book was a revelation to me; here was an Army Ordnance officer who tried to speak up for the GIs with integrity and courage, only to be silenced. Fittingly, after retiring from the Army, Col. Jarrett (who as a teenager amassed a huge collection of Great War militaria) was placed in charge of the Army's tank and ordnance collection at Aberdeen Proving Ground, Maryland. Yet to the best of my knowledge, his part in the tank scandal has never been widely told until now.

Beyond the boasts and denials of career generals and Roosevelt administration officials was another hero of the scandal: the lowly American draftee GI tanker who fought on to victory in the face of his leaders' lies and obstinacy.

The Sherman tank scandal is still eerily relevant; decades later, GIs are again sent off to far away wars with inferior equipment while their flag-waving political and military leadership assure the American public that all is well from the comfort of their Washington offices.

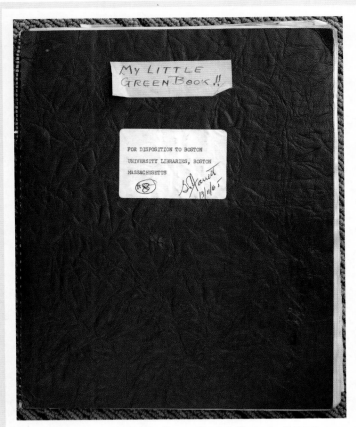

Col. George Jarrett's "Little Green Book." *Photo by Robert Coldwell Sr., courtesy of the US Army Military History Institute, Carlisle Barracks, Pennsylvania.*

Compared to his Great War predecessors, the soldier of the 1940s was notoriously unsentimental, but a poem by British Infantryman Herbert Read, "To A Conscript of 1940," in which the ghost of an old soldier addresses a new generation, could apply to the Allied tankers of WWII:

> We went where you are going, into the rain and the mud:
> We fought as you will fight
> With death and darkness and despair;
> We gave what you will give—our brains and our blood.
>
> …But you my brother and my ghost, if you can go
> Knowing that there is no reward, no certain use
> In all your sacrifice, then honour is reprieved.
>
> To fight without hope is to fight with grace.[64]

Paul Fussell observed that an honest book about WWII should offend the critics for "damaging numerous sentimentalities and exposing many merely patriotic certainties."[65] As the seventieth anniversary of the war's end was celebrated in 2015, I heard the same tired old numbers, statistics, and figures. While they are not to be discounted, I hope to bring to life another set of figures of which war correspondent Ernie Pyle wrote in notes found on his body after he was killed by a Japanese sniper on tiny Ie Shima Island in April 1945.

After years of covering the war in Europe and the Pacific, Pyle wrote in a draft of his uncompleted last column of "the unnatural sight of cold dead men scattered over the hillsides and in the ditches along the high rows of hedge throughout the world…. Dead men by mass production…in such familiar promiscuity that they become monotonous…. These are the things that you at home need not even try to understand. To you at home, they are columns of figures."[66]

These are the "figures" I hope to bring to life with this book: the over 60,000 American armored division men (including tank crewmen, but excluding casualties in the bloody Italian theater tank fighting) that Gen. George Marshall reported to Congress as killed and wounded in the European Theater of Operations.[67]

In 1945, at the height of Marshall's fame as the "Architect of Victory," he submitted a detailed "Report on the Winning of the War" to Congress and the American people. Marshall inspired such George Washington–like awe that he could make kings, prime ministers, field marshals, generals, and admirals jump to their feet just by walking into Allied conferences. Yet even the humble Midwestern American press sensed something amiss in his "explanations" for the tank scandal.

"Human nature being what it is," observed "Omissions in the Record," an October 21, 1945, *Kansas City Star* editorial, "a record written by one of the leading participants is bound to show omissions, to gloss over certain mistakes, and to be less than candid in some of its comments."

> There are certain obviously important points which General Marshal did not feel free to discuss…. The question of the quality of the American tanks is passed over rather lightly by the Chief of Staff…he avoids the real points at issue…the men who operated our tanks were acutely aware of their deficiencies…but why they were not cured earlier remains a mystery.

"These points," concluded the *Star*, "will require discussion by future historians."[68]

With these questions in mind, an old US Cavalry tanker will examine the many complicated factors—technical issues, Army and civilian politics, confusion over evolving armor doctrine, the experience of frontline GIs, intelligence failures, and the role of the stateside civilian press—in the first comprehensive survey of the Sherman tank scandal of WWII.

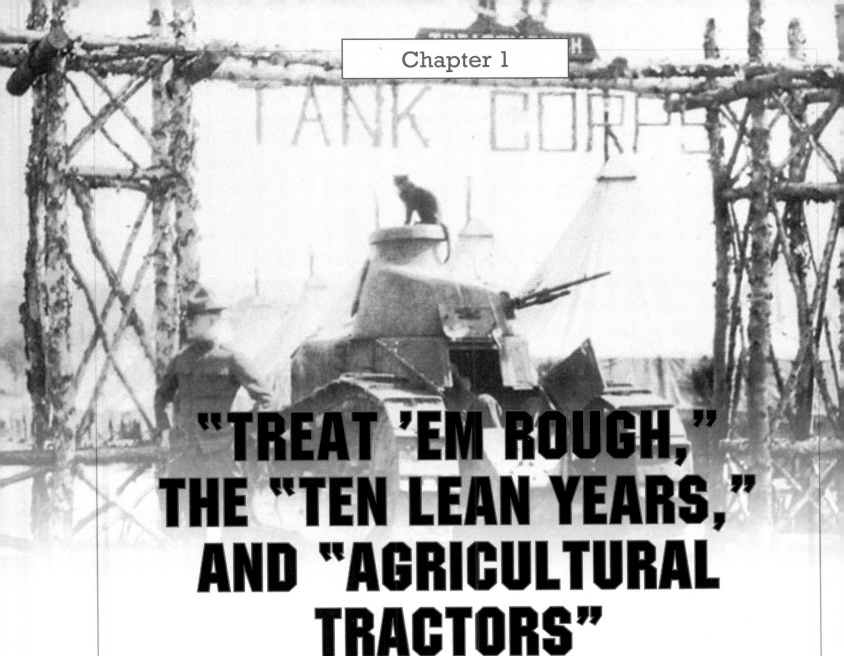

# Chapter 1

# "TREAT 'EM ROUGH," THE "TEN LEAN YEARS," AND "AGRICULTURAL TRACTORS"

## Beginnings: "Treat 'Em Rough"

In WWII, the mere presence of a German Tiger or Panther tank could rout American or British troops, but during WWI, when British tanks made breakthroughs at Cambrai (November 1917) and other battlefields, it was terrified *German* Infantry that fled in confusion. Recalled German veteran Erich Maria Remarque in *All Quiet on the Western Front*:

The tanks have become a terrible weapon. Armoured, they come rolling on in long lines, and more than anything else embody for us the horror of war. We do not see the guns that bombard us; the attacking lines of enemy Infantry are men like ourselves; but these tanks are machines, their caterpillars run on as endless as the war, they are annihilation, they roll without feeling into craters and climb up again without stopping, a fleet of roaring, smoke-belching, armour-clad, invulnerable steel beasts squashing the dead and the wounded- we shrink up in our thin skin before them;

The Tank Service should be under the general supervision of the Chief of Infantry, and should not constitute an independent service.[1]
—A War Department board on the future of tanks, 1919

against their colossal weight our arms are sticks of straw, and our hand-grenades matches.[3]

Today, it is hard to appreciate the sense of awe the new weapon inspired. British Capt. Richard Haight, MC, was one of the first tankers:

TANKS! To the uninitiated…the name conjures up a picture of an iron monster, breathing fire and exhaling bullets and shells, hurling itself against the enemy, unassailable by man and impervious to the most deadly engines of war; sublime, indeed, in its expression of indomitable power and resolution.[4]

"We were different," recalled an American tank pioneer, then-Capt. Dwight D. Eisenhower. In early 1918, he arrived at Camp Meade, Maryland, to lead the 301st Heavy Tank Battalion, hopefully to France. "The men dreamed of overwhelming assault

Over the Top, 1918: British troops ride on the back of a Mark IV tank.

A rare British Mk. IV tank under restoration. *Author photo courtesy of the National Armor and Cavalry Heritage Foundation*

Col. George S. Patton Jr., 1919. *US National Archives*

LITTLE WILLIE
-1915-

## JOIN THE TANKS
### SEE SERVICE SOON
Treat 'em rough!

Capt. Dwight Eisenhower, Camp Colt, Gettysburg, Pennsylvania, 1918.

Camp Colt, the Army's new Tank Corps training center:

My orders were specific, indeed rigid. I was required to take in volunteers, equip, organize, and instruct them and have them ready for overseas shipment when called upon. The orders warned that my camp was not only a point of mobilization, but of embarkation. This meant that the troops sent from Gettysburg would go directly to a port without any intermediate stops.[6]

But Eisenhower and his tankers would never get "over there." For the United States in the Great War, although politicians boasted of sending a tidal wave of then-unbuilt American weapons to the battlefields, even predicting the manufacture of 23,405 light and heavy tanks,[7] tank production was too little, too late. To save time, the Army would copy the French Renault FT-17 light model and the British Mark V heavy. Ford Motor Company—experts at mass production of automobiles—contracted to deliver 15,015 light tanks.[8]

on enemy lines, rolling effortlessly over wire entanglements and trenches, demolishing gun nests with their fire, and terrorizing the foe into quick and abject surrender."[5] Soon after, Capt. Eisenhower was assigned to Gettysburg, Pennsylvania, to set up

But not a single American-designed or -built tank reached the front. Only fifteen of the small, two-man "6-Ton Tank M1917s" (a license-built FT-17) were completed in the US before the war ended.[9] Historian Dale Wilson has shown that even with shortcuts like copying Allied designs, US tank production was plagued by production delays and bureaucratic infighting—problems that would be repeated during WWII.

It was planned to mate thousands of American-built Liberty V-12 aircraft engines to new Mark VIII "International" or "Liberty" heavy tanks assembled in France, but not a single engine made it overseas before the Armistice. Foreshadowing the WWII failure to get decisive numbers of the T26 heavy tank to the front, in 1918, the Mark VIIIs did not arrive in Europe until after the guns fell silent. Designers could not even agree on the right machine gun (the Marlin-Rockwell, made for aircraft use, was chosen, then abandoned after months of testing), or whether the gauges in American tanks should measure speed and distance in miles or kilometers.[10]

The promised flood of American arms to rescue exhausted European Allies evaporated in failure. To Dale Wilson, it was "one of history's great ironies" that "the nation that spawned the technology from which the tank was created did not play a role in the vehicle's conception. It is equally ironic that the United States, which later became known as the 'Arsenal of Democracy,' was unable to produce a single armored vehicle that saw combat with its Tank Corps."[11]

The US Tank Corps saw action late in the war in the Saint-Mihiel and Argonne offensives of September–October 1918. Adopting the motto "Treat 'em Rough," its men had an aggressive black cat as a mascot, shown on vivid recruiting posters as sweeping the battlefield of German tanks. America's first tankers hoped to fulfill the predictions of British theorists J. F. C. Fuller and Basil Liddell-Hart, who envisioned masses of Allied tanks bursting into the enemy's undefended rear areas with shock and surprise, opening holes for waves of Infantry behind them. In Fuller's proposed "Plan 1919," thousands would lead the charge into Germany.

In spite of the valor and dash of tank pioneers like Col. George S. Patton Jr. (who led the 304th Tank Brigade equipped with light Renault FT-17s), their French and British vehicles were plagued by breakdowns; more were lost to mechanical failure than to enemy fire. There was also the inevitable confusion that comes with learning to use a new weapon. The American 301st Heavy Tank Battalion, using borrowed British Mark V heavy tanks, supported Allied attacks on the Hindenberg line. As a rueful after-action report observed, "Due to the fact that the 27th Division had never had an actual operation with tanks, the Infantry commanders did not seem to grasp the idea of tanks cooperating with Infantry."[12]

In July 1917, Col. Patton wrote to his staff that the new machines were "not worth a damn."[13] By January 1918, his outlook had improved: "I feel sure that tanks in some form will play a part in all future wars,"[14] he wrote home to his wife Beatrice. He had attended British and French tank schools, and set up an American training camp close to Langres, France, with twenty-two borrowed Renault FT-17 two-man light tanks. In a February 21, 1918, letter to Beatrice he was more optimistic: "The tanks have attracted a lot of good men, and I get requests from them to transfer into tanks nearly daily."[15]

After the Armistice, tank pioneers Eisenhower and Patton served together at Camp Meade. They shared a "strong belief in tanks," Eisenhower recalled,

> a belief derided at the time by others. George and I and a group of young officers...believed that tanks could have a more valuable and spectacular role. We believed

# Join the Black Toms
### *( The Tanks )*
TANK CORPS RECRUITING OFFICE
19 W. 44th STREET      NEW YORK
# They Treat 'em Rough

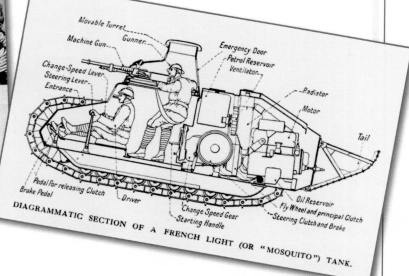

DIAGRAMMATIC SECTION OF A FRENCH LIGHT (OR "MOSQUITO") TANK.

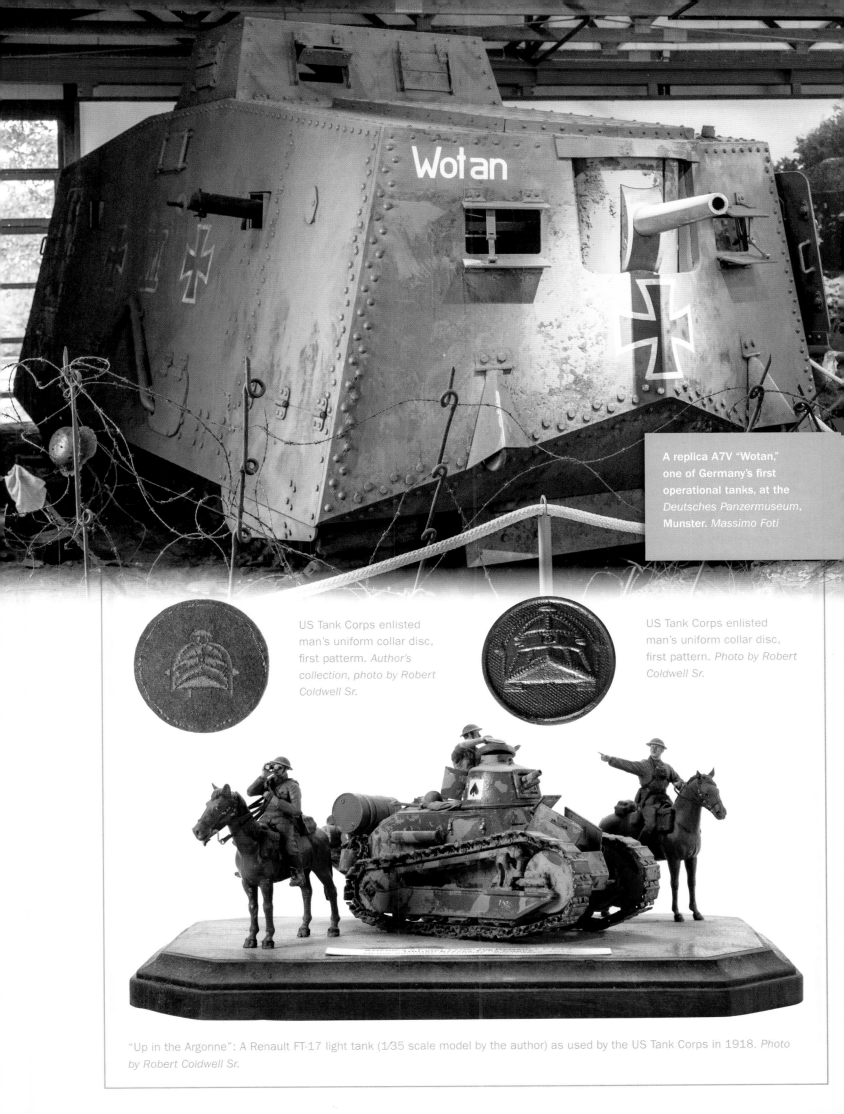

A replica A7V "Wotan," one of Germany's first operational tanks, at the *Deutsches Panzermuseum*, Munster. *Massimo Foti*

US Tank Corps enlisted man's uniform collar disc, first pattern. *Author's collection, photo by Robert Coldwell Sr.*

US Tank Corps enlisted man's uniform collar disc, first pattern. *Photo by Robert Coldwell Sr.*

"Up in the Argonne": A Renault FT-17 light tank (1/35 scale model by the author) as used by the US Tank Corps in 1918. *Photo by Robert Coldwell Sr.*

Detail of the track on a preserved Mk V "Star." *Courtesy of the National Armor and Cavalry Heritage Foundation*

Restored British Mk V "Star" heavy tank used by the American 301st (Heavy) Tank Battalion in 1918. The red and white markings were used to distinguish companies within the unit. *Courtesy of the National Armor and Cavalry Heritage Foundation*

would be proof against machine guns and light field guns, but not so heavy as to damage mobility.[16]

they would attack by surprise and in mass. We wanted speed, reliability, and firepower. We wanted armor that

In September 1919, Patton was selected to serve on the Tank Corps Technical Board of Officers, whose members, noted

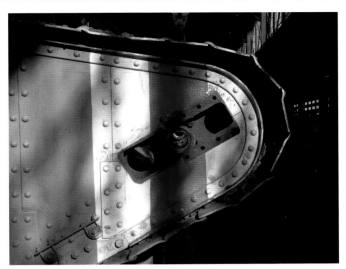

Rare British Mk V "Star" used by the American 301st Heavy Tank Battalion in 1918. *Author photo courtesy of the National Armor and Cavalry Heritage Foundation*

Captain Dwight Eisenhower and Renault FT-17 light tank.   *US National Archives*

TREAT 'EM ROUGH

Slam them, bang them.
Show you're tough,
To lick the Boches.
Treat 'Em Rough.

*Courtesy U.S. Army post museum, Fort Meade, Maryland*

As decades passed and WWII loomed, Patton grew more optimistic. Along with his US Cavalry colleagues Adna Chafee and Daniel Van Voorhis in the US, and fellow officers like Charles DeGaulle in France, Mikhail Tukhachevsky in the Soviet Union, and Heinz Guderian and Erwin Rommel in Germany, Patton recognized that once armor technology caught up with the promise it had shown in 1917–18, the tank would become a decisive weapon.

The irony is that a generation after Cambrai, the possibilities suggested there came to fruition, but not through the tank's British inventors, nor their American allies; instead, the Germans turned Fuller's ideas into the blitzkrieg that shocked the world in 1939–40.

WWI ended before the role of armor could be discerned by the major powers. In the US Army, the argument went on for decades through WWII, and was not settled until that war ended in 1945. After more than twenty-five years, competing branches within the Army could not agree on how to use the "new" weapon, nor even who should control it.

historian Martin Blumenson, "visited repair shops, studied preventive maintenance, recommended changes in the ammunition storage system, the driver's location, the engine, the eye slits, the foot accelerator, the ground clearance of the axles, the movable roof, the pistol ports, the antiaircraft protection, the seat suspension, the small-arms ammunition racks, and the placement of tools."[17] But after reading Fuller's 1920 *Tanks in the Great War*, Patton (celebrated today as an innovator in the use of armor) concluded that Fuller's "entire views are extreme and though sound, will not be realized in our generation."[18]

The spectacular promise of the tank—created to break the stalemate of trench warfare and restore mobility to the battlefield—had not been realized, partly due to the crude state of tank technology. After WWI, generals from older, rival branches threatened by the new invention viewed the inconclusive results as "proof" that the tank would not live up to its dazzling potential.

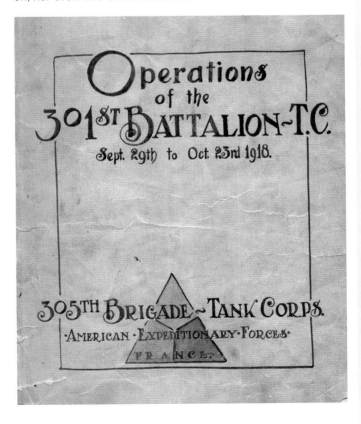

Operations of the 301st BATTALION-T.C.
Sept. 29th to Oct. 23rd 1918.

305TH BRIGADE~TANK CORPS.
·AMERICAN·EXPEDITIONARY·FORCES·
FRANCE.

In French Renault FT-17 light tanks, pioneer American tankers advance "Up the Argonne" to the climactic battles of the Great War.

HUNS DON'T LIKE THESE TANKS NOW, AND IF YOU BUY MORE LIBERTY BONDS THEY WILL LIKE THEM LESS

US Tank Corps wool sleeve patch: The "Armored Triangle" represents the mobility and dash of the Cavalry (yellow), the ground-holding tenacity of the Infantry (blue), and the firepower of the Artillery (red). *Author photo*

Enlisted man's collar disc, US Tank Corps, second pattern. *Author's collection, photo by Robert Coldwell Sr.*

US Army Great War Sergeant's rank insignia. The doughboy Army was so short-handed of basic issue items that often only one would be worn on a single sleeve. *Author's collection, photo by Robert Coldwell Sr.*

Camp Meade, Maryland: US Tank Corps soldiers pose around Mk VIII "Liberty" heavy tanks, 1921. Maj. George S. Patton Jr. (circled left) is next to Capt. Dwight D. Eisenhower (circled right).

In rearranging the US Army for peacetime after Armistice Day, the question arose what to do with the infant Tank Corps. The older Cavalry, Infantry, and Artillery branches were jealous of their turf. They viewed the new mechanical monster and its supporters with suspicion and hostility, much as they did the new US Army Air Service and its pugnacious apostle Gen. "Billy" Mitchell. The Tank Corps "should not be a large organization," testified General of the Armies John J. Pershing before Congress in 1919; it should be placed "under the Chief of Infantry as an adjunct to that arm."[19] Through the National Defense Act of 1920, rivals abolished the Tank Corps. Pershing's desire to put tanks under the thumb of Infantry control was followed, and Congress appropriated a mere $500 for tanks.[20] To rival branches, any hopes for a future independent Armored Force were seemingly destroyed.

Between the world wars there were three major American schools of thought on the tank's future role, which was hotly disputed within the Army. These competing theories and their

A British Mk IV tank (left) and an American Mk VIII "Liberty" International tank (right). *Author photo courtesy of the National Armor and Cavalry Heritage Foundation*

*Author photo courtesy post museum, US Army, Fort Meade, Maryland*

Gen. John Pershing. *Colorized portrait courtesy Mads Madsen*

powerful advocates would influence tank design and doctrine, and lead to the Sherman tank scandal of the 1940s.

Wanting to maintain its dominant position, the officers of the Infantry branch viewed the tank as a mere adjunct to soldiers on foot, existing only "to facilitate the uninterrupted and economical advance of the rifleman in the attack."[21] They restricted tanks to accompanying marching soldiers at foot-slogging speed. Tanks might stumble upon and engage stationary targets delaying the Infantry's advance, but were not to seek out or fight enemy tanks on their own. Supporters of this "Infantry tank" position saw the tank as a pillbox on wheels, and favored tank designs with lots of armor mounting machine guns rather than cannon. Critics of the Infantry's "rolling pillbox" position argued it nullified the tank's best attributes: speed, mobility, firepower, and shock.

Cavalrymen espoused a relatively moderate position; since tanks shared some of the best traits of the horse-mounted US Cavalry, traditional Cavalry doctrine could be transferred to them. Tanks could use speed and mobility for reconnaissance as cavaliers had done for centuries, probing ahead of the main force, scouting enemy weaknesses, and leading the main body to them

*The tank is new and, for the fulfillment of its destiny, it must remain independent. Not desiring or attempting to supplant Infantry, Cavalry, or artillery, it has no appetite to be absorbed by any of them…as an independent corps, we may assist any one of the arms as directed. Absorbed by any one of them, we become the stepchild of that arm and the incompetent assistant of either of the others…. Like the air service, tanks are destined for a separate existence.[2]*
*—Col. George S. Patton Jr., "Tanks in Future Wars" (1920)*

in surprise attacks. Speed and mobility were favored over firepower and armor protection. Tanks could be used to greatest effect by applying them to the enemy's weakest points: outposts, supply lines, and rear areas. Rather than duel one-on-one with enemy tanks—likely his most powerful weapon—the greatest destruction could occur at the least cost by hitting the enemy where he was most vulnerable. Supporters of this middle-ground view favored lightly armed and armored "Cavalry tanks," and this would be the prevailing doctrine going into WWII.

The most radical and contentious position espoused by a few prophets (which ultimately became official Army doctrine after WWII and beyond) went farther than moderates in the Cavalry. The advocates of this school of thought, rejecting Infantry control, held that tanks were a decisive new weapon that should be cut loose to aggressively seek out the enemy and destroy his tanks. Armor should be a fully independent branch not tied to and controlled by the Infantry.

Far from avoiding a fight with enemy tanks, if American tanks with powerful guns and decent armor protection could be massed they could act as a spearhead, leading the way for the Infantry and crushing all opposition. The best design for this role would

Gettysburg, Pennsylvania: A bronze plaque dedicated in 1954 by Tank Corps veterans to commemorate the previous site of Camp Colt in 1918. *Author photo*

combine firepower and armor with speed and mobility. Tank design is an eternal conflict between these factors; reducing or increasing one affects the others, so the ideal model is a balanced compromise between them.

After the 1918 Armistice, apostles of an independent tank branch were told to keep their radical ideas to themselves. The older arms (especially the Infantry and Artillery) sought to maintain their traditional dominance of the Army by marginalizing the threatening new upstart. Only three years after tanks led the American offensive in the Meuse-Argonne, a 1921 Army training manual, *Doctrines, Principles and Methods*, asserted the primacy of the Infantry, not even mentioning tanks.

In 1920, the influential *Infantry Journal* featured some predictions by Maj. Dwight Eisenhower. In a future war, the Kansan wrote, "tanks will be called upon to use their ability of swift movement and great fire power...against the flanks of attacking forces."[22]

Many years later, Eisenhower recalled a small group of tank officers who preached a gospel in which "tanks could have a more valuable and more spectacular role":

> We believed that they could be speedy, that they should attack by surprise and in mass. By making good use of terrain in advance, they could break into the enemy's defensive positions, cause confusion, and by taking the enemy frontline in reverse, make possible not only an advance by Infantry, but envelopments of, or actual breakthroughs in, whole defensive positions.[23]

For expressing such blasphemy, Eisenhower was threatened with court martial by Chief of Infantry Gen. Charles Farnsworth, and warned not to publicize his radical ideas again. As his biographer Carlo D'Este notes, Ike fell in line: "While a student at the Command and General Staff College, Eisenhower wrote that it was apparent that tanks could never take over the mission of the Infantry, no matter to what degree developed."[24]

Future general Bradford Chynoweth was friendly with Patton and Eisenhower. He observed that while the confrontational Patton was more outspoken in questioning Army doctrine, when Eisenhower was selected for and graduated from the prestigious Command and General Staff College, "Doctrine was his religion.... Ike had been 100 percent conformist, never deviated, and stood first in his class."[25]

The Army's higher levels had a stodgy climate that not only discouraged innovation and introspection, but—as Gen. "Billy" Mitchell learned—persecuted dissenters. A typical excuse for crushing rebellious ideas was that independent thinking was bad for morale. Officers attempting to question Army doctrine or equipment in professional journals not only had to get their commanding officer's blessing, but also faced censorship from journal editors. As the *Infantry Journal* cautioned in 1922:

> The Infantry Board will review certain classes of articles that pertain to Infantry equipment, prior to their publication in the *Infantry Journal*. This applies only to those articles that have a tendency to bring into the infantry-man's mind a suspicion that the equipment he is supplied with is not the very best that can be had for him. It can readily be seen that the army that does not believe in its equipment, weapons especially, is equal to, or superior to that of a possible enemy, will suffer to some degree in morale.[26]

The small, interwar peacetime Army was strapped for funding and stingy with promotions. It would take a brave man to publicly rock the boat on tank doctrine, and it would not be George S. Patton Jr. Initially, like Eisenhower, Col. Patton also published articles on the tank's potential and called for making them an independent branch. Also like Eisenhower, Patton received threats to keep silent. But he was careful to straddle the fence; as a recent biographer noted, "In a lecture at Fort Myer in 1933," Patton "articulated the many virtues of mechanized forces, both armored vehicles and tanks. In his conclusion, however, he

*Photo by Robert Coldwell Sr.*

Gen. Adna R. Chaffee recalled his "earliest experiences with the old Infantry Tank Board, when it was under General (Samuel) Rockenbach" in a 1941 letter to Gen. Marshall: "I used to see them standing around arguing about the size of a bolt hole, to the point where they never got any tanks built, and never thought about tactics."[30]

This legacy of bureaucratic infighting for decades enabled the later failure to address the Sherman tank's inadequate main gun. It also contributed to the delay in producing and fielding the desperately needed T26 heavy tank until the last weeks of WWII in Europe.

In June 1928, a temporary "Experimental Mechanized Force" (dubbed the "Gasoline Brigade" by the press) was established at Fort Meade, Maryland, using obsolete M1917 Renault (light) and Mark VIII "Liberty" (heavy) tanks. Historian Mildred Gillie wrote of the two-man M1917, "it went 5.5 miles an hour maximum, and required incessant repairs from the day they left the factory until they were junked."[31] Surprisingly, the hulking Mark VIII tank—a virtual land battleship—could outrun the nimble little Renault, attaining speeds of up to 6.5 miles an hour. But as Gillie quoted "tank equipment expert" Maj. C. C. Benson, the "Liberty" tank vibrated so much its "engine bolts must be tightened after each three hours of running time."[32]

While the theories behind the mechanized force were modern, and a step in the right direction, it needed new equipment to realize them—and decent funding. To the *Washington Post*, the experiment showed "that a motorized force is superior to one that is not. But a force mounted on broken-down equipment cannot prevail against an enemy mounted in modern, up-to-the-minute machines. It has been demonstrated that the need is imperative for increased appropriations for mechanization. Congress should not refuse any request for such funds."[33]

undercut much of what he had just said by outlining the new weapons' vulnerabilities and by restating the perpetual need for a horse Cavalry."[27]

Fearing career retribution, Patton transferred out of the Infantry (then the home of the tanks) and back to the horse Cavalry, where he began to toe the line on tanks. As his biographer Ladislas Farago wrote, "The man who only a few months before was outspoken in his advocacy of armor could now be heard deprecating the tank in forceful and graphic language."[28]

Yet a 2012 biography spins Patton's weaseling into something admirable:

> Like his friend Eisenhower, Patton backed down from his advocacy of the tank in the face of threats to his military career. Adna Chaffee assumed the role of visionary champion of the tank, while Patton enjoyed a comfortable and secure existence in the Cavalry. It is arguable that Patton's only retreat was an example of admirable (if uncharacteristic) discretion. He preserved his ability to lead troops to victory in World War II.[29]

Between the world wars, the inefficiency of the Army's awkward tank design process worsened. Repeating errors that kept American models from reaching the front in 1917–18, bureaucracies became entrenched as competing spheres of power and influence, each one jealously guarded by their chiefs. The process became so convoluted that often, the tank's end user—the soldier—was not involved until the last stages, when the prototype was delivered for final testing.

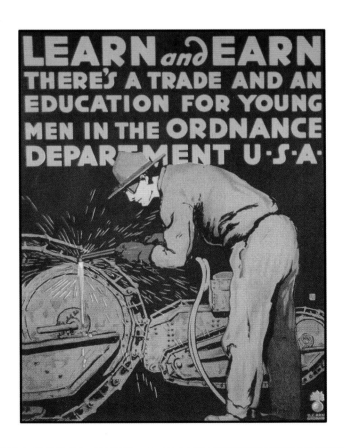

Mark VIII International ("Liberty" heavy tank) 1/35 scale
model by the author. *Photo by Robert Coldwell Sr.*

Lt. General Daniel Van
Voorhis, a godfather of
American armor.

But the Experimental Mechanized Force, even equipped
with leftover tanks, posed a
threat to older branches. When
Maj. Gen. Frank Parker (the
Army's assistant Chief of Staff
1927–1929) suggested in a
study that the EMF be made
permanent, the angry response
epitomized the interwar estab-
lishment's hostility towards tanks. "The tendency in this study
to set up another branch of the service," shot back Chief of Infantry Maj. Gen. R. H. Allen, "is heartily opposed. It is as
unsound as it was for the Air Corps to separate itself
from the rest of the Army.... The tank is a
weapon and as such it is an auxiliary to the
infantryman, as is every other arm or weapon."[34]

Armor supporters took hope in late
1930, when the EMF became the "Mechanized Force" under Col. Daniel Van
Voorhis, one of the fathers of American
armor. Based at Fort Eustis, Virginia,
the approximately 600

soldier organization included a tank company.[35] But as historian
John Wilson wrote, "the Infantry, Cavalry, and other arms and
services opposed the use of scarce Army funds to finance the
new organization. With limited amounts of new wine available,
customers wanted their old bottles filled first."[36]

Barely a year later (October 1931), Army Chief of Staff Gen.
Douglas MacArthur disbanded the Mechanized Force, ordering
the Infantry and Cavalry branches to separately devise their own
distinctive tanks and rules for their use. The resulting "Infantry
tanks" would accompany men on foot at a slow pace while light,
under-gunned "Cavalry tanks" conducted reconnaissance and
exploited enemy weaknesses.

Mildred Gillie, who wrote a pioneering 1947 history of the
US Armored Forces, believed MacArthur's actions had disastrous
consequences for the future: "When MacArthur saw fit to split
the development of mechanization, the association of the two
branches automatically resolved into an internecine competition
for money, men, and equipment."[37]

While the cause of an independent American tank arm
had been set back, a remnant of the Mechanized Force
(about 175 men under Col. Van Voorhis) transferred to Camp
Knox, Kentucky, becoming the nucleus of a new armored
Cavalry unit, the 7th Cavalry Brigade.[38] Though reduced
to claiming tongue-in-cheek that their mounts were
not actually tanks, but rather "combat cars" (to
circumvent the anti-armor restrictions of the
National Defense Act of 1920), these troopers
resolved to keep the armor cause alive.

"Tornado": A Christie T3 medium
tank 67th Armored Regiment 1/35
scale model by the author. *Photo by
Robert Coldwell Sr.*

Tank designer J. Walter Christie looks down on an Army officer. Given his cantankerous personality, the feeling was mutual.

Shoulder sleeve insignia of the 67th Infantry (Tank), which was equipped with pioneering tanks such as the "Liberty" and "Christie convertible" models. *Photo by Robert Coldwell Sr.*

Even as forward thinking American tankers were forced to resort to such a silly subterfuge, in Germany, Hitler was encouraging and accelerating tank development. The bitter debate over the role of the tank (and which branch would control it) continued in the US Army, and the unresolved arguments and ill feelings between competing branches would contribute to the inadequacy of US tanks in WWII.

The stifling bureaucratic inertia and lack of foresight that crippled American interwar tank design and the procurement process is exemplified in the treatment of eccentric inventor J. Walter Christie. One of the most important figures in tank design, Christie was described by armor historian Ian Hogg as "Either an unrewarded mechanical genius or a dangerous lunatic, depending on your point of view."[39]

Christie's ideas included a "convertible" tank able to run on or off road by using either large wheels or caterpillar treads. His designs were so advanced, according to Dr. Russell Weigley:

> Christie's tank of the early 1930s traveled 42½ miles an hour on tracks, compared with the 18 miles an hour of contemporary Ordnance Department tanks; it was well armored and performed spectacularly well over fields and across hills.[40]

Yet a parsimonious Congress- and Infantry-dominated Army leadership rejected it. Fighting for what little funding they could beg from Congress for their own pet projects, they had little desire to advance the upstart cause of armor at their expense.

Rejected by his own government, the cantankerous Christie took his designs to the Soviets, who were happy to apply them to their BT (fast tank) series, and to the T-34, one of the best all-around tanks of WWII. The T-34, which has been called the grandfather of all modern tank design, was such an effective counter to Germany's Panzers that it accelerated the tank arms

A rare Christie T-4 "convertible" medium tank.
*Author photo courtesy of the National Armor and Cavalry Heritage Foundation*

One of Christie's more exotic ideas was a flying tank.

race by generations—"arguably the most influential tank ever developed."[41] In response, the Germans designed the Tiger, King Tiger, and Panther, models that rendered American tanks obsolete.

Because the T-34 spurred the creation of more powerful German tanks, the interwar Army establishment's rejection of Christie's ideas contributed to the Sherman tank scandal. Christie's stubborn personality aside, had Army leaders been more receptive to innovative tank designs, America might have entered WWII with better tanks. Instead, tankers were issued mediocre models that became outclassed by the Tiger and Panther. In the ensuing race to catch up, US armor lagged behind Germany's until 1945. The older Army branches' pettiness, bureaucratic dysfunction, and desire to prevent an independent armor branch contributed to the loss of American tankers 1942–1945.

## "The Ten Lean Years" and the Horse Cavalry's Demise

Along with unresolved doctrine and bureaucratic infighting, two other factors that impeded US tank development were miserly peacetime budgets and the slow, painful death of the horse Cavalry. The traditional élan of flashing sabers and trumpet-heralded charges notwithstanding, realists could see the internal combustion engine, machine guns, trenches, and barbed wire had ended this glorious era of military history. Mechanization was inevitable, and the Cavalry's future depended on whether its leaders would adapt or resist. "Modern firearms have eliminated the horse as a weapon," warned Army Chief of Staff Gen. Douglas MacArthur in 1931, "and as a means of transportation he has become, next to the dismounted man, the slowest means of transportation. The time has therefore arrived when the Cavalry arm must either replace or assist the horse as a means of transportation, or else pass into the limbo of discarded military formations."[44]

Cavalryman Gen. Robert Grow referred to the 1930–1940 decade of thin budgets as "The Ten Lean Years." Gen. Chaffee wrote of this period:

> When war is over, the country at large thinks no more of the means and methods of making war. Its object is to lick its wounds, and to recover its loss in life and money. The natural tendency is to put aside the weapons with which the last war has been fought, as the main supply for the next.[45]

The interwar Army was one of the world's smallest. On August 28, 1939, three days before the German blitzkrieg on Poland began the war in Europe, a *Newsweek* article called "Gaps in US Preparedness" ranked it number seventeen in "effectiveness," behind Romania.[46] Taking stock of the Army's tanks in 1934, Chief of Staff MacArthur had listed a grand total of twelve "modern" (built after WWI) ones in the arsenals, and they were not even standardized (finalized designs able to be mass produced), but one-of-a-kind, practically hand-built prototypes. To MacArthur, they were "inadequate even for limited forces…and, such as they are, manifestly obsolescent."[47]

Along with up-to-date models, American tankers lacked funding; their 1934 training budget was so small that other than to and from the firing ranges, it actually forbade them to move their vehicles. An *Infantry Journal* cartoon depicted a doughboy pushing himself along on a child's scooter labeled "1st Tank Company" with the caption "Lost my gas and oil allowance for training, but thank God I still have the old initiative!"[48]

In late 1935, Gen. Malin Craig replaced MacArthur as Army Chief of Staff. He chose to build up manpower rather than weapons for a future emergency, leading to the Protective Mobilization Plan. In an era of tight Congressional funding, more soldiers could be obtained by spending money on personnel instead of research and development for expensive new weapons such as tanks.

To do this, Gen. Craig froze existing weapons designs, contributing to the production and fielding of obsolete weapons that the soldier in the field did not want,[49] i.e., the M3, a towed 37mm anti-tank gun adopted in 1940. The M3's performance was known to be inadequate before Pearl Harbor, and it was known that Germany was building more powerful anti-tank guns that outclassed it, along with tanks whose armor protection reduced the M3's effectiveness at stopping tanks to little more than nuisance value.

"The poorest product gotten out by the Ordnance Department at this time," Gen. Marshall admitted to his biographer Forrest Pogue in 1956, "was the 37mm cannon an anti-tank gun…. This was archaic when it was issued to the troops."[50] Yet due to interwar attempts at penny pinching, the toy-like M3 was produced in large numbers and was used with little success throughout WWII. 37mm guns were fielded as a towed anti-tank gun (the foundation of Gen. Lesley McNair's tank destroyer concept) hitched to jeeps, used as the main armament on the ill-fated M6

**Restored Soviet T-34 medium tank.** *Author photo courtesy of the National Armor and Cavalry Heritage Foundation*

Issue US Cavalry Saber, 1906 pattern. *Author's collection, photo by Robert Coldwell Sr.*

Mounted trooper wearing his campaign hat and jodhpurs, circa 1941.

The classic US Cavalry "Montana Peak" campaign hat worn in the late 1930s–early WWII period by the author's 1/104th Cavalry. The 104th Cavalry motto on the brass crest reads, "Over, Under, or Through." *Author's collection, photo by Robert Coldwell Sr.*

*Photo by Robert Coldwell Sr.*

*Photo by Robert Coldwell Sr.*

The prime mover of the German attack [on Poland] may be said to have been the gasoline motor in the air and on the ground; the basis of the Polish defense was the man, propelled only by his legs or by a horse.... The army whose destructive, striking effort was based on mechanization, aviation, and motorized Infantry swept the enemy from the battlefield...40 regiments of regular Cavalry, aware of the threat of enemy mechanization and therefore presumably trained to fight it, were unable to delay the enemy.... Somehow, German mechanization managed to push the Polish army and its Cavalry all over the map. It's time we developed an aggressive defense that will prevent the same fate from overtaking us...it's time to wake up.[43]

—A Cavalryman under the pseudonym "Earnest Grouch" in "Time to Wake Up," a November–December 1939 *Cavalry Journal* editorial

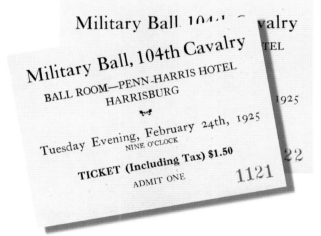

In the interlude between world wars, historic horse Cavalry units such as the author's First Troop Philadelphia City Cavalry—part of the 1/104th Cavalry—were known for social events as much as for heritage and military prowess. *Author's collection, photo by Robert Coldwell Sr.*

4th Cavalry troopers at the Louisiana Maneuvers of 1941.

US Cavalry "combat car." Note the proud display of the Cavalry guidon and crossed sabers plaque (near the tanker's hand) on the turret.

US M1 37mm towed anti-tank gun. *Photo by Robert Coldwell Sr.*

still carried a weak 37mm gun that even the Ordnance Department's postwar official history concedes was "obsolete before it was even standardized."[51] Prewar newsreels depicted an M3 37mm anti-tank gun towed by an early jeep in midair, seemingly flying over hills, as an answer to the blitzkrieg. Today, their small size and light weight make them good decorations for VFW and American Legion posts, looking more like a July 4 toy pop gun than a serious anti-tank weapon.

Fargo tank destroyer and the M3 and M5 Stuart light tanks, and as an auxiliary weapon on the M3 Lee medium tank.

Thus, while in 1945 Germany had tanks with modern, high-velocity guns (Panther and Tiger), British tankers were receiving the powerful new Comet tank, and Russia had excellent models like the T-34 and JS-2 Stalin, American M5A1 light tanks

The emphasis on building up Army manpower at the expense of updated weapons led to darkly humorous scenes in training. From the depths of the Great Depression until 1942, American soldiers trained with bags of flour substituting for hand grenades. Broomsticks and logs took the place of rifles, machine guns, and cannon, and old trucks bearing hand-painted signs reading "TANK" filled in for the real thing.[52]

Jeep in midair with towed M1 37mm AT gun

"My God," recalled then-Col. Dwight Eisenhower, "we were carrying some wooden machine guns, and all kinds of damn [simulated] mortars that were nothing but logs."[53] Meanwhile, Germany embraced modern tank design and production, and thanks to the Spanish Civil War tested armor theories under combat conditions and worked out mechanical bugs in their designs in the field. All this would have disastrous future consequences for Allied tankers.

Even as opponents of independent armor like Chief of Infantry Gen. Steven Fuqua insisted, "There is no such animal as 'armored Cavalry' in these modern days. Remove the horse, and there is no Cavalry,"[54] realists such as Gens. Chaffee and Van Voorhis recognized that "Cavalry" could be defined by *how* a soldier fought as much as by *what* he rode in to battle. If properly used, tanks possessed attributes that had made horse-mounted Cavalry successful for centuries: shock, speed, and mobility. By bowing to the inevitable to embrace a different mount, the US Cavalry could continue in the same spirit with the same techniques now made exponentially more effective.

Prominent among the Cavalrymen willing to adapt old methods to new technology was Gen. Adna Romanza Chaffee. "Those fellows," he responded to critics of mechanization at the Cavalry School, Fort Riley, "ought to understand that the definition of Cavalry now includes troops of any kind equipped for highly

General Adna Romanza Chaffee: the first leader of the Armored Force, he is considered the father of American armor. *U.S. National Archives*

mobile combat, and not just mounted on horses. The motto of the Cavalry School says, 'Through Mobility We Conquer.' It does not say, 'Through Mobility on Horses Alone We Conquer.'"[55]

To historian Russell Weigley, Chaffee "saw the tank now as neither an Infantry nor a Cavalry weapon but the core of a new arm, capable of striking with the speed and shock power of Cavalry, but with some of the staying force of Infantry as well."[56]

*Photo by Robert Coldwell Sr.*

Due to the success of the 1970 film *Patton*, the general public's image of Gen. George Patton is of a tank genius and an outspoken rebel unafraid to challenge authority, but at times he took a cautious position in the horse versus mechanization debate. He had been muzzled after publishing pro-mechanization views and left the fledgling Tank Corps to return to the horse Cavalry. To protect his career while waiting to see where the chips would fall, Patton claimed to see a future for *both* horses and tanks on the battlefield. "It is my opinion," he stated in the September–October 1933 *Cavalry Journal*, that an independent role for tanks, separate from horses, "will be the exception rather than the rule and that, in general, mechanized and horsed Cavalry will operate together…think, for example, of the possibilities of a combat car (i.e., tank) charge instantly exploited by horsemen…for night marches, machines will *always* be preceded by horsemen, or else become victims of ambush."[57]

Combat cars in line

While Patton straddled the fence in the bitter debate, leading the reactionaries was the Army's last Chief of Cavalry, Gen. John Herr. Gen. Herr is mocked for his rigid devotion to the mounted Cavalry cause, but before Pearl Harbor, as Paul Fussell has written, "the Cavalry itself still seemed a not implausible arm of the service":

In 1941 the United States War Department announced with satisfaction that the Army had just supplied itself with 20,000 horses, the most since the Civil War, and in April, 1941, *Life* magazine devoted its cover to a photograph of an earnest "U.S. Cavalryman," Pvt. Buster Hobbs, standing at attention steel-helmeted beside his horse Gip. Inside, an eight-page "photo

> Any further attempt to encroach on my horse Cavalry will meet with bitter opposition.... Under no circumstances will I agree to any further depletion of my horse Cavalry. To do so would be a betrayal of the national defense.[42]
> —Chief of Cavalry Gen. John K. Herr, February 1940

essay" celebrated the United States First Cavalry Division, then training at Fort Bliss, Texas. Over half its 11,600 men were mounted, the rest driving armored cars, jeeps, and motorcycles. Their anti-tank defense was the 37mm gun. At the moment the *Life* reporter visited the division, the troops were hoping for the ultimate delivery of "heavier" equipment—thirteen light tanks.[58]

While acknowledging in fall 1941 (when it was too late) that "the pressure was on from certain quarters to eliminate the mounted service,"[59] Gen. Herr vowed not to give up a single man to mechanization. His stubbornness led to Cavalry tanks being transferred to the new Armored Force in July 1940, where control of them was splintered: some former Cavalry tanks went to the new Armor branch, while others went to the Infantry, assigned on a piecemeal basis. Ultimately, Gen. Herr's refusal to evolve contributed to the abolition of the horse Cavalry in 1942.

An understandably bitter Gen. Robert Grow would later write that Gen. Herr had "lost mechanization for Cavalry," that the US Cavalry had "lost a prestige that it can never regain again."[60] Grow mocked Herr for predicting a future for the saber on the battlefield, even as he opposed mechanization. While it is easy for modern readers to ridicule such obstinacy in hindsight, before rushing to judgment and ridicule over Gen. Herr's stand, one must consider the powerful emotional bond between man and horse that existed for centuries. (I can relate to Gen. Herr, having served and ridden with the historic First Troop Philadelphia City Cavalry founded 1774, which preserves the horse Cavalry tradition by continuing to ride horses for ceremonial purposes.)

In the summer of 1937, the Cavalry received fair warning of things to come from a surprising source: Lt. Col. Adolph von Schell of the German *Wehrmacht*. Visiting Gen. Daniel Van Voorhis's Seventh Cavalry Brigade at Fort Knox, von Schell talked shop with his American counterparts. The .50-caliber machine

guns on the Cavalry's small "combat cars," he warned, would not stop heavier, well-armored German tanks. Van Voorhis responded that in a future war, following current Army tank doctrine that prevailed well into WWII (favoring lightly armed and armored tanks), American tanks would avoid direct tank-versus-tank battles. Ideally, they would play a "breakthrough" or "exploitation" role, only attacking soft targets in the enemy's rear like men on foot and trucks, while somehow eluding his tanks.

Col. Von Schell pointed out the likelihood of enjoying such ideal conditions on the battlefield was slim, and even warned the Americans that Germany would use a mixture of four heavy tanks to every light tank. On July 23, 1937, Gen. Van Voorhis reported the conversations to the Office of the Adjutant General. Germany's tank armor doctrine for a future war, he wrote, was designed to

> hurl thousands of tanks against the enemy position to overcome the hostile resistance. After this mass of tanks has disposed of the main elements.... German Infantry will then follow through, protected at close quarters by a small number of additional tanks which will mop up any chance machine gun nests or strong points which may have escaped the initial mass tank assault.[61]

In August 1939, just weeks before the Nazi invasion of Poland, articles syndicated by the International News Service reported bitter dissension within the US Army between the Cavalry's armor proponents and their Infantry rivals. Reporters covering large-scale Army maneuvers around Plattsburg, New

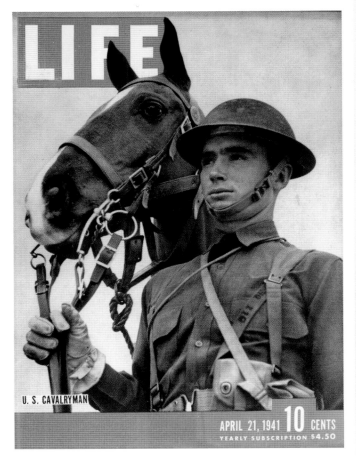

U. S. CAVALRYMAN

*Author's collection, photo by Robert Coldwell Sr.*

GOGGLES

CRASH HELMET

BINOCULAR CASE

CARTRIDGE CLIPS

BINOCULARS

FIRST AID KIT ON SIDE

PISTOL

MAP CASE

**ABOVE:** Typical US WWII Army issue binoculars used by tank commanders. This example was made by Nash-Kelvinator (formerly producers of refrigerators) in 1943. *Author's collection, photo by Robert Coldwell Sr.*

**BELOW:** The Cavalryman and tanker's trusted standby—the Colt Model 1911 automatic, with issue pistol belt, Cavalry model holster, magazine pouch, early "two-tone" finish magazine, and wooden .45 ammunition crate. *Photo by Robert Coldwell Sr.*

The well-dressed US Cavalry tank commander, 1941. Note the issue jodhpurs (traditional riding breeches) and riding boots. In this instance spurs are not worn, but the horse Cavalry's sartorial traditions died hard. *Author's collection, photo by Robert Coldwell Sr.*

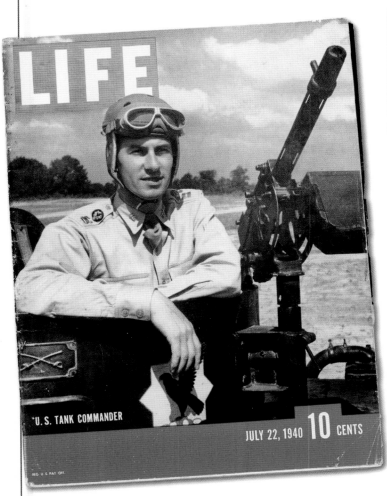

*Author's collection, photo by Robert Coldwell Sr.*

Khaki cotton "overseas cap" with Cavalry yellow piping and brass 1/104th Cavalry insignia proudly worn by the author's A Troop in the late 1930s–early WWII era. *Author's collection, photo by Robert Coldwell Sr.*

A typical US Cavalry unit marking proudly displayed on the side of vehicles in the 1930s-early WWII period. In this case, the author's A Troop, 1/104th Cavalry, on a wheeled scout car. *Photo by Robert Coldwell Sr.*

July 1941: Troopers of the 1/104th (Mechanized) Cavalry meet their new mounts at the American Car and Foundry Corporation, Berwick, Pennsylvania. While the classic campaign hat has been replaced by the more practical overseas cap—cocked jauntily to one side in the Cavalry style—the traditional jodhpurs and riding boots remain.

Regulation US Cavalry Model 1930 riding boots worn with standard issue M1911 spurs. Upholding the long Cavalry tradition—from J.E.B. Stuart to Theodore Roosevelt—of affecting a jaunty appearance, some Troopers favored fancier, private purchase versions of these uniform items. *Author's collection, photo by Robert Coldwell Sr.*

Officer's shirt collar insignia, First Troop Philadelphia City Cavalry. *Photo by Robert Coldwell Sr.*

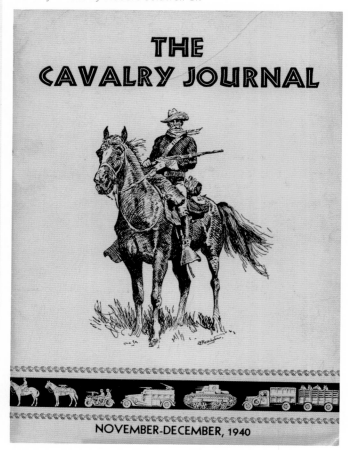

NOVEMBER-DECEMBER, 1940

*Author's collection, photo by Robert Coldwell Sr.*

York, described the controversy swirling around tanks. Was the armored Cavalry then attracting the public's attention

a valuable Army unit, or a pretty toy? It is agreed by the entire Army that the mechanized Cavalry puts on a dashing and impressive show with its hundreds of motor units, but the agreement ends there.... Mounted Cavalry would as soon discuss the devil as its rival on wheels, and the Infantry has a low opinion of the mechanized brigade, which it terms "the men from Mars" [perhaps because they wore comical leather crash helmets made by sporting goods manufacturer Rawlings with donut-shaped padding, resembling those in the popular Buck Rogers comic strips].[62]

The Pennsylvania National Guard medal for Mexican Border service (left). For historic mounted units like the author's First Troop Philadelphia City Cavalry (founded 1774), Pershing's Punitive Expedition into Mexico would be "the last (mounted) campaign." On the right is the Pennsylvania National Guard Medal for victory in the Great War of 1917-1918. *Author's collection, photo by Robert Coldwell Sr.*

Less than two weeks after this article, Germany unleashed its blitzkrieg on Poland. On September 1, 1939, Gen. George Catlett Marshall was sworn in as Army Chief of Staff. He would make further headlines in December, warning that "the Army machine," if called upon, "is probably less than twenty-five percent ready for immediate action."[63] Addressing the American Historical Association and American Military Institute, Marshall lamented that "historians had been inclined to emphasize victories and gloss over mistakes, leaving people with a comfortable belief in our invincibility";[64] words which, in light of the sanitized "Good War" version of WWII that most American popular culture perpetuates, could apply to the Sherman tank scandal.

It would take some ten months for the Army to respond to the Panzerwaffe (German Army tank force) by organizing the new Armored Force under Gen. Chaffee, but Chaffee's diligent efforts until his death from cancer three months before Pearl Harbor could not undo decades of bitter disunity within the Army.

The cost of generals' bureaucratic rivalries would be borne by young tankers killed and wounded fighting in vehicles that were obsolete almost as they rolled off assembly lines— the flawed products of those disastrous "Ten Lean Years."

Shoulder sleeve insignia of the Second Cavalry Division. *Photo by Robert Coldwell Sr.*

Cutaway view of a Cavalry "combat car" or light tank. *Photo by Robert Coldwell Sr.*

July 1938: At Fort Oglethorpe, Georgia, 6th Cavalry Regiment troopers practice anti-aircraft defense using Browning machine guns mounted on a Cavalry scout car. *US Army Signal Corps*

Detail of the instrument panel in a preserved scout car. *Author photo courtesy of the National Armor and Cavalry Heritage Foundation*

## "Agricultural Tractors": German Tank Development

"That's what I need! That's what I want to have!"[65]
—German Chancellor Adolf Hitler viewing a 1933 tank demonstration

Late in fielding tanks in WWI, Germany caught up in the interwar years, using secret treaties with the Soviet Union to establish tank schools and proving grounds. Hitler appreciated the Panzer's potential; as early as 1929, he noted in Nazi weekly

*Illustrierter Beobachte*, "The significance of this weapon can best be seen from the fact that the Treaty of Versailles expressly prohibits Germany from using it."[66]

Even as small budgets and dissension handicapped the US Army, Germany violated the Versailles treaty by building new tanks claimed to be mere *Landwirtschaftschlepperen* (agricultural tractors), as well as new towed anti-tank guns. Inspired by the ideas of Gen. Heinz Guderian and others, Germans also developed innovative armor and combined arms doctrine and tactics.

Tiger and Panther tanks did not appear out of thin air in 1942–1943; there were warning signs. Years before WWII, the Germans had been steadily improving their tank designs and combat-testing them in Spain. The *Panzerkampfwagen I* (PzKpfw I or Panzer I) first appeared in 1934, mounting a pair of 7.92mm machine guns. The next year brought the Panzer II with a 20mm main gun and the Panzer III with a larger 37mm main gun. Looking ahead, designers gave the Panzer III a roomy turret to facilitate future upgrades, which were added in the form of more powerful short and long-barreled 50mm main guns that saw service in the final phases of the French campaign.

The Panzer IV carried a short-barreled 75mm main gun that would be further refined into a long-barreled, high-velocity 75mm weapon. (GIs called tanks equipped with this main gun the "Mark IV Special.") Produced throughout the war, the dependable Panzer IV (whose importance has been overshadowed by the more notorious Tigers and Panthers) became the backbone of the German tank arm, a workhorse used from 1939 Poland to 1945 Berlin.

In spite of the *Panzer IV's* 75mm main gun, the Allies assumed thinly armored tanks carrying machine guns only—or small, towed 37mm guns—would be adequate to fight Germany's new tanks. There were exceptions, decent tanks such as the British Matilda II and the French *Char B* (*Char de Bataille*, or battle tank, armed with a powerful, short 75mm gun mounted in the hull), but often when the British and French met up with German tanks, although the Allies had intelligence information on them from Spain and onward, the firepower of their main guns came as a nasty shock.

In late 1942, GIs and British Tommies in North Africa were amazed by the ability of the "Mark IV Special" to penetrate Allied armor plate. But as Army Ordnance Col. George Jarrett (one of the Army's most knowledgable authorities on worldwide tank ordnance) noted, Germany's 75mm tank main gun should have come as no surprise, nor that the Germans would later adapt their 88mm anti-aircraft artillery piece to fit inside a tank turret.[67]

Far from coming out of the blue, the Panther's and Tiger's use of the devastating "88" was the next logical step in the steady progression of German tank development.[68]

American industry would eventually churn out thousands of tanks with inadequate firepower and armor protection, but Germany trumped it throughout the war with more powerful models. They also developed effective anti-tank guns and artillery before the US entered the European war, including the small 37mm PaK 35/36 towed gun and the notorious "88." Years after the Germans debuted the "88" in Spain as a "dual purpose" (used against air or ground targets), freestanding artillery piece, the Allies, stunned by its destructive power, lacked a counter to it.

To Col. Jarrett, the Allies missed red flags that had been waving for years:

> The Germans made a most detailed evaluation of the use of their armored vehicles while in Spain, together with their new 88mm gun and certain shells…. They were well aware of the coming role of the tank and anti-tank gun, and set out to develop weapons capable of delivering a decisive effect—to win the battles sure to come in the near future…. Many evaluating engineers of the Allied countries had equal opportunities to arrive at similar reasoning, but most of them treated with contempt the rumblings of war, which consistently came from well-informed observers and other agencies, all of which indicated the need for superior material.[69]

This intelligence failure continued from the mid-1930s to the last days of the European war. The Allies were repeatedly surprised by better-armed, better-protected German tanks, and failed to adapt their existing weapons in large numbers to defeat them. The British Firefly and American M36B1 were feasible solutions: the M36B1 could have been mass produced, and

Panzer I in 1939 Polish Campaign markings, 1/35 scale model by the author. *Photo by Robert Coldwell Sr.*

Panzer II in *Deutsche Afrika Korps* (German Africa Corps) markings, 1941, 1/35 scale model by the author. *Photo by Robert Coldwell Sr.*

**Restored Panzer I Ausf. (Model) A at the Deutsches Panzermuseum, Munster.** *Massimo Foti*

Restored Panzer III Ausf. (Model) F at the Musée des Blindés, Saumur, France. *Massimo Foti*

Restored Panzer II at the Tank Museum, Bovington, Dorset, UK. *Massimo Foti*

Restored Pzkpfw. IV Ausf. J, (Panzer IV, Model J) at the Musée des Blindés, Saumur, France. *Massimo Foti*

Panzer II Ausf. (Model) C.

existing M4s could have been adapted to carry the Firefly's powerful British 17-pounder main gun, but Army leaders rejected them.

Col. Steven Fuqua served as Chief of Infantry and as military attaché in Spain. The reports he cabled home exemplify the Army's prevailing anti-armor bias; rather than warn of the quality of German weapons, Fuqua dismissed the Spanish Civil War as having little relevance to future conflicts between the US and major European powers. This was done at the risk—which became a brutal reality—of American tanks falling behind Germany's in quality.

Col. Truman Smith (serving as a military attaché in Berlin) and Maj. Albert Wedemeyer (attending the *Kriegsakademie* in Berlin 1936–1938) gave notice of German innovation, but to little avail. Smith's warnings were also diluted when he became embroiled in a media controversy that overshadowed the intelligence value of his observations.

While visiting Germany, legendary aviator Charles Lindbergh—who also gave notice of German mobilization—became the victim of a carefully staged Nazi prank: the shy, cordial "Lone Eagle" was abruptly presented a medal from Nazi *Luftwaffe* leader Hermann Göring. As Lindbergh was a prominent and respected critic of Roosevelt's interventionist foreign policy, the pro-Roosevelt American media seized the chance to attack the idolized "Lucky Lindy." To Col. Smith, the unsuspecting, polite Lindbergh had been ambushed by the German's photo opportunity, but in the course of defending Lindbergh, Smith's warnings of a resurgent German military were brushed aside.

Panzer III in Yugoslavia, 1941.

According to the Army's original wartime caption, "In 1943 he was simply a young Lieutenant assigned the new Foreign Materiel Branch of the Ordnance Corps. Today he is probably the greatest expert in military ordnance available anywhere in the world. In spite of his great love of weapons, Jarrett is a deeply religious man. This is George Burling Jarrett at his desk at the Aberdeen Proving Grounds." *Courtesy US Army Military History Institute, Carlisle Barracks, Pennsylvania*

The truth about Lindbergh would emerge later: far from supporting Hitler as a jealous FDR claimed, Lindbergh—smeared as a Nazi sympathizer—had secretly volunteered to put his

Close-up of instruments on a preserved "88" field piece. *Author photo courtesy of the National Armor and Cavalry Heritage Foundation*

prestige and fame to work for the good of the US military. At the request of the US Embassy in Berlin, he used his unprecedented access as an international celebrity and aviation icon to tour German arms factories from 1936–1938, the better to spy for the US government. Returning from trips to Europe, he would pass on detailed reports warning of German re-armament.

The press in thrall to FDR painted the "Lone Eagle" as a dupe of the Nazis, exploited for their own sinister purposes, even as Lindbergh—who went on to secretly fly some fifty combat missions in the Pacific, strafing barges and downing a Japanese aircraft, though a civilian at the time—passed on technical details on German arms that most countries' intelligence agencies could only dream about possessing.

The Lone Eagle. Accused of treason by FDR and his partisans, Charles Lindbergh used his fame to observe and report on German weapon developments. Barred from serving overseas by a petty Roosevelt, he flew dozens of combat missions as a civilian "consultant" in the South Pacific, even downing a Japanese aircraft in aerial combat. Here he chats with top P-38 Lightning fighter ace Maj. Thomas McGuire. *US National Archives*

The notorious "88": a restored German "dual purpose" (used against air and ground targets) artillery piece. *Photo by Lindsay Fraschilla, courtesy of the National Armor and Cavalry Heritage Foundation*

German Pzkw (Panzer) IV

Gen. Albert Wedemeyer, who warned of a resurgent Germany. Gen. Marshall referred to him as "that long-legged [then] Major in War Plans." *US Army Signal Corps*

When Maj. Wedemeyer wrote a 100-page document on what he had seen in a resurgent Germany, he was dismayed to find high-level officers on the Army's general staff more concerned about gossip of "Hitler's personal peculiarities and the love lives of Joseph Goebbels and Hermann Göring."[70] Thankfully, Wedemeyer's observations were eventually appreciated by Army Chief of Staff Gen. George Marshall, who referred to him as the "long-legged major in War Plans."[71]

In July 1941, Marshall had Wedemeyer put his suggestions in a memorandum, in which he called for "Highly maneuverable tank divisions, lots of tank divisions, capable of striking deep into enemy territory,"[72] but it was too late; in the late 1930s, Wedemeyer's warnings, along with Smith's and Lindbergh's, seemed to fall on deaf ears.

Attachés' reports were dismissed as too fantastic to be true, or pigeonholed by enemies of armor who wanted to preserve older branches' dominance over the small tank arm. Competing for a share of stingy peacetime budgets and unwilling to buck the establishment on which their promotions depended, Infantry and Artillery officers short of modern equipment were not likely to call for greater funding for new tanks. According to Col. Jarrett:

> Valuable information was accumulated by the Allies during this period on German developments, but few people would believe that there was any reason for extensive military preparedness, and money for adequate development was scarce. Tank development agencies were starved for funds. Many military personnel were also of the opinion prior to 1939 that war was a long

Rare M2 medium "Infantry tanks" with a lackluster 37mm main gun. Bristling with machine guns for Infantry support, these rolling pillboxes were obsolete almost as they left the factories, but inspired the M3 and M4 mediums. *Author's collection, photo by Robert Coldwell Sr.*

Soldiers contemplate a "Mae West" of the 2nd Tank Company, attached to the 2nd Infantry Division—note the famous "Indian Head" shoulder patch insignia on the turret. *US Army Signal Corps*

way off...they really had no tactical plans upon which to base requirements for new and really modern and powerful ordnance.[73]

As historian Mildred Gillie wrote:

On the plains of the Catalan and the Basque, Germany successfully employed in test tube proportions the *blitzkrieg* tactics that Germany used in full-scale war to conquer Poland. The tragedy was that only Germany and Russia profited from the laboratory demonstration.[74]

Maj. Percy Black, like Col. Smith, was another military attaché whose alarm bells were drowned out by the static of domestic politics and scandal. While acting military attaché at the American Embassy in Berlin, Black had observed and reported on the *Wehrmacht* in the field during the 1939 invasion of Poland. When Black returned to the US in late November, Brig. Gen. Chaffee, leading the 7th Cavalry Brigade (Mechanized) at Fort Knox, Kentucky, recognized the benefits of disseminating Black's first-hand experiences and observations. "Let us draw from him as much professional information as we can," Chaffee suggested to Marshall, who responded that Maj. Black should lecture to audiences at seven Army posts.[75]

But Black was silenced when some of his public remarks caused what Marshall termed "a violent Jewish reaction."[76] Black told the media that during the Polish campaign, *Wehrmacht* soup kitchens had fed hungry Polish civilians and refugees, adding, "I do not believe any of the atrocity stories."[77]

The politically astute Marshall knew that Roosevelt would court Jewish-American voters in 1940. Objecting to "advertising" Maj. Black and his controversial views, he canceled the lectures.[78] Black may have shown a disconcerting lack of objectivity towards

the invading Germans, but by allowing domestic politics to silence his first-hand observations of Germany's new tank arm in Poland, Marshall made a bad intelligence situation worse.

On the eve of the blitzkrieg in France, the Americans had not addressed the growing threat of German armor. Along with lacking a coherent tank or anti-tank doctrine, the Army was handicapped by a meager peacetime budget.

Lt. Belton Cooper, who would join the future Third Armored Division, recalled in his memoir *Death Traps*:

As a young Army ROTC cadet in August 1939, I was shocked to find that our total tank research and development budget for that year was only $85,000. How could the greatest industrial nation on earth devote such a pittance to the development of a major weapons system, particularly when World War Two was to start in two weeks?[79]

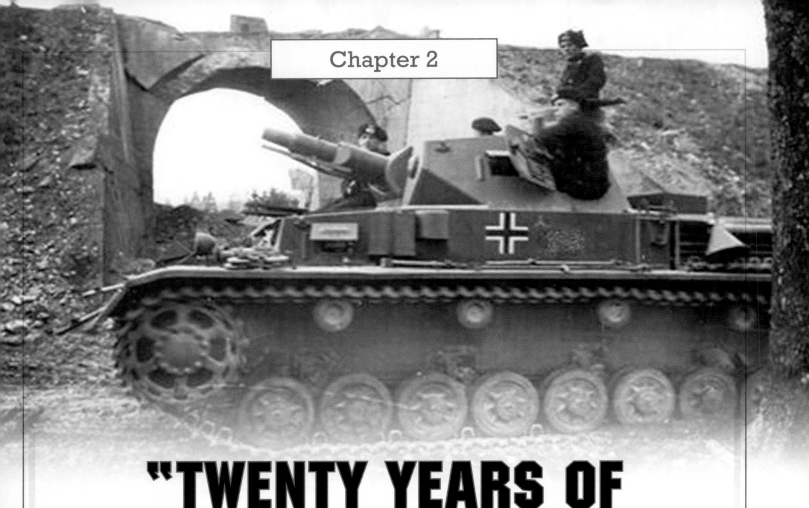

# "TWENTY YEARS OF NEGLECT"

## "Arsenal of Democracy": America Responds to the Blitzkrieg

The blitzkrieg of 1939–1940 caused great panic among the Allies and a desperate realization that they must catch up. While America was exalted for its automobile industry and Great Britain had invented tanks and used them first, both had been left behind by Germany, which was well ahead in quality and quantity.

But there was an unwillingness to believe in the extent of German tank superiority. "Some British propaganda published before the German attack," notes a historian of the Dunkirk campaign, "suggested that Germany was passing off cardboard, mocked-up tanks as the real thing, to make her *Panzer* divisions appear more powerful than they really were."[4] True, back in the early days of their revamped tank program the Germans had used wooden and fabric dummy tanks to simulate the real thing for training purposes, flimsy frameworks mounted on top of civilian cars. But that was in 1929. In 1939 Poland, and in 1940's Operation Yellow (the German invasion of France and the Low Countries), the Allies were in for a rude shock; instead of flimsy mock-ups, the new Panzers were all too real.

A young driver of a French *Somua 35* tank named Jean-Marie de Beaucorps of the *3ieme Division Legere Mecanique* (3rd

> There is danger ahead—danger against which we must prepare…. We must produce arms… with every energy and resource we can command…. We must be the great Arsenal of Democracy.[1]
> —President Franklin Roosevelt, radio address to the nation, December 30, 1940

DLM Light Mechanized Division) recalled being attacked by an estimated 200-plus German tanks and artillery pieces near Merdorp in 1940. "Smoke, dust. I cannot see much. I try to drive in a straight line, and then there is a terrible crash":

Our tank is lifted off the ground, and then falls back down again on its tracks. My legs are slammed into the inner tank shell and I fear that they might be broken. Behind me, the light has gone out. The turret has been torn off. It was probably hit by a large shell. In front of me, the curtain of dust and smoke is still thick. I don't know where I am, nor where I can find friend or foe. I turn around. Our gunner has been flattened at the back of the tank. He must have been crushed when the turret fell off. The lieutenant [de Beaucorps' tank commander] has completely disappeared. He has flown away along with the turret…

Then all of a sudden a German tank appears close to mine, about twenty meters away. The presence of my tank, immobile, half destroyed, does not deter him. A second tank joins him…. They are smaller than my tank. Their guns are relatively small caliber; they must be

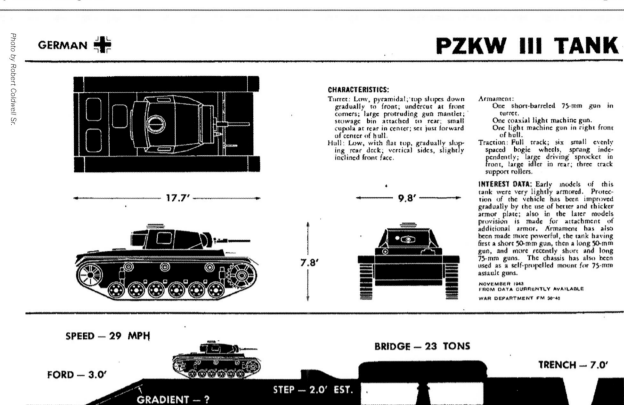

GERMAN ✠

Photo by Robert Caldwell Sr.

# PZKW III TANK

**CHARACTERISTICS:**

Turret: Low, pyramidal; top slopes down gradually to front; undercut at front corners; large protruding gun mantlet; stowage bin attached to rear; small cupola at rear in center; set just forward of center of hull.

Hull: Low, with flat top, gradually sloping rear deck; vertical sides, slightly inclined front face.

Armament:
One short-barreled 75-mm gun in turret.
One coaxial light machine gun.
One light machine gun in right front of hull.

Traction: Full track; six small evenly spaced bogie wheels, sprung independently; large driving sprocket in front, large idler in rear; three track support rollers.

**INTEREST DATA:** Early models of this tank were very lightly armored. Protection of the vehicle has been improved gradually by the use of better and thicker armor plate; also in the later models provision is made for attachment of additional armor. Armament has also been made more powerful, the tank having first a short 50-mm gun, then a long 50-mm gun, and more recently short and long 75-mm guns. The chassis has also been used as a self-propelled mount for 75-mm assault guns.

NOVEMBER 1943
FROM DATA CURRENTLY AVAILABLE
WAR DEPARTMENT FM 30-40

17.7'    9.8'    7.8'

SPEED — 29 MPH    BRIDGE — 23 TONS

FORD — 3.0'    TRENCH — 7.0'

GRADIENT — ?    STEP — 2.0' EST.

Restored French Somua S-35 tank at the Tank Museum. Bovington, Dorset, UK. *Massimo Foti*

Restored French Somua S-35 tank at the Tank Museum. Bovington, Dorset, UK. *Massimo Foti*

light tanks, Mark Is or Mark IIs. I start my motor…I engage the clutch. My tank must have jumped forward, because without the turret I can go much faster. They have no time to move and I crash into them. All I can hear is the sound of my tracks grinding into their metal. They cannot escape. As if in a dream, I light my burning grenade and place it on my seat. In five seconds it will emit flames and intense heat, and burn my tank. After it has been turned into a burning torch, it will in its turn burn two enemy tanks. I scurry to the rear of my tank. One jump and I am outside.[5]

On May 13, a French captain of Infantry in Maisoncelle observed:

A wave of French lorries, cars, cyclists, motorbicyclists, horse riders, and artillery vehicles, as well as troops on foot without any weapons passing at top speed down the main road…. This panic has been caused by a lieutenant engineer, or someone who claimed to be a lieutenant engineer, mounted on a side car who shouted again and again in the middle of the crowd which surrounded him, "Save your lives. They are coming! They are chasing us from Bulson."[6]

The Army has about 500 tanks, one-half of which are obsolete. It has ordered one heavy tank, but at the moment it does not own even one.[2]
—Arthur Krock, *New York Times* editorial page, October 1, 1940

Near Fond Dagot, staff officers of the French 55th Division standing outside their headquarters witnessed what was delicately called "an unexpected and unpleasant incident" that would become familiar in years to come: Allied soldiers retreating in terror before rapidly advancing German tanks:

They speed past, with clusters of men hanging on to the vehicles like grapes. They are panic-stricken, and shout that the enemy and their tanks have just arrived at Bulson. Some of the retreating soldiers are completely out of control and fire their guns in all directions. Shots whistle through the branches of the trees at the very moment when Gen. Pierre Lafontaine [commander of the 55th Division] comes out of his headquarters on hearing the commotion…most of the fleeing soldiers have no weapons and many of them are clutching suitcases.[7]

The French had failed to understand the changing nature of warfare. In understandable reaction to devastating losses in WWI, they also fell prey to a defensive, static mentality epitomized by the Maginot Line fortifications. But not all Frenchmen failed to foresee the tank coming to maturity; in 1934, an obscure French Army Lt. Col. Charles DeGaulle published *Vers L'Armee de Metier* (translated into English in 1940 as *The Army of the Future*), advocating the modern organization and deployment of tanks:

"Twenty Years of Neglect"

And then suddenly the internal combustion engine becomes armored. Crawling along on its caterpillars, carrying light guns and machine guns, it advances into the frontline, climbs over mounds and ditches, and beats down trenches and barbed wire entanglements. However faltering and awkward it may have appeared at first, the tank completely upset the science of tactics. Through the tank was reborn the art of surprise, to which it added the relentlessness of machinery. Through it the art of maneuvering was restored in detail, since it could deliver either a frontal or flank attack under fire, move and fire at the same time, and advance in any direction. Through it, above all, detachments of fighting men recovered the mobile protection which they appeared to have lost forever.[8]

German Waffen SS *Panzertruppen* inside the turret of their vehicle. *Courtesy German Federal Archives*

But the book was little noticed, selling a mere 750 copies in France.[9] As war clouds loomed, according to one biographer DeGaulle became "almost obsessed with the theory of tank warfare, to the point where, even in maneuvers, he was prepared to disobey orders to demonstrate his point."[10] But DeGaulle, like tank advocates in America, was seemingly butting his head against a brick wall of obstinate bureaucracy.

A British Expeditionary Force officer's anonymously published 1940 diary gives a sense of the shock and awe of the new tank and combined arms warfare. From May 14–19, he wrote:

All the dash and drive is left to the Germans…. The Panzer divisions seem insatiable. [Late on May 17,] with the bit between their teeth, they are going as strong as ever." On May 19 came "news that the Panzers are in Amiens. This is some ridiculous nightmare. The BEF (British Expeditionary Force) is cut off. Our communications are gone…the Germans have taken every risk… and they have got away with it."[11]

On May 21, 1940, an awed *Beromunster Radio* of Switzerland commented:

This grand offensive has achieved massive victories in the ten days since it began…at the moment there is nothing to indicate that the Allied forces have succeeded in halting it…it must be said that rapid victories by the Germans are due to a fighting method that had never been used before the Polish Campaign of last September: complete mechanization of the attacking forces. Technology has taken over warfare. The offensive

A rare, restored British A13 Cruiser Mk III tank at the Tank Museum, Bovington, Dorset, UK. *Massimo Foti*

French Renault R-35 at the Musée des Blindés, Saumur, France. *Massimo Foti*

French Somua S-35 at the Musée des Blindés, Saumur, France. *Massimo Foti*

French Renault Char B1 bis heavy tank and crew, 1940.

is not unfolding along one continuous front, but takes the form of countless spearhead thrusts by armored divisions.[12]

In September 1939, the German Army magazine *Die Wehrmacht* bragged:

Irresponsible propaganda had persuaded Polish soldiers that our tanks were not much more than tin mock-ups… leading to an almost grotesque attack on some of our tanks by a Polish lancer [i.e., Cavalry] regiment, with what annihilating consequences one can easily imagine…. In one battle a single German heavy tank annihilated two anti-tank gun crews with a single shot, and then crushed the guns themselves under its heavy track chains…the tank driver, a very young second lieutenant, shortly afterward stopped a railroad train loaded with Polish reservists, forced them to climb out, and herded them along—400 men in all—in the van of his tank.[13]

In vivid Nazi propaganda, endless columns of Panzers raced towards Warsaw and Paris:

Our spearhead rapidly reached the hills on this side of the river…enemy artillery fired, but our tanks rolled undeterred toward their targets…. As the sun sank toward the west they had penetrated the city…. While the armored spearhead was still securing the river

Manufacturer's data plate on a preserved French Renault Char B1 bis heavy tank at the Tank Museum, Bovington, Dorest, UK. *Massimo Foti*

crossing, the second wave of our tanks was already rolling up—reinforcement Panzer units in an irresistible train over twelve miles long.[14]

From the Allied countries came speculation that contributing to this success were large numbers of mysterious "assault" or "breakthrough" (*durchbruchwagen*) tanks. But the British and French had more armor during the Battle of France, some of good design. The French Renault *Char B1 bis* heavy tank was one of the best armed and armored tanks of any army at the time of the blitzkrieg on Poland, and the British Matilda II's armor could stand up to most Panzers until mid-1941. While most of Germany's best models carried only a 37mm gun, the French *Char S-35*

German *Neubaufahrzeug* heavy tanks, Norway, April 1940. *Courtesy German Federal Archives*

(Somua) medium tank carried a 47mm main gun, the L34 SA35—"the most powerful of its class on the Western front."[15]

The French Army's *Char B1* goliath went one better than many tanks by mounting two guns: a 47mm gun in a turret and a short, powerful, 75mm gun (L 17) in the hull. It also carried impressive armor compared to the *Panzer IV*. To armor historian Zaloga: "The *Char B1 bis* offered superior armored protection to that offered by the *Pzkpfw IV*, (with) 60mm armor on the front and sides and 55mm of armor on the rear, which made it essentially invulnerable to the 75mm gun of the *Pzkpfw IV*."[16]

While official Nazi propaganda was contemptuous of French weapons, respectful German tankers called the *Char B1* the *Kolasse* (giant).

Although the Allied press noted the power of Germany's towed anti-tank guns, such as the small *Pak 35/36*, the *Char B1*, Somua, and British Matilda II could shrug off hits from them. Soon, German gun crews began to deride their own *Pak 35/36* as "the door knocker" for its inability to punch through French and British tank armor.

Yet German propaganda created an exaggerated sense of Allied tank inferiority in the 1940 campaigns that persists today. When Hitler invaded Norway in April 1940, German photos showed monster tanks with three separate turrets carrying multiple

cannon and guns (one 75mm cannon, one 37mm, and three 7.92mm MG13 machine guns) rolling through the streets of Oslo, leading a frightened British War Office to warn of a giant new "Panzer V." In lurid newspaper and magazine stories of the day that attempted to envision an invasion of Britain or of France, illustrators featured roads clogged with columns of the new monster tank.

The giant Panzers with a six-man crew did exist, but there were only three of them. The intimidating land battleships pictured in Oslo in 1940 were prototypes of a failed heavy tank built in 1934, the *Neubaufahrzeug* (NbFz), or "New Construction Vehicle." Tests revealed it to be too slow and unwieldy to warrant mass production, but Nazi propagandists appreciated the shock value of its huge size and multiple turrets and guns. Proudly displaying one at the 1939 International Automobile Exposition in Berlin, they sent the three prototypes to Norway the next year. What in Allied newspapers appeared to be long lines of monster tanks were, in fact, the same three models dramatically posed and photographed again and again.[17]

The rumors of such monsters panicked American ambassador to France William Bullitt. "The German tanks," he reported to Roosevelt from Paris on May 14, "have crossed the River Meuse as if it did not exist. They have run through the French anti-tank defenses, which consisted of railroad rails sunk deep

April–May 1940: Neubaufahrzeug in Norway. *Courtesy German Federal Archives*

Restored British Matilda I light tank at the Tank Museum, Bovington, Dorset, UK. Some claim the nickname came from a cartoon character, "Matilda the Duck." *Massimo Foti*

**Matilda I Tank
Infantry Mark I A11** (253)

in concrete and protruding from the ground, as if the rails were straw. They have crossed the anti-tank traps and completely demolished the concrete fortifications by which the Maginot line had been extended."[18]

"At this moment," French Premier Paul Reynaud told Ambassador Bullitt, "there is nothing between those German tanks and Paris."[19] Bullitt then requested Thompson submachine guns for a last stand at the American embassy. On June 8, the Army's Ordnance Department received orders to rush a dozen "Tommy guns" (a.k.a. "Chicago Typewriters") to Paris by way of the Atlantic Clipper flying boat, but it was too late: the "City of Light" fell six days later.[20]

On the topic of German armor, gossip characterized Allied press. According to an American article datelined "Paris, May 24, 1940":

Yesterday a new German weapon was deployed for the first time: flame throwing tanks whose crews are equipped with asbestos suits. The tanks are said to have been transported through Flanders as far as the English Channel, and assisted the German motorized units which were halted in their push to the sea."[21]

One might expect such hyperbole from the civilian press, but even usually staid US Army publications caught the prevailing whiff of panic. In the summer of 1940, with a Nazi amphibious invasion of Britain using secret weapons expected any day, the *Field Artillery Journal* for July–August 1940 incorrectly reported

that the Germans not only had 70-ton monster tanks, but that they were amphibious as well.[22]

The response to the "breakthrough tank" rumor exemplifies Army intelligence failures that continued until 1945. Though charged with knowing enemy weapons so American tanks could match or surpass their abilities, Ordnance had been blindsided. Seeking excuses, they embraced wild rumors of unstoppable phantom "assault tanks."

In 1940, America also lacked heavy tanks; the preference among many Army leaders was for small, nimble ones. As far back as 1933 (when tanks were under Infantry branch control), then-Chief of Infantry Maj. Gen. Edward Croft had written, "it seems to me that light, inexpensive tanks, with not too much armor or armament, and stout-hearted soldiers manning them,

November 1940: A "Mae West" conquers iron obstacles at Ft. Belvoir, Virginia. *US Army Signal Corps*

A German recruiting poster for the occupied Netherlands showing stylized, imaginary monster tanks.

will better serve our Infantry purpose than will tanks that are heavy and expensive and calculated to meet every contingency."[23]

This opposition to heavy tanks would prevail until the last months of WWII. But what if other countries began to field bigger, more powerful tanks, as Germany had with the few *Neubaufahrzeugs* in 1934, and would do so in larger numbers with the Tiger, Panther, and King Tiger? In the fearful climate of 1940, Roosevelt ordered the Army to attempt to make up for years of neglect by fielding a heavy tank quickly: 500 of them in 1942 and 5,000 in 1943.[24] The result was a nearly 60-ton white elephant: the M6. When it was introduced, the December 15, 1941, issue of *Time* magazine (which also covered the Japanese attack on Pearl Harbor) ran an impressive photo of the mechanical monster captioned "New Heavy: In quickness, a destroyer; in power, a battleship." To *Time*, it was the "Ideal Tank?":

> In time for a new war, the best heavy tank in the world was unveiled at Eddystone, near Philadelphia, this week. A joint product of Baldwin Locomotive Works and U.S. Army Ordnance, it weighs 57 tons, and is heavily armored with welded and cast (armor) plate. Its contours are rounded to deflect hits, and even its traction gear is protected by steel. Its turrets are power driven, its silhouette cut down. It totes a three-inch double-purpose anti-tank and (anti) aircraft gun powerful enough to stop any tank in existence, and is equipped with a secret

device that gives its gunners 500% more accuracy than can be had in any other tank today. Powered by a 1,000-h.p. Wright Cyclone-type airplane motor, the new tank is as speedy as the M-3 medium (top, 25 mph), and in comparison with smaller types rides as smoothly as a limousine.

> Because the new tank wastes no space and carries a lot of its weight in armor, it looks almost as small as a medium. Only 75s and 105s loaded with armor-piercing shells would be effective against it. Although many a layman was skeptical of the new machine, figuring that few bridges could bear its weight, Army men knew it could be utilized with devastating effect in open country. In action against other tanks, it is expected to have the power of a battleship and the maneuverability of a destroyer.[25]

> American production of guns and ammunition rested on a solid foundation of more than a century of development and use, but production of tanks in World War II was based on twenty years of neglect.[3]
> —*Official History of the Army Ordnance Department in World War Two*, 1960

Perhaps one of the few heavy tank designs available at the time, the Army was pressured into developing the M6 by the "assault tank" panic of 1940. Reflecting the Army establishment's rejection of heavy tanks in theory (as well as the M6's specific mechanical faults), the prototype was not completed until December 1941, more than a year after the shock of the French campaign. The M6—slow, awkward, and prone to breakdowns—would never be mass produced. As 1942 proceeded, trouble with the transmission, suspension, wheels, and other components doomed it from receiving a proper evaluation by the Armored Board for possible standardization and large-scale production, never mind sending it to foreign battlefields.

The M6's poor performance and political pressure from Roosevelt to rush into production a flawed design increased opposition to more powerful tanks within the Army hierarchy. Ordnance briefly reconsidered mass-producing the clunky M6 as

For more than a century the name "Baldwin" has meant "locomotive" to railroad men throughout the world. Baldwin still serves the railroads, meeting their demands for modern power. Baldwin steam locomotives are helping the railroads to handle greater tonnage—at higher speed—than ever before in history. Baldwin Diesel-Electric switchers are speeding freight movements in yards and terminals from coast to coast.

But, today, Baldwin is more than a builder of railroad motive power. The skill and experience of the Baldwin organization is being applied to the building of tanks, guns and many other things needed by our armed forces and by industries essential to the war program.

Today, as in the First World War, Baldwin is devoting its efforts to this dual task of producing ordnance materiel and, at the same time, meeting the demand for its regular products so urgently needed to help achieve victory.

**BALDWIN**

The Baldwin Locomotive Works, Philadelphia, Pennsylvania: Locomotive & Ordnance Division; Baldwin Southwark Division; Cramp Brass & Iron Foundries Division; Standard Steel Works Division; Baldwin De La Vergne Sales Corp.; The Whitcomb Locomotive Co.; The Pelton Water Wheel Co.; The Midvale Co.

**BALDWIN SERVES THE NATION WHICH THE RAILROADS HELPED TO BUILD**

*Courtesy Henry Smith, photo by Robert Coldwell Sr.*

late as August 1944, when tankers were desperate for anything heavier than the M4.[26] But when the tank scandal broke in the stateside press in early 1945, with GIs overseas demanding more powerful tanks with heavier armor to confront Tigers and

King Tigers, the brass that had feted the M6 in 1941 as "the best heavy tank in the world" now pointed to it as "proof" that heavy tanks would fail.

While an awkward behemoth was not needed in 1941, neither was the other extreme of the tank design debate: a too small, too lightly armed and armored tank. Instead, the solution was a compromise, like the T-34: a medium tank that balanced speed, firepower, and armor protection.

Speaking to the House of Commons in May 1941, Prime Minister Winston Churchill reflected a prevailing bitterness among the Allies: Germany's success with tanks was not due to foresight and technical prowess, nor to decades of meager Allied defense budgets. Instead, he implied the wily Germans had cheated:

In the last war, tanks were built to go three or four miles an hour and to stand up to rifle or machine-gun bullets. In the interval the process of mechanical science had advanced so much that it became possible to make a tank which could go 15, 20, and 25 miles an hour and stand up to cannon fire. That was a great revolution, by which Hitler has profited...a simple fact which was perfectly well known to the military and technical services three or four years before the war. It did not spring from German brains. It sprang from British brains...and it has been exploited and turned to our grievous injury by the uninventive, but highly competent and imitative Germans.[27]

The "secret" of the blitzkrieg's success was that, instead of spreading tanks out thinly to support Infantry as the Allies had

"Junior" Meets "Mr. Big."  M-6 Heavy Tank with M-5 Light Tank of U. S. Armed Forces

*Courtesy Henry Smith, photo by Robert Coldwell Sr.*

Summer 1940: "Mae West" light tanks of the 28th Tank Company—attached to author's 28th "Keystone" Infantry Division—battle through smoke at the First Army Maneuvers in New York State. *US Army Signal Corps*

done during WWI, the Germans massed them in a spearhead role. And unlike the Americans (who since 1917 could not even agree on which branch of the Army should control tanks, let alone how to use them), the Germans learned to coordinate armor, infantry, artillery, and airplanes in a mutually supportive fashion for maximum speed, flexibility, and firepower.

When Germany invaded Poland, the US owned 70% of the world's automobiles.[28] Although American industry had mastered mass production techniques that could be applied to tanks, US tanks were obsolete and small in number. Gen. Marshall, who had been sworn in as Army Chief of Staff that eventful September 1, 1939, warned listeners in a February 1940 radio address that complicated modern weapons often needed one or two years to go from drafting board to battlefield.[29]

But over two years later, shortly after Pearl Harbor, America's tank force remained "plodding...a joke to the Germans":

> The Army was so short of tanks that French Renaults from World War I had to be towed behind trucks in maneuvers, to afford the soldiers an idea of what tanks really looked like. When even these did not total up to impressive numbers, ranks were filled out by Ford trucks with big cardboard placards: TANK. The more cynical sergeants and corporals obtained the impression that these signs, no matter how big or how black the letters, would not fool the Nazis.[30]

In May 1940, as Hitler invaded the Low Countries, Massachusetts Senator Henry Cabot Lodge addressed the Senate after observing large Army maneuvers in Louisiana:

> I have recently seen all the tanks in the United States, about four hundred in number, or about one finger of the fanlike German advance about which we have read, or about the number destroyed in two days of fighting

in the current European War. The Germans have a rough total of 3,000."[31]

Compared to the elite, tough *Panzerwaffe*, wisecracked *Time* magazine, "the U.S. Army looked like a few nice boys with BB guns."[32]

In August 1940, Maj. Dwight Eisenhower led a battalion of the 15th Infantry Regiment in the massive Fourth Army Maneuvers around Washington State. In October, he expressed a preference for his next assignment to his old friend Col. George Patton, leading the new Second Armored Brigade at Fort Benning, Georgia. "It would be great to be in the tanks again once more, and even better to be associated with you again."

"I will be delighted," Eisenhower also wrote to future Gen. Mark Clark in Washington, DC, "to serve in the Armored Corps in almost any capacity." He elaborated in a November letter to Clark, "It is my hope that I may get one of the armored regiments next spring [1941]." "George Patton has told me," he confided to another friend, "that at least two new armored divisions are to be formed early next year [1941], and if he is assigned to command one of them he intends to ask for me, possibly as one of his regimental commanders."[33]

While Eisenhower may have hoped to come back to tanks, as Panzers rolled towards Paris in June 1940, the United States Army's tanks were in a woeful state. Some had been mothballed since 1918, and were more suitable for museums than motor pools. Just 28 were even marginally combat effective.[34] President Roosevelt announced in his January 6, 1941, State of the Union Address, "The immediate need is a swift and driving increase in our armament production." Ironically, even while forcing the Army to freeze and mass produce obsolete tank designs to meet his demands, he also insisted that "today's best is not good enough for tomorrow."[35]

Motivated German tankers, using decent tanks combined with arms tactics (working in close coordination with their artillery

and infantry), had swept aside powerful British and French designs like the Matilda, Somua, and Char B1. Had America entered the war in 1940 or early 1941, the possibility of her mothballed antiques standing up to the Panzerwaffe was highly unlikely.

By 1941, Germany had combat-proven high-velocity 75mm tank main guns in France and Russia, establishing a new standard for tank armament. Soon they would advance to the next generation, adapting the freestanding 88mm anti-aircraft cannon used in Spain to fit inside a medium or heavy tank turret. But in the US, a Cavalry School manual insisted as late as 1937 that "the light tank…as it stands today, is one of the most redoubtable weapons of modern armies."[36] That year, the Cavalry's M1 and M2 "Combat Cars" (light tanks so named to circumvent the provisions of the National Defense Act of 1920, which forbade the Cavalry from having tanks) entered service carrying only one .30-caliber (light) machine gun and one .50 (heavy).

Weeks after the invasion of Poland, the Army's first order for mass production tanks since 1919 was placed with American Car and Foundry: 329 small, light M2A4s mounting a 37mm main gun.[37] Two earlier light tanks—the M2A2 (1934) and the similar M2A3—had an unusual design: two oval turrets seated side by

side (which inspired GIs to nickname the tanks "Mae Wests"). But like the Cavalry's M1 and M2 "Combat Cars," they were armed with just a single .30-caliber machine gun in one turret and a .50 in the other.

A cocky German tank crew. *Courtesy German Federal Archives*

October 1941: A "Mae West" light tank shows off for members of Congress at Ft. Belvoir, Virginia. *US Army Signal Corps*

Restored US M2A1 medium tank. *Courtesy of the National Armor and Cavalry Heritage Foundation*

In the spring of 1940, as Panzers with powerful 75mm main guns blazed through France, the just-ordered M3 Stuart light and M2 medium tank exemplified the flaws in American tank design: weakly armed with 37mm main guns (though the M2 bristled with eight pugnacious looking .30-caliber light machine guns) and lacking adequate armor. In May 1940, as German tanks descended on France and the Low Countries, Marshall admitted to the Senate Appropriations Committee that the Army had only

M2 Medium tanks at the 1941 Louisiana Maneuvers. Note the early model jeeps.

A late 1930s–early WWII American tanker wears the padded Rawlings "donut" tanker helmet and M1938 "Resistal" protective goggles. The resulting look inspired rival Infantrymen to mock tankers as "Men from Mars" and "Buck Rogers." *US Army Signal Corps*

The 3rd Army Maneuvers, 1940: An M2A1 medium tank of the 67th Infantry Regiment. *US Army Signal Corps*

The real Mae West displays two of her most prominent assets. For obvious reasons, admiring tankers affectionately nicknamed their twin-turreted light tanks after the buxom Hollywood star.

ten light and eighteen mediums.[38] A thousand M2 mediums were on order in June 1940, but they were canceled in favor of the M3 medium tank to arrive in June 1941. While the M3 (inspired by the French Char B1/bis design) did carry a 75mm main gun in a hull sponson (as well as the ubiquitous 37mm gun in a powered turret), it was inadequate to take on Germany's best. It would be a rude awakening when Lees confronted Tigers in the sands of North Africa and Tunisia.

Another belated American response to the blitzkrieg was the April 3, 1940, creation of the Armored Force under Gen. Chaffee after a laconic George Marshall scrawled a simple "O.K., GCM" on a proposal.[39] After more than two decades of internal strife, tanks and the doctrine for their use were removed from under the thumb of the resentful Infantry branch. Chief of Staff Marshall's act (along with his forming the new Tank Destroyer Force) reflect-ed dissension at the Army's highest levels. Rather than a direct response to what equipment and doctrine was needed at the time, it was a political compromise, an attempt to reconcile feuding branches and doctrines. Even the term "armored" was a pacifier, chosen to avoid the Infantry's preferred term "tank" and the Cavalry's "mechanized." While a much-needed start, the Armored Force perpetuated the dominance of small, light "Cavalry tank" doctrine when the Army needed a medium tank that balanced firepower, armor protection, and mobility.

An M3 Stuart struts its stuff. Even as the Germans were moving towards powerful, well-armored medium tanks with 75mm or potentially 88mm main guns, American tank design reflected the prewar emphasis on small, lightly armed and armored vehicles. While a decent light tank design by late 1930s standards, by 1942- when faced with more powerful German tanks in North Africa- the outclassed M3 was retired from frontline American service. *US Signal Corps via Ralph Riccio*

Today, the idea of vast American material abundance in WWII is taken for granted, yet the Armored Force was so short handed in its first years tankers were ordered to *imagine* they had medium tanks and 75mm main guns. They trained on light models with a white letter "M" painted on the turret and "75mm GUN" chalked onto their 37mm weapons.[40] Thousands of men would die because firepower and armor protection (qualities in which the Tiger and Panther were superior to the Sherman) were downplayed in favor of the "breakthrough" role popularized by J. F. C. Fuller. Designers built light, weakly armed and armored tanks instead of anticipating and preparing for heavier, future German ones that might appear on the battlefield.

Drive (forward) wheel of a restored M3 Stuart. *Author photo courtesy of the National Armor and Cavalry Heritage Foundation*

Fort Benning, Georgia, February 1940: An M2 medium tank approaches infantry in 1918-style trenches during field exercises. *US Army Signal Corps*

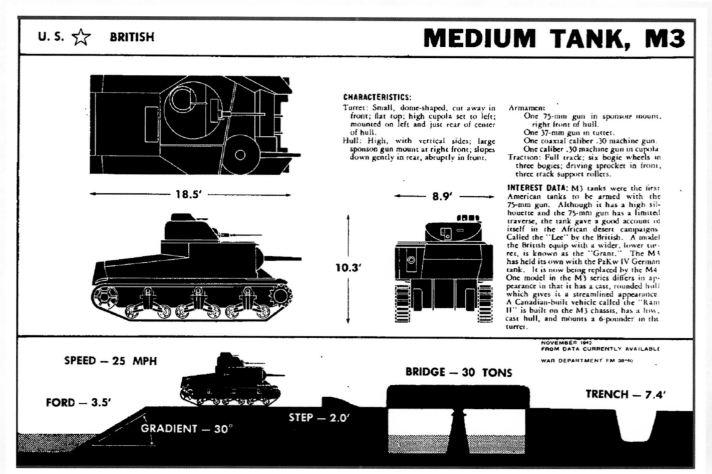

# MEDIUM TANK, M3

18.5'

8.9'

10.3'

**CHARACTERISTICS:**

Turret: Small, dome-shaped, cut away in front; flat top; high cupola set to left; mounted on left and just rear of center of hull.
Hull: High, with vertical sides; large sponson gun mount at right front; slopes down gently in rear, abruptly in front.

Armament:
One 75-mm gun in sponson mount, right front of hull.
One 37-mm gun in turret.
One coaxial caliber .30 machine gun.
One caliber .30 machine gun in cupola.
Traction: Full track; six bogie wheels in three bogies; driving sprocket in front, three track support rollers.

**INTEREST DATA:** M3 tanks were the first American tanks to be armed with the 75-mm gun. Although it has a high silhouette and the 75-mm gun has a limited traverse, the tank gave a good account of itself in the African desert campaigns. Called the "Lee" by the British. A model the British equip with a wider, lower turret, is known as the "Grant." The M3 has held its own with the PzKw IV German tank. It is now being replaced by the M4. One model in the M3 series differs in appearance in that it has a cast, rounded hull which gives it a streamlined appearance. A Canadian-built vehicle called the "Ram II" is built on the M3 chassis, has a low, cast hull, and mounts a 6-pounder in the turret.

NOVEMBER 1942
FROM DATA CURRENTLY AVAILABLE
WAR DEPARTMENT FM 30-40

SPEED — 25 MPH

FORD — 3.5'

GRADIENT — 30°

STEP — 2.0'

BRIDGE — 30 TONS

TRENCH — 7.4'

Photo by Robert Coldwell Sr.

The author with an M3 medium tank of the former Aberdeen Proving Ground collection. An interim design, the M3 was a stopgap attempt to mount a 75mm main gun on an American tank. Many of the more successful elements of its design (the turret, 75mm main gun, and suspension) would be incorporated into the next generation of American medium tank: the M4 Sherman. *Photo by Pete Johnston*

"Break-Through Tanks: Will They Bring Freedom of Action to Armored Divisions?," written by Captain C. R. Kutz over a year before Pearl Harbor, showed the prevalence of the "assault tank" myth, although Germany had no heavy tanks at the time:

One weapon used by the Germans, the heavy breakthrough tank, came as a surprise to many military men as well as civilians. Judging by the comments of the news correspondents, it can be assumed the breakthrough tank was the German Army's much-discussed "secret weapon." On May 10, 1940, "German breakthrough tanks, estimated to weigh seventy tons and armed with 77mm or 155mm cannon and flamethrowers, opened up a hole in the Little Maginot Line. Through this gap poured...massed armored divisions closely backed by Infantry in trucks. The age of mechanization came into its own."[41]

"The American Army," Kutz noted, "as yet has no modern heavy tanks. The closest thing to them is the one hundred Mark VIII tanks that have been out of service for nearly a decade."[42]

American lethargy contrasted with German vigor. In 1935, the US M2 "Mae West" light tank carried only machine guns and was lightly armored, but an Austrian tank expert wrote that year, "The more recent development of...anti-tank guns and the use of 75mm field pieces for defense against tanks makes heavy armor imperative. Modern heavy tanks have greatly increased armor protection. The best will protect against some hits from a 75mm weapon"[43]—precisely what the Sherman would carry seven years later.

The lesson for the Americans, concluded Kutz, was "don't send a boy to do a man's job...in a break-through tank, fire power plus armor protection [qualities Germany stressed in the Tiger and Panther, and which the M4 would be found wanting] are more important than battlefield speed."[44] In spite of warnings

October 1941: A lineup of Company D, 192nd Tank Battalion M2A2 "Mae West" light tanks at the Third Army (Carolina) maneuvers. *US Army Signal Corps*

"*Never before have we had so little time in which to do so much.*"

like this, American tanks remained under-gunned and under-armored until 1945. When the US entered the war, surprisingly, the job of its tanks was *not* to fight the enemy's tanks. Instead, "the main purpose of the tank cannon is to permit the tank to overcome enemy resistance and reach vital rear areas, where the tank machine guns may be used most advantageously"[45] in Fuller's breakthrough role.

"Operations" in *Army Field Manual 100-5* (May 1941) declared the armored division's primary role was "offensive operations against hostile rear areas,"[46] i.e., against soft targets like Infantry and trucks—not enemy armor.

By late 1941, as the new M3 Stuart light tank began rolling off assembly lines, the need was recognized for a medium tank with more powerful armament. The insufficiently armed M2 medium design (a rolling machine gun pillbox that reflected Infantry preference for tanks used to support men on foot) evolved into the M3 medium, with an unconventional approach to mounting a 75mm main gun inspired by the French Renault Char B heavy tank.

The M3 Lee's turret was too small to hold a 75mm gun. In an expedient measure that duplicated the Char B's layout, de-

**FARM SCRAP BUILDS TANKS & GUNS**

*18 tons of Scrap Metal goes into a Medium Tank*

signers positioned the main gun far down on the hull at the viewer's left front corner, restricting the gunner's field of fire. Since the 75mm gun could only traverse fifteen degrees from side to side (and only elevate and depress 0 to 20 degrees), engaging an enemy anywhere other than at the right front of the tank required turning the entire vehicle. Naturally, as French Char B tankers learned to their sorrow in the May–June 1940 campaign, this gave an advantage to modern German models with revolving turrets able to cover 360 degrees. In fairness, when the first Char B prototypes appeared with this lopsided layout in 1929–31, a tank mounting a 75mm main gun was innovative. Almost twelve years later, although the recent, disastrous French campaign showed the obvious limitations of this design, American tank designers repeated it on the new M3 medium, which Gen. Chaffee rated as having "barely satisfactory performance characteristics."[47]

British tankers were happy to receive the M3 (which they called the Grant, a Lee with British-requested modifications, including a smaller turret to reduce its too-high profile) through Lend-Lease aid, along with the new M3 Stuart light tank (which they affectionately nicknamed the "Honey"). Both were improvements over what they had been using.

A transitional stopgap design, the Lee was a step forward; it mounted a larger (75mm) main gun than previous tanks and was the first American model with an electrically powered turret and a "gyrostabilizer" for shooting on the move. But it was not good enough to take on Germany's best; nearly *half* of the 167

M3s sent to the British were destroyed by German tank or anti-tank fire.[48]

Publicly, Army and Roosevelt administration officials praised the new tanks rolling out of factories, but privately they recognized them as inadequate. Work soon began on the next generation of American medium tank, the M4 Sherman.

## Army Bureaucracy and FDR'S Numbers Racket

Amidst the panic of May 1940, Roosevelt tried to calm public fears by claiming on the radio that the US could respond to a future emergency with 792 tanks, 744 anti-tank guns, and other weapons "on hand or on order."[51] Critics mocked this "popgun defense," because most of the weapons were "on order," far from being ready for action, they were still not built. And the tanks in question were light models not likely able to counter the heavy "breakthrough" models Germany was believed to have.

As France fell in June 1940, another target number was thrown around: 1,741 American medium tanks to be built in the next eighteen months.[52] The same month, Chrysler opened the massive Detroit Tank Arsenal to build the new M3 medium and the British Tank Commission arrived, hoping to buy thousands of then-unbuilt US tanks of any kind.

M2A3 light "Infantry tanks" parade near the US Capitol, 1939. Note the Infantry guidon and crossed rifles plaque on the turret and the rare "donut" tanker helmet worn by crews. *Courtesy US National Archives*

November 1939: Shortly after German tanks spearheaded the invasion of Poland, a "Mae West" light tank of the 66th Infantry (Tank) Company, based at Ft. Meade, Maryland, makes short work of an anti-tank log obstacle at Ft. Belvoir, Virginia. *US Army Signal Corps*

US wooden storage box for belted .30-caliber machine gun ammunition as used from the Great War (1914–1918) to the late 1930s. *Author's collection, photo by Robert Coldwell Sr.*

Secretary of War Henry Stimson in 1929.

No American heavy tanks then existed or were on order. When the press estimated some might be built by a year later (June 1941), Gen. Marshall revised even this far-off date to the fateful December 1941. "I am terribly disappointed," a senator responded, "in the attitude of the Army. Their ambition is to get ready in a period of 18 to 24 months when we are living in a period of wars being settled in 30 days."[53]

Roosevelt ordered tank production in response to the blitzkrieg in what he called in March 1941 "a constantly increasing tempo of production—a production greater than we now know or have ever known before—a production that does not stop and should not pause."[54]

Were his politically minded goals realistic? If not, who was going to tell him? "It was frequently said in those days by politicians who had seen Mr. Roosevelt," remembered Marshall, "that they never got a chance to state their case. He was quite charming and quite voluble, and the interview was over before they had a chance to say anything."[55] Author Jonathan Jordan cites Gen. Marshall complaining to Treasury Secretary Henry Morgenthau of Roosevelt's "impulsiveness—his inability to sit still long enough to think through the whole picture." According to Marshall:

> First the President wants five hundred bombers a month, and that dislocates the (rearmament) program. Then he says he wants so many tanks, and that dislocates the program. Then the President will never sit down and talk about a complete program, and have the whole thing move forward at the same time."[56]

Secretary of War Henry Stimson was equally caustic in condemning Roosevelt's habit of making defense policy through improvisation. In summer 1941, Roosevelt complained in a cabinet meeting that his impulsive scheme to fly American P-40 fighters to Russia (which Marshall also opposed as being beyond the P-40's range) was not being carried out. "I didn't get half a chance with him," Stimson wrote in his diary of attempting to reason with FDR. "He was really in a hoity-toity humor, and wouldn't listen to argument." Lend-Lease aid to the Soviets ("This Russian munitions business,") noted Stimson, in words that could apply to the tank scandal, "has shown the President at his worst. He has no system. He goes haphazard and he scatters responsibility among a lot of uncoordinated men, and consequently things are never done."[57]

Garet Garrett, a staunch critic of Roosevelt's New Deal, deplored his rearmament program in the October 4, 1941, *Saturday Evening Post* for its "Enormous waste, great bungling, afterthinking, alphabetical confusion, free wheeling, conflict of authority; all that is true and very serious and has yet to be dealt with.... In their anxiety to see it dealt with, many are saying... that America is failing. The program is bogged down." But to Garrett, "There has never been a program. There is not now a program for which it is possible to make any definite outline. In place of a program there has been a progressive intention, bounded only by the unknown."[58]

> It appeared inexcusable to me that our troops were furnished with such a deficient main battle tank. The M4 Sherman appeared to have been designed by a committee, and many young Americans bled and died as a result.[49]
> —Lt. Belton Cooper, *Death Traps*

Coupled with Roosevelt's fickleness and lack of organization, the Army's tank design and building agencies had been decentralized and inefficient since 1917. As far back as 1929, an officer had lamented in the *Infantry Journal* how this impeded the development of new weapons such as tanks:

> Our Army is lacking a suitable agency for general research, experimentation, and development. We have branch boards (The Infantry Board, Tank Board, Air Corps Board, Field Artillery Board, etc.), each of which can make studies, within limits. But these minor agencies are severely limited as to what they may do, and they have, individually, scant resources with which to operate. And most important of all, they are isolated from one another.... Criticism that attributes our slow progress to ultra-conservatism is unjust. The fault lies not there but in the lack of a suitable agency. The missing element should be supplied.[59]

More than two years before Pearl Harbor rumors of powerful German tanks beginning during the 1939 blitz on Poland brought the issue of military preparedness to the American public's attention. But until the key role of Panzers in the German invasion of Russia forced reform on the US Army, there was no independent tank design and building office within the Ordnance Department. Instead, the responsibility came under the Artillery branch, which had the most experience designing and producing cannon and large guns.

This changed in July 1941, with the establishment of the separate Tank and Combat Vehicle Division under Lt. Col. John Christmas. Soon after, another scattered tank bureau operating within the civilian Office of Production Management was brought into the Ordnance Department. While these were steps in the right direction, an inefficient government bureaucracy with cobwebs dating back more than two decades would soon be confronted with Roosevelt's demands for 45,000 tanks in 1942.[60]

The Army agencies involved in tank design included the Ordnance Department, under Chiefs of Ordnance Gens. Charles Wesson (1938–1942) and Levin H. Campbell (1942–1946); Ordnance's Research and Design Service, led by Gen. Gladeon Barnes (1938–1946); Gen. McNair's Army Ground Forces; and the Armored Force headed by Gen. Chaffee until his death in August 1941, then by Lt. Gen. Jacob L. Devers.

Though tasked with the same goal, these agencies operated apart, in competition. They duplicated efforts, squabbled for money and influence, and allowed little input and feedback from the end user, the tanker. His mount was presented to him as a *fait accompli*:

> One of the major causes of the tank scandal was that within the Army, after decades of acrimony, the role of tanks (and even the definition of a tank, as opposed to tank destroyers, "gun motor carriages," self-propelled guns, etc.) remained unresolved. Thus, there was little consensus on the most effective tank designs. Before

Gen. Gladeon Barnes of Army Ordnance.

neuver, and shock. As a result of the different mentalities that have been brought to bear on our question, our present doctrine contains all of these ideas. It is a compromise, and thus open to the weaknesses of all compromises.[62]

Throughout the war, Army organizations responsible for tank design and production butted heads behind the scenes. The lack of consensus ensured GIs would be handicapped with inadequate weapons until the last months of the European war as interagency squabbles delayed better tanks at the cost of Allied lives.

Another factor that impeded tank design and production was bureaucratic inertia. Gen. Marshall complained of the War Department's "Civil War institutions" in late 1941, which were racked by inefficiency and petty jealousy over who ran which fiefdoms. His general staff was tasked with planning and coordinating Army-wide efforts to prepare for future wars, but it had "lost track of its purpose of existence. It had become a huge, bureaucratic, red-tape-ridden operating agency. It slowed down everything."[63]

Gen. Joseph McNarney was no stranger to red tape; appointed to the War Plans division of the War Department General Staff in early 1939, in June, he joined the Joint Army-Navy Planning Committee. He rose to become Deputy Chief of Staff of the Army under Gen. Marshall in March 1942, and later recalled of those days:

the war, the majority view was that speed and mobility should outweigh firepower and armor protection. Army Ground Forces was the most outspoken on this, wanting tanks for an exploitation, "Cavalry tank" role: lightly armed and armored, but fast and mobile.

As to demand for heavy tanks at this early stage of the war, while it was believed at the time that the Germans had them, and although the M6 heavy tank had appeared days after Pearl Harbor, Army Deputy Chief of Staff General Richard Moore (second only to Marshall) insisted in February 1942, "I haven't found an officer yet in the U.S. Army that proposes that we get these heavy tanks.[61]

As the war progressed and steadily more powerful German models debuted, the Armored Force began to call for more firepower. From 1943 onward, Ordnance also recognized the need for better guns and armor, possibly at the expense of speed and mobility.

But Gen. Lesley McNair remained firm, insisting tanks were not to fight other tanks. Instead, the job should go to his pet project, tank destroyers. He used his considerable influence to reject and obstruct heavier and up-gunned models.

In June 1941, Col. K. B. Edmunds of the Army's Command and General Staff College pointed out the dangers of bureaucratic and doctrinal squabbling and rivalry:

An engineer presented with the problem [of stopping enemy tanks] will think of obstacles and mines. An artilleryman will think of the fire of cannon. An Infantryman or Cavalryman will first consider movement, ma-

If a decision had to be made that affected an individual doughboy, it had to be referred over to the Chief of Infantry, get his recommendation on it, and back to the General Staff section; it then went up to one of the secretaries, General Staff, and they had at least eight assistant secretaries …who did nothing but brief papers so that they could be presented to the Chief of Staff and…three Deputy Chiefs of Staff.[64]

It requires little imagination to predict how inefficient bureaucracies would handle a task as complicated as designing and manufacturing new tanks, a process involving thousands of individual parts and extensive testing and revision of mechani-

Typical ration stamps issued to stateside civilians to buy food items. *Author's collection, photo by Robert Coldwell Sr.*

Photos by Robert Coldwell Sr.

Photo by Robert Coldwell Sr.

cally complex components like engines, transmissions, suspensions, and guns. And the Army would have to coordinate with civilian firms converting to wartime production. Charles Kettering, in charge of research at General Motors, complained to the *Saturday Evening Post* in January 1941 that some might not have appreciated the extent of the challenge.

In the public mind, the key to output lay in mass production; an easy phrase that most people knew, although they had no real understanding of what it meant. Detroit and the automobile industry had long been the heart and soul of American mass production, and the public expected miracles from its companies doing defense work. But few people realized how much preliminary work was required to set up mass production of anything:

> "Guns aren't windshield wipers," growled [Kettering]… he recalled being asked, "You fellows know how to make eight thousand automobiles a day, don't you? Well, then, why can't you make one thousand tanks a day without all this stalling around?"[65]

Compounding the problems were the pettiness and jealousy among officers in the interwar Army, competing with rival branches for scarce promotions and meager congressional funding. Marshall's biographer Dr. Forrest Pogue observed:

> For decades the Chiefs of Infantry, Cavalry, Field Artillery, and Coast Artillery—major generals—had exercised great power in training and equipping troops assigned to their particular arm. Jealous of their rights, they insisted on being consulted about any order that might conceivably pertain to their special preserves. They stood for hallowed service loyalties and a special parochialism that made change and speed and development especially difficult to achieve.[66]

In March 1942, greatly influenced by Gen. McNair's ideas, the Army underwent a major reorganization, including the creation of Army Ground Forces and Services of Supply. While Marshall hoped to make it more efficient, the changes added more layers of control and authority, more squabbling agencies, and more red tape to a decades-old bureaucratic nightmare. Army Ground Forces, the Armored Forces, Army Service Forces, the Ordnance Department, and other competing bureaucracies all became involved in tank design, and continued to bicker and work at cross purposes throughout the war.

Ordnance resented newcomers attempting to move in on its bureaucratic turf. In 1949, Col. John Raaen, Ordnance Chief

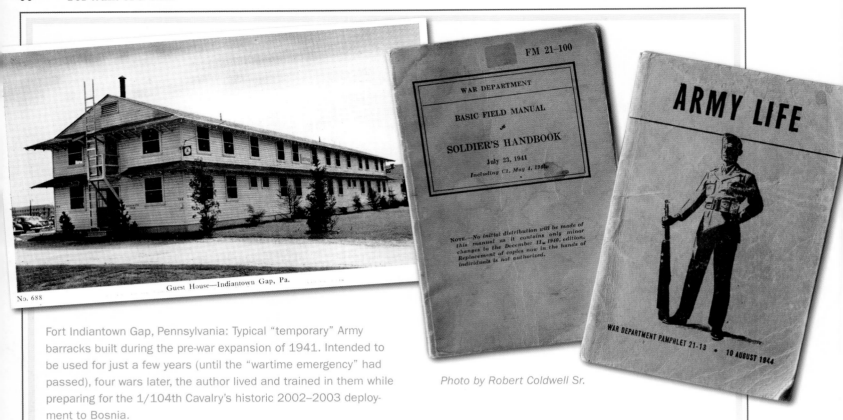

Fort Indiantown Gap, Pennsylvania: Typical "temporary" Army barracks built during the pre-war expansion of 1941. Intended to be used for just a few years (until the "wartime emergency" had passed), four wars later, the author lived and trained in them while preparing for the 1/104th Cavalry's historic 2002–2003 deployment to Bosnia.

*Photo by Robert Coldwell Sr.*

Campbell's executive officer, gave the department's point of view. Given after the fact, it should be taken with a grain of salt:

> The Ordnance Department had been a procuring service over a period of some 130 years. During that time it had developed a certain know-how concerning procurement and manufacture. Very few of the members of the ASF headquarters had any experience in the procurement or manufacture of Ordnance items.... There was a group of some two or three thousand in the ASF headquarters with little or no experience along our specialized line who were continually telling us just how to do our job in the minutest details. We resented this, and I think rightly so.[67]

Col. Clinton Robinson of ASF gave the other side of the dispute in an April 1942 memo to Lt. Gen. Brehon Somervell, who led Army Services of Supply, and many in the Armored Force would agree with his view:

> There appears to be a decided fraternity or clique feeling among the majority of Ordnance officers.
>
> There is apparently a belief that there is something "mysterious" about the design and production of Ordnance munitions; that Ordnance officers are specialists in this, no one else knows anything about it, and no one should interfere. Apparently there is the feeling that the way the organization should operate is to give the Ordnance Department the job, and complete authority for production of Ordnance munitions, and then for any higher headquarters to forget about it and assume that the job is being done.[68]

*When it came to designing the Sherman, Ordnance hurriedly handed out pieces of the project to various committees, crossed its fingers, and wished hard.[50]*
*—Geoffrey Perrett, There's A War To Be Won*

Until the late 1930s, the Army had little experience mass producing standardized tanks. The few completed between the wars (some of them one-of-a-kind prototypes) were virtually hand built by craftsmen. In 1938, with the passage of the Education Orders Act, Congress provided funds for small orders of weapons like tanks from civilian firms to give them experience and identify production problems should large numbers of tanks be needed in a future war.

As Ordnance's official history concedes, although tanks were vital weapons of the future, they "were given scant attention" in the Educational Orders program because "the using arms had not adopted a clear statement of desired tank characteristics, nor assigned tanks a high priority." Thus, "Ordnance did not consider it advisable to attempt much by way of educating industry in their manufacture."[69]

Another limiting factor was their high cost, from $25,000 to $50,000.[70] The Educational Orders Act was intended to improve preparedness by allowing firms to get experience and practice building complicated weapons. As they required much trial and error to build, tanks would seem ideal subjects. But only two minor orders were placed: one for light tank hulls and another for a mere ten M2A4 light tanks by the Baldwin Locomotive Works. Production was delayed until after Pearl Harbor, and by then the still-unbuilt tanks were already obsolete. "In terms of production preparedness," Ordnance admitted, "the two orders brought no significant results."[71]

In May 1940, Chief of Ordnance Gen. Charles Wesson responded to criticism by pointing out that no country's armies had heavy tanks—as if this excused America from preparing to field them. Germany would introduce heavy tanks on the battlefield ahead of the US with the Tiger tank of 1942. In hindsight, it is interesting to ponder, what if the US had taken the lead and introduced powerful, effective heavy tanks first?

U.S. Armored Regiment

Photos by Robert Coldwell Sr.

Blindsided by German success, Army leaders responded to a fearful American public by attempting to spin unpreparedness into a virtue. The excuses in "Tank Service Becomes A Main US Arms Target" (*United Press International*, 04 February 1941), are not very convincing:

> The U.S. Army tank arm has begun to carry out an enormous expansion program, based on plans which have been developed, continuously improved, and modernized since 1928. The Army always realized the striking power of rapid-moving tanks but, armored officers explain, considered it wiser to avoid spending billions of dollars for the production of tanks that would have then had to be stored in giant depots until the day they were mobilized, and that might by then have become outdated. The Army trusted in the geographic position of the USA to give it time to assemble, whereas the European nations are compelled to keep their armies and arms always ready to deploy.[72]

"The U.S. Army," wrote historian Martin Blumenson, "started far too late to prepare seriously for World War II. As a result, the training program, the procurement of weapons, and virtually all else were hasty, largely improvised, almost chaotic, and painfully inadequate throughout the intensely short period of mobilization and organization before and after Pearl Harbor."[73]

Col. George Jarrett noted years later that while Americans froze existing obsolete designs, the Germans were quick to steadily upgrade theirs:

> A strange situation prevailed, and continued until the end of the war. Some of the Allied designers seemed to be satisfied to know that, perhaps on their drawing boards, they had designed an improvement in some type of ordnance. They were content to rest on their oars. Meanwhile, at the front, the enemy was already using a similar innovation, or a better one...the fact that the enemy was using such improved materiel as compared with our designers' drawing board marvels never disturbed these people at all. Usually, the defenders of such action had not even the education afforded

the proof directors at a testing station, who smelt cannon smoke from some proving ground.[74]

Another problem was the tug of war between quantity versus quality—delaying mass production to update designs. If Ordnance was to keep up with Germany, would its models not require constant modification as feedback on them came in from overseas? Unlike Roosevelt, Assistant Secretary of War Louis Johnson appreciated in July 1940 that production "obviously cannot be frozen either as to quantities or types.... A happy compromise must be effected between the two opposites of production and perfection in order to obtain most effective results."[75]

An M3 Lee medium tank rolls through Center City Philadelphia, near Broad and Locust Streets. To the left of the drug store sign is the old Philadelphia Academy of Music.

*Photo by Robert Coldwell Sr.*

But Johnson, perhaps not coincidentally, was replaced soon afterward. The next month, his successor, Robert Patterson, attempted to address this conflict with a secret memo to Chief of Ordnance Gen. Wesson: in order to meet Roosevelt's demands for large numbers of any tanks, now the Army would "freeze" obsolete designs. To Assistant Secretary Patterson, "The best is the enemy of the good.... Germany has demonstrated that thousands of imperfect tanks on the battlefield are better than scores of perfect tanks on the proving ground."[76]

This decision had some short term merit, but as Ordnance's official history points out, it was unreasonable; how could Ordnance be expected to keep up with constantly evolving advances in German tanks if already out-of-date designs were frozen? "Everyone agreed," Ordnance's history says, "that a thousand 'imperfect' tanks on the battlefield were better than scores of 'perfect' tanks on the proving ground, but whether they were better than 500 'more-nearly-perfect' tanks on the field of battle was a moot question."[77]

Coupled with a willingness to mass-produce designs known to be dated, observed Col. Jarrett, was a hesitation to update them. The Germans:

were always so quick to take advantage of the slightest [improvements], while our designers at home would fool and fiddle with this or that. Meanwhile, troops in the field had to carry on with only the courage God gave

An M2-series medium tank during stateside maneuvers. Note the side-mounted machine gun in the "barbette" (small turret), Great War-style doughboy helmets worn by GIs, and the row of extra fuel cans. Wanting to demonstrate armor's potential to detractors, tank crews intended to move far and fast. *US Signal Corps*

Typical US Army sergeant's stripes for the summer Cotton Khaki Chino (CKC) uniform. *Photo by Robert Coldwell Sr.*

Typical "sweetheart jewelry" that a tanker in training would send home from Fort Knox, Kentucky. *Photo by Robert Coldwell Sr.*

them to do the best job with the means at hand. The countless dead, with their crosses, were mute testimony of the power of German weapons.[78]

While the Americans froze designs and "Our own developing agencies would wrangle for weeks or months over any change," recalled Jarrett, the Germans "would put new ideas into effect at once, with little loss of time. Sometimes the testing of a piece was at the front, not at a proving ground. While such a procedure cannot remove 'bugs,' nor hardly reveal them properly, in an emergency it is a time saver, and if the item had any good points, they might be revealed and contribute to a military success."[79]

Observing this process first hand in Detroit and Washington, DC, Chief British Technical Liaison to US Army Ordnance Brig.

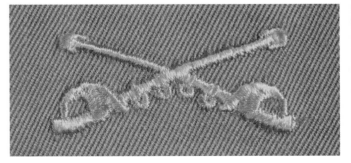

US Cavalry officer's insignia for warm weather uniform. *Author's collection, photo by Robert Coldwell Sr.*

Tank in Armored Force Division, Fort Knox, Ky.

*Photo by Robert Coldwell Sr.*

Roosevelt had willed it, therefore, it must be done. As Clementine Churchill recalled a postwar conversation with Gen. Marshall, Roosevelt, said Marshall, "would direct his mind like a shaft of light over one section of the whole subject to be considered, leaving everything else in outer darkness. He did not like his attention called to aspects he had not mastered, or which, from lack of time or indolence or disinclination, he had disregarded."[82]

To historian Geoffrey Perret, FDR's political gestures sacrificed quality to quantity:

> The Army relinquished... putting the best possible weapons into the hands of its fighting men...in order to arm millions of men quickly, it chose as a matter of policy not to aim for superiority in tank versus tank.... Instead it set its sights on adequacy—and crushing, smothering numbers. Weight and quantity of arms were accepted as being decisive over quality.[83]

Armor officer's collar insignia for the winter uniform. *Photo by Robert Coldwell Sr.*

Gen. MacLeod Ross described the prickly relationship between Ordnance and the Armored Force:

> Ordnance objectives seemed far removed from Armored Force requirements, so that even when we influenced the latter, they still cut no ice with Ordnance. The Armored Force did not have the strong lobby that Ordnance enjoyed, and so the latter continued in paternal fashion to dispense to the user what they considered good for him...the problem was compounded by a somewhat complex organization, divided into two parts, one in Washington, the other in Detroit...either due to deliberation or ignorance, no effective U.S. tank gun designed by Ordnance throughout the war took its place in battle.[80]

A little-appreciated aspect of the Sherman tank scandal is the influence of domestic politics: Roosevelt's desire to make dramatic gestures in response to the blitzkrieg impeded American tank design. "I frankly was fearful," Gen. Marshall told his biographer Forrest Pogue in 1957, "of Mr. Roosevelt's introducing political methods, of which he was a genius, into a military thing.... You can't treat military factors in the way you do political factors."[81]

When Roosevelt pressured the Army to realize his huge production numbers in 1940, since designing modern tanks from scratch might take years, his demands were met by halting proposed improvements to outdated designs. Regardless of their inferiority, production of any tanks would begin immediately.

While there is some truth to this view, it implies that Army leaders' negligence was a well-thought out, intentional policy. But to argue that American factories had no alternative to churning out inferior guns is not correct; the generals rejected available solutions. Factories could just as easily have cranked out thousands of M4s with powerful 90mm or 105mm main guns instead of the inadequate 75mm guns that continued to be built well after frontline tankers warned of their lackluster performance against German tanks. The means to build better tanks was there, but far from having their hands tied by impersonal forces, Army leaders refused to do so.

Until Operation Barbarossa, American medium tanks had a low priority production rating of A-l-g.[84] Spurred by the shock of German armor's initial successes, Roosevelt ordered the Army to speed up tank production, "with the only limiting factor...the ability of American industry to produce tanks."[85]

In April 1941, Roosevelt's new Joint Tank Planning Committee had proposed to build 1,000 tanks of all types each month; by July, in the midst of the dramatic success of seemingly unstoppable German armor on the Russian steppes, this target was doubled.

After Roosevelt conferred with Churchill, he raised production goals to 25,000 medium tanks in 1942, then 45,000 in 1943.[86] In September 1941, as the Ordnance Department's official history puts it, FDR "dropped a bombshell" on the Army. Not only would the production rating of medium tanks be increased to a higher priority (A-1-a), but at a White House conference the president reviewed current military production plans. When he came to the schedule calling for production of 1,000 medium tanks and 400 light tanks per month the president paused,

placed a cigarette in his famous long holder, lit it, and then calmly issued this cryptic directive: "Double it!" Monthly production was to be 2,800, or 33,600 per year. The cost would be close to a billion dollars for one year's production.[87]

In his 1942 annual message to Congress on January 6, Roosevelt then handed the Army an even larger goal:

> To increase our production rate of tanks so rapidly that in this year, 1942, we shall produce 45,000 tanks (including 25,000 mediums), and to continue that increase so that next year, 1943, we shall produce 75,000 tanks (including 50,000 mediums).[88]

In delivering this news to his advisers, Roosevelt "told his staff not to fall out of their chairs," joking he had "arrived at the figures...by my usual rule-of-thumb method."[89] As Eleanor Roosevelt once stated, "The president does not think. He decides."[90] Observed author Jonathan Jordan:

> Having started his draft speech with production targets supplied by his advisers, Roosevelt blithely penciled through the numbers and boosted them as he thought proper, asking no input from either military or industrial experts. His numbers were not based on what had been possible in the past; they were based on what America needed to defeat three enemy empires that had swallowed nearly one-third of the world's strategic resources and population.[91]

Biographer Jean Edward Smith gives possible explanation for Roosevelt's preposterous numbers, which he says FDR "had drawn more or less out of a hat." According to Smith:

> Roosevelt relied on the guesswork of [Churchill's advisor] Lord Beaverbrook, who cautioned against underestimating US production capacity. Taking the projected Canadian production for 1942 as a base, Beaverbrook estimated that the excess of American resources over Canadian resources should permit the United States to produce fifteen times as much. According to Beaverbrook's calculations, this would mean 45,000 tanks... figures that FDR relied on in drafting his speech.[92]

Roosevelt had written to Secretary of War Stimson that victory would come from "our overwhelming mastery in [sic] the munitions of war. The concept of our industrial capacity must be completely overhauled under the impulse of the peril to our nation." Furthermore, "We must not only provide munitions for our own fighting forces but vast quantities to be used against the enemy in every appropriate theater of war, wherever that may be."[93]

In other words, not only would the Army need thousands of tanks for its own soldiers, it would supply the British and Soviets, too. When Army officers expressed concern about the feasibility of such lofty goals, Roosevelt's response was a typically airy, "Oh, the production people can do it if they really try."[94] To historian Jordan, "The experts were appalled by Roosevelt's naiveté. Incredulous War Department officers could only joke that Roosevelt had 'gone into the numbers racket.'"[95]

A US matchbook solicits American public support for British war relief, 1941. *Photo by Robert Coldwell Sr.*

The Ordnance Department's official history observed:

The President's letter to the Secretary of War, and his address to Congress three days later, constituted a striking example of the lack of coordination between the White House and the Army staff. The President apparently drew up his plans in consultation with a few close advisors and with the British delegation that had come to Washington soon after Pearl Harbor, but without consulting his own generals. Reaction in Ordnance to these goals was not favorable, for they were regarded as unbalanced, and in some cases unattainable.[96]

"Lack of coordination" was polite understatement describing Roosevelt's working style, since he "treated lines of responsibility with a benign neglect, to be used when convenient and disregarded when they got in the way":

He would dole out overlapping projects to sworn enemies, bypass chains of command, and refuse to bind himself to any precedent that might not suit him in the future. A master of the art of ignoring problems until they solved themselves, FDR encouraged dissent and talked out of both sides of his mouth. Lines would remain fuzzy, opportunities would be seized as they stumbled across his desk, and a film of unpredictability would shadow the American high command.[97]

Roosevelt's generosity with tanks was at the U.S. Army's expense. To historian and retired Army colonel David Johnson:

Roosevelt's policy of supplying war materiel to the Allies, often over War Department protest, exceeded production capacity. The large-scale production of existing models was emphasized—at the expense of further development—to equip the rapidly expanding U.S. Army and its hard-pressed Allies.[98]

Army officers, administration officials, and tank designers and manufacturers were forced to stress quantity over quality, motivated by the "Fear of incurring Roosevelt's indirect wrath,

which seemed ever at the back of some officers' minds...they would pass weapons unfit for battle rather than break the production promises which the Chief of Ordnance had put into the mouth of the President."[99]

At times, the brass's willingness to please the Commander in Chief assumed comical proportions. At March 1942 meetings, instead of telling Roosevelt his production goals might be unrealistic, some generals proposed renaming non-tanks to sound more like tanks; in this way, Roosevelt could claim to have met his promised numbers. A self-propelled gun, suggested Gen. Lucius Clay, could be transformed into an "artillery tank." Wheeled armored cars, Gen. Charles Harris helpfully added, might be dubbed "light tanks," while Gen. Brehon Somervell pushed for adopting a new system of nomenclature for Army combat vehicles, the better to enhance the verbal shell game.[100]

Roosevelt needed a realistic assessment, not subterfuge. Instead, career-minded generals resorted to chicanery and wishful thinking, labeling a light truck a tank, a broomstick a rifle, or a wooden log an artillery piece.

Would the brass speak up? While Gen. Somervell (Assistant Chief of Staff [G-4] on the War Department General Staff, who would eventually head the Army's Services of Supply) was unwilling to do so, to his credit, Chief of Ordnance Gen. Wesson "was less restrained, bluntly declaring that the program should be 'balanced' and 'in line with actual requirements,' even if it meant informing the President that 'his objectives were unsound.'" But politics reared its ugly head; Assistant Secretary of War Robert Patterson "stated that he could not report to the White House that certain items in the program were superfluous and not useful."[101]

Meanwhile, the "Arsenal of Democracy" rolled on. In July 1942, the *New York Times* exulted that "throughout the land, a mighty revolution is in progress":

American industry is beating the ploughshares of peacetime—the autos, electric refrigerators, the toasters and the washing machines—into the swords of total war: planes, tanks, and high explosive bombs. It is a revolution to which there can be but one end: The doom of Nazidom.[102]

After Roosevelt promised Prime Minister Winston Churchill the latest tank models, British Col. Ross helped prepare new M4s for shipment to North Africa in the summer of 1942. To Ross, Ordnance Department officials were more concerned with obeying FDR's demands for *any* tanks, *now*, than with supplying adequate ones. When British experts (who, unlike the Americans, had years of first-hand knowledge fighting German designs) pointed out weaknesses, Ordnance insisted on shipping them regardless:

The new Chief of Ordnance, General Levin Campbell, had presumably given a promise to get out tanks to the number asked by the President, and he had impressed on his underlings that it was do or die. The impression was that their very promotion depended on turning out the promised tanks, whether fit for battle or not.... The trouble was that Ordnance wished to be able to say,

"We have complied with our Commander in Chief's order. The tanks have sailed."[103]

Thus, American tankers entered the war in 1941 with mediocre weapons, about to be blindsided by Germany's—a situation that continued until 1945. Although the M3 medium was already obsolete as it clanked out of factories by the thousands in late 1941 (while Roosevelt spouted impressive-sounding production figures for it), it was represented as a "Fort On Wheels" in Dodge advertisements. A week after Pearl Harbor, *Time* magazine readers read how:

> Dodge men are producing guns…. And they are producing tanks…these 28-ton "Forts On Wheels" roll daily off the triple assembly lines at the huge Chrysler Tank Arsenal. Dodge Division is producing forgings and machine parts for these tanks on a continuous three-shift basis…. These, it has been said, are real production miracles.[104]

Photo opportunities at Detroit's new Chrysler Tank Arsenal showed M3 mediums effortlessly crushing telephone poles—much as more powerful German tanks would crush the under-gunned M3 Lees in North Africa and Tunisia barely a year later. There, GIs would suffer some of the worst American routs of the war.

In November 1942, not long before the M3's combat performance in American hands showed the need for a better medium tank, the Army's newest supply program figures were issued. The lofty tank production goals for 1942 had not been met; only some two-thirds of the target number had been built.[105] Roosevelt in his 1942 State of the Union Address had demanded a dramatic increase in tank production, but now reversed himself, cutting medium tank production almost in half, from 46,500 Shermans in 1943 to 24,582.

Roosevelt's Secretary of the Navy Frank Knox, a Spanish-American War Army veteran who served with D Troop of Col. Theodore Roosevelt's First US Volunteer Cavalry, had personal experience with military unpreparedness. In 1898, although British soldiers had been issued practical cotton "kharkhi" summer uniforms for almost two decades, Knox had arrived in tropical Cuba wearing a thick, dark blue wool uniform shirt because the Army supply system had been blindsided by the war with Spain.

"There have been many mistakes," Knox acknowledged in December 1942, speaking to the National Association of Manufacturers. "There has been timidity, hesitancy, inefficiency, confusion, waste, and all the other things the critics say, but contrasted with what's been accomplished, I marvel there have not been more."[106]

Tankers were routed in North Africa and Tunisia, but FDR was able to spout his big numbers. After the humiliating defeat

New M3 Lee medium tanks at the Detroit Tank Arsenal.

M3 Lees (left) are joined by early Sherman tanks (right) at the Detroit Tank Arsenal, 1942.

at Sidi-bou-Zid, the M3 Lee—the "Fort on Wheels" star of press releases and propaganda newsreels—was withdrawn from frontline service. It had served a political purpose at the cost of soldiers' lives.

All these factors—decentralization of design agencies, disagreement over armor doctrine, petty bureaucratic rivalries, peacetime inertia, and domestic civilian politics—combined to produce a bitterly ironic situation: the nation behind mass production of the automobile remained years behind Nazi and communist dictatorships who built better tanks, got them to the battlefield, and steadily updated them as the state of tank technology advanced. Roosevelt's boasts notwithstanding, the world's leading industrial giant muddled along by rushing flawed designs into production.

Before the war, bureaucrats failed to see that German tanks and anti-tank guns were years ahead of Allied models. During the war, they brushed aside warnings from men actually fighting them. Col. Jarrett served in the Middle East, helping the British maximize the effectiveness of their American Lend-Lease equipment. Although he sent many captured German weapons home to Aberdeen Proving Ground for evaluation:

The Allied agencies charged with keeping abreast of the needs at the front...with only thought for their trends...would not place sufficient weight on reports from the front. Endless discussions over policies, with personalities playing a huge part in the delays, would at times hold up urgently needed improvements... eventually, an improvement would be developed, but... by the time it reached the frontlines, the Germans would have a more advanced design already in action. Then, the Allied piece would be obsolescent, if not obsolete.[107]

When stateside technicians were slow to address shortcomings in American armor protection, tankers overseas began to improvise solutions in the field, hoping to increase their chances of survival. Eventually, the GIs' unauthorized quick fixes were approved and incorporated into new tanks rolling out of the factories. But until the last days of the war, the dictatorships rolled out better tanks than FDR's vaunted "Arsenal of Democracy."

A British tank attack in the Western Desert

# BACK THEM UP!

PROPERTY U. S. ARMY AIR FORCES

MF'D. BY FOTOSHOP, N. Y. C.

General Grant, American

T307     Medium Tank M3     17

*Photo by Robert Coldwell Sr.*

# Chapter 3

# "AVOIDING ACTION"
## The Tank Destroyer Sideshow

In a July 1940 study, Chief of Infantry Gen. George Lynch pondered how to stop German tanks. The just-defeated French, he wrote, had overemphasized towed anti-tank guns. In a prescient warning, Gen. Lynch cautioned against taking the same course. Favoring towed guns over tanks would "fail wholly to apply the proper remedy, and waste our resources in the development of ineffective means."[4] Better tanks were needed to counter German armor: "the best anti-tank defense lies in the defeat of hostile forces by our own armored units."[5]

But Gen. McNair disagreed. Soon-to-be Chief of Staff of Army General Headquarters and ranked close to Gen. Marshall in Army hierarchy, he had been impressed by Germany's use of towed guns in Spain, Poland, and France. To McNair—an old artilleryman—towed guns, not tanks, were the answer; American tanks should not fight Germany's, but merely "secure immunity from small arms fire"[6] for accompanying Infantry. This zeal for towed guns would lead to a detour in the Army's anti-tank doctrine: ineffective, awkward 37mm, 57mm, and three-inch towed anti-tank guns.

> To even the most inexperienced second lieutenant tank platoon leader, it was obvious that if our Armored Force doctrine said that tanks were not supposed to fight tanks, the Germans would do just the opposite, and oppose our tanks with their heavier tanks whenever possible.[1]
>
> —Lt. Belton Cooper, Third Armored Division

Gen. McNair's defensive ideas assumed that friendly tanks could avoid battling enemy tanks and fight on their own terms. France's anti-tank guns had failed, McNair argued, because they were used incorrectly. He was very familiar with French artillery, having been assigned to France in 1913, to observe their use of it. He had also written a guide to using artillery in battle decades ago, before WWI.

"The tank's natural and proper victim," McNair was certain in 1940, "is unprotected personnel and materiel."[7] Furthermore:

If the [towed anti-tank] gun outmatches the [enemy] tank, then not only is the gun superior to the tank in anti-tank defense, but *employing armored units against other armored units positively should be avoided whenever possible* [author's emphasis]. The gun, supported properly by foot troops, should defeat hostile armored units by fire, and free the friendly armored units for action against the [rear area] objectives which are vulnerable to them.[8]

"McNair's Folly," a 3-inch towed M5 anti-tank gun. *Photo by Lindsay Fraschilla, courtesy of the National Armor and Cavalry Heritage Foundation*

Influenced by the success of small German 37mm towed guns like the PaK 35/36, McNair wanted an American version built. The resulting unpopular 37mm M3 entered service in 1940.

Gen. McNair, whose intense gaze led *Time* magazine to call him "cave-eyed,"[9] was regarded in the Army as an intellectual, "noted for prodigious and sustained mental exercise."[10] In his US Military Academy graduating class of 1904, he "stood eleventh in a class of a hundred and twenty-four."[11] The usually reserved George Marshall, not known for hyperbole, called him "the brains of the Army."[12] Significantly, in light of the coming tank scandal that pitted frontline tankers against stateside officers, McNair never held a combat command. Instead, he was responsible for overseeing the domestic training of Army ground troops.

His biographer, E. J. Kahn of *The New Yorker* fame, titled his book *Educator of an Army*. Writing of McNair's way with paperwork, Kahn noted his distress over "any wording that did not come up to his exacting standards, and he personally rephrased many of the directives that emanated from his headquarters."[13] Furthermore, observed Kahn, "Proof of his constant interest in precise wording is furnished by the large dictionary he invariably kept within arm's reach."[14]

Constantly updating American tank designs to compete with Germany's required flexibility, and a willingness to reconsider prewar tank doctrine and adapt to the situation in the field. This is a quality that soldiers acquire through the hard, unforgiving school of overseas deployment conditions where, faced with an immediate, life-threatening situation, one may not have the time to reach for a manual to apply the approved "textbook" solution.

In the years to follow, Gen. McNair would become a key figure in crucial tank production decisions and in the tank scandal itself. But his fastidiousness and rigidity (he came from a dour Scottish Presbyterian background, "regulated his life strictly," and was known to "always [keep] a fly swatter not only in his office but in his car as well")[15] ill prepared him for revising anti-tank doctrine that, while seeming ideal on paper, may not have suited the real world situations GIs faced.

During WWI, Lesley McNair served as a staff officer (Operations) with the First Infantry Division, where he came to the attention of Gen. John Pershing, leader of the American Expeditionary Force. At thirty-five, McNair became the youngest Brig. Gen. in the AEF. He had been commissioned as an Artillery officer, and in four decades of Army service led many commands and posts connected to that branch, including assistant commandant of the Field Artillery School.

To armor advocates, McNair's preference for artillery fueled what they perceived as an anti-armor, pro-towed gun bias. Perhaps he harbored resentment toward the flashy, cocky Cavalry as well; as Kahn writes in his 1945 biography, when Army Ground Forces was established in 1942, McNair not only abolished the office of Chief of Cavalry, he ended the separate "training and schooling functions" that the Cavalry had enjoyed. This was the tradition of training their own men in the pride, dash, and élan of the Cavalry trooper. "This new trend against segregation [in training

M6 "Fargo" Gun Motor Carriage tank destroyer (1/35 scale model by the author, pictured here as used in North Africa and Sicily), a weapons carrier (light pickup truck) with a 37mm gun mounted in the bed. With the M10 GMC, the TDs became near-tanks, thinly armored, open-topped poor substitutes for the real thing. Tank Destroyer men joked what they needed was not a "tank killer," but simply a "killer tank." *Photo by Robert Coldwell Sr.*

*Author photo courtesy of the National Armor and Cavalry Heritage Foundation*

soldiers]," wrote Kahn, "for a while rather offended old Cavalrymen, who were proud of their exclusiveness and dismayed at having to associate so fraternally with pedestrians, but it delighted General McNair, a firm believer in teamwork."[16]

Tanks were not the first revolutionary new weapon that McNair had stoutly resisted; in 1925, he was a witness for the Army establishment against air power crusader Gen. William Mitchell. McNair, at Mitchell's court martial, had dismissed his predictions of a surprise, Sunday morning Japanese aerial attack on Pearl Harbor as highly improbable.

By the time of the blitzkrieg on France, McNair's decades-long preference for towed guns over tanks, the need to respond to German armor, and his great influence with Army Chief of Staff Marshall combined to create his pet project: the ill-fated Tank Destroyer forces that would impede American tank design and doctrine, and delay the adoption of a more powerful and protected heavy tank.

McNair was leading the Command and General Staff School at Fort Leavenworth, Kansas, in September 1940, when Marshall chose him to become Chief of Staff of the Army's new General Headquarters. Gen. McNair was now the Army's number two man, and this power and influence ensured that his preferences would have a central role in the future tank scandal.

On paper, the "TD" (tank destroyer) concept seemed reasonable. With little time to match years of German tank development, a fast American response to the blitzkrieg was needed, and now. As biographer Kahn put it, the general's attitude was, "you may do the *wrong* thing, but do *something*."[17]

Instead of waiting for all new tanks, why not use an existing design—simple towed guns—against the Panzers? It was good economics; towed guns could be mass produced faster than expensive, complicated tanks, and were easier and cheaper to replace when lost. As Gen. McNair told a July 1941 conference at the Army War College in Washington, DC:

I do not quarrel with the assertion that the best defense against tanks is by other tanks; possibly it is correct. However, it is questionable economy to employ a tank costing $35,000 to destroy another tank of substantially the same value, when the job could be done by a gun costing but a fraction of that amount. It seems more logical to employ our guns to counter the hostile Armored Force while saving our own Armored Forces for use against profitable targets to which they are vulnerable.[18]

Beginning in 1940, the 37mm M3 was adopted as the standard US towed anti-tank gun. Modeled after the German Pak 35/36 (though not a direct copy, as some have written), it was similar to the German gun and used a 37mm shell, which was considered adequate when used in the French tanks of 1918.

Rather than get an edge on the Germans by building a model with a bigger gun than their Pak 35/36 (which German gunners in the 1940 French campaign derided as a mere "door knocker"), mobility was favored over firepower in the M3. It was intended to be easily transported by a jeep or weapons carrier (light truck), then manhandled into firing position by two or three soldiers. Some 18,702 were built 1940–1943, when it began to be supplanted by the larger 57mm M1 towed gun.

But scrutiny would reveal troubling news about the M3. Although much hope for the success of Gen. McNair's plans to stop tanks were pinned on this quick-fix expedient, according to the Ordnance Department, the M3 "had been obsolete from the day it was accepted" in 1940.[19]

The new M3 Stuart light tank (beginning to clank off assembly lines in 1941) had 1.5-inch thick armor in some spots—less than or equal to the armor on many German tanks. But as *Time* magazine warned in "Is it Good Enough?" (June 1941), Ordnance

Department tests found the 37mm towed gun could not punch through even an inch of tank armor from a short 100 yards.[20]

Like the M3 towed gun, the M3 light tank also lagged behind German designs. While the Germans were pioneering effective use of tank-to-tank radios and intercoms for crew communication inside noisy tanks, that was not the case with the Stuart tank that then-Lt. Al Irzyk, who had started in the horse Cavalry, was introduced to in summer 1942:

I found myself standing on a narrow plank above and behind where the driver sat… Standing on the plank enabled the tank commander to have his head out of the tank…to signal the tank driver, the tank commander used his foot. To tell the driver to go right, tap his right shoulder—a hard right, a hard tap; to go left, tap the left shoulder; to slow down, a gentle tap on the middle of the back. To stop, a firm push on the center of the back. It was pretty rudimentary stuff. America had been poorly prepared for World War II, and much of its equipment was still somewhat primitive.[21]

Along with its tanks, American armor doctrine, hampered by bureaucratic turf wars, also lagged behind Germany's. During the

> The separate Tank Destroyer is not a practical concept on the battlefield… the weapon to beat a tank is a better tank. Sooner or later the issue between ground forces is settled in an armored battle—tank against tank.[2]
> —Gen. Jacob Devers, January 1943

June 1941 Tennessee Maneuvers, Gen. George Patton's tanks performed so well that an angry Gen. McNair (seeking to prove that towed guns could stop tanks) stopped the exercises. As Ladislas Farago wrote:

Right off the bat, Patton cut behind the lines of the 5th Infantry Division, "decimated" it, and then captured its command post. The "hell buggies" of the 2nd Armored Division continued to run wild, and were winning hands down when McNair ordered the umpires to cut Patton down to size. After that, every decision went against him. But so devastating were his tactics that in the end McNair was forced to call off the exercises 12 hours ahead of their allotted period, because Patton had wrapped them up and left nothing more to do.

Nevertheless, the anti-armor crowd presented the experience as a tremendous victory for towed guns. In a letter from the maneuvers, McNair wrote to a friend that he had gained "considerable encouragement" for his advocacy of anti-tank units. "It can be expected," he added, "that the location of hostile armored elements will be known practically constantly, thus permitting

"The pea shooter": An M3 Stuart light tank crew scrubs the bore of their 37mm main gun, then and now an essential part of tank maintenance. When GIs in North Africa and Tunisia realized how ineffective it was against German Panzer IV "Special" tanks with high-velocity 75mm main guns, their (printable) nicknames for it included "pea shooter" and "door knocker." *US Army Signal Corps*

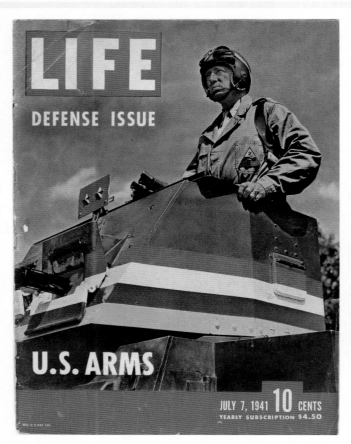

July 1941: Maj. Gen. George S. Patton, scowling for *LIFE* magazine, rides high in his colorfully painted M3 combat car command tank. *Author's collection, photo by Robert Coldwell Sr.*

Gen. George S. Patton directs Louisiana maneuvers from his M3 combat car. Note the two-star general's pennant on the left hull and top of the turret. *US Army Signal Corps*

anti-tank opposition to be moved correspondingly, and massed at the proper point—" a conclusion that was unsupported by the exercises.[22]

In fall 1941, the Army held further massive maneuvers in Louisiana and the Carolinas, the largest ever held in the United States. Gen. McNair named as "the outstanding question"[23] of the Carolina Maneuvers "to see...if and how we can crush a modern tank offensive" with his towed guns.[24] At first glance, AT guns appeared to be a great success; in an after-action review, McNair claimed 983 tanks had been knocked out in the Carolina maneuvers alone, 90% of them by anti-tank guns.[25]

Impressive numbers, until one learns that under the rigged rules of the game—literally written by McNair—tanks could be knocked out by such unrealistic means as simulated .50-caliber machine gun fire alone. And while small towed guns could knock out one tank per gun per minute, those tanks could not disable them with gunfire, only by overrunning them.[26]

Shortly before the Carolina maneuvers began, McNair issued a memo that further rigged the game's rules to favor anti-tank forces: Infantry would be able to disable or destroy tanks with bags of flour simulating hand grenades.[27] Said Maj. Gen. Charles Scott, an angry Cavalry tanker, "If hand grenades would destroy tanks, we would quit building them."[28]

To many tankers, the final indignity from Gen. McNair came late in the Louisiana maneuvers, at the September 28 "Battle

> The tank destroyer should be one of our principal means of avoiding tank versus tank action.[3]
> —Gen. Lesley McNair, July 1942

for Shreveport," a legendary chapter in the history of American armor. There, Patton's aggressive tankers performed so well and soundly refuted armor's opponents that McNair suddenly called a halt to the games, stopping the whole exercise at the height of its pivotal "battle,"[29] which motivated tankers were clearly in the process of winning.

Angry armor proponents felt that instead of holding an impartial test, Gen. McNair had tilted the rules against tanks, ensuring the game's umpires decided in favor of his anti-tank theories. Gen. Jacob Devers, Chief of the Armored Force, spoke for many: "We were licked by a set of umpire's rules."[30]

The tankers' rage was understandable; McNair had essentially written the skewed rule book for the war games, personally supervising the preparation of the *GHQ Umpire Manual* that came out in February 1941.[31] Yet in his 2015 biography of McNair, author Mark Calhoun fails to see a conflict of interest in a general literally rewriting the rules to favor his personal prejudices. While acknowledging that "McNair's authoring of the umpire manual...can give the impression that McNair sought to ensure that the Manual reflected his and Marshall's confidence in specific doctrinal and equipment related issues like AT guns and tank destroyers," Calhoun insists "there is no evidence that McNair intentionally favored AT guns."[32]

Buoyed by the apparent success of his anti-tank theories in the Louisiana and Carolina Maneuvers, Gen. McNair called for the establishment of a new Army branch to implement them, and fast, light new vehicles to mount anti-tank guns.

By March 1942, with Marshall's approval, the Tank Destroyer Command was created at Camp Hood, Texas. Instead of as-

An experimental fit of a 37mm gun and Browning water-cooled machine gun to an early jeep (US Cavalry jeeps were known as "peeps" for their reconnaissance role). These improvised, slapdash TDs led to broken windshields from the gun's recoil, but the idea may have influenced the equally ineffective M6 Fargo GMC. *US Army Signal Corps*

signing the job of stopping enemy tanks to the Armored Force's tanks, in a political compromise, Marshall gave it to the "TDs," which would use towed guns and the yet-to-be-built near-tanks still on the drawing board. He was appeasing armor's Infantry and Artillery opponents, who sought to prevent tanks from becoming independent, thus lessening the influence of *their* branches. In a counterintuitive reversal, the proposed TDs—light, small non-tanks—would tackle the enemy's heavier and more powerful tanks, while the Armored Force's tanks, rather than fight their enemy equivalents, would instead seek soft targets in the rear, such as trucks and soldiers on foot.

These roles rested on a dangerous assumption: that the enemy would not oppose light tanks with heavier, more powerful ones, or counter a small towed gun with a heavily armored tank. In fairness to Gen. McNair, until 1945, US armor doctrine reflected the interwar school of thought that tanks existed to support Infantry, and the Cavalry's preference for using them as weapons of exploitation to hit the enemy's weak rear. According to an AGF manual issued in September 1943, "the primary role of the tank" was not to fight enemy tanks, but "to destroy enemy personnel and automatic weapons."[33]

The TD concept's supporters also assumed that the Germans would conveniently mass their armor in large, easy-to-find columns

The pugnacious shoulder sleeve insignia of the Tank Destroyers: in tribute to the "Black Toms" of the US Tank Corps in WWI, a fierce cat devours an enemy tank. Their motto was "Seek, Strike, Destroy." *Author's collection, photo by Robert Coldwell Sr.*

as in Poland and France, so that American towed and self-propelled tank destroyers, passively waiting in reserve, could be rushed to the decisive point. Reacting rather than acting, they conceded the initiative to the enemy.

In 1939–1941, the Allies fought defensively, reacting to Nazi offensives, but when Americans reached the battlefield in late

1942, the Germans were on the defensive; massed columns of their armor were becoming a thing of the past. The reactive anti-tank doctrine of 1940 was out of date by 1943, and adherence to it would result in lost Allied lives.

Rather than consider if textbook theories matched battlefield reality, stateside doctrinaires under McNair claimed GIs at the front were not properly applying the approved solutions. They also seemed confused over the TD's hazy role. "Tank Destroyer units are especially designed for offensive action against hostile enemy forces,"[34] stated FM 18-5, the *Tank Destroyer Field Manual* (1942). A poor substitute for a true tank was expected to stop the enemy's best tanks, and "The tank destroyer," claimed Gen. McNair in July, "should be one of our principal means of *avoiding* [author's italics] tank versus tank action."[35]

In 1942, 639 TDs were built. The next year, even as troubling questions were raised over tank destroyer doctrine, design, and performance in North Africa, Tunisia, and Sicily, the true believers seemed to double down. The year 1943 was the war's peak for American tank destroyer production, with some 6,879 rolling off assembly lines.[36]

To author Robert Citino:
This solution to the problem of antiarmor defense was

unique to the United States—and for good reason. Tank destroyers simply were not the answer. The U.S. Army would have been better off with more Shermans.[37]

After hard battlefield lessons, official TD publications began to include footnotes describing unofficial techniques that—while contradicting the official doctrine—had been found effective in stopping German tanks. As late as 1944 (after combat showed the enemy's use of tanks had clearly changed since 1939–1940), on some pages of the TD School's "Tank Destroyer Combat Reports from Theaters of Operations," the frontline GIs' informal but effective methods outnumbered the stateside theorists' approved (but ineffective) classroom solutions.[38]

The TD concept's flaws can be seen not only in its fuzzy doctrine, but also in the development of its actual weapons. Starting out small, they grew steadily larger as the war went on; bloated and overweight, but never as effective or protected as a true tank.

The idea began in 1940, with the M3 37mm gun towed by a jeep and with little protection for the crew. It was soon realized that for better mobility and armor protection the gun should be mounted directly on a vehicle. This led to the M3 Gun Motor Carriage (GMC), a stopgap measure until purpose-built TDs could

Ft. Knox, Kentucky, circa 1942: A posed GI in training pits an early half-track against an imagined enemy; some would be fitted with 75mm guns and used as *ersatz* tank destroyers. While still wearing an M1917A1 WWI-style "Kelly helmet," at least he has the Army's new M1 rifle (note the shiny gas tube characteristic of early M1s). The vehicle exhibits yellow star and unit markings that were changed to white after the North African and Tunisian campaigns. *Alfred Palmer*

Photo by Robert Coldwell Sr.

be designed and mass produced. The M3 used a 75mm gun on an existing, thinly armored half-track. Cpl. Harry Dunnagan, 813th Tank Destroyer Battalion, called them "Clumsy.... The M3 half-track we used in Africa resembled a huge, awkward monster. It was big and heavy with about 3⁄8 inch armor plate on it, but there was no power steering, and it took about half a block to turn it around. That lack of maneuverability sometimes put us in a precarious spot." Adequate against light Japanese armor in the Philippines in 1941–1942, facing German tanks in North Africa it was no contest. Added Dunnagan, "It was scary defensively."[39]

Thin-skinned half-tracks designed to transport troops, not fight Panzers, could not withstand hits from them, let alone expect to destroy them: "employed in a number of roles for which they were neither intended nor equipped to function…they suffered severe losses."[40]

Another 1941 design was the Dodge M6 Gun Motor Carriage (the "Fargo"), with a 37mm gun mounted in the bed of a three-quarter-ton weapons carrier—a light pickup truck. The M6 not only had *less armor* than the M3 half-track, but also a weaker gun compared to the M3 half-track's 75mm.

Why it was thought a small pickup truck designed for light cargo duties could take heavy tanks on and survive is a mystery. Even a memo from the Chief of Ordnance conceded, "The sending of such a patently inadequate tank destroyer into combat can at best be termed a tragic mistake."[41] The TDs may have sported the aggressive motto "Seek, Strike, Destroy," but "Used in combat in North Africa, the M6 proved to be a total failure as a tank destroyer…and was quickly withdrawn from service."[42]

A line was irrevocably crossed with the M10 Gun Motor Carriage (GMC) tank destroyer. The first newly designed self-propelled TD (rather than a quick-fix modification of an existing vehicle), it mated a Sherman tank chassis to a new, lighter hull (body) and turret. It had thin, vulnerable armor on the sides, and the turret was open and uncovered on the top, exposing the crew to enemy fire.

Reflecting the slapdash design of the vehicle, when the heavy 3-inch gun was installed the turret became unbalanced, requiring the addition of crude counterweights. To simplify production the turret was not powered; the gunner had to hand crank it to engage his targets.

TD supporters reasoned that a near-tank was easier to produce than the genuine article. Echoing the prewar concept of lightly armored "Cavalry tanks," they argued that skimping on armor protection for the crew added speed. But here was anoth-er flaw of the TD concept: unless the vehicle could get a lucky first shot at a heavy tank with thicker armor and firepower, if it could not survive return fire from a true tank, speed mattered little. M10 crews suffered deaths and wounds because of its thinly armored turret; as they entered European cities, the open top made them vulnerable to snipers, grenades, bazookas, and artillery.

Fighting near the German border in late 1944, TD man Cpl. Harry Dunnagan recalled:

We had one man standing up in the turret [of an M10], on guard. The rest of us were lying down in the tank, sleeping. Shortly after dark, a large explosion shook me awake. That was a time explosion [tree burst] shell directly over the open turret, and it was on its mark. Fortunately, I was not hit. As I looked up, the man in the turret, Clancy A. Jordan, was sinking down, saying "Mother" and other words I couldn't understand. I reached for him and tried to see if I could give him some penicillin. There was no time; by the time he reached the floor he was dead. I put my hand on our Sergeant, George A. Richey, to try to wake him; he was dead, too. The Lieutenant's legs were also chopped up. We had to get the tank out of this position and unload the bodies. Since it was dark, I climbed out and sat outside on the front of the tank and directed the driver back to headquarters. There, we unloaded the bodies, got the Lieutenant out, and waited for daylight so we could clean out the tank.[43]

To historian David Johnson, "The European campaign demonstrated that tanks fight tanks."[44] Soon after VE Day, an Army general board convened to record the lessons of the ETO came to the same conclusion. Armor leaders as well as Infantry generals (who had opposed tank development for decades) agreed on the need for better, more powerful tanks, not TDs. Their final report recommended the Tank Destroyers be disbanded.[45]

M10 tank destroyer at the Musée des Blindés, Saumur, France. *Massimo Foti*

October 1944: Two 703rd Tank Destroyer Battalion TDs, both thinly armored and open-topped: the M10 (left) and M36 Jackson (right). *US Signal Corps photo via Ralph Riccio*

What was obvious in 1940 had taken five years for Army establishment to recognize, especially Gen. McNair, who had continued to insist since the blitzkrieg on Poland and France that "It doesn't take a tank to knock out a tank. It takes a gun (i.e., a towed cannon or artillery piece)."[46]

Instead of adapting to the changing battlefield with better tanks to counter Germany's, Army leaders stuck with an obsolete quick fix of 1940. A decent medium or heavy tank was needed, but they continued to build poor substitutes for a true tank—from 1942 until the war's end some 9,400 of them.[47] By impeding

development of a tank that could compete on equal terms with Germany's best and saddling GIs with ineffective equipment, the "TD" debacle would cost the lives of thousands of young Americans.

# Tank-Eating Tiger!

OFFICIAL INSIGNIA
TANK DESTROYER FORCES
UNITED STATES ARMY

Oldsmobile respectfully dedicates this page to the Army officers and enlisted men who wear these colorful shoulder sleeve insignia.

HERE'S A TOAST TO THE MEN OF THE ARMY TANK DESTROYER FORCES, *one of the newest branches of the service, yet one that has already built up its traditions of high courage, gallant conduct and brilliance in combat action. The Tank Destroyer Forces do just what their name implies—seek out enemy armor and destroy it . . . utterly. Their chief weapons are speed and Fire-Power—speed to out-maneuver enemy tanks—Fire-Power to out-range and out-slug them. In Africa, in Sicily, in Italy . . . Hitler's once-boastful Panzers have learned to respect—and to fear—America's Tank Destroyer Forces!*

## FIRE-POWER
### is Our Business!

"Seek!—Strike!—Destroy!" is the official motto of the Tank Destroyer Forces. And it's our job at Oldsmobile to help give them Fire-Power to carry out that

mission. In full co-operation with the United States Army Ordnance Department, Oldsmobile is building both cannon and shell for the Tank Destroyers—long-barreled, high-velocity cannon which can knock out any tank that's built—plus the high-explosive and armor-piercing shell these deadly guns fire. Oldsmobile also builds automatic cannon for fighter planes, cannon and shell for tanks, and shell for the artillery and Navy.

### BACK UP THE BOYS
### WHO WEAR THESE INSIGNIA

You can help provide the Fire-Power our Tank Destroyer Forces need—by investing in U. S. War Bonds and Stamps. Buy now and keep buying, until the last Axis tank has been destroyed!

## BUY WAR BONDS!

# OLDSMOBILE DIVISION OF GENERAL MOTORS
#### KEEP 'EM FIRING

*Courtesy Henry Smith. Photo by Robert Coldwell Sr.*

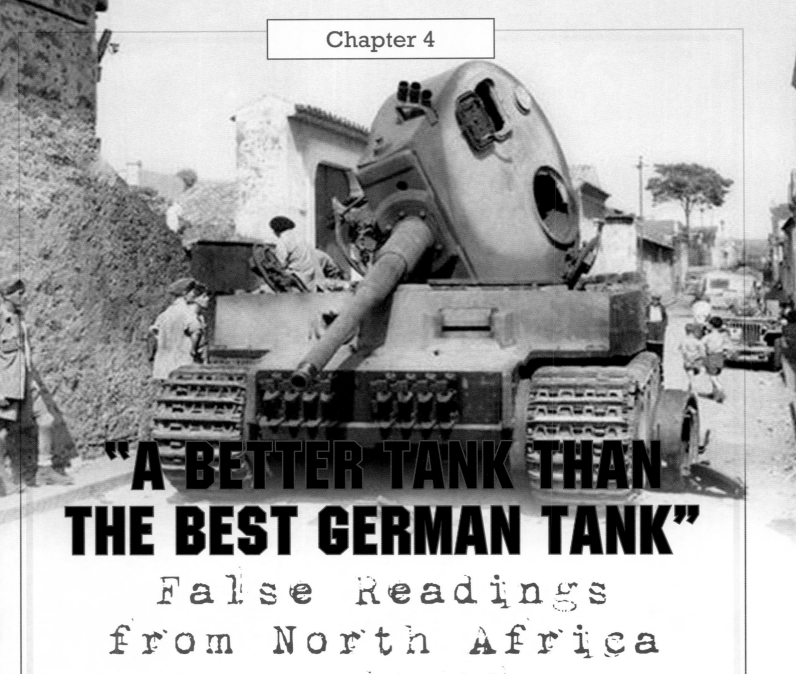

# Chapter 4

# "A BETTER TANK THAN THE BEST GERMAN TANK"

## False Readings from North Africa and Sicily

### The Sherman's Debut

On September 18, 1942, the Detroit Tank Arsenal received a special visitor: FDR in a convertible. According to author Maury Klein's 2013 history of wartime production:

> The party observed every phase of production from materials to final assembly, then moved on to a testing ground where the new M4 Sherman tank was put through its paces before rumbling at top speed toward the presidential car. Roosevelt's eyes widened as the tank screeched to a halt barely ten feet short of his car. "A good drive!" he laughed. He was deeply impressed by the plant's ability to shift from manufacturing M3 medium tanks to M4s without losing a single hour of production.[3]

They overcame every tank which they opposed.[2]

—Gen. Gladeon Barnes, who led Army Ordnance's Research and Design Service, in 1943 congressional testimony about the Sherman tank in North Africa

While the new M3 medium tank was already being phased out barely four months after its first combat use, some GIs would still be stuck with it. Ironically, when American tanks dueled Germany's for the first time they had British crews.

The US supplied Stuart light tanks to the British, as well as the new M3 Grant medium tank. In May 1942, the M3 mediums fought decently around the Gazala Line in North Africa, but were overwhelmed. By the time Gen. Erwin Rommel's *Afrika Korps* took Tobruk in June, almost half of the 167 Lend-Lease Grants had been destroyed by German anti-tank guns and tanks.[4] On the eve of the battle of El Alamein, to compensate for their tank losses at Tobruk, the British were given some of the first M4 Shermans by Roosevelt. While the gesture was appreciated, it hurt under-equipped American tankers. "Mr. President, the [Shermans] have just been issued to the [US] First Armored Division," cautioned Gen. Marshall. "It

*Photo by Robert Coldwell Sr.*

British Crusader III tank in desert paint scheme at the Tank Museum, Bovington, Dorset, UK. Note the Italian medium tank to the right. *Massimo Foti*

is a terrible thing to take weapons out of a soldier's hand, but if the British need is so great, they must have them."[5]

The Sherman's origins can be traced to the T5 medium tank of 1938 that was built in small numbers. The T5 led to the more advanced M3 Lee, the Sherman's father. The M4 design owed much of its origins to the Lee, and was recognized as a stopgap measure even before it was built. It was decided to address some of the M3's shortcomings (such as its high profile and main gun's limited traverse) in a newer design that would incorporate the Lee's more successful components: the suspension, engine, transmission, and turret.

A wooden mockup called the T6 Medium Tank was prepared in May 1941, followed by a steel prototype in September—just in time for Roosevelt's "double it!" demand for 2,000 tanks a month in 1942. By October 1941, although the M3 Lee had just begun to roll out of factories, it was already planned to replace it with the Sherman.

May 1942: one of the earliest Lend-Lease Shermans to arrive in England—nicknamed "Michael" after the head of the British Purchasing Commission—is displayed at the Horse Guards Parade in London. *Courtesy US National Archives*

*Courtesy Henry Smith. Photo by Robert Coldwell Sr.*

Large scale Sherman production began in July 1942, at Chrysler's Detroit Tank Arsenal. Eventually, eleven different firms[6] would crank it out, including the Fisher Body Division of General Motors. Before the first M4 left the factory, owing to pressure from Roosevelt it was decided that thousands would go to the British. One of the first was named *Michael*—with a brass plaque on its side—in honor of Michael Dewar, head of the British Tank Purchasing Commission that had arrived in the states in 1940. Today, this pioneer M4 resides at the British Tank Museum in Bovington Camp, Dorset.

By the November 1942 Allied invasion of North Africa, the Sherman began to replace the M3 as the Allies' main medium tank. American Maj. Herbert Hillenmeyer, commanding Company A of the 1st Armored Regiment, 1st Armor Division in Tunisia and Italy, left a detailed description of the new tank:

> The General Sherman, or M4 as we knew it, was the backbone of Allied armored formations in World War Two.... It weighed thirty tons, and had armor plate from an inch and a half to three inches thick. There was a crew of five. There were four entrances and exits [the early models—later ones added another escape hatch to the turret]. The driver had his hatch; the assistant driver had his hatch. There was a hatch in the turret [a single hatch for the commander; when the difficulty of four men climbing out of one hatch if hit was realized,

a second one was added on later models, above the loader] and an escape hatch in the bottom of the tank. The last was more useful than you might suppose... many tankers used it as a more or less protected avenue of exit if it became necessary to abandon a tank, say, that was burning and still subject to enemy fire.

Since the war, they have developed tanks to such an extent that driving them is child's play, but at that time it took a real man. The assistant driver didn't have much to do, and his seat was the warmest spot in the tank. We used to take turns in that seat during long, cold night marches. He had a gun to fire, a machine gun...it rested in his lap on a ball and socket mount, and there was no way he could aim it. About all he could do was sort of spray the bullets around in much the same manner as you would a garden hose.

The gunner, loader, and tank commander were in the turret. The turret could be traversed 360 degrees by the gunner, either by a hand wheel or with a power mechanism, but the latter lacked the fine adjustment he needed to bring his gun on the target.... he also had a telescopic sight in his periscope... He fired the gun, and also a machine gun mounted co-axially alongside [the main gun]. There were two foot switches, which fired these guns electrically. He could fire them singly or together.

The big gun was a 75-millimeter, or about 3 inches in diameter. A "basket" was hung from the turret, and in this the gunner, loader and tank commander revolved with the turret, which had a .50 caliber machine gun mounted on top for mostly AA [anti-aircraft] use. All around this basket were racks containing ammunition for both the machine gun and the 75. Needless to say, this ammunition was a constant source of danger in case of a direct hit on the tank.

The tank commander had his hands full. He usually had a map to follow. He had field glasses he had

*Photo by Alfred Palmer*

The Sherman tank commander sat or stood in the open turret, a very vulnerable position. Later models of the M4 added a second (loader's) hatch in the turret, but only after many crew members in the earlier models were burned to death, unable to exit the single tank commander's hatch in time.

to use. He had to direct the gunner on to targets. He wore earphones, which were plugged into a jack box on the side of the turret. He had a microphone through which he could talk to any member of his crew or, by flicking a switch over the radio to other tanks in his formation. He had a push button FM radio, through which, by pushing various buttons, he could listen or talk to other units on his "net."

The tank commander stood directly behind the gunner, usually with his head sticking out of the turret. When in a combat area, we usually operated "buttoned up," that is, with all hatches closed. However, we learned long before we got into battle that the tank commander just couldn't see enough buttoned up, and consequently he usually peeped out, even when under direct fire. Each hatch had a periscope through which the occupants peered when buttoned up; thus they were not exposed to direct fire.

...we carried about 180 gallons of gasoline, and that was good for about 100 miles of operation. On a clear highway we could run at forty miles per hour, but twenty was more nearly the usual speed.[7]

German tanks, Hillenmeyer recalled:
had the better gun. In the flat desert country where there was no cover, that hurt. It was merely a matter of who had the longest reach, and the Germans had it. You get a sinking feeling when you poop around out there and see [your shells] bounce off the enemy tank, and about that time you see his gun wink, and the tank next to you bursts into flame. When we later got into country where we could sneak around in the hills, our better maneuverability paid off."[8]

Hillenmeyer well described one of the Sherman's worst characteristics that earned it the German nickname "Ronson":

Our tanks had a tendency to catch fire when hit, or "brew up," as the British said. We always had a private opinion that it was because we used gasoline, whereas the Germans used diesel fuel [Sic—they did not; this was a common Allied misconception]. Regardless of the reason, I knew we lost no time in "bailing out" when the tank went up in flames.

Very few men could tell you how they got out. The first thing they remembered was that they were on the ground and running. This was such a common occurrence that one of our soldiers, Tommy Stinsill, carried on his belt what he called a "bailout kit": a little packet containing razor, toothbrush, and change of socks."[9]

4x5 neg rec'd from BPR, 3/27/43. Used in Press
Release, "Axis Planes, Tanks & Ammunition Captured in North Africa".

War Theatre #15 (North Africa)
CAPTURED MATERIAL    (over) tured in North Africa".

C-23289AC.

The infamous "88," the notorious German field piece captured by Allied Forces in North Africa. *US Army Air Force*

Sgt. Jim Rothschadl, 712th Tank Battalion tank gunner, described his station in the Sherman:

I had control of the turret and of the gun going up and down…manual control and electrical control. I had two buttons I could push to fire…one for the 75mm main gun and one for the .30-caliber [coaxial machine gun, parallel to the main gun]. I also had manual [control of the guns], in case the electric went off. There were manual triggers for both the 75 and the .30. The turret had a toggle in it that was electrical, but it also had a little wheel there, so you could traverse it manually. There was another wheel: one for traversing the turret, and the other for raising the gun up…. And I had two gun sights in there. The .30-caliber and the 75 were co-axial.[10]

Rothschadl described the loader's job:
He was sitting in a position near the breech on these 75 cannons…a huge breech. The shells were about two feet long, so that breech was big. And when you

> We don't yet know exactly how to handle the Mark VI [Tiger] tank.[1]
> —Gen. Dwight Eisenhower to Gen. George Marshall after the Sidi-bou-Zid, Faid Pass, and Kasserine disasters, February 1943

fired, it went back almost to the back wall of the turret. It made a hell of a racket. The loader was sitting back there, on the side of the gunner and tank commander. He had a little porthole on the side of the turret… he could open it to throw out the spent shell casing. His job was also to feed the belt if the .30 was firing, and to load the 75. It was a hell of a position for another reason: the danger of trying to get out of the tank. And of course, the danger of that recoil.[11]

The new American light and medium tanks were a welcome step up from what British tankers had been using. As Gen. Erwin Rommel wrote of El Alamein, "There was a surprise awaiting us here, one which was not to our advantage—the new M3 medium tank."[12]

But they were not good enough; the Sherman had some fatal flaws. "Their engines ran on high-octane petrol," an account of El Alamein noted, "and a white-hot round could send them up in seconds."[13] A British Tommy watching an M4 saw "its turret swing round, and then it suddenly shook and vibrated. Then there was a loud explosion, and flames burst through the hatch like a blowtorch. All I could think of was, 'Christ help those poor sods inside it.'… Those things were absolute death traps."[14]

The British learned, as the Yanks would all too soon, that the Sherman, Lee, and Stuart were outgunned. American armor Col. William Triplett recounted a British tanker's lecture that nicely captures the perception Allied tankers held of their German opponents—one of contemptuously relaxed mastery of the battlefield:

It is quite difficult when we are outgunned. The Jerry tank waddles up to fifteen hundred yards and stops. The gunner dismounts and dusts off the lens of his telescopic sight, then climbs back in and begins to dot off our chaps one by one. And we have to move in to half that range before our shot will take effect on him.[15]

Though the Americans were latecomers to the desert war, the Ordnance Department was kept informed through the efforts of advisors and observers. Captain Joseph Colby and five technical sergeants arrived in the desert in late summer 1941. In December, Colby reported home that German 88mm guns with armor piercing ammunition had knocked out the majority of 47 out of 51 British tanks lost to artillery—and Rommel had done this while possessing only for-

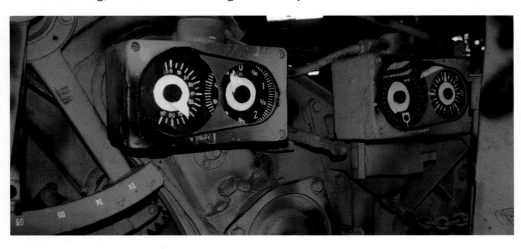

Operator's instrumentation on a captured German "88." *Author photo courtesy of the National Armor and Cavalry Heritage Foundation*

# AMERICAN TANK CALLED BEST ON BATTLEFIELD

NEW YORK, Feb. 25 (*AP*).—General Jacob Devers, commander of United States Armored Forces who returned recently from the North African war theaters tonight termed the American General Sherman tank "the best tank on the battlefield" and the self-propelled 105 porting light artillery weapon on the battlefield."

Speaking from Louisville, Ky., over radio station WAVE on the "March of Time" program (NBC), Gen. Devers said the superiority of these two American weapons was confirmed by North African commander generals, line and field generals and enlisted men.

He said, "American troops are well-trained and splendidly equipped. They know and have confidence in their weapons and you may have confidence in them."

"It is a grim truth, however, he declared, "that the final seasoning of a soldier must come on the battlefield. There will be dark moments."

A captured Italian M13/40 medium tank. Luckily for American tankers, Italian unwillingness to fight and die for Mussolini and Hitler assured their armor was not a significant threat.
*US Army Signal Corps*

ty-eight of the notorious weapons.[16]

More warnings came from an Army technical team known as the Military North Africa Mission (MNAM), arriving in Cairo, Egypt, in February 1942. MNAM's members were tasked with helping the British get the best out of their Lend-Lease equipment, and with studying British and German ordnance.

Cpt. George Jarrett (soon to be promoted to major) was a particularly effective member of MNAM. Originally an ammunition advisor to the British, he examined captured German weapons, sending them and data home to Aberdeen Proving Ground, Maryland, for study.

Today, George Jarrett emerges as an unsung hero of the Sherman tank scandal. Born in Haddonfield, New Jersey, in 1901, and raised in a prep school background, he just missed WWI. He began a collection of helmets, bayonets, and small arms that grew to earn nationwide recognition; long before his WWII Army service, a 1928 New Jersey newspaper article pictured him at home next to walls covered with captured German weapons. As the caption joked, few burglars would dare to invade Jarrett's bedroom. Eventually he became an Army Ordnance Department officer, assisting the British in the Middle East and running the foreign materiel (i.e., captured weapons) branch at Aberdeen.

While stationed at Aberdeen, Jarrett was able to examine many captured enemy weapons—from pistols to tanks—and perform comparative tests. He gave talks throughout the country about American equipment, but was censored and even accused of being pro-German for acknowledging that some enemy weapons might be better than their American equivalents. When the tank scandal was exposed in the stateside press in early 1945, Jarrett kept a scrapbook of newspaper clippings on it, which he filled with pungent criticism and marginalia. Today, his "Little Green Book" is preserved at the Army Military History Institute at Carlisle Barracks, Pennsylvania.

Jarrett's liaison work with the British in the Middle East was so effective, the Ordnance Department's official history calls him "the one-man technical section of the MNAM Ordnance section."[17] He helped send one of the first German 88mm field pieces—abandoned by the Germans near Sidi Rezagh—home to the US from the Western Desert.

To the grateful British, the Sherman tank was an improvement, but when they won at El Alamein, they exaggerated its effectiveness. "The M4 is a better tank than the best German tank," British generals exulted. Oliver Lyttelton, Britain's Minister of Production, called it a "match for the best armor Rommel has."[18] British Gens. Charles Norman and Richard McCreery claimed the M3 Lees "had stopped the Germans at the El Alamein line, and that the M4 tanks defeated the Germans in the breakthrough."[19]

But after examining burned-out wrecks on the battlefield, George Jarrett found that most Panzers had been stopped by British artillery, not tanks, and that their own crews, not M4s, often destroyed them after running out of fuel. When Shermans, Lees, and Stuarts dueled tanks like the Panzer III "Special" (with a 50mm main gun) and Panzer IV "Special" (armed with a high velocity, long-barreled 75mm gun), Jarrett concluded "The Germans had out-gunned us."[20] But back home, desperate for good news after the fall of Bataan and Corregidor, the American press repeated British praise of the M4 and added their own exaggerated claims.

Gen. Jacob Devers, who led the Armored Force at Fort Knox, toured the North African front from December 14, 1942, to January 25, 1943. His goal: to "examine the problems of Armored Forces units in the European Theater of Operations." After speaking with British and American officers and enlisted tankers and examining Allied and Axis equipment, Devers stated in an extensive report that the Sherman "could easily defeat any German tank." Its armor piercing (AP) ammunition "was found capable of penetrating all German tanks at ranges as great as 2,500 yards." The Sherman, Devers concluded in his influential January 1943 report, was "the best tank on the battlefield."21 Articles then appeared across the country touting the M4; the Del Rio, Texas, *News Herald* reported that Gen. Devers, speaking on the "March of Time" radio show, boasted that "American troops are…splendidly equipped…they know and have confidence

DAK (German Africa Corps) Panzer IV "Special."

### Sherman Tank Best On Tunisian Front, General Devers Says

NEW YORK, Feb. 26. (AP)— Gen. Jacob Devers, commander of United States armored forces who returned recently from the North African war theatres last night termed the American General Sherman tank "the best tank on the battlefield" and the self-propelled 105 mm. Howitzer Priest "the best supporting light artillery weapon on the battlefield."

Speaking from Louisville, Ky., over radio station WAVE General Devers said the superiority of these two American weapons was confirmed by North African commanding generals, line and field generals and enlisted men.

He said, "American troops are well - trained and splendidly equipped. They know and have confidence in their weapons and you may have confidence in them."

"It is a grim truth, however," he declared, "that the final seasoning of a soldier must come on the battlefield. There will be dark moments."

in their weapons." Said Devers, according to the *News Herald*, "The superiority of the M4 was confirmed by North African commander generals, line and field generals, and enlisted men."[22]

A dangerous complacency arose among Army and civilian leaders, setting the stage for a rude awakening. Though touted as a war-winner, the latest American medium tank began to fall behind Germany's; even the Panzer IV of 1939 had been updated with a 75mm gun more powerful than the new M4s. And yet, because the new Tiger tank would first be encountered in small numbers, often handicapped by the mechanical bugs common

The "GI Jive," Fort Benning, Georgia, April 1942: like mules at the plow, soldiers in training drag Gen. McNair's beloved 37mm M1 towed anti-tank gun. *US Army Signal Corps*

to a new weapon, and could be knocked out by lucky shots from towed guns and artillery, it would be underestimated.

Even George Jarrett—a later critic of US tank gun development—seemed to drop his guard, perhaps ordered by his Ordnance Department superiors to toe the Allied propaganda line. "Most Of America's Weapons Better Than Those Of The Enemy: 'Box Score' Comparisons are Given By Tester; Nazi Equipment Rated High," appeared in April 29, 1943, papers like the Danville, Virginia, *Bee*. Jarrett, now a colonel, was identified as "Chief of the

*Courtesy Henry Smith. Photo by Robert Coldwell Sr.*

Shoulder insignia of the multinational II Corps, which fought in some of the disastrous battles in North Africa and Tunisia. The eagle on the left represents American troops; the lion on the right is for British elements. *Photo by Robert Coldwell Sr.*

A typical German vehicle marking, in this case on a Marder self-propelled gun. *Author photo courtesy of the National Armor and Cavalry Heritage Foundation*

Foreign Materiel Branch at Aberdeen [Proving Ground, Maryland]," tasked with "keeping up to the minute on the limit or effectiveness of the enemy weapons."[23]

Jarrett was off the mark concerning the US 37mm towed anti-tank gun, calling it "far superior" to its German counterpart. As to the "General Sherman" tank, he asserted it was "far superior to anything the Axis has to offer.... They have a 62-ton tank, called the Panzer Mark VI (Tiger), which has been blasted by our standard medium-caliber anti-tank guns and which has yielded up its secrets to us. We have nothing to fear from the Tiger or any other tank the Axis has developed." The Sherman's main 75mm gun, Jarrett stated, "will pierce the armor of any known enemy tanks at battle ranges," while "our latest tanks, with their cast hulls, increased armor, and rivetless makeup, have built into them all the lessons that were learned in the Western Desert."[24]

Given such overconfidence in the M4 medium, not surprisingly, there would also be bad news for crews of the light M3 Stuart tank. Lt. Freeland Daubin, 1st Armored Regiment, 1st Armored Division, fought the Battle of "Happy Valley," the first large tank-versus-tank duel between Germans and Americans, on November 26, 1942. Daubin and his Stuart crew had "a great

Restored Panzer IV in DAK markings at the Deutsches Panzermuseum, Munster. *Massimo Foti*

A preserved M3 Stuart at the National Museum of Cavalry and Armor refinished in typical 1942–1943 North Africa/Tunisia theater markings. *Courtesy of the National Armor and Cavalry Heritage Foundation*

*Alfred Palmer*

and abiding faith" in the prowess of their M3's 37mm "cannon" until they came up against a Panzer IV Special armed with an improved, high-velocity main gun:

> The 37mm of the little American M3 light tank popped and snapped like an angry cap pistol…. The Jerry seemed annoyed by these attentions. Questing about with his incredibly long, bell-snouted, "souped-up" 75mm Kw K40 rifle, the German commander spotted his heckler. Deciding to do the sporting thing and lessen the extreme range, he leisurely commenced closing the 140-yard gap between himself and the light tank, but keeping his thicker, sloping frontal plates turned squarely to the hail of 37mm fire.
>
> The crew of the M3 redoubled the serving of their piece. The loader crammed the little projectiles into the breech and the commander (who was also the gunner) squirted them at the foe…. The German shed sparks like a power driver grindstone. In a frenzy of desperation and fading faith in their highly touted 37mm weapon, the M3 crew pumped more than eighteen rounds at the Jerry while it came in. Through the scope sight the

tracer could be seen to hit, then glance straight up. Popcorn balls thrown by Little Bo Peep would have been more effective.[25]

To one armor historian:
> The skirmish made the inadequacies of the M3 light tank painfully clear…. A captured German tanker later mocked his captors saying that the Americans would lose the war because they built such poor tanks.[26]

In the Allies' November 1942 invasion of North Africa, the M3 Lee was the main US medium tank. Its 75mm gun was surely better than the Stuart's 37mm, but was still inadequate. Col. Henry Gardiner, who led the 2nd Battalion, 13th Armor Regiment of the 1st Armored Division, recalled:

> The Second Battalion was equipped when it landed in Africa with the M3 Lee…. While the M4s or General Shermans were being supplied to the armored divisions at home, we never had a full complement of them until after the fighting had ended. The M3 was a much inferior tank. It had a limited traverse on its 75mm gun, which meant the tank could only fire in the direction in which it was headed.

An early Tiger I (1⁄35 scale model by the author) as it appeared during its debut against Allied forces in North Africa and Tunisia. *Photo by Robert Coldwell Sr.*

An M3 Lee in motion. *Alfred Palmer*

Moreover, the gun was set so low that almost the whole tank had to be exposed before it could be brought to bear on a target. There was no slope on the side armor [i.e., it was straight, thus more likely to be penetrated, while sloped armor could sometimes deflect shots and gave the crew more protection] and the .30-caliber light machine gun in the cupola, which was for defense against aircraft, was worse than useless.[27]

Gardiner also encountered a mysterious new German heavy tank when he and his crew were "hit hard by what later proved to be an 88 [mm shell] fired from a Tiger tank I had not seen… the driver and gunner were killed, the assistant driver badly wounded, and I got some shrapnel in my left arm."[28]

The Allies first encountered the Tiger when British gunners with towed cannon knocked one out around Pont-du-Fahs in January 1943.[29] The massive new tank had a lower silhouette compared to the Lee and the Sherman, devastating firepower, and armor that deflected Allied shot with ease. Gen. Eisenhower's aide, Capt. Harry Butcher, in his diary entry for April 17, 1943, wrote from Algiers of British Gen. Kenneth Anderson inviting Eisenhower to "see three Mark-6, or Tiger tanks":

These were three of the twenty-seven destroyed by the British when the Germans made a push March 26. While Ike was interested in seeing the tanks, he was more concerned with familiarizing himself with the terrain over which American troops soon would operate.… Because of possible presence of booby traps, there was a noticeable reluctance to prod into the innards of the Tiger tanks or to touch the articles lying around them.… I filled my pockets with burned-out machine

He used to say jokingly, "Less noise, please; I'm telephoning!" Now he speaks from the bedlam of one tank to another. The tiny microphone at his throat hears—not the clamor—but only his words. Out of the din, it sends his commands. Out of his commands come battles won. Out of battles won come peace and our new world.

*Courtesy Henry Smith. Photo by Robert Coldwell Sr.*

US M1938 tanker helmet with goggles. This example was made by the Rawlings Sporting Goods company. *Photo by Robert Coldwell Sr.*

Hand-held type T-17 ("Lollypop") hand microphone used by American tank commanders. *Photo by Robert Coldwell Sr.*

T-30 throat microphone and SW-141 "push-to-talk" intercom switch as worn by American tankers. *Photo by Robert Coldwell Sr.*

gun cartridges from one of the tanks, pilfered a seven-foot copper whip antenna from another, and got away with an 88-mm. projectile. The size of the Tiger, its armament, and especially its 88mm gun were impressive.[30]

The initial shock of the Tiger's debut has been represented as a great surprise to the Allies, but George Jarrett, with the British Eighth Army, had warned Ordnance in early 1942 that American tank ammunition could not penetrate existing German armor. Tests comparing M61 Armor Piercing, Capped (APC) ammo to captured Panzer IV rounds showed Germany's to be superior. They easily punched through US armor, exploded inside the crew compartment, and caused further catastrophic damage by igniting ammunition stored there.

Ingeniously, the British Royal Army Ordnance Corps adapted German tank ammo for use in the M3 Grant. Approximately

15,000 rounds were ready by May 1942; Col. Jarrett (whose assistance with the project earned him a medal from the British government) sent home samples and data. Thus, months before Operation Torch, Army Ordnance not only knew their tank ammunition was inadequate, but they had a solution at hand.[31]

Thanks to George Jarrett, Aberdeen Proving Ground also captured examples of the feared "88" for testing. Although it was just a matter of time until Germany mounted the devastating artillery piece in a tank, the Americans persisted with a weaker 75mm main gun in their medium tanks. As to the M3 medium's 37mm auxiliary gun, combat revealed it to be superfluous; to historian Christopher Gabel, "at ranges over a thousand yards, the 37mm gun could not penetrate even two inches of armor."[32]

M4 Sherman and M3 Lee medium tanks in stateside training, 1942.

Because the M3 medium's main gun was hull mounted at a man's height instead of high up in a turret, the tank could not be hidden behind obstacles to fire from protected positions. Its conspicuous profile (over ten feet tall) also made it vulnerable. And while the armor plate on German tanks was solidly welded, the Lee's used large rivets. Tearing loose when hit, they flew around inside the tank at high speed, injuring the crew as effectively as German bullets.

When the US 1st Armored Division's M3 Lees met Panzers for the first time around Oran, Tunis, and Bizerte, it was a disaster. Col. Henry Gardiner's 13th Armor Regiment helped slow a German offensive, but lost so many tanks and men in doing so that just weeks later in December 1942, they were declared *hors de combat*. "We were losing tanks and taking casualties every day," recalled Gardiner, "and morale was far from high":

> We were within eleven miles of our objective, Tunis, before the mounting German resistance brought us to a stop. A period of confused and bitter fighting followed.... When the Battalion pulled out of the line on 10 December, it only had twelve M3 Lee tanks left, the other forty-two having been lost in actions around Djedeida and Tebourba.[33]

Facing such steep odds, American tankers placed high hopes in the Lee's replacement, the new M4.

The Sherman's little-known combat debut in American hands occurred near Djebel-bou-Aoukar on December 6, 1942. An entire Second Armored Division platoon—five out of five tanks of the 66th Armor Regiment—was "wiped out" by concealed German anti-tank guns and tanks, including the soon-to-be notorious Tiger.[34] As M4s were picked off from afar, GIs realized that German tank and anti-tank guns were so powerful they could destroy M4s with a few long-distance hits before the Shermans could even approach to take a shot. And often, unless scoring a rare lucky hit to the thinly armored rear, American shells literally bounced off the Panzers' thick hide.

"We are going to go all out for the total destruction of the Americans," boasted German Gen. Albert Kesselring.[35] The first large-scale US/German tank battle occurred at Sidi-bou-Zid on Valentine's Day, February 14, 1943, and "A less auspicious battle debut for American armor could scarcely be imagined."[36] In stories datelined March 1, 1943, *New York Times* and *Newsweek* magazine reporters wrote of American tank destroyer soldiers and Infantry fleeing "to their foxholes" as:

> the German tanks sped up in V formation, with great 52-ton Mark VIs [Tigers] spearheading them...the American [anti-tank] gunners were overrun before they had time to fire a round. The Nazi units thus sliced through the thin American lines in all directions.[37]

Alfred Palmer

In one day, the First Armored Division alone lost over 100 tanks. According to Eisenhower biographer Jean Edward Smith, "Of the fifty-two Sherman medium tanks the First Armored had deployed, only six survived."[38] The number of Americans killed, wounded, and captured exceeded 3,000. Afterward, "the American Army was in panicky, headlong flight, leaving scores of tanks burning on the battlefield."[39]

"Scarcely had the first shells left our guns," Lt. Kurt Wolff, leading a tank company, told a German propaganda magazine:

the first three enemy tanks were on fire.... There were at least 15 burning tanks ahead of us, and the most advanced of our tanks were already making their way between the destroyed American tanks in the rear. [My battalion commander], laughing like a boy, went from

Syndicated war correspondent Ernie Pyle.

Courtesy Henry Smith. Photo by Robert Coldwell Sr.

The M3 (GMC) TD, a thinly armored, open-top half-track with a 75mm gun. After severe losses in North Africa they were phased out of frontline Army service and in time-honored fashion passed second-hand to the US Marines. *US Army Signal Corps*

**A restored Panzer IV.** *Courtesy of Paul Hannah*

A restored Panzer IV. *Author photo courtesy of the National Armor and Cavalry Heritage Foundation. Photo enhancement by Robert Coldwell Sr. Inner photo courtesy of the German Federal Archives*

company to company asking himself and us too: "Did you ever see anything like it? Did you ever see anything like it?" I could still see the long line of fires in front of which our tanks cruised up and down, their engines humming, calm yet proud after a good day's work.[40]

Cpl. James Hagan, 1st Armored Regiment, First Armored Division, fought in the Valentine's Day battle of Faid Pass, where at least fifteen tanks fell to Tigers. In a February 23 story called "A Humiliating Predicament," syndicated columnist Ernie Pyle wrote:

hordes of German tanks and troops…swarming out from behind the mountains around Faid Pass…we didn't

know so many tanks were back there…. The attack was so sudden nobody could believe it was in full force…. Our forward troops were overrun before they knew what was happening… All that these men and vehicles could do was duck and dodge and run like hell…. The accompanying tanks fought until knocked out, and their crews then got out and moved along on foot. One tank commander whose whole crew escaped after the tank caught fire said that at least the Germans didn't machine-gun them when they jumped from the burning tank.[41]

A deadly aura soon surrounded the German mystery tank, a fear that remained for the rest of the war and beyond. Lt. Franklyn Johnson, with the storied First Infantry Division ("The

GERMAN ✠

# PZKW IV TANK

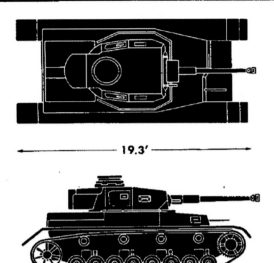

**CHARACTERISTICS:**

Turret: Pyramidal; top slopes down gradually to front; undercut at front corners; large stowage bin attached to rear; high cupola at back in center; set just to rear of center of hull.

Hull: Low, with flat top gradually sloping down at front; shallow, nearly vertical front face.

Armament:
One 75-mm gun mounted in turret.
One coaxial light machine gun.
One light machine gun in right front of hull.

Traction: Full track; eight small evenly spaced bogie wheels sprung in pairs; driving sprocket in front; large, low idler in rear.

**INTEREST DATA:** This is the standard German medium tank. Early models mounted a short-barreled 75-mm gun which has been replaced by a more powerful, long-barreled 75-mm weapon in later types. This tank appears in quantity on the battlefield. It was used in France in 1940, and by Rommel in Africa.

NOVEMBER 1943
FROM DATA CURRENTLY AVAILABLE
WAR DEPARTMENT FM 30-40

‹— 19.3' —›    ‹— 9.6' —›    8.8'

SPEED — 30 MPH    BRIDGE — 25 TONS

FORD — 3.5'    TRENCH — 9.0'

STEP — 2.0' EST.

GRADIENT — 27°

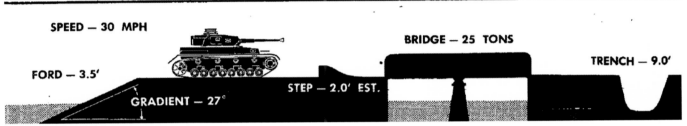

*Photo by Robert Coldwell Sr.*

Big Red One"), recorded in his diary for Friday, February 19, 1943, how it had "Rained half the goddam [sic] night, but strangely my tent stood up." What was of more immediate concern took place around 10:30, when:

> a German tank attack came at the English about 1 mile from our position.... Biggest damn tank in the world, a Mark VI (63 tons) appeared on a hill. Unbelievably huge. Proceeded to shell the English area; joined by a second Mark VI. The British sent up 5 tanks—2 knocked out before they even got close, others withdrew.

Johnson then witnessed a second attack by eight Tigers that "shelled my area, blew up my CP (three 88 shells direct hits), wounded Holmes (later found he died the next day), killed Cahill and Castle." Ironically, Lt. Johnson—who punctuated the dead soldiers' names in his diary by drawing crosses next to their names—was serving in an Anti-Tank company charged by Gen. McNair with stopping German tanks with towed guns.[42]

In an article dated March 3, Pyle told stateside readers of examining a battlefield "riddled by the wide, spooky tracks of the almost-mythical Mark VI [Tiger] tanks."[43] Attempting a counter-attack the next day, forty more Shermans were lost.[44]

Cpl. Hagan, who called American tanks "death traps," wrote in his diary of seeing "13 of our 17 tanks destroyed." Of the remaining four:

> two were [being repaired], but had to be burned [during the American retreat]. There were only two tanks to get

out safely with full crews...we had to retreat about 35 miles, where we re-equipped and started again, two months later. When we came back through the Faid Pass, there were our tanks, with most of the bodies in them.[45]

"If we saw a shadow," recalled Lt. A. Robert Moore, "we fired at it...men went by without guns, just running. It was panic. Anybody who calls it anything else just doesn't know what panic is."[46] To Capt. Bruce Pirnie, it was "a rat race. The Americans were just running away, and the Germans were just running after them."[47]

These disasters were followed on February 19 by the Battle of Kasserine Pass, another embarrassing US defeat and a victory for Rommel. There, notes Eisenhower biographer Jean Edward Smith, "The US Second Corps lost more tanks (235) than the Germans had deployed at the outset of the battle (228)."[48]

To 1st Armored Division platoon Sgt. Lloyd Haas, Kasserine Pass was:

> a nightmare. It was all 88s along our right flank, with a big valley between them and us. An 88mm hit our tank, but bounced off. A second shell hit us—an armor-piercing shell that went right through our armor plate. When an 88mm goes in one side, it doesn't come out the other. Fragments stay inside, bouncing around and knocking stuff loose.
>
> I was hit. It was white-hot where the shell went through and the shrapnel went in. I got all the hair burned off my face and hands, but I was able to move.

"Georgie" and "Ike": The old pals and tank pioneers are all smiles as Patton receives a third star. *US Army Signal Corps*

A Sherman in Tunisia, in original 1943 color.

Three of us got out, but the other two didn't make it—our assistant driver and machine gunner didn't get out. The loader got out, but they machine-gunned him down. I made it out of the tank and didn't realize I was so badly burned until I looked at the other guys and said, "God, you guys got burned." Then they informed me, "You should see yourself."[49]

Dillard Oakley, of Sgt. Haas' tank crew, finished their story:

We could see our tanks just burning all around, in every direction. Our own... had been hit in the rear, and the gas tank started burning.... We started running to a ditch about 40 yards away.... I must have sucked in a lot of the smoke, because I was coughing and hacking and could hardly keep up with the rest. I made it to the ditch and lay there a little while before I looked up... the rest decided to make a run for it, but I stayed with another guy from another tank. It was about 5 p.m. by then and I told him, "It'll get dark in about 40 minutes. That'd give us a better chance to get out of here."

While we were waiting, I could see German infantry in the distance gathering up our boys as prisoners. And here comes three German tanks, followed by troops on foot. So my friend and I played dead. They passed us right by; we got out after dark. Only 14 of us from the company [of about 120 men] made it back without getting captured or killed. All the tanks were lost.[50]

In later fighting around El Guettar, on March 23, men of the 601st Tank Destroyer Battalion were fortunate to receive advance notice of approaching German armor that helped them knock out thirty tanks, including two Tigers. Even with fair warning to position and conceal their guns they lost twenty-one out of thirty-one M3 75mm gun-equipped halft-rack TDs.[51]

Weeks earlier, Ernie Pyle had witnessed "One of our half-tracks, full of ammunition, which was livid red, with flames leaping and swaying. Every few seconds one of its shells would go off, and the projectile would tear into the sky with a weird whanging sort of noise."[52]

To Weldon Adams, 813th Tank Destroyers, "Those half-tracks we used in North Africa—they weren't too good. Shooting from them was about like throwing a rock at a German tank."[53]

The TD men also found the M3 towed gun in which Gen. McNair had placed so much confidence was little more than a doorknocker, as the Germans nicknamed their own 37mm guns. "The troops in this theater," wrote Gen. Walton Walker in a June 1943 report, "have lost confidence in the 37mm anti-tank gun.... Many enlisted men complained that they were told that this weapon would stop a tank, but found out it would not do so." Added a 1st Armored Division armored infantry officer, "In my opinion, the 37mm is useless, unless you have gun crews with the guts to stand and shoot from 100 yards. I think we are placing faith in a false reed here."[54]

Col. William Triplett, judging the M3 "pitifully light armament for use against modern German tanks," described techniques American gunners might use if they were to have a chance of stopping them:

The turret and frontal armor of the German tanks is thick and sloped, impossible for 37mm shot to pene-trate—might as well throw pebbles at it. The side armor is thinner and more vertical. You have a chance of getting through the side. The rear armor is even thinner. And any time you get a shot through the armor, you have a good chance of hitting the engine, a fuel tank, or ammunition. So try to hit them on the side or rear—hit-ting the front or the turret would be like slapping Jack Dempsey.[55]

During the Battle of El Guettar (March 23–April 7, 1943), a Mark IV tank disabled Lt. A. Robert Moore's Sherman. Suddenly a second hit "came through the drivers' hatches. They had their hands on both sides of the holes, lifting their bodies out, when I told 'em to bail out and run":

The second round came between the thumb and the forefinger of the driver's hand. He had about 140 pieces of steel taken out of his hand when he got back to the hospital. He didn't stop running until he got there. The driver and the assistant driver got out. The third round bounced off of the top of our turret...it hit the beveled edge and it shattered the gun sight. The gunner looked up and said, "The sight's gone." I said, "Let's bail out."

Typical Army issue, early-WWII GI metal flashlight. *Photo by Robert Coldwell Sr.*

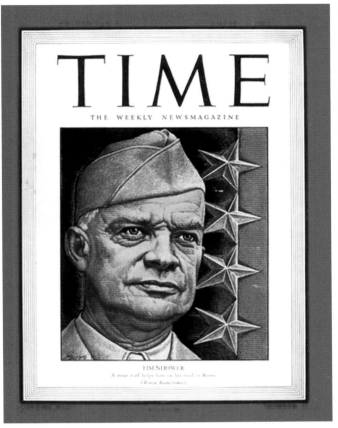

I got out and when the fourth round came through the gun sight...the loader...was on his way out.... It cut him in half and it took the gunner's head off. So I lost two men there. Three of us got out. That tank burned. I went back that night and got the half a body [of the loader]. He was still breathing, but he died before we got him to the hospital. The other guy, the gunner; the biggest piece of him we found was the hip. The rest of him burned in the tank.[56]

War correspondent Ernie Pyle surveyed damage from the El Guettar debacle in April 1943. "You see dark objects sitting far off on the plain. These are burned-out tanks of both sides":

A certain two sit close together like twins, about a mile off the road. The immense caterpillar track is off one of them and lies trailed out behind for fifty feet. The insides are a shambles. Seared and jumbled personal and mechanical debris is scattered around outside. Our

Robert Benney, *American Tank Man*.

soldiers have already retrieved everything worthwhile from the German debris, but you can still find big wrenches, oil-soaked gloves, and twisted shell cases.[57]

In his memoirs, Gen. Omar Bradley recalled how the new M4 earned the bitter "Ronson" moniker, after the cigarette lighter guaranteed to light up the first time. "At Faid (Pass) alone, more than 90 (First Armored Division) tanks were left burning on the valley floor":

I learned that our gasoline-driven Shermans had already established a bad reputation among US troops at the front. Because their high-octane fuel blazed too easily when the engine was hit, the crews pleaded for diesel engines to "replace these firetraps." Sergeant James H. Bowser of Jasper, Alabama, a tough young veteran of 23, spoke for his crew. "General," he said, "this is my third tank.... We were burned out of the other two. If they were diesels, it wouldn't have happened. But these gasoline engines go up like torches on the first or second hit. Then you've got to barrel out and leave 'em burning.[58]

Though known to Ordnance from eyewitness battlefield reports, the fire hazard would not be addressed until 1944, through the improved "wet stowage" (antifreeze or water protected) ammo storage system.[59] And the high loss rate among Sherman loaders—expected to exit a burning tank in seconds (often while wounded) through a single hatch on the far side of the turret after the gunner and tank commander preceded them—would not decrease until the introduction of a second hatch in late 1943–early 1944, more than a year after the first casualties in North Africa and Tunisia.

A GI contemplates a destroyed Panzer IV.

"The material and personnel losses in the First Armored Division," Gen. Eisenhower wrote from the front to Gen. Marshall:

> are very severe…112 medium tanks…most of this stuff was destroyed in actual battle…however, some of it was overrun through surprise action [i.e., the Americans abandoned their equipment without a fight].… I do not believe that any of our (captured) tanks will be particularly valuable to the enemy.… We are cannibalizing the Second Armored Division and the Third Infantry Division to rebuild as necessary, while we get ourselves established to stop further advance and get our units sorted out all along the line.[60]

Eisenhower did not seem unduly alarmed, "In the broad aspect of the campaign, I realize that this affair [the Kasserine Pass disaster] is only an incident."[61] But as to American armor, "I've heard some really discouraging reports about our M3 (medium) tanks."[62]

Prophetically, Eisenhower added to Marshall, almost in passing, "We don't yet know exactly how to handle the [Tiger] tank."[63]

Until the 1944 Ardennes offensive, Sidi-bou-Zid, Faid Pass, Kasserine Pass, and El Guettar were the worst American defeats in the war against Germany. "At moments," even as censors attempted to downplay the extent of the losses for the stateside public, Gen. Marshall "seemed angrier at the press for reporting the fiasco then at his generals for causing it. In a memo to General Alexander Surles, head of the Army's public relations office, he complained at the frequent references in the newspapers to "green troops," a label he considered an aspersion on his training policies."[64]

Eisenhower also condemned the civilian press coverage in an April 16, 1943, letter to Marshall written from Algiers. Marshall

had referred to "adverse stories published concerning certain of our American units." To Eisenhower:

> the knowledge that such stories had gotten out in such a definitely critical vein was practically a body blow, because many weeks ago I had foreseen the effect at home of discouraging reports and had been working like a dog to insure a reasonable utilization of American troops and the presentation of a proper perspective in reports. Moreover, I have made [his British subordinate Gen. Harold] Alexander and others concerned see the great damage that would result from unfair or caustic criticism of any tactical failure of the kind indicated.[65]

In a syndicated column dated February 23, 1943, Ernie Pyle wrote from North Africa:

> Personally, I feel that some such setback as this…is not entirely a bad thing for us. It is all right to have a good opinion of yourself, but we Americans are so smug with our cockiness. We somehow feel that just because

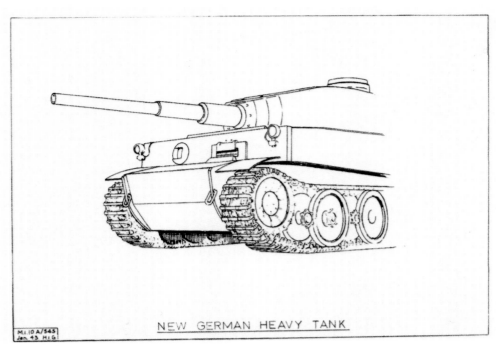

NEW GERMAN HEAVY TANK

A British conjectural drawing of Germany's new tank, January 1943. As rumors leaked out of Tunis, the Allies attempted to gather more information. When *Newsweek* ran one of the first photos of the Tiger in July 1943, speculating it might carry the powerful 88mm artillery piece converted for use in a tank, US Army Ordnance insisted the "88" was too big to fit inside a tank turret. The rumors were all too true. *Photo by Robert Coldwell Sr., courtesy US Army Military History Institute, Carlisle Barracks, Pennsylvania*

we're Americans, we can whip our weight in wildcats. And we have got it into our heads that production alone will win the war.

He also saluted the scrappiness of the American tanker, after seeing "crews that have had two tanks shot out from under them, but whose only thought was to get a third tank and "have another crack at them blankety-blanks."[66]

Instead of recognizing warning signs of flawed tanks, armor, and anti-tank doctrine, Army leaders dismissed them as a natural result of raw GIs going up against Rommel's battle-hardened *Afrika Korps*, or read into them confirmation of their own views. To Gen. McNair, "Developments in Africa only serve[d] to demonstrate the soundness" of his tank destroyer project: "...if they had piled in tank destroyers instead of armored units [i.e., tanks], the 1st Armored Division would still be intact."[67]

While the general public today is familiar with the triumphant Normandy invasion, few recognize names like Sidi-bou-Zid and El Guettar. Since the war, historians mesmerized by the "Good War" narrative have neglected coverage of these American defeats. If they are mentioned at all, it is to repeat the wartime Army leaders' explanation: "Bad generalship, not obsolete equipment, was the First Armored Division's greatest problem in Tunisia."[68]

Lt. Lawrence Robertson, First Armored Division, rejected this view:

Historians have failed to understand the cause of our initial defeat in Central Tunisia, [stating] that our failure was due to "green American troops." Other historians have followed suit, like so many parrots. I was there in the thick of combat, leading a medium tank platoon,

and I know that the officers and men of the First Armored Division were... highly trained, well-disciplined, and well-led.... We failed because the Germans introduced...new high-velocity tank guns, and...the new Tiger tank, equipped with the famed and feared 88mm gun. With that advantage, they could pick off our tanks long before we, with our popguns, could score a penetration.[69]

German propaganda gloated on their triumphs. According to Lt. Wolff:

In a roaring attack, we took the town of Sidi-bou-Zid from the occupying Americans. We rode to the rear of their batteries, annihilated a row of tanks, and by late afternoon we had reached our prescribed target.... The enemy evidently had retreated a long way: Even his usually active artillery was silent...we stood on the turrets of our tanks and counted the torches [burning American tanks] on the horizon.[70]

Shortly after the November 1942 invasion, Gen. Devers led officers on an inspection tour of American units in North Africa. On returning to the states he declared, "The M4 medium tank is the best tank on the battlefield."[71] Not to be outdone, Gen. Gladeon Barnes testified to Congress that in the desert battles, the Shermans "overcame every tank which they opposed."[71]

The success of the Germans' 88mm field piece in the desert appeared to support Gen. McNair's conviction that the best answer to a good German tank was a towed gun, not a better American tank. This led to emphasis on the tank destroyer concept over updating flawed tanks, "a conviction that to some extent hindered Ordnance in developing a more powerful tank than the Sherman." As Ordnance would later admit, this was "one example of a tendency among U.S. Army planners to apply the early experience of the Allies without enough imagination or flexibility."[72]

December 1942: One of the first photos to appear of the new Tiger tank (here rolling into Tunis) from the German newspaper *National Zeitung*. The first ones wore a green paint scheme but were later repainted tan to match desert conditions. The *British Daily Mail*, reporting on the mystery tank a month later, referred to them as "monsters" and "land battleships."

In spring of 1943, to check on the progress of the TDs, Gen. McNair also made a brief trip to the North African/Tunisian front. His comments to the press hint at the dissention between supporters of his theories (his career generals and subordinates at home) and the frontline soldiers doing the fighting who were forced to follow those theories. There was a disconnect, a gap that would steadily widen throughout the war.

As his biographer Kahn describes it, McNair "explained to the press that he had made [the trip] to check on certain matters about which his Ground Forces combat observers had disagreed. 'You get dizzy from trying to reconcile divergent views,' he said."[73] "I went there not from a sense of getting into the fray and swinging a club," he told reporters, "but from a sense of duty to these young men in training back home."[74] It is an enlightening comment that shows McNair's stateside frame of reference; what about his duty to the young men at the North African and Tunisian fronts forced to follow his erroneous theories on pain of death? Stateside training was rigorous, but blind adherence to failed doctrine overseas killed men.

Ironically, Gen. McNair—who never held a combat command in four decades as an Army officer—was wounded on his first day at the front. At the time he was "our highest-ranking casualty, and our only lieutenant general to be wounded in action in this war; he was struck, and nearly killed, by fragments of a German shell."[75]

Reacting to the North African and Tunisian debacles, some stateside commentators were full of doom and gloom. "The

dominance enjoyed by Armored Forces in 1939 and 1940," insisted *The Cavalry Journal*, "is over.... It is another example of the old story of firepower versus armor. Firepower always wins in the end." Correspondent Jack Belden, in *Time* magazine, sighed, "Tanks! How futile they appear face-to-face…with ambush-emplaced guns."[76]

Reading of the disasters, the American public had the "reverential awe with which they regarded [tanks]…sharply jarred."[77] Clearly, there were problems with US equipment. But Roosevelt, instead of ordering high-priority production of improved tanks in great numbers, now lowered the position of tanks on the priority list for military manufacturing. Though tanks with better firepower and armor protection were needed, the president was de-emphasizing their manufacture.[78]

"In 1942," gushed Roosevelt in his January 7, 1943, State of the Union Address, "we produced 56,000 combat vehicles, such as tanks and self-propelled artillery. We produced 21,000 anti-tank guns, six times greater than our 1941 production."[79] This figure included the 37mm M3 towed gun, which soldiers from private to general agreed was little better than a "pea shooter" ineffective against tough German tank armor. Yet they were cranked out in droves enabling FDR to spout his superficially impressive numbers.

Even while claiming "The Arsenal of Democracy is making good…we have achieved a miracle of production," and "What matters most in war is results," Roosevelt also conceded, "Our 1942…tank production fell short, numerically, of the goals set

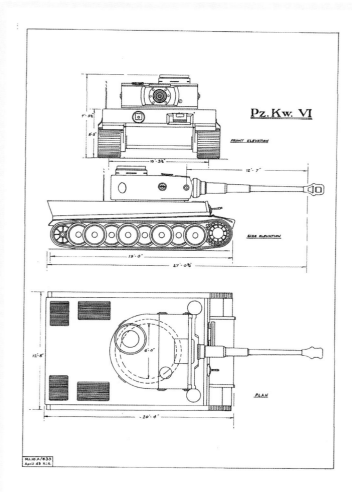

A British conjectural drawing of the new German "land battleship." Not surprisingly the overhead view is a bit sparse. *Photo by Robert Coldwell Sr.*

a year ago." This was said minutes after he boasted, "A year ago we set certain production goals for 1942 and 1943. Some people, including some experts, thought that we had pulled some big figures out of a hat just to frighten the Axis. But we had confidence in the ability of our people to establish new records. That confidence has been justified."

Tank production for 1943 would now be lowered, Roosevelt explained euphemistically, to build near-tanks—substitutes for genuine tanks. "In tank production, we revised our schedule—and for good and sufficient reasons. As a result of hard experience in battle, we have diverted a portion of our tank producing capacity to a stepped-up production of new, deadly field weapons, especially self-propelled artillery [i.e., tank destroyers].[80]

## Enter the Tiger

The Panzer VI (Tiger I) tank debuted around Leningrad in August 1942. Months later, in the North African and Tunisian campaigns, American M4 tank crews first grappled with the Sherman's great nemesis. Germany's new heavy tank was a response to the T-34, Russia's successful blend of firepower, crew protection, and mobility.

Gen. Heinz Guderian conceded that while Germany had enjoyed an edge over Russian armor before the T-34, "from now on the situation was reversed."[81] Acknowledging "the marked superiority of the T-34 to our Panzer Mark IV," Guderian wrote

that officers "at the front were of the opinion that the T-34 should simply be copied, since this would be the quickest way of putting to rights the most unhappy situation of the German Panzer troops."[82] The disparity fueled a tank arms race with the Soviets, resulting in two of the best German tanks of the war: the Tiger and Panther.

Allied intelligence, in another stumble, did not know the Tiger had debuted three months before on the eastern front. A secret British telegram dated November 3, 1942, noted a "captured German diagram" of "a new...[heavy tank] known as the [Panzer Type 6] being built... We have asked [Allied forces in the Middle East] to take urgent steps to obtain precise information on its characteristics."[83]

Another November telegram graded "Most Secret" revealed that data on the "New German Super-Heavy Panzer 6 Tank" came "from a delicately placed, reliable source." It included impressive performance estimates, "NOT to be generally circulated or reproduced in a summary."[84]

After German authorities allowed a dramatic photo of a Tiger rolling into Tunis to appear in the newspaper *National Zeitung* on December 11, 1942,[85] the *British Daily Mail* reported on January 30, 1943:

62-TON GERMAN TANKS ARRIVE - Germany's new 62-ton monster "Tiger" tanks, equipped with dual purpose 88mm guns, have now appeared in Tunisia. Their numbers at present, however, are small.

The "land battleships," though not much bigger than the German Mark IVs, are about twice the weight—the difference being entirely due to the tremendous armour of the "Tiger."

Seven-inch armour plating protects the "Tiger's" turret, the front of which is additionally strengthened with a further inch of armour.

The sides of the tank are protected by 5in. plating.

The tanks are still in an experimental stage, and have apparently been brought here to boost the morale of the Axis troops.

Three Tigers are believed to have had their tracks—their most vulnerable point—blown off last week when they ran over French mines.[86]

British armor historian David Fletcher has written that when early reports suggested a tank generations ahead of Allied designs—which in his view were "a feeble travesty of the German achievement"[87]—one reaction was the same resignation as in 1940, when the success of the blitzkrieg was credited to phantom "assault tanks."

This willingness to accept the Tiger, wrote Fletcher, as "outside the accepted parameters of tank design as understood in 1941...was all part of the general surrender of technological initiative...that allowed Germany to outstrip Britain and her Allies so decisively for the rest of the war."[88]

Army Ordnance's reaction to the Tiger was the opposite of the 1940 "assault tank" panic. Back then they had believed German propaganda on non-existent monster tanks, but now (1943) Ordnance dismissed a real danger. When *Newsweek* published a rare photo of the mystery tank and speculated it

Lt. Gen. George S. Patton Jr. wears an Army Air Force flyer's heavy, sheepskin-lined high-altitude flight jacket in the hot North African/ Tunisian desert, perhaps contributing to his scowl. Note the eyeglasses in his right pocket. *US Signal Corps*

might be armed with an 88mm gun, Ordnance officials were quick to reject this; the 88, they insisted, was too large to be fitted into a tank turret—precisely what the Germans had done.[89]

Because only some nineteen Tigers appeared in North Africa,[90] the danger they posed was not immediately appreciated. When British anti-tank gunners knocked out a few, this seemed to "confirm" the Tiger was no threat. In a February 15, 1943, secret report, British Brig. T. Lyon Smith stated it had been "proven conclusively (to me anyhow) that the 6-pounder Anti-Tank gun can deal most effectively with the Mark VI tank." Prophetically added Brig. Smith, "I hope I may not be proved at a later date to have been wrong."[91] The Allies also underestimated the new tank because it experienced breakdowns—not unusual for a complicated weapon developed under pressure and rushed to the battlefield.

Today, the Tiger enjoys a popular reputation as one of history's best tanks, but at the time the mystery tank first appeared, British journalist Philip Jordan belittled it as "a legendary flop."[92] The British *Daily Telegraph* insisted on February 5, 1943, "The legend of their invulnerability has been completely dissipated by the fact that the six-pounders (towed anti-tank guns) were able to knock out two of them from a distance of between 400 and 500 yards."[93] In the American press, nationwide headlines appeared, such as "Tiger Outmatched" in the Uniontown, PA *Morning Herald* of June 19, 1943. Speculating on "Will Russia Seize the Summer Offensive?" the *Herald* claimed, "Already the Germans have been let down by their much-touted Mark VI Tiger

tank, this season's surprise which was counted upon to subdue the Red Army." The new Tiger, it was claimed, had already been rendered inferior by the advent of heavy new Soviet tanks like the KV-1.[94]

One of the first captured Tigers was sent home to the US soon after the tanks' arrival on the Tunisian front in April 1943, by a pioneering Ordnance Department technical intelligence team. According to a press release, "Ordnance Intelligence Officers Exercise Ingenuity on Battlefields," the disabled metal monster was stuffed into a homeward-bound Liberty Ship by Capt. George Bennett and two GIs using "an improvised block and tackle"—quite an impressive feat if true, since the behemoth weighed sixty tons.[95]

The personal papers of Col. George Jarrett at the Army's Military History Institute at Carlisle Barracks, Pennsylvania, include a memo signed by Capt. George Drury, "Ordnance Technical Intelligence Team No, 1, APO 230," referring to a captured Tiger being sent home for study to Aberdeen. The subject line is "Panzer VI Tiger Model B Design Study, Technical Analysis, and Tests":

1. This tank, delivered to you at Aberdeen Proving Ground, represents more than just a runner Tiger Model B. It represents thousands of man-hours of work performed by the men who risked their lives to evacuate it from the scene of capture and those who prepared and shipped it to the United States. The cost in dollars of this evacuation far exceeds its cost of production.

2. The men who have done so much to bring you this splendid example of German ordnance are deeply interested in its complete technical study. They have seen its performance in the field and are cognizant of its ability to deal with all American tanks, but the overall picture of its advantages can only be learned from laboratory and field tests conducted by experts with the finest of testing equipment.

3. It would be criminally wrong for this tank to be pounded to pieces on the proof ranges without first being studied for performance and maneuverability. A hull has been previously shipped for the purpose of plate tests, and every effort to deliver a runner was put into this tank. The men of this Team are proud, and profoundly so, of their accomplished part in this project. They charge you to equal their contributions.[96]

After the hard lessons of the desert war were absorbed, the options for improving American armor included updating existing

M4 in the Sicilian hills, 1943

Italian M14/41 medium tank in desert camouflage at the Tank Museum, Bovington, Dorset, UK.
*Massimo Foti*

An M4A1 named "Eternity" moves out from a Sicilian beach-head in July 1943. Note the variance in the circle around the white US star national marking, caused by cut-out stencils; the absence of white paint around the circle shows where the stencil was attached. The "T" shape below the name is a unit marking, which came in various geometric shapes instead of numbers to hopefully confuse the enemy.

M4s with more powerful guns and thicker armor, or designing and building all new, heavier tanks. But the prewar preference for light, nimble "Cavalry tanks" lingered.

While Armored Force Chief Gen. Jake Devers remained a critic of the Tank Destroyer concept, and questioned its combat effectiveness after his inspection tour of North Africa, he also objected to building a new heavy tank. Perhaps recalling the failed M6 white elephant of 1941, he dismissed this option in a December 7, 1942, letter to Gen. McNair. "Due to its tremendous weight and limited tactical use, there is no requirement in the Armored Force for a heavier tank. The increase in power of the armament of the heavy tank does not compensate for the heavier armor."[97]

Other armor generals, including Patton, agreed with Devers. Coming from a Cavalry background emphasizing speed and mobility over firepower and armor protection, they favored designs approaching obsolescence even when first built back in 1941.

But even as Germany introduced bigger, more powerful models like the Tiger and Panther, American armor doctrine still envisioned the ideal use of tanks as weapons of exploitation to sneak into enemy rear areas, attack his most vulnerable points, and get away.

An M6 Fargo TD used in Sicily and North Africa. While some of its stark, straight lines have been broken up with mud, the large white star surely defeats the attempt at camouflage.

Eisenhower's private correspondence with Marshall after the North Africa disasters also shows the prevalence of the passive, reactive Tank Destroyer doctrine. Rather than striking first, tanks would be held back in reserve, conceding the initiative to the enemy. "Among other things," Eisenhower wrote, "our troubles came about because we are still too weak in A.T. [anti-tank weapons]…my great effort was to…station the bulk of the First Armored Division in the rear…so as to be ready to launch a vigorous and powerful counter-attack against any force thrusting its way through the hills…[but it] was held out of action until considerable portions of its forward detachments had been used up, and this naturally resulted in piecemeal action."[98]

After the 1942–1943 Guadalcanal campaign in the Pacific theater Marshall ordered GIs to be interviewed, and their hard-earned, first hand wisdom compiled for distribution. "Soldiers and officers alike should read these notes and seek to apply their lessons," Marshall wrote in the forward to *Fighting In Guadalcanal*. "We must cash in on the experience which these and other brave men have paid for in blood."[99] Would the same hold true with the painful lessons learned about the inadequacies of American tanks and TDs, and the validity of the outdated doctrine for their use?

Following the North Africa and Tunisia campaigns came the July 1943 Allied invasion of Sicily. There, reporting on a battle between American "'Chutists" (paratroopers) and "Eyties," *Chicago Tribune* reporter John "Beaver" Thompson (so nicknamed for his prominent beard) wrote of "many strange sights here during the past several days" in a story appearing in the Amarillo, Texas, *Daily News* on July 16, 1943. For example, "the lush green fields of tomato plants or unripened grapes, and in their center, a squat, ugly Tiger tank belching smoke and shells."[100] Associated Press reporter Harold Boyle filed a story that ran with the headline "American Colonel Single-Handedly Slays Giant

52-Ton Tiger Tank in Sicily." Boyle elaborated on the "battle of the vineyards," where "One Colonel stepped to within a few paces of a giant 52-ton Tiger tank and single-handedly knocked it out of the battle with a lucky shot from his anti-tank gun. Such a deed can be compared only to David Slaying Goliath."[101]

In the aftermath of the Sicilian campaign, a conclusive assessment of the use of tanks was difficult because atypical conditions prevailed. The campaign was unusually short; Sicilians and Italians had little desire to fight Americans, and less to die for Hitler and Mussolini. As reporter Boyle described pamphlets issued to GIs:

> One card, which contained a full-length picture of an Italian soldier, gave these as his characteristics: "The Italian is emotional, excitable, and proud. He responds best to gentle treatment. Unlike the German the best results are got from the Italian by kindness."
>
> One soldier read this paragraph aloud to his fellow soldiers.

Anti Tank Gun and Crew, Fort Custer, Michigan

textbook-style duel of massed tanks over open ground; the ideal conditions writers of armor doctrine had hoped and prepared for.

But warning signs that tank and TD doctrine might need revision were present; on the morning of July 11, the Americans were nearly thrown off the landing beaches and back into the sea by seventeen Tigers of the Hermann Göring *Panzer Division*, who destroyed an entire platoon of Second Armored Division Shermans.[104] "It was reported that an enemy tank column was moving south astride the Ponte Olivo-Gela road," recalled Paul Skogsberg, First Infantry Division:

> There was a gap between the 1st Division and the Rangers, and this column was headed right for this opening.... I set out towards Gela on a route that paralleled the beach.... I was able to locate myself at a dinky little railroad overpass, which afforded me excellent cover. I could see the tanks clearly from under the bridge…there was, at that moment, nothing to stop the Tigers from driving directly to the beach…had they continued on, they could have raised havoc.[105]

But according to Gen. Marshall in his postwar *Report on the Winning of the War*, "General Eisenhower wrote me on 17 July 1943 [that] all the initial invasion moves were carried out smoothly, and an astonishing lack of resistance was encountered on the shoreline."[106]

Landing on the invasion beach near Gela, Gen. John Lucas saw "Several German Mark VI Tiger tanks. Unbelievable monsters, over 60 tons, and each mounting an 88mm gun. The armor plate looked to be well over 3 inches thick. Splashes [minor gouges] could be seen where [American 37mm guns] had hit. The crew probably didn't even know they were under fire. The 37mm gun," concluded General Lucas, " is useless against the front armor

Gen. Patton on the beach at Gela, Sicily, in July 1943. *US Army Signal Corps*

"Sure," said one of them, patting his rifle, "kill them with kindness."[102]

The Second Armored Division had just twelve days of combat on Sicily,[103] and the rugged, mountainous terrain precluded a

Side view of a US M5 3-inch towed anti-tank gun.
*Author photo courtesy of the National Armor and Cavalry Heritage Foundation*

of any German tank. It must be used against the flanks, or preferably, the rear."[107]

While a general on the invasion beaches recognized the growing Tiger threat with his own eyes, others downplayed it. The morning of July 11, tankers and infantry pinned down on the beaches by Tigers were rescued by offshore naval gunfire. This lucky escape saved them from disaster, but also hid problems with American equipment and doctrine. That afternoon (D-Day plus one), Shermans and self-propelled artillery were able to knock out more panzers, including ten Tigers, inspiring more complacency; writing to a West Point classmate, on July 22, Gen. Vernon Pritchard Eisenhower called the Sherman tank "one of the finest weapons on the battlefield."[108]

A British journalist judged the Tiger in Tunisia "a legendary flop" because it had experienced teething problems. Now, in Sicily, July 11 successes against German tanks also led to an Allied assumption that this new Tiger could be tamed. Thus, another chance to address problems with American armor—and to match or surpass this new generation of German design—was lost. As in North Africa and Tunisia, some read into the Sicilian campaign lessons or conclusions that supported their pet theories, accentuating the positive while ignoring danger signs.

When the Second Armored Division traveled a hundred miles in four days to capture Palermo, to the powers-that-be it seemed to validate current armor design and doctrine. But some overlooked a major reason for the happy ending to the "Race to Palermo": unlike on the beachhead, the 2nd AD met little or weak opposition from German armor.[109] Had Stuart light tanks been confronted with Tigers, the "race" may have ended differently. But to Gen. Patton, who captured headlines with his aggressive spirit, all was well. "I believe that this operation," he confided to his diary, "will go down in history, certainly at [Fort] Leavenworth [the US Army's Command and General Staff College] as a classic example of the proper use of armor."[110]

Unlike many soldiers, Patton also had good words for the despised 37mm towed gun:

If a projectile can be developed for the 37mm gun with more penetrating effect, it is superior to the 57mm (towed gun) as an offensive anti-tank weapon…it can be pulled by the…1/4-ton truck [while] the 57mm cannot, and must be towed either by a half-track or a…3/4-ton truck. Second, with limited crews available, the 57mm cannot be manhandled any distance over bad country, while the 37mm can. Even with the present ammunition, the 37mm is deadly against tanks up to 400 yds.[111]

"Patton's views, however," author Zaloga has noted, "were not widely shared by the Infantry."[112]

Pondering the effectiveness of the self-propelled TDs in Sicily, Gen. Lucas wrote in an influential report, "The tank destroyer has, in my opinion, failed to prove its usefulness…. I believe the doctrine of an offensive weapon to "slug it out" with the tanks is unsound." But like Gen. Devers, Lucas did not consider more powerful tanks to be the answer. Instead, "the only successful anti-tank weapon is…a towed gun of great power and low silhouette."[113]

Soon after the Kasserine Pass disaster, Army Ground Force observers also reported (on March 5, 1943) on the towed 37mm gun with which Gen. McNair had hoped to stop enemy tanks. According to Lucas:

Two general officers condemned this gun as useless as an anti-tank gun, and strongly recommended that it be discarded. They stated that it would not penetrate the turret or front of the German medium tank; that the projectiles bounced off like marbles, and that the

German tanks over-run the gun positions. The G-3 of the Allied Forces informed me that the above recommendation had been approved, and they do not want the 37mm gun.[114]

Concerning both types of TDs (self-propelled vehicles and towed guns), one author has concluded with admirable understatement, "The circumstances for which [the TDs] had been formed were rarely encountered... Designed as a means of stopping hordes of German tanks which had ruptured a defensive line, it slowly became apparent that this was not occurring."[115] After severe losses, the slapdash 75mm gun-equipped M3 half-tracks and tiny M6 Fargo TDs were quietly withdrawn from frontline service.

But Gen. McNair continued to call for towed guns to stop enemy tanks. He now advocated the use of a new 57mm model and an upcoming 3-inch (90mm) version that would be mocked by GIs as "McNair's Folly": large, heavy, and awkward for men on foot to move and emplace. "We would tow it with a half-track," Cpl. Jack Myers, 692nd Tank Destroyer Battalion, recalled to the author. "We needed four men to move it and dig it in, using picks and shovels. We'd emplace it, then park the half-track about 50 yards behind it."[116]

This 3-inch towed gun, like the earlier 37mm and 57mm models that McNair had also championed, was not the best solution to stopping tanks, yet it was inflicted upon GIs until 1945. "McNair stubbornly persisted," wrote Zaloga, "and argued that experiences in the North African campaign indicated that the towed anti-tank gun had been proven a successful adversary of the tank. Rank won out and McNair's opinions triumphed, even if his assessments of the North African campaign were dubious."[117]

Back home, Gen. McNair maintained that all was well, rejecting the possibility that TDs might be poor substitutes for true tanks. He remained "a supporter of his pet project, despite the flaws which had been found in both tank destroyer equipment and doctrine."[118] Doubling down, he ordered TD units originally equipped with self-propelled guns to convert to towed guns. According to Steve Zaloga:

On January 1, 1943, McNair ordered [Tank Destroyer Force commander Gen. Andrew Bruce] to test a towed battalion, and the 801st Tank Destroyer Battalion served as the guinea pig...on March 31, 1943, McNair ordered the conversion of 15 self-propelled battalions into towed battalions.... In November 1943, McNair [would order] that half of all tank destroyer battalions would be converted to towed configuration in time for the forthcoming campaign in France.[119]

Along with disregarding Tank Destroyers' lack of success in the North African and Tunisian campaigns, Army leaders also misread the use of armor in Sicily. Instead of heeding warnings that Germany was upping the ante in the tank design competition, they made too much of two fortunate anomalies: the Allied naval gunfire that rescued tanks on the landing beaches (something unlikely to recur in future, inland tank-versus-tank combat in the crowded hedgerows and forests of Western Europe) and the "race to Palermo," which owed as much to Italian soldiers' contempt

for Mussolini and Hitler as it did to Patton's skill using tanks. Many Italian soldiers despised their German allies and viewed the Allies as liberators. But would such a fortunate political situation repeat itself when American tankers met die-hard, experienced SS fanatics in tank-to-tank combat deep in *das Vaterland*?

Gen. Alvin Gillem, who led the Armored Command, told of his visit to the Sicilian front in the August 9, 1943, *Armored News*, Fort Knox's official newspaper. "Throughout the Sicilian campaign," he exulted—while neglecting to mention the Tiger:

the tanks have contributed to the success obtained... [their] characteristics have been exploited by General George S. Patton, Jr., using tanks ahead of or behind the Infantry.... The capture of Palermo furnishes a perfect example.... During the first week of the operation, an armored division was held in reserve. Infantry divisions on the flank were ordered to breach the defenses of one of the Sicilian valleys running north from the southern coast. The Armored Division was on a six hour alert. When the opportunity presented itself, the Corps commander shot the Division through the hole, turned it north into the valley, and Palermo was captured almost per schedule. The speed and force of this one blow assisted materially to knock out all Axis defenses in the Western half of the island.[120]

Gen. Gillem gave some misleadingly optimistic figures: "Up to the time I departed Sicily, the total box score, American tanks versus Axis tanks, read 21 American tanks lost and 81 Axis tanks lost."[121] While these numbers seem impressive, note that Gillem—perhaps restricted by censorship—did not specify *types* of tanks; a more accurate way to gauge their respective effectiveness.

July 1943: On the road to Messina, Sicily, Gen. Patton looks down on Lt. Col. Lyle Bernard, who led the 30th Infantry Regiment, Third Infantry Division. Note the yellow circle variation around the US white star national marking. *US Army Signal Corps*

TD men of the 636th Tank Destroyer Battalion, with "Jinx," their M10 GMC. In September 1943, they helped turn back a German attack around Salerno, Italy, by destroying multiple tanks and vehicles and were awarded Silver Stars in Fifth Army General Orders. *US Army Signal Corps*

The Axis losses he cited include small, obsolete Italian designs crewed by demoralized men and older, lighter German models. Both types fell to heavier, better armed and armored Sherman medium tanks. Recall that when Shermans fought Tigers crewed by aggressive, motivated tankers of the *Hermann Göring Panzer Division*, an entire platoon of five tanks from the 2nd AD was wiped out.[122] Gen. Gillem neglected to discuss the potential odds in a Tiger vs. Sherman duel.

While praising American tanks to the public, behind the scenes, Gen. Gillem was calling for up-gunned Shermans. At one point in August, Armored Command called for production of all 75mm gunned Shermans to end, to be replaced with models with the more powerful 76mm gun in a new turret. But the 76mm gun was only a slight improvement over the 75mm, and its larger rounds would reduce the amount that could be carried in the M4. American tank guns were designed to be "dual purpose": able to fire high explosive rounds (to fight soft targets) or armor piercing rounds used against tanks. According to Charles Baily, "Despite the smaller size of the 75mm round, its high-explosive projectile carried almost twice as much explosive filler as the 76mm projectile."[123]

When it was realized the 76mm gun was not a major improvement, Gen. Gillem modified his request, now calling for roughly one-third of the M4s in US tank units to be equipped with the new 76mm gun. On September 4, 1943, he also wrote to Gen. McNair, requesting that the Sherman be up-gunned with a 90mm main gun:

> He argued (to McNair) that combat experience had proven American tanks sometimes had to engage German tanks to carry out their primary mission, and the Germans were introducing tanks with increasingly heavy armor. The 90mm gun was needed to defeat those tanks, and the only way to get that gun into a tank by June 1944 was to mount it in a Sherman.

> But McNair refused Gillem's request. He argued that combat experience had shown that tanks should

not engage other tanks, and that no theater had requested tanks with 90mm guns. Still retaining his faith in tank destroyers, McNair believed enemy armor should be the target of US anti-tank guns. In addition, the Ordnance Department had convinced McNair that Gillem's idea "would result in a heavy tank…" [Gen. Barnes] did not explain his objections in detail, but Gillem's proposal was an obvious rival to the T25 and T26:

> Many officers at Fort Knox believed that Gillem should have gone to General Marshall with the idea, but Gillem, torn between desire for the tank and loyalty to his commander, elected not to go over McNair's head. This marked the end of an idea that promised to provide a 90mm tank gun to American troops during 1944.[124]

Capt. Harry Butcher, Eisenhower's public relations aide, recounted in his diary for August 25, 1943:

> We had Generals [Sir Harold] Alexander and [Bernard] Montgomery…for lunch on Monday. Both Alex and Monty said that the Germans are getting ahead of us on tank design, particularly gun power. Montgomery said that our tank designers apparently build a tank and then stick a gun in it, rather than design a gun and build a tank around it. He claims we are outshot by the German tanks.[125]

When the fighting moved to the Italian mainland, the First Armored Division had a long, tough campaign, receiving little credit for difficult battles such as those in support of the February 1944 Anzio landings. Against Tigers and Panthers M4 losses were heavy; for example, in the little-known May 1944 battle of Campoleone, the 1st AD lost twenty-one Shermans.[126]

M4A1 Medium Tank: The first production version of the M4 was distinguished by the rounded, turtle-like cast hull. Later versions had a welded hull made of slab-sided, flat armor plates. The M4A1 was the first model of the Sherman to see combat in North Africa—with British crews. It was such an improvement over previous British and American models that its flaws were not immediately apparent. While stateside press releases called it a war winner, tank crews nicknamed it the "Ronson," after the cigarette lighter guaranteed to light up on the first try. *Author's collection, photo by Robert Coldwell Sr.*

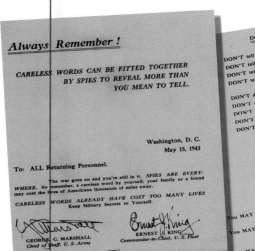

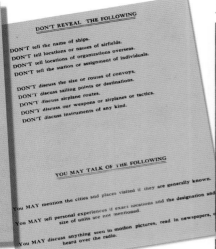

# KEEP 'EM FIRING!

*Courtesy Henry Smith. Photo by Robert Coldwell Sr.*

Italy, 1944: A captured Tiger dwarfs a New Zealand Sherman tank and crew.

On May 25, 1944, Pvt. Robert Dodge of the Third Infantry Division watched a desperate tank duel "taking place in a broad valley" on the road to Rome:

> I could see four Tiger tanks, sitting on knolls, firing at our Sherman tanks. Our tanks would sit behind knolls, revving their engines, dash to the top, fire, and be on their way down en masse at once.
>
> It was like a shooting gallery; the Jerries kept picking off our tanks. I watched the Shermans make hits in the Tigers, but the shells just ricocheted into the clouds. When one of our tanks was hit, it just sat there and burned. Sometimes survivors got out and made a run for cover, sometimes not. At one time, four of our tanks were burning.[127]

As to the ability of towed guns to stop tanks, after a November 1944 Fifth Army tank destroyer conference in Florence, Italy, the attendees were "unanimous in the opinion that the towed battalion was unsatisfactory and grossly inferior to the SP-gun [self-propelled gun, i.e., M10 and M18 tank destroyers]. It cannot

be manned effectively in the forward combat area. Men cannot and will not stay with towed guns as they will with the M10 or M18."[128]

Yet even as the Tiger threat grew, the American public was assured their Army's weapons and equipment were some of the world's best.

Gen. Adna Chaffee, emphasizing the importance of "timely execution of adequate manufacturing programs," had warned against falling behind the enemy in a statement read to the US House of Representatives days after his death in August 1941:

> It is essential that we manufacture the most modern type of fighting equipment for today and, concurrently, develop more efficient types for tomorrow. We are all too familiar with the long and precious time required to develop, tool for, and manufacture new types of critical items of equipment. We are also familiar with the uselessness of an army which is second best in materiel.[129]

But high-level complacency and public praise of the M4 continued. The Americans approached the invasion of Hitler's "Fortress Europe" with inadequate tanks and flawed armor and anti-tank doctrine, and little awareness of the impending disasters awaiting them on the Normandy beaches and beyond.

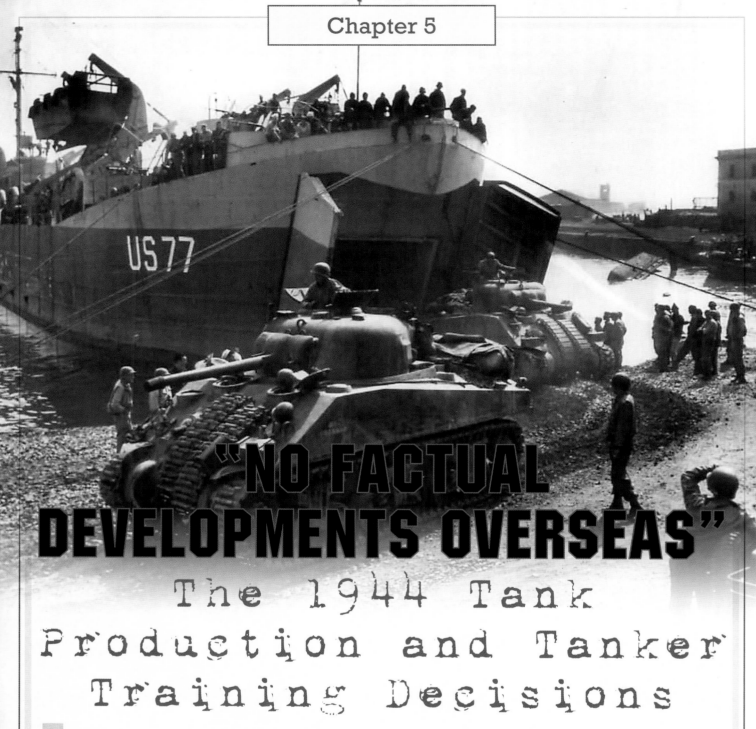

# Chapter 5

# "NO FACTUAL DEVELOPMENTS OVERSEAS"

## The 1944 Tank Production and Tanker Training Decisions

In 1945, when the Sherman tank scandal was exposed in the civilian press, Army leaders claimed tankers were not requesting heavier or more powerful models. "German tank successes," argues the Ordnance Department's history of tank production, "were due more to skilled tactical use, and the employment of heavy German tanks against Allied mediums, than to any failure of American industry to produce in quantity the tanks desired by the using arms [notice the careful wording excludes Ordnance from criticism]."[3]

This claim implies that Ordnance "succeeded" at building flawed tanks it was *ordered* to build by stateside leaders while evading its failure to build the up-gunned, better-armored tanks *needed* by GIs fighting the tank war overseas. Ordnance was supposed to evaluate Germany's

> [In 1943] the decision was made to de-emphasize production of the T26 heavy tank, and concentrate instead on the M4 medium tank. This turned out to be one of the most disastrous decisions of World War II, and its effect on the upcoming battle for Western Europe was catastrophic.[1]
>
> —Lt. Belton Cooper, Third Armored Division, *Death Traps*

best tanks, updating US designs to not just match, but *defeat* them. It stumbled on both counts. By the time the press exposed the controversy it was too late to make a difference.

Senior Army leaders steadily obstructed adoption of the T26 heavy tank. Had it been delivered to the ETO before the Ardennes offensive, it might have contributed to shorter casualty lists and fewer tank losses; from September to mid-December 1944, the Twelfth Army Group (First, Third, and Ninth Armies) lost nearly 1,000 tanks—a figure that excludes the Ardennes fighting that began on December 16 and continued into January 1945.[4]

The tank design and building process continued to be racked by power struggles between Army Ground Forces (AGF), the Ordnance Department, and Armored Forces (which, thanks to

McNair, had been reduced in status, and was now known as Armored Command). In hindsight, since Ordnance Gens. Campbell and Barnes were opposed to various quick fixes, it is tempting to single them out as culprits, but much is not as it seems.

A closer look shows the two generals resisted stopgap changes to the M4 because they wanted to adopt a new tank—the T26—instead, but were blocked by Gen.l McNair. In late 1943, observes Ordnance's official history, Gen. Barnes was "in the thick of a fight which he hoped to win, to get a better tank than the M4 to the battlefield in 1944." In October, Barnes requested 500 prototype T26s be produced immediately, in time for the Normandy invasion, but his request was rejected by Gen. McNair's AGF.[5]

Ordnance was aware of the M4's deficiencies through front-line tankers' feedback. In October 1943, Capt. A. Robert Moore, First Armored Division, wrote from the Italian theater.[6] Endorsements on the original document, "Suggested Design Improvements [for] Medium Tank," imply that it went up the command ladder: "All personnel of the Ordnance Department concerned with the development matters discussed by Captain Moore are being supplied with a copy of this letter."[7]

Moore noted his "considerable experience with tanks and tank weapons in actual combat." "Having been in the Armored Force for about three and one-half years," and with "ample opportunity to watch and study the development of our tanks," he felt qualified to state that "…in my opinion, the present German armored equipment excels ours in many ways."[8]

In three sentences Capt. Moore pinpointed the major problem with American WWII tanks that many higher ranking Army leaders failed to appreciate:

The German has concentrated on developing a gun, with the means of moving it, and the maximum amount of protection for the crew. We…have concentrated more on the means of movement than on the gun itself. In my opinion, the gun should be given the most attention, and everything else rated secondary.

Having studied much "German equipment on the battlefield of Tunisia," Capt. Moore realized "any German armor-piercing shot, regardless of caliber, can penetrate any or all of our armor at reasonable ranges." The enemy's bore sighting tools, gunners' sights for the main gun, and sight reticles, in his experience, were also superior:

As for the gun itself, practically any of the German anti-tank guns [47mm, 75mm, or 88mm] will penetrate all of our armor at greater range than we can knock out their armored vehicles. I have seen too many of our Armor Piercing shots bounce off Tiger tanks, while they punch clean holes in our M4s. The new US 57mm and 3-inch [towed anti-tank] guns are definitely an improvement [over the towed 37mm gun], but in my opinion, these guns just about put us at par with the Germans. I am highly in favor of getting way ahead of them for a change. Something like the 90mm gun, at least, is desired, something that will punch a hole in at least 10 inches or better of armor at 1,000 yards.[9]

Noting a shortage of the new M61 Armor Piercing round, Moore was "convinced that we should have a high percentage

KEEP 'EM SHOOTING!

*Photo by Robert Coldwell Sr.*

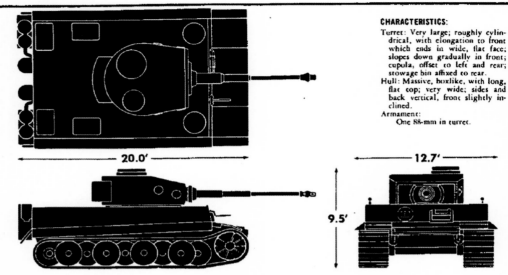

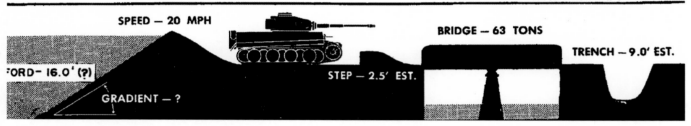

US data (estimated): Information on the new Tiger from US Army Field Manual FM 30-40, "Recognition Pictorial Manual on Armored Vehicles," November 1943. Notice the assumption that a tank heavier than the Sherman must have poor traction and mobility. *Photo by Robert Coldwell Sr.*

*Courtesy Henry Smith. Photo by Robert Coldwell Sr.*

of it in our basic load (it's only 5% at present)."[10] This little-known tank ammo shortage continued until VE Day. Later, when small numbers of 90mm-gunned TDs reached the ETO, their crews often lacked even a "basic load" of ammunition—the minimum for combat.

Addressing the M4's tendency to catch fire after being hit, Capt. Moore observed, "When a tank is penetrated by an AP shot, invariably it burns, and the fire usually starts in a matter of seconds, rather than in minutes... In my case, about three seconds after first penetration, the entire turret was ablaze."[11]

One proposed solution was adopting less flammable diesel fuel. Americans experimented with diesel engine equipped Stuarts, and small numbers saw combat with the Marines on Guadalcanal. With a few more seconds to climb out wounded Allied tankers might have escaped their "Ronsons," but concern over different fuel types causing logistical problems led to the continued use of gasoline-engined tanks. They "brewed up" (as the British called it) so quickly that men with minor injuries burned to death, unable to exit their "iron coffins" in time. Capt. Moore suggested that future tanks have at least four fire extinguishers, "with the outlets from the third and fourth large units protecting the ammunition racks. All these units to be equipped with an automatic device for discharging...a system like this would possibly enable the crew to remove wounded crew members before they burned to death."[12]

Returning to the want of a better gun, Capt. Moore closed his letter on an optimistic note: if a future tank had "particular attention paid to the mounting of a 90mm gun in the turret, the

Tennessee, 1944: Cpl. Jack Myers, 692nd Tank Destroyer Battalion, and his M10 GMC crew in training.

design of the sight and the sight bracket, and bore sighting equipment, it would be the last word in tanks."[13] Moore's report was disseminated to designers and technicians, and perhaps to Gen. Barnes, who headed Ordnance's Research and Design Service. After receiving such feedback, how could Ordnance later deny knowledge of the problems in 1945, or deny receiving pleas for better tanks and tank guns?

By late 1943, Army leadership was at a crossroads. With the Normandy invasion coming, they had major decisions to make: which model tanks and TDs should be produced in 1944? How many? The possibilities included modifying existing Shermans, adopting a replacement for the M4, or both. The Shermans in service could be upgraded with a more powerful gun and thicker armor, while simultaneous development and mass production of the T-20 series heavy tanks could be given the highest priority.

Apologists for the tank scandal have claimed that by 1944, there was no alternative to retaining the M4 because fielding a successor would take too long. But by late 1943, the Army had new turrets mounting more powerful guns able to be retrofitted to older Shermans; this discounts the idea that an entirely new tank was the only alternative. Second, since 1942, designers had been working on the T20 series of heavy tanks, incorporating advances in firepower, armor protection, and mobility. Had T26s been mass produced in 1943–1944, they could have landed on Norman beaches, or helped repulse the Ardennes attacks, but Army leaders opposed their adoption and failed to ensure the highest priority was placed on building and fielding them.

In fairness to leaders like Marshall and McNair contemplating requirements for future tank production and tanker training in late 1943, we need to compare and contrast the frequency of

tank combat and the state of tank design on the Eastern Front versus the western Allies' situation. The Russians and Germans had engaged in epic tank battles, some involving hundreds of tanks. The frequency and intensity of this tank combat had forced them into a tank design war, in which advances in firepower and armor protection leaped ahead by generations. The Germans and Russians were forced to steadily introduce bigger, more powerful, better armored models, as well as anticipate the enemy's next advances, and to have newer models in the works even as their latest tanks were being fielded.

In contrast, the US Army had experienced relatively few large-scale tank-to-tank slugging matches in North Africa, Tunisia, and Sicily. The Tiger had been marginalized as only appearing in small numbers, mechanically unreliable, and seemingly able to be stopped by Allied anti-tank guns. The Sherman tank had been a good design when introduced in 1942, mechanically reliable and able to be mass produced. By late 1943, thousands were in service worldwide, and—if one believed the propaganda—seemed to be doing the job.

FM 30-40

# RECOGNITION
## PICTORIAL MANUAL
## ON ARMORED VEHICLES

This manual supersedes FM 30-40, 9 January 1943, including C 1, 19 August 1943,
FM 30-41, 27 May 1941, and FM 30-42, 3 October 1942.

*Dissemination of restricted matter. The information contained in restricted documents and the essential characteristics of restricted materiel may be given to any person known to be in the service of the United States and to persons of undoubted loyalty and discretion who are cooperating in Government work, but will not be communicated to the public or to the press except by authorized military public relations agencies. (See also par. 18b, AR 380-5, 28 Sept. 1942.)*

UNITED STATES GOVERNMENT PRINTING OFFICE · WASHINGTON · 1943

U. S. ☆    BRITISH    RUSSIAN ★        # MEDIUM TANK, M4A1

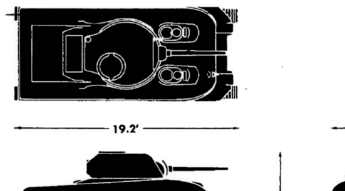

- 19.2'
- 8.6'
- 9.3'

**CHARACTERISTICS:**
Turret: Large, dome-shaped; flat top; radio bulge in rear; set at center of hull.
Hull: Cast; well streamlined; slopes down gently in rear, abruptly in front.
Armament:
    One 75-mm gun in turret.
    One coaxial caliber .30 machine gun.
    One caliber .30 machine gun in right front of hull.
Traction: Full track; six equally spaced bogie wheels, suspended in pairs; three track support rollers; driving sprocket in front.

**INTEREST DATA:** The M4A1 is similar to the other tanks of the M4 series in performance and appearance, but can be distinguished from them because of its smooth cast hull. It is not as important as the later models of the series, which will be much more numerous on the battlefield.

NOVEMBER 1943
FROM DATA CURRENTLY AVAILABLE
WAR DEPARTMENT FM 30-40

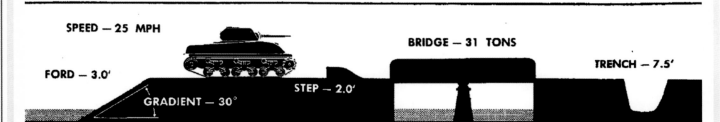

SPEED — 25 MPH

BRIDGE — 31 TONS

TRENCH — 7.5'

FORD — 3.0'

STEP — 2.0'

GRADIENT — 30°

A dangerous complacency had arisen. British Brig. Ross, observing American tank design and production first hand, described the mentality that arose early in the war among high ranking Ordnance officials as "win the war with the M4," and lamented, "Someone with authority over U.S. Army Ordnance should have ensured that modification of the Sherman received first priority. In fact…no priority whatsoever was established."[14] Army leaders not only rejected the adoption of a more powerful, better armored tank until the last weeks of the war, they also failed to implement expedient upgrades to the primary Allied tank, which was flawed but plentiful.

In spite of the evidence coming in, Gen. McNair argued that a more powerful tank was not needed; that his beloved Artillery, towed, and self-propelled tank destroyers and the M4 could handle German tanks. "Tank destroyers"—he insisted in a January 1943 letter to Gen. Marshall just weeks before the disastrous Valentine's Day tank battles—had been "provided for the defeat of armored attacks, and demonstrated their effectiveness for this purpose."[15] Later, after disasters in North Africa and Tunisia and close calls in Sicily, McNair continued to argue, "I see no reason to alter our previous stand…that we should defeat Germany by use of the M4 series of medium tanks. There have been no factual developments overseas, so far as I know, to challenge the superiority of the M4 Sherman."[16]

High level meetings were held in late 1943 to decide tank production for 1944, and to evaluate the performance of existing tanks and tank destroyers. Now was the time for an honest assessment of American weapons and doctrine, especially on the part of Gen. McNair, who once admonished his subordinates in a "round robin" letter, "The truth is sought, regardless of whether pleasant or unpleasant, or whether it supports or condemns our present organization or tactics."[17]

Gen. McNair could have pushed for upgrades to the M4s in service, or to replace them through high priority production and adoption of the T26. Instead, the father of the Tank Destroyer concept used his considerable power and influence to convince the Army to stick with the deficient M4.

In 1940, when Gen. McNair promoted expedient measures to stop German tanks, they had begun with a simple 37mm towed gun—faster and cheaper to build then a tank, and able to be transported and positioned by a few soldiers with a jeep. But by 1944, the resulting tank destroyers, although lacking armor protection, had become so bloated that the newest TD design (the M36 Jackson) was almost the same size and weight as a Sherman—the true tank the TDs were supposed to be augmenting. Often the TDs, with hand-cranked, unprotected, open turrets and thin armor, could only destroy German tanks under ideal conditions. And even if a "TD" was faster than a Panzer, with better firepower and armor (because the TD design sacrificed armor protection to gain speed), one or two shots from a Panzer's harder punching gun (possibly mounted in a faster, powered turret) could knock it out, nullifying the speed advantage gained by inadequate armor.

I see no reason to alter our previous stand…that we should defeat Germany by use of the M4 series of medium tanks. There have been no factual developments overseas, so far as I know, to challenge the superiority of the M4 Sherman.[2]
—Gen. Lesley McNair, Chief, Army Ground Forces, November 1943

692nd Tank Battalion men in stateside training. Note the TD black cat mascot painted on the back of the M10 turret—"Seek, Strike, Destroy!"

Even as they grew bigger and heavier, the TDs remained a shadow of what was needed: a genuine tank with more firepower and armor protection for the crew. Instead of improving the M4 in large numbers or adopting a replacement to match Germany's best, Army leadership under McNair's influence stuck with the TDs: a half-measure, flawed near-tank. The TD men's frustration is summed up in their bitter quip that they needed not a "tank killer," but a "killer tank."

"Victories," Gen. McNair once stated in a speech, "are won in the forward areas by men with brains and fighting hearts, not by machines."[18] Having been saddled with one inadequate machine after another, TD men would surely agree; they often had to substitute guts for better weapons. After facing the possibility of fighting a Tiger tank with a puny 37mm gun mounted in a light pickup truck (the M6 Fargo), they can be excused for taking a dim view of their senior leaders back home. Yet, insisted McNair while addressing Officer Candidate School graduates, "The Army's peerless soldiers will follow you, believe in you, trust in you, need you, and fight for you."[19]

For 1944, it was decided to build the new M18 Hellcat TD with a 76mm gun. Reflecting the design doctrine of speed over firepower and armor protection, the Hellcat could exceed 50 mph because its armor had been reduced to as little as half an inch thick in some spots. Gen. McNair and his sycophants assumed M18s could simply avoid one-on-one combat with bigger, better armed German tanks.

It was decided the M18 would be followed in mid- to late 1944 by the new M36 Jackson tank destroyer, mounting a modified 90mm anti-aircraft gun and better armor. Built in small numbers, while relatively successful, the open-topped M36 was still not as good as a true tank with a 90mm gun and adequate armor, and it was often rendered ineffective by tank ammunition shortages.

Trying to inspire an aggressive spirit, Gen. McNair had chosen the name "Tank Destroyer" rather than "Anti-Tank," and the pugnacious motto "Seek, Strike, and Destroy." But on Armistice Day 1942, his attempts to whip up martial fervor brought him notoriety among stateside civilians, and soon ridicule from frontline tankers who had just landed in North Africa three days before.

That November 11, the intellectual, fastidious general who kept a dictionary at arm's reach gave a bloodthirsty radio speech. "We must hate with every fiber of our being. We must lust for battle; our object in life must be to kill," exhorted McNair, who had never seen combat. "We must scheme and plan day and night to kill...there need be no pangs of conscience...it is the avowed purpose of the Army to make killers of all of you."[20] Afterward, he may have returned to his quarters at the Army War College in Washington, DC, described by his wartime biographer E. J. Kahn as "perhaps the most beautiful Army post in the country...handsome officers' quarters...rows of huge elm trees, tennis courts...and a flood-lighted swimming pool."

There, the McNairs lived in "a stately, colonnaded house on the edge of the...golf course.... In front of the house was a bandstand...their home was furnished with a great many oriental tapestries."[21] A photo in Kahn's book[22] is almost a parody of upper-middle-class WASP respectability: Gen. McNair, his wife Clare, son Col. Douglas McNair, and his wife and baby daughter pose in front of a blazing fireplace. A stuffed bear rug, candlesticks, large mirrors, drapes, and fresh flowers all testify to living conditions far removed from those endured by weary tankers and TD men sleeping on the ground in places like North Africa, Sicily, Italy, and Normandy. Up front, GIs wore the same sweat-soaked, greasy uniforms for months, eating cold "meals" out of cans, lucky to enjoy a monthly bath or rare field shower.

Safe in his plush AWC surroundings, Gen. McNair apparently saw no hypocrisy in scolding troops for what he perceived as a lack of aggression. "Many of our boys," he once told an interviewer, "are too much like Ferdinand the Bull. They just want to smell the pretty flowers."[23] He also demanded, "troops must be toughened mentally, so that adverse conditions will not divert them from their mission. Fatigue, loss of sleep, limited rations, adverse weather conditions, and other hardships must not weaken their determination to find and destroy the enemy."[24]

Attempting to encourage more volunteers for the Infantry, he praised that branch, inspiring a "lady song-writer" to write a jaunty ditty called *Nothing in Front of the Infantry But the Enemy*. From the safe, manicured parade grounds and golf courses of the Army War College, Gen. McNair declared, "It is the Doughboy who will give the battle cry of victory."[25] The reaction of cynical GIs overseas to such pompous sloganeering from a stateside general can be imagined.

"If you have a son or husband in uniform," a fawning *Saturday Evening Post* profile told families, "you may owe his welfare or even his survival to 'Whitey' McNair...the mild-mannered

# 76-MM GUN MOTOR CARRIAGE, M18

U. S. ☆

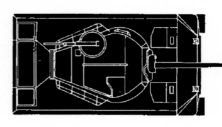

← 17.4' →

← 9.2' →

8.5'

**CHARACTERISTICS:**

Turret: Low, conical, with large undercut projection in rear; set at center of hull; open top; has ring mount for AA machine gun at left rear.

Hull: Flat top, with slight upward bulge in rear of turret; extends beyond tracks in rear; sides flat, inclined slightly at top; front flat, slopes down gently; front corners beveled.

Armament:
One 76-mm gun.
One caliber .50 AA machine gun on ring mount on turret.
76-mm gun, extending well beyond front of carriage.

Traction: Full track; five equally spaced, medium-sized bogie wheels, independently sprung; four track support rollers; driving sprocket in front.

**INTEREST DATA:**

Formerly designated as the T70, this vehicle is the successor to the 3-inch gun motor carriage M10, as the standard tank destroyer weapon. It is much faster than the M10, but is lightly armored. It has been a star performer on the battlefield with its 76-mm weapon and top speed of 55 mph. It was the first U. S. armored vehicle with the torsion bar suspension system to go into action.

C 4, FEBRUARY 1945
FROM DATA CURRENTLY AVAILABLE
WAR DEPARTMENT FM 30-40

SPEED — 55 MPH

FORD — 4.0'

GRADIENT 31°

STEP — 3.0'

BRIDGE — 19 TONS

TRENCH — 6.1'

*Photo by Robert Coldwell Sr.*

# THE HELLCATS ARE ON THE PROWL

Lieut., Pa.- spoiled two Germans in burg, Pa.- who told us they had a bridge - who told us they had been left as outpost guards for an ammunition dump a couple of miles ahead.

In less than a minute, 76-mm shells of our tank destroyers were whistling overhead and there was a tremendous release and plume of smoke marked the end of the dump. Our marvelous fire, at times, we ran into shellfire from 88's due to on the other side of the town. Our tank destroyer guns went to work and in half an hour had wiped them out.—From a battlefront dispatch in the New York News datebook Magazine to the U. S. 3rd Army at Orleans, Aug. 31 (Outsiuse)

THE Army calls them 76-mm. Gun Motor Carriages — designation M-18. But to Buick men who designed and built them, in cooperation with Army Ordnance — and to Tank Destroyer Command forces who fight in them — they're Hellcats.

The name fits.

They are tank-killers with the pace of a panther and the lethal strike of the king cobra.

They're so fast they run rings around anything but their brothers, and they master obstacles that stop other vehicles cold.

They can split an enemy tank at several miles — and thanks to springing born of Buick's work on your car, they can romp down roads at passenger car speeds.

And now they're on the prowl.

It has been twenty-odd months since we started work on these sluggers as answers to the vaunted Tiger tank. Twenty-odd months of designing, building, testing, perfecting.

More than a year ago they went into production, and several months ago we knew they were on their way, in quantities, to undisclosed battlefields.

They have shown what they can do there. They've added their force to the Great Effort — and because of them, American men have had benefit of a harder-hitting weapon against tanks, pillboxes, strong points and machine gun nests.

We're mighty glad that's so. Not just because this is a Buick baby. But because it's a good American weapon, built in our way, for use of our own kind.

More power to it, say we — and to those gallant men in uniform for whom we sweated it out!

**WHAT IS THE "HELLCAT"?**

*The Hellcat is a 76-mm. Gun Motor Carriage bearing the Army designation, Model M-18. With 55 mph speed, maximum maneuverability, high fire power, and all-steel, center-guided tracks, it can smash tanks at several miles.*

*Designed and built by Buick in cooperation with the Ordnance Department, it has proved superior to latest versions of the German Tiger tank in actual battle and is 30 mph faster. Special Buick-designed suspension, including knee-action principles, enables the Hellcat to fight running battles when necessary. It masters obstacles that stop other vehicles, fords water traps and streams and is almost as easy to run as an automobile.*

*Ordered on January 28, 1943 after demonstration of pilot models, the Hellcat has been in regular production since July, 1943. All allies have asked to be supplied with it.*

YOU LEND A HAND WHEN YOU LEND YOUR DOLLARS ★ INVEST IN MORE WAR BONDS

*Buick will be glad to furnish, without cost, a full-color reprint of this advertisement to those interested in this important new weapon. Write to Buick Motor Division, Flint 2, Michigan*

**BUICK** DIVISION OF **GENERAL MOTORS**
*Every Sunday Afternoon—GENERAL MOTORS SYMPHONY OF THE AIR—NBC Network*

**BUICK** BUILDS THE **HELLCAT**

WHEN BETTER AUTOMOBILES ARE BUILT
BUICK WILL BUILD THEM

The Army-Navy "E" proudly flies over all Buick plants.

*Courtesy Henry Smith, photo by Robert Coldwell Sr.*

M4A3 Shermans disembark onto the beachhead at Anzio, Italy, 1944. Note the spare treads on both M4s used as improvised armor protection. The M4A3 was the most produced version of the Sherman, easily distinguishable from the M4A1 by its flat, slab-sided cast hull. The interior ammo storage bins (on the sides, below the gun) were particularly vulnerable to fire. *US Army Signal Corps*

general with the blue eyes and sandy hair is hell on 'metallic generals.' A 'metallic general' is described as a gentleman who has silver in his hair, lead in his teeth, and lead in his pants.... 'It's plain murder,' says the general, 'to send boys into battle under incompetent officers. You can't live with your conscience and you can't win that way.'"[26]

Knowing the odds of taking on heavy German tanks with inadequate equipment, GIs overseas saw through the armchair bravado of their desk-bound leadership at home. One night in late 1944, when the 636th Tank Destroyer Battalion was fighting up in the Vosges Mountains, "Sergeant Tom Sherman had to drive a new Lieutenant forward to one of the [towed] gun platoons":

> Crawling up a winding mountain trail with no lights, Sergeant Sherman just made out a hand waving him to stop. The Sergeant recognized one of the outfit's old campaigners, a veteran of every fight since Salerno. The soldier motioned Sherman and the new Lieutenant to silence.
>
> "See those lights over there?" he whispered in a voice tight with fear, "That's a German tank."

"Why don't you go get it?" queried the new Lieutenant quietly.

"I don't want it," replied the old soldier.[27]

Years after the blitzkrieg's tide had receded, independent TD battalions were still being farmed out for use against 1939-style massed armored spearheads that rarely arrived. The Germans failed to act as outdated textbooks said they would. The reality on the battlefields of 1944 was not matching the script of Gen. McNair's rigged 1941 war games for which he had written the rules.

Unable to fulfill their original role—remaining flexible and moving quickly to decisive points when needed to counter large enemy concentrations—idle TDs were misused as static artillery, little better than Gen. McNair's beloved French cannons of the pre-great war era. Rather than consider if the 1940-style defensive doctrine underlying the tank destroyer concept remained relevant, Army leaders reinforced failure, calling for *more* TDs.

Instead, Allied soldiers needed a better-armored true tank with a more powerful gun. The proposed T26 mounted a 90mm gun, more armor, and an improved suspension. But along with

A restored Sherman Firefly with 17-pounder main gun at the Tank Museum, Bovington, Dorset, UK. *Massimo Foti*

the decision to stay with Gen. McNair's lackluster TD concept in 1944, in late 1943, the brass rejected large-scale production and adoption of the T26 as an M4 replacement. The Armored Force generally supported mass production of it, but McNair objected. His November 1943 policy statement to Gen. Marshall shows not only how disconnected some leaders at home were from conditions at the front, but also arrogance toward our British allies who, unlike the Americans, managed to field an up-gunned Sherman in time for Normandy—the Firefly.

Gen. McNair's opposition to large-scale T26 production would have consequences during the campaign for Western Europe. "There can be *no basis* for the T26 tank," he insisted to Marshall, "other than the conception of a tank vs. tank duel, which is believed to be unsound and unnecessary. Both British and American

battle experience has demonstrated that the anti-tank gun in suitable numbers and disposed properly is the master of the tank.... There has been no indication that the 76mm anti-tank gun is inadequate against the German Mark VI Tiger tank."[28]

He also opposed upgrading Shermans in the field with a 90mm gun, citing the M4's alleged superiority:

The recommendation [to build or modify] a limited portion of tanks carrying a 90mm gun is not concurred in for the following reasons: The M4 tank has been hailed widely as the best tank on the battlefield today. There are indications even the enemy concurs in this view. Apparently, the M4 is an ideal combination of mobility, dependability, speed, protection, and firepower.

September 1943: Marshall and Ike are all smiles in Algiers. *US Army Signal Corps*

Other than this particular request—which represents the British view [sic- Americans, including Ordnance's Gen. Gillem, also called for a new or up-gunned tank]—there has been no call from any theater for a 90mm tank gun.

Gen. McNair concluded these sweeping assertions with one that would have stupefied Allied tankers: "There appears to be no fear on the part of our forces of the German Mark VI Tiger tank."[29]

The American commanders overseas who were calling for an up-gunned tank included Eisenhower. Gen. Marshall had ordered him home for a two-week furlough before he took up his duties in England as commander of the upcoming Normandy invasion. Just as Eisenhower had written privately to Marshall in early 1943 that the US had no answer to the then-new Tiger, now (January 1944), in personal talks with him at the new Pentagon, Ike mentioned to Marshall the need for a more powerful American tank.[30]

Gen. Marshall overruled McNair in December 1943, ordering modest T26 production to begin for test and evaluation purposes, but the resulting numbers would be too little, too late. As Army Service Forces warned (also in December 1943), unless the delays and red tape in the T26 program were eliminated, "It is... apparent that this tank will not be available for the early

part of planned major operations in the ETO," i.e., the Normandy invasion.

Army Service Forces Director of Materiel Maj. Gen. Lucius D. Clay noted the dangers of "the usual difficulties attendant upon putting a pilot model in to assembly line production," including the T26's advanced new transmission, which Clay considered "a radical departure" from past designs.[31] The T26 needed to be given the highest priority for mass production and eventual adoption as a Sherman replacement; instead, it was obstructed and delayed until the war's last months.

Today, Gen. McNair's obstinacy seems particularly hard to justify. He championed outdated anti-tank theories after battlefield conditions had changed, dismissed GIs' warnings of the Tiger, and argued that giving tankers a better gun would encourage them to hunt German tanks. According to old artilleryman McNair, this violated prewar doctrine; as he saw it, the job of tank hunting belonged to Artillery and TDs, not the upstart armor branch. Author Steve Zaloga called this refusal to acknowledge the idea that tanks fight tanks "a fossilized view appropriate to World War I tank combat, but now completely out of date."[32]

Gen. McNair still thought of armor in 1920s terms: a slow, passive weapon of exploitation, supporting the Infantry at their pace. Gen. Barnes (who preferred replacing the M4 with the T26 to upgrading it) also did not help the tankers' plight when he argued that adding a bigger or heavier main gun to an M4 hull

Gen. Gladeon Barnes of Army Ordnance.

might create an "unbalanced design."[33]

To one author, Gen. Mc-Nair's "arguments had an air of academic unreality about them, since they largely omitted to address what the Germans might field in the summer 1944 battles":

There had been a continual arms race in tank guns, anti-tank guns, and tank armor on the Eastern Front. The Panther had been developed in response to the Soviet T-34, and was arguably the finest tank of the war. U.S. Army intelligence was aware of the technical specifications of the Panther, since the military attaché in Moscow had been allowed to inspect a captured example at an exhibit.[34]

By January 1944, Ordnance had begun limited production for testing of the new T25 tank turret with a 90mm gun—six months before Operation Overlord. But mass production and adoption of it was rejected. Had this been made a high priority, up-gunned Shermans might have landed in France. Even if one argues in hindsight that six months was not sufficient time to upgrade large numbers of M4s, certainly some could have reached the front by December 1944, eleven months after the new turret and gun began to be produced and in time to help repulse the German counteroffensive in the Ardennes.

"U.S. Officers Inspect Russian Trophies," reported papers like the Pottstown, Pennsylvania, *Mercury* on July 1, 1943, in-

cluding a photo of the giant tank "radioed from Moscow to New York."[35] As Zaloga elaborated, "Details were contained in widely distributed Army technical intelligence reports published in the fall of 1943":

Although the Panther was not as thickly armored as the Tiger in the front, its armor was better angled, giving it greater effective armor thickness in front. Its glacis plate was 80-85mm thick, giving it an equivalent thickness of 185mm. As a result, the Panther's gun mantlet was vulnerable to the U.S. Army's 76mm gun only at ranges of 100 m or less, while its hull front was essentially invulnerable at any range.

Although the technical features of the Panther were correctly noted, the U.S. Army ignored the new tank's importance. At first the Panther was seen as a heavy tank that would be deployed in separate battalions like the Tiger, implying that it would be fielded in modest numbers. This was completely wrong. The Panther was intended as a medium tank to replace the PzKpfw IV. Unlike the Tiger, it would be manufactured in very large numbers so that by the time of the Normandy invasion, in June 1944, Panthers made up almost half the German medium tank force in France. Instead of being encountered on relatively rare occasions, which had been the US experience with the Tiger in 1943, the Panther would become a major threat to US tank units in France.[36]

Also in January 1944, Gen. Barnes inspected the British Firefly, a modified M4 with a powerful 17-pounder (76.2mm) main gun in a new British-designed turret. The Abilene, Texas, *Reporter-News* had run a story on October 11, 1943, headlined "British Gun Answer To Nazi Tiger Tank." Datelined from London, it called

A restored *Panzerkampfwagen V* (Panther) under wraps. While the Tiger has always had a deadly mystique around it, the later Panther was a better tank. Designed, like the Tiger, to counter the Russian T-34, the Panther was an ideal combination of firepower, maneuverability, and armor protection. *Author photo courtesy of the National Armor and Cavalry Heritage Foundation*

the 17-pounder "capable of blasting the turret off a tank at 1,500 yards" and "Britain's newest secret weapon and her answer to the powerful and heavily-armored Tiger tank recently introduced by the Germans."[37]

Until the T26's debut, the Firefly or "Mayfly" (so named because of the "muzzle blast" of flame it gave off when firing) was one of the Allies' most effective tanks for fighting Tigers and Panthers, with a high-velocity gun capable of penetrating their armor. The British not only rushed it into production in time for the Normandy invasion, they offered it to the Americans, but US brass refused it, and also rejected better American turret and gun designs and combinations.

Once again, Ordnance and AGF officials led by Gens. McNair and Barnes (who wanted to mass-produce the T26) rejected opportunities to correct the M4's major deficiencies, problems pointed out by combat veterans like Capt. Moore in late 1943.[38] And even as their propaganda newsreels and radio broadcasts boasted of superior industrial potential, the Americans were trumped by the strained but resourceful, pragmatic British.

This refusal to up-gun the M4 is particularly frustrating in light of the M36B1 Jackson TD, which combined a stock Sherman hull and suspension with a 90mm gun in a new turret. When a shortage of hulls held up M36 production, it was discovered the Jackson's new turret and 90mm gun could be fitted into the body of a standard M4A3. Rather than wait for the M36 bodies to arrive, M4A3 hulls pulled right off assembly lines were mated to the new turret and gun. Far from being an "imbalanced" design as Gen. Barnes argued, when firing high-velocity, improved 90mm ammunition this ad hoc up-gunned Sherman (officially labeled a "gun motor carriage," or TD) was effective in the Battle of the

Bulge, and was one of the few Allied weapons able to challenge Tigers and Panthers with a reasonable chance of success.

Photo by Robert Coldwell Sr.

But in a sign of the Army's ongoing doctrinal confusion, the M36B1 was not recognized for what it was: an up-gunned Sherman and a practical antidote to the gun problem.

Instead, the M36B1 was considered merely an expedient TD, a substitute to keep assembly lines moving while waiting for delayed M36 hulls. Only 187 were produced, and those few were handicapped by a little-known ammo shortage.[39] Another chance had been missed to upgrade the M4's flawed main gun, a relatively straightforward solution that discredits the apologists' argument that by 1944, the only option was a totally new tank, such as the T26.

Meanwhile, the Germans recognized a good design in their new Panther. Even as they began large production of it, planning to make it the most numerous tank in their armored units, in the US—as newsreels depicted factories cranking out endless lines of Shermans—Army leaders decided to decrease tank production for 1944.

In the summer of 1943, the War Department convened a procurement review board under Maj. Gen. Frank McCoy ("the McCoy Board") to review requirements for future munitions production. In a dramatic departure from Roosevelt's extravagant "Double it!" order of 1940–1941, the McCoy Board concluded production goals had been reached, and that enough reserve stocks of replacement weapons and materials were available for future use. The board's members recommended decreasing tank production, assuming those on hand would be enough to finish the war.

The McCoy Board's findings led to complacency among stateside war workers with deadly consequences for GIs overseas. To Gen. Lucius Clay, this was "the worst thing that ever happened around here [in 1944]. They came out with a report telling the world that we had too much of everything, and the emphasis went over to economy instead of 'man-don't-you-be-short.'"[40]

Influenced by the board's findings, Gen. McNair and other Army leaders met to estimate the numbers of tanks needed for 1944, which entailed predicting future combat losses of tanks and tankers. They decided to decrease tank production and tanker training at the Armor School, Fort Knox. Like the McCoy Board's conclusions, these reductions were ordered after assuming lesser numbers of flawed Shermans and fewer tankers could muddle through another year of combat with more powerful German designs. Sir Max Hastings called this "a fundamental error:":

The US War Department…recognized the weakness of American tank guns and protective armour against those of the enemy. But they concluded that the Allies' quantitative advantage was so great, the qualitative issue did not matter. The fact that losses were readily replaceable reflected the Allies' huge resources. But, for men obliged to contest the battlefield against panzers, awareness of the inadequacy of their own tanks against those of the enemy profoundly influenced their combat behavior. After painful early experience, most U.S. armoured units gave orders for platoon commanders to ride third in a column, not first.

For a tank crew, it was irrelevant to know that their own army possessed an overall superiority of anything up to ten to one. They were confronted only with the immediate reality that if they fired at a German Tiger or

TANKS need clean air, too!

... and AAF EQUIPMENT supplies it!

SPECIALLY designed Roto-Clones assure needed ventilation and heat dispersion inside our tanks so that crews are more comfortable; especially during battle maneuvers when openings must be closed against enemy shell fire. The Roto-Clone brings in outside air from which it removes dust and dirt.

AAF's contributions to war production are widely varied. Deck houses and hull sections for LST boats . . . air intake filters for airplane engines . . . special filters for submarine and cargo vessels . . . in addition to all types of air cleaning equipment for war industries.

If you have a dust problem, write for "AAF in Industry", a booklet which describes our complete line of dust control and air filtration equipment.

AMERICAN AIR FILTER CO., INC.
388 CENTRAL AVE., LOUISVILLE 8, KY.
In Canada: Darling Bros., Ltd., Montreal, P. Q.

*Special Roto-Clone for tank ventilation*

*Air filters for Airplane engines*

ENGINEERED DUST CONTROL

*Courtesy Henry Smith. Photo by Robert Coldwell Sr.*

even a Panther, their shell was likely to bounce off, unless it struck a weak point below the gun mantlet or the flank. Meanwhile, if an enemy's shell hit a Sherman, the notorious "Ronson" or "Tommy cooker," it was likely not merely to stop, but to burn. "The Sherman was a very efficient workhorse, but as a fighting tank it was a disaster," said Captain David Fraser. The first time Corporal Patrick Hennessy fired his Sherman's gun at a Tiger tank, he watched the shell hit its hull, then ricochet straight up into the air. "I thought 'To hell with this!' and pulled back."

"Who," concluded Hastings, "could blame Allied armour units for displaying caution amid such realities?"[41]

In his January 11, 1944, annual message to Congress, President Roosevelt spoke of aircraft production shortages in words that also apply to the failure to produce tanks and train the tankers that would be needed to finish the war—the smug attitude of "Win the War with the M4": "Those who failed to make them…were merely saying, 'The war's in the bag—so let's relax.' That attitude on the part of anyone—government or management or labor—can lengthen this war. It can kill American boys."[42]

A result of these 1943 decisions was a dire shortage of American tanks and replacement crews. As depicted in the 2014 movie *Fury*, untrained men were culled from rear-echelon units and thrown into hastily repaired M4s. In some of them, daylight shone through holes punched in their sides while the blood of their previous crews stained the white-painted interiors. The strain on all involved can be imagined—not only on the rookies, but on tight, cohesive tank crews that had been working together for months or years, only to have amateurs dumped on them as poor substitutes for their dead or wounded comrades. "I remember one man—he must have been thirty-five if he was a day—who wet his pants and then wept in shame," recalled tank commander Sgt. Nate Frankel of the Fourth Armored Division, a highly motivated, experienced outfit:

Then there was one kid—and I mean kid—from the Quartermaster who was up in the turret with me. I was screaming instructions at him because the shelling was deafening, and he kept jumping, particularly when he heard the sound of our tank pummeled with bullets. I felt like sitting on him. I shouted to him to load and fire himself. Then he shouted something else at me. I couldn't hear him the first or second time, but the third time I knew what he was saying. "I might get killed," he was saying. His exact words.[43]

While Gen. Marshall acknowledged the "very serious…replacement shortage," he gave a litany of excuses:

This shortage of replacements at such a vital moment [as the Germans sprung their surprise Ardennes offensive] was the final effect of long accumulating circumstances. The Army's manpower balance had been disturbed in the fall of 1943 by shortages in deliveries of inductees by the Selective Service System…a second factor was the miscalculation after North Africa that resulted in too many men being trained for the Armored Forces…. Another factor was our failure in the early stages of the war to compensate in the over-all strength ceiling for the number of men who would be required to fill the long overseas pipelines and the time involved between the completion of the training of the individual in the United States and his final arrival in the division. Still another was the heavy pressure brought to bear on the War Department to hold down or reduce its demands for manpower. It will be recalled that for more than a year a rather vigorous attack was maintained against the War Department's estimates of manpower

Sgt. Smith depends on five of them to keep his General Sherman tank rolling

1.

Seaman Jones depends on two of them to carry his landing craft through a curtain of fire straight for a beachhead...

G. I. Joe depends on one to power his fire fighter...one to pump his drinking water ...one to keep his truck moving...

3.

2.

What is it they depend on?... Chrysler engines in tanks, landing craft, welders, tractors, pumps, fire fighters!...

4.

Like the engine in your Chrysler car...the moving parts in these engines are Superfinished, which means they've got the smoothest surface in the world... and that's important to men whose lives depend on an engine.

WAR PRODUCTS OF CHRYSLER DIVISION • Industrial Engines • Tank Engine Assemblies • Marine Engines • Tank Parts • Navy Pontoons • Harbor Tugs • Gun Boxes • Anti-Aircraft Cannon Parts • Marine Tractors • Air Raid Sirens • Navy Searchlight Reflectors • Fire Fighting Equipment • Airplane Wing Panels

**CHRYSLER**

DIVISION OF CHRYSLER CORPORATION

THE NATION-WIDE CHRYSLER DEALER ORGANIZATION OFFERS OWNERS SERVICE FACILITIES TO MEET THEIR TRANSPORTATION NEEDS

24

*Courtesy Henry Smith. Photo by Robert Coldwell Sr.*

Both American tanks stood their ground.... One tank, called "The Bouncer," was commanded by Sergeant Oscar Smith, who used to pitch hay down in Jacksonville, Texas. The other, "Old Blood Hound," was run by Private T. Spruill, who once had a milk route in Battle Creek. Those General Shermans stood there and dished it out.

One, two, three Nazi Tiger tanks were knocked out by the guns from "The Bouncer" and "Old Blood Hound." Then American Artillery rushed up and knocked out two more of the enemy tanks.

By that time, more American tanks had arrived on the scene, and the surviving Tigers decided it was time to make tracks.

Packard reports that "The Bouncer" did not come out unscathed. One of the German shells bounced off her caterpillar tread and mussed it up, but the crew was uninjured, and she still was pouring lead at the enemy when the Nazis broke off the fight.

Packard tells of another American tank crew that escaped injury by a hair—in fact, by several heads of hairs. It seems that a stray shell hit their tank. The blast burned the hair off every one of the five crew members, but otherwise, they didn't suffer a scratch.[45]

re-quirements. This limited our ability to get the men we needed when we needed them.[44]

An already deficient tank was now further handicapped with inferior crews up against battle-hardened professionals that had fought in Poland, France, Russia, North Africa, Tunisia, Sicily, and Italy who crewed two of the war's most powerful tanks. But according to the press, the M4 was a war-winner. "Two General Sherman Tanks Rout 14 Nazi Tigers in Italy," blared headlines in papers like the Neosho, Missouri, *Daily News* for November 2, 1943:

With The Fifth Army In Italy - It was two General Sherman tanks against nine Tiger tanks that were high-tailing it in retreat. That's right—the other five enemy tanks were out of action.

United Press correspondent Reynolds Packard tells about the battle, which took place Wednesday. He terms it the most important armored engagement since our forces crossed the Volturno [River] in Italy.

Packard says the 14 Tiger tanks jumped our two General Shermans in an effort to cut them off from the rest of our forces, but the Nazis didn't reckon with the fighting spirit of a Texas farmer and a Battle Creek, Mich. milkman.

Another command decision with fateful consequences for tankers came in January 1944, and involved leaders with combat experience bullied by a man said to be one of the Army's most knowledgeable tank experts: Gen. George S. Patton, Jr.

Demonstrations were held at Tidworth Downs, England, for generals involved in the upcoming invasion of Fortress Europe. As weapons from pistols to tanks were shown, Ordnance asked the brass their requirements. Armor leaders were offered upgraded Shermans with a 76mm gun to supplement in small numbers the existing 75mm model. The generals also saw diagrams, photos, and films of the T26 and its advantages over the M4 were explained: increased firepower, armor protection, and maneuverability. Armor leaders with combat experience such as Gen. Maurice Rose criticized the standard 75mm M4; perhaps the T26 with a 90mm main gun should replace the M4 entirely. At the very least, the 76mm Sherman could be mass produced, not distributed piecemeal.

But Patton outranked the critics. Surprisingly, the general with a bulldog reputation argued the stock M4 was adequate, and that up-gunning it might encourage tankers to aggressively seek out and destroy Tigers and Panthers.[46] Patton, in contrast to his pugnacious image, also argued the powerful T26 violated prewar armor doctrine, in which American tanks were to avoid fights with enemy tanks, instead seeking soft targets in the enemy's rear areas. As to adopting the new 76mm Sherman on the eve of an invasion, Patton's objections were on more solid ground; for example, he was concerned to do so would invite logistical problems. On this issue, Patton erred on the side of caution. In refusing large numbers of the new tank, he also argued it had not yet been combat proven when the only way to do so was to field it. To tankers in 1944, a slightly improved main gun was preferable to the inadequate one that they had been using since 1942, in North Africa.

Patton's objections are reasonable on closer examination; on April 20, 1944, his trusted friend and Chief of Staff Gen. Hugh Gaffey sat on a board that examined the "Distribution of Medium Tank, M4 Series (76mm) Gun." Gen. Gaffey had reservations about mechanical "bugs" to be worked out, and over the lack of training time and practice to bring tankers up to speed on a new weapon before Operation Overlord. More seriously, the board found that "the gun's high-explosive performance was inferior to the 75mm, and its severe muzzle blast...obscured the tank commander's view of a target 1,000 yards away for three to six seconds, despite a stiff breeze." The Board declined to issue the new tank since training problems and muzzle blast were "... an excessive price to pay for an additional inch of armor penetration."[47]

While Patton did concede to accept small numbers of the M4 (76mm) on a trial basis, as to requesting the T-26, in spite of the objections of Gen. Rose and other like-minded armor leaders, Patton's rank and views won out; it was refused six months before the Normandy invasion. Had it been mass produced and sent to the ETO in 1944, perhaps tank losses might have been lower and casualty lists shorter. Instead, the Allies invaded France with under-gunned Shermans.

Meanwhile, the vast buildup for the invasion continued. Fort Knox's March 6, 1944, *Armored News*—official newspaper of the Armored School—told of Eisenhower, Air Chief Marshall Sir Arthur Tedder (Ike's deputy for Overlord), and British Gen. Montgomery "inspecting Armored Forces training for the invasion." The Supreme Commander spent some three hours observing M4 gunnery practice and talking with US tankers about their equipment.[48] A few weeks later, the newspaper reported on another visit by the invasion's three top leaders. "As might be expected," in discussing tanks with the GIs, Ike was said to be "interested in everything."[49]

Eisenhower, a tank pioneer since his 1918 Camp Colt days, had big plans for armor in the upcoming campaign. "Three weeks before the invasion," recalled Gen. Marshall in 1945, Eisenhower had written to him. "In forecasting future possibilities," Ike stated, "it is, of course, necessary that we seek ways and means to bring to bear those factors in which we enjoy a great superiority over the enemy," including armor. "I am trying to visualize

England, 1944: Shortly before the Normandy invasion, Supreme Allied Commander Eisenhower and his deputy, Air Chief Marshal Arthur Tedder (in RAF flight jacket), observe Sherman tank gunnery practice.

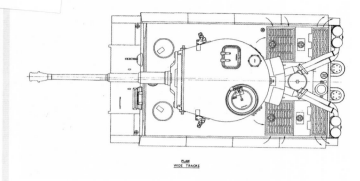

Overhead view of a Tiger I. *Photo by Robert Coldwell Sr.*

an operation in which we would bring in behind the initial beach-head a great strength in armor, and seek an opportunity to launch a big armored attack in conjunction with a deep and very heavy penetration by airborne troops."[50]

But when offered the new M18 Hellcat TD (with a 76mm main gun) in February 1944, and the new, 90mm M36 Jackson in May, Eisenhower refused them. Like Patton's views on the new T-26, Eisenhower reasoned that re-equipping and retraining tank crews and mechanics that were comfortable with their old M4s would complicate things—a surprising view for a man who praised the flexibility and "can-do" spirit of American soldiers. In fairness, converting to new weapons can be troublesome, as the author's unit learned many decades later when his Apache Troop, 1/104th Cavalry switched (much to his regret) from the M1A1 Abrams tank to the Stryker wheeled armored fighting vehicle (AFV).

Ideally, commanders like Ike and Patton wanted all new units equipped with new weapons, composed of soldiers that had been training on the new vehicles from the beginning in the states, rather than attempting to convert and retrain old units with older weapons already overseas.

Even after the dismal performance of the M3 anti-tank gun in North Africa, Tunisia, and Sicily, Gen. Bradley (who would share responsibility for invasion ground forces as the leader of the First United States Army Group [FUSAG]) still preferred towed guns to self-propelled gun motor carriage TDs like the M18 and M36. In addition to ordering the number of self-propelled tank destroyer battalions to be reduced, Bradley also prepared to create from scratch and convert more units equipped with towed guns until there were equal numbers of self-propelled and towed TD units.[51]

Reviewing wartime articles today, there is a disconnect between the powers-that-be and the enlisted GIs who would do the actual fighting in the upcoming invasion. "Tankmen Stage Firepower Show for Visitors" (March 27, 1944) boasted of a Fort Knox demonstration in which "General Sherman tanks...crushed enemy installations, and complete neutralization was speedily accomplished."[52] Just weeks later at Fort Knox—after wishful thinking had collided with battlefield reality in Normandy—tankers desperate to address the M4's inadequate firepower and armor would bitterly suggest Germany's impressive new Panther tank be copied outright for Allied use.[53]

Almost a year previous, George Patton had written home to his wife Beatrice from Sicily, including photos he had taken of a knocked-out Tiger tank. "In my opinion," he wrote, "their so-called Tiger tank with their 88mms are a flop. They are too slow." While dismissing one of Germany's deadliest tanks, he also used his

35mm Leica to capture a knocked-out M4. Wielding a grease pencil, Patton drew black Xs on the photo, emphasizing where the Sherman's armor had been violently penetrated by 88mm guns. Apparently, Patton saw no contradiction in ridiculing a German tank able to inflict such punishment on the M4.[54]

Back home at Armored Command, Fort Knox, recognition was dawning of the growing Panther threat. "While it is conceded that the primary objective of our armor is to engage the enemy infantry, artillery, and rear installations," stated an April 17, 1944, report,

experience has shown that the enemy will always counter an armored penetration with his own armor. Therefore, in order to operate successfully against re-munerative and desirable enemy installations, we shall first have to defeat the enemy armor. To do this, we must have a fighter tank which is superior to the fight-er tank of the enemy. Available information on charac-teristics of German tanks compared to those of our nation show that no American tank can equal the German Panther in all-around performance.[55]

Also in April 1944, weeks before the invasion, Gen. Barnes proclaimed American weapons the best in the world.[56] He also quoted Gen. Jacob Devers, commanding Army forces in the Mediterranean: "I note that there is a lot of interest in the German Tiger tank."

"I note also that the Russians don't think any more of it than I do. I also note that the Germans think very highly of our Sherman tank, and only recently, General Montgomery remarked when he saw pictures of the new tanks [possibly the 76mm equipped Sherman], 'That is the tank that will do the job.'"[57]

Days before Operation Overlord, in a May 28 letter to Ordnance Chief Campbell, Gen. Devers also belittled the Panther, soon to wreak havoc in Normandy and beyond. Echoing Patton's charac-terization of the Tiger as big and clumsy, Devers wrote of an M5 Stuart light tank knocking out a Panther with its small 37mm main gun, firing "before the lumbering Panther could swing its big gun into action."[58]

On May 23 in Essex, England, the Americans and British tested their 75mm, 76mm, 90mm, and 17-pounder guns against slabs of armor representing German tanks. The results showed the 75mm gun, as tankers had been warning, was inadequate, and the much-touted new 76mm main gun could only penetrate German armor an inch deeper. The most effective Allied gun for punching through the simulated German armor seemed to be the British 17-pounder.

Later, it was discovered some test results were invalid due to flawed testing conditions. The true ineffectiveness of some of the guns (when firing standard ammunition rather than "souped up" HVAP rounds) was even worse than results appeared to in-dicate, because the Ordnance officers who had set up the tests used armor slanted at only 30 degrees, but Panther tanks carried metal plate tilted at a 55-degree angle, thus making them hard-er to penetrate.[59]

Just two weeks before the invasion confidence was the order of the day. In June, Chief Ordnance Officer of the European Theater Brig. Gen. Henry Sayler assured Gen. Campbell the US

A program for one of Col. George Jarrett's many speeches on captured enemy weapons made to civilian audiences around the country. As Jarrett wrote in his private papers, he was frequently "in hot water" with his superiors for answering audience questions truthfully and ordered to "toe the line" that American tanks were far superior to Germany's. Photo by Robert Coldwell Sr., courtesy US Army Military History Institute, Carlisle Barracks, Pennsylvania

First Army making the assault was "probably the best equipped fighting force in the history of warfare."[60] As to the Sherman specifically, the Associated Press's William White told stateside readers in "M4 Tank Reassuring, Says Writer" of a ride during live-fire exercises in England. Small arms fire, he raved, bounced off "the Sherman's tough sides" while "the crew ignored it." White's "outstanding impression was of reassurance…these men were plainly ready to go in every sense—in equipment, training, and morale."[61]

Unfortunately for tankers then fighting in Italy, they could not "ignore" enemy fire. Ernie Pyle sent home "a sad story" dated April 17 about "a tank driver named Corp. Donald Vore, a farm boy from Auxvasse, Missouri":

> The corporal had a girl back home he was crazy about. After he came to Italy she sent a beautiful new photograph of herself. Like most tank men, he carried it with him in his tank.
>
> The other day a shell hit the tank. It caught fire, and the whole crew piled out and ran as fast as they could. Corp. Vore had gone a little way when he suddenly stopped, turned, and went dashing back to the tank.
>
> Flames were shooting out of it and its heavy ammunition was beginning to go off. But he went right into

the flaming tank, disappeared a moment, and came climbing out with his girl's picture safely in his hand.

> A few hours later the crew came trudging back to home base. Mail had arrived during their absence. There was a letter for Corp. Vore from his girl. He tore it open.

Original US Signal Corps wartime caption: "A tank of the 1st Armored Division, 5th US Army passes down an Italian street, April 1945." Note the Italian flag with the King's House of Seville crest, soon to be removed. *US Signal Corps photo via Ralph Riccio*

The letter was merely to tell him she had married somebody else.

They said that if it hadn't been such a long walk back, and he hadn't been so tired, Corp. Vore would have returned to his tank and deposited the picture in the flames.[62]

Back home, tankers' loved ones read headlines like "U.S. War Equipment Superior to Others: Glance at Record of Captured Enemy Material Proves It: Gives Some Facts." So stated reporter Martha Kearney in papers like the Bristol, Pennsylvania, *Daily Courier* on May 4, 1944. "The myth of enemy super weapons is dispelled in the following article," assured the *Daily Courier's* editors, "one of a series of exclusive stories on the Army's Proving Ground at Aberdeen, Md. The writer was the first correspondent permitted to make comparative tests of American and Axis equipment":

As "D" day approaches and American troops engage in pre-invasion maneuvers, the time is ripe for exploding the myth of Axis super-weapons and scientific ingenuity.

A look at the record in the form of captured enemy materiel at the Aberdeen Proving Ground shows that American equipment is superior in any way to anything used by the Axis up to and including the Italian campaign.

…German equipment is for the most part a polyglot assortment of parts which are too heavy for mobile warfare, too vulnerable for success, and too dangerous to the crews for safety.

A typical latest-design German tank at the Proving Ground is made up of a Russian turret gun, French chassis, and Czechoslovakian engine. The problem of replacing parts is an all but insolvable one.

The highly-publicized German Tiger tank is impressive, but immobile and particularly vulnerable by reason of a poor wielding job. Captured Tiger tanks show that a single hit can rip the welding apart and incapacitate the tank.

All American ammunition today is armor-piercing. The armor plate used on American tanks is carefully tested at the Proving Ground, to make sure it stands up against enemy ammunition.

Col. George G. Eddy, director of the Aberdeen Research Center, returned from Italy recently to report that American soldiers are superlatively proud of their equipment.

An elated tank crew told him of an incident at Cassino where a General Sherman tank moved up to a German-occupied house and opened fire on it with armor-piercing ammunition.

When the house was demolished the crew discovered that a Tiger tank, which had been lying in wait in back of the house, had been hit by an armor-piercing projectile which had passed through the house and set the tank ablaze.

…Darned clever, these Americans.[63]

Boasts like these would soon be proven horribly wrong in the hedgerows of Normandy.

US training ammunition in "disintegrating" metal links. The crimped top and lack of bullets indicate these are blank training rounds. *Photo by Robert Coldwell Sr.*

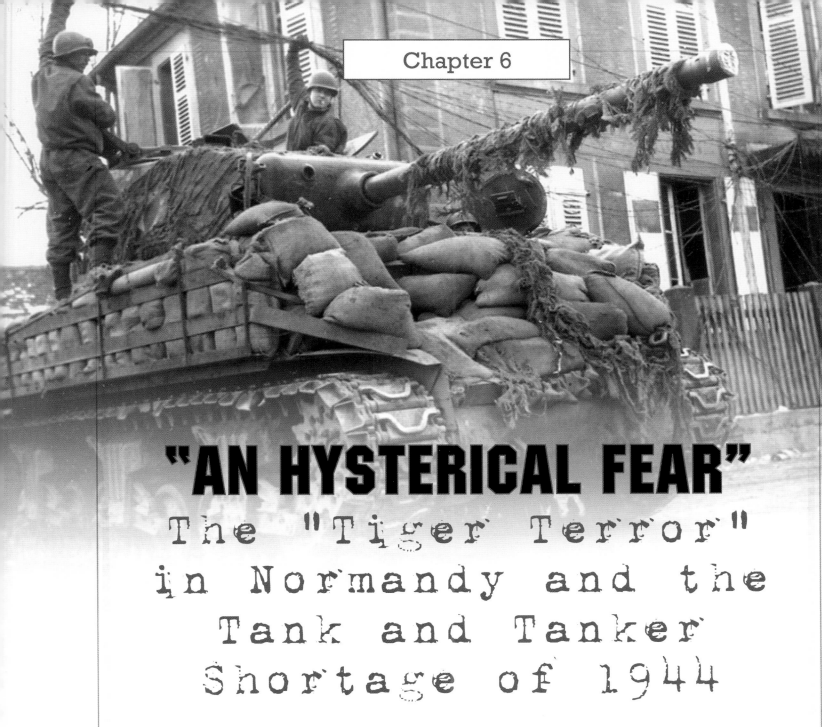

# Chapter 6

# "AN HYSTERICAL FEAR"

## The "Tiger Terror" in Normandy and the Tank and Tanker Shortage of 1944

The Allies had dismissed danger signs in North Africa, Tunisia, Sicily, and Italy, from the poor performance of the early tank destroyers to the Tiger's debut nearly two years before Operation Overlord. Hopefully, Normandy would be a proving ground for decades of unresolved tank doctrine, the long-awaited, decisive showdown with German tanks under Western European conditions, unlike the atypical circumstances of North Africa (flat desert) and Sicily (mountainous terrain). To one historian, "Only the Normandy campaign offered tank commanders the opportunity to demonstrate the validity of armor as an arm of operational and strategic decision."[4]

But Normandy "pitted an inferior Armored Force against a technologically vastly superior force,"[5] a contest in which outgunned Allied tankers would pay the price. "By the summer of 1944 Western armor had evolved, in theory, in direct reaction to German

A certain mythology persisted among GIs that German technology had produced tanks that were almost invincible. I had heard this view in advance of my first contact with German armor, and it had worried me greatly.... I could not free myself of the fear of the giant Tiger, Germany's awesome heavy tank.[1]

—Cpl. John Irwin, Sherman tank gunner, 33rd Armored Regiment, 3rd AD

armament. [But] in fact, it reflected the personal biases of general officers in key positions, who, rather than answer clear calls from the battlefield, ensured that their personal philosophies prevailed."[6]

Lulled by their leaders' boasts and reassurances, untried tankers arrived in France with an inflated opinion of the M4's capabilities.

Cpl. Bert Close departed England in mid-June, assigned to the crew of Staff Sgt. Lafayette Pool, Third Armored Division, the top American "tank ace" of the war. The rumble as he watched his company's sixteen M4s pass by sounded "like aircraft engines. When the order was given to start them and all 16 engines began roaring, it sent chills through me.... How could the Germans ever stop those tanks?"[7]

Lt. Belton Cooper, also with the Third Armored Division, recalled a similar optimism:

*Photo by Robert Coldwell Sr.*

Before we went into Normandy we had been led to believe that the M4...was a good tank, thoroughly capable of dealing with German armor on an equal basis. We soon learned that the opposite was true. The Third Armored Division entered combat in Normandy with 232 Sherman tanks. During the European Campaign, the Division had some 648 Sherman tanks completely destroyed in combat, and we had another 700 knocked out, repaired, and put back into operation. This was a loss rate of 580 percent.[8]

To prepare for the invasion, instead of improving the standard M4 in large numbers, the Allies built rare, specialized versions (known as British Gen. Percy Hobart's "Funnies") for jobs like bulldozing, bridge laying, and mounting flamethrowers.

The "DD" (Duplex Drive, nicknamed the "Donald Duck") Sherman, with a canvas hood and propellers, was supposed to swim its way to the hostile Norman shore. Apparently, few Allied leaders saw the irony in designing oddball variants built in small numbers whose overall impact would be minimal while the thousands of M4s that would bear the burden of armored combat lacked adequate firepower and armor protection.

Epitomizing the black comedy of the situation, the swimming tanks were a failure on Omaha Beach. Launched too soon and swamped by the tide, many sank before reaching shore. Their crews drowned without firing a shot in anger; in the 741st Tank Battalion alone, 27 "DD" tanks, each carrying five men, were lost in the heavy tide on June 6.[9] Yet today, the simplistic cliché of Allied technical and material superiority remain; "the logistical buildup before D-Day," claims a recent best-selling biography of Eisenhower, "not only left nothing to be desired, but provided an abundance of everything the Allies needed to take them to Berlin."[10]

Cpl. Close recalled waiting out his company's first battle near Villiers-Fossard as a still unassigned replacement. He expected "good news," and thought the war "was going along pretty well...the 16 tank crews [of four or five men each] left that morning of June 29th with their engines roaring, supremely confident they could do it all."[11] Later he was shocked to see wounded tankers returning in small groups—not mounted in their M4s, but riding in trucks or walking.

*Photo enhancement by Robert Coldwell Sr.*

The real "War Daddy": Sgt. Lafayette Pool, 3rd Armored Division, legendary tank commander and top American "tank ace" of WWII. An amateur boxer before the war who wore non-regulation cowboy boots into combat, Pool was nicknamed "War Daddy" by his fellow tankers.

Among tankers, having to slink away on foot after losing your mount is the ultimate indignity, similar to a knight in the age of chivalry being rudely "unhorsed" in battle. Decades after Cpl. Close, I joined a new generation of Army tank crewmen, graduating M1 Abrams tanker school weeks before the September 11 attacks. In my training, abandoning your tank was viewed with horror: "Death Before Dismount," we were told.

But in the bitter summer 1944, fighting in Normandy, recalled Cpl. Close, far more than the GIs' dignity was injured:

> What happened after the tanks had made their way through the hedgerows and into the open fields was an absolute shock. A German bazooka brigade, supported by mortar teams hidden in the hedgerows, ambushed the tanks. 12 of the 16 tanks were destroyed in a matter of minutes. The tanks burned, and as the crews jumped out, they were fired upon with machine guns and mortars. Several crewmen were killed, and many others were badly burned and wounded.

> I (Eye) Company crews went into their first battle feeling invincible in their Sherman tanks. They came out sobered with the realization that they, and their tanks, were highly expendable.[12]

The M4s had not fallen to Tigers or Panthers, but to German Infantry with *Panzerfaust* (the German equivalent of the American Bazooka anti-tank weapon) and mortars.

Cpl. Close soon revised his opinion of the M4, calling it "a disgrace to the U.S. Army. They were greatly inferior in armor and firepower to German tanks. I lost four destroyed by enemy guns."[13]

In bland, bureaucratic language, even Army Ordnance's postwar official history concedes the desperate situation of the Allied tanker in Normandy. He was often bogged down in the bocage with his vision and mobility restricted; Shermans would sink into soft ground while German tanks, with a lower ground-to-weight ratio, were more maneuverable.

"Because the M4s would bog down in the fields," lamented Maj. Al Irzyk, "out of necessity they would be forced to stick primarily to the roads":

> The front would narrow to single tanks in a column, and the tanks would have to attack in a column. The front would be one road wide. What a field day for the defender, knowing that he could focus his attention and all his effort on the roads…. This he would do with apparent relish…. He would mine the roads, set up roadblocks, and zero his longer range, high-velocity weapons on the bends in the road, and on the [American tankers'] blind spots.[14]

**Poughkeepsie New Yorker**   **EXTRA**

A Newspaper for the Home — Information and Entertainment for Every Member of the Family

*Continuing and Succeeding the Poughkeepsie Star-Enterprise, Established 1882, and the Poughkeepsie Eagle-News, Established 1785*

Vol. LXIII, No. 4    Poughkeepsie, New York, Tuesday, June 6, 1944    Price Five Cents    THE WEATHER: Fair and warmer.

# INVASION STARTS, ALLIED TROOPS HIT COAST OF FRANCE

SUPREME HEADQUARTERS, ALLIED EXPEDITIONARY FORCE-(AP)- American, British and Canadian troops landed in northern France this morning, launching the greatest overseas military operation in history with word from their Supreme commander, General Dwight D. Eisenhower, that "we will accept nothing except full victory" over the German masters of the continent.

The invasion, which Eisenhower called "a great crusade," was announced at 7:32 a. m. Greenwich mean time (3:32 a. m., eastern war time) in this one-sentence communique No. 1:

"Under the command of General Eisenhower, Allied naval forces supported by

*Photo by Robert Coldwell Sr.*

Panther Ausf. A at the Deutsches Panzermuseum, Munster. *Massimo Foti*

Along with mobility problems in mud, rough terrain, and snow, the Sherman's main gun and armor were inferior to the best Panzers. Thus, in all three of the crucial factors for successful tank design—mobility, firepower, and armor protection—the M4 was deficient.

To shore up its weak armor plate, in time-honored fashion GIs improvised. According to Ordnance's 1960 history, "Many of the tanks equipped with hedgerow cutters also carried on their fronts piles of sandbags or extra pieces of armor plate, for the crews knew that the tank did not have armor thick enough to withstand the German guns. This had been discovered in North Africa."[15] As to firepower, "neither the 75-mm gun on most of the Shermans nor the 138 new 76mm guns that arrived in Normandy on 20 July would penetrate the frontal armor of the German Tigers and Panthers."[16]

After three campaigns, experience showed the M4's gun and armor were not even equal to Germany's best. "The scandal of the European campaign," one historian would write, "was the inability of Western democracies to produce armor, and perhaps doctrine, that was at least on a par with that of their opponents."[17]

We have had no difficulty in dealing with German armour.... We have nothing to fear from Panther and Tiger tanks...provided our tactics are good we can defeat them without difficulty.[2]
—Gen. Bernard Montgomery, July 4, 1944

In the July 1944 First United States Army Tests held in Normandy, soldiers fired weapons from rifle grenades up to 105mm howitzers against a captured Panther. The results showed the new 76mm main gun, while slightly better than the 75mm, could not penetrate a Panther's frontal armor. The 105mm howitzer could, but only at a dangerous 500 yards or less.

The best American tank main gun was the 90mm firing improved "HVAP" (High Velocity Armor Piercing) rounds, as mounted in the rare new M36 Jackson tank destroyer and in the T26 heavy tank back home, whose mass production and adoption the brass continued to obstruct.[18] This was the same 90mm gun in a new turret that could have been added to existing Sherman hulls and was being used on the M36B1 expedient TD.

Among the fatalities in Normandy that summer was Gen. McNair. During a brief visit to observe Operation Cobra (the Allied breakout from the beachhead), he was killed near St. Lo on July 25, when American bombers dropped their deadly cargo too short. Coincidentally, in his only other overseas inspection visit (to the Tunisian front in Spring 1943), McNair was injured on the first day of his trip, becoming the Army's highest ranking "WIA" (wounded in action) soldier up to that time.

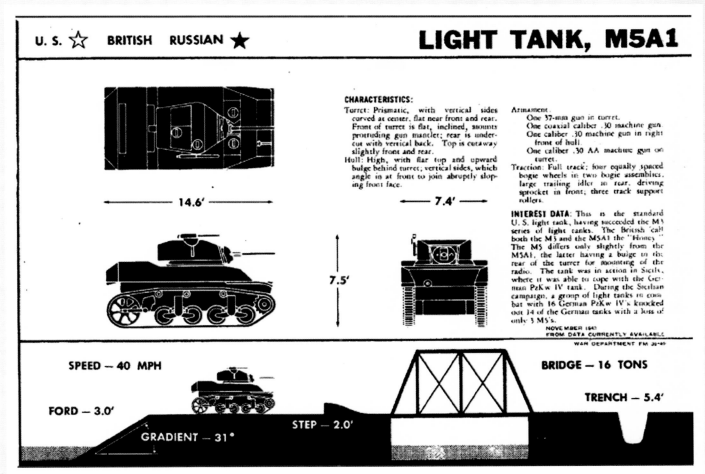

## U. S. ☆　BRITISH　RUSSIAN ★　　LIGHT TANK, M5A1

**CHARACTERISTICS:**

Turret: Prismatic, with vertical sides curved at center, flat near front and rear. Front of turret is flat, inclined, mounts protruding gun mantlet; rear is undercut with vertical back. Top is cutaway slightly front and rear.

Hull: High, with flat top and upward bulge behind turret; vertical sides, which angle in at front to join abruptly sloping front face.

Armament:
One 37-mm gun in turret.
One coaxial caliber .30 machine gun.
One caliber .30 machine gun in right front of hull.
One caliber .30 AA machine gun on turret.

Traction: Full track; four equally spaced bogie wheels in two bogie assemblies, large trailing idler in rear, driving sprocket in front; three track support rollers.

INTEREST DATA: This is the standard U. S. light tank, having succeeded the M3 series of light tanks. The British call both the M3 and the M5A1 the "Honey." The M5 differs only slightly from the M5A1, the latter having a bulge in the rear of the turret for mounting of the radio. The tank was in action in Sicily, where it was able to cope with the German PzKw IV tank. During the Sicilian campaign, a group of light tanks in combat with 16 German PzKw IV's knocked out 14 of the German tanks with a loss of only 3 M5's.

NOVEMBER 1943
FROM DATA CURRENTLY AVAILABLE

WAR DEPARTMENT FM 30-40

14.6'　　7.4'　　7.5'

SPEED — 40 MPH　　BRIDGE — 16 TONS

FORD — 3.0'　　TRENCH — 5.4'

GRADIENT — 31°　　STEP — 2.0'

Photo by Robert Coldwell Sr.

A sixty-one-year-old stateside trainer—one of the Army's most intellectual generals who never held a combat command in four decades—was killed at the front by his own men. Initial reports blamed German fire, but the truth could not be suppressed. On August 1, an angry Gen. Marshall cabled Eisenhower of his intention to silence McNair's staff (including his personal pilot) who were exposing the scandal back home. "We are endeavoring to suppress the story here, in line with your desire to avoid any air-ground antagonism."[19] As *Time* reported on August 14, "U.S. Army press officers had insisted that [McNair]...had been killed by the enemy. But too many people knew better, and last week the tragic truth came out."[20]

Lesley McNair had attained the dubious distinction of being the Army's first three-star general to die on a battlefield, and one of the highest ranking Americans killed in the war (Army Lt. Gen. Simon Bolivar Buckner Jr. would be killed in action by Japanese fire on Okinawa in 1945). On July 13, twelve days before McNair's death, the War Department announced that he was moving from command of Army Ground Forces at home to a position in the European Theater, possibly command of all US ground forces there. While speculation is idle, one wonders how he would have responded, had he lived, to the growing tank scandal.

The tank destroyer concept had lost its most ardent supporter, a man with Gen. Marshall's ear. Yet GIs continued to be burdened with towed guns as a result of Gen. McNair's pet project. Gen. Manton Eddy, commanding the US VII Corps, wrote home to Washington on July 3, 1944, reporting some of the first lessons of the Normandy fighting. The towed 57mm anti-tank guns, he warned, "Were virtually useless in the close country

encountered. Such weapons assigned to the [regimental] anti-tank companies certainly should be some type of self-propelled mount, and probably those assigned to battalions. The present [57mm towed] gun cannot be placed into position sufficiently promptly, except along roads."[21]

Would the accidental death of Gen. McNair, whose influence had been felt throughout the Army, lead to a reassessment of armor and anti-tank doctrine, a fresh start to address the problems exhibited in the Normandy tank fighting?

Not surprisingly, considering M4 medium tanks were inadequate against Tigers and Panthers, M5 light tanks (an improved M3 Stuart) suffered as well. Steve Zaloga observed:

The M5 light tank was used most intensively in the first months after the Normandy landings. Patton's Third Army, for example, lost 308 M5A1 tanks during the 1944–45 fighting, of which nearly half were lost in

Gen. Leslie J. McNair. With irony worthy of a Greek tragedy, this powerful staff officer was killed by friendly fire from American heavy bombers during a short July 1944 inspection trip to the ETO. He was one of the war's highest-ranking American casualties.

Some typical tanker gear on top of an M4A3 turret. *Author photo*

August and September 1944 alone. A similar pattern was repeated in Hodge's First Army, which suffered the majority of its light tank casualties in June–September 1944. The heavy casualties in light tank companies led tank commanders to exercise caution in employing the M5A1 light tank, and the diminishing casualties in later months was due in no small measure to restricting the missions of the light tanks to reduce their vulnerability.

By September 1944, heavy M5A1 losses in Normandy led the Armored Section of Gen. Bradley's 12th Army Group headquarters to request that the new M24 Chaffee light tank replace all M5A1s as soon as possible. But the War Department in Washington failed to concur, citing shipping and logistics problems.[22]

Weeks after the invasion, wrote British historian John Ellis, American M4 losses alone in Normandy ran "around 500 medium tanks per month."[23]

"My dear General," Eisenhower wrote Marshall in a July 5 "secret" cable:

I have just returned from a visit to the First Army where I found them deeply concerned over the inability of our present tank guns and anti-tank weapons to cope successfully with the German Panther and Tiger tanks.

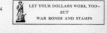

Photo by Robert Coldwell Sr.

None of our present ammunition…can penetrate the front armor of the Panther or Tiger tanks and, due to the restricted terrain and narrow roads in which we are fighting, we are unable consistently to attack these tanks from a favorable angle. Moreover, even from the flanks, our present weapons and ammunition are not adequately effective.

…at least a percentage of our tanks must have a powerful gun, if we are to conduct successful armored attacks. Outside of the possibilities of improving ammunition, it appears that the 90mm gun on the M36 [tank destroyer] and 90mm Tank T26, would materially improve our anti-tank defense, as well as our capabilities in attack. In the absence of early improvement of ammunition, the delivery of these weapons must be expedited in every way practicable to this theater to replace less efficient guns.

The urgency of this manner is such that I am sending Brig. Gen. Joseph A. Holly to you by air in order to amplify this urgent request and give you the benefit not only of information from the battle-field but his own personal experience in tank design and development.

I cannot emphasize too strongly that what we must have now is effective ammunition at the earliest practicable date. We cannot wait for further experimentation.[24]

In his diary for July 7, Ike's aide, Capt. Harry Butcher, referred to "The Holly Mission":

One of the things [Eisenhower] learned first hand in France was the inadequacy of firepower of American tanks against Tigers and Panthers. [Ike] set all hands to work by a special message to [his Chief of Staff Gen. Walter "Beedle" Smith] while he was in Normandy, and today had "all hands on deck."

The result was a special letter to General Marshall, carried by Brigadier General Joseph A. Holly in person. Holly, a tank expert, said he had made six trips across the Atlantic in the last six months, dealing with this and related problems.[25]

Marshall responded on July 13, assuring Eisenhower:

*photo by Robert Coldwell Sr.*

Restored Tiger I at the Deutsches Panzermuseum, Munster. *Massimo Foti*

CREW CASUALTIES BY POSITION

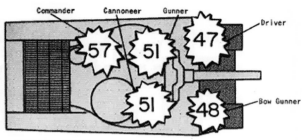

MEDIUM TANK

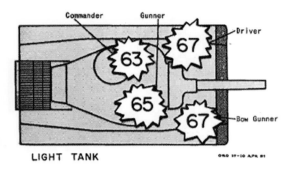

LIGHT TANK

Figure 8. Percentage cf tank crew casualties broken down by crew position.

From a secret postwar report for the Army, Coox and Naiswald, *Survey of Allied Tank Casualties in World War Two* [1951]. *Photo by Robert Coldwell Sr., courtesy US Army Military History Institute, Carlisle Barracks, Pennsylvania*

Your letter…which dealt with your concern over the inability of our present tanks and anti-tank weapons to cope successfully with the German Panther and Tiger Tanks, has resulted in action being taken to expedite the shipment to you of 90mm Gun Motor Carriage M36, together with 90mm APC ammunition…additional [M36s] will be made available for shipment as a result of expanding and expediting the manufacturing program. This action on the program has already been initiated and the highest priorities have been assigned to it. You will be advised of the further schedule of availability as soon as the production schedule is firmed up, which will be about 20 July.

As you have been advised by cable, it will be necessary that your shipping people assign top priority to these shipments to assure their movement to your theater as quickly as the equipment becomes available. I am having these shipments followed here to certain that no delay develops at this end.

The 90mm Tank T26 has only recently been released to production. Shipment of these new tanks to you should begin the end of this year. This production is also being expedited with the highest priority.[26]

As to improved TD, tank, and anti-tank gun ammunition, while "90mm high velocity ammunition will be available for shipments starting in September"

improvement in the armor piercing performance of the 57, 75, and 76mm. gun projectiles and 105mm howitzer projectiles has been continuously under development…. As our cables have indicated, results have not been particularly promising and no improvement is in sight in these calibers in the immediate future. Holly is taking over additional information on this.[27]

As will be seen, in spite of Marshall's promises of "expedited production," "expedited shipping," and "highest priorities," all the items mentioned in this cable and requested by Eisenhower in July 1944 would be delayed, experience dire shortages, or arrive too little, too late.

From June 6 to August 5, the US First Army in Normandy lost some 647 tanks, including 463 M4 Shermans with the standard 75mm gun, and 144 M5A1 light tanks.[28] On August 9, Gen. Bradley ordered his Twelfth Armor Group's Armor Section to request the British Firefly, emerging as one of few Allied tanks able to defeat German tanks and AFVs at long range. But there was a shortage of completed Fireflies and (as a result of the high-level decisions to decrease M4 production and combat losses) standard American M4s to be converted into Fireflies. Even while Allied propaganda trumpeted American industrial capacity, this shortfall was so acute that Bradley's request went unfulfilled.[29] "Losses of Ordnance equipment," Eisenhower admitted to Marshall around September 1944, "have been extremely high. For example, we must have as replacement items each month…500 tanks."[30]

The next month, Gen. Holly had opportunities to take the British up on their offer to convert American M4s to Firefly con-

*Portrait of a Medic* by Howard Brodie.

figuration. But as he wrote to Army Ground Forces in Washington on September 17, he feared the chance had "slipped into the background because of…no apparent accumulation of tank reserves…battle losses consumed our 75mm gun tank reserves."

In other words, so many standard American M4s were being lost that none could be spared to upgrade to Fireflies. Yet shortly before this, Gen. Holly had also optimistically predicted to a coworker, "Probably the problem of the Panther will no longer be with [the] U.S. for the remainder of the war. The German, we believe, has lost most of his armor."[31]

Given high Sherman losses, what was to be done in the interim? The use of sacrificial decoy tactics—M4 crews would bait Tigers or Panthers in the hope that while distracting them other tanks could attempt shots at their vulnerable points. This terrible arithmetic led to many deaths. At first, losses were "replaced" by shuffling men around to form complete companies; a private driving a tank one day might find himself replacing a dead tank gunner (a corporal or sergeant's position) the next. Losses were particularly high among officers and sergeants serving as tank commanders because they were exposed while standing in the tall, open cupola (the small turret above the main one, from which they directed drivers and fire).

In an attempt to cover losses, wounded tankers were sent back to their vehicles before full recovery. In the 743rd Tank Battalion there were so many losses each company had to be rearranged daily. "Reorganizing Company," the 743rd's after action report for July 14 reads, "is a difficult problem, as all platoon sergeants and leaders [usually lieutenants] have become casualties. New crews have to be established and trained."[32]

Jim Gifford arrived as a replacement with the 712th Tank Battalion in mid-July 1944 and recalled his "first contact with the 712th." He was ordered to search the hulks of burned out Shermans from a recent battle:

I had the shitty job of going back to those tanks and getting the dog tags of those that had died. We made up a little box. If you found anybody's remains, you always put their dog tags in that box. They went with the body.

These guys had all been incinerated, because the tanks were like a furnace. It was like getting into a furnace after something's been destroyed. I'd go where the tank driver was supposed to be sitting, and I'd find only a dog tag. I wouldn't even find the body. This is the way it was. A very horrible experience, especially when you're gonna get in a tank yourself the next day.

Gifford remembered "one tank in particular" where the gunner "had survived a little bit" after his tank was hit:

It's a gruesome story…. He was still sitting in the gunner's seat. There was nothing left of him but maybe his hips. And when I was looking for his dog tags, I pushed this thing. I thought it was a piece of the machinery, and a piece of it came off…like the skin on a turkey, it came off, this big black crust, and then I realized it was what was left of him.

Those guys never knew what hit them. Those tanks exploded. You've got all that hundred-octane gasoline—nobody had a chance.[33]

Ironically, even while a deadly aura surrounded the small numbers of near-mythical Tigers and Panthers in Normandy, the *Panzer IV* remained the backbone of Germany's armor divisions. Contrary to postwar myth, Tigers were relatively rare in the American sectors; more of them opposed British troops in their assigned areas with unfortunate results. Sir Max Hastings wrote of "a shocked British tank officer after his Cromwell was hit by an 88mm shell from a Tiger":

A sheet of flame licked over the turret and my mouth was full of grit and burnt paint. "Bail out," I yelled, and leaped clear…. There were my crew, hiding under a currant bush, miraculously all safe. Joe, the driver, white and shaking, crouched with drawn revolver. He looked like a cornered rat…. The Tiger drove off undamaged, its commander waving his hat and laughing…. Our hands shook so much that we could hardly light our cigarettes.[34]

Among frontline soldiers, fear of the Tiger reached epidemic proportions; GIs and Tommies imagined them everywhere. To British tanker David Holbrook, the Tiger inspired "an hysterical fear…. Soldiers were quickly dismayed to find that a burning Sherman would emit mocking smoke rings as well as shouts and monstrous gouts of fire."[35] This fear was "hardly surprising," observed historian Russell Hart, "when experience had established sending five tanks to knock out a Tiger, and expecting only one to return."[36]

Maj. Al Irzyk wrote of being fired upon by German "88s"—both the towed artillery pieces and those mounted in the Tiger:

Guided by the flashes [of American tanks firing], some of these rounds would bury themselves in the ridge just below the crest. Others would spank the top of the ridge just vacated [by American tanks]—a direct hit, if it had been a second or two sooner—and ricochet screaming overhead and onto the rear. This was the most God-awful, frightening sound imaginable.

Normandy, June 1944: A British Sherman tank crew of C Squadron, 13th–18th Royal Hussars, takes a break: a quick letter home, then perhaps a "brew up" of some "char" (tea).

*End of a Busy Day* by Franklin Boggs.

tornado or locomotive. When it hit the ridge the ground trembled, and its ricochet was the most deafening, terrifying, throaty, horrible, fearful, screeching sound I had ever heard.

I would never again hear a sound that came even close to producing such fear, terror, shock, and alarm. It was absolutely staggering, and brought chills and shivers to these veterans who had already experienced terror during their many weeks of combat. After one of these frightening close calls, it would have been so easy to just hunker down, cowering in safety.

It spoke volumes for the courage and guts of those tankers to climb back up to the crest of the hill, to resume firing and take another chance at the fury of an "88mm."[37]

While the phrase "post traumatic stress disorder" did not exist in the 1940s, "shell shock" or "battle fatigue" was a debilitating factor in armored combat. According to British historian John Buckley, tankers "displaying symptoms of battle exhaustion would typically suffer from tremors, profound loss of confidence, odd behavior patterns and withdrawal from everyday life."[38] Buckley quoted Lt. Stuart Hills of the Sherwood Rangers:

Our gunner…was carried off in an ambulance. Nobody quite knew what had happened to him, but for some reason he would not come out of the tank. He slept in it, ate in it, refused the opportunity even of a game of football, which he loved. Perhaps he had drawn too deeply on his own particular well of endurance, had seen too many terrible sights, suffered too many vivid nightmares.[39]

The 88mm was particularly dreadful. Its flight from gun to target could hardly be clocked—how do you measure an instant? It was on you like the roar of a

**British Cromwell IV tank at the Tank Museum, Bovington, Dorset, UK.** *Massimo Foti*

Trooper Joe Ekins, Northants Yeomanry, served with "one bloke" who "every time he got within two yards of his tank, was sick. He was carted off, and we never saw him again. I didn't blame him, though."[40]

Max Hastings described a British tank officer's long, frightening night in July 1944, "spent on the Bourguebus Ridge during one of the most bitter armored clashes." The officer conceded, "We were all rather frightened. Two men from my troop corporal's tank came up and said they would rather face a court-martial than go on. I explained that we all felt much the same, but were not given the option."

Two days later, when one of this officer's tanks was hit, the crew baled out:

I never saw the gunner and wireless operator [British Army radioman] again. They were cases for the psychiatrist, and the M.O. [medical orderly] sent them away. These fellows had been in nearly every battle the regiment fought, and each had bailed out [of a burning tank] at least twelve times before."[41]

It seems unlikely this officer would have embraced the views of British Gen. Miles Dempsey, who told historian Chester Wilm-

*Eye [I] Company crews went into their first battle feeling invincible in their Sherman tanks. They came out sobered with the realization that they, and their tanks, were highly expendable.[3]*
*—Cpl. Bert Close, US Third Armored Division*

ot after the war that while he (Dempsey) knew the Bourguebus Ridge fight "would be costly," he had been "prepared to lose two or three hundred tanks" in the course of the battle.[42]

Appearing before the Panther, the Tiger's imposing size and firepower inspired an aura of invincibility that grew in the following decades, eclipsing the Panther's. Yet the Panther was built in larger numbers and became Germany's best tank of the war, a better balance of firepower, armor protection, and mobility.

Col. William Triplett recalled an American officer's description of the Panther as "probably the best tank built":

It's fast, agile, and has a low ground pressure.... Frontal armor sloped, so that we see our shells bounce off. That high-velocity 75mm will go through our apron [thin side armor] or turret on the M4, and the muzzle brake shoots the smoke to each side, so the gunner can shoot as fast as the loader can shove in the ammunition. The only way we can take a Panther or Tiger is to keep him interested in front and sneak a tank or tank destroyer around to hit him in the side or rear.[43]

**Restored German Panzer V ("Panther").** *Author photo courtesy of the National Armor and Cavalry Heritage Foundation, photo by the author*

Artist unknown, from a book by James Jones. *Photo by Robert Coldwell Sr.*

The Tiger was relatively slow and mechanically unreliable, yet its iconic status remains; as one historian observed, "In Normandy in the summer of 1944, the legendary 'invincibility' of the Tiger was found 'paralyzing' by the Allied soldiers who knew that their Shermans were, in the German phrase, "Tommy Cookers" [soldier's stoves] by comparison.[44]

An account of a 4th Armored Division M4 dueling a Panther hints at the bitterness of the Normandy tank fighting. Commanding was Capt. Murray Farmer, CO, 25th Cavalry Reconnaissance Squadron. Rolling down an Avranches street, they saw a Panther thirty yards away:

Captain Farmer ordered the Sherman's driver to ram the Panther before it could bring its high velocity gun to bear. The two armor-plated giants crashed together with a metallic clangor. The Sherman struck the Panther full in the flank, and the muzzle of the [M4's] 75 almost touched the German turret. The Panther's crew tried vainly to swing their tank gun against the Sherman, but the long barrel would not clear it.

Sergeant Edward A. Rejrat...fired four 75mm HE and AP shells point blank into the Panther. The explosions rocked the men in the Sherman, but as the dazed survivors of the Panther's crew tried to climb out of their tank, Captain Farmer shot them with a submachine gun. With one last heave, the Sherman tried to push the heavier Panther over and knock it completely out of the fight. Instead, the straining Sherman overturned into a

ditch with its tracks in the air. The [M4] began burning, but the crew wriggled away from the two tanks and dodged safely through scattered German Infantrymen.[45]

Max Hastings wrote of British tanker Peter Hennessy, "ordered to investigate the fate of another tank of his Sherman squadron which had halted immobile a few yards ahead,"

his driver dismounted, clambered up the hull, glanced into the turret and ran hastily back. "Christ," he said, "they're all dead in there. What a bloody mess." An 88mm round had ricocheted around the interior, killing the entire turret crew and terminating in the co-driver's back. A few moments later a shocked and emotional figure lifted the driver's hatch of the stricken tank and emerged, the sole survivor.[46]

General Fritz Bayerlein commanded the *Panzer Lehr Division* in Normandy. "So far," he observed, "[Allied] tank crews have not shown much enthusiasm for fights between tanks."[47]

In a June 16 letter leaked to the British War Office and Allied civilian press, British Brigadier Harold Pyman, Chief of Staff of XXX Corps, described the "Tiger terror":

Tiger and Panther tanks now form a higher proportion of the equipment of German armoured regiments. The result is that while 75mm shot has been failing to penetrate the front face of the Tigers and Panthers at ranges down to 30 yards, they can knock Shermans and Cromwells out at ranges up to 1,500 yards with ease...it cannot be stressed too strongly that we are fighting with inadequate equipment.[48]

The civilian press began to suspect problems with Allied armor in Normandy. Broadcasting to the states on June 17, CBS News radio correspondent Douglas Edwards questioned the high tank losses in the invasion, numbers that contradicted the cheery, official press releases praising the M4. Edwards returned to the theme on June 20; ten days later, fellow CBS correspondent William Henry—also telling stateside listeners of large tank losses—suggested a formal congressional investigation.

One response of Allied military leaders was more censorship. Gen. "Freddy" de Guingand, Chief of Staff to Field Marshal Montgomery, wrote to him June 24 of the growing "Tiger terror":

If we are not careful, there will be a danger of the troops developing a Tiger and Panther complex.... P.J. Grigg [Percy James Grigg, Churchill's Secretary of State for War] rang me up last night and said he thought there might be trouble...as regards "the inadequacy of our tanks compared with the Germans."

"Naturally," de Guingand reassured Monty, "the reports are not being circulated."[49]

Eisenhower's aide Harry Butcher referred to this "report from Monty" in his diary for July 1, noting "indications in the report of censorship cuts in newspaper stories filed from the front, which indicate that our tanks are inferior to those of the Germans."[50]

Col. George Jarrett, as an expert on captured enemy weapons, was often invited to address the public on his work at Aberdeen Proving Ground, but his speeches had to be submitted to a general for approval, and Jarrett felt the hand of censorship when he attempted to tell civilian audiences the truth. As he described it in hand-written notes he left for posterity:

> I was continually being asked to give talks on the captured [enemy] materiel—but always forced to "toe the line" that U.S. Ordnance materiel was superior to, especially, the German items—which in many instances, they were not. I was usually in "hot water," as I would answer queries honestly.[51]

His superiors "gave me a hard time," Jarrett wrote, "I was accused of being partial to German equipment, and that I thought it was better than ours—which it often was." Memos preserved in his papers at the Army's Military History Institute show routing slips between Jarrett and his superiors who reviewed his speeches. He was warned not to publicly compare US and enemy weapons—difficult to do, as this was his job. When he did so, Jarrett was warned "don't make it a habit" by Gen. Barnes who, shortly before the Normandy invasion, had assured the public American weapons were the world's best.[52]

British tanker Jack Thorpe of the 2nd Fife and Forfar Yeomanry described a column of knocked out tanks:

> Along the column of our tanks I see palls of smoke and tanks brewing up, with flames belching forth from their turrets. I see men climbing out, on fire like torches, rolling on the ground to try and douse the flames. The tank twenty yards away from us is hit. Flames shoot out of its turret. I see a member of its crew climbing out through the flames. He is almost out, putting one foot onto the rim to jump down. He seems to hesitate, and he falls back inside. Oh, Christ![53]

British tanker Les Taylor of the Northamptonshire Yeomanry learned quickly why experienced tankers avoided inspecting destroyed tanks if they could:

> I climbed up to look inside the turret. The stench was indescribable.
> I saw the loader-operator, his hands frozen in the act of feeding a belt of ammo into his machine gun, his head resting sideways on his arm. The appalling thing was, the body was black as coal. The gunner was just a shapeless mass of decomposition on the turret floor, but the most horrific sight of all was the tank commander...the projectile on entry had decapitated the poor man. I scrambled down from that cham-

ber of death and corruption and lit a cigarette...and vowed never again to look inside a k.o.'d tank.[54]

But Allied generals continued to feed the press boastful stories of the M4's alleged superiority; in a July 4 public letter to British Secretary of State for War P. J. Grigg, Gen. Bernard Montgomery insisted:

> We have had no difficulty in dealing with German armour, once we had grasped the problem. We have nothing to fear from the Panther or Tiger tanks; they are unreliable mechanically, and the Panther is very vulnerable from the flanks...provided our tactics are good, we can defeat them without difficulty.[55]

WWII Allied reporters were censored; civilian media who asked probing questions or refused to play along could be uninvited from generals' press conferences, or lose their press credentials and be sent home. Ernie Pyle, witnessing a tank on fire, put a happy spin on it in a column appearing in stateside newspapers datelined "In Normandy, July 15, 1944." He had been standing in a doorway, "peeking out at the tank":

> It started backing up. Then suddenly a yellow flame pierced the bottom of the tank and there was a crash of such intensity that I automatically blinked my eyes.

Photo by Robert Coldwell Sr.

The tank, hardly fifty feet from where I was standing, had been hit by an enemy shell.

A second shot ripped the pavement at the side of the tank. There was smoke all around, but the tank didn't catch fire. In a moment the crew came boiling out of the turret.

...I have never seen men run so violently. They ran all over, with arms and heads going up and down and with marathon-race grimaces. They plunged into my doorway.

I spent the next excited hour with them. We changed to another doorway and sat on boxes in the empty hallway. The floor and steps were thick with blood where a soldier had been treated within the hour.

What had happened to the tank was this:

They had been firing away at a pillbox ahead when their 75 backfired, filling the tank with smoke and blinding them.

They decided to back up in order to get their bearings, but after backing a few yards the driver was so blinded that he stopped. Unfortunately he stopped exactly at the foot of a side street. More unfortunately there was another German pillbox up the side street. All the Germans had to do was take easy aim and let go at the sitting duck.

The first shot hit a tread, so the tank couldn't move. That was when the boys got out. I don't know why the Germans didn't fire at them as they poured out.

While rightly celebrating the tankers' resilience after their tank was knocked out, Pyle did not question why this was happening with disturbing frequency:

The escaped tankers naturally were excited, but they were as jubilant as June bugs and ready for more. They had never been in combat before the invasion of Normandy, yet in three weeks their tank had been shot up three times. Each time it was repaired and put back in action. And it can be repaired again this time. The name of their tank, appropriately, is Be Back Soon.[56]

"Frontline Fighters Prefer Sherman Tank To Mark V Panther of Germans" appeared in newspapers like the Lincoln, Nebraska, *State Journal* on August 5, 1944. Reporter L. S. B. Shapiro, "With the British and Canadian Forces in Normandy," quoted a "high ranking Allied officer in command of a major tank formation now engaged in the Normandy front." Asked a "point blank question," the unnamed officer insisted, "If I were given the opportunity of exchanging all my Sherman tanks for German Panther tanks I would certainly refuse, and so would my tank commanders. We are absolutely firm on that point."[57]

For most of the war, the press seemed to follow the government and military leaders' playbook. "Introducing the "Hole Puncher," gushed a caption in the August 14, 1944, *Baltimore Sun*. "Used for the first time in the invasion of France, the Army today lifted the curtain on the new 'Hole Puncher' 76mm gun which fires a 15-pound projectile and which achieved tactical surprise. It won the nickname 'hole puncher' because its high muzzle velocity packs a hard wallop in piercing German armor."

Col. George Jarrett, who had witnessed the effects of German armor on Middle Eastern battlefields, was not convinced. "Only 2,600 [of them built]," he wrote on a clipping of the article, "and [it] barely matches the obsolescent Panzer IV 75mm gun [with a muzzle velocity of] 2,600 fps. It took from El Alamein to Normandy to create this, and by then the Panzer IV was obsolescent, and the Germans had the Mark V Panther in big quantities, with a 75mm KWK 42 gun [3,200 fps]. The Panther was first used in Russia in fall of 1943."[58]

Reading the boasts about American armor in the press, one notices a glaring omission: the opinions of the GIs actually using these tanks at the front. Articles often quoted stateside generals, whose views on the combat effectiveness of tanks derived from press releases or drawing board estimates, rather than real experience; Gen. McNair, wrote his biographer E. J. Kahn, was "an accomplished mathematician passionately attached to his slide rule."[59]

When the press—fed statistics of German tank losses—exulted that a certain amount of Panzers were destroyed, they may not have realized that for each one, multiple Shermans may have gone up in flames with attendant deaths and injuries among their crews.

Col. Sidney Hinds, Second Armored Division, understood quantity was being thrown against quality. "In my opinion, the reason our armor has engaged the German tanks as successfully as it has is not due by any means to a superior tank, but to our superior numbers of tanks on the battlefield, and the willingness of our tankers to take their losses while maneuvering to a position from which a penetrating shot can be put through a weak spot of the enemy tank."[60] The "willingness" of young draftee GIs to "take such losses" is debatable, while the brass's decision "to expend Shermans," wrote Gen. Bradley after the war, "offered little comfort to crews who were forced to expend themselves as well."[61]

Bradley acknowledged in his memoirs:
In Europe, as well as in Africa two years before, the Tiger could both outgun and outduel any Allied tank in the field.... Originally, the Sherman had come equipped with a 75mm gun, an almost totally ineffective weapon against the heavy frontal plate of these German tanks. Only by swarming around the panzers to hit them on the flank could our Shermans knock the enemy out. But too often American tankers complained it cost them a tank or two, *with crews*, to get the German. Thus we could defeat the enemy's panzers but only by expending more tanks than we cared to lose."[62]

The M4 could not beat the Panther or Tiger "in a direct frontal attack." However, "in dependability...the American tank clearly outclassed the German. This advantage, together with our U.S. superiority in numbers, enabled us to surround the enemy in battle and knock his tanks out from their flanks."[63]

At the time, Bradley was writing without wartime censorship. His candor was needed 1942–45, when Army and civilian leaders were making inflated claims of the M4's alleged superiority. And

Typical example of tankers' attempts to improve the Sherman's inadequate side and front armor, along with their odds of survival. Spare tracks, sand bags, and even chicken wire filled with poured, hardened concrete were some of the methods. *US Army Signal Corps*

Photo by Robert Coldwell Sr.

brations of production figures and industrial might, while the Sherman's lack of armor protection and inability to fight Germany's best tanks on an equal level is glossed over. A recent book on the Ardennes Campaign, while noting the improvised armor and decoy tactics that GIs adopted in response to their tanks' shortcomings, offers as compensation the idea that "the Sherman was a multifaceted vehicle that could move swiftly and be adapted for various purposes."[64]

After failing to provide GIs with armor able to take on Germany's best, generals and politicians sacrificed men and tanks as so many decoys to fight an enemy with more powerful models. As the situation worsened, bureaucrats continued to obstruct adoption of a Sherman replacement, the T26.

The M4's armor was so inadequate, GIs piled on anything to increase their odds of survival, hoping to deflect deadly 88mm shells, including layers of cement behind chicken wire, metal track links, road wheels, wooden planks, and sandbags. Photos show M4s covered with so many sandbags they resemble pillboxes. The enlisted tankers' "efforts and modifications to improve [tanks]," wrote Maj. Al Irzyk, "never ceased." In February 1945, his 4th Armored Division's "126th Armored Ordnance Maintenance Battalion...sent out crews to weld chicken wire on the front,

although few tankers would agree that the M4's mechanical reliability excused its deficient firepower, this wartime excuse for the tank scandal has been repeated for decades.

All tank designs attempt to balance firepower, armor protection, and mobility. Although the M4 failed in at least two out of three of these vital categories, for decades, we have read cele-

Souvenir de France, 1944: A handkerchief sent home by tankers from the ETO. *Photo by Robert Coldwell Sr.*

sides, and turrets of light and medium tanks, so that tank crews could insert in them natural camouflage material."[65]

But Shermans continued to blaze. Sgt. Kenneth Titman, a tank commander with the 712th Tank Battalion, was wounded in the July 1944 Battle of Hill 122 while supporting the 90th Infantry Division:

We were all coming together in an open field. When we got in there, the German 88s got us. They hit my tank, and it exploded…we dropped the escape hatch (in the floor)… the driver put it in reverse, and the driver and assistant driver went through the escape hatch…the gunner and the loader went out through the turret, and they were on fire.

I hollered, "Abandon tank!" and they all jumped out…. Cohron got killed right in the tank; an 88 hit him. The assistant driver went out of the top and down the side. He was on fire when he hit the ground…I went out of the turret and got hit in the leg…I looked around and I saw all these American tanks running away. One tank ran in front of me and hit the one on the left, and both exploded. That's what I saw. I just told my crew to abandon tank…I jumped out of the turret and hit the back deck, and on my combat boot, the blood was coming out of the top.

When I got down off the tank and looked up, I saw the loader coming out of the turret, and there were sparks. That was Wojtilla. And Cohron, I knew he didn't come out, because I had some of his flesh on my helmet…then Morrison put the tank in reverse, and the assistant driver dropped the escape hatch…the tank had enough power to back off, and the guys got out from under the tank. I don't know where they went after that. I know I got in a slit trench, and the Germans

"In The Mood," 1944: one of the few known photos of Sgt. Lafayette "War Daddy" Pool's Sherman. Pool was a platoon sergeant in Item Company, 3rd Battalion, 32nd Armored Regiment, 3rd Armored Division, and likely the top American "tank ace" of the war. He commanded several M4s named "In The Mood"; this one, with a 76mm main gun, served as the lead or "point" vehicle for columns of tanks some twenty-one times. In a short but spectacular eighty-four-day combat career, Pool and his crew (from July-September 1944: gunner Cpl. Willis Oller, loader T/5 Delbert Boggs, driver T/5 Wilbert "Bunny" Richards, and assistant driver PFC Bertrand "Bert" Close) destroyed an estimated 258 enemy vehicles and killed or captured hundreds of Germans. This Sherman was eventually knocked out, killing replacement loader PFC Paul King and wounding Cpl. Oller and Sgt. Pool, who lost his right leg. "War Daddy" Pool soldiered on in the postwar Army, retiring as a Chief Warrant Officer.

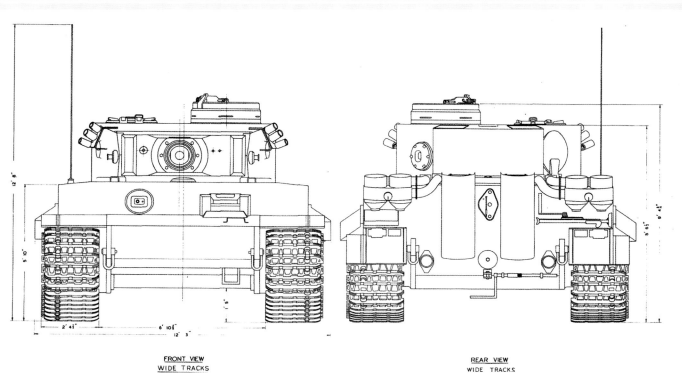

FRONT VIEW
WIDE TRACKS

REAR VIEW
WIDE TRACKS

Two views of a Tiger I from an Allied intelligence report. *Courtesy US Army Military History Institute, Carlisle Barracks, Pennsylvania*

picked me up and put me on a litter, because they knew I was hit.

I was standing there in the turret when the tank got hit. See, it went through the front end and exploded, and that got me in the leg…and the rest of the guys, Cohron got hit in the face…the loader, he jumped out of the turret, and he was on fire…I looked back at the tank, and it sounded like popcorn popping. That makes a hell of a noise.[66]

After seeing GIs' attempts to improve the armor on their Shermans, Gen. Patton complained to his diary, "I noticed that all the tanks were covered with sandbags. This was very stupid. In the first place, it made the soldiers think they could get hurt; in the second place, it overloaded the machinery; and in the third place, it provided no additional protection. I ordered their removal at once."[67]

Privately, the same General who forbid his scared GIs from attempting to raise their chances of survival wrote bloodthirsty poetry. Perhaps he was able to show such aggression on paper because, unlike his own soldiers, he was not confronting Tigers or Panthers:

So let us do real fighting
Boring in and gouging, biting,
Let's take a chance now that we have the ball.
Let's forget those fine firm bases
In the dreary shell-raked places,
Let's shoot the works and win!
Yes, win it all![68]

Sandbags and other improvised armor may indeed have "overloaded the machinery," as Patton claimed, but did they protect the men inside, who did the "real fighting?" Far removed from Patton's safe headquarters world of immaculate uniforms, spit-shined boots, and gleaming helmet liners, the 67th Armored Regiment reported:

Technical Sergeant Heyd, Maintenance Sergeant of Company E, 67th AR, has seen and retrieved all tanks of this company that have been hit by enemy tank and anti-tank guns. Of a total of 19 tanks hit, 17…had been penetrated, while only 2 tanks had withstood the force of the enemy high-velocity shells and ricocheted…due to the added protection of sandbags and logs used to reinforce the armor plate in front of the tank.[69]

But as to the one-inch-thick extra side armor plate M4 tankers added to the hull, over ammo storage areas, according to a British *Analysis of 75mm Sherman Tank Casualties Suffered Between 6th June and 10 July 1944*, "It should be recognized that in no recorded case in our sample has the extra applique armor resisted any hit." Another British study claimed, "There does not seem to be a very strong argument for these plates. It seems doubtful whether the fitting of these plates is justified."[70]

Although unknown to most of them at the time, there was a slight consolation for Allied tankers in the Normandy campaign: the death of Michael Wittmann near Saint Aignan. The battle in which he was killed epitomizes Allied and German differences in the use of armor: the Allies stressed quantity, the Germans quality. Wittmann and his SS Tiger crew had destroyed hundreds of Russian vehicles on the Eastern Front, but found themselves outnumbered by aggressive Canadian tankers in M4s who stopped a German attack cold.

While it is believed Trooper Joe Ekins (a Firefly gunner with the 1st Northants Yeomanry) killed Wittmann, he regretted the notoriety attached to his name: "I had never heard of Wittmann; didn't know who he was. It was six to seven years after the war before I knew what had happened."[71] One of Germany's best tank commanders had fallen to superior numbers, but it took multiple

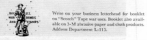

*Courtesy Henry Smith, photo by Robert Coldwell Sr.*

Allied tankers and M4s to stop him. Wittmann's end brings to mind a joke among GIs, lines supposedly spoken by a captured German officer, "One of our Panzers is worth ten of your Panzers—but you always have *eleven*!"

Constant tank warfare took an emotional toll. Nerves were stretched taught in a state of permanent alert. Sgt. Nat Frankel wrote of the "thousand-yard stare," an "anesthetized look, and the wide, hollow eyes of a man who no longer cares. I wasn't to that state yet, but the numbness was total."[72]

Sergeant Lafayette Pool's 76mm Sherman "In The Mood" often led the way in columns, serving as the point tank for M4s with the standard 75mm gun. "It was not possible to relax," recalled Cpl. Bert Close, one of Pool's assistant drivers and bow gunners. "I rode with the hatch usually closed, with my eyes on the periscope and one hand on the trigger of the bow gun. If there was a blind corner, a group of trees, a clump of bushes, a farmhouse, a barn or shed, there could be a hidden tank, anti-tank gun, bazooka team, or sniper waiting for us. They were not spotted until they fired the first round. When they were…they caught hell from us, and from every tank in the task force. The blasts from [gunner] Oller's 76mm cannon and coaxial machine gun firing over my head got to be deafening."[73]

The Normandy battles blended together in Close's mind. "Do I remember specific 'In The Mood' tank battles during these days? I do not. There were days, and there were days and nights, at places like Couptrain, Ranes, and Fromentel, where Oller fired his cannon and machine gun and I fired my bow gun. Times when I had to be careful not to burn the barrel of my machine gun from constant firing. The days ran together. As each day passed and the action was repeated, it became a blur."[74]

Sgt. Frankel wrote that tankers developed a mixture of fear and numbness that kept them going. "After Avranches…I would learn what it meant to actually adapt to combat":

I saw five Germans on foot, and an American tank gunner cut them down. I saw men wiggle out of burning tanks, only to die a moment later. …and I saw Infantrymen running and ducking and falling and sometimes getting up again. Suddenly I wasn't afraid. Something had tightened in my gut, and I continued shooting. Then fear returned again, and then another tightening, another personal push against the enemy, and death was so close I couldn't fear it. The scar tissue had formed around my heart, and what would happen would happen.[75]

In late 1943, Army leaders decided to muddle through the invasion of France with the M4s and tankers on hand. In planning for it, historian John Ellis has observed the generals assumed a tank loss rate of only six percent a month, later upped to nine percent. Influenced by Gen. McNair, they chose to stick with the deficient M4 and the flawed TD concept over fielding the Sherman's replacement T26 or a mass upgrade of existing M4s. For 1944, they also cut Sherman production and tanker training at Fort Knox, gambling the numbers on hand would be enough. All these decisions led to maintenance and personnel nightmares and increased casualties for the rest of the war.

While Overlord planners had estimated a loss rate of 6–9% for Allied tanks, the actual numbers that summer were 26.6% in June 1944, 24.4% in July, and 25.3% in August.[76] "Losses of Ordnance equipment have been extremely high," Eisenhower reported to Marshall in September. "We must have as replacement items each month…500 tanks." The figures, Marshall wrote soon after V-E Day, "indicate the severity of the campaign in France."[77]

So many tanks and trained crews were lost that when a shortage of both arose, untrained "replacements" with no armor experience were hastily brought up to the frontlines to be thrown into combat. Sgt. Jim Rothschadl, a Sherman gunner with the 712th Tank Battalion, was wounded in a July 1944 tank battle. Evacuated to an English hospital, he was surprised to see a cook from his unit:

I said, "What the hell happened to you?" He had a big cast all the way down his leg." "Well," he said, "Them sonsabitches. One day they got short a loader and they stuck me in a tank." He was never in a tank [before]. He said, "They showed me what to do," and he got his knee in the way of the recoil from the breech [when the M4's main gun fired], and it smashed his leg."[78]

"Between July 26th and August 12th," conceded Ordnance's official history in 1960, "one of the 2nd Armored Division's tank battalions had lost to German tanks and assault guns 70 percent of its tanks destroyed, or evacuated for 4th echelon repairs."[79] In July alone, the 743rd Tank Battalion lost 38 out of 54 light and medium tanks in Normandy. Sixteen tankers were killed in action, ninety-eight wounded, and nineteen missing. This was the equivalent of losing roughly twenty-six complete tank crews in a month in a war lasting over three and a half years.[80]

But according to Gen. Marshall, "By the spring of 1944, as most of the shortcomings of the replacement system had become evident, the War Department took vigorous corrective action. A directive was sent to every theater requiring the establishment

of retraining centers so that every man in the Army would be put to his most efficient use."[81] The Army Chief of Staff's words would come as a surprise to cooks, bakers, and clerks abruptly thrown into M4 tank crews with little or no training, a practice that continued until the last days of the war.

What was the mental toll on these men? During the August 1944 battle of Falaise-Argentan Gap, Sherman gunner Cpl. Steve Krysko accidentally fired on American troops when his tank commander "screwed up" their orders. "I fell back onto the gunner's seat, laid my head on my arms, and cried. As far as I was concerned, the war was over for me. It hit me that not only was I killing human beings, which in itself is traumatic, but I was killing our own men":

> I refused to fight on, and had to be sent back to A Company's [A Co, 712th Tank Battalion] rear "safety zone." I crawled under a disabled tank and lay there for the rest of the day. No one said anything to me. I tried to convince myself that I was a Section 8—mentally disturbed—and would be sent back to the States because of battle fatigue. By dusk, however, I realized that faking a mental breakdown was something I couldn't do.[82]

Capt. Jack Sheppard led a company in Krysko's 712th TB. Battling for Normandy's Hill 122 in July, his tank was hit and his company reduced to seven out of seventeen tanks:

> I went up in a jeep and looked in the tanks, and there was nothing but ashes down on the bottom.... Sometimes you would find dog tags, because they didn't burn....

I'll tell you something you'll never forget...the smell of those burning tanks. Barbecued people. You could smell it a long way off, and it is horrible.[83]

As the Allies broke out of the Normandy beachhead and approached Germany, the increasing pace of armor operations caused rest and maintenance to be neglected, diminishing tanks and men. Maj. Al Irzyk noted that by September 1944, "Gone were the confident, cocky, winning tankers" in his Eighth Tank Battalion, 4th Armored Division:

> Instead, the men appeared somewhat beaten, and their eyes had a different look, as though they had been kicked in the stomach...the staff at [Combat Command B, 4th AD] had a report from the division psychiatrist indicating that the combat exhaustion incidence in the division had been rising rapidly. He surmised that this trend was due to numerous causes, such as length of time in combat, constant activity day and night, little rest, incessant rain, lack of hot food, and a holding, defensive mission—not what Armor was designed for.[84]

The pace was particularly hard on men in the independent tank battalions shuffled around to support various Infantry divisions with little rest or breaks in between assignments. "Sufficient time must be allowed for maintenance of equipment during sustained operations," noted the commanding officer of the 191st Tank Battalion. "Tanks cannot continue to pass through Infantry battalion after battalion, leading the attack day after day. Three days of sustained operations has been found to be the

*Photo by Robert Coldwell Sr.*

maximum time without maintenance. After three days, efficiency is greatly reduced due to (tank) breakdown." As to his men:

> Coupled with maintenance on vehicles, tank crews must be allowed some time to rest. It must be realized that tank crews usually must reservice after dark. Radio watches must be continually maintained. Therefore, tank crews do not get as much rest as Infantry troops. If these factors are not considered, battle exhaustion will take a high toll of good tank officers and men. During the past month [September 1944], eight tank platoon leaders were evacuated for battle exhaustion. This could have been practically eliminated, had tank crews been given a day's rest after three or four days' operations.[85]

All men had their breaking points; Capt. Sheppard, who admitted suffering from "battle fatigue" for a week, later spent time in an Army mental hospital in Germany. He remembered one tanker who returned to the ETO after a very uncommon furlough back to the states. "The next tank he got in, they got under artillery fire, and he tore all his fingernails off trying to dig his way through the inside of the tank with his bare hands. Coming back was too much for him."[86]

In the midst of combat Capt. Sheppard, as a tank company commander, had to submit paperwork when his men were wounded and killed in action. Not surprisingly, the Army bureaucracy also required forms when desperate men injured themselves to get out of combat, known as SIWs (Self-Inflicted Wounds). "I'm not going to name names, times, places, or dates, but one man took a hand grenade and stuck his hand out of the turret, released the pin and spoon, and then held onto the grenade. He got evacuated." But on the inevitable paperwork, the cause "went on the records as an enemy mortar":

I did lots of men favors that way, stretching the truth a little bit. There's no advantage to being real truthful about it; it had nothing to do with anything...another time, I had a tank presumably hit by a German mortar and set on fire. But actually, what had happened was they were firing up the little cook stove in the bottom of the tank, and it caught the tank on fire...I let it go as a [wound from an enemy mortar]. We were losing tanks so fast and furious, what's one more tank?"[87]

Reporting to Congress and the public soon after the war, Gen. Marshall acknowledged such "casualties," claiming, "Extreme care is taken to insure that men suffering from mental and nervous disorders resulting from combat are not returned to civil life until they have been given every possible treatment and regained their psychological balance."[88]

Broken tanks, like damaged men, also needed help. "This is not a war of ammunition, tanks, guns, and trucks alone," wrote Ernie Pyle. "It is as much a war of replenishing spare parts to keep them in combat as it is a war of major equipment.... The gasket that leaks, the fan belt that breaks, the nut that is lost...will delay GI Joe on the road to Berlin just as much as if he didn't have a vehicle in which to start."[89]

As brutal tank fighting continued attrition ground down Sherman numbers. By September 1944, the Third Armored Division was down to just 75 running tanks out of its full authorized strength of 232, "a shortfall," observed Max Hastings, "matched in most other formations."[90]

At the same time, damaged M4s sat idle for lack of spare parts, although the Norman roads were littered with salvageable hulks. Mechanics were forbidden to cannibalize the wrecks for usable components. Instead, they were ordered to leave disabled tanks untouched by the side of the road for eventual formal survey (inspection) and recovery, with all the paperwork and red tape that this entailed.

When combat necessity made this delay intolerable GIs refused to wait. Parts were stripped from knocked out tanks to

M4s in action, Belgium, 1944. The tank commander is spotting with binoculars.

*Moving Up* by Howard Brodie.

make others run. Maintenance Sgt. Jim Driscoll, 712th Tank Battalion, recalled "trying to keep the tanks going" in this way. "You could take, say, an oil pressure line off of one and put it on the other one and go with it. So, they kind of fussed at me one time for leaving a tank stripped, but, by stripping that one tank, we had three or four other tanks that were kept going."[91] To maintenance officer Lt. Cooper, "One tank in combat was a lot better than two on the dead line, waiting for spare parts."[92]

Not only tank parts were stripped from burned-out hulks; Max Hastings wrote of GIs "clearing human body parts from damaged tanks":

> In the U.S. Third Armored Division, the repair crews one day balked at addressing a mess of twisted steel and charred flesh that had been towed into the depot. A tall, weedy soldier from the maintenance battalion stepped forward, and surprised his comrades by doing the job single-handed. He said afterward, "I figured somebody had to do it. I have a younger brother who's a rifleman in the First Infantry Division somewhere forward of us. If he was killed, I would like someone to recover his body so it could be given a decent Christian burial."[93]

Two weeks before Operation Overlord, the Army Service Forces Requirements Division warned of the consequences of reducing tank production. A May 22 memo stated, "We should push at once for as many additional medium tanks as we can get in 1944."[94] But Sherman producers like the Fisher Tank Arsenal, the Chrysler Tank Arsenal in Detroit, and the Pressed Steel Car Company were ordered to slow down or stop assembly lines.

In light of the growing supply crisis in France, Gen. Hugh Minton, head of the ASF Production Division, suggested "applying all possible pressure to the producers" to get 300–500 Shermans built by the close of 1944,[95] but it was too late; the shortage would continue until VE Day. Brigadier Ross wrote of a dangerous situation in his October 24 diary entry. "General Holly, in Detroit from Europe, says the U.S. lost 1,400 tanks completely destroyed;

90 percent being burnt out. Tank battalions are down from 54 tanks to ten. It is rather pathetic that the U.S., which at one time was able to produce 4,000 tanks a month, should have its A.G.F. grossly underestimate their probable wastage in battle."[96]

By late 1944, with Roosevelt gifting huge numbers of Lend-Lease weapons to Britain, Russia, France, China, Canada, and others, the American tank shortage had become so acute tanks already assigned to the British had to be repossessed. "General Alexander Gatehouse [of the British Supply Mission]," Ross wrote in his diary for December 12, 1944, four days before the German surprise attack in the Ardennes would further deplete US tanks,

> reports extraordinary goings-on at the International Aid Committee meeting in Washington. The U.S. has grossly underestimated their wastage of tanks. The British reserve has been built up to 90 per cent, while the American is down to only 7 percent.
>
> As a result, our British demands for a further 150 M4s for modification in the U.K. to mount the 17-pounder gun are strenuously opposed. General Gatehouse describes the most "sanguinary" scenes; American brigadier generals banging the table and screaming they will not give the British another tank. The British, having foregone three months' assignments [of tanks], consider 150 a small request.[97]

In the European Theater, the Supreme Commander was feeling the heat. "Don't forget that I take a beating every day," Eisenhower wrote to his wife Mamie on November 12, from Gueux, France. "Entirely aside from my own problems, I constantly receive letters from bereaved mothers, sisters, and wives that are begging me to send their men home, or at least out of the battle zone…it's all so terrible, so awful, that I constantly wonder how 'civilization' can stand war at all."[98]

But as bad as the losses and shortage of tanks and tankers in the ETO was, the worst was still to come.

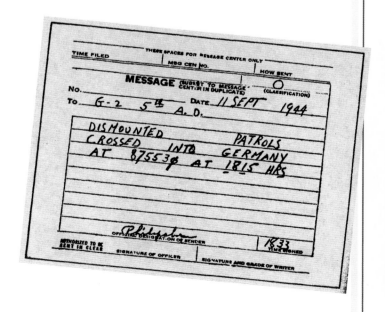

# Chapter 7

# "WIN THE WAR WITH THE M4"

## How American Armor Was Represented to the Wartime Public

Today, a cursory glance at wartime advertisements, press releases, newspapers, and magazines depicting American tanks shows that for the sake of home front morale, truth was the first casualty of war. While dismissing or suppressing warnings from GIs overseas using inferior equipment, War Department officials, politicians, manufacturers, and civilian journalists depicted American weapons as the world's best. They celebrated the vast numbers of tanks being built while avoiding the fact they were years behind Germany's, and fell down in at least two of the three elements of successful tank design. This was the essence of Roosevelt's "Arsenal of Democracy" propaganda: quantity over quality and form over substance.

By 1939 standards, the M3 Stuart light tank was a decent design, but by 1943, under-gunned and under-armored, it was withdrawn from first line service after losses in North Africa and Tunisia. Yet the 1944 book *American Tanks and Tank Destroyers* boasted light tanks were still being

> Our fighting men…are the best judges of the weapons with which American industry is supplying them. They know just how fast the General Sherman M4 medium tank will go—how accurate that seventy-five gun is—and whether or not direct hits will bounce off the armor plate. The test of action in actual service gives them the final answer—the only one that matters.[1]
>
> —Wartime advertisement by Fisher Body Works, one of the M4's builders

"manufactured in great numbers. Right now, in just one company, the American Car and Foundry Company, fourteen light tanks are being made every day. In that company a light tank is rolling out every forty-five minutes."[4]

On another page, while conceding the M3's "37mm gun is not powerful enough for fighting medium tanks,"[5] the author praises its "splendid record."[6] Earlier books bragged of Stuarts "being turned out in unbelievable numbers…. They'll have to [be], if American industry is to reach President Roosevelt's goal of 45,000 tanks in 1942."[7]

In magazine advertisements, Cadillac depicted the M5 light tank—a slightly improved version of the M3—as a world beating "surprise weapon." Assigned one during stateside training, Capt. Al Irzyk was impressed by its "twin Cadillac engines and automatic transmission," but "on the verge of combat" he had second thoughts:

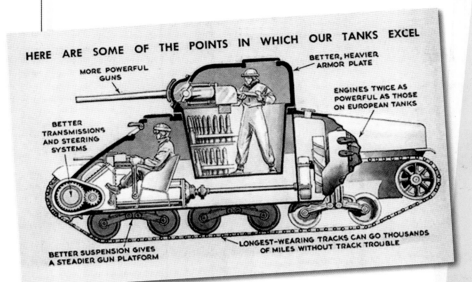

HERE ARE SOME OF THE POINTS IN WHICH OUR TANKS EXCEL

MORE POWERFUL GUNS

BETTER, HEAVIER ARMOR PLATE

ENGINES TWICE AS POWERFUL AS THOSE ON EUROPEAN TANKS

BETTER TRANSMISSIONS AND STEERING SYSTEMS

BETTER SUSPENSION GIVES A STEADIER GUN PLATFORM

LONGEST-WEARING TRACKS CAN GO THOUSANDS OF MILES WITHOUT TRACK TROUBLE

# Loaded for War

Take a good look at the picture below. It shows a Santa Fe train loaded for war.

That war train is ready to roll. It is *going through*.

In railroad language, it has the right-of-way over everything else on the line.

So it must be with *all* American transportation until this war job is done.

## Victory Rides on Wheels

For this is essentially a war of rolling wheels . . .

Millions of men and millions of tons of vital foods, raw materials, and finished products must be moved swiftly and surely, where and when they are needed.

*Stop the wheels that move them,*

*and we stop all that floats and flies as well.*

That is why, on the Santa Fe, movements essential to the war effort are topping the greatest transportation job in all our history. They *must* come first, beyond argument or selfish interest.

★ During 1942, *with 26% fewer locomotives*, Santa Fe moved 122% *more freight ton-miles*, and 79% *more military and civilian passenger-miles* than in 1918, during the First World War. The War Department, the ODT, and civilian shippers and travelers everywhere are cooperating 100% with the railroads of America in making records like this possible.

True, it was very mobile, fast, and could still run like a scared rabbit, and would enable me to get around the battlefield quickly. But being light and fast, it was also very thin-skinned, and would protect only from small arms fire and shell fragments. Any heavier projectile would zip through it like the proverbial knife through butter.

The greatest shortcoming was its gun. It was a poor excuse for the main gun of a tank. The gun was only a 37mm, with a small projectile, low muzzle velocity, and consequently, a very limited armor piercing capacity.[8]

So many M5s would be lost in Normandy that other than scouting and reconnaissance duties it was pulled from the frontlines. For stateside audiences, it was depicted as an exceptional tank. Similar praise was heaped on the M8, an M5 variant with a short-barreled 75mm howitzer:

Under the direction, and with the cooperation of Army Ordnance, Cadillac has developed, and is building, what have proved to be two of the most effective pieces of armament in the Arsenal of Democracy.

One is the M5 Light Tank, a fast, quick, highly maneuverable weapon, armed with a high velocity, 37mm cannon. This tough, speedy, hard-hitting tank is one of America's great "surprise weapons" ideal for upsetting enemy formations. Like a speedy halfback, it darts through the slightest opening in the line, or "runs the ends," as the need may be. It is almost as fast as a motor car.

The other is the M8 mounting the Army's 75mm Howitzer cannon. Utilizing the same chassis as the M5, it gives to demolition artillery a degree of mobility it has never known before. With this weapon, big guns can follow their targets—keep the position from which they can do the most good.

...The quickness with which these peacetime units were sent to war not only attests to their inborn quality of design and construction, but it indicates the splendid

SERVING THE SOUTHWEST FOR 75 YEARS

Santa Fe

*Courtesy Henry Smith. Photo by Robert Coldwell Sr.*

manner in which Army Ordnance has utilized the nation's resources to astound the world with its armament program.[9]

While one would expect a tank builder to engage in such hyperbole for civilian consumption, the Army joined in as well.

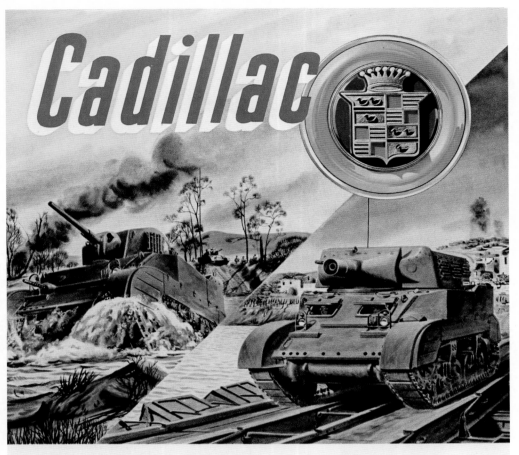

## Some go Through – Some go Over !

Under the direction, and with the cooperation, of Army Ordnance—Cadillac has developed, and is building, what have proved to be two of the most effective pieces of armament in the Arsenal of Democracy.

One is the M-5 Light Tank—a fast, quick, highly-maneuverable weapon, armed with a high velocity, 37 mm. cannon. This tough, speedy, hard-hitting tank is one of America's great "surprise weapons"—ideal for upsetting enemy formations. Like a speedy halfback, it darts through the slightest opening in the line,

or "runs the ends," as the need may be. It is almost as fast as a motor car.

The other is the M-8 mounting the Army's 75 mm. Howitzer cannon. Utilizing the same chassis as the M-5, it gives to demolition artillery a degree of mobility it has never known before. With this weapon, big guns can follow their targets—keep the position from which they can do the most good.

The two units that give these weapons their power and maneuverability were developed by Cadillac in peacetime: the Cadillac V-type

engine and the Hydra-Matic transmission.

The quickness with which these peacetime units were sent to war not only attests their inborn quality of design and construction—but it indicates the splendid manner in which Army Ordnance has utilized the nation's resources to astound the world with its armament program.

*Every Sunday Afternoon . . . GENERAL MOTORS SYMPHONY OF THE AIR—NBC Network*

CADILLAC MOTOR CAR DIVISION     GENERAL MOTORS CORPORATION

LET'S ALL

BACK THE ATTACK

BUY WAR BONDS

*Courtesy Henry Smith. Photo by Robert Coldwell Sr.*

rounds among cynical GIs that the only way to hurt a German with the 37mm gun was to give him an enema with it). But here, readers were assured it could "pierce the thick hide of the dinosaur of the modern battlefield."[12]

Perhaps for civilian consumption, *He's In The Armored Force Now* included the story of an experimental 37mm shell being tested that flew so high and so far that it left the confines of Fort Knox, crossing Kentucky state lines to impact in an Indiana farmer's barnyard. Thus, a French weapon that originated in the last war recently withdrawn from frontline service is depicted as a war winner: "Unofficially, when it was found exactly how far away from Fort Knox the farmer lived, there was much glee and praise from the military at Knox for the performance of the 37mm gun."[13] It is unlikely survivors of the Battle of Sidi-bou-Zid, during which American Stuart light tanks with 37mm guns were almost powerless against the German opposition, would share that "glee."

The M3 medium tank, while an improvement over past designs, was a hastily designed stopgap measure until the Sherman could be introduced,

Shortly before Germany—recognizing that small, lightly armed and armored light tanks were obsolete—introduced the Tiger heavy tank, a book about the US Armored Forces hailed the M5 as "nearly mechanically perfect a vehicle as modern military science has yet designed."[10]

While acknowledging "the increased power of anti-tank guns has made it necessary to use heavier guns as well as heavier armor on tanks," long after the Germans had adapted powerful 88mm and high-velocity 75mm guns for tank use, the authors praised the M3 and M5's 37mm main gun—derided by GIs as a "pea shooter" or "door knocker"—as "a weapon of high power to give it armor penetration."[11] This "high-powered weapon" was similar to the gun that Gen. McNair had embraced in its towed, two-wheeled form with disastrous results as the basis of the tank destroyers.

*He's In The Armored Force Now* outlined the training and equipment a new tanker would receive and use. Tankers in the North African theater watched 37mm shells bounce off German tanks, good for little more than nuisance value (a joke made the

but when some of the first ones rolled out of Chrysler's Detroit Tank Arsenal in 1941, they were depicted as seemingly unstoppable. In staged photo opportunities reproduced in newspapers across the country, dramatic pictures showed them crushing logs and other obstacles.

The M3 was a much needed step forward in American tank design, but its crews suffered when American tankers met Rommel's Afrika Korps. Yet according to Chief of Ordnance Campbell in a 1944 mass market book *American Tanks and Tank Destroyers*, "The Germans who have faced our M3 mediums would be the first, I am certain, to state that we have in the M3 medium a tank which makes the going uncommonly rough for them. We know by actual test what our high-velocity 75mm shell can do to German medium tanks. We blast big holes in them at ranges beyond which their guns can reach."[14]

This would be news to tankers who survived debacles in North Africa and Tunisia, burned out of their Lees by the fire from a "Mark IV Special" powerful main gun. Note that Campbell also refers to German *medium* tanks—not heavies like the Tiger.

# 30 TONS—geared for fast action!

*MACK BUILDS AN 8,000 POUND TRANSMISSION GIVING THIS MONSTER TANK A 35 M.P.H. SPEED!*

Army M-3 tank, "land battleship" of America's modern mechanized army. Armed with cannon and machine guns.

**T**he Army had to have a transmission—one capable of converting the speed of a 400 h.p. airplane engine into the smashing force of a 30-ton tank. *Mack is building it* —a mighty 8,000 pound gearbox, the largest ever manufactured in quantity production—more than 300 times the weight of a passenger car transmission.

The largest trucks in Army service are gigantic six-wheel Macks. Great fleets of Mack dumpers are clearing the way for air-base construction at defense outposts. Mack skill and resources contribute in more than a score of ways to America's military might.

*The Tough Jobs Go to Mack!*

MACK TRUCKS, INC., NEW YORK, N. Y.

## Mack
### TRUCKS
### 1 TO 45 TONS

**MAKERS OF WORLD-FAMOUS GASOLINE AND DIESEL-POWERED TRUCKS, BUSES, FIRE APPARATUS AND MARINE ENGINES**

7

*Courtesy Henry Smith. Photo by Robert Coldwell Sr.*

Presumably he is referring to the Panzer Mark IV and not the Mark V (Panther); a comparison between the Panther and the Lee could not be made, because the outclassed M3 medium was retired from frontline service before the Panther's debut. Campbell's careful word choice allowed him to avoid how American tanks were faring against the Tiger, as well as the lack of American heavy tanks. Thus spoke the Chief of Ordnance, charged with keeping up with enemy advances and supplying GIs with the best weapons.

As to the Sherman, *American Tanks and Tank Destroyers* assured readers that it "has often engaged and defeated the far heavier Mark VI [Tiger], which was the pride of the Nazis in Tunisia."[15] Furthermore, "With its up-to-date equipment and its heavy gun, the M-4 is a tank of exceptional power. In battles and maneuvers it has again and again proved its sturdiness. We heard of one M4 mishap in the African desert. The tank commander radioed headquarters that he had run into a German mine. Headquarters asked, 'What's happened, much damage?' The tank commander replied, 'Not a thing, but it knocked my hat off.'"[16]

Regarding the Sherman's risk of fire, surviving crews who had been burned out of their tanks would be surprised to read, "the M4 is equipped with modern devices for safety and comfort. It has, for instance, an excellent fire detector, which flashes a red warning light. At this signal the driver knows that a flame has touched one of the detectors in the engine compartment. He pulls the fire extinguisher and puts out the fire before it can do any real damage."[17]

While Elizabeth Conger's book does recognize "the need for heavier armor or greater speed and bigger guns,"[18] it also claims, "This need is being satisfied in large measure by the introduction of tank destroyers." "Beyond a doubt," the book also asserted, "the tank destroyer is the answer to the tank."[19]

After the war, one would hope for more honesty, since the need to prop up home front morale had disappeared. According to the Chrysler Corporation's self-congratulating 1946 retrospective, the M3 medium they had built became "The tank which whipped Rommel... the tanks which first turned the tide of the war in North Africa for the British."[20]

Fisher Body Works built Shermans and boasted about them in a magazine advertisement:

Our fighting men have a tough job to do, and they are doing it. They are finding out, in all parts of the world, what they have to work with. They are the best judges of the weapons with which American industry is supplying them.

They know just how fast the General Sherman M-4 medium tank will go, how accurate that seventy-five is, and whether or not direct hits will bounce off the armor plate.

The test of action in actual service gives them the final answer—the only one that matters.

Here at Fisher, we want to make sure it's the right answer. That's why we give our tanks, bombers, and anti-aircraft guns the best we've got in us. We're using every craft we've mastered, every special skill we've developed, and they add up to an impressive number to give our armed forces that all-important edge.

*Courtesy Henry Smith. Photo by Robert Coldwell Sr.*

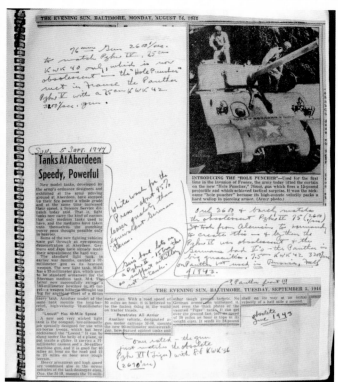

A page from Ordnance Colonel George Jarrett's "Little Green Book" on the tank scandal, in which he damns Army and Roosevelt administration propaganda as "White wash for the press." *Courtesy US Army Military History Institute, Carlisle Barracks, Pennsylvania, photo by Robert Coldwell Sr.*

Come the pinches, craftsmanship always counts. And it's only natural that our fighting men should rate such craftsmanship as "better than a rabbit's foot."[21]

On September 5, 1944, "Tanks At Aberdeen Speedy, Powerful" appeared in the *Baltimore Sun*. To Col. George Jarrett—then evaluating captured weapons at Aberdeen—the article's boastful figures were a "whitewash for the press." Surely exaggerating, a frustrated Jarrett rated US weapons as "about 95% lesser quality than equivalent German items."[22] By April 1945, little had changed in what Jarrett privately derided as "our sales program." An Aberdeen press release appeared in the *Baltimore Sun* as "M-36 'Sluggers' Favored By 10 To 1 In Combat." In it, Aberdeen's Director of Ordnance Research and Development Col. George Eddy boasted that "When M-36 'sluggers' go into action against German *Panzer* tanks, the enemy has only one chance in ten to win." Eddy claimed the 703rd Tank Destroyer Battalion, attached to the 3rd Armored Division, "had destroyed ten enemy tanks for each M-36 tank destroyer loss."[23]

Notice the article does not specify which model Panzers. While the M36 was the best-armed TD of the war, with a 90mm gun that could beat the Mark IV and challenge the Tiger (when firing improved HVAP ammunition, frequently in short supply), dueling well-armored Panthers or King Tigers was another story. Frontline tests made by the same 703rd Tank Destroyer Battalion on captured tanks found that under some conditions, the Jackson's

The Armored Force is the most powerful of America's Army Ground Forces…. America's answer to blitz war is the Armoraider and his tank…the best craftsmanship has gone into making the guns with which soldiers fight…generally speaking, our guns are the best that can be put together.[2]
—Capt. Addison F. McGhee Jr.

gun had problems punching through the Panther's armor, especially the King Tiger's.[24]

TD men finally had a gun able to take on the Tiger, but the M-36 was only built in small numbers. Through much of its short service career it was handicapped by a serious ammunition shortage. Even as home front newsreels celebrated American industry, depicting busy factories with long assembly lines bristling with weapons for Allies around the world, those same factories were unable to supply GIs with the required numbers of improved ammo they needed. The same "Arsenal of Democracy" able to build hi-tech atomic bombs and B-29s failed its tankers in something as basic as adequate production of tank ammunition.

Publications written for civilian consumption inadvertently reflected the Army's internal confusion and debate over the role of tanks. Even as one book recognized that "with the widespread use of armor-piercing shells comes the need for heavier armor or greater speed and bigger guns,"[25] it repeated the high-level prejudice against heavy tanks like the T26. According to *American Tanks and Tank Destroyers* (which tactfully described the failed M6 heavy tank of 1941 as "rarely seen by the public, because it is not in constant use"[26]), "We have been slow to introduce our heavy tanks…. Our roads and bridges are not strong enough to support their weight, and so far, these tanks have not been needed. The mediums have been doing the work successfully."[27] This "bridge excuse" became one of the "explanations" for the tank scandal, especially after Gen.Marshall used it in 1945. After the war and

An M4 crosses a temporary bridge.

over decades, the myth that heavy tanks were not needed or too heavy hardened into "fact." This view presumes that adding a more powerful gun and better armor would make a tank slow or awkward, which was not necessarily the case. And if heavy tanks were unable to cross bridges and roads, one wonders how the Germans were able to use Tigers and Panthers on the roads and bridges of North Africa, Tunisia, Sicily, Italy, Normandy, and Germany.

That such fallacies and contradictions could appear in a mass market book reflects the confusion over armor doctrine and design that characterized American tanks in the war. Quoting an *American Magazine* article "American Workers Licked Rommel," the same book states "early in the [North] African campaign" Winston Churchill personally informed Roosevelt "that the 75mm gun was no match for the German 88mm… gun."[28] Then why, observant readers must have wondered two or three years later, were the majority of Sherman tanks in action still armed with the inadequate "75"?

Overseas, confusion over the role of tanks led to their occasional use in a passive, indirect fire role, lobbing shells from a distance. Back home, they were presented as aggressive, of-

> The patriotic baloney that the Sherman was the best tank in the world was widely bandied about in orientation lectures and in the press. It was demoralizing for the tank crews to listen to such nonsense, after they had paid a high price to learn otherwise.[3]
>
> —Armor historian Steve Zaloga

fensive weapons. According to Gen. David Barr of the General Staff Corps in 1944's *The Armored Forces of the United States Army*:

> American Armored fighting units…strike hard, powerful, mechanized blows at our Axis enemies. Striking through weak points made in the enemy's defenses, they seek more and more points of weakness to overwhelm Axis forces with their tremendous speed, drive, and crushing power. The Armored Forces have increased the whole power of our great fighting teams of the ground more than any other recent development of warfare…. Speeding into battle…the Armored Forces soldier has already overrun some of our Axis foes.[29]

Another book asks, "What role does the Armored Force play in the scheme of things?"[30] According to *War Department Training Circular No. 4* (1940), "The primary role of an Armored Force… is offensive operations against vital objectives in rear of the hostile main battle positions, usually reached by a penetration

*Courtesy Henry Smith. Photo by Robert Coldwell Sr.*

*Photo by Robert Coldwell Sr.*

## MORE POWER FOR TANKS TODAY— CHEAPER POWER FOR AMERICA TOMORROW!

America's tanks pack a powerful push as well as a powerful punch. And more times than most people know, this push comes from a General Motors Diesel Engine.

What's more, you'll also find these rugged, hard-working power plants in landing barges, patrol vessels, military trucks, construction tractors and many other wartime jobs where sturdy dependability is required.

They burn cheaper fuel and use less

of it—operate with a minimum of attention.

Of course the needs of war are taking every engine that even our expanded production can make, but when peace comes America will profit—through low-cost power for many new applications.

So while now GM Diesels are adding strength to America's fighting arm, they will be one of the important contributions to better days after victory is ours.

*With each war there seems to develop a new era in transportation. And in this one there is the epoch-making General Motors Diesel Locomotive, tried, proved and providing a new pattern of transportation, keyed to the greater days ahead.*

| | |
|---|---|
| **ENGINES** .....15 to 250 H.P..... DETROIT DIESEL ENGINE DIVISION, Detroit, Mich. | |
| **ENGINES** ..150 to 2000 H.P... CLEVELAND DIESEL ENGINE DIVISION, Cleveland, Ohio | |
| **LOCOMOTIVES** ..................... ELECTRO-MOTIVE DIVISION, La Grange, Ill. | |

*Courtesy Henry Smith. Photo by Robert Coldwell Sr.*

of a weak portion of the front, or by the encirclement of an open flank." The book continued, "The Armored Division is not suitable for defensive action and, as such, should be relieved of this type of mission as soon as possible."[31] But even as these words saw print, American armor was handicapped by obsolete doctrine and defensive tactics that ceded the initiative to the enemy, seeking ever elusive ideal conditions to position tanks and TDs like pieces on an orderly chess board. American armor was being misused, held back instead of cut loose to aggressively fight German tanks.

Decades later, hindsight is 20/20, but the author, Capt. McGhee (a tanker himself), inadvertently noted of one of the biggest problems with the Army's anti-tank and armor doctrine in WWII, "All plans can be drawn up in secrecy, filed away in a strong-box, guarded constantly; then when you bring them out, you often find there is absolutely no correlation between the 'perfect' plans and the situation at hand."[32]

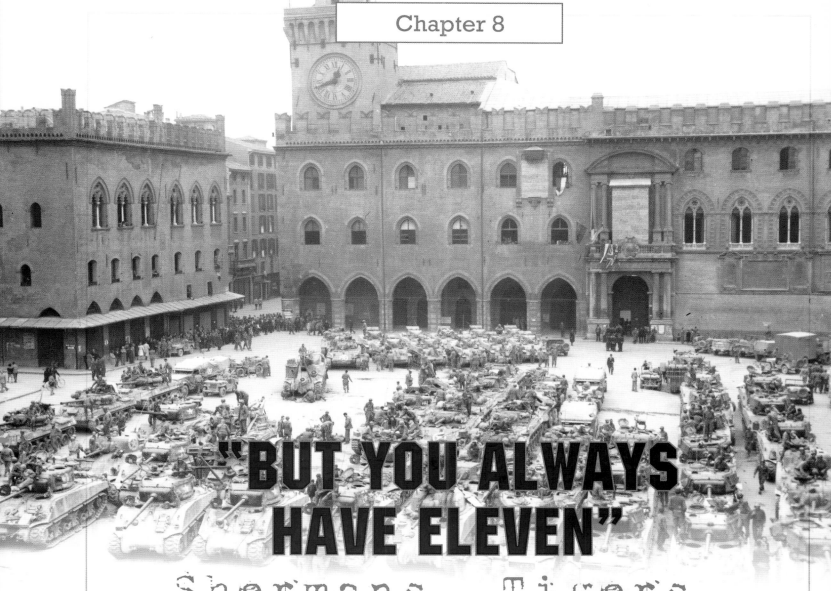

# Chapter 8

# "BUT YOU ALWAYS HAVE ELEVEN"

## Shermans, Tigers, and Panthers: Some Comparisons

Today, the Sherman is inevitably compared to the Tiger and Panther as if they were equal contemporaries, but a more accurate German equivalent would be the workhorse *Panzer IV*: like the M4, an unglamorous but versatile medium tank that was built in large numbers and served throughout the war. Yet most civilians born generations after 1945 know the powerful cats, not the Panzer IV.

The Tiger evoked an aura that the Sherman and Panzer IV failed to inspire, a combination of fear and admiration that has never dissipated. To British armor historian David Fletcher:

One does not have to go far to find the reasons for this. In the first place, it was for nearly three years the biggest and most powerful armoured fighting vehicle in service anywhere in the world. It fought a galaxy of Allied armies on four major fronts and usual-

If such a choice were possible, I would prefer to fight in the Tiger or Panther tank rather than the present U.S. Sherman medium tank.[1]
—Lt. Col. Wilson Hawkins, CO 3rd Battalion, 67th Armor Regiment

ly came off best. And what is more, it looked the part. Broad shouldered and apparently irresistible, it seemed to crush, or blow to smithereens, everything in its path while, gathered about it, was the sinister, impersonal martial efficiency of the German war machine.

"The Tiger," concluded Fletcher, "was the armoured manifestation of the Jackboot."[4]

Complicated and costly to build and maintain, Tigers existed in far smaller numbers than the M4 and *Panzer IV*. "Consider whether it is worthwhile," asked a captured German document dated March 21, 1944, evaluated by the British, "to employ heavy tanks, or whether you couldn't do the job just as well and more cheaply with other weapons! Every Tiger costs the German people 300,000 work hours."[5] Their 55-ton weight, largely due to thick armor, made them

Photo by Robert Coldwell Sr.

At the Henschel factory, Kassel, Germany, a new Tiger I is lowered onto a flatcar for shipment to the front. *Courtesy German Federal Archive*

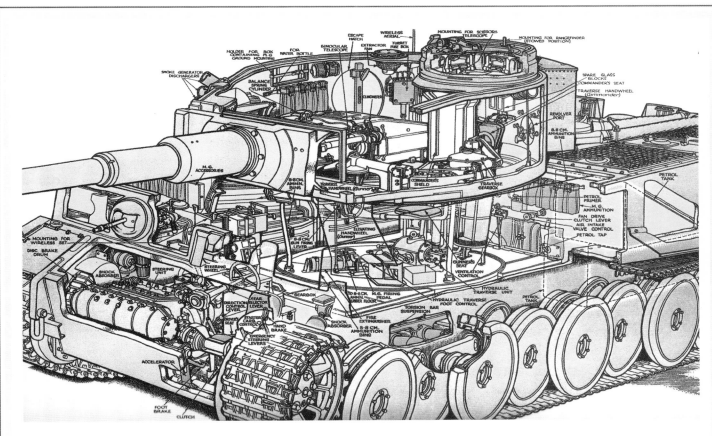

Interior of a Tiger I: Cutaway view showing crew positions and ammo storage. While the Sherman used two vertical levers to steer and turn, the Tiger had a steering wheel. Unlike the M4's powered turret, the Tiger's was traversed manually, one of the few advantages an M4 gunner had over his German counterpart in a duel- that powered turret might give him a few extra seconds to get off the first shot. But as many Allied tank gunners found, even if they got the drop on a Tiger or Panther, the round might bounce harmlessly off of the effective German armor plate. *Photo by Robert Coldwell Sr., courtesy US Army Military History Institute, Carlisle Barracks, Pennsylvania.*

sluggish; German tankers called them "the furniture van."[6] But in the minds of Allied soldiers their invulnerability grew to epic proportions. To frightened GIs, the Tiger's main gun barrel seemed as long as a telephone pole. As a British Infantryman recalled, "In a tank-against-tank battle, we were decidedly mercenary and bet on the Jerries, unless our tanks outnumbered them something fierce. A Tiger could sit all day just like a chunk of solid steel, soaking up the punishment, and then blast off one 88 round and put paid to the pestering Sherman."[7]

Cpl. John Irwin described the "Tiger terror" that struck new tankers arriving in the ETO. Feeling "extremely vulnerable" riding on top of a Sherman, he feared the Tiger's "super-versatile cannon with such muzzle velocity, even without armor-piercing ammo, it could send a shot in one side and out the other of a Sherman...I had seen only a dormant example of an 88 at Fort Knox, and had never even heard one fire. And I did not desire that pleasure at this time."[8]

"Those German 88s," recalled Tank gunner Sgt. Jim Rothschadl, "They could hit the front of a tank, and that 88 shell would come right out the back end. They had double the muzzle velocity of our 75s. Double. The 88 was a powerful thing."[9] Coupled with the Tiger's firepower was its impressive armor protection. Sherman commander Sgt. Nat Frankel wrote of the Moselle River fighting:

The Sherman tanks were a disgrace to the U.S. Army. They were greatly inferior in armor and firepower to German tanks. I lost four destroyed by enemy guns.[2]
—Cpl. Bert Close, who served in the tank crew of Sgt. Lafayette Pool, 3rd AD, the top American tank ace of the war

A monster of a Tiger was pivoting not thirty yards in front of me. We fired three shots at it, figuring to force it backward.

All three shots bounced off the side and ricocheted harmlessly. What do I see but a German officer sticking his head out of the turret and smiling at me! He then proceeded to pull a white handkerchief out of his pocket and wipe it against the side of his machine, where our bullets had skidded. He smiled again as if to forgive me for scratching his property; then he replaced his handkerchief in his pocket.[10]

Capt. Jack Sheppard recalled dueling a Tiger:

Though we weren't looking for tank battles...we were coming over a hill down towards this shallow valley with a creek in the bottom. Up on the other bank, almost to the top of the hill, was a German Tiger tank shooting its 88 at anything that moved on our side of the hill, and our powers-that-be decided that we had to knock it out.

So we fired everything we had at it. The Artillery fired everything they had; the corps artillery, which included 155-millimeter and eight-inch guns, fired them

Konigstiger at the Tank Museum, Bovington, Dorset, UK. Notice the rough-textured Zimmerit anti-magnetic coating. *Massimo Foti*

at it. It never moved, and it continued to shoot. Eventually it quit shooting, and when we finally took the area, I personally climbed into the Tiger. It was out of gasoline. It was still usable, and the forest was cleared for a hundred yards all the way around it. There wasn't a tree left standing. There were only dents in the Tiger where our rounds had hit the metal and ricocheted off. We didn't even break the track. They just let it sit out there as a pillbox, used up their ammunition, and left.[11]

Although only some 500 were built, the rare *Konig* (King or Royal) Tiger inspired still more fear, especially in the Ardennes. It was "virtually invulnerable to frontal attacks,"[12] and GIs imagined them everywhere. "Anyone running into a big enemy tank, " Col. Jarrett noted, "at once assumed it was a King Tiger," although "German factories were unable to supply them in adequate numbers…. The King Tiger was in effect a scaled-up Panther," so they were mistaken for each other.

The Panther's [high-velocity 75mm KwK 42 L/70] gun was so capable of astonishing destructive effect on a Sherman, that it was just naturally assumed to be the work of a King Tiger. The same kind of destruction was possible from the 88mm gun on the King Tiger, but due

to its heavier projectile, it could accomplish this at greater distances. Many instances exist where 88mm shells fired by the King Tiger went completely through a Sherman tank, side-to-side, or front to back.[13]

But the King Tiger's intimidating bulk came at a price. Although "the heaviest and most powerfully armed tank to see combat in significant numbers in the war, with a weight of 69 tons, 150mm of armor on the glacis, and 185mm on the front of the turret," it was slower than the Tiger I and "its power-to-weight ratio, maneuverability, and ground pressure were all significantly worse. Hauling all that weight, too, resulted in reliability problems for the overtaxed engine and transmission."[14] A December 6, 1944, article in the US press (appearing days before King Tigers wreaked havoc in the Ardennes) noted the King Tiger's "additional weight has two distinct disadvantages. It forces the tank to be slower than the Shermans, and it creates the necessity of reinforcing bridges over which the tank must pass."[15]

By the Normandy invasion, while the Tiger I may have attracted more notoriety, there were far more Panthers, and they were more advanced than the Tiger, essentially a scaled-up *Panzer IV*. First encountered by GIs in the Anzio campaign, War Department publications called the Panther "probably the most successful tank [the Germans] have produced."[16] Its long-barreled, high-velocity main gun fired at 3,066 fps, compared to the 75mm Shermans' paltry 2,050.[17] Although weighing almost 45 tons, it could exceed 30 miles an hour under ideal conditions, and its slanted armor (80mm in front, 50mm on the flanks) could shrug off hits.[18]

Col. Bill Triplett, Second and Seventh Armored Divisions, praised the "neat lines of the Panther," with its muzzle-braked 75mm gun, as "even more attractive than the Tiger. This one looks like it could move as well as shoot," he told a captain:

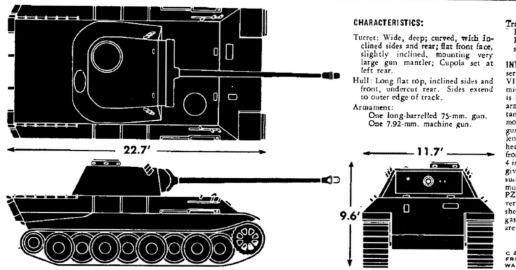

**GERMAN** ✠    # PZKW V TANK "PANTHER"

**CHARACTERISTICS:**

Turret: Wide, deep; curved, with inclined sides and rear; flat front face, slightly inclined, mounting very large gun mantlet; Cupola set at left rear.

Hull: Long flat top, inclined sides and front, undercut rear. Sides extend to outer edge of track.

Armament:
One long-barrelled 75-mm. gun.
One 7.92-mm. machine gun.

Traction: Full track; eight (double) large, overlapping bogie wheels; large driving sprocket in front, small idler in rear.

**INTEREST DATA:** The German tank series is finally completed from I to VI with the appearance of the long-missing PZKW V. The new vehicle is fast, well armored, and powerfully armed. It resembles the Soviet T-34 tank. The "Panther" has the same motor as the 63-ton "Tiger." The gun is a new weapon with an over-all length of 18 feet 2 inches. The heaviest armor—the gun shield and front of the turret—is approximately 4 inches thick. Sharply sloping armor gives increased protection on many surfaces. The Soviets find this tank much easier to knock out than the PZKW VI, despite its good maneuverability. Incendiary armor-piercing shells are especially effective against gasoline tanks and ammunition which are just in rear of the driver.

C 2, 22 APRIL 1944
FROM DATA CURRENTLY AVAILABLE
WAR DEPARTMENT FM 30-40

22.7'    11.7'    9.6'

SPEED - 31 MPH    BRIDGE - 45 TONS
FORD - 16.0'    TRENCH - 10.0'
GRADIENT - 38°    STEP - 2.5'

*Photo by Robert Coldwell Sr.*

Restored Panther in running condition at the Musée des Blindés, Saumur, France. *Massimo Foti*

Yes, Sir. The Panther is probably the best tank built. It's fast, agile, and has a low ground pressure.... Frontal armor sloped, so that we see our shells bounce off. That high-velocity 75 will go through our apron or turret on the M4, and the muzzle brake shoots the smoke to each side, so the gunner can shoot as fast as the loader can shove in the ammunition. The only way we can take a Panther or Tiger is to keep him interested in front, and sneak a tank or tank destroyer around to hit him in the side.[19]

To Maj. Al Irzyk, 8th Tank Battalion, 4th Armored Division:

The Panther was an absolutely outstanding tank with an outstanding gun. It had a 75mm gun as did the Sherman medium tank, but there the similarity abruptly ended. The Sherman 75mm gun had a short barrel with an extremely low muzzle velocity, while the Panther's 75mm gun had a very long barrel with a very high muzzle velocity.

The armor on the Panther front slope plate and turret was thicker than that on the Sherman. The Panther, thus, won handily on both counts. It had a more powerful gun, and less metal to penetrate in the Sherman.

Conversely, the Sherman had a far less powerful gun, and more metal to penetrate in the Panther. As an example, the Panther high-velocity twenty-three inch shell (over a third longer than the Sherman's) could penetrate the Sherman's three-inch turret armor at far greater ranges than the low velocity, fourteen-inch 75mm Sherman round could pierce the Panther's four-inch thick turret. Face to face, the Panther could knock out a Sherman before it could get close enough to fire effectively.[20]

According to Col. Jarrett, "When the Sherman encountered a Panther in Italy and the ETO, it was so hopelessly outclassed as to be worse than a sitting duck...the Panther roamed at will with a 75mm gun that frankly outclassed the gun on the Sherman tank by a velocity of approximately 1,230 feet per second. It is hard for one to appreciate such a fact, but it meant, in simple language, practically 2 German shells could be on their way for every one American."[21]

Maj. Brendan Phibbs, MD, a field surgeon with the 714th Tank Battalion, described a duel between a Panther and a Sherman equipped with the new 76mm main gun. The M4 fired three rounds first that landed "swiftly and accurately, right on the Panther's front slope-plate." But the hits bounced off:

A Panther in Paris, 1944. *Courtesy German Federal Archives*

As an angry tanker yelled "Ping-Pong balls! Goddamn fucking Ping-Pong balls!" over the radio network, the Panther fired a shot that penetrated the Sherman. It continued to rake the M4 with fire from front to rear, knocking it out and killing one man. Phibbs, recalling the horror of walking up to knocked out American tanks and being hit with the smell of burning flesh, learned to approach them upwind.[22]

The Panther combined firepower, armor, and mobility, with advanced features like hydraulically operated brakes and synchromesh gears. Yet Germany's best tank, physically larger than the Tiger, "was always portrayed as the lesser tank. It was one of the curiosities of the war that the Tiger's legend grew faster than its kills. There were only three weak Tiger battalions in all of France, but they were reported to be everywhere. Panthers outnumbered Tigers by at least four to one, knocked out more Allied armor, and overran more Infantry, but never inspired quite the same terror."[23] Sgt. Henry Giles, a combat engineer, recorded in his wartime journal a tank commander's insistence that while "it took four of our Shermans to equal one of their Panthers," the notorious Tiger tank was worth "about eight" Shermans.[24]

Although far heavier than the M4, the Panther was maneuverable. "I saw where some Panther tanks crossed a muddy field," Cpl. Emery Fazzini observed, "without sinking the tracks more than five inches, while we in the M4 started across the same field, the same day, and bogged down."[25] To Col. Jarrett, "The Germans had realized the importance of track design, and as their tanks became heavier, a well-thought-out track was developed. This afforded an excellent ability to move over poor ground; in fact, better than the track designs of many Allied vehicles. The 47-ton Panther could move over any terrain, and in many instances over ground which mired Sherman tanks of only 30–35 tons."[26]

Even in rough terrain, Tigers and Panthers could turn quickly along their tracks, setting up for long distance shots at mired Shermans. Gen. James Gavin, who led the 82nd Airborne Division, wrote of the wrecks on the narrow, crooked Kall Trail during the infamous Hurtgen Forest battle in Germany, "a shambles of wrecked vehicles and abandoned tanks. The first tanks that had attempted to go down the trail had evidently slid off and thrown their tracks. In some cases, the tanks had been pushed off the track, and in the bottom of the canyon there were four abandoned

REPORT ON

# Pz Kw VI
*(Tiger)*
## Model E

### PART I.
*General Description*

*Military College of Science*
**SCHOOL OF TANK TECHNOLOGY**
Chobham Lane   Chertsey

*January 1944*

tank destroyers and five disabled and abandoned tanks."[27] Eventually, the M4A3E8 ("Easy Eight") Sherman was fielded with an improved Horizontal Volute Spring Suspension (HVSS), but it arrived late in the war, and in small numbers.

German tanks combined destructive ability and crew protection. In 1942, according to Max Hastings, Germany's Minister of Production Albert Speer had reasoned the Nazis could not match America's vast industrial potential, so while the US mass produced obsolete designs, Germany stressed quality over quantity.[28]

Tank commander Otto Carius, who allegedly destroyed 150 Soviet tanks, called the Tiger "the most ideal tank that I was acquainted with.... The strength of a tank lies in its armor, its mobility, and finally, in its armament. These three factors have to be weighed against each other so a maximum in performance is achieved. This ideal appeared to be realized in our Tiger."[29]

Many Allied models (and the Tiger) used flat, vertical plates of side armor, but the Panther's, copying the Soviet T-34, were slanted at a thirty-degree angle for more protection. Shots that would penetrate a Sherman bounced off a Panther. American armor, on tanks designed with speed and mobility rather than protection in mind, was also too thin. The Tiger's main gun rounds, recalled Sgt. Judd Wiley, 712th Tank Battalion, "went right through our tanks. Our tanks were like tin compared to theirs."[30]

German designs were better in many areas. While most US tanks had exhaust pipes facing the ground, stirring up plumes of dust that gave their position away, the Germans avoided this by facing them skyward. Panthers also had special "flame trap" mufflers to conceal exhaust at night. German tanks had excellent optics and sights; *Panzer* gunners could switch from low to high power by just flipping a lever, helping them see farther than Sherman gunners faster, which helped them get off the crucial first shot at long range.

IMAGINATION IS THE DIRECTING FORCE AT CHRYSLER

## IMAGINATION AND IMPROVEMENTS

HOW THEY WORK FOR YOU—IN WAR—IN PEACE

*Courtesy Henry Smith.*

Searching for targets, M4 gunners inside the turret could become disoriented as they rotated independently of the hull. A gunner might be scanning to the rear (six o'clock) while the hull was at twelve o'clock, rolling forward, and hear a hasty command from the TC, "Tiger- two o'clock." Because his view was limited to a narrow periscope, a Sherman gunner had to rely on the eyes of the TC above him to lay the main gun on the target. Should he under- or over-compensate valuable seconds would be lost. In battle, this could mean the difference between life and death, because Tigers and Panthers could fire first: their gunners had a simple gauge near their position—a silhouette of the hull and turret that rotated in unison with the real thing—showing where the two were in relation to each other. At a glance, German gunners could aim quickly and more accurately than Americans.

Although generals like Patton praised the M4's gyrostabilizer (supposed to enable firing on the move without the barrel being jarred and taken off the aiming point), GIs distrusted it, finding it too complicated; they often turned it off in battle. They also complained the M4's internal compass was frequently off by as much as plus or minus twenty degrees.[31]

Another German innovation was the tank commander's cupola, the small turret in which he stood to guide the gunner and driver. On Shermans, the hatches for it were two half moon-shaped slabs of iron. For the best view, the tank commander had to open these hatches and stand straight up, exposing his body from the waist up. His options were limited to closing them ("buttoning up") and relying on a small periscope with limited vision or opening them, thus vulnerable to small arms, artillery, and tank fire.

As a result, being a Sherman TC was one of the most hazardous jobs in the ETO. Recalled assistant driver O. J. Brock, a

> If we had a tank like that Tiger, we would all be home today.[3]
>
> —Sgt. Clyde Brunson, tank commander, 2nd Armored Division

replacement with the 712th Tank Battalion, "The first person I saw get killed was in my tank," his tank commander, Lt. Hank Schneider. As they rolled toward a small French village, Schneider was standing in the open hatch, studying maps and directing his driver. A shot rang out and "Hank was hit in the head with a sniper's bullet, and he fell down through the top of the tank. We radioed back, and the gunner [who took command of the tank if the TC was injured or killed] said 'Turn around,' and told us where the aid station was. But Hank was dead immediately, shot through the head.... We had to clean the tank out, all the blood and stuff...that was certainly a shocking experience."[32]

In contrast, German tanks had an ingenious cupola using periscopes and an armored hatch that could rise up, swivel, and be locked into several optional positions. The tank commander had a choice of seeing out with it fully closed, raising the hatch slightly while still remaining inside (enabling him to see all around while still unexposed and protected from overhead fire), or opening it fully for the best view. Innovations such as these were later incorporated into American postwar designs; sixty years later, the M1A1 Abrams the author used as a US Cavalry tank gunner had a commander's cupola similar to the Tiger and Panther.

Some postwar literature implies German armor superiority was a given, highlighting exotic designs from the ironically named Goliath (a small, remote-controlled, rolling land mine on treads) to the gigantic Maus (a massive experimental tank, perhaps the largest of the war). But little known today is that behind the small numbers of advanced new tanks emphasized in Nazi propaganda was a mixture of captured Allied models. Throughout the war, the Wehrmacht used everything from French Renault FT-17s circa 1918 to various mid-1930s Czech designs, making the already complicated maintenance of their tanks (German tankers joked that they must have been designed by watchmakers) a logistical nightmare. In contrast, the US simplified by fielding relatively few models with standardized ammunition and parts.

Postwar embellishment of wartime myths simplistically depict the Tiger and Panther as all powerful. In fact, they were excessively complicated, fragile, and hard to maintain. In the first batch of Panthers (appearing in the July 1943 Eastern front Battle of Kursk) every one failed mechanically. Reporting from Russia that month, *Oberstleutnant* von Grundherr wrote, "At a range of 7,900 yards, a Soviet T-34 was knocked out with the first round [from a Panther]." However, he regretted "a very sad story": the new tank was mechanically unreliable. In the Oberstleutnant's opinion, there was "no shadow of a doubt that the majority of technical deficiencies resulted from substitute [*ersatz*] materials which simply did not measure up to standard."[33]

The effects on German morale were predictable. "There were a great many who expected a decision to come from the new, untried weapon," said von Grundherr. "The initially complete failure [of the first Panthers] therefore had a somewhat depressing effect, particularly since... special expectations had been aroused."[34]

The Oberstleutnant nicely illustrated a great irony in German vs. American tank design. Although the Americans dropped the ball on firepower, armor protection, and to some extent maneuverability, reflecting their talent for mass production of automobiles, they got many of the automotive basics right on the Sherman, producing better tank engines, tracks, and transmissions. In contrast, while German designers excelled at intricate, precise technology like gun sights, range finders, and optics (even beginning to install infrared night sights in some tanks by 1945), they failed to perfect the mundane but crucial elements. As Oberstleutnant von Grundherr put it, "So long as one builds such

a valuable weapon, one must not build in an unusable gasoline pump or deficient gaskets."[35]

Like the early Panther, the Tigers also suffered breakdowns. "The Tiger engine requires very skilled…maintenance to get the best performance," observed a 1945 War Department guide, "and in the hands of insufficiently trained crews, mechanical troubles are apt to appear. This characteristic has been the tank's principal disadvantage."[36] Author John Ellis observed that in

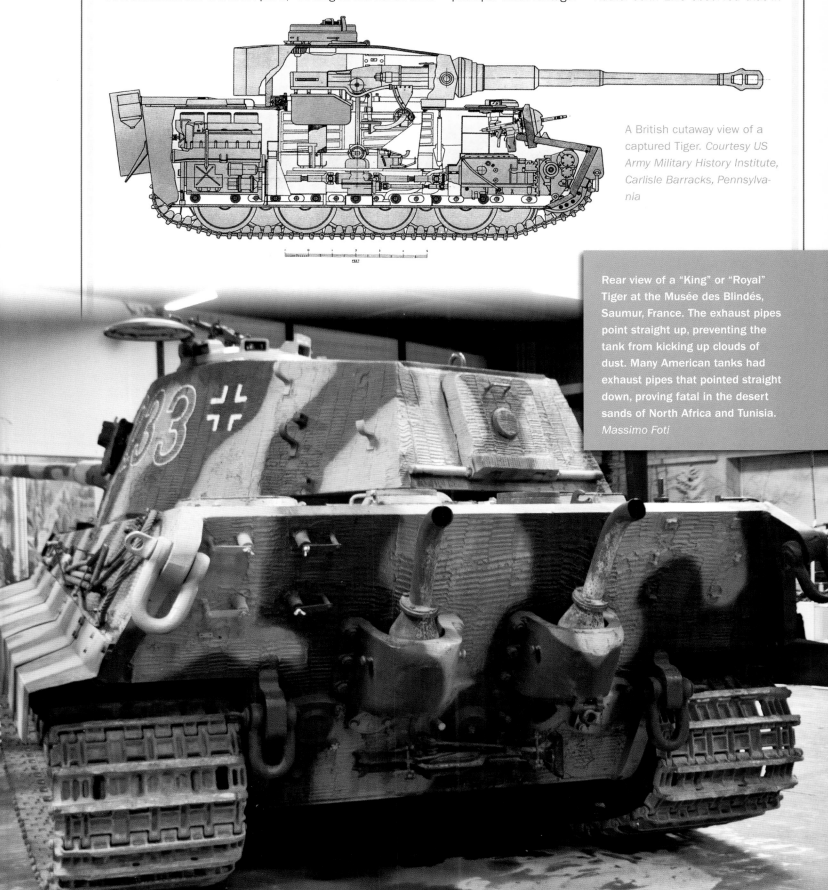

A British cutaway view of a captured Tiger. *Courtesy US Army Military History Institute, Carlisle Barracks, Pennsylvania*

Rear view of a "King" or "Royal" Tiger at the Musée des Blindés, Saumur, France. The exhaust pipes point straight up, preventing the tank from kicking up clouds of dust. Many American tanks had exhaust pipes that pointed straight down, proving fatal in the desert sands of North Africa and Tunisia. *Massimo Foti*

Restored Panzer 38 (T)—a captured Czech design—at the Deutsches Panzermuseum, Munster. *Massimo Foti*

Normandy on June 15, 1944, all 38 Tigers in the First SS Panzer Corps were unserviceable: 30 needing short-term repairs and 8 requiring extensive work. Two weeks later, *SS Panzer Abteilung 101* had only 3 out of 28 Tigers ready to fight, with 25 awaiting repairs.[37] On August 27, the First SS Tigers were still mostly red-lined, with 33 out of 43 under repair.[38] While the Tigers were sidelined many Shermans rolled on.

Though superior in terms of firepower, armor, ground handling, and innovative design, the small numbers of powerful tanks Germany fielded were defeated in the end by far larger numbers of mediocre but mechanically dependable American designs. Tigers and Panthers often had to be transported to the battlefield by rail because they could not be relied on to travel long distances on their own—distances an M4 would take in stride. Many King Tigers became inoperable due to engine failure rather than

Allied fire, destroyed or abandoned by European roadsides by their own crews. Towards the end, the *Panzerwaffe* was desperately short of fuel and oil. "Imagine those enormous panzers, laborious at best, now having to rely on coal and wood for the least bit of movement," wrote Sgt. Frankel. "That rendered them all the more primitive: the fetid odor of burning wet lumber, the ejaculations of dark smoke—all in order to push a gigantic steel idol forward, inch by excruciating inch. The more primitive those traps became, the more certain was their doom."[39]

Sgt. Frankel recalled a disturbing and symbolic incident:

We had just left Koblenz. Alongside the road was a smoldering Tiger, apparently the victim of American artillery. I saw Bob Saville inspecting it, so I jumped from my own tank to say hello.

Inside the panzer was a little bundle of logs and a dead German. His clothes had been shorn right off by fire, but his face was relatively whole. His body was propped up against the side; Bob nudged him down, and when he fell, his penis shriveled, dropped to the floor, and landed in miniscule fragments of foreskin. Ouch![40]

During the Ardennes offensive, although Panzers terrified GIs in temporary routs, they were stopped by running out of gas and spare parts. Entering La Glieze toward the last stages of the campaign, the US 743rd Tank Battalion found some thirty immobile Tigers and Panthers—not destroyed or damaged, but parked intact for lack of fuel.[41] Meanwhile, the lackluster but mechani-

Restored Panzer 38 (T) at the Deutsches Panzermuseum, Munster. "Wilde Sau" is German for "wild boar." *Massimo Foti*

A disabled Panther, Italy 1944.

cally reliable Sherman, with an extensive fuel and supply network, rolled on to Berlin. In photos of tank parks in Italy from 1945, M4A1s from 1942 rest beside the latest model M4A3E8s ("Easy Eights") of 1944.

For all the fear they inspired, the deadliest Panzers lacked the decisive impact of the humble Sherman. To Col. Jarrett, a testament to American automobile expertise and mechanical reliability is that more Panthers were lost to mechanical break-downs than to Allied firepower:

Assembly line of Tiger I tanks, Germany 1944. *Courtesy German Federal Archive*

The Germans, because of their lack of a well-organized automotive industry as compared to the Americans, never built a tank with a highly satisfactory power plant.... It was almost a rule that their tanks required so much adjusting and repairs that very often in action they had to be destroyed by their own crews to avoid capture. In fact, far more were destroyed by their own crews than were ever destroyed by Allied tank or anti-tank gunfire during battles.[42]

Maj. Al Irzyk described a long road march his Shermans completed through Germany near the war's end, exulting that the M4 "rolled, sped, climbed, forded, chugged, and labored across three hundred and ten miles in less than thirty days.... The only maintenance it received during that period was on the fly by its crew, during very rare pauses. It was an amazing, uncomplicated, unbelievably durable, faithful workhorse."[43]

It is not commonly known that when not on the move or fighting, tank crews spend hours that other soldiers use for sleep on maintenance and resupply of their tanks. "Armored soldiers," wrote Maj. Irzyk, "are always performing maintenance and cleaning weapons." Walking around his unit's parked tanks in France, he saw laid out for cleaning "parts of the coaxial machine guns, bow machine guns, grease guns [a GI's personal weapon, the M3 subma-

The Ardennes, January 1945: 7th Armored Division M4s fire on the enemy near St. Vith.

Bologna, Italy, April 1945: Tanks of the 752nd Tank Battalion in Plaza Emanuel. Although suffering from inadequate armor, firepower, and ground handling, the M4 was a mechanically reliable design; early versions rolled on until VE and VJ Day and beyond. *US Army Signal Corps*

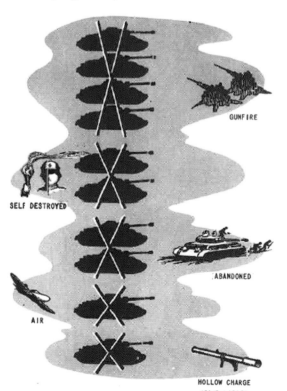

Figure 7. An analysis of German tank losses due to various causes inflicted by US, Canadian, British, and French forces.

**LEFT:** From a secret postwar report, Coox and Naiswald, *Survey of Allied Tank Casualties in World War Two* [1951].

chine gun] together with the ever-present oil, rags and patches… spread out on sleeping bags or GI blankets. Occasionally one saw a couple of crew members with the long staff and brush cleaning out the bore of the tank main gun, while another greased the bogie wheels."[44] At night, while Infantry soldiers not on operations or guard duty attempted to sleep, tankers waited for resupply trucks, then spent hours taking on fuel and ammunition:

> After stopping for the night, and realizing it would be some time before the trucks showed up, the tankers' initial priority was food. They quickly prepared coffee and heated rations…they were tired and emotionally drained…but they knew the day was far from over, and there was much more hard work yet to come. So they stretched their legs as much as they could within the narrow confines of the tank, and tried to catnap. Those who dozed never did so for very long, for they were soon shoved awake.
>
> The trucks had arrived…. It took teamwork by the whole tank crew. Gasoline came in five-gallon jerry cans, and each can had to be lifted off the truck, and either carried to the tank or passed to it as in a bucket bri-

Fort Benning, Georgia: Restored M4A3E8 as attached to the 3rd Infantry Division during the Korean War. The tiger face artwork was used to scare allegedly superstitious Chinese and North Korean soldiers. *Author photo courtesy of the National Armor and Cavalry Heritage Foundation*

Restored M4A3E8 ("Easy Eight") in Korean War markings at Fort Benning, Georgia. *Author photo courtesy of the National Armor and Cavalry Heritage Foundation*

Right side drive (forward-most) wheel. *Photo enhancement by Robert Coldwell Sr.*

Three views of a Tiger I from an Allied Intelligence report.
*Photo by Robert Coldwell Sr., courtesy US Army Military History Institute, Carlisle Barracks, Pennsylvania*

American early to mid-war K ration meals. The "K" honors the inventor, Dr. Ancel Keys. *Photo by Robert Coldwell Sr.*

gade...[once the fuel was poured in from the can], this process was repeated from eight to fourteen times, depending on how dry the tank had become. The cans were heavy when full, so this task was tiring work...it was pitch-black and there were no lights, so the tankers relied completely on feel, which had come with experience.

As soon as the tank was topped off, the gasoline truck moved out and the ammunition truck moved in. The crew shifted its attention to the loading of ammunition, as great if not a greater challenge. The machine gun ammunition posed no problem. It was belted, and came in metal boxes. Loading these was easy and quick.

It was the tank main gun shells that presented the truly exacting task. These rounds were big, long, and heavy. They came in pairs, and were secured in a small wooden crate. A hammer and an iron bar had to be used to extricate the rounds from the crate…the round had to be carefully carried and handed up to the man on the tank's rear deck, who in turn handed it to the man in the turret, who placed it gently and cautiously in its receptacle in the turret ring and clamped it into place. Each round was handled almost as tenderly as a newborn babe. Each man knew that the slightest mishandling could cause a dent in the semi-hard, susceptible brass casing. If that occurred, there could be hell to pay.

The bore of the gun was carefully and expertly machined. Its surface had a system of spiral grooves called rifling that caused a fired projectile to rotate about its longer axis, thus increasing its power, distance, and muzzle velocity…the shell which was shoved into the bore of the gun was likewise carefully and expertly machined so that it would fit absolutely snugly within the bore. The shell and the bore matched so tightly that even a slight dent could prevent the shell from sliding home. A dented live shell had to be discarded, and that meant one less round available and the waste of many dollars, as these pure brass shells did not come cheap.

The greatest fear was to have a shell just slightly dented, so it escaped the caress of the loader's hand as he shoved it into place, and jammed in the bore too tightly to pull back out, and not far enough to be fired. When this happened, the gun and tank instantly became

useless and dangerous. The round had to be removed without delay. Extricating the jammed shell out of the bore without having it explode in the tube was a ticklish, dangerous, frightening experience. Any tanker who wrestled with a jammed shell vowed, "Never again." That explained the cuddly care each round received until it was finally fired.

As they loaded the shells in the darkness, the tankers also had to recognize and distinguish between and properly stow the high explosive [HE], armor piercing [AP], and the occasional white phosphorous [WP] rounds. Altogether it was twenty or forty more rounds that were loaded into the tank turret, depending on the intensity of the day's activities. So like the loading of gasoline, the loading of ammunition required great teamwork by the tank crew, and was a demanding and exhausting task following an exhausting, pressure-packed day of combat.[45]

In contrast to the M4's ability to keep rolling with minimum maintenance, the Tiger I had a range of only about 70 miles before needing repairs and adjustments. Even a German propaganda magazine, *Die Wehrmacht*, acknowledged in March 1943 that a captured Sherman made "a journey of some 210 miles, lasting four and a half days, which testifies well to the overall march capacity of this steel colossus…. Preliminary investigation in Tunisia had already revealed that this rolling steel mine is not a bad product."[46]

In seemingly mundane but crucial areas the Sherman came out on top. For example, its tracks lasted some five times longer than German steel ones; with identical rubber blocks on both

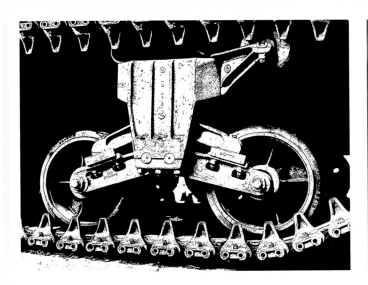

**ABOVE:** *Photo enhancement by Robert Coldwell Sr.*

**RIGHT:** Typical American tank tread with "chevrons" for traction. While German treads were often metal, tearing up roads and not as long lasting, American ones used two-sided rubber that could be flipped when worn to extend the life of the tread. *Author photo courtesy of the National Armor and Cavalry Heritage Foundation*

sides, when the outer surfaces became worn they could be flipped over to expose a new surface. And while complex German engines often took days to disconnect, remove, and repair, American ones could be exchanged in one piece. To Col. Jarrett, the Sherman's engine was one of its best features. "The American tanks had remarkable power plants, and could continue in operation with little if any repairs, outside of battle damage. These qualities were possible by virtue of the long and worthwhile experience of the American automotive industry. They put in all American vehicles, combat or cargo, the finest power plants obtainable."[47]

Yet when compared with Germany's most powerful designs, Allied armor has been derided. Certainly one can question the wisdom of placing the M3 medium tank's main gun off to one side, severely restricting its field of fire, but a closer look is required. In condemning American tanks as lighter and smaller than the most notorious German ones, it needs to be appreciated that the Germans could field bigger, heavier tanks because they sent them to the battlefield using interior supply lines. In contrast, American tanks were subject to size and weight restrictions because they had to sail overseas in tightly packed landing craft.

The size or weight of a tank's hull does not mandate the effectiveness of its main gun, but at the height of the 1945 tank scandal, generals and politicians seeking to duck criticism cited it as justification for inferior firepower. After the war, this "landing craft" excuse became an article of faith repeated by Gen. Marshall and generations of gullible historians. "It is crucial," insists a 2003 article on the M4, "to remember that the Shermans had to be transported across oceans…and fit on existing naval tank transports, one reason they were smaller and lighter than German late war armor."[48]

The hull dimensions of US tanks were valid concerns, but why would they determine the potency of the main gun? As

early as 1942, when the M4's debut in Operation Torch showed it unable to duel with Germany's best (and Army tests had concluded that a 90mm main gun could be fitted to the M4), the Shermans in the field could have been up-gunned with little effect on their ability to fit in a landing craft, or to cross bridges. Yet wartime "landing craft" or "size" excuses are repeated as historical "truth."

Though inferior in at least two of the three vital elements of tank design (firepower, armor protection, and maneuverability), the M4 was easily adaptable; its many variants included mine layers and rollers, flamethrowers, rocket launchers, and "swimming" tanks. And it could also be built in large quantities (over 50,000, compared to just 1,800 Tigers and 6,000 Panthers) and easily repaired and maintained. To Col. Jarrett, American tanks "were quite superior mechanically. They never required the repairs that those of the Germans did."[49] The M4 became a war winner not only through sheer weight of numbers built, but also through politicians' and generals' willful, callous expenditure of young soldiers' lives.

Like the mounted trooper with his horse, tankers bonded with their machines. Maj. Al Irzyk, 4th Armored Division: "A particularly close kinship developed between the troops and these inanimate objects. Tank crews named their tanks and lettered the names on the sides for all to see. Ironically and surprisingly, tank crews became as fond of their steel mounts as Cavalrymen had been of their horses."[50] Tanks became home, where GIs rested, slept, and cooked and ate their meals. Irzyk wrote of them, "Each tank had its own five-gallon water containers and a Coleman burner. In addition, the experienced, resourceful tankers had acquired a basic load of cooking utensils such as a frying pan, boiling pan, coffee pot, spatula, and big spoon."[51]

Correspondent Ernie Pyle described living conditions in and around a tank in a column datelined "With Allied Beachhead Forces in Italy, April 15, 1944":

One day I sat around with a tank crew.... This crew has its metal behemoth hidden behind a small rise, half obscured by oak bushes. The men were cooking a pot of dried beans when I got there in the mid-forenoon. They had coffee boiling as usual, and we drank coffee as we talked.

When tank men are out like this, ten-in-one rations and C-rations are brought up to them at night by jeeps. They do all their own cooking, and sleep in the tank for safety. They aren't supposed to smoke inside the tanks, but everybody does. Some crews even burn their little cook stoves right in the driver's compartment.

A tank and the territory around it are a mess after five men have lived in it for eight days. The ground is strewn with boxes and tin cans and mess gear. The inside of the tank looks as though a hurricane hit it.

This tank had everything in it, from much-handled comic books to a pocket edition of the Bible. You found old socks, empty tobacco cans, half cups of cold coffee. The boys used the top of the tank for table and shelves, and this too was littered.

Sleeping five nights in a tank isn't too comfortable, for space is very limited. They spread their blankets around the interior, sleep in their clothes, and nobody gets completely stretched out. The worst spot is around the gunner's seat, where the man really has to sleep halfway sitting up, so they take turns sleeping in this uncomfortable spot.[52]

Today one can see restored, spotless tanks in museums with glossy paint jobs and spurious markings, stripped of the usual mix of eclectic gear and souvenirs on the outside. But as the author can well attest, having crewed US Cavalry M1A1 Abrams tanks in diverse environments, real tanks loaded up under operating conditions are a chaotic sight. Lt. Col. George Rubel, 740th Tank Battalion:

In the attack, a tank was a strange looking object. There were usually from ten to twenty men riding on top of it...in addition, the tankers had placed sandbags on the front slope [armor] plate of the tank, the sides, and sometimes around the turrets for protection against Panzerfausts.

Add to this conglomeration the tankers' housekeeping tools, which usually included a liberated heating stove, three or four joints of stovepipe, two or three frying pans, and two or three ordinary black pots. The pots were multipurpose articles. They were used for converting snow into drinking water, washing clothes, cooking food, and pouring gasoline. They were also used as carriers for other smaller articles while en route. The load on the back deck of the tank usually included, in addition to all the other items mentioned, several extra boxes of .30 and .50 cal ammunition and, occasionally, the carcass of a deer or cow that had been killed while "attacking" the tank.[53]

Sgt. Nat Frankel wrote of tank fighting in Rennes, France, where some "Eleven American tanks were lost, the heaviest

damage inflicted against the 4th Armored since the beginning":

It was very strange, but the skeletons of our tanks were somehow more frightening to me than the torn-up corpses and the occasional arm or leg lying about without an owner. I suppose it was because we were more and more becoming extensions of our machines. Our whole lives were tied in with them. If I were to die, it would probably be in the turret, or I would probably be burned up inside. Yet the thought of being without the tank was like the thought of certain death. They were our cock and balls. The site of them devastated, clumped in a heap and leaking oil, was like the aftermath of some grizzly, primitive castration rite, considerably more frightening than a scattered limb.[54]

America, Britain, Canada, Australia, France, Poland, the Soviet Union, and China all used the M4, but their victory came at a cost to tank crews. While "mechanically reliable," as George Jarrett observed, "compared to the German tanks, on a gun-to-gun basis, the American tanks were always under-gunned."[55]

Years after GIs warned of the M4's shortcomings, an April 1945 official report on "Combat Data on the M4 Sherman" from Maj. J. B. McDivitt, 4th Tank Battalion, First Armored Division, to the division Ordnance officer shows the human cost of the M4's inferiority. Dated April 9, 1945, from "Headquarters, In the Field," it relays data derived from "personal experience of this unit in combat." In businesslike language, dispassionately reporting tanker deaths by decapitation and amputation, it is a graphic demonstration of the deficiencies of American armor after three years of war:

**Tank hits**. Most hits are made on the front slope plate, with the German gunner usually concentrating at close range on the forward portion of the driver's hatch, or on the sponson sides, well forward, where the largest, flattest surface is found.

**Cause**. Armor piercing projectiles fired from 75mm or 88mm guns... Penetrations made at ranges up to and including 3,000 yards, at an angle of impact of 20 degrees or less from the perpendicular.

**Effect**. All penetrations, with a minor number of exceptions, cause immediate burning of the tank and total loss. Hits on the turret usually effect penetration of both sides. Few hull penetrations have succeeded in piercing both sides.

**Personnel casualties**. Most casualties are caused by burning. Men shocked or injured by penetration of a shell, with the amputation of a limb or severe lesions from flying fragments, are usually fatally burned before aid can reach them. Average casualty is one man killed for each tank knocked out by AP [Armor Piercing] fire. Additional casualties vary from slightly wounded to seriously wounded, depending on location of penetration and violence of resulting fire. Amputations are frequent. Decapitation by hits on the side sponson and turret.

Limb amputations by miscellaneous penetrations, ricochets of projectile within the tank, and flying gear. The extreme velocity of AP projectiles, however, does minimize most flying fragment injuries, because the tendency is for the projectile to cut cleanly through the tank equipment with slight disturbance, rather than tearing housings loose, or free, with impact.[56]

The Germans called M4s "Tommy Cookers," after a British portable cooking stove. According to US statistics, 65% of them "brewed up" when hit.[57] Sgt. Frankel wrote of his fear of fire:

The best you could hope for in the event of a hit was that only the treads would be scored. This would immobilize your machine, but you could stay inside [and hope that the Germans would uncharacteristically relent their fire], or you could jump out and run for cover of some sort."

But when that gas got hit, your options were, to say the least, limited. Oh, we had a fire extinguisher, but that was for overheated motors; it was useless for an exploded tank. Now, there were two ways to get out: One was via the turret; the other was through a trapdoor on the opposite side of the driver from the bow machine gun. Often the turret would be inaccessible to anyone inside the tank; if the machine was hit badly, particularly if it was knocked on its side, the trapdoor would jam as well. At best you would have ninety seconds to get out that door; if it jammed, you would need fifty of those seconds to push it open. That would leave forty seconds for three men to squeeze out. Tick, tick, tick, boom!

And what would happen if both the turret and the trapdoor were inoperative? What would happen is, you'd die! It takes twenty minutes for a medium tank to incinerate, and the flames burn slowly, so figure it takes ten minutes for a hearty man within to perish. You wouldn't even be able to struggle, for chances are, both exits would be sheeted with flame and smoke. You would die like a dog. Steel coffins, indeed![58]

While many blamed the gasoline engine, more likely the M4's vulnerability to fire was due to how main gun ammunition (which could cause secondary explosions and fires if the tank was hit) was stored. Often "Scattered throughout a tank's interior," recalled Maj. Irzyk, would be "tank gun and small arms ammunition. There is always gun cleaning material, oil, grease, and oily rags. It's combustible, to say the least. It does not take too big a spark in the right place to start a fire, or cause an explosion."[59]

Flaunting the regulations, crews carried extra main gun ammunition loose and unprotected inside the hull, contributing to "brew ups." Units who stored it only in the proper armored containers had significantly less fires. Eventually, an improved "wet stowage" storage system using antifreeze or water was introduced on later variants. Ironically, although the M4 is more notorious for its vulnerability to fire, the Panther, which lacked protected ammo storage bins, had similar problems.[60] Yet the Sherman's lackluster main gun almost *required* Allied tankers to carry extra ammo. They faced a grim choice: go into battle without it, following textbook safety procedures dreamed up by stateside technicians at the risk of being hit and burning after running out of ammo, or augment their supply against regulations and possibly burn up if the loose ammo caught fire when hit.

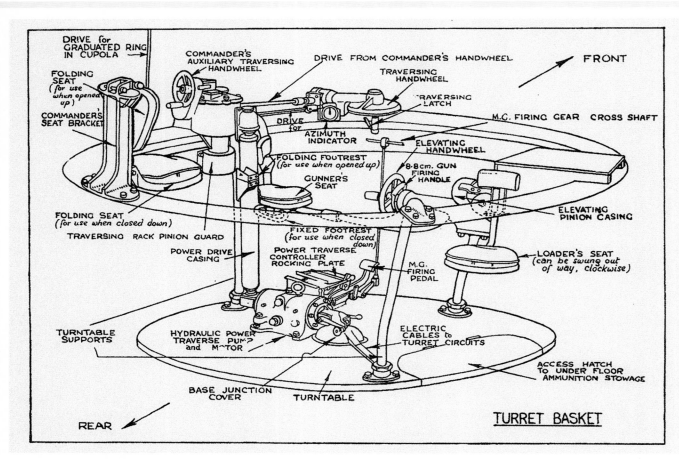

Cutaway view of a captured Tiger turret's lower interior, or "basket."

As for German tank ammunition, Col. Jarrett found it:

well-made, and shot from powerful guns…it made sieves of our tanks. It seemed that these projectiles had been made to tackle even heavier armor than we carried on our tanks…there was no question that they would penetrate, and at ranges advantageous to them… throughout the evolution of Allied tanks, Jerry put out some very excellent tanks with more powerful guns. His guns always kept us at bay. They were faster in velocity, and shot heavier and better quality shells… in the final analysis, he often wrecked our tanks before we could even get in close enough to hurt him.[61]

German tank guns had muzzle brakes to diffuse the gas and flames that resulted when firing. This reduced recoil, giving the gunner a steadier platform (and thus better aim), allowing him to fire more rounds faster because his targets were not obscured by clouds of kicked-up dust or sand. In contrast, American gunners had to wait for the clouds to blow away, delaying their subsequent shots and revealing their position to the enemy. Even as Army engineers on the Manhattan Project were deciphering the secrets of the atom, most American tanks lacked such an elementary improvement, although its benefits had been noted on captured German tanks sent back to Aberdeen for testing.

The Panzers' main gun ammunition also used smokeless gunpowder that did not leave a telltale plume when fired. At the turn of the century, Americans fighting in Cuba had a rude awakening: the Spaniards could fire their German Mauser rifles (using smokeless powder) without being seen, while the ammunition

used in the US Infantry's standard "trapdoor Springfield" rifle marked them for the enemy. Four decades later, the Army had not adopted this common sense advance to tank ammunition. According to Lt. Demetri Paris, a platoon leader with the 14th Tank Battalion, 9th Armored Division,

Every time we fired, we revealed our position with both smoke and flame.

One of our lieutenants received one of five new tanks with the 105mm gun [sic—although they were standard M4s with more powerful guns, Army leaders insisted on calling them "assault guns," a sort of self-propelled artillery]. Shortly after, we were adjacent when he fired. The smoke and flame could be seen for miles. When I questioned why we did not use smokeless powder, the answer was that the chemical salts in that kind of explosive would corrode the barrel, damaging the lands and grooves. Yet I once went to an area in France where I saw hundreds of disabled tanks, many with a single hole in the body. They had perfect gun tubes that could have replaced any damaged by the chemical salts.[62]

One vulnerability GIs found with the Tiger's gun was its manually rotated turret; the Sherman's powered version spun faster. Cpl. John Irwin, a tank gunner, exulted when he "learned of one of the Tiger's weaknesses: its slow turret traverse…a weakness I learned to exploit."[63] Maj. Al Irzyk elaborated:

The Sherman gunner could hold in front of him a metal grip like a handle, turn his wrist to the right, and hydrau-

*Photo by Robert Coldwell Sr.*

lic pressure would instantly swing the turret to the right. If he turned his wrist to the left, the gun would swing to the left. He could control the speed by the angle of his wrist. If he turned his wrist sharply, the turret swung around rapidly. The gunner could stop the turret instantly, with the gun pointing exactly where he wanted it, by straightening his wrist.

So the M4's power traverse enabled the gunner to swing rapidly and lock on to his target, and to adjust immediately after a shot was fired. Thus, he could get his shots off quicker, better, and faster than the German gunner. Often a good American gunner spotting a German tank at the same time he was spotted could get off three to four rounds before the first German round. This didn't help the German's aim when he did fire.[64]

The American failure to keep pace with German armor led to morale problems. "The lack of confidence," author Michael Green wrote, "in the armor protection fitted to the Sherman is best described by a grim inside joke among American tankers during the war: if you took a hammer or helmet and hit the side of an M4, it was guaranteed that the vehicle's crew would jump out...before you could strike the tank a second time."[65]

After the 191st Tank Battalion saw two weeks of combat, its commanding officer, Maj. Welborn Dolvin, warned in August 1944:

The Sherman tank equipped with the 75mm gun is no match for...the German Mark IV, Tiger, or Panther.

On numerous occasions, hits were obtained on German tanks with no noticeable results. On the other hand, German high-velocity tank guns never failed to penetrate the Sherman. This situation has a tremendous effect on the morale of the tank crews. This was evidenced by the reluctance of crews to fire on German tanks, feeling that it would do no good, and would result in their being promptly knocked out. Crews soon became ultra cautious where German tanks were in the vicinity.[66]

For tankers who survived their vehicle's destruction, the psychological effects were serious. "The Army found out that the typical tanker could stand two or three tanks being destroyed under him before suffering a mental breakdown. A few stood up to six or eight Shermans being destroyed under them without being psychologically affected. This only happened, however, when two or three of their vehicles were destroyed in the same day."[67]

While Roosevelt boasted of production statistics, the tank scandal took a grim toll on GIs. The press and Hollywood liked to highlight glamorous, elite troops such as rangers and airborne, some Army jobs went less publicized. Slowly riding in a jeep near the French town La Ditinais, "a rural village in rolling country," Ernie Pyle saw:

Just a few feet ahead of us...a brick-red American tank, still smoking, and with its turret knocked off. Near it was a German horse-drawn ammunition cart, upside down. In the road beside them was a shell crater.

Fearful of going into the unknown [I was] just ready to turn around and go back when I spied a lone soldier at the far side of the field.... He turned out to be a second lieutenant—Ed Sasson, of Los Angeles. He is

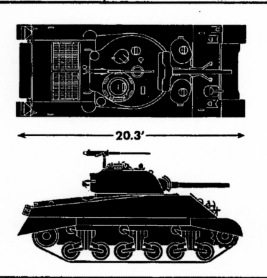

## U.S. ☆ MEDIUM TANK, M4A3 (75-MM GUN)

← 20.3' →    ← 8.6' →    9.5'

**CHARACTERISTICS:**

**Turret:** Large, dome-shaped. Flat top, with cupola on the right, second hatch on the left. Radio bulge in rear. Set at center of hull.

**Hull:** Angular, but has streamlined appearance from the side. Slopes down gradually in rear, abruptly in front. High and square-cut as seen from the front because of steep forward plate and vertical sides.

**Armament:** One 75-mm gun in turret. One coaxial caliber .30 machine gun. One caliber .30 machine gun in bow. One caliber .50 AA machine gun on turret.

**Traction:** Full track. Six equally spaced bogie wheels suspended in pairs in prominent brackets. Three support rollers. Driving sprocket in front.

**INTEREST DATA:** This latest production model of the dependable M4 tank has several improvements over previous models. A vision cupola gives better visibility from the tank commander's position. An extra turret hatch and larger hatches in the hull speed mounting and dismounting of the crew. The steep front plate of the hull is new. A flame thrower may be fitted in the bow of the tank for special operations.

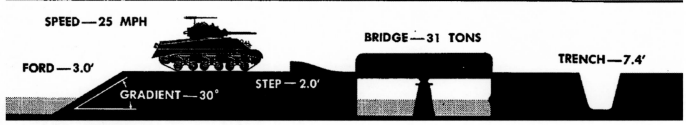

SPEED — 25 MPH          BRIDGE — 31 TONS

FORD — 3.0'          TRENCH — 7.4'

GRADIENT — 30°     STEP — 2.0'

*Photo by Robert Coldwell Sr.*

a Graves Registration officer for his armored division, and he was out scouring the fields, locating the bodies of dead Americans. He was glad to see somebody, for it is a lonely job catering to the dead.[68]

A tanker's death was gruesome; according to *Death Traps*:

When a tanker inside a tank received the full effect of a penetration, sometimes the body, particularly the head, exploded and scattered blood, gore, and brains throughout the entire compartment. It was a horrible sight. The maintenance crews had to get inside and clean up the remains. They tried to keep the body parts together in a shelter half [GI pup tent] and turn them over to the Graves Registration people. With strong detergent, disinfectant, and water, they cleaned the interior…as best they could, so men could get inside and repair it.

After the repairs were completed, the tank's fighting compartment would be completely painted. In spite of this, the faint stench of death sometimes seeped through. A new crew might hesitate to take a tank assigned to them because they were very superstitious about tanks in which their buddies had been killed.[69]

The Sherman's flaws ground down the nerves of its crews. Sgt. Jim Rothschadl, a gunner, recalled a "commotion" in Normandy in June 1944, as a platoon of four tanks were about to roll into battle. "Here was this tank driver, and he refused to drive. I couldn't believe it…we had been taught that in the rules of war, if you disobey an order at the front, you don't have to be court-martialed, they could shoot you right there…. He was just

saying, 'I'm not gonna go…the hell with you, I'm not gonna go.' And they put him in a jeep, and away they went. And we thought, well, they're going to take him back and shoot him, he's a dead duck. If you refuse an order like that on the frontline…"

But the frightened soldier was not shot. He was taken to the rear for treatment, while a Sgt. Bailey—not a trained, experienced tanker, but a communications sergeant whose primary job involved maintaining radios and field phones—volunteered to take the broken man's place in the attack. That day, along with nine out of twenty 712th Tank Battalion men, dutiful Sgt. Bailey was killed in action.[70]

PFC Michael Vona also fought in Normandy. He was burned out of his tank, wounded by grenade fragments, and engaged in hand-to-hand combat with a German soldier who put a Luger pistol to his temple that failed to go off. Later, American medics "operated on me three times. But then, in those days, they didn't give a damn…they sent me back…to the line, where I didn't belong…let's face it, how much can I take?":

So I got sick. I said, aw, the hell with it. I didn't say that, I just got sick. I thought…I'm not gonna take it any more…. After they sent me back to the outfit, I got sick, I went berserk. I got the jitters. 'cause I'd had too much of it…I saw too much…I couldn't stand it…I still get medication…I was in a straitjacket…they had me tied up, with all these damn things, my arms and all that crap. Straps right across to hold me there…

When they sent me back to the line…I knew I wasn't right…. Then one day I just…not quit, I said, "I just can't take it,"…and just lay down…I started shaking. My mind went berserk on me. I didn't know what the hell was happening…I still have nightmares. That's why now, I

sleep alone, and my wife sleeps alone. It's unbelievable, but you live with it. Well, you can't cry about it, you know what I mean?[71]

The human cost of facing Panthers and Tigers was grim. According to Sir John Keegan, "The U.S. Army's rule of thumb was that it took five Shermans to knock out one Panther."[72] By war's end, over 5,000 Panthers had been built. Since M4s carried a four- or five-man crew, theoretically, to knock out 5,000 Panthers might entail not only the loss of thousands of Shermans, but putting thousands of GIs at great risk of injury or death as well. According to an extensive, classified 1951 Johns Hopkins University study for the Army examining a sample of some 274 US First Army medium tanks (and 1,370 crewmen), when a Sherman was hit by "major weapons" such as gunfire, "about 2.5 men per medium tank became casualties." In other words, "This sample also shows that the casualty rate for these 274 medium tanks was 51 percent of all the crewmen involved."[73]

The Johns Hopkins study was able to break down casualties by crew position:

The First Army sample of 274 medium tanks revealed that the tank commander suffered the heaviest casualty rate, 57 percent. The driver had the lowest percentage for this sample, 47 percent. The remaining three crew positions all hovered near the 50 percent mark. The higher casualty rate among the commanders is no doubt due in part to the fact that it was frequently necessary for them to expose themselves, either partially or wholly, in fighting their vehicles. In so doing they became extremely vulnerable to the Germans' two main casualty-producing weapons: gunfire and bazooka attacks.[74]

Little wonder that in secret reports requested by Gen. Eisenhower GIs expressed a preference for fighting in the Tiger or Panther over their own American-designed and built Sherman, and that those reports were suppressed from the American public.

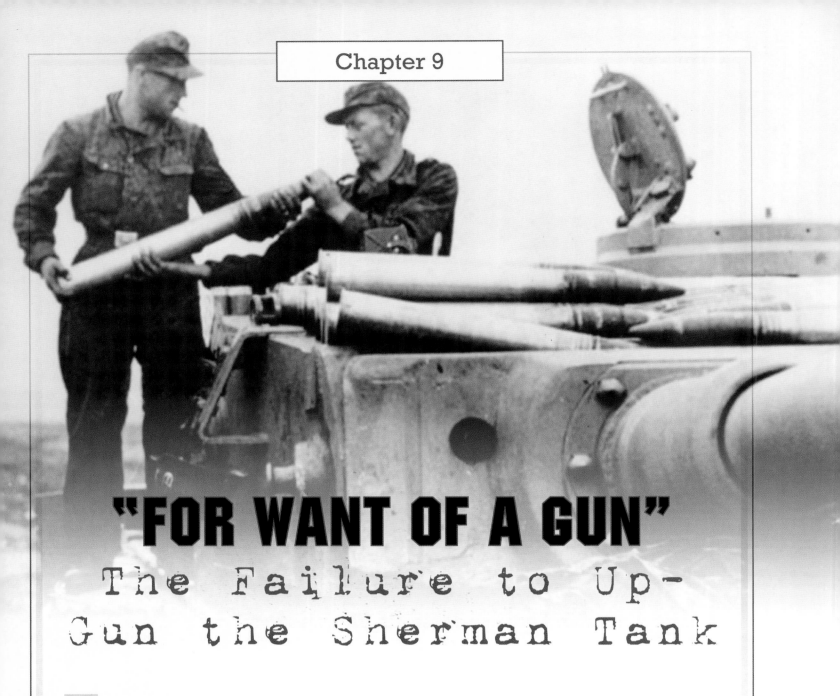

# Chapter 9

# "FOR WANT OF A GUN"
## The Failure to Up-Gun the Sherman Tank

Allied tank guns had lagged behind Germany's since the Spanish Civil War (1936–39). Until the last weeks of WWII, little large-scale, decisive action was taken to address the imbalance. According to Col. George Jarrett, "Throughout the evolution of Allied tanks, Jerry put out some very excellent tanks with powerful guns. His guns always kept us at bay. They were faster in velocity, and shot heavier and better quality shells… in the final analysis, he often wrecked our tanks before we could even get in close enough to hurt him."[4] To Col. Wilson Hawkins, commanding the 3rd Battalion, 67th Armored Regiment, "We have been outgunned since Tunisia, when the Germans brought out their Mk IV 'Special' with the long-barreled 75mm gun and higher muzzle velocity."[5]

During the war, Gen. Omar Bradley downplayed problems with the M4 as ordered by Eisenhower, but in his postwar memoirs Bradley changed his tune to agree with Hawkins. Starting in North Africa and Tunisia:

The German has concentrated on developing a gun, with the means of moving it, and the maximum amount of protection for the crew. We have concentrated more on the means of movement, than on the gun itself. In my opinion, the gun should be given the most attention, and everything else rated secondary.[2]
—Capt. Robert Moore, 1st Armored Division, detailing the Sherman tank's flaws to Army Ordnance and suggesting improvements, October 1943

The German 88 had already become the nemesis…of the tankers…. It easily outranged our Shermans with their 75mm guns. In their first engagement, the American tankers learned that tank for tank, their General Grants and Shermans were no match for the more heavily armored and better-gunned German panzers. Two years later, in the Battle of the Bulge, this disparity had not yet been corrected…at no time could [the M4] engage the enemy's Panthers and Tigers in a direct frontal attack.[6]

Would upgrading Shermans in the field with more powerful guns, or replacing them with the new T26, have caused a logistical nightmare, as apologists for the tank scandal have argued? American industry constantly debuted complicated new weapons, trained soldiers on their use and repair, and set up a worldwide distribution network to maintain them. In light of the logistical accom-

On the Eastern Front, a German soldier keeps track of his kills on a self-propelled gun. Little known to most westerners, the USSR used thousands of Lend-Lease M4A2 Shermans.

plishments in the Normandy invasion alone, it strains credibility to assume improving the gun on existing tanks—perhaps a field modification done overseas—was an insurmountable challenge.

Charles Baily has examined the feasibility of fielding 90mm gun Shermans:

> The new T25 turret could have been mounted in the M4. This was possible because the turret rings of the M4 and T20 series [tanks] were both 69 inches, and the T23 and T25 turrets were interchangeable…. A Sherman with the T25 turret could probably have been available in 1944. Adapting the T23 turret began in July 1943, and the M4 [76mm] entered production only seven months later.[7]

Since the T25 turret was complete in January 1944, it seems reasonable Shermans with that turret could have been in production by September. Production experience with the M4 (76mm) indicated a 90mm version could have been rapidly produced in large numbers. These tanks could probably have been available in Europe in time for the Battle of the Bulge.[8]

Clearly, GIs would have welcomed expedient methods to improve their tanks; they often took the initiative to better their odds of survival. When the thick Norman *bocage* restricted their mobility (forcing them to expose thinly armored M4 bellies to climb over it), Sgt. Curtis Culin of the 102nd Cavalry Reconnaissance Squadron designed the "Culin Cutter" or "Rhino." It used salvaged German beach obstacles cut into a plow shape and welded to a tank's nose to break through Norman hedgerows. Like a later generation of enterprising GIs adding scrap armor to their vulnerable Humvees in Iraq and Afghanistan, WWII tankers welded iron slabs on the Sherman's outer hull. Placing it over the ammo storage area they hoped might reduce the chance of fire on impact.

Later, stateside brass got around to approving these simple improvised armor slabs. Eventually, they would be standardized and added to M4s on the assembly lines. At the time, although this quick fix was not authorized (which might have taken months of red tape), mechanics toiled around the clock to install them. Given the tankers' resourcefulness, they would have embraced the chance to add a more powerful main gun to their tanks had leaders at home mass produced better guns to be shipped and installed overseas.

The Army Air Forces did this throughout the war; B-17 Flying Fortress and B-24 Liberator bomber crews worldwide unofficially installed extra .50 caliber machine guns to increase their firepower, improvements that were later approved and done at the factories at home. Apologists today may reasonably argue that adding more .50 caliber machine guns to an aircraft is an easier task than upgrading a tank's heavy, bulky, main gun, yet there is an Army Corps precedent: B-25 Mitchell bomber crews in the Pacific theater added 75mm cannon (originally intended for ground force use against ground targets) to their airplanes for strafing Japanese targets by the notorious 345th Bomb Group, the "Air Apaches."

# THE "HOLE-PUNCHER"!
## (76 M.M. CANNON)

### It's America's Hard-Hitting Tank Cannon—with Fire-Power to Punch Holes in Heavy Concrete!

*Pinned down by murderous fire from a pillbox, all we could do was hug the ground—and hope for a miracle . . . Then it came!—a 76 mm. "miracle" that smacked into that pillbox with a force not even reinforced concrete could withstand. WHAM!—another shell found its mark. And as those earth-shaking explosions continued, we knew that our tanks were right behind us. Those good old Shermans, with their long-nosed, long-range "Hole-Puncher" guns, were pounding the enemy's defenses to pieces, so we could move forward again.*

THE man who first called America's 76 mm. tank cannon a "Hole-Puncher" really knew his Fire-Power. Hundreds of riddled enemy vehicles and shattered enemy fortifications bear witness to the effectiveness of this versatile weapon, which Oldsmobile has been producing for over two years. Oldsmobile also builds automatic cannon for planes, aircraft rockets, aircraft engine parts, heavy-duty axles for military vehicles . . . plus that most critically needed war product of all, *heavy-caliber ammunition* . . . 90 mm., 105 mm., 155 mm. shell. Fire-Power is our business—*our urgent business*—until Victory is final!

**YOUR MOST POTENT WEAPON IS A DOLLAR BILL!**

Don't let it burn a hole in your pocket. Let it help *punch* holes in enemy armor. Put it with other dollars . . . to buy an extra Bond . . . that will help buy a "Hole-Puncher" cannon!
**BUY WAR BONDS!**

# OLDSMOBILE DIVISION OF GENERAL MOTORS
### *FIRE-POWER IS OUR BUSINESS*

*Courtesy Henry Smith. Photo by Robert Coldwell Sr.*

Vierling, the Sherman, "a basically good implement of war," was handicapped by "overwhelming disadvantages":

The greatest deficiency lies in its firepower, which is most conspicuous by its absence. Lack of a principal gun with sufficient penetrating ability to knock out the German opponent has cost us more tanks, and skilled men to man more tanks, than any failure of our crews—not to mention the heartbreak and sense of defeat I and other men have felt when we see twenty-five or even many more of our rounds fired, and they ricochet off the enemy attackers. To be finally hit, once, and we climb from and leave a burning, blackened, and now useless pile of scrap iron. It would yet have been a tank, had it mounted a gun.[9]

The press praised the M4 as a war winner, but often it could barely scratch the paint on a Tiger. Sgt. F. W. Baker, Second Armored Division, commanded a Sherman with the 76mm main gun. In a secret 1945 report to Eisenhower, he described a duel with three or more Panthers: "Ordering my gunner to fire at the closest tank…approximately 800 yards away, he placed one right in the side, which was completely visible to me. To my amazement and disgust, I watched the shell bounce off…. My gunner fired at least six more rounds at the vehicle, hitting it from the turret to the track…but I was completely surprised to see it moving after receiving seven hits from my gun."[10]

After seeing "combat several times in a tank," Cpl. James Miller, a gunner with the 67th Armor Regiment, Second AD, concluded, "it is silly to try to fight the German tank." One November 1944, morning, "about daylight" in Puffendorf, Germany:

I saw several German tanks coming across the field toward us. We all opened fire on them, but…. We might as well have fired our shots straight up in the air, for all the good we could do. Every round would bounce off,

Aircrews working under primitive conditions were able to upgrade their aircraft by installing 75mm cannon without major logistical support from home. Throughout the war the Army Air Forces, responding to feedback from men at the front, would manufacture and distribute modification "packs" or "kits" to be installed by local mechanics. Since these upgrades were successfully carried out in places at the end of the AAF logistical chain like the China/Burma/India (CBI) Theater, the South and Central Pacific, and the Aleutian Islands, it is not unreasonable to suggest that tank mechanics in the ETO—backed by a supply line stretching stateside to London, Paris, and Brussels—would have been able to field install 90mm tank main guns in new turrets on to existing tanks.

Adding improvised, thicker armor to the hull was a small start, but the main gun's shortcomings remained. To Cpl. Francis

and wouldn't do a bit of damage. I fired at one 800 yards away; he had his side towards me. I hit him from the lap of the turret to the bottom, and from the front of the tank to the back, directly in the side, but he never halted. I fired one hundred and eighty-four rounds at them, and I hit at least five of them several times. In my opinion, if we had a gun with plenty of muzzle velocity, we would have wiped them out. We out-gunned them, but our guns were worth-less.[11]

Except at close range, the 75mm gun could not penetrate the best German armor and the 76mm was little better. Even as generals from Patton to Montgomery praised the M4 and expressed contempt for the Tiger and Panther, "Secret trials quickly proved that…there was not an Allied tank in the inventory [the Red Army excepted] that could kill a Tiger. In fact, British Royal Ordnance scientists discovered to their horror that the Tiger could not be penetrated at any range. Point-blank engagements at under 100 yards proved that the 6-pound-er and 75mm tank guns could not defeat the Tiger's frontal armor. The rounds simply bounced off."[12]

Even young draftee privates recognized the Sherman's greatest fault: an inadequate main gun. In contrast, German tanks could punch through the M4's front, rear, and flanks like a hot knife through butter. When the Second Armored Division first fought Panthers in Italy, the story quickly spread of an M4 "knocked out, with the German 75mm round going through the transmission, through the ammunition rack on the hull floor, through the engine, and out the rear."[13] Little wonder that bitter crews called them "Iron Coffins" and "Purple Heart Boxes."

Perhaps the most straightforward method to address the problem was to install a more powerful 90mm gun. Many accounts imply the 90mm-gunned T26 tank was a late-war invention, but as early as 1940, the US possessed a 90mm anti-aircraft (AA) gun (the M1) that could be fitted inside a tank, just as the Germans would successfully mount their "88" AA gun in the Tiger. To Gen. Richard Moore, chief of AGF's requirements section, it was "time we got to thinking about our 90mm to match this 88—it would be fine if we could get ahead of the Germans just once."[14]

In February 1942—six months before the Tiger's Eastern Front debut and the same month the battle of Sidi-bou-Zid exposed the inadequacy of US tank guns—Ordnance tests confirmed the 90mm M1 gun would fit inside an M4 turret. Had the brass acted decisively and pushed for large scale, priority production of improved 90mm High Velocity Armor Piercing (HVAP) tank ammunition, the war's most powerful tanks might have been American. Instead, the Army's most effective tank gun only ap-peared in small numbers on the M36 Jackson TD, and on small numbers of the long-delayed T26 tank—over three years after Ordnance confirmed the feasibility of this relatively simple solu-tion. The few 90mm equipped armored vehicles that reached the front suffered from a recurring shortage of HVAP ammunition.

Throughout the war the M4's gun was improved sporadical-ly, when it should have been done on a grand scale. Instead, flawed tanks rolled out by the thousands and tankers died while

*The most important point, upon which there is universal agreement, is our lack of a tank gun…with which we can effectively engage enemy armor at the required range.[1]*

*— Gen. Isaac White, commanding the 2nd Armored Division, in a secret report to Gen. Dwight Eisenhower, March 1945*

politicians cited production figures. In 1941, American industry had answered Roosevelt's politically motivated call to mass produce near-obsolete tanks to be seen responding to the blitzkrieg. Although Ordnance knew of the threat posed by Ger-many's 88mm gun for years, for most of the war they failed to field a gun even equal to it. Propaganda aside, FDR's "Arsenal of Democracy" failed to de-liver a decent tank gun for dueling Tigers and Panthers until the final weeks of the war in Europe.

In March 1945, as newspaper and mag-azine headlines trumpeted public denials from Gens. Eisenhower, Patton, and Bradley, Col. George Jarrett added some handwritten "personal notes" to his "Little Green Book" on the ongoing tank scandal. The excuses Col. Jarrett was reading in blazing headlines did not square with his years of firsthand experience as one of the Army's top captured enemy weapons experts, who had been warning of the inadequa-cy of Allied tank guns and armor for three years. Surely with an eye to posterity, perhaps hoping some future historian would come forward to dismantle the tangled web of the tank scandal, Col. Jarrett wrote:

1. I first reported the effectiveness of the German 75mm AP-HE shell [1,650 fps] from the Western Desert in March 1942 [When Jarrett was serving as a liaison to British forces in Egypt and Libya, examining captured enemy Ordnance and sending it home for testing.] I tested the effectiveness at APG [Aberdeen Proving Ground] in March 1943, and proved their superiority over the U.S. M61 [tank round] in performance.

2. I reported the new German 75mm AP-HE [shell] in August 1942, from the Qattara Depression battles in Egypt. This shell traveled 950 ft./sec. faster than the original German AP-HE [tank round]. I made the first drawings for both shells in Cairo…

3. Jan 1943: I talked before the Development Section [General Barnes' Research and Development Section] of the Office of the Chief of Ordnance [OCO] at the Pentagon building, and stirred up much comment—no action was taken, save to stop me—I was told it was too controversial an issue! I also stressed the point that our tank sights, tank guns, and armor were inferior.

*Photo by Robert Coldwell Sr.*

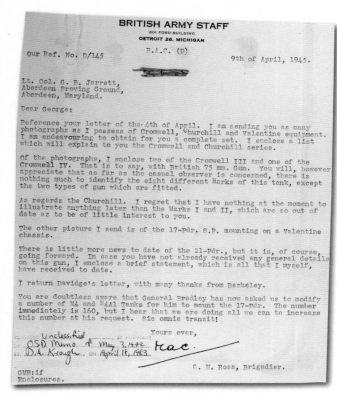

Brig. Ross letter to Col. Jarrett: Note the mention of Gen. Bradley's urgent request for Fireflies. *Photo by Robert Coldwell Sr., courtesy US Army Military History Institute, Carlisle Barracks, Pennsylvania*

I was severely criticized by Gen. Barnes and then Col. Eddy [George Eddy, who led Aberdeen's Ordnance Research and Development Center] told [me] I'd conform to Ordnance Department policy.

I questioned the value of the 76mm [gun]—new at the time. I told the OCO that in Egypt, 8 out of 10 of our tanks hit when burned due to the superiority of the German AP-HE shell, and that their higher velocities increased the chances of their shells getting a hit and going thru. In our case, when we disabled a German tank, we had to send the Engineers out to blow it up—our shells seldom completely destroyed the enemy tanks.

4. March to June 1943 saw tests at APG which confirmed the above remarks—even Col. Eddy phoned Col. Haller that our M61 [round] was 5 years behind the first German 75mm AP-HE.

5. In subsequent [testing of German] 75mm PAK 40 vs. U.S. 3" AP-HEs, both Col. Eddy and Gen. Barnes agreed, "We don't need HE, the M62 is so good." This was a comparative test against an M3 medium [tank] hull. I was amazed, as after all of the above, I realized that the push for a decent AP-HE shell was seriously delayed.

6. To support [Jarrett and his staff], Bethlehem Steel made up some sample rounds just like the [German] PAK 40 [round] and improved the performance of the [US] 3" gun tremendously. This was in August 1943.

Within a few weeks, pressure was brought to bear on us, as we had acted without Pentagon [approval], and the program was stopped. M61 and M62 design [remained] as was, and would be continued—to hell with a better shell...[Therein] lies a basic fact of the poor performance of U.S. hits on German armor during the battles to come in France.

7. Early in 1944, the British offered us the 17-pounder, then coming into its own, for use in the U.S. M4A3 tank.

Gen. B. [Bradley or Barnes?] refused this, as he hated anything British. The 17-pounder was the only gun at the time capable of matching the new Panther's 75mm gun soon to be met. The British put 350 [of these guns] in their M4A3s, and raised merry hell with Jerry—June 1944.[15]

One of the first attempts to improve the M4's firepower was the 76mm gun, produced in small quantities compared to the standard 75mm model. Gens. McNair and Patton rejected opportunities to field large numbers of 76mm Shermans. While at first glance this seems easy to criticize, the new gun was not much of an improvement over the 75mm M3 model already mounted in the M4. "The 76mm Gun, M1 as a tank weapon," wrote Gen. Alvin Gillem, who headed the Armored Force, to McNair on September 1, 1943, "has only one superior characteristic to the 75mm gun, M3":

This superior characteristic is in armor penetrating power. The 76mm gun will penetrate on average one inch more armor than the 75mm Gun, M3 at the same range. The high-explosive pitching power of the 76mm gun is inferior to that of the 75mm gun...the exterior ballistics generally of the 76mm gun are less satisfactory for a general purpose Medium Tank than the 75mm gun.... The characteristics of the complete round of the 76mm gun makes it possible to stow only approximately 70% as many rounds in the Medium Tank, M4 as can be stowed for the 75mm gun...in view of these facts, it is considered unwise to equip an armored division or separate tank battalion entirely with 76mm guns to the exclusion of the 75mm gun. It must be remembered in making these comparisons that the 75mm Gun M3 is not entirely helpless against enemy armor.[16]

Using the new, rare HVAP rounds made with a tungsten and carbide core, tankers firing the new 76mm gun had a slight chance to "penetrate the front belly plate of the Panther at 300 yards, and at 200 yards, had a sporting chance (about one to four) of penetrating the front slope plate."[17]

These were the odds under ideal conditions, often using decoy tactics. But the new gun, as Gen. Bradley wrote after the war, frequently only "scuffed rather than penetrated" the armor on German tanks.[18] When it was able to penetrate, it only did so an inch deeper than the standard 75mm gun.[19] When firing, the 76mm gun emitted clouds of smoke visible to the enemy that obscured the gunner's vision. "The 76mm gun," *New York Times*

### Plan no changes in Sherman tank

WASHINGTON. (NANA). The war department is not planning any immediate changes in the design of the General Sherman tank to meet the superior features of the German Royal Tiger, an official spokesman here indicated Tuesday.

The new German tank has been acclaimed by members of the Twenty-second armored division, now fighting in Germany, as the best tank in battle today.

The war department spokesman said that the Royal Tiger is undoubtedly a good machine, and that it has some features that would make it appear the better weapon. However, he added, the fact remains that the Royal Tiger can be stopped, even by two soldiers with a bazooka, and the General Sherman tank now used by the allies is still capable of handling the work assigned to it.

The Royal Tiger is far heavier than the General Sherman, weighing between 60 and 70 tons, while the American weapon weighs only 42 tons. Most of the additional weight of the nazi tank is accounted for by the heavy armor on the front of the machine, where it is reported capable of resisting 75-mm. and 76-mm. shells at ordinary distances.

#### Weight Disadvantage.

The additional weight has two distinct disadvantages. It forces the tank to be slower than the Shermans, and it creates the necessity of reinforcing bridges over which the tank must pass.

Should our tanks be as heavily armored as the German ones, this would bring up almost insurmountable difficulties in transportation, since many of the tanks now are still being landed on beaches. Another factor to be considered is the fact that allied weapons are being made for use in many theaters of war, while the nazi material is for use inside Germany, for the most part. Thus, changing a design for only one theater of the war might endanger the success of the drives in still another.

### 'U. S. to Keep Same Tanks'

#### 'Criticisms Based on Sketchy Operations'

(INS)—The War Department Monday was disclosed to be determined to keep the same tanks now in use on all war fronts, despite complaints by tank operators in the European theater that this offensive armor is inadequate.

The American tank has been criticized as incapable of holding its own against Germany's heavy Royal Tiger tank, which is armed with 88 mm. high velocity guns.

War Department officials feel that repeated criticisms in America of the present Sherman tank have been based on piecemeal operations.

American tank warfare planning provides for the use of anti-tank guns, more powerful and more mobile than tanks, as a match for any tanks which the Germans may throw into the battle, and it assertedly never was contemplated that the American tank should face the heavier German tank.

The Germans, it was observed, developed the Royal Tiger tanks as a defensive weapon to be used in retreats—not as an offensive weapon. As an offensive weapon the tank was said to be too heavy to negotiate such obstacles as the Rhine, which American armor must now cross.

In a dispatch from east of the Rhine, Frank Conniff, International News Service correspondent, said that American tankmen he interviewed were convinced that American armor is no match for the Nazi panzers.

He quoted Sgt. Adam Subach of Girardville, Pa., as saying:

"It's all right for people in Washington to sit back and turn out stories saying that our tanks are a match for the jerries'. They don't have to sweat it out against the Tigers and Panthers like we do. We just can't handle the German tanks, and that's all there is to it."

---

culties in transportation, since many of the tanks now are still being landed on beaches." Appearing just days before King Tigers were at the forefront of a surprise German counteroffensive in the Ardennes, the article told how War Department officials, while conceding the Royal Tiger's "superior features…that would make it appear to be the better weapon," refused to make "any immediate changes in the design of the General Sherman tank to meet…the King Tiger."

The new German colossus, they acknowledged, "has been acclaimed by [tankers] now fighting in Germany as the best tank in battle today." However, claimed the War Department spokesman, "the Royal Tiger can be stopped, even by two soldiers with a bazooka." Further whistling in the dark, he insisted, "The General Sherman tank used by the Allies is still capable of handling the work assigned to it."[22]

To facilitate American tanks being shipped around the world, their ability to fit into landing craft, and to cross hastily built or repaired temporary bridges, Army Regulation 850-15 set size and weight limitations on tank designs. But improving the main gun inside a tank's hull, or adding better armor, though likely adding weight, would not necessarily keep it from fitting into a landing craft.

This is borne out by the M4A3E2 "Jumbo," an up-armored Sherman built in small numbers and sometimes referred to as an "assault tank," a US version of the mythical German "breakthrough tanks" of 1940. Bigger and heavier (42 tons) than the standard M4, though it had seven inches of armor added to the gun mantlet and six inches on the turret sides, it had no trouble fitting into landing craft or crossing bridges. But while the Jumbo carried better armor, it still used the underpowered M3 75mm main gun. This was a reversion to the prewar idea of an "infantry tank"; a "moving pillbox" to support Infantry by parking and bombarding fixed fortifications.

The best-gunned Sherman of the war was British: the Firefly, with a 17-pounder main gun in a larger, British-designed turret. Though a tight fit (the gun had to be mounted sideways), it worked, and was able to penetrate a Tiger's frontal armor. British Lt. Bob Boscawen, Coldstream Guards, recalled the first time he fired a Firefly's main gun:

> There was a blinding flash. My beret was whipped off and out, through the open turret hatch above. As the hot air and fumes subsided, I just caught a sight of the tracer round hitting the target, and pulling it right out of the ground.
>
> A cheer went up from outside the Officers Mess, and the staff sergeant put his head into the turret and called out, "Are you alright in there?"
>
> An answer to the enemy's superiority in armour had arrived.[23]

Fireflies often led columns of vehicles, attracting German fire with their distinctively longer barrels, but there were too few of them; only a quarter of the tanks in British armored units. Just 109 Fireflies were in Normandy by late June 1944.[24]

The British offered the Firefly to American brass, who promptly refused it. One is tempted to suspect xenophobia on the part of tradition-bound Army Ground Forces leadership and

---

columnist Hanson Baldwin wrote, "is a useless weapon, for due to its terrific muzzle blast, it is impossible to observe or adjust fire."[20] And even when improved HVAP rounds for it were introduced in fall 1944, they were hard to get; Ordnance's official history concedes production problems so severe, "receipts of HVAP before 1 March 1945 were less than two rounds per gun per month."[21]

One wartime and postwar excuse given for the M4's inadequate armor protection involves the size and weight of US tanks. "Plan No Changes In Sherman Tank," an article appearing on December 6, 1944, cited an unnamed "War Department Official Spokesman." "Should our tanks be as heavily armored as the German ones, this would bring up almost insurmountable diffi-

A British-crewed "Firefly" Sherman, with its powerful 17-pounder gun, exhibits an admirable example of improvised camouflage. The nickname was due to the main gun's tendency to flash and spark when firing. This shotgun marriage of a British gun with an American tank resulted in an answer to the Panther and Tiger.

RA PD 335631

Happy accident: When a shortage of hulls (bodies) for the new M-36 Jackson tank destroyer arose in factories, the result was the improvised M36B1: rather than hold up assembly lines, the M-36's new turret, with a powerful 90mm main gun, was mated to a standard M4A3 hull. The simplicity and speed with which the M36B1 was produced sheds doubt on the argument that by 1944 it was "too late" to field a more powerful US medium tank. The M36B1 could have been built in large numbers, or the improved turret and gun retrofitted to existing M4s. Instead, just 187 M36B1s were built- another missed opportunity to address the Sherman's inadequate main gun. Though the M36B1's formal nomenclature was "Gun Motor Carriage" or "Tank Destroyer," it was in fact, an upgunned Sherman tank.

A restored Sherman Firefly in Canadian markings. A similar M4 of the 1st Northants Yeomanry killed Germany's top Panzer ace, Michael Wittman. *Author photo courtesy of the National Armor and Cavalry Heritage Foundation*

speculate on what could have been: one of the best US fighter planes of the war, the P-51 Mustang, was a winning combination of American airframe and British engine. The more progressive Army Air Force, rather than squabble over who designed what, embraced an innovative design with British help and reaped great results. But within McNair's hidebound Army Ground Forces such co-operation did not extend to better tanks; a contemptuous Ordnance Department dismissed the Firefly—perhaps the most effective M4 variant at fighting Germany's best tanks—as a "nuisance."[25]

But after the 76mm gun Sherman failed to meet expectations, the brass reversed their position. At the height of the 1944 Normandy tank losses and when the tank scandal reached its apex in stateside media in early 1945, the Americans were begging for Fireflies. Gen. Bradley was publicly attempting to downplay the tank scandal to the stateside press,

An M36B1 at a stateside proving ground. While the more powerful 90mm gun was a great improvement over the standard Sherman's 76mm gun, the vulnerability of the TD's thinly-armored, open-topped turret remained. All tank designs seek a balance between firepower, armor protection, and speed and mobility; the "TDs" sacrificed armor protection for speed with disastrous results for their crews.

Some of the General Sherman tanks (medium tank M-4) in action in Normandy and Brittany are armed with 105-mm howitzers. Such a tank is seen in this photograph. This is the first time that a field artillery piece with the punching power of a 105-mm howitzer has been successfully installed in a medium tank. It represents the maximum firepower thus far achieved in the fast-moving, highly maneuverable vehicle. The new General Sherman is the master of any German tank in the field today. It weighs approximately 33 tons, has a speed of 24 miles an hours, and carries a crew of five.

August 1944.

Signal Corps Photo.
Copy neg made from enlarged print received from OCSigO HQ, SOS, European Theater of Operations, USA thru BPR, August 1944.
Released by BPR, August 11, 1944.        lmd
4x5 copy neg          Lot 9244

*A 105mm M4 "howitzer" used as mobile artillery to lob shells from afar while parked and immobile, rather than duel tanks on the move. US Signal Corps Photo via Ralph Riccio, photo enhancement by Robert Coldwell Sr.*

as requested by Eisenhower, but behind the scenes was a different story. "You are doubtless aware," wrote British Brigadier G. M. Ross on April 9, 1945, from the "British Army Staff" offices at "801 Ford Building, Detroit 26, Michigan" to "Lt. Col. G. B. Jarrett, Aberdeen Proving Ground," "that General Bradley has now asked us to modify a number of M4 and M4A1 Tanks for him, to mount the [British] 17-Pdr. The number immediately is 160, but I hear that we are doing all we can to increase this number at his request. *Sic omnia transit!* [Latin for roughly "it all passes," i.e., "it's now or never!"].[26]

Records show that when Gen. Bradley's Twelfth Army Group requested 160 Fireflies in February 1945, the number had to be halved due to shortages. A few may have arrived in the ETO, but it is uncertain if they ever saw combat. US Ninth Army records also mention the hoped-for delivery of 40 modified Shermans with the British gun in the last weeks of the war, but not whether they arrived before VE Day.[27]

Like the Jumbo, the M36B1 expedient version of the Jackson TD shows the fallacy of the "weight" or "bridge" excuse for the tank scandal: that shipping requirements and weight restrictions dictated an inadequate gun. As designed, the M36 featured a new hull and turret with a powerful 90mm main gun. But when a production shortage of the hull arose, it was found the improved turret and gun could fit on a standard Sherman. This fortunate accident led to another opportunity to address the M4's inadequate 75mm gun. Rather than wait for delayed M36 hulls, M4A3

Sherman bodies were pulled off assembly lines. Fisher Automotive then simply replaced the usual turrets and guns with the new 90mm ones from the M36. The modification went off without a hitch. With HVAP ammunition (in short supply due to a shortage of tungsten and carbide), the hybrid vehicles, designated M36B1s, were better able to take on German tanks. This improvised quick fix resulted in a vehicle with a much better main gun and (by using the hull of a true tank) the thickest (but still inadequate) armor protection of any American TD.[28]

The accidental success of the M36B1 illustrates the lack of clarity in the tank destroyer concept. The TDs had begun with a small, simple towed gun in 1940, a quick-fix substitute for costly real tanks. They then morphed into the disastrous M6 Fargo and M3 half-track expedient TDs in 1942–43. Adding improvised anti-tank guns to existing designs not created to stop tanks clearly failed, leading to the M10 TD, the first entirely new, purpose-built TD design, but it was an open-topped, vulnerable tank substitute lacking decent armor. By 1944, the best armed and best armored American "tank destroyer," the M36B1, was in fact a genuine tank, an improved Sherman with a 90mm gun that was needed for years.

Ordnance belatedly developed special 90mm tank rounds, the T30E16 HVAP and the T33 AP. These rounds were not only able to punch through Tigers and Panthers, but also penetrate (albeit at short range) the frontal armor of the monstrous King Tiger, Germany's best-armored tank.[29] But the M36B1—a solution at hand—became another lost opportunity. Although thousands were needed, only 187 were built.[30] Tank destroyer officers, reflecting the lack of consensus among Army agencies, viewed the M36B1 not as the improved Sherman it was, but merely a substitute TD until the production delay with the new M36 hulls was overcome.

T26 supporters like Gens. Campbell and Barnes objected to such quick fixes to the Sherman, arguing partial solutions would delay production and adoption of what they saw as the best solution, a new heavy tank. And the improved ammo the M36B1 used did not reach frontline tankers until March 1945, in small numbers.[31]

Another possibility was an M4 with a 105mm main gun also produced only in small numbers and used for static "indirect artillery support." Internal Army squabbling over tank doctrine doomed it to be another tank misused as a cannon, parked behind the lines to passively fire on distant targets and rarely moving or pursuing the enemy.

The doctrinal confusion is also reflected in the refusal to call a tank a tank. Army leaders designated the M36B1 (an up-gunned Sherman, with better armor than the thin-skinned tank destroyers) a TD. Similarly, although the 105mm Shermans only differed from standard M4s by having a more powerful gun, parochial Army leaders insisted they were static "assault guns" for

Infantry support, not tanks. They also refused to use them as tanks, because this would conflict with various textbook doctrines. Thus, another possible solution to the under-gunned Sherman was restricted to a reactive, passive role, firing indirectly and immobile behind Allied lines.

The more powerful main guns of the Firefly, M36B1, and the 105mm Sherman refute the excuse that up-gunning the M4 required heavier tanks unable to negotiate European bridges. New turrets with more powerful 90mm or 17-pounder guns could have been added to existing M4 hulls (as was done with the M36B1 and the Firefly), but still more chances were missed. While Gens. Marshall, Eisenhower, and Patton were not directly involved in the tank design process, had a leader of their stature heeded warning signs and demanded action, large numbers of up-gunned tanks could have arrived overseas before the Normandy invasion.

When the 76mm Sherman was offered to Patton in January 1944 for the Normandy invasion he refused it, not wanting to introduce new equipment on the eve of battle. Months later, the tank and tanker shortage forced a reversal of Patton's decision; the 76mm Sherman arrived, but still in small numbers. In September 1944, of the American 12th Army Group's 1,913 tanks, only 250 had the new M1A1 76mm gun.[32], and the improved HVAP ammunition for it remained in perpetual short supply.

Fall 1944: Crossing the West Wall, or Siegfried line. Note the notorious "dragon's teeth"—concrete anti-tank obstacles.

Restored Tiger I at the Deutsches Panzermuseum, Munster.
*Massimo Foti*

As noted, the 76mm Sherman was a slight improvement, but not good enough. In his memoirs, Bradley depicts an angry Eisenhower's outrage over its lackluster performance in the Summer 1944 "First Army Tests": "You mean our 76 won't knock these Panthers out? Why, I thought it was going to be the wonder gun of the war.... Why is it that I am always the last to hear about this stuff? Ordnance told me this 76 would take care of anything the Germans had. Now I find you can't knock out a damn thing with it!"[33]

When considering improvements to US tanks, rather than up-gunning M4s in service, some viewed the problem as requiring a completely new tank. This, they argued, might take years. Yet as early as 1942, one was in the works that might have been produced before Normandy: the T26. But Gen. McNair and other Army leaders obstructed its adoption. These missed opportunities demonstrate the provincialism and bickering between Army agencies working at cross purposes that plagued American tank design, production, and doctrine since 1917. The powers-that-be supported building

*There can be no excuse for the abysmal ignorance of tank tactics generally, and tank operations in Europe in particular... the simple answer was to design a better gun, something infinitely easier than to design a new tank.[3]*
*—British Army Brigadier Gavin MacLeod Ross, The Business of Tanks*

specialized tank destroyers, the exotic Normandy "Funnies," "Infantry tanks," and indirect fire, pseudo-artillery "assault guns" in small numbers, for very specific jobs. At the same time, they opposed making expedient improvements to the thousands of existing M4s that bore the brunt of the tank war—modifications that addressed the flaws of US armor.

One of the tragedies of the Sherman tank scandal is available solutions went unheeded. Americans could have used one of their greatest strengths—massive industrial production—to help tilt the balance of the tank war. The November 22, 1944, *New York Times* reported an exhortation to home front workers by Gen. Marshall, in which he called for more weapons, including tanks: "The very speed of our advance has created new production problems that demand Herculean effort on the part of all our people in the months ahead. Every hour of delay means hundreds of lives and millions of money. A prodigious effort is being made by the Army. An equally prodigious effort must be made here at home."[34]

STATISTICAL AFTER ACTION REPORT OCTOBER 1944
746th TANK BATTALION

'RICTED
1. No. and kind of enemy tanks destroyed.

MK 4 - 2
MK 5 - 4
MK 6 - 2

2. Other enemy vehicles, pillboxes or weapons destroyed.

Half tracks - 5
Trucks - 5
AT Guns - (47MM) - 6
AT Guns - (75MM or over) - 5
AT Guns - (Bazooka on wheels) - 8
AT Rocket Guns - 8
Machine Gun - (Open emplacement) - 134
Pillboxes - (With machine gun) - 50
Pillboxes - (Without machine gun) - 35

3. Our tanks lost.

Tank Medium, M4 (75MM gun) - 10
Tank Medium, M4A3E2 - 1
Tank Light, M5A1 - 1

Lost to AT gun fire - 3
Lost to AT rocket fire - 5
Lost to mines - 3
Lost to artillery fire - 1

*Photo by Robert Coldwell Sr., courtesy US Army Military History Institute, Carlisle Barracks, Pennsylvania*

**ABOVE:** An M3 Lee medium tank crew in North Africa/Tunisia (1942–1943) poses with assorted tank ammunition; note the spent shell casings on the ground.

By the fall of 1944, the Allies began to approach the borders of Germany, coming up against Hitler's vaunted Siegfried Line defenses. Recalled Sgt. Wayne Robinson, 743rd Tank Battalion, who would later publish a novel of the tanker's war variously titled *Barbara* (1962) and *Hell Has No Heroes* (1964):

So much has been written about the complex fortifications of the Siegfried Line that a stranger to it might suppose it was nothing but one pillbox after another, with bands of steel and concrete jutting out of the earth. This is a false impression.

Much of the Siegfried Line looked deceptively like normal countryside. The massive barriers, a favorite subject for war photographers, were only a part of it. There were long stretches of green countryside...with sleepy, normal-looking villages spotted through it. There was nothing sleepy and nothing normal about them... every village was part of the fortress system. The countryside might appear normal because the pillboxes built by the hundreds into its woods and contours were carefully concealed and camouflaged. Some of them were built so as to hide in the ground—when they went into action, they rose out of the ground, and then after firing, sank back into the ground, out of sight again. Every house seemed to have its quota of snipers and gunmen.[35]

While the image of a lone Sherman dueling multiple Tigers and Panthers makes for dramatic video games, television documentaries, and Hollywood epics, in fact, Shermans fought an array of enemy weapons, not only tanks. This can be seen in the composition of the M4's typical "combat load" of ammunition. While it included Armor Piercing (AP) rounds for fighting enemy tanks, most of the rounds carried were High Explosive (HE) for

## Ike Losing Tanks at Rate 500-900 Month

WASHINGTON, Nov. 14 — (P) — General Dwight D. Eisenhower's forces are losing 500 tanks and 900 trucks a month, says Under-secretary of War Patterson.

And Eisenhower is in "imperative need" of more artillery ammunition than we are producing, Patterson told a news conference, explaining that the general should have 3,600 tons a day for adequate support.

*Photo enhancement by Robert Coldwell Sr.*

engaging relatively "soft" targets like enemy trucks, towed guns, and machine gun positions. The Siegfried Line fighting also highlights the fact that the typical M4 had a "dual purpose" 75mm or 76mm main gun, used not only for occasionally engaging enemy tanks with AP but more frequently for firing HE rounds when serving in the less glamorous "Infantry support" role.

This is illustrated in the work of the 741st Tank Battalion, which supported the author's[36] 28th Infantry Division, "The Bloody Bucket," in its costly entrance into Hitler's Siegfried Line. On September 14, 1944, 2nd Lt. Joseph Drew, commanding the 1st Platoon of the 741's C Company, led his tanks to batter the West Wall. Lt. Drew was one of the replacements for C Company's platoon leaders, all of whom had been killed or wounded in the breakout from Normandy:

On 14 September, we moved into position at 0840 hours southeast of Großkampenberg. The 1st Platoon moved up on the right side of the road to the edge of the dragon's teeth and placed direct AP and HE fire on two pillboxes, at four hundred yards. We then placed a few HE on a small clump of trees just over the dragon's teeth, and then placed fire on three pillboxes to the left front at ranges from 700 to 1,200 yards. We waited until 0915 for the engineers to come up and blow a way through the dragon's teeth. When they failed to arrive, my tank pulled within a few feet of the concrete pillars, and fired AP point blank at them. About 0925 my tank went through, and the rest of my platoon followed.

We moved up to the pillboxes and fired AP and HE at them, point blank. Then we moved ahead and over the hill. There were two pillboxes on our right, at about two o'clock, and we fired on them. I heard AP whistle around the tank, and then saw an anti-tank gun directly ahead of us, by a building about eight hundred yards away. We blew that one up and swung towards the town. We saw another anti-tank gun by the corner of the building, and blew the corner off the building firing at it, but I'm sure we didn't hit the [AT] gun, for I saw it pull back.

Then Captain Young called me and said an anti-tank gun had knocked out one of my tanks behind me, so we pulled back to get him. The gun that got the tank was in the woods to the right, and we put three rounds of HE at it at four hundred yards, and blew it up. We covered the wounded until they were dragged behind the pillbox, and the other tank of my platoon sat by the other one. We waited until 1230 for the Infantry to come up and take the pillboxes, because they were full of Heinies. But the Infantry didn't come up, and finally it got so hot with AP that Captain Young pulled us out of there.

Before we pulled out, Lieutenant Covington came up and removed the wounded men, on his tank. Then

Typical German tank rounds. *Author photo courtesy of the National Armor and Cavalry Heritage Foundation*

we took up positions back of the dragon's teeth, and didn't do much, except sit there and sweat out enemy artillery from the woods, about two thousand yards to our left flank. We were out of HE rounds in my tank, and had just a few AP rounds left. About 1700, we pulled into a better position, about three hundred yards to our left rear and waited until 2200, when we were relieved.[37]

By October 1944, the Allies were in Germany. Optimists hoped the war would end by Christmas. Gen. Marshall made a brief trip to the ETO at Eisenhower's request to discuss the growing manpower and ammunition shortages face-to-face. "It was apparent from the Chief of Staff's opening conversations," Gen. Bradley recalled, "that the chill which had caused us to revise our rosy September estimates on the end of the war had not yet filtered through to Washington and the War Department...I made it quite clear that the war could not be brought to an end by Christmas."[38]

In just a week, Gen. Marshall visited "five army, eight corps, and sixteen division headquarters, and shook hands with the commanders and staffs of eight other divisions."[39] He questioned them: "How was the winter clothing? What about the condition of the men? How about their morale? Were the new boots any good; why were they experiencing high rates of trench foot?"[40] Like Eisenhower during his well publicized visits with his troops, Chief of Staff Marshall—the most powerful man in the Army hierarchy—had a chance to hear first hand his tankers' views on the effectiveness of American armor.

Had he read a letter Lt. Lewis Sasser, 66th Armored Regiment, wrote home to his wife Celeste from Germany on December 1, he would learn of a young armor officer lamenting the loss of his wife's namesake—a Sherman tank.

Am not in El Celeste, as she is kaput as of last Tuesday. Was a good tank and hated to lose it after it had been as lucky as it was, but her luck ran out, and mine damn near did with it.... We'd made our attack and were in the process of holding, when some of the brass decided to send a reconnaissance over the hill to see what was there. So my platoon won out and I took off, with my platoon on line and El Celeste in the middle. Went over the hill with all guns blazing away, eyes open to see what was in store for us. We found out in a hurry... they opened up on us coming at them with their armor piercing shells interspersed with high explosive [shells]. I could see the gun flashes and put my gunner on them, but our stuff is a little light on their tanks, and they had the advantage.

I looked right down the line of fire of one AP [armor piercing shell] that barely missed the tank, and then the next one hit a glancing blow that failed to penetrate. It felt just like a big sledge hammer had hit the tank and sparks flew, which gave the impression a welder had struck the metal with his blow torch, only on a grander scale. We were giving shells back to Jerry as fast as he was throwing them at us, but he lucked out the next shot, and that AP came right on inside.

I had already told the other tanks over the radio when I first got hit and we were starting to back off, but when that shell came inside, things came to a standstill. The drivers' and assistant drivers' hatches flew open, and I threw my turret hatch open at the same time. The loader and gunner were pushing me out the turret, and at the rate I was going, I didn't need pushing. Lifted myself up by my arms on the doors and swung to the ground in one motion. For a fraction of a minute the whole crew was standing there on the ground outside the tank, and then we took off as the flames from the exploding ammunition inside the tank started pouring out of the turret.

Once Lt. Sasser reached safety behind another tank:

I could see El Celeste burning on the other side of the hill, and every few minutes she would explode.

Seemed that at first only flames came up, then white smoke would belch forth and then black smoke, after which there would be another explosion, and more fire would pour out. It burned and exploded for over two hours and although I haven't got up there again to see it, I know what it will look like—the paint will be completely gone and the metal will be rusted; the bottom will be blown out, and you won't be able to make out exactly what any of the charred remains therein were in their previous form. Maybe it'll just sit there indefinitely, or maybe one of these days Ordnance will load

## GENERAL DESCRIPTION

As compared with other A.F.V's in service, the "Tiger" is outstandingly well armed and protected. Designed to carry an 8.8 cm. gun and constructed of very heavy armour plate, the vehicle is naturally of exceptional size and weight and it is therefore somewhat surprising to note how it is, to a certain degree, dwarfed by the main armament.

Viewed from the side with the turret at 12 o'clock, the 8.8 cm gun extends beyond the nose of the tank by about a quarter of its length, and the length from the muzzle brake to the mantlet is rather over half the total length of the vehicle.

From the front aspect the great width and extremely wide tracks present a clean formidable appearance, whilst from the rear, the abnormal height of the flat tail plate carrying the large cylindrical silencers and air pre-cleaners, present by contrast an ungainly and untidy appearance.

it up for the metal that's left, or the tracks, or some part of the outside that might still be usable.

Anyway, it was a good tank. It killed a lot of Germans and it went a good many miles through France, Belgium, Holland and Germany.... But I'll get another El Celeste and I'll have the same crew, and I suspect we'll kill a few more Germans before this is over with.[41]

It was not uncommon for crews to be shot out of multiple tanks; Lt. Sasser's fellow 66th Armored officer Don Critchfield lost five of them from Normandy to VE Day.[42] Lt. Sasser and his crew got a replacement tank, but he was killed in Belgium the next month by German artillery shrapnel during the Ardennes attack. "The Jerries," he had written home to his wife on December 29, "don't seem to have the concentration of artillery everywhere [here in Belgium] that they had up there [in Germany]. I've gotten to the place where I quit worrying about ever being sick, and if I can just keep missing those armor piercing shells, I think I'll make out OK. Medical science has developed to the place where they can pretty much patch up any hole if it's just not too big."[43]

In the inevitable dreaded letter home, one of the 66th Armored's chaplains assured Mrs. Sasser that "when hit by an enemy artillery shell and killed in action...he did not suffer, but was killed instantly."[44]

"The German Army," Gen. Marshall would concede in his postwar "report" to Congress and the public, "held an advantage almost to the end of the war" in its "triple threat 88mm gun, which our troops first encountered in North Africa":

As a result the 88 was a powerful German weapon, ahead of ours in quality and technique almost to the end of the war. In the Spanish Civil War the Germans were careful to conceal the role of the 88 as an anti-tank and antipersonnel weapon, revealing it only as an antiaircraft piece. When we first encountered it, it was serving all three purposes with deadly effect. A single 88 could fire several rounds of armor-piercing shells at our tanks, then suddenly begin firing air-bursting fragmentation shells at our Infantry following their tanks, and a few minutes later throw up anti-aircraft fire at planes supporting the ground operation. The 90mm gun had no such flexibility. It could not be depressed low enough for effective anti-tank fire. Our technique of handling the gun had not been sufficiently developed...and we did not have the numbers of weapons the Germans had.[45]

Troubling questions are raised here. How did Gen. Marshall think the Germans had "developed" their "techniques" to use the 88mm gun as artillery and mounted in tanks? By getting it to the battlefields and then working out the bugs. Contrary to his confessions of ignorance, US military attachés from Wedemeyer to Black had warned of Germany's powerful 88mm gun well before Pearl Harbor. Army Ordnance had shown as early as 1942 that the US 90mm anti-aircraft gun could be adapted to

American M4 medium tanks enter Cologne, Germany, 1945.

fit in a tank turret, but it was not done in enough numbers to make a difference. If the Germans could work out the bugs with the 88mm gun in the field "over a period of years," why did the US fail so dismally at a similar task? And all the "Arsenal of Democracy" propaganda notwithstanding, and the theme of overwhelming numbers that continues to this day, why did the Allies "not have the numbers of weapons the Germans had?"

Marshall knew of the Tiger threat since at least early 1943. Before the tanks hit the Normandy beaches in the summer of 1944, up-gunned American tanks with better armor protection should have been built in large numbers. But politics and doctrinal confusion prevented this; generals and politicians refused to admit their mistakes, protecting pet theories and careers.

When the M4 was introduced in early 1942—before the Tiger and Panther's debut—it was adequate for taking on Germany's late 1930s model tanks, up to the "Mark IV Special." But in Fall 1944, as Sherman tankers rolled into Germany to confront Tiger and Panther crews aggressively defending their homeland, the M4 was showing its age; in terms of firepower and armor protection, it was generations behind Germany's best.

Would a leader like Gen. Marshall coordinate the available piecemeal solutions and improvements and unite the various squabbling agencies to upgrade the Shermans in the field, or place the highest priority on mass production of the Sherman's replacement, the new T26?

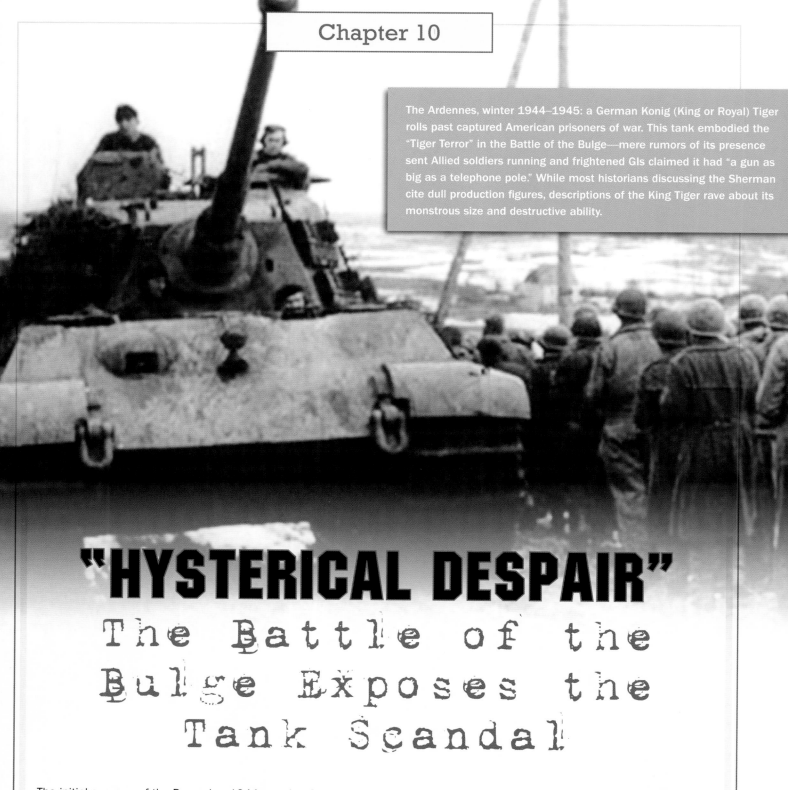

The Ardennes, winter 1944–1945: a German Konig (King or Royal) Tiger rolls past captured American prisoners of war. This tank embodied the "Tiger Terror" in the Battle of the Bulge—mere rumors of its presence sent Allied soldiers running and frightened GIs claimed it had "a gun as big as a telephone pole." While most historians discussing the Sherman cite dull production figures, descriptions of the King Tiger rave about its monstrous size and destructive ability.

# "HYSTERICAL DESPAIR"
## The Battle of the Bulge Exposes the Tank Scandal

The initial success of the December 1944 surprise German offensive in the Ardennes showed the Third Reich's tanks at their finest—and often America's at their worst. Inspiring tales of tankers holding back the Nazi swarm at St. Vith and of Creighton Abrams' Shermans riding to the rescue of besieged Airborne Infantry at Bastogne—in the finest US Cavalry tradition—made for good copy, but they were exceptions. Perhaps more typical was a Sherman crew "completely out of armor piercing shells" and facing three Mark IV Panzers. They "rained shells on the hulls of the enemy tanks as fast as (they) could shoot, but each explosion on the thick armor plate only served to knock the tanks back a few feet."[4]

Now all my lies are proved untrue
And I must face the men I slew.
What tale shall save me here among
Mine angry and defrauded young?[3]
—Rudyard Kipling, "A Dead Statesman" (1924)

Col. William Triplett took over a 7th Armored Division combat command during the December 1944 Ardennes fighting and recalled, "too much talk about…the invincibility of the Tiger tanks" and the penetrating power of the 88mm gun: "hell of a clank. Went right through that M4, through the half-track behind it, wrecked a jeep and kept right on going."[5]

The contrast in performance of the two nations' armor was the most striking since the North Africa/Tunisia debacles of 1943, and German soldiers reveled in it. A Lieutnant Rickhammer wrote to his wife from the Ardennes on December 22:

Tanks of an independent tank battalion (here attached to the US 75th Infantry Division) conduct a "relief in place" for the 82nd Airborne during the Ardennes campaign.

You cannot imagine what glorious hours and days we are enjoying.

Today, we overtook a retreating column and flattened it…we got past them by taking a back road through the wood; then, as if we were on maneuvers, we lined up along the road with 60 Panthers. This endless American column approached us, their vehicles side-by-side, hub-to-hub, and filled to the brim with men. We were able to concentrate the fire of 60 tank guns and 120 machine-guns on them. It was a glorious bloodbath, vengeance for our devastated homeland…. We shall throw these arrogant big-mouthed apes from the New World into the sea…. The snow must turn red with American blood.[6]

"The roads are littered with wrecked American vehicles, cars, tanks," a German lieutenant of artillery exulted to his diary on December 20. "Another column of prisoners passes. I count over a thousand men. Nearby there is another column of 1,500, with about 50 officers, including a Lieutenant Colonel who has asked to surrender."[7]

"NAZI OFFENSIVE PIERCES FIRST ARMY LINES; CHUTISTS AND LUFTWAFFE SUPPORT PUSH," read the *New York Times* for December 18, 1944. "It now looks like the real thing," admitted reporter Harold Denny.[8]

A shaken FDR refused to comment at a December 22 press conference, other than acknowledging the obvious: "the end is not in sight." The extent of his despair can be seen in the fact that afterward, Roosevelt asked Secretary of War Stimson and the Manhattan Project's Gen. Leslie Groves if still unbuilt atomic bombs could be used against German strong points in the "Bulge."[9]

For 1944, from the Normandy beaches in June to December's first two weeks of the Ardennes campaign, the Army's tank losses in the ETO included 2,270 M4 Shermans (main gun caliber not specified), 768 M5A1 light tanks, and 369 tank destroyers (264 M10s, 77 M18 Hellcats, and 28 of the new M36 Jacksons).[10]

In towns that had recently welcomed American tankers as liberators, French and Belgian civilians now watched them pull out in the face of the staggering German offensive. According to the 781st Tank Battalion's unit history, "The French flags weren't hanging from the windows anymore, and no little kids waved. Moving back was a new and unwelcome experience."[11] The 781st, an independent tank battalion that supported Infantry units, would be assigned to five different ones during the Ardennes campaign. On January 9, 1945, backing up the 70th ("Trailblazers") Infantry Division, some of their tankers engaged the enemy in the Alsace region of France:

At 0600, Company A's tanks were warmed up in the cold Alsatian dawn. There was a foot of snow on the ground, and the air was misty. A carefully coordinated tank-Infantry attack had been worked out at 0200 that morning. At a few minutes before 0700, tanks and infantry arrived together at the edge of Sessenheim, as planned. It was still dark but, in spite of the mist and darkness, they could see the town. Several buildings in it had been set afire by the artillery.

A few minutes after 0700, they were a bare four hundred yards from a group of buildings on the outskirts of the town. At that moment every tank radio carried Sergeant Sexton's voice saying in tense amazement,

January 1945: As the tank scandal exploded in the press, Col. George Jarrett added clippings to his "Little Green Book," adding his own caustic, handwritten comments. Here, on one of *New York Times* reporter Hanson Baldwin's articles, Col. Jarrett—who had been warning of problems since 1942—damns Army Ordnance generals' "blind refusal to face the reality of the situation." *Photo by Robert Coldwell Sr., courtesy US Army Military History Institute, Carlisle Barracks, Pennsylvania*

Restored Konigstiger at the Deutsches Panzermuseum, Munster. Notice the main gun ammunition in the lower left corner. *Massimo Foti*

Luxembourg, 1945: Tankers "punch the tube" on a 105mm gun-equipped Sherman. Even in brutal winter temperatures (as the author would learn decades later) basic tank maintenance must go on.

*Photo by Robert Coldwell Sr.*

The White House: Standing room only at a wartime press conference. The Sherman tank scandal exploded on page A-1 of major newspapers across the country, forcing Roosevelt to address it in his 1945 State of the Union Address.

GIs examine a disabled Panther.

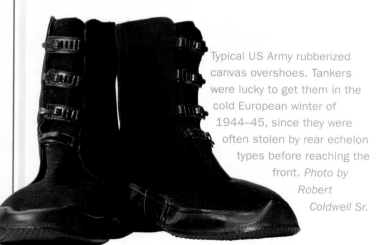

Typical US Army rubberized canvas overshoes. Tankers were lucky to get them in the cold European winter of 1944–45, since they were often stolen by rear echelon types before reaching the front. *Photo by Robert Coldwell Sr.*

"My God, it's as big as a house!" "It" was one of four German Mark VI Tiger tanks, dug in and painted white, that had been brought into the town secretly during the night. A moment after the Sergeant spoke, 75mm shells from our Shermans found their way to the Nazi tanks, but as Sergeant Johnson put it, "They bounced off like tennis balls."

It wasn't long before German shells from 88s, anti-tank, and self-propelled guns were everywhere. Technician Grade 5 Huya saw one shell hit to the right of Johnson's tank, then to the left, then one left a trail of sparks as it scraped harmlessly along the belly of the tank. Eight American tanks out of eight were hit in

as many minutes. The attack on Sessenheim ended with eleven men killed or MIA, fifteen seriously wounded, and with six of our tanks left burning in the snow at the edge of the town.[12]

The failure of American armor to stop the initial stages of the German offensive was such a shock to morale that the press, blind to the problem for three years, now splashed it across front pages. Associated Press correspondent Kenneth Dixon, "With the AEF on the Belgian Front, Jan. 3," wrote of captured German "news pictures," including "graphic pictures of blazing American tanks, some obviously taken in the midst of intense action":

One is especially graphic, even cruelly so. It shows a Sherman tank still smoldering, its tread knocked off and the turret askew. Hanging partly out of the turret are the remains of the American tank commander. It is not a picture you care to look at long, but it probably got quite a play in Berlin newspapers.[13]

"Must We Defeat Germany with Inferior Weapons?" asked *Newsweek's* Roland Gask in February 1945. "During the Battle of the Bulge, I learned of countless incidents illustrating the inferiority of our Sherman tanks to German machines…during the battle for Samree, north of Bastogne, an entire task force of the Second Armored Division was held up two hours at a crossroads by a lone King Tiger. The German tank stood up to everything the Americans could slam at it, including artillery, before lumbering off unscathed."[14]

Tankers add foliage to an already whitewashed Sherman. They have cotton cold weather caps designed to be worn as a liner under the usual tanker helmet; the long flap in back was an attempt to keep cold winter air out.

In a later, secret report to Gen. Eisenhower, tank gunner Cpl. Herman Gillen told of dueling a Tiger in the Ardennes. "After firing on it at a range of 300 yards and getting five hits on the turret, the German tank turned and fired on mine. With one shot it penetrated the turret, disabled the 75mm gun, and froze the turret completely. In my opinion, the Tiger and Panther are far superior to any of our tanks."[15]

"Fighting a tank in the depths of winter," observed Max Hastings, "was almost as tough as living in a foxhole. The Sherman's air intake sucked a constant icy blast into the turret, causing the commander and gunner to suffer special misery. Periscopes frosted. Condensation formed into icicles inside hulls. Starting up was often a major operation, and crews had to use 'Little Joe' portable generators to keep batteries charged when their engines were still."[16]

On January 14, 1945, tank commander Lt. Joseph Couri wrote near Bellevaux, "This was the coldest night that I experienced in the war":

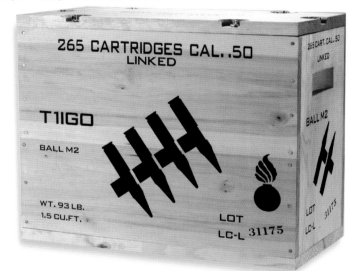

After going through the forest with the turret open and the snow tumbling down from the trees, I was completely wet. The tank…was a Frigidaire, and we were going to try and sleep in it. We were better off than the Infantry, for it was impossible for them to dig a foxhole.… They asked if they could bed down under our tanks, and they did. There was not much sleep that night. The shelling from both sides was continuous.[17]

The next day, *Time* magazine featured a "Post-Mortem on the Ardennes" that referenced the *New York Times*'s Hanson

A crate of belted .50-caliber ammunition for the M2 heavy machine guns used on the Sherman tank. Although dating from the Great War era, John Browning's trusty "Ma Deuce" was such a reliable design that sixty years after VE Day, the author used it as an M1A1 Abrams tank gunner. His unit even trained with leftover 1942-dated live rounds for service in Bosnia after the September 11, 2001, attacks. *Author's collection, photo by Robert Coldwell Sr.*

Baldwin's tough questions. At Aberdeen Proving Ground, George Jarrett pasted the article in his growing tank scandal scrapbook, writing in the margins, "I think we have kidded ourselves for the past 3 years, and Normandy and Germany have proven it."[18]

Even some Germans pitied American tankers in the M4. Entering Clervaux, Belgium, during the offensive, Hans Hejny of the Fifth Panzer Army noticed:

Another "Ronson" lights up, Oberkirchen, Germany, 1945.

a huge fire rages in the middle of the roadway, obstructing any passage.... Dense clouds of smoke float above our heads. Because of the dark smoke, I could not make out what was burning until a gust of wind, for an instant, provided sight of the street.

About 50 meters away, an American Sherman tank was fully aflame. Behind it some Americans sought cover, but these poor devils had no escape left. There was no possibility of flight. There were too many eyes, too many rifle barrels waiting tensely for them to step forward. Dense smoke clouded the scene almost completely, and the enormous heat exploded the ammunition inside the tank. Now, certainly, the Americans could not last too long behind the tank, and would have to leave...

A massive detonation wave shook the street. Whole pieces of steel were hurled into the air. The windowpanes of neighboring houses burst with loud cracks. A terrible gust of fiery wind threw me back, choking and coughing. Then I saw, for the first time, an American soldier, and he was jumping for his life (from the tank)...but no sooner did he make his

daring leap, than rifle and machine pistol shots whipped the pitiful man. Mortally wounded, he fell to the ground. A comrade took off to help him, risking his life. As he bent down to the fallen one, he, too, was dropped by murderous bullets.[19]

The American press had been repeating British propaganda claiming the Sherman was a world beater since 1942. Now they reversed themselves, conflicting with generals and politicians who attributed the Nazis' success to bad weather. On December 28, with all the candor of his eighty years, long-retired Gen. Peyton March (the Army's Chief of Staff during WWI) told the *New York Times* that such a flimsy excuse made him "just fall on my knees and weep."[20]

In one of its first combat actions, the independent 740th Tank Battalion supported the 82nd Airborne Division on the north side of the "Bulge." On January 7, its Second Platoon, Company A was near Arbrefontaine, Belgium:

The stories of some of these battles are sheer tragedy. American tankers, drilled to believe that the first to get his shot home was the victor, saw six or eight of their shells bounce off the enemy armor. They have been known to crawl out of their tanks and beat the ground with their fists, tears streaming down their cheeks in hysterical despair. Then they would see a Jerry "88" get the range, and pierce a Sherman with one shot.[1]

—The Baltimore *Evening Sun*, December 16, 1944

At about 0830 hours, word came down that a [Royal Tiger] was shooting hell out of things not very far down the road. Staff Sergeant Hendrix and Sergeant Fasoli advanced to take it out.

While Staff Sergeant Hendrix covered him, Sergeant Fasoli fired five rounds, which were all direct hits. They apparently jammed the King Tiger's turret, but the tank could not be destroyed. Seeing this, Lieutenant Tribby called up two tank destroyers, which carried 90mm guns. The King Tiger swung his gun on them, knocked them both out, and they both burned. Lieutenant Tribby then called up another TD and a 57mm towed AT gun. Lieutenant Tribby and Sergeant Fasoli led these guns into position, on foot. The TD fired fifteen rounds into the side of the King Tiger at a range of a little over 150 yards, but no rounds penetrated. However, the King Tiger finally did catch fire, and the crew bailed out. With this tank out of the way the attack was resumed, with Sergeant Fasoli spearheading and Sergeant Hendrix and Lieutenant Tribby following.

Sergeant Fasoli entered the town [probably Goronne, Belgium], where he encountered the second Panzer VI [Royal Tiger]. He fired twice at this tank at about fifty yards' range, backed up into the cover of a building, and fired three more rounds. They just glanced off. The Royal Tiger fired three rounds at him, and missed with all three. A US bazooka team armed with captured German Panzerfausts was called up to engage it, but while it was coming up, the Panzer VI withdrew. Sergeant

Fasoli then knocked out three machine-gun nests to the right of his tank.[21]

After years of cheery propaganda, it must have been confusing to civilians to read in the January 15, 1945, *New York Times*, "German Tanks Have Edge: Superior Maneuverability is Revealed in Bad Weather." While repeating the excuse that American setbacks were due to the weather, the *Times* also noted, "American armor is at a distinct disadvantage in dealing with German armor that already has proved itself superior in some respects…. Sherman tank crews…are now finding it impossible to get off the roads to maneuver. This is where German superiority in firepower and armor protection has shown up in all categories—medium and light tanks as well as tank destroyers."[22] The article told of a duel between two Shermans and a Panther near Houffalize, Belgium. Although the M4s had a powered turret (in contrast to the Panther's hand-cranked one), the Sherman could only get off two shots to the Panther's seven before retreating.

"Were German Armored Vehicles Better Than Ours?" asked Col. Albin Irzyk, veteran of the Ardennes, in a March 1946 *Army Ordnance* magazine article. In the "Bulge," he admitted, "the American tank was impotent when running into the German tank head-on."[23] Col. Irzyk later wrote of American tankers belatedly adopting a common sense German practice—whitewashing their tanks. In January 1945, his 8th Tank Battalion "received orders to begin whitewashing all vehicles…it made sense. With the

white, frozen landscape, the white vehicles would blend in better.... Apparently white vehicles had worked successfully for the Germans, who had pulled out all the stops in their Ardennes attack. Now the Battalion would be emulating them. Why not? Always go with a good idea, even if you have to borrow or steal it."[24]

While wartime news written for civilian consumption was often slanted to paint a rosy picture, one would expect the Army's internal publications to give a more realistic view. Instead, the Army Ordnance Association's bulletin bragged in a typical release, "The powerful new 90mm [M36 Jackson] tank destroyer is

hanging up an excellent record in mauling monster Royal Tiger tanks in fierce armor battles inside Germany... [crews] have found that the high-velocity 90mm gun is a deadly weapon against the Nazi giants." Firing improved HVAP ammunition, the M36 could succeed at close range, but there were too few of them, they suffered from a severe ammo shortage, and the M36 lacked the armor of a true tank.

TD gunners firing standard ammunition instead of hard-to-get HVAP rounds were disappointed:

**ABOVE:** Whitewash paint thrown on an M-36 Jackson tank destroyer. Luxembourg, January 1945. *US Signal Corps Photo via Ralph Riccio*

**LEFT:** Maj. Al Irzyk, who started out in the horse Cavalry, became one of the 4th Armored Division's best combat commanders.

Tests conducted by the 703rd Tank Destroyer Battalion in early December 1944 using captured Panthers indicated that the Panther's frontal armor could defeat some shots fired from as little as 150 yards. The Battalion concluded that the M36 should still maneuver for side shots against the Panther...if that were not possible, two TDs should engage the target...the M36's 90mm gun cannot penetrate the frontal armor of the King Tiger at any range. The Battalion called for better ammunition, rather than a bigger gun.[25]

While highlighting the rare M36 slowly reaching the ETO in small numbers, the Ordnance Association story overlooked the larger problem: the insufficient firepower of the Shermans when fighting Tigers and Panthers. Ironically, the article was dated December 15, 1944, the day before German tanks spearheaded an offensive that overnight made such cheery pronouncements about "mauling monster Royal Tiger tanks" seem ludicrous even to civilians at home.

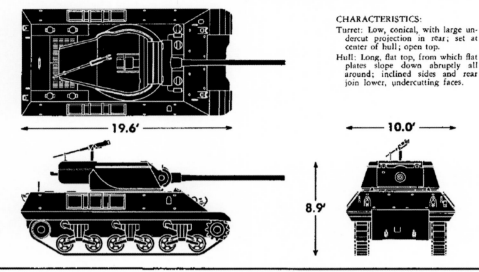

U. S. ☆                          **90-MM GUN MOTOR CARRIAGE, M36**

CHARACTERISTICS:
Turret: Low, conical, with large undercut projection in rear; set at center of hull; open top.
Hull: Long, flat top, from which flat plates slope down abruptly all around; inclined sides and rear join lower, undercutting faces.

Armament:
One 90-mm gun in turret.
One caliber .50 machine gun on rear of turret.
Traction: Full track; six equally spaced bogie wheels suspended in pairs; driving sprocket in front; three track support rollers.

INTEREST DATA:
This is the tank destroyer weapon that is stopping the newest German 67-ton "Royal Tiger" tank. It is a modified 90-mm AA gun mounted on a chassis similar to that of the M10. Its main distinctive features are the extreme length of the 90-mm barrel, the large undercut projection in rear of the turret, and the modified M3 medium tank running gear.

C 4, FEBRUARY 1945
FROM DATA CURRENTLY AVAILABLE
WAR DEPARTMENT FM 30-40

— 19.6' —          — 10.0' —          8.9'

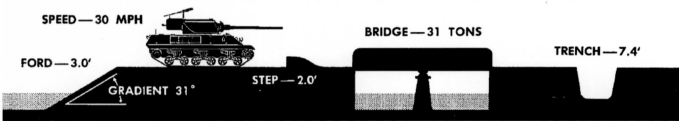

SPEED — 30 MPH          BRIDGE — 31 TONS          TRENCH — 7.4'
FORD — 3.0'
GRADIENT 31°     STEP — 2.0'

*Photo by Robert Coldwell Sr.*

In spite of its unequivocal title, "Shermans Defeat Nazi Tigers," appearing in newspapers on December 16, 1944—the first day of the "Bulge"—told a sad story of tank battles in Germany, with the same problems as in Belgium: tankers had to face better-armored, more powerful heavy tanks with underpowered main guns. Correspondent Jack Bell described the 70-ton Royal Tiger, "with its high-velocity barrel 88mm gun, also new and considered the finest in the business."[26] After meeting and narrowly defeating masses of Tigers, the US Second Armored Division was "licking its wounds."[27] Bell's article contradicts claims that Ordnance was unaware of the gun problem, or that GIs did not call for a more powerful tank until it was too late.

While failing to address the M4's greatest shortcomings, generals from Patton to Marshall would soon claim the Sherman was more maneuverable than Tigers and Panthers, as if this made up for an inadequate gun and decent armor. But Bell's article also discounts this "mobility excuse":

American tanks cannot beat Germany's in open combat. The Panther and Tiger armor will repel our tank-gun shells, while their 75 and 88mm. guns will shoot through our best armor. "We won because of sheer numbers," one tank officer said.... In mud, the usual condition here, a Sherman will sink half a foot deeper than the Tiger. Tigers moved across ground where Shermans were mired, despite the fact that the Tiger is 70 tons, the Sherman half that weight. The Americans won by feinting and sparring.[28]

**U. S.  ARMY  FIELD  RATION  D**
To be eaten slowly (in about a half hour). Can be dissolved by crumbling into a cup of boiling water if desired as a beverage.
INGREDIENTS: Chocolate Sugar, Skim Milk Powder, Cocoa Fat, Oat Flour, Artificial Flavoring, 0.45 mg. Vitamin B₁ (Thiamin Hydrochloride).
4 OUNCES NET..........................600 CALORIES

The infamous "D-Bar." A hard chocolate bar packed with nutrients and intended for emergencies, when GIs ran out of regular rations in the field. While GIs joked they broke one's teeth, they learned to shave off pieces and boil them into ersatz hot chocolate. *Photo by Robert Coldwell Sr.*

Eventually, Army leaders would claim better tanks were not wanted nor requested. But at the front, tank commander Sgt. Louis Weir of Detroit left no doubt: "I want a tank with a 90-mm gun. A tank officer nodded approval, as did 30 tank fighters."[29]

Even when small numbers of the marginally improved 76mm Shermans and more powerful 90mm M36 Jacksons reached the ETO, they faced a serious shortage of tank ammunition. Gen. Eisenhower had requested up-gunned tanks and TDs in July 1944, but the enhanced new HVAP rounds did not reach the European Theater until September, and in small quantities. The improved ammo gave GIs a chance of punching through German armor from close range (if the Germans did not pick them off first from a distance), but was delayed by production problems and tungsten and carbide shortages.

"Monty" meets the press, flanked by "Ike" and "Brad." During the war, all three attempted to tamp down the growing scandal in the civilian press over problems with the Sherman tank's inadequate firepower and armor protection.

Along with a dearth of ammunition and replacement crews, tankers also lacked fuel. "Not only didn't we get the human resources we needed," wrote Sgt. Nat Frankel, "but supplies couldn't keep up with us either. So what do you do? You walk, that's what you do. We'd bivouac at night, and then carry our gasoline and ammunition back to the line with us. Not one tank was allowed to double back, not one tank could leave its hard-won clod of stinking earth, to pick up supplies."[30]

According to Gen. Marshall's postwar *Report*, "In this country, an urgent demand was made for maximum production; fast rail and water transportation was utilized to make shipments direct from the production lines...and rationing to less active theaters, as well as stabilized fronts in the European theater itself, became rigid. Only by these measures was it possible... to secure an adequate supply of ammunition for the final battles against Germany."[31]

Marshall's postwar assurances notwithstanding, not only was the US unable to field a tank with adequate gun and armor protection, but during the Army's largest European battle it failed to provide GIs with decent tank ammunition, a basic necessity. As late as March 1945, weeks before V-E Day, tankers told Eisenhower in the secret White-Rose Reports of having to go into battle with only four rounds of the new ammo.[32]

The December 27, 1944, New York *Herald Tribune* was frank about what was happening in the Ardennes, which (in terms of numbers of Americans captured) ranked with Bataan and Corregidor as one of the worst US defeats, eclipsing even the North

Belgium, winter 1945: GIs stand next to nicely parallel parked captured Panther tank. *USAAF*

Africa-Tunisia routs. "Superior Tanks Get Credit for Nazi Advances: U.S. Ordnance Experts Call Army Far Behind Enemy in Armored Equipment," blared the headline on reporter Don Cook's story.[33]

Since "Ordnance Experts" had been missing warning signs for three years, this about face contradicted the reassurances of Army and Roosevelt administration officials. "Failure of the Army to receive tanks comparable to the latest German models such as the Royal Tiger," the *Herald Tribune* reported, "was said today by Ordnance experts to be responsible in a large degree

An American officer inspects an abandoned Panther.

HEADQUARTERS
THIRD UNITED STATES ARMY

O each officer and soldier in the Third United States Army, I wish a Merry Christmas. I have full confidence in your courage, devotion to duty, and skill in battle. We march in our might to complete victory. May God's blessing rest upon each of you on this Christmas Day.

*G S Patton Jr.*

G. S. PATTON, JR.
Lieutenant General,
Commanding, Third United States Army.

PRAYER

ALMIGHTY and most merciful Father, we humbly beseech Thee, of Thy great goodness, to restrain these immoderate rains with which we have had to contend. Grant us fair weather for Battle. Graciously hearken to us as soldiers who call upon Thee that armed with Thy power, we may advance from victory to victory, and crush the oppression and wickedness of our enemies, and establish Thy justice among men and nations. Amen.

for the success of the Nazi counter-offensive." Although "All figures on American tank losses in the fighting on the Western front are being withheld," wrote Cook, headlines now screamed what GIs had been saying since 1943, and what the administration had been denying:

> A point-by-point comparison of American and German armored equipment, obtained from an authorized source, left little doubt that the superiority is on the enemy side.
>
> Not only are the Germans putting superior tanks into the field, but they have been able to improve their

armor steadily in the last two years, despite the pounding their factories have taken from the air. The latest model Royal Tiger, with a completely redesigned turret and an improved version of the 88-millimeter gun which proved so deadly in the African campaign, made its appearance in the early fall.

**No U.S. Heavy Tank:**

Although the first of the German Tiger tanks…made its appearance in the spring of 1943 in North Africa [sic, against the British and Americans—the Tiger actually debuted in Russia in late 1942], American forces still rely on the M4 medium tank…as their basic armored equipment… No specially designed American heavy tank is in the field…

…The Tiger was re-designed and improved in the winter of 1943–1944. The present Royal Tiger weighs sixty-seven tons, compared to the fifty-four tons of the original Tiger model…it has an improved turret, and a heavier 88-millimeter gun with a double-cast barrel to give it higher velocity and consequently greater power.… The M4…is outclassed by the 88.

**M4 Weak in Armor:**

The M4 falls down in its armor. The tank must go into action against twice its weight, and is much more easily knocked out by the German 88 than the Americans

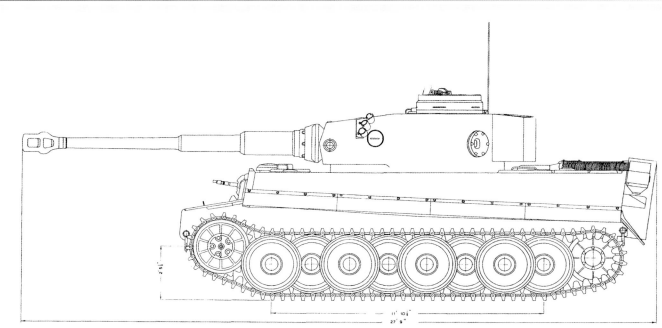

Profile of a Tiger I. *Courtesy US Army Military History Institute, Carlisle Barracks, Pennsylvania*

Gen. George S. Patton in an Army Air Force sheepskin jacket.

A 692nd Tank Destroyer Battalion GI poses with the notoriously large, bulky 3-inch towed anti-tank gun derided as "McNair's Folly." Imagine having to move and set one up in the ice and snow of the Ardennes; "TD" man Cpl. Jack Myers of the 692nd recalled with the author it was not a pleasant task.

can knock out the Royal Tiger.... Not only is the M4 outclassed by the enemy heavy tank…but in the medium-tank class it must match a faster, more heavily armored German model in the Panther. Weighing forty-five tons in action, the Panther can travel thirty miles an hour, and carries frontal armor of four and a quarter inches—slightly heavier than the M4.... As a result of the superior armor and heavy firepower of the enemy tanks, Americans have been forced to resort to flanking attacks, rather than direct and quicker frontal assaults, in armor combat on the Western front.[34]

The *New York Sun* concurred the next day, January 28, 1945, adding:

Only superiority in numbers and better maneuvering of Armored Forces have allowed American tanks to meet German tanks in battle on anything like equal terms. It is not characteristic of Americans to receive such an unpleasant truth as inevitable. They will wish to know why something was not done to give the American armies

a tank that would match the Tiger, which first made its appearance on the front in Africa almost two years ago.

The unidentified Ordnance experts have not gone far enough. They have put a finger on one of the main reasons for the success that the Germans have had, but they have not put a finger on the reasons for American failure to deprive the Germans of their advantage in armor.[35]

Another disaster was the ineffectiveness of Gen. McNair's towed guns to stop tanks:

The towed tank destroyer battalions were doomed by the combat in the Ardennes. One study concluded that self-propelled tank destroyers were five to six times more effective than the towed guns, and that the towed 3-inch guns were successful in only two out of nine defensive actions. In contrast, the self-propelled M10

Photo by Robert Coldwell Sr.

3-inch tank destroyers had a favorable exchange ration of 1:1.9 when operating without Infantry support, and an excellent ratio of 1:6 when integrated into an Infantry defense. The M10 tank destroyer units were successful in 14 out of 16 defensive actions against German tanks. The First Army report noted that tank destroyer battalion losses totaled 119, of which 86 were towed guns; a clear disproportion that revealed the glaring vulnerability of the towed guns…. It is clear that during the battle of the Ardennes, the self-propelled battalion again proved its superiority over the towed battalion for both offensive and defensive action.[36]

A look at the 692nd Tank Destroyer Battalion around this time shows the confusion that plagued the use of "TDs" throughout the war, and the persistence of Gen. McNair's bias towards towed anti-tank guns over self-propelled vehicles or tanks—a dispute not resolved until the war's end. According to a secret January 1945 combat report submitted from Germany and signed by Lt. Col. Samuel Morse, commanding officer of the 692nd, from the period January 1–10, the unit was equipped with the awkward 3-inch towed anti-tank gun called "McNair's Folly" by GIs because it was difficult to move and emplace. The 692nd

GIs of the 773rd Tank Destroyer Battalion and their whitewashed mount, January 1945. The personal gear, tarps, sleeping bags, etc., strapped onto the side of the open turret give an idea of the crowded living conditions for a four-man crew.

was "continuing to support the Infantry Regiments and to deliver reinforcing Artillery Fire in support of organic Field Artillery Battalions" and "indirect fire positions, in support of the artillery."[37] In other words, a static role; the towed guns would be pulled into place by a half-track, then dug in (emplaced) to fire from one position. This continued from January 11–20, with the men also "preparing additional "Dummy positions"[38]; digging in, a reactive role in which tank hunting was not encouraged, nor easy to do.

But from January 21–31, the unit prepared to turn in their towed guns, as "the Battalion began preparation for possible conversion to Self-Propelled Tank Destroyers," i.e., the M-36 Jackson. "A program of training was coordinated with the 702nd Tank Destroyer Battalion (SP)…in the vicinity of LINCE, Belgium.… Selected personnel from this Battalion attended classes being held on maintenance, employment of Self-Propelled Tank Destroyers, and observed range practice of M-36 Self-Propelled Tank Destroyers. As of 31 January 1945, this Battalion had sent four (4) officers and forty-two (42) EM (enlisted men) to such classes."[39]

While better equipment was welcome, imagine the confusion among soldiers who had trained with one weapon for years, only to have it taken away as they converted to a new one as battles raged inside Germany. And as the unit was reorganized, not every GI was lucky enough to be assigned to the new M-36. The TD men not selected, recalled Cpl. Jack Myers to the author, often found themselves shipped off to the Infantry. So in this example of just one unit, in a one month period, the unresolved TD debate caused such disruption that the 692nd TD men went from manning towed guns, to possibly converting to the new Jackson self-propelled TD, to potential reassignment to the Infantry.

Ironically, amid embarrassing US defeats in the Ardennes, the controversial self-propelled tank destroyers (M10s, M18s, and new M36s) showed some success. The TDs had been created to respond to 1939–1940-style blitzkrieg massed formations of German tanks on the offensive, but by 1943–1944, the Germans were mostly on the defensive until their Ardennes counterattack. There, for once, the Panzers conformed to the elusive "textbook" conditions for TD deployment that stateside theorists had been awaiting for years. Attempting to repeat their old 1940 successes, the Germans hoarded many of their best tanks to attack in long, massed spearheads towards Allied lines. At last, it seemed, the TDs could play their long-anticipated role: defensive, reactive, and ceding the initiative to the enemy.

The *Saturday Evening Post* told of a duel near Noville, close to Bastogne. "Like the curtain on a winter snow scene, the fog lifted with startling suddenness. There, deployed in an open field on the edge of Noville, sat six more German tanks. Three American tank destroyers opened fire. The enemy tanks tried to scoot over the brow of a nearby hill, but the unerring tank destroyers picked them off one by one, like ducks in a shooting gallery."[40]

With their high speed (due, unfortunately for their crews, to thinner armor) and more powerful guns than standard M4s, the TDs helped blunt the massed German assaults at Bastogne and St. Vith. Master Sgt. Theodore Brush called the new M18 Hellcat "a tanker's dream: an electric turret with a 76mm gun with a muzzle brake, radial aircraft engines, and—the best thing we

US five-gallon "Jerry" (fuel) can. GIs in the ETO were probably surprised to receive "USMC" stamped cans, which stood not for US Marine Corps, but merely noted the manufacturer: US Metal Container Company of Miami, Oklahoma. *Photo by Robert Coldwell Sr.*

liked about them—automatic transmission. They were real quiet, and very fast."[41]

Another TD man, Howard Lutz, described the "shoot and scoot" tactics that used the Hellcat's speed and mobility to best advantage:

When in a firefight, I wanted to be able to outmaneuver my opponent. With the M18, we were certainly able to do this better than with the M10. We liked to pop over a hill with only our gun snouts exposed and knock off several rounds until we were under fire, then slide back out of sight and pop up elsewhere to knock off a few more…we were always moving, as a moving target is much harder to hit than one sitting still. With the M18, many times we were able to outflank the enemy.

We did not like a frontal attack on a lot of German tanks due to the heavy armor they carried up front, but their suspension and track systems made a good target as well as their motor carriage. Much less armor there, and of course, they were practically blind in an attack from this direction, as they had to turn their vehicles to face us, or slow down, or even stop to turn their turret in our direction, and by that time, we were off to another site.[42]

When issued an adequate supply of HVAP ammunition, the rare M36 Jackson was also impressive—the best armed TD of the war, with a powerful 90mm main gun. Author Steve Zaloga judged it "the only American AFV [armored fighting vehicle] capable of dealing with the new generation of thickly armored German panzers."[43] Cpl. Jack Myers was a gunner with the 692nd Tank Battalion. Though trained on towed guns, he was happy to convert to the new "TD." With it, "We could knock out tanks, vehicles, bunkers," he recalled proudly to the author. "The only thing I couldn't knock out was the Tiger—it was built tough, with that thick armor!"[44]

American tanks cannot meet latest-model German tanks on even terms…the failure to equip American armed forces with tanks that are the equal of the German Tiger or Panther is in great measure responsible for the success of the German drive [in the Ardennes].[2]
—The New York *Sun*, December 28, 1944

December 26, 1944, 1650 hours: "Cobra King," an M4A3E2 "Jumbo" Sherman, becomes the first tank to break into embattled Bastogne. Her crew included Lt. Charles Boggess (tank commander), Cpl. Milton Dickerman (gunner), Pvt. James Murphy (loader), Pvt. Hubert Smith (driver), and Pvt. Harold Hafner (bow gunner). As the "4" and the triangle (the symbol for an Armored Division) proudly indicate, she was attached to the 37th Tank Battalion of the 4th AD.

Close up of side markings on "Cobra King." Typically on US Army tanks, this included the vehicle's War Department individual serial number (under the "USA") and shipping data (on the left), such as height and weight restrictions—always a concern in fighting a global war. *Author photo, courtesy of the National Armor and Cavalry Heritage Foundation*

"The trouble with the TDs," explained armor historian George Forty, "was that they were continually being used as tanks, a role for which they had never been designed. Their thin armor and open tops did not lend themselves to tank-versus-tank engagements."[45]

And there were too few of them; by December 20, only 306 M18s and 236 M36s were in all overseas combat zones. Even if more had been available for the Ardennes fighting, the TDs, like the Shermans, lacked a decent supply of the promising new HVAP rounds.

While the Pentagon attempted to downplay problems, pushing stories that presented American armor in the best light (such as the 4th Armored Division rolling to the rescue of surrounded paratroopers in Bastogne), Sherman and TD losses piled up. From December 20, 1944, to January 20, 1945, alone, 614 Shermans (75mm, 76mm, and 105mm main guns), each with a

The real "Cobra King" under restoration. The wooden plank across the bow (front) was a GI improvisation, a simple shelf for gas cans, ration craters, etc. It also minimized the too visible white star. *Author photo courtesy of the National Armor and Cavalry Heritage Foundation*

**RIGHT:** Mug shot for war crimes trials; Peiper's SS troops committed the notorious Malmedy Massacre, executing Belgian civilians and unarmed GIs after they surrendered (including medics). Peiper spent almost twelve years in prison; after moving to France, he was killed by unknown avengers on Bastille Day 1976.

four- or five-man crew, were lost in the ETO. Among the TDs, 122 M10, M18, and M36 tank destroyers were destroyed.[46]

But the upbeat stateside press releases on the Ardennes fighting could not silence angry tankers at the front. The poor performance of American armor during "the Bulge" finally exposed the Sherman tank scandal that erupted in the stateside media in early 1945.

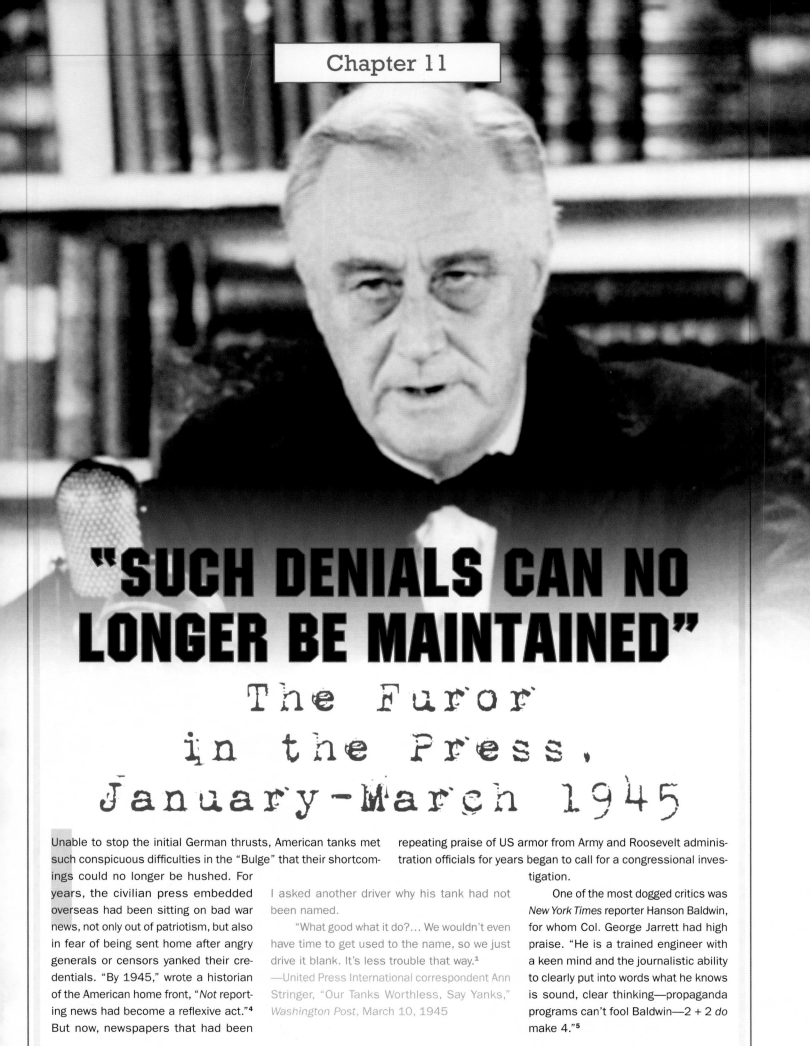

# Chapter 11

# "SUCH DENIALS CAN NO LONGER BE MAINTAINED"

## The Furor in the Press, January-March 1945

Unable to stop the initial German thrusts, American tanks met such conspicuous difficulties in the "Bulge" that their shortcomings could no longer be hushed. For years, the civilian press embedded overseas had been sitting on bad war news, not only out of patriotism, but also in fear of being sent home after angry generals or censors yanked their credentials. "By 1945," wrote a historian of the American home front, "*Not* reporting news had become a reflexive act."[4] But now, newspapers that had been repeating praise of US armor from Army and Roosevelt administration officials for years began to call for a congressional investigation.

One of the most dogged critics was *New York Times* reporter Hanson Baldwin, for whom Col. George Jarrett had high praise. "He is a trained engineer with a keen mind and the journalistic ability to clearly put into words what he knows is sound, clear thinking—propaganda programs can't fool Baldwin—2 + 2 *do* make 4."[5]

> I asked another driver why his tank had not been named.
>
> "What good what it do?... We wouldn't even have time to get used to the name, so we just drive it blank. It's less trouble that way.[1]
>
> —United Press International correspondent Ann Stringer, "Our Tanks Worthless, Say Yanks," *Washington Post*, March 10, 1945

February 1945: hit and on fire, a 76mm gun-equipped M4A3 of the 1st Armored Division does a slow burn.

Photo enhancement by Robert Coldwell Sr.

In his January 5 article "The German Blow III: New German Tank Proves Superior to Ours—Inquiry by Congress Urged," Baldwin asked:

Why, at this late stage of the war, are American tanks inferior to the enemy's? That they are inferior the fighting in Normandy showed, and the recent battles in the Ardennes have again emphatically demonstrated. This has been denied, explained away and hushed up, but the men who are fighting our tanks against much heavier, better-armored and more powerfully armed German monsters know the truth. It is high time that Congress got to the bottom of a situation that does no credit to the War Department. This does not mean that our tanks are bad. They are not; they are good. They are the best tanks in the world—next to The Germans.[6]

"YES!!!," Jarrett wrote in all upper case letters on the article, adding it to his private scandal scrapbook—"ASK THE TANK CREW!" He damned a "refusal to realistically face tank facts...our blind refusal to face the truth of the situation," that in spite of an ongoing

"sales program" of propaganda, "We are little better off than at El Alamein," where the M4 had debuted. While German tank technology moved steadily forward, Jarrett observed, it was "Always the same story.... I've seen this day by day...we never beat Jerry, but catch up to last year's model, next year."[7]

A controversy that had been suppressed for years now reached government's highest levels. As public and press outrage demanded answers, Roosevelt's administration went into full "damage control" mode. The occasion he chose to concede the problem was his 1945 State of the Union Address.

On January 6, 1945, President Roosevelt spoke to the nation. Back in 1940, to counter charges of unpreparedness with impressive production figures, he had ordered the Army to freeze obsolete designs and start rolling *any* tanks out of the factory gates. After years of pressuring the Army and American industry to produce ever more tanks, Roosevelt now lamented...a shortage of them. Though he did not explain it to the country, the 1944–45 tank shortage was not caused solely by tanks destroyed in combat, as might be assumed. It also stemmed from too optimistic estimates of future tank losses, and from the late 1943 decision to reduce tank production in the hope of muddling through with the flawed tanks on hand.

Calling tanks one of the Army's "most important" needs, a "critical production program with sharply rising needs," Roosevelt admitted, "Present production is behind requirements." But as in 1940, he emphasized quantity rather than an honest assessment of the quality of American tanks. "Although unprecedented production figures have made possible our victories, we shall have to increase our goals even more in certain items."[8]

And who would pay the price of the tank shortage? The GIs Roosevelt praised: "the average, easy-going, hard-fighting young American, who carries the weight of battle on his own shoulders.

M1A1 Thompson .45-caliber submachine gun, better known from gangster movies as the "Tommy Gun." Along with the Colt M1911 pistol, it was a favorite personal weapon of Sherman tankers because inside a crowded tank turret, its compact size was a better fit than a long M1 rifle. *Photo by Robert Coldwell Sr.*

It is to him that we, and all future generations of Americans, must pay grateful tribute. But it is of small satisfaction to him to know that monuments will be raised to him in the future. He wants, he needs, and he is entitled to insist upon, our full and active support—now."[9]

As to the quality of American tanks and the heart of the scandal, Roosevelt scaled new heights of hypocrisy. "In the continuing progress of this war we have constant need for new types of weapons, for we cannot afford to fight the war of today or tomorrow with the weapons of yesterday."

He referred to the T26, delayed and obstructed for years. "For example, the American Army now has developed a new tank with a gun more powerful than any yet mounted on a fast-moving vehicle. The Army will need many thousands of these new tanks in 1945."[10]

Ever the politician, this was the same man who had promised voters in October 1940, "Your boys are not going to be sent into any foreign wars,"[11] then demanded hordes of obsolete tanks ("the weapons of yesterday") that contributed to the deaths of thousands of those "boys." With stunning hypocrisy, he also scolded the country: "If we do not keep constantly ahead of our enemies in the development of new weapons, we pay for our backwardness with the life's blood of our sons."[12]

Roosevelt implied to millions of radio listeners—many with sons at the European front—that a problem brushed under the carpet for years would be addressed by "many thousands" of new T26s on their way to the battlefields.[13] Most of them would never arrive.

His words on the "hard-fighting young American" who "carries the weight of battle on his own shoulders" bring to mind an aspect of the scandal that, with all the furor over the technical details of machines, has been overlooked: the shortage of trained tanker replacements. The disastrous 1943 command decision to lower the numbers of tank crewmen to be trained in 1944— based on optimistic predictions of tank "wastage" and the war's

duration—caused replacements with little or no armor training to be hastily thrown into the tank war as so much cannon fodder. Replacement O. J. Brock: "I was in combat less than a week after I was brought in from headquarters" after arriving in France.[14]

This tragedy is epitomized in the story of 18-year-old PFC Billy Wolfe, a handsome Virginian who joined the 712th Tank Battalion as a replacement Sherman loader on March 4, 1945. He wrote home the next day to his family, "I have joined an outfit. As a lieutenant told us, 'the best goddamned outfit in the world'…it played a major part in smashing the Siegfried Line, and has fought since D-Day, and drove the Nazis from France. It is the 712th Tank Battalion. I am in Company C and in Germany now."[15]

Sgt. Otha Martin, tank commander, recalled Pvt. Wolfe and another new replacement dropped off at the 712th with him as "just youngsters…. The first or second day they got there, they were talking to me. They were concerned about how they would do in combat." Martin told them, "Boys, I don't know how you'll do, but the fact that you're concerned about it, I believe you'll be all right." Well, they both got killed in just ten or twelve days, but they didn't get killed because they were bad soldiers…. When one of those big shells hits you, you're dead; it's not your fault either."[16]

Pvt. Wolfe's letter arrived in Virginia on March 16. "You can be glad you are not boys," he teased his twin sisters, "or there would be the possibility of you getting into this mess, although I don't think (and hope) it won't last that long."[17] As Wolfe's family read his letter that day, his Sherman was nearing Pfaffenheck, Germany.

Billy Wolfe would enter combat just twelve days after joining his battalion.

"I hardly know how to start this letter," tank platoon leader Lt. Francis Fuller wrote to Pvt. First Class Hubert Wolfe (Billy's brother, serving in the Infantry) in July 1945,

> as you don't even know who I am…Lieutenant Seeley, the adjutant of our battalion, received a letter from you asking the facts about your brother, Billy Wolfe. As I was

---

I am a tank platoon leader, at present recovering from wounds received during the Battle of the Bulge. Since I have spent three years in a tank platoon doing everything, and at one time or another held every position and have read everything on armor I could get my hands on during this time, I would like to get this off my chest. No statement, claim, or promise made by any part of the Army can justify thousands of dead and wounded tankmen, or thousands of others who depended on the tank for support.[3]

—an anonymous "2nd Lieutenant of Cavalry," *New York Times*, March 19, 1945

1942 dated canvas pouch full of 20-round Thompson SMG "stick" magazines. *Photo by Robert Coldwell Sr.*

his platoon leader and was there when he was killed, Lt. Seeley has asked me to try to give you the facts you requested. Captain Sheppard has already written your mother, but perhaps he has not told her exactly how he died. But I am trusting that since you are a soldier, I can tell you the true facts, and then perhaps you can tell your folks what you think they ought to know.

Your brother joined my platoon on the 4th of March while we were driving to the Rhine River, following up the 11th Armored Division…on the evening of March 14, we crossed the Moselle River and found that the Infantry that had preceded us had gotten into a jam and lost over half of their men and gotten cut off, so we were called upon to rescue them.

On the morning of the 16th, we were told to attack the town of Pfaffenheck…. The TDs started into the town first, but as they rolled over the crest of a hill, the lead tank destroyer was knocked out by an anti-tank gun. They withdrew, and succeeded in knocking out the gun and another.

We were then ordered to try to enter the town…. Your brother was in the No. 2 tank, which was commanded by Sergeant Hayward, with Johnny Clingerman as gunner, William Harrell as driver, Koon Moy as bow gunner, and your brother as loader...all of the tanks got into the town okay except No. 3, which encountered a 40mm AA gun, which killed the tank commander.

We took all but three houses, when the Infantry got stopped by firing from the woods east of the town. In order to knock out the gun that was holding up the Infantry, the tanks started to move out to get a firing position. I sent the second section along the backs of the houses, while I took the first section into an orchard. My tank was in the lead, and the tank your brother was in was on my left flank, slightly behind.

Just after we had passed an opening between two houses, my loader told me No. 2 tank [PFC Wolfe's] had been hit. I looked over, and the men were piling out. The tank was blazing. The shot had gone through the right sponson, puncturing the gas tank.

I didn't know then how many men had gotten out, so I tried to get my tank into position to rescue the men. But as I moved into position, my tank received a direct hit through the gun shield, killing my loader. Fortunately for the rest of us, my driver was able to move the tank before the Heinies could fire again.

After giving Clingerman [Wolfe's gunner] first aid and getting the rest of the boys calmed down, I took my gunner with me and we crawled out to where Sergeant Hayward [Wolfe's tank commander] lay wounded. I found that he would have to have a stretcher to be moved.

I went back to the medics, and then I learned from the rest of the crew that your brother never got out of the tank. As the tank was burning all this time, we could not get near it. I don't know if you have ever seen one of our tanks burn, but when 180 gallons of gas start burning, and ammunition starts to explode, the best thing to do is keep away.

When the medics got back out to Sergeant Hayward, I found he had been killed by a sniper.... Your brother's tank continued to burn all that night, but in the morning we were able to go out to investigate. We determined that your brother had been killed instantly, as the shell had hit right above his seat. There was nothing visible but a few remnants of bones that were so badly burned that if they had been touched, they would have turned to ashes.

As for personal effects, you could not recognize anything because the intense heat and the exploding ammunition had fused most of the metal parts together.

Maybe I have told you more than I ought to, but I really would like to help you in any way I can. Your brother was very well liked by all the rest of the crew, but he was so doggone quiet that we hardly ever knew he was around. Of the other members of his crew, driver William Harrell is still with me, as is Koon Moy [bow gunner/assistant driver]. Clingerman, the gunner, lost his eye and had his legs filled with shrapnel, and is now back in the States.

"That was the worst day I had in combat," concluded Lt. Fuller. "I lost three tanks, I had four men killed and three wounded.... Incidentally, you will have to use your judgment as to how much of this story you want to pass on to your mother.... There is no use in trying to tell you how sorry I feel, because you've been through the same things yourself, so I'll just say so long and good luck."[18]

The January 15 issue of *Newsweek* featured "Decision to the Tiger: Doubt in Caliber of US Arms Raised by New German Weapons." The magazine recalled printing a rare photo of an early Tiger back in 1943, quite a scoop at the time, "the first picture of the now famous Nazi Tiger tank to be published in the United States."[19] *Newsweek* had speculated that the mystery tank might be armed with an 88mm main gun. When asked for

A Tiger tank commander surveys the field in Russia, March 1943. *Courtesy German Federal Archive*

## Army Ordnance Chief Says Our Weapons Top Enemy's

By FRANK CAREY
(Associated Press Science Writer)

WASHINGTON, Feb. 3.—The army chief of ordnance, answering critics of American armament, says he has this assurance from top ranking generals and scores of enlisted men: "We need not only have no apology for any item of American ordnance in comparison with that of the enemy—but we're leading them all the way."

**Not Enough Shells**

Returning from a tour of inspection of ordnance in the European and Mediterranean theaters, Major General Levin H. Campbell told the Associated Press:

"The only real criticism of American ordnance which was made by General Eisenhower and the rest is they haven't as much ammunition as they'd like to have—but I can assure the American public that matter will be adequately cared for under the stepped up program dating from December 1st.

**Answers Critics Of Tanks**

Referring particularly to published reports our tanks are not big enough to cope with the Nazis' vaunted Royal Tiger and Hunting Panther tanks from the standpoint of armor and firepower, Campbell asserted:

"I could build a tank as big as the Pentagon if the generals in the field said they wanted one, but there is no evidence to date that they want or need tanks larger than those we now employ. Those men know what they want—they're good judges of horse flesh!

"General Eisenhower told me that to date the Germans have lost two tanks to every one of ours. How could we have such a record if our tanks were inferior?"

He said our generals have requested—and have received—"tanks of great maneuverability designed for rapid developing offensive tactics and capable of deploying like a lot of rattlesnakes."

General Campbell said the 73 ton Nazi Royal Tiger which packs an 88 millimeter gun is "big and clumsy, with a lack of maneuverability, plagued by a great deal of engine trouble and subject to being caught in soft mud where it's like a sitting duck—capable of being knocked off from the side by even a bazooka."

**Sherman Best In World**

General Patton, he said, told him during his trip that our tanks, in combat with German Tigers, have proved to be the "best tanks in the world." He said Patton declared our 35 ton General Sherman, with its electrically controlled gun turret, is able to fire several rounds while the Tigers with hand powered turrets, were able to get off one.

Campbell reported we also have a new "assault tank" which is a development of the Sherman, with double its armor and about five tons heavier.

### Eisenhower Says We Need More Men, Guns

WASHINGTON, Feb. 3. — (AP) — General Dwight D. Eisenhower, declaring we have a "general superiority" in weapons and ammunition over the enemy in Europe, said "What we need is more of both, as well as men, to finish the job."

The general made his statements in a letter from his headquarters in the European theater to Major General Levin H. Campbell, Jr., army chief of ordnance.

The text of the letter dated January 18th and given to the Associated Press by General Campbell, is as follows:

Dear General Campbell:
Battlefield reports from every front in the European theater of operations continue to tell of the splendid quality of our weapons and ammunition. What we need is more of both, as well as men, to finish the job.

Last Summer, the enemy was defeated in Normandy by our firepower, and the teamwork of our

action is an interesting question: particularly interesting, we should think, to various American supply and statecraft geniuses who were telling us before the [1944 Presidential] election that our fighting gear was the world's best, and have been berating us for complacency since shortly before the election."[22]

As the scandal's intensity rose in the press, Army and administration leaders issued a flood of denials and obfuscation. "We need not only have no apology for any item of American Ordnance in comparison with that of the enemy," Chief of Ordnance Campbell claimed in early February, "but we're leading them all the way."[23] Cleverly but inaccurately (since Campbell privately supported production of the T26 heavy tank), he noted armor leaders had been offered a heavy tank (the lackluster M6 behemoth) but refused it back in 1940. He did not clarify that their rejection was of that particular model, not of all better gunned or better armored tanks. Gen. Campbell also claimed, as if it were 1939, that what the *generals* (not the tankers at the front) wanted was "lighter, nimbler armor."[24]

Campbell produced statements from Eisenhower and his subordinates Patton and Devers, downplaying problems with the M4 and insisting they were satisfied with it, as Gen. Eisenhower had requested they do. For all his easy grin and likable manner, Ike was no babe in the woods when it came to public relations; after watching him interact with some 200 reporters in Paris on February 26, 1945, FDR's White House press secretary Steve Early—no stranger himself to fielding probing questions—called it "the most magnificent performance of any man at a press conference that I have ever seen."

Merle Miller, writing for *Yank* magazine, admired Eisenhower's ability to deflect politically dangerous questions; asked about his difficult relationship with British Gen. Bernard Mont-

an opinion, the Ordnance Department had responded this was impossible; the 88, they said, was too big to be mounted in a tank turret. To *Newsweek*,

> That little incident symbolized the attitude of the War Department toward the new German tanks—and toward other military developments where observers thought the Nazis had achieved technical superiority. Correspondents have time and again written that the big German tanks were better than the 30-ton American Shermans, but the Washington reply has nearly always been that the American machines were more maneuverable.[20]

"Why Don't We Have Big Tanks To Combat Nazis?" asked a January 28, 1945, story by North American Newspaper Alliance reporter Victor Jones, overseas with "Advanced Headquarters, 7th Army." Jones quoted a tanker captain, "You know, a lot of good men are getting killed because we haven't a tank big enough to handle the German tanks. We found that out in Africa. For God's sake, how long is it going to take to do something about it?"[21]

On February 5, newspapers ran a story (syndicated from the *New York Daily News*) on the Soviets' new Josef Stalin heavy tank, which German radio allegedly conceded "is more than a match for our best tank, the Royal Tiger." Asked the *Daily News*, "Why both the Russians and the Germans should turn up at this stage of the war with more powerful tanks than we have yet put into

*Sergeant Joe Eaz*, by Howard Brodie.

Ike faces the press.

gomery, Ike "took about five minutes to say absolutely nothing." Miller elaborated to his diary, "Ike is a master, though for my taste he smiles too much and says too little. Sometimes, when he chooses, he uses a great many words to say nothing at all, but the boys and girls of the press acted as if they had heard Einstein explain relativity."[25]

On February 2, newspapers across the country carried headlines like "U.S. Weapons Superior, Says Eisenhower." Back on May 22, 1944, he had assured reporters attached to his headquarters for the invasion of Europe (including Ernie Pyle), "Our countries fight best when our people are well informed. You will be allowed to report everything possible, consistent, of course, with military security. I will never tell you anything false."[26]

Now, in support of Gen. Campbell's denials, the Supreme Commander stated in a public letter to him, "Battlefield reports from every front in the European theater of operations continue to tell of the splendid quantity of our weapons…throughout the war there has been a noticeable and steady improvement in the quality of many of our weapons and equipment. Such improvement is mandatory always; the alternative is stagnation and eventual disaster…we have a general superiority in quality and quantity of ordnance."[27]

Eisenhower's testimonials contradicted his July 1944 requests to Ordnance for better armed tanks, his January 1944 request to Gen. Marshall at the Pentagon for tanks with more firepower, and his early 1943 letter to Marshall from the North African front noting the Tiger's seeming invulnerability to American tank and anti-tank guns. When necessary, the Supreme Commander was able to spin the truth for the sake of morale; back in August 1942, referring to worries over the upcoming invasion of North Africa, he had written to Marshall, "It seems to me that the rougher the prospects, the more necessary it is that superior commanders allow no indication of doubt or criticism to discour-

age the efforts and to dampen the morale of subordinates and of troop units."[28]

Trying to deflate the "Tiger terror," Gen. Campbell ignored the Panzer VI's firepower, instead calling it "big and clumsy, with a lack of maneuverability… subject to being caught in the mud, where it's like a sitting duck."[29] This description, the top secret White-Rose Reports to Eisenhower would soon show, could also apply to the Sherman.

Campbell read a boast from George Patton: the M4, insisted "Old Blood and Guts," was "the best tank in the world."[30] He also cited a claim of Gen. Eisenhower's used in a *Time* magazine article: "We have knocked out twice as many tanks as we have lost."[31] These numbers, impressive at first glance, were used to deflect criticism of the M4.

But as GIs at the front pointed out, the figures being circulated were not an accurate mea- sure of the M4's effectiveness versus German tanks; instead of indicating German tanks destroyed by Shermans *alone*, they reflected German tank losses from *all* causes: mortars, bazookas, artillery, and fighter bombers, as well as M4s.

*Time* magazine received a letter from Gen. Patton, acting on Eisenhower's orders to try to tamp down the growing tank controversy. "We've got the finest tanks in the world!" he insisted, not only backing Gen. Campbell's claims, but outdoing him in assuring readers, "We just love to see the German King Tiger come up on the field."[32] But Patton knew better. As recently as Christmas Day 1944, after ordering that a hot turkey dinner be delivered to every soldier in the Third Army, he visited his troops in the field. "We left at six o'clock in the morning," recalled his driver, Sgt. John Mims. "We drove all day long, from one outfit to the other… General Patton would stop and talk to the troops."[33]

Patton's men were fighting the biggest battle in Army history, spearheaded by German tanks. Given a rare opportunity to convey their observations directly to their commanding general, it is unlikely that no-nonsense old sergeants and embattled, outspoken draftees jittery from imagining King Tigers everywhere confined their talk to platitudes about the day's menu.

On February 7, 1945—just days before Ordnance Chief Campbell's boast (backed with statements from Eisenhower,

> We need not only have no apology for any item of American Ordnance in comparison with that of the enemy, but we're leading them all the way.[2]
> —Chief of Ordnance Gen. Lewin Campbell, February 2, 1945

**U. S. Tanks Fill Bill**

One question which now seems to have been answered with reassuring finality concerns the quality of American tanks. There has been considerable discussion on the subject, with some military observers asserting that American tanks were inferior to German tanks. The reply to this criticism comes from General Eisenhower, several field commanders and Maj. Gen. Levin H. Campbell, jr., army chief of ordnance.

In a letter to General Campbell, General Eisenhower reports that German battle losses have been far greater than those of American forces, that in pieces of artillery the Germans have lost eight to one American gun lost, and that American armies have knocked out twice as many tanks as they have lost.

"We have a general superiority in quality and quantity of our ordnance," wrote General Eisenhower, "a superiority that must always be maintained."

General Campbell quoted field commanders such as Gen. George S. Patton, jr., and Gen. Jacob L. Devers as saying they don't want any better tanks than they have now. The Sherman tank, they said, is entirely satisfactory. They want fast, mobile tanks, and that is what they have. They emphasize that they are on the offensive and want offensive weapons, not slow, ponderous machines which would destroy the accent on speed.

The field commanders pointed out that the German use of heavy tanks when the German defensive period began and that when the nazis were racing through Poland, Belgium, and France on the offensive their reliance was on lighter tanks. As to critics of American tanks, General Devers commented: "Ask them to take a look at who's retreating—we or the Germans?"

American commanders in the field are in the best position to know what they want and what they have in the matter of equipment. If they are satisfied, comparison of American tanks with others on a purely technical basis loses most of its meaning.

ORO-T-117                                                                 Appendix E

**TABLE XXXV**
**GERMAN TANK LOSSES BY CAUSATION – 1944-1945**
(Sampling)

| CAUSE OF IMMOBILIZATION | | NO. OF TANKS | PERCENT OF TOTAL KNOWN |
|---|---|---|---|
| **GUNFIRE:** | | | |
| 75-mm or 76-mm AP | | 66 | 12.5 |
| 75-mm HE + AP | | 2 | 0.4 |
| 90-mm AP | | 6 | 1.1 |
| Tank | | 125 | 23.6 |
| Tank + Artillery | | 100 | 18.9 |
| TD | | 24 | 4.5 |
| TD + Artillery | | 7 | 1.3 |
| Artillery | | 14 | 2.6 |
| AP | | 127 | 24.0 |
| APC | | 7 | 1.3 |
| AP (TD) | | 2 | 0.4 |
| HE | | 18 | 3.5 |
| 57-mm AT | | 3 | 0.6 |
| SP | | 1 | 0.2 |
| "Gunfire" | | 26 | 4.9 |
| | TOTAL | 529 | 43.8 |
| **HOLLOW CHARGE WEAPONS:** | | | |
| Hollow Charge Weapons | TOTAL | 53 | 4.4 |
| **AIR:** | | | |
| Rocket | | 35 | 38.5 |
| Cannon | | 4 | 4.4 |
| Bomb | | 7 | 7.7 |
| "Fighters" | | 7 | 7.7 |
| "Air" | | 38 | 41.7 |
| | TOTAL | 91 | 7.5 |
| **MINE:** | | | |
| Mine | TOTAL | 3 | 0.2 |
| **MISCELLANEOUS, ENEMY ACTION:** | | | |
| Multiple Action: AP + HC | | 5 | 55.6 |
| Grenade | | 1 | 11.1 |
| Captured | | 3 | 33.3 |
| | TOTAL | 9 | 0.7 |
| **MISCELLANEOUS, NON-ENEMY ACTION:** | | | |
| Mechanical or Terrain | | 49 | 9.4 |
| Abandoned (lacked parts, gas, recovery; under attack, etc.) | | 222 | 42.5 |
| Self-destruction | | 251 | 48.1 |
| | TOTAL | 522 | 43.2 |

87

*From a secret postwar report, Coox and Naiswald,* Survey of
Allied Tank Casualties in World War Two *[1951].*

Bradley, Patton, and Devers) that "we're leading them all the way" made nationwide headlines—Army historian Col. Kent Greenfield sat down to interview Maj. Gen. James Christiansen, Chief of Staff of the Army Ground Forces, previously commanded by the late Gen. McNair.

As a result of Gen. McNair's reorganization of the Army, his AGF bureaucracy had taken over armor and TD training and doctrine, while tank design was parceled out to separate, rival offices in the Army Service Forces (ASF). Col. Greenfield described this disconnect with the GI customer at the front as having "cut back and smothered the Armored Force, reducing it to a Center."[34]

Even as newspapers and radio across the country featured denials of the tank scandal, Gen. Christiansen—knowing his comments were for posterity, and that he would not likely face immediate public scrutiny—admitted to historian Greenfield:

The Germans have two tanks that have outgunned, out-armored, and out-floated our M4. Our light and medium tanks are superior to anything in use by other armies, but we have nothing with which to stop, tank for tank, the new German heavies.

The AGF must share in the responsibility for this. Our decision to concentrate on Shermans goes back to General McNair's concept of exploitation. General McNair was right at St. Lo and in the sweep from Normandy to the Rhine. Our tank men there benefited by the superior mobility, mechanical dependability, and accurate fire of the Sherman. It has been argued that

if the Germans had been armed with similar tanks, they would have broken through in the Ardennes offensive.

But because of his concept for the role of tanks, General McNair never pushed Ordnance for a tank gun with punch. Neither did General Devers or General Gillem.[35]

In mid-February, Gen. Bradley was privately asking the British to convert American Shermans to the Firefly, mounting a powerful British 17-pounder gun. Yet for public consumption, Eisenhower's dutiful subordinate made headlines such as "Bradley Defends Sherman Tanks," filed from "Headquarters United States 12th Army Corps" and appearing on March 26, 1945, in papers like the Portland *Oregonian*. While he conceded the Tiger and Panther "have some advantages when meeting a Sherman tank head-on," Bradley, who had followed Ike's request to the letter by "[making] his remarks about tanks in attempting to refute published statements that the American Sherman is no good," created a straw man to duck the gun problem. The M4, he told reporters, "had always been better at out-maneuvering," while "...our

## Tank Critics Hit by Blast Of Gen. Patton

WASHINGTON —(P)— Lieutenant-General George S. Patton Jr. has fired a high-velocity volley of words and figures at "certain misguided or perhaps deliberately mendacious individuals" who criticize American tanks.

The War Department made public today a letter from the Third Army Commander to Lieutenant General Thomas T. Handy, deputy chief of staff, in which Patton attacked criticism that American tanks are not comparable with the German Panther or Tiger tanks. This, said Patton, "is wholly incorrect for several reasons."

One he cited is that since the Third Army started fighting the Germans last August German tank losses have been virtually double those of the Third—2,287 to 1,136.

"These figures of themselves refute any inferiority of our tanks," Patton wrote, "but let me add that the Third Army has always attacked, and therefore better than 70 per cent of our tank casualties have occurred from dug-in anti-tank guns and not enemy tanks, whereas a majority of the enemy tanks put out have been put out by our tanks."

Patton conceded that if an American Sherman medium tank were to engage in a fixed-place duel with a Tiger the medium "would not last." But he insisted the purpose of the American tank is not to engage in a slugging match but to attack from the rear.

ORO-T-117        Annex 7, Appendix E

5. Discussion: The value of mobility over heavy armament is borne out by the fact that 83 percent of the Mark V and VI German tanks were destroyed by gunfire as compared to 67 percent for American M4 and 59 percent for German Mark III and IV. The minor importance of shoulder rocket guns is evidenced by the low percentage of tanks destroyed by their use, both American and German. The American tank appears to be more susceptible to fire when hit than the German. The recognizable groups of hits as shown in Figures 28 and 30 show that the German and American gunner is shooting for the driver and assistant driver on his front shots. The American aims more for final drive than the German. On the side shots, the German is still shooting at the spot on the forward sponson in which ammunition was stored in early M4 tanks. It is evident from this study that either the American 75-mm gun or the 76-mm gun is capable of destroying any German tank.

      For the Army Ordnance Officer:

                    K. R. DANIEL
                    Lt Col, Ord Dept
                    Asst Ordnance Officer

4 Incl:
  Incl 1 - Statistics, Mk III & IV German Tanks
  Incl 2 - Plot of All Hits, Mk III & IV German Tanks
  Incl 3 - Statistics, Mk V & VI German Tanks
        - Plot of All Hits, Mk V & VI German Tanks

ORO-T-117        Appendix E

ANNEX 7

HEADQUARTERS
THIRD UNITED STATES ARMY
Office of the Ordnance Officer
APO 403               KRD/rfc
                      19 March 1945

SUBJECT: Examination of Causes for Rendering Tanks Inoperative.

TO   : Chief of Staff, Third US Army

       ...

3. 100 German Mark III and IV tanks examined.

    59 - Tanks or 59% were destroyed by enemy
           gunfire as follows:

        8 - Hit by rockets
        4 - Hit by 90-mm AP
       47 - Hit by 75-mm or 76-mm AP
    1 - Tank destroyed by mine.
    40 - Tanks or 40% were destroyed by terrain
           obstacles or mechanical deficiencies.

  Of the 59 tanks destroyed by gunfire, 20 or 34% burned.

  For details of location of hits on tanks see Figure 28.

4. 30 German Mark V and VI tanks examined.

    30 - Tanks or 83% were destroyed by enemy gunfire
           as follows:

        9 - Hit by rockets
        2 - Hit by 90-mm AP
       19 - Hit by 75-mm or 76-mm AP
           No tanks destroyed by mines.

    6 - Tanks or 17% were destroyed by terrain
           obstacles or mechanical deficiencies.

  Of the 30 tanks destroyed by gunfire, 12 tanks or 40%
  burned.

  For details of location of hits on tanks, see Figure 30.

                101

**LEFT:** Mixed messages: While Patton—as ordered by Ike—was denying any problem with the M4 to the stateside press, behind the scenes his own Third Army Ordnance experts conceded, "The American tank appears more susceptible to fire when hit than the German," something Sherman tankers had known since the 1942–1943 North African and Tunisian battles. *Photo by Robert Coldwell Sr., courtesy US Army Military History Institute, Carlisle Barracks, Pennsylvania*

*Photo by Robert Coldwell Sr.*

## Patton Says US Tanks Infinitely Superior to Others

Washington, March 27 (AP) Lt. Gen. George S. Patton Jr., has fired a high-velocity volley of words and figures at "certain misguided or perhaps deliberately mendacious individuals" who criticize American tanks.

The War Department made public today a letter from the Third Army commander to Lt. Gen. Thomas T. Handy, deputy chief of staff, in which Patton said "It has been stated at home' ' that American tanks are not comparable with the German Panther or Tiger tanks. This, said Patton, "is wholly incorrect for several reasons."

One he cited is that since the Third Army started fighting the Germans last August German tank losses have been virtually double those of the Third—2,287 to 1,136.

Patton conceded that if an American Sherman medium tank were to engage in a fix-place duel with a Tiger the medium "would not last." But he insisted the purpose of the American tank is not to engage in a slugging match but to attack from the rear.

The text of Patton's letter, written from 3rd Army headquarters under date of March 19 and referring to the presence of the Army at Mainz, Germany, follows:

"My dear General Handy:

"It has come to my knowledge that certain misguided or perhaps deliberately mendacious individuals, returning from the theatre of war, have criticized the equipment of the American soldier. I have been in command of fighting units since the 7th of November, 1942 and may therefore claim some knowledge of the various types of equipment.

### WHOLLY INCORRECT

"With reference to the tank, either Mark V (light) or Mark IV (medium), it has been stated at home that these tanks are not comparable with the German Mark VI, the so-called Panther and Tiger type tanks. This statement is wholly incorrect for several reasons:

"Since August 1, 1944, when the 3rd Army became operational, our total tank casualties have amounted to 1,136 tanks. During the same period we have accounted for 2,287 German tanks, of which 808 were of the Tiger or Panther variety, and 851 on our side were Mark IV.

"These figures of themselves refute any inferiority of our tanks, but let me add that the 3rd Army has always attacked, and therefore better than 70 per cent of our tank casualties have occurred from dug-in antitank guns and not enemy tanks, whereas a majority of the enemy tanks put out have been put out by our tanks.

### MADE FOR REAR ATTACKS

"It is patent that if a Tiger tank with an enormous thickness of armor were put at one end of a village street and engaged in a fire fight with a Mark IV at the other end, the Mark IV tank would not last. However, the great mobility of the Mark IV tank usually enables it to circumvent the slow and unwieldly Tigers and not to engage in a slugging match but to attack them from the rear.

"With the advent of the heavy, cumberson Tiger tank, the German, in my opinion, lost much of his ability in armored combat. These tanks are so heavy and their road life is so short that the German uses them as guns and not as tanks—that is, he uses them on the defense against our armor, whereas we invariably try and generally succeed in using our armor on the offense against his infantry which is the proper use of armor.

"Had the armored divisions which accompanied the 3rd Army

HUGH KIDNEY URINE

## The Tank Argument

General Patton gets into the argument over the quality of the American tanks by denying what he terms the "wholly incorrect" statements of "misguided or mendacious individuals" that the United States weapons are inferior to the German Panthers and Tigers. In a letter to the deputy chief of staff at Washington he reports that the Third Army had destroyed up to a recent date twice as many enemy tanks as the number of its own tank losses.

Indirectly General Eisenhower defended United States tank abilities recently by reminding the chief of ordnance that the Americans had "knocked out twice as many tanks as we have lost."

But the weight of the evidence, nevertheless, seems to run against the idea that we have kept abreast of the Germans in tank development. Experienced correspondents have shown pretty conclusively, by comparing various abilities of the German and American weapons, that not until we built the T-26 (the General Pershing 45-tonner), of which few are yet in action, did we approach the German Panther and Tiger models. United States army tankmen themselves support the correspondents.

Until now the United States tanks have been outgunned—88-millimeter rifles for the Germans against 75-millimeters for most of ours. German tanks have outweighed ours—about 55 to 72 tons compared with 35 tons for the General Sherman. Hanson Baldwin of the New York Times disclosed that German models carry larger supplies of ammunition, use wider treads and employ a lock-tread mechanism that enables them to "turn on a dime." Several tankmen quoted in the Paris edition of the Stars and Stripes relate that their 75-millimeter shells merely dropped off the heavy armor of the German tanks when they were hit from certain angles.

The new General Pershing carries a 90-millimeter gun which is a shade larger than the German 88s, but probably has a slightly slower muzzle velocity. The weight of the Pershing is 45 tons against the Sherman's 35. Mr. Baldwin concludes that, "all things considered, the Sherman is a much inferior tank to the German Panther and Tiger models, and there is yet no certainty that the new T-26 General Pershing, though it is a much better tank than the Sherman, will be a match for the Panther, much less for the Tiger."

General Patton himself seems to concede something to the critics when he says that in a fixed-place duel the Sherman could not match the Tiger, and goes on to argue that the purpose of the United States tanks is not to engage in slugging, but attack from the rear.

One of the regrettable aspects of the matter is that there might not be enough General Pershings in battle before the European phase of the war is over to actually determine whether we have overtaken the Germans in tank-building.

---

mechanics were able to maintain more of our tanks in action than the Boche." Complaints "against other types of American equipment," insisted Bradley, "are due more to the nature of human beings, who always think the other fellow's jacket or automobile is best."[36]

Bradley's private request for up-gunned British Shermans was never fulfilled, due to tank and ammo shortages on both ends. The British were unable to give the Americans completed Fireflies because they lacked enough of them to supply their own units. And even while Roosevelt spoke of the importance of "the development of new weapons," the Americans were losing so many standard M4s they were unable to pull them off the frontlines to get them to the British for conversion.

Even if the Allies had been able to mass produce Fireflies, there was a critical shortage of improved ammunition for them.[37] "If we do not keep constantly ahead of our enemies in the development of new weapons," Roosevelt had told the nation when the United States could not even match German tank design, never mind surpassing it, "we pay for our backwardness with the life's blood of our sons." In the case of the promising but scarce Firefly Sherman, which mounted one of the most effective tank main guns to see action, this is precisely what happened.

A February 23, 1945, article was interesting for its origin and audience. "Shells Bounce Off Tigers, Veteran Tankmen Say" appeared in the GIs' own newspaper, the *Stars and Stripes*. Though one would expect higher-ups to squash the story, livid combat tankers with two or three campaigns under their belts disputed the recent statements of Gens. Campbell, Devers,

**BELOW:** A cold but smiling M10 TD crew poses with Thanksgiving turkeys, Italy 1944. Given the danger of most TDs' thinly armored, open-topped turrets, they might have joked bitterly about "sitting ducks" or "cooked geese." Resourceful GIs added unauthorized but effective armored top covers to the turret for extra protection from overhead fire and shrapnel.

Gen. Omar Bradley. Like Patton, he tried to downplay the tank scandal to the civilian press, as ordered by Eisenhower.

Patton, Bradley, and Eisenhower.[38] Just three days later, *Newsweek* stoked the flames with "Must We Defeat Germany with Inferior Weapons?"[39] Added the *Baltimore Sun* two days later in "German Tanks Tops—Yanks: Said to Be Superior Both in Guns, Armor":

What this inferiority means to men who are called on to fight for their lives against inexcusable odds is graphically apparent today to anyone riding through the roads of the Bastogne-Houffalize area, where some of the biggest tank battles of the war were fought during the Germans' December breakthrough…the exact figure of our losses is still secret. But on a recent trip through one small sector of "the Bulge," I saw one bit of open land where sixteen burned and exploded tanks—American ones—were scattered along less than a mile of road. In another pocket were twelve—American. At a crossroads a few miles farther on were five more—also American. And this is just a small part of the battlefield.[40]

March 7 saw one of the most candid syndicated articles allowed by censors to appear nationwide on the tank scandal, by United Press correspondent Ann Stringer—datelined "With the Third Armored Division, Germany." When the story appeared in the *Washington Post* on March 10, it was headlined "Our Tanks Worthless, Say Yanks." Stringer began:

Don't talk about the superiority of American tanks to men of this Third Armored unit.

"Our tanks are not worth a drop of water on a hot stove," said Staff Sgt. Robert Early, of Fountain, Minn., who commanded the first tank to enter Cologne. "We want tanks to fight with, not just to drive over the countryside."

Early was tired and he was shaking. So were the rest of the men in his company.

LACK PLENTY

"It makes us feel pretty bad to have everyone at home talking about having the best equipment when we know our tanks lack a lot of being the best," chimed in Corporal Charles Miller, of Kansas City, Mo.

In one field alone, this company lost half its tanks. Altogether, it has been assigned three times as many tanks as normally allotted to a tank company.

"We pushed into this town in our old M-4 tanks, which the Nazis have been knocking around all through France," said tank commander Sergeant Sylvester Villa, of St. Louis. "It makes us feel pretty blue." Added tank driver T/5 Virgil Sanders, of Pomona, Calif.:

"They gotta keep giving us more because the Jerries keep knocking them out."

I asked another driver why his tank had not been named.

"What good what it do?" he asked in reply. "We wouldn't even have time to get used to the name, so we just drive it blank. It's less trouble that way."[41]

As this article appeared across the country on March 7, Gen. Marshall wrote privately to Eisenhower to commiserate over the scandal. "We are under attack of course…for the charge that 75 per cent of our materiel is inferior to that of the Germans. They grant that the jeep and the Garand rifle are all right, but

Restored Königstiger at the Deutsches Panzermuseum, Munster. *Massimo Foti*

Tigers in Russia, July 1943. *Courtesy German Federal Archive*

everything else is all wrong. Making war in a democracy is not a bed of roses."[42]

"The German 88," Eisenhower responded, "is a great all around gun, and as a separate weapon has caused us lots of trouble. But his artillery as a whole is far behind, and the 90mm gun will match the 88." As to the tank scandal, "It is my opinion," Ike cabled Gen. Marshall on March 12, "that when we have the new T26 in sufficient numbers, and especially when we get the even newer model that has the souped-up 90mm gun, our tank force will be superior in slugging power as well as in maneuverability and in numbers."[43]

Secretary of War Henry Stimson entered the fray on March 8, with an unintentionally humorous press conference. Eight weeks before the end of the war in Europe, he called the long-delayed new T26 heavy tank "an answer to the German Royal Tiger." Administration and Army officials had been praising the Sherman for years, reporters noted, and claimed that armor leaders overseas did not want a heavy tank. So why did this allegedly superior medium tank now need to be replaced—and with a heavy tank, at that? Could Secretary Stimson explain these contradictions? But Stimson stuck with his story, insisting "there is no actual conflict between these statements."[44]

A week later appeared "Better Tanks, Less Talking Asked By Army," by Associated Press Correspondent Wes Gallagher, "Just returned from the U.S. Ninth Army Front." Stateside editors informed readers that "Seventeen words [have been] censored from this paragraph," and that "Gallagher apparently was not permitted to say whether the Pershing has been in action in Europe." Gallagher noted that while confirming the T26 was "just coming into production," Chairman W. A. Krug of Roosevelt's War Production Board carefully "side-stepped any discussion of relative merits of the General Sherman tank and the heavier German tanks," adding that "he had high regard for General Campbell." When "asked why this country had not put a heavier tank, such as the Pershing, into production sooner, Krug said it was not WPB function to decide upon types, but merely to see that they

are produced when the military services order them."[45]

"It has long been a mystery," reporter Clifton Daniels wrote in the March 10 *New York Times*, "to those who have lived and worked with the Army, why the higher ranks persisted in denying evidence repeated over and over again by men actually engaged in combat that American tanks were individually inferior to the German Tigers and Royal Tigers that they were meeting. Now it appears that such denials can no longer be maintained."[46]

Gen. Patton was assailed by reporters on March 17, while giving a press conference in Luxembourg, as Ike had ordered him to do in an attempt to put out the flames of the tank scandal. There, "the question of our tanks versus German tanks came up," Patton blandly recalled to his diary.[47] According to his wartime diaries (later sanitized to create his posthumously published memoir *War As I Knew It*), Patton responded "by saying that in the course of the fighting so far, we had got two German tanks for every one we lost. I stated also that all of our equipment… was superior to anything the Allies or Germans had."[48]

(Please Turn to Page 7, Column 1)

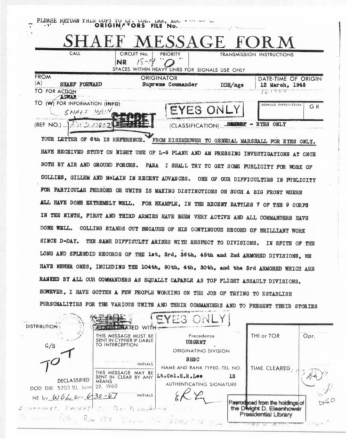

March 12, 1945: In a secret "Eyes Only" message to Gen. Marshall, Eisenhower- even while referring to criticism of American equipment as "pure bosh" - predicts that "our tank force will be superior in slugging power" if only "sufficient numbers" of the Sherman's replacement, the T-26, can be shipped to the ETO in time. *Courtesy Kevin Bailey, Dwight D. Eisenhower Presidential Library and Museum*

Patton followed up his "move along—nothing to see here" press conference with a public letter to Deputy Chief of Staff of the Army Lt. Gen. Thomas Handy, Marshall's number two man. "Thinking over the criticism of the tanks as a result of the discussion with the war correspondents," he later recalled, "I wrote a letter...restating what I told the correspondents."

Patton—who angrily forbade his soldiers to add improvised armor to their tanks—now attempted to represent himself as their protector. "This letter was given wide publicity and had considerable effect in stopping the foolish criticism, which was not only untrue, but was also having a bad effect on the morale of our soldiers."[49] Notice that Patton fails to address that criticism of the M4 was coming not only from the press, but also from his own tankers actually using it at the front, many with years of first hand experience on two continents with the M4's lack of firepower and armor protection.

A fawning Gen. Campbell responded to Patton with a letter on March 30. "There has been so much talk based upon opinion rather than facts with respect to tanks.... Your letter...to General Handy has certainly cleared the air with respect to tank characteristics and vicious criticism which is going around in this country about tanks in the way nothing else possibly could. It is a great service to the country to send the letter as you did!"[50]

Privately Patton held a different opinion of the tank scandal, one at odds with the public statements being fed to home front

audiences. "Ordnance takes too Goddamn long seeking perfection at the expense of the fighting men," he told a visiting representative soon after the Ardennes embarrassment (who soon passed it on to the Chief of the Research and Development Service within the Office of the Chief of Ordnance), "and you can tell that to anyone at Ordnance."[51]

On that same Saint Patrick's Day 1945, headlines in the Philadelphia *Record* and many other papers gave the frontline tanker's view, starkly contradicting the public boasts of Patton, Ike, and Bradley through Associated Press correspondent Wes Gallagher's "U.S. Tankmen to Washington: Give Us Tanks Instead of Talk."[52] Gallagher asked GIs to react to the comments of the generals in the ETO, as well as those of Campbell at home, Secretary Stimson, and other officials.

Not surprisingly, soldiers actually fighting the tank war hotly disputed the brass hats. Gallagher agreed with the GIs that Eisenhower and Patton's figure of two Tigers and Panthers destroyed to every Sherman lost was inaccurate and misleading, because it reflected German tanks destroyed by *all* American weapons, including airplanes and artillery, not just Shermans.

After Gallagher filed his story, government and military censors (perhaps more vigilant after the recent, unusually candid *Stars and Stripes* piece) deleted some words.[53] The published version contained three bold-faced notices: "25 words censored...107 words deleted before and after this paragraph...165 words censored."[54] But what remained directly contradicted the Army and Roosevelt Administration leaders' denials:

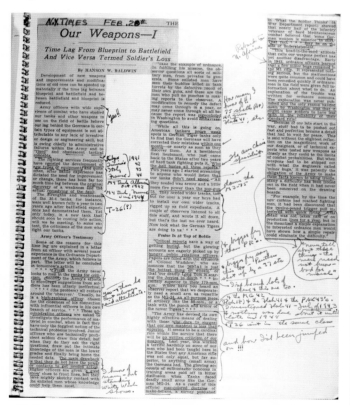

Col. George Jarrett's "Little Green Book;" on a New York Times article by reporter Hanson Baldwin, Jarrett accurately notes that his superiors—whom he calls "arm chair specialists"—buried critical reports and "jumped on" him for "daring to suggest that our materiel is less than superior." *Photo by Robert Coldwell Sr., courtesy US Army Military History Institute, Carlisle Barracks, Pennsylvania*

Fighters Ask Better Tanks, Less Washington Boasting

Photo by Robert Coldwell Sr.

The reaction of American tank soldiers who have had to do the fighting is that they want new tanks on the battle line, and less talk about them in Washington…"Give us enough gun to knock out the Tiger, and we will carry it around on trucks," is the tank man's answer…. Men and officers alike who have fought in Shermans for two years say they are fed up with the statements coming out of Washington praising American equipment…. American tank men say they feel that the Germans have been using Tigers and Panthers for two years, and that only as the war is nearing an end are the American armies able to produce their equal, and that only in driblet form [165 words censored].[55]

The GIs overseas were unaware that behind the scenes Gen. Campbell was trying to send them the new T26. But in one of the many ironies of the controversy, Campbell became a focus of soldiers' wrath: "Arousing the most ire was a dispatch…which quoted the American Army Chief of Ordnance as saying the Germans lost two tanks for every one the Americans lost, and that American equipment was superior in every department."[56]

One might be tempted to chalk up their anger to the American enlisted citizen soldier's tradition of healthy griping, but on this issue, draftee private to career general agreed. Gallagher quoted an angry tanker colonel "who has fought across Western Europe" and retorted, "I would like to have [General Campbell] in the lead tank during one of our attacks some day. He would damn soon change his tune."[57]

Like the *Stars and Stripes* piece, Gallagher's is atypical because of his sources; often the enlisted tanker's voice was suppressed while his coached officers "spoke" for him. Gallagher ended his dispatch by noting that in the GIs' opinion, in spite of the recent torrent of denials from the brass, their tanks had been inferior to Germany's since at least 1943. And far from resolving the problem as FDR had implied to the country in his State of the Union address, the new T26—Secretary Stimson's "answer to the German Royal Tiger tank"—was only arriving in "driblet" form.[58]

How did candid articles slip through censorship? Often, author and war correspondent John Steinbeck wrote, "the foolish reporter who broke the rules would not be printed at home, and in addition, would be put out of the theater by the command."[59] But in Gallagher's case, while conspiracy theorists like to picture the federal government as omnipotent, the story's publication could have been a simple oversight on the part of overworked censors. While forbidding some 165 words that were presumably even more incendiary than what the American public ultimately read, they let most of the story pass in modified form. Perhaps sympathetic censors, resenting years of obfuscation, passed it in a rare attempt to let the frontline, enlisted GIs' authentic voice be heard back home.

The *New York Times* for March 19 also fanned the flames; reporter Hanson Baldwin quoted one tanker, "German tanks have more firepower and more protective armor than any American tank ever used in combat." To this GI, "It is criminal for a nation to permit its supporting weapons to be inferior to those of the enemy." Concluded Baldwin: "Whoever was responsible for supplying the Army with tanks is guilty of supplying material inferior to its enemy counterpart for at least two years or more. How anyone can escape punishment for neglecting such a vital weapon of war is beyond me."[60]

How would the Army's leadership respond to the scandal? With newspaper and radio correspondents calling for a congressional investigation, would Roosevelt, Marshall, Patton, and Eisenhower finally address a problem denied for years?

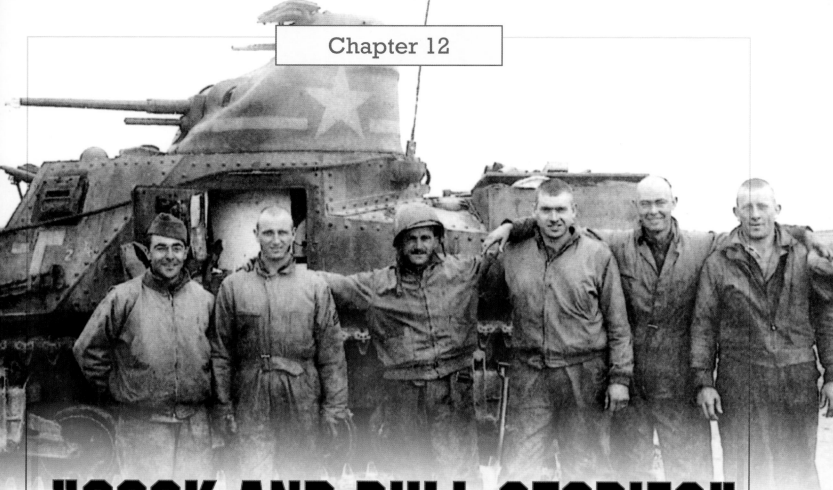

# Chapter 12

# "COCK AND BULL STORIES"

## What the GIs Thought: The Secret White-Rose Reports to Eisenhower

At the height of the tank scandal, during the Army's worst defeat since Bataan and Kasserine Pass—a surprise winter offensive spearheaded by German tanks—Army and Roosevelt administration leaders not only denied problems with the Sherman, they doubled down, proclaiming its superiority.

Many of these statements, rather than quoting combat tankers' views of equipment they had been using for years, came from men with no experience against Tigers and Panthers. As Patton and Eisenhower learned in the 1920s, career officers publicly challenging doctrine could jeopardize said careers. In contrast, the opinions of draftee citizen soldiers (who could speak more frankly because most had little desire to make the Army a career) were conspicuously absent from the stream of press releases coming from Army and Roosevelt administration leaders.

Correspondents in Europe questioned Eisenhower. As the Supreme Commander, he had the power to address problems at the top through Marshall and Roosevelt. Why, reporters asked,

> I haven't any confidence in an M4. Jerry armament will knock out an M4 as far as they can see it.[1]
> —Sgt. Robert Early, tanker, nine months combat experience

were civilian and Army leaders' opinions of the M4 so different from those of frontline GIs actually using the Sherman in combat?

On March 18, 1945, Eisenhower asked Gens. Isaac White and Maurice Rose, commanding the Second and Third Armored Divisions, respectively, to survey their men. He wanted their candid opinions of the Sherman, and their views on how the T26 (if it arrived in time and in decisive numbers) might fare against Germany's best tanks. In his letter, Eisenhower expressed annoyance to Gen. White that in spite of denials from top generals, the press was running "stories where some reporter is purportedly quoting non-commissioned officers in our tank formations to the effect that our men, in general, consider our tanks very inferior in quality to those of the Germans."[4]

Eisenhower's reasoning as to why "our men" held these views is a far cry from today's sentimental image of a caring Ike, eyes watering as he watches "his boys" take off from an English airfield to begin the Normandy invasion. To the Supreme Com-

An M3 Lee driver in training at Fort Knox, Kentucky, 1942. *Photo by Alfred Palmer*

mander, the tankers' scathing opinions of the M4 derived not from years of hard-earned battlefield experience, but rather "... from the human tendency to make startling statements in the hope that out of them will come a bit of publicity and self-notoriety."[5]

Contradicting his own public statements (as well as those of Patton, Bradley, Devers, Barnes, and Campbell), Eisenhower recounted his "mere impressions I have gained through casual conversations" with tankers. From "my own experience in talking to our junior officers and enlisted men in armored formations," Eisenhower conceded privately to Gens. White and Rose, "the Sherman is not capable of standing up in a ding-dong, head-on fight with a Panther...neither in gun power nor in armor is the present Sherman justified in undertaking such a contest."[6]

Some of Eisenhower's statements show him to be far removed from the enlisted tanker's world: "Most [GIs] realize we have a job of shipping tanks overseas, and therefore do not want unwieldy monsters; [and] that our tank has great reliability, good mobility, and that the gun in it has been vastly improved."[7]

"Most" GIs would have disagreed and begged for "unwieldy monsters" to take on Germany. Men in mortal peril were hardly concerned with esoteric shipping regulations. "The war effort of

An M4 and crew of the First Armored Division, Lucca, Italy, March 1945.

Gen. Isaac D. White

the United States," Gen. Marshall said in February 1942, "will be measured by what can be transported overseas."[8] But to frontline tankers, the Germans—using "unwieldy monsters" in North Africa, Sicily, and over the roads and bridges of France, Belgium, and Germany—had conquered most of Europe. To GIs, the overriding problem was simple: the most numerous American tank was inferior to German opponents in firepower and armor protection. And as Ike privately admitted to Gen. Bradley, the Sherman's supposedly "vastly improved" 76mm gun still was not good enough.

In mentioning size and weight limits on the hull (body) of a tank—which did not necessarily preclude the effectiveness of the main gun—Ike set the stage for a postwar excuse for the tank scandal that Gen. Marshall would also cite. And by referring to waiting for heavy tanks ("unwieldy monsters") to arrive, rather than addressing the possibility of upgrading the M4 medium tanks already in the ETO, he voiced another questionable justification for the scandal repeated to this day: the implication that correcting the M4's shortcomings could only be done with a whole new tank (perhaps a behemoth like the lackluster M6 heavy of 1941) that would take too long to develop and deliver.

The "new tank" argument claims that to mass produce and field a new heavy tank might take years, but the T26, waiting in the wings, could have been produced and fielded in massive numbers had it received Roosevelt and Marshall's full support. This argument also ignores the possibility of adding a main gun with more punch, such as a 90mm or British 17-pounder, to M4s a gun firing improved HVAP ammunition if Army and administration leaders would make the production of better tank ammo a top priority. As to armor protection, building on the field expedient extra armor GIs had added against regulations, experiments were being carried out stateside to create better tank armor, including the use of advanced plastics. And to address the Sherman's off

road mobility problems, by 1945, the M4A3E8 ("Easy Eight") variant was being fielded in small numbers with an improved suspension for better handling on rough terrain.

Rather than wait for a wholly new tank, these expedient improvements in firepower, armor protection, and mobility could have been combined and incorporated into a new variant of the M4, whether through modification "kits" or "packs" field installed on existing tanks, or through new M4s rolling off stateside assembly lines that would incorporate these upgrades.

By 1945, Eisenhower was aware of ad hoc solutions like the 17-pounder Sherman Firefly, the 105mm equipped Sherman, and the M36B1 Jackson. A year earlier, during his January 1944 two-week stateside furlough, he had personally discussed the need for better tanks with Gen. Marshall in the Pentagon. Gen. Eisenhower was the top man in the ETO, with the authority and influence to decisively address the tank scandal—so why didn't he do more? Historian David Johnson has suggested that Ike's subordinates may have shielded him from the full extent of the problem, although Eisenhower personally boasted of his well-publicized informal chats with thousands of GIs.

In his March 18 letter to Gens. White and Rose, Eisenhower gave a private opinion that, contrasting with his popular image, shows a disconnect with frontline GIs: "Most of them feel …that we have developed tactics that allow them to employ their superior numbers to defeat the Panther tank."[9] This might have been the view at the safe, comfortable heights of SHAEF (Supreme Headquarters, Allied Expeditionary Force) HQ, but did Eisenhow-

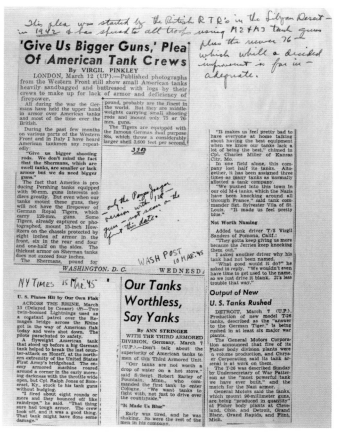

Another page from Col. Jarrett's "Little Green Book" on the Sherman tank scandal, noting that Allied soldiers were expressing concerns about the M4's firepower as early as 1942. *Photo by Robert Coldwell Sr., courtesy US Army Military History Institute, Carlisle Barracks, Pennsylvania*

Spring 1944: Tiger tank of the 1st SS *Leibstandarte Adolf Hitler Panzer Division* in northern France. *Courtesy German Federal Archive*

er truly believe that at the front (among men he called "the real fighters" in a letter home to his wife Mamie) GIs favored decoy tactics that sacrificed them like so many eggs thrown against a brick wall? He added a very vital qualifier: "As long as they are not surprised, and can discover the Panther before it has gotten in three or four shots."[10]

This is the sort of wishful thinking behind the flawed Tank Destroyer doctrine: "as long as" the Germans conveniently massed their tanks in textbook-style, large formations to be surprised, and "as long as" they did not use powerful tanks against TDs, the TDs would do just fine. Combat tankers well knew the Sherman's odds of surviving "three or four good shots" from a Panther, Tiger, or King Tiger; as they detailed in the ensuing secret reports to Eisenhower, they watched American shells bounce off of them, while Tigers and Panthers could set an M4 ablaze by contemptuously snapping off shots from afar. Eisenhower seemingly assumed US tanks could avoid being surprised by Panzers with longer-reaching guns and better optics, and that conversely, M4s, though less maneuverable, could surprise German tanks able to negotiate hills and muddy fields that left M4s bogged down and helpless.

In fairness to Ike, he had personally emphasized the need for up-gunned tanks to Marshall face-to-face in January 1944, and sent the Holly Mission back to the States in July to repeat the request. But almost a year later, T26s were only trickling overseas in small numbers. Most remained on the Antwerp docks or in rear depots, awaiting unpacking, final preparations such as installation of radios and machine guns, and delivery to the front. Far from "thousands" of T26s arriving as FDR had implied in his address to the nation, most GIs never saw them. Alluding to the hoped-for T26, Eisenhower ended his letter to Gens. White and Rose on an optimistic note: "most... [GIs] know also that we have improved models coming out which even in head-on action are not helpless in front of the Panther and the Tiger."[11]

Gens. White and Rose, encouraging their men to speak frankly, had interviews conducted with tankers of all ranks, quickly returning the responses to Eisenhower. The resulting reports gave such damning evidence of the M4's flaws that they were promptly suppressed and denied to the civilian media. The final 76-page classified document, "United States Versus German Armor: As Prepared for the Supreme Commander, Allied Expeditionary Force," contained the no-holds-barred opinions of some

An M3 Lee crew in North Africa.

150 combat tankers. It is powerful evidence against the civilian and Army leadership responsible for the tank scandal, coming from men whose first-hand knowledge of American and German tanks came through years of combat. Their responses were devastating; the GIs' condemnation of the Sherman was unanimous. The White-Rose Reports, little known to the general public, are the "smoking guns" of the tank scandal.

"I haven't any confidence in an M4," declared Sgt. Robert Early, with "nine months of combat." "Jerry armament will knock out an M4 as far as they can see it."[12] Alluding to tankers' attempts to increase their chances of survival (methods Patton forbade), tank commander Sgt. Joseph Posecoi asked, "If our tanks aren't out-armored and out-gunned, why does every outfit that has ever been up against a German Mark V tank use 100 to 150 sand bags for added protection?"[13] Capt. Joseph Roberts, 66th Armored Regiment, "after having interviewed both the enlisted men and officers whose statements are attached," summed up their views as "Give us German armor and tank guns, and nothing could stop us."[14]

Sergeant Nick Moceri, Second Armored Division, saw through the cooked statistics that Patton used to credit German tank losses to Shermans only. In truth, they were destroyed by a combination of tanks, aircraft, artillery, land mines, mortars, and bazookas. "The only reason we've gone as far as we have is summed up in 'Quantity' of tanks and 'Cooperation of Arms,' [i.e., Artillery and fighter-bombers, working with Shermans and attacking Panzers]," said Sgt. Moceri. "Until such time as the Army puts out a tank gun that can knock out a Panther from the front at 1,500 yards, or adds enough armor to stop a shell from the same distance, we'll continue to lose a heavy toll of tanks, men, and equipment."[15]

There is a gulf in all armies between soldiers up front and high-ranking officers safe in the rear with little knowledge of actual conditions. From the staff officer's perspective—the comfort and detachment of the rear area—colonels and generals condemn what they view as the frontline GI's excessive griping; his tendency to accentuate the negative and blame his superiors for shortages and discomfort. Conversely, the scruffy, tired GI—lacking a bath, warm food, and laundry, opining from a narrow

view with limited knowledge of the big picture—damns the pampered generals to the rear, running battles from a dry, warm, well-lit map room, quick to criticize men in a situation they know little about.

But the White-Rose Reports lack this gulf. In them, tankers from private up to commanding generals of armored divisions condemn the Sherman while praising the Tiger and Panther. The career officers' candid views are all the more impressive than those of the enlisted draftees, because they had more to lose in challenging the claims of powerful men like Gens. Marshall, Eisenhower, Bradley, Patton, Barnes, and Campbell.

Speaking from his "experience with U.S. Army equipment in combat…two years, five months, [including] North Africa, Tunisia, Normandy, Northern France, Belgium, Holland, and Germany to date," Lt. Col. Wilson Hawkins, who led the 3rd Battalion, 67th Armor Regiment, chose candor over tact:[16]

> If such a choice were possible, I would prefer to fight in the present German Panzer VI Tiger or Panzer V [Panther] tank rather than the present U.S. M4 medium tank…. The feeling among the tank crews, men who have four, five, and six campaigns to their credit, is the same…. Our M4 tank does not compare favorably with the German Mk V or VI in armor plate. Theirs is much thicker than ours and sloped so as to prevent strikes against it…
>
> I have inspected the battlefield at Faid Pass in Tunisia, being with the force that retook it [in early 1943]. Inspection of our tanks destroyed there indicated that the 88mm gun penetrated into the turret from the front, and out again in the rear. Few gouges were found, indicating that all strikes had made penetrations. Our tanks were penetrated by 88mm, 75mm, and 50mm caliber in this engagement, in all parts of the hull and turret. I personally measured many of the holes.
>
> The tank gun is the most vital factor in tank fighting. I know of many cases to prove the fact that the German 75mm and 88mm will penetrate our tanks, while our weapons will not penetrate theirs at the same range…. We have been outgunned since Tunisia, when the Germans brought out their Mark V with the long-barreled 75mm gun.[17]

During the scandal in the press, Army leaders like Ordnance Chief Gen. Campbell claimed tankers were not asking for bigger, more powerful tanks, but Hawkins' account, like others, negates this flimsy defense:

> Following the Tunisian Campaign and in England and France, I was interviewed by War Department representatives who were gathering facts concerning our equipment. Many of the enlisted men who had considerable experience were interviewed at the same time. The same points considered most vital to tank personnel, and those needing urgent improvement at this time,

*You know, our morale would be a lot better if there weren't so many cock-and-bull stories in the papers about how our tanks are world-beaters…when the layman reads that we've knocked out twice as many Jerry tanks as they have of ours, he doesn't realize that it's not our tanks alone that did the job. It's tanks plus artillery plus planes—plus guts.[2]*
*—Capt. James Burt, 66th Armored Regiment*

and which are stated above, were told to representatives of the War Department and Ordnance representatives almost two years ago.[18]

Col. Sidney Hinds, who led Combat Command B, Second Armored Division, disputed Patton's contention that US tanks should not fight German ones. While desirable on paper, such a textbook situation was often unavoidable: "In spite of the oft-quoted tactical rule that one should not fight a tank-versus-tank battle, I have found it necessary—almost invariably—in order to accomplish the mission."[19]

Hinds noted the human cost of sacrificial decoy tactics the Allies were reduced to adopting:

> Our tanks' armor does not withstand German direct fire weapons of 75mm or larger…in a head on, one-against-one tank fight, ours always comes out as a casualty. In my opinion, the reason our armor has engaged the German tanks as successfully as it has is not due by any means to a superior tank, but to our superior numbers of tanks on the battlefield, and to the willingness of our tankers to take their losses while maneuvering into a position from which a penetrating shot can be put through a weak spot of the enemy tank.[20]

While not naming names, Brig. Gen. John Howell Collier (who led 2nd Armored Division's Combat Command A) alluded to Patton and Campbell's boasts: "It is my opinion that press reports of statements by high-ranking officers to the effect that we have the best equipment in the world do much to discourage the soldier who is using equipment that he knows to be inferior to that of the enemy.… The fact that our equipment must be shipped over long distances does not, in the opinion of our tankers,

*If our tanks aren't out-armored and out-gunned, why does every outfit that has ever been up against a German Mark V tank use 100 to 150 sand bags for added protection?[3]*

*—Sgt. Joseph Posecoi, 2nd Armored Division tank commander*

justify our inferiority. The M4 has been proven inferior to the Tiger in Africa before the invasion of Sicily, July 10, 1943."[21]

As to the new T26, although Roosevelt had spoken in January of the Army needing "thousands" of them in his State of the Union Address, "It is not possible to comment on the M26 tank," Gen. Collier (who would lead the Armor School after the war) lamented, "as we have had no experience with it."[22]

Gen. Isaac White, commanding officer of the Second Armored Division, said the new M4A3E8 ("Easy Eight") was beginning to appear an improvement, but still not good enough; its inadequate 76mm gun was further handicapped by serious ammunition shortages. "The 76mm gun," he wrote to Eisenhower, "even with HVAP ammunition, is not effective at the required ranges at which we must be able to effectively engage enemy armor…the main armament of our tanks, including sights, is not comparable to that of the Germans."[23]

One of few non-West Point graduates to earn four stars, Gen. White confronted the problem that Patton, Eisenhower, and other generals attempted to spin in their statements to the press: no matter how mechanically reliable the M4, or how many obsolete tanks could be rolled out of factories, the bottom line was the inadequate gun. For want of a better tank gun thousands of GIs died needlessly. Gen. Isaac White:

> The most important point, and upon which there is universal agreement, is our lack of a tank gun and anti-tank gun with which we can effectively engage enemy armor at the required range.… The correction of this deficiency has made progress, but the problem has not as yet been satisfactorily solved.[24]

As to the much-anticipated T26 tank, White echoed other tankers waiting in vain: "The T26…has not yet been issued to

Gen. Maurice Rose, commanding officer 3rd Armored Division.

this division, and consequently, no comments can be made."[25]

Third Armored Division commanding Gen. Maurice Rose, in the five-page March 21, 1945, cover letter to Eisenhower that accompanied his secret report, agreed with Gen. White. "It is my personal conviction," Rose stated unequivocally, "that the present M4A3 tank is inferior to the German Tiger."[26] An unsung American armor leader of the war (and the highest ranking Jewish-American in the US Army at the time), Gen. Rose knew of what he wrote.

Tragedy seems to follow high-ranking actors in the tank scandal, from Gen. McNair's "friendly fire" death in Normandy, to the loss of his son on Saipan two weeks later, to Marshall's tanker stepson being killed in action in Italy. In Germany, nine days after writing Eisenhower, Gen. Rose was killed in action by a Tiger crew. Leading from the front near Paderborn on March 30, he was trapped and surrounded after the Panzer crashed into his jeep.

"U.S. General Was Murdered By Nazi Tankmen Captors," headlined the Sacramento *Bee* on April 3, 1945, which called General Rose "one of the outstanding tankmen of the war." His aide, "Major Robert Ballinger, White Plains, N.Y. said Rose already had surrendered to the crew of a German Tiger tank when tankmen with a 'burp' gun [German submachine gun] shot him."[27] While Rose's last moments are unclear, apparently he was murdered after surrendering as he reached down to unbuckle his pistol belt to hand over his personal weapon. While gossip claimed he had been targeted as a Jewish-American general—the son and grandson of rabbis—Sir Max Hastings calls him "merely a victim of the chance of battle."[28]

Within Gen. Rose's report Col. Matthew Kane, commanding the 1st Battalion, 32nd Armored Regiment, 3rd AD, acknowl-

edged—unlike the Secretary of War, Chief of Ordnance, and Gens. Marshall, Patton, McNair, and Eisenhower—that GIs were smarter than their patronizing leadership assumed. "Crews recognize the deficiencies in our tanks, and know that success on the battlefield is only attributable to our superiority in numbers of tanks, and to our resolve to sustain heavy casualties in men and tanks in order to gain objectives."[29]

Citizen soldiers from an educated democracy also rejected praise of decoy tactics that killed Americans, sometimes sacrificing three or four Shermans and their crews to destroy one or two German tanks. Col. Kane's battalion had "lost 84 tanks through enemy action in nine months of combat."[30] His verdict on the Sherman? "In a tank versus tank action, our M4 tank is woefully lacking in armor and armament when pitted against the super-velocity 75mm or 88mm gun of the German tank. Greater maneuverability and speed have failed to compensate for this deficiency, and our tank losses in the Belgian Bulge were relatively high, even when we were in defensive positions."[31]

These were the views of career Army officers whose advancement might depend on Army leaders involved in the scandal. Not surprisingly, draftee citizen soldiers were even more critical. To "Sergeant Moore and crew," Second Armored Division, "All of this stuff we read about German tanks knocked out by our tanks makes us sick because we know what price we have to pay in men and equipment to accomplish this." Though they had "never seen the M26 with the 90mm gun on it," it would be "the answer to a tanker's prayer...with our added firepower, we would have some chance of living."

Instead, "As things go now, every man has resigned himself to dying sooner or later because we don't have a chance against the German tanks.... Our tanks are no match for the Panther and Tiger tanks, and it is just suicide to tackle them. Even our tank destroyer with the 90mm gun cannot match themselves against the more powerful German tanks."[32]

Technician 4th Grade William Marcheski, a tank gunner, told of "moving down the road in a Sherman with a 75mm gun" at two in the morning one moonlit night. Suddenly:

> We saw a Mark IV tank, twenty yards away, back off to permit a Mark V [Tiger], thirty-five yards away, to fire on us. We fired AP at the Mark V and hit him on the front slope, left side—and it bounced off. He then hit us twice. The first shot hit just below the driver's hatch, went through two layers of sandbags, the armor plate, and exploded inside. The second shot hit slightly below the first, with the same effect. The tank behind us, a Sherman with 76mm gun, fired upon the Mark V and hit him on the front part of the turret, but the AP shell bounced off. The Tiger then hit the 76mm Sherman on the front plate, just to the right of the driver. The German shot went through a single layer of sandbags, and pierced the armor plate.[33]

"One day," recalled tank commander Sgt. Clyde Brunson, "a Royal Tiger got within 150 yards of my tank and knocked me out. Five of our tanks opened up on him from ranges of 200 to 600 yards, and got five or six hits on the front of the Tiger, but they all just glanced off.... The Tiger backed off and got away." Con-

A Tiger tank of the 1st SS Leibstandarte Adolf Hitler Panzer Division and a *Schwimmwagen* in northern France, spring 1944.
*Courtesy German Federal Archives*

Tanker Sergeant Hobart Drew, B Company, 37th Tank Battalion. Although the *Stars and Stripes* accidentally named him as the winner of their "Man of the Year 1944" contest, the actual "winner" was a photo of his fellow tanker, an exhausted Sgt. John Parks. Given the weariness on Sgt. Drew's face, surely he also qualified for the dubious "honor"—voted by his fellow GIs—of being named one of the most tired GIs in the ETO.

cluded Sgt. Brunson, "If we had a tank like that Tiger, we'd all be home today."[34]

Tankers like Technician 4 Melvin Evans took hit after hit. If they survived, knowing the risks, they still climbed back into their Shermans day after day:

> On 7 August 1944, in the vicinity of St. Sever, Calvados, France, I was driving the second tank in a column when it was hit by a Tiger. This shell penetrated through the gunner's sight. Another shell hit and penetrated the gun shield and the tank itself.... On 17 November 1944, in the vicinity of Puffendorf, Germany, I witnessed five rounds of 75mm AP hit a Tiger. Four of these ricocheted, with only one penetrating. All of these shells hit broadside.... On 8 January 1945, in the vicinity of LaBatty, Belgium, a German 75mm self-propelled gun fired six rounds. Five of these rounds penetrated the turret, and one hit the top of the tank and ricocheted.[35]

Sturmgeschütz (Stug) at the Musée des Blindés, Saumur, France. *Massimo Foti*

Sergeant Harold Fulton once fought "a column of six Panthers...and two Mark IVs. As gunner, I fired thirty-eight rounds from the 75mm gun of our M4 tank. Some were HE, some smoke [used to mark targets and to obscure American tanks to help them escape], and the rest AP":

> Each time one of the APs hit the tanks, you could see them ricocheting two and three hundred feet into the air. Along with my gun firing, there were four more tanks of my platoon. Two or three M4 tanks from another company, and two M7s [self-propelled guns] were firing at the same column. The range from my tank to the targets was five to eight hundred yards. Two days later, having a chance to inspect these vehicles, we found the Mark IVs with large holes in the front, but of all the Tigers, there was only one penetration in one tank, on the back of the turret. In the numerous places where the other projectiles hit, there were just grooves or penetrations part way through the armor.
>
> I have seen our M4 tanks with holes in any part a person would want to name. These holes are clean, just like they had been melted through the armor. I saw two M4 tanks mounting the 76mm, and one M4 mounting a 75mm gun, knocked out in less time than I can write it. All three tanks were hit in the front, our heaviest armor. One 76mm M4 was hit on the sloping part of the armor, next to the ground, just in front of the transmission. This projectile didn't stop until it reached the transmission.
>
> I could write all day telling of our tanks I have seen knocked out by more effective guns. Our best [anti-tank] weapon, and the boy that has saved us so many times, is the P-47 [Thunderbolt fighter-bomber, used to support Allied tanks].[36]

The secret reports to Eisenhower left no doubt the standard 75mm Sherman was inadequate to fight Germany's best tanks. And not only were the "improved" 76mm guns little better, they were short of ammunition. So what *was* needed? "What the American tanker wants," tank commander Sgt. Rains Robbins and tank driver Cpl. Walter McGrail told interviewers, "is a high-velocity weapon, as high or higher than the Germans,' mounted on a tank of equal maneuverability, and added armor plate."[37]

Sgt. Leo Anderson, "a tank commander and a veteran of Africa, Sicily, France, Belgium, Holland, and Germany," wanted Eisenhower to know "some things I have seen in combat that were disturbing and disgusting to any tanker.... Many times I've seen our tanks engage German tanks in tank duels. Their tanks have the ups on us. Their guns and armor are far better than ours." He recalled:

> Just north of Wurselen, Germany, our column was advancing toward its objective when suddenly we began to draw direct fire from German tanks. At once we located two Tiger tanks at about 2,800 to 3,000 yards away. At once our tank destroyers and tanks opened fire on them. The gunners had the eye to hit, but our

guns didn't have the power to knock them out. I saw our tank destroyers and self-propelled guns get several direct hits on the Kraut tanks, but the projectiles just bounced off the Jerries. The Jerries' guns didn't fail—they knocked out three of our tank destroyers and one Sherman tank at 2,800 to 3,000 yards. If our tanks had been as good as the German tanks, they would never have scored a hit.

"Give us the tanks," Sgt. Anderson pleaded, "that compare with the Jerries' tanks, and we have the rest. No soldier could ever have fought with better spirit than our boys have, full knowing that we were facing better equipment than that which we were using ourselves."[38]

Tank commander Sgt. Stephen Hill: "I don't think there's any comparison whatsoever between our armor and the superior German armor." Sgt. Hill described fighting "a large force" of Tigers and Panthers near Gilenkirchen, Germany. The American tankers made "innumerable direct hits on them with our 75mm guns at 1,200 yards, only to have them bounce off with no effect—while on the other hand, the enemy tanks were able to knock us out at the same range, and even greater distances. There is nothing that will lower the soldier's morale more than a situation similar to this. I see no reason why we can't have a better tank, or at least an equal one, than the Germans can make."[39]

After receiving this explosive feedback from Gens. White and Rose, Eisenhower replied to them on March 27, 1945. "I feel your conclusions…should go at once to the War Department, and I am sending them on to General Marshall without delay."[40] Earlier in the war, Marshall had shown willingness to learn from men in the field, and to publicize their hard-earned wisdom. He had arranged for veterans of the Solomon Islands campaign, for example, to be interviewed, with their comments compiled and disseminated throughout the Army. "Soldiers and officers alike," wrote Marshall in a forward to the resulting *Fighting on Guadalcanal*, "should read these notes and seek to apply their lessons."[41]

Gen. Marshall also made a tragically ironic comment in light of the failure to decisively address the tank scandal: "We must cash in on the experience which these and other brave men have paid for in blood."[42] He ordered a million copies of *Fighting on Guadalcanal* to be printed and widely circulated to help soldiers apply its lessons, but the inflammatory White-Rose Reports were censored, hidden from the press and public. Even if they had not been suppressed, the war would have been over in just seven weeks.

Today the question remains: are we to believe that Gen. Eisenhower—whose reputation for decency toward his soldiers paved his way to the White House, making him (after Marshall) the war's most respected American general—was blindsided by the findings of these reports? Eisenhower, an amiable man, wrote home to his wife Mamie of how he enjoyed escaping the rear-echelon political games at SHAEF to visit ordinary GIs. While his relaxed Midwestern manner encouraged their trust and candor, seeing the intensity and unanimity of their views on the tank scandal in print may have come as a shock.

Was Eisenhower unaware of the severity of a worsening problem that he had personally identified to Marshall two years

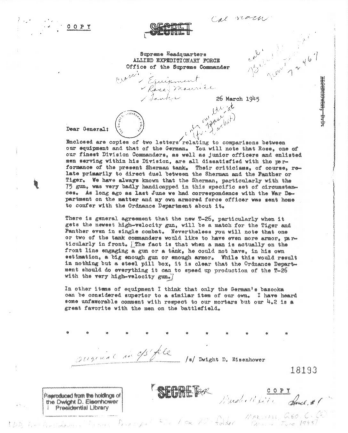

March 26, 1945: In an "Eyes Only" cable to Gen. Marshall, even as Roosevelt administration and Army officials attempted to minimize the Sherman tank scandal to the press, Eisenhower concedes, "We have always known that the Sherman, particularly with the 75mm gun, was very badly handicapped… It is clear that Ordnance should do everything to speed up production of the T-26." This secret message was Ike's cover letter for the White-Rose Reports. *Courtesy Kevin Bailey, Dwight D. Eisenhower Presidential Library and Museum*

before? Historian David Johnson, a retired Army colonel, suggests Eisenhower may have been insulated by some of his top armor commanders like Devers and Patton, who issued boasts and denials.[43] Author Stanley Weintraub has noted Ike's "ongoing tendency to distance himself from awkward matters for which deputies fronted for him."[44] But what of his personal interaction with his GIs, including pre-Overlord visits to tank units in England, where his soldiers had the opportunity to evaluate their weapons and equipment while he observed Sherman tank gunnery?

Even if we allow, as Johnson suggested to the author, that many of these GIs were rookies without battlefield experience, the Supreme Commander was present at the January 1944 weapons demonstrations at Tidworth Barracks, England, where armor officers with combat experience defied Patton to request the T26. To Johnson, Eisenhower neglected the tank crisis, postponing a reckoning because "it never became a crisis in and of itself"[45] until 1945, when it was far too late—when the press exposed the GIs' concerns and demanded congressional investigations. During the Ardennes fighting and "faced with the destruction of an Army," Johnson concluded, "tanks were a marginal issue" to Eisenhower. "Only when the press paraded the irate comments of his soldiers before him did Eisenhower turn his attention to tanks. By then, it was too late for significant material correction."[46]

The 1944 armor casualties in France, and the later stalemate as the Allies approached Germany, had nearly exposed the tank scandal to full civilian and media criticism; the press had noted heavy tank losses just weeks after the Normandy invasion that contradicted the rosy official views coming from the top. But once the Army had broken out of the Norman hedgerows through Gen. Bradley's Operation Cobra embarrassing questions were swept under the rug, replaced by colorful headlines about Patton's glamorous dash across France—an advance made possible by relatively light resistance from Hitler's Panzers, coupled with the Germans' lack of basic supplies.

In the Ardennes, the Americans had been saved from disaster by GIs' tenacity and sacrifice, and when SS and Wehrmacht armored spearheads of King Tigers, Tigers, and Panthers ran out of gas and supplies. It was a close-run thing, but once again, Army leaders hoped to muddle through to the finish line as they had in North Africa, Tunisia, Sicily, and Normandy.

Now, in early 1945, as German resistance crumbled and the Allies advanced farther into the Third Reich, the generals assumed (just as they had when decreasing M4 production and tanker training numbers for 1944) they could make do with the tanks and tankers on hand. Perhaps things would work themselves out; American and British armor might make a romantic, overwhelming dash into Berlin along the lines of pioneer armor theorists like Liddell-Hart and Fuller, whose dramatic "Plan 1919" envisioned tanks leading the charge in an epic sweep across Germany.

The explosive White-Rose Reports were never released; the findings were suppressed, classified for many years. To this day, this devastating "smoking gun" of the tank scandal remains little known to the public. Back home, administration officials continued to deny GIs' assertions finally appearing in the press, but they protested too much.

The last hope for American tankers in the ETO was the arrival in large numbers of the long-obstructed T26 heavy tank. In January, FDR had spoken of "thousands" of them presumably on the way, but just weeks before VE Day, frontline tankers lamented to interviewers in the White-Rose Reports:

As for the M26, all we have seen of it is pictures.... No comment can be made on the M26...as none have been seen by this crew as yet. However, a more heavily armored vehicle would be very desirable, and if the M26 tank lives up to its publicity releases, it should be the answer to the [Tiger and Panther] problem.... So far we have only seen pictures of it, but a high velocity 90mm gun is what we need to penetrate the armor of a Tiger or Panther. With such equipment we would at least be a match, instead of having the odds against us.... None of us have ever seen a T26. But from what we understand, it is certainly a step in the right direction. It sounds like it gives us a gun and armor that can at least begin to compare with what we are fighting against."[47]

Nazi Germany had fielded the monstrous Tiger since 1942, then followed it up with the Panther, Germany's best tank. Soviet Russia had been building the T-34, probably the finest all-around tank of the war, since 1940, and Stalin's designers had steadily upgraded the T-34's firepower and armor to keep pace with German technological advances. Unlike the Germans, whose complicated tanks possessed qualitative but not numerical superiority over the Americans and British, the Soviets designed the simple T-34 to be quickly built in massive quantities.

By 1945, both dictatorships were fielding powerful, mobile, well protected tanks generations ahead of American designs.

Would FDR's "Arsenal of Democracy" finally catch up to the dictators before the war's end?

*Photo by Robert Coldwell Sr.*

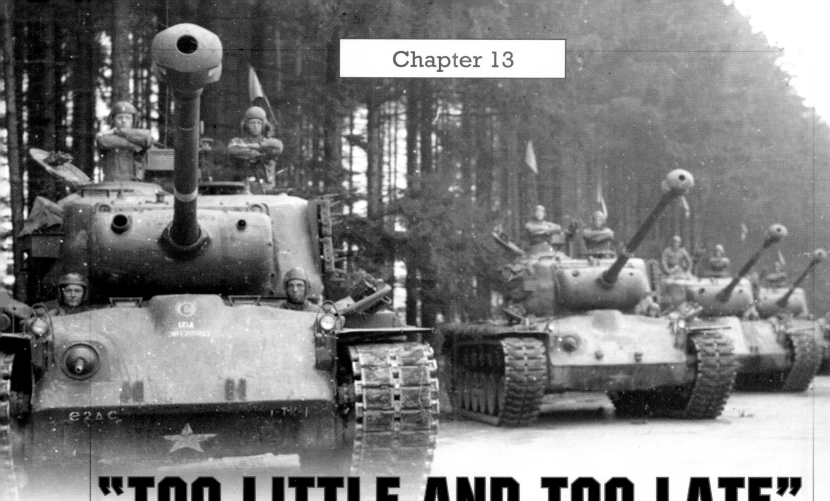

# "TOO LITTLE AND TOO LATE"
## The T26 Heavy Tank

The T26 heavy tank was a generational leap forward for American tank design, with innovations in firepower, armor protection, and maneuverability. It influenced successive models for four decades, from the M48 and M60 tanks used in the Cold War and Vietnam War to the Army's current M1 series Abrams main battle tank that was so successful in the Persian Gulf and Iraq Wars, a tank the author was proud to crew.[4] But the Pershing (ironically named for an opponent of an independent Tank Corps who insisted to Congress that tanks must remain under the Infantry's thumb) failed to reach the frontlines until the last weeks of the war in Europe, and then only in minimal numbers.

In the last days of March 1945, Lt. Don Critchfield, 2nd Battalion, 66th Armored Regiment, 2nd Armored Division, was ordered to a rear area on Germany's Rhine River with a scratch platoon of tankers and maintenance men. Their happy task: to take delivery of some of the few T26s to arrive overseas in time. The lieutenant's new tank was formally designated "F-15" (F Company, 15th vehicle), but in the finest tanker tradition it would be nicknamed "Fancy Pants."

To Critchfield, the T26's "90mm gun made all the difference. Instead of bouncing projectiles off their armor, we could penetrate. Alas, it came too late."[5] His enthusiasm for a Sherman replace-

President Roosevelt told Congress in his State of the Union message that the T26...mounts a gun more powerful than any yet carried.... The President said the Army "will need thousands of these new tanks" in 1945. But apparently they are still in the factories, on the proving grounds, or aboard ship; no report has yet come from the battlefields of an American heavy tank in action.[1]
—"Decision to the Tiger," *Newsweek*, January 15, 1945

ment was understandable, as just weeks before he had lost "his fifth and final tank since landing in Normandy."[6]

Although desperately needed, the T26's adoption and mass production were obstructed by bureaucratic infighting, and by doctrinal disputes that had hampered American tank design since 1918. "Toe to toe," observed *Time* magazine in "New Tank," a March 1945 article, "the Shermans never could [match the Tiger]. They had to count on getting around the Tiger's flanks, where the Germans are more vulnerable. In the kind of confined fighting the U.S. Army ran into four months ago [in the Ardennes], end runs were seldom possible. The smaller Shermans were badly battered.... Where was the T26 when it was most needed?"[7]

While Germany and Russia steadily advanced the state of tank design, US Army leaders from McNair to Patton insisted the old preference for light, under-gunned, under-armored "exploitation" tanks remained valid. As early as fall 1942, the Ordnance Department had completed a prototype of the T23, a medium tank with a 90mm main gun. Ordnance Chief Campbell and Gen. Barnes (heading Ordnance's research and development service) were in favor of mass producing it; surprisingly, an influential tanker—Maj. Gen. Jacob Devers, who led the Armored Force—

tank, and (unlike the lackluster M6 behemoth of 1941) a successful one. Design work began in December 1942, shortly before the Sidi-bou-Zid debacle. As the Tiger threat grew and information about its capabilities leaked out, T26 blueprints were steadily updated; the new American model was planned to trump the Tiger tank.

But opposition from powerful Army leaders delayed the arrival of a Sherman replacement. In October 1943, Gen. Barnes made an "urgent recommendation" for priority, "immediate" production of 500 90mm equipped T26E1 tanks—essentially, the tank finalized as the M26 Pershing.[9] But Gen. McNair's Army Ground Forces refused the request seven months before the Normandy campaign, preventing GIs from invading Western Europe with a more modern tank.

Col. Robert Icks worked at Aberdeen Proving Ground and in the office of the Chief of Ordnance, Detroit. Evaluating a prototype T26 in May 1944, he rated it "an impressive tank":

Compared with the M4, the ride was firm and smooth. The engine power was adequate, and the transmission smooth. But impressive as the ride was, it was not as impressive as its main armament. I had fired tank

opposed a tank with a more powerful gun—the 1930s light "Cavalry tank" doctrine died hard. The T23 medium remained an experimental model only built in small numbers.[8]

In light of the Tiger's success, the T26's designers bucked the conventional wisdom that prevailed among generals like Devers and McNair. They intended the T26 to be a large, heavy

A restored M26 Pershing Heavy tank. *Author photo courtesy of the National Armor and Cavalry Heritage Foundation*

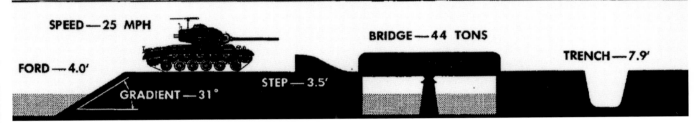

## HEAVY TANK, M26

U.S. ☆

**CHARACTERISTICS:**

**Turret:** Massive, irregular. Very large, undercut bulge in rear. Sharply curved, very prominent mantlet in front. Vision cupola on the right, and second hatch on the left. Set well forward of center of hull. In travelling position gun is turned to rear.

**Hull:** Long, low, set deep between tracks. Inclined front plate is sharply undercut. Long rear deck slopes down gradually to rear and sides.

**Armament:** One 90-mm gun in turret. One coaxial caliber .30 machine gun. One caliber .30 machine gun in bow. One caliber .50 AA machine gun on turret.

**Traction:** Full track. Six large, independently sprung bogies. Five very large return rollers. Driving sprocket set low in rear. Large high-set idler in front. Very wide tracks.

**INTEREST DATA:** This is the first important heavy tank of American manufacture. It is a formidable tank embodying many battle-tested characteristics. The 90-mm gun is a tremendous weapon. The turret is very large to afford ease of movement for the crew; observation from the turret is aided by the vision cupola. The very wide tracks and torsion bar suspension give the tank excellent performance. This is the first American tank with a drive sprocket in the rear.

20.2' — 11.2' — 9.2'

SPEED — 25 MPH — FORD — 4.0' — GRADIENT — 31° — STEP — 3.5' — BRIDGE — 44 TONS — TRENCH — 7.9'

weapons many times, but never any of this caliber.... The 90mm rounds hit exactly where they were aimed, and gave one confidence that soon, we would have a tank equal to anything the Germans had to offer.[10]

The T26 was the heaviest US tank of the era, but unlike the awkward M6 of 1941 (or the M4, which could sink into muddy ground that heavier Tigers and Panthers took in stride), it could maneuver thanks to wider, larger tracks and a new "torsion bar" suspension descended from J. Walter Christie's advanced ideas that were rejected by 1930s Army leadership. The resulting lower ground pressure made the T26 more mobile off road and across country, and less likely to get stuck in mud—a complaint of M4 crews who watched Panzers run circles around them in rough terrain.

A vulnerable spot on the Sherman was the turret sides, typically with only two inches of armor. This vulnerability can be observed in wartime photos. American M4s landed on the French coast with bright white stars (a standard US vehicle insignia) painted on their front slopes and turret sides, but after realizing the bold markings were ideal aiming points for German gunners, tankers splashed mud on them or obscured them entirely with fresh green paint.

Arriving in Normandy, Maj. Al Irzyk discovered a knocked-out Panther "sitting on the edge of a wooded area, with its gun pointing out over some open ground toward another wooded area":

I climbed up on the back deck, behind the turret. Once on top, I glanced along the length of the gun, out across the open field, to the woods on the other side of the clearing. What I saw was absolutely unreal. There, ap-

parently approaching me, as I'd seen dozens of times on Tennessee maneuvers...were five American Sherman tanks, pointing straight at me. I waited a moment for some movement, for something to happen. There was nothing. Then I suddenly realized to my great shock and dismay that they would not be moving—they, too, were knocked out. I couldn't believe what I was seeing—five perfectly normal looking tanks that were new, unmarked, and so very real. What had happened?

I jumped to the ground and raced across the open ground. I was stunned by the answer to my question; what I saw just could not have happened. Every American tank had, for identification purposes, a large white star in the middle of the front slope plate of the tank, and a smaller white star painted on each side of the turret.

*Photo by Robert Coldwell Sr.*

As I examined the tanks, I found that each had been destroyed in an identical manner. I came to the sickening realization that the big white stars on the front of the tank had served as a huge, perfect aiming point. Each of the five tanks had one hole in the white star from the powerful Panther that had killed them. I turned back to the knocked out Panther, and sure enough, I could see the snout of the Panther's gun pointing straight at me. I knew without doubt that one Panther had knocked out five M4s before someone eliminated it. My stomach churned; I felt sick. What a waste of five American tanks, and American lives. Except for the one hole, they looked good enough and fresh enough to have just rolled out of the motor pool.[11]

When the M4 was on the drawing board, its armor protection was decent by 1941 standards—but had fallen behind by 1945. In a departure from the prevailing US tank design doctrine of thinly-armored tanks that sacrificed protection for speed, the T26 had thicker front and side armor. For example, the turret side armor—typically 2" on the M4—was increased to 3" on the T26.[12]

American designers had also noted the Panther's effective mantlet, the armored shield around the base of the main gun barrel. Curved instead of flat, it deflected hits up or to the sides, away from the crew compartment. The T26's was similar but thicker, with 4½" of armor.

Tankers used to seeing German shells punch holes through Sherman armor (sometimes literally going in one side and out the other) were in for a surprise. Inspecting the damage to his T26 after an April 1945 tank duel, gunner Cpl. John Irwin saw only "chinks and gouges in the heavy armor plate on the front and the turret," hits that would have penetrated an M4. To Cpl. Irwin, "it was the extra armor that had saved us."[13]

The T26 featured an innovative, boat-like hull that lowered its overall silhouette, making it less conspicuous; a new engine; and at last, a powerful 90mm main gun. The Sherman's tendency to catch fire when hit was addressed with improved fire suppression and ammunition stowage systems. The Americans had also learned from the Germans to position exhaust pipes high up on the hull away from the tank, rather than pointing toward the ground, where they whipped up clouds of visible dust.

Here at last was the tank that had been called for since the North Africa and Tunisia disasters. Finally, GIs could take on Germany's best with confidence. Gen. McNair, true to his Artillery branch roots, had insisted that towed guns should be used to counter strong German tanks. A more muscular American tank, he argued, might inspire tankers to aggressively hunt Panzers. Gen. McNair "would have been appalled," noted historian and former Army officer Charles Baily, "to learn that when the troops received a T26 with a special, high-velocity 90mm gun, the tankers immediately welded more armor on it, and went looking for a Royal Tiger."[14]

*There is no doubt that the T26 will prove superior to the Sherman, but it is premature, despite official readiness to do so, to compare them in superlative terms with the German Tiger and Panther…the demand of the tankers, now almost two years old, for a better tank than the Sherman has at last been satisfied… but the introduction of the T26 is prima facie evidence, despite misleading statements from some of our generals, that the Sherman tank is not equal, tank for tank, to the German Panther and Tiger models…. The "General Pershing" has at length been produced— but too little and too late.*[3]

*—Hanson Baldwin,* New York Times, *January 1945*

Instead of getting the new tank to the front in large numbers, the three major Army agencies involved in tank production engaged in another bureaucratic squabble. In June 1944, as the tank fighting in Normandy exposed problems with the M4, the T26 was being tested at Fort Knox, Kentucky. Instead of this Sherman replacement—the next generation of American tank—being given the highest priority for mass production and shipment to the combat zones, the testing was delayed by a lack of spare parts:

On 30 June 1944, the Armored Board complained of delays in getting spare parts for the tanks being tested [at Fort Knox]. One T26 had been inoperable for a week, and lack of parts remained a problem for the Armored Board throughout the summer and fall. In September, the Board complained that one T26 had been inoperable for seventy-two out of 109 days. Although AGF protested the delays and ASF admonished the Ordnance Department, the problem was not solved. It is surprising, given the importance of the service tests to the future of the tank, that the Ordnance Department did not see that they were completed as rapidly as possible. The involvement of major headquarters such as ASF and AGF in such a petty manner as spare parts for an individual tank revealed the increasingly caustic relationship between Gen. Barnes and AGF.[15]

While agreeing the T26 should be produced, they argued over numbers. Ordnance called for 1,500 right away. The Armored Force, while agreeing T26 production should have a high priority, only wanted 500. Army Ground Forces, still influenced by the late Gen. McNair's opinions, rejected both numbers and continued to obstruct the adoption of the T26. As if unaware of the gun problem, AGF even argued the T26's 90mm gun should be ditched in favor of the lackluster 76mm model. Mass production of the new tank would remain delayed until November 1944; by mid-December, as the Germans began their Ardennes surprise offensive on December 16, led by powerful tanks, just twenty T26 prototype models existed.[16]

It was the shock and ferocity of the Bulge fighting that broke the impasse among the bureaucracies; there, when Second Armored Division commander Ernest Harmon begged for a tank able to take on Germany's, enlisted tankers agreed and repeated his request "prayerfully or profanely—wherever the enemy Panzer divisions appeared out of the Ardennes hills and forest."[17]

To General Harmon, the ideal tank would balance "First: gun power; Second: battlefield maneuverability; Third: as much armor protection as can be had after meeting the first two requirements, still staying within a weight that can be gotten across obstacles with our bridge equipment."[18]

By January 1945, outrage over the Ardennes disaster caused Army bureaucrats at home who had obstructed the T26 for years

Under Secretary and later Secretary of War Robert Patterson. *Courtesy US National Archives*

to call for immediate production of 10,000 of them, but this would require reactivating assembly lines that had been slowed down or stopped by the late 1943 decisions to lower tank production. Although Ordnance Chief Campbell demanded "every…known means of stimulating tank production,"[19] Gen. Thomas Hayes Jr., who led the Industrial Service within Campbell's office (until departing soon after in May 1945), called this goal "extremely doubtful."[20]

The T26's belated debut added a further element of black comedy to the tank scandal: bureaucrats who had been praising American armor for years (while T26 mass production was rejected) now bragged the T26 was the solution or "answer" to the Tiger! On February 5, Ordnance Chief Campbell (who privately wanted to replace the Sherman with the T26) publicly rejected concerns the Sherman might be out of date. "U.S. Weapons [Are] Tops," he insisted, and "We're leading them all."[21]

When speaking to the public, the Chief of Ordnance contradicted his true views; as small numbers of the new heavy tank trickled into Europe, Gen. Campbell told newspapers generals overseas—never mind the enlisted men, NCOs, and junior officers actually doing most of the tank fighting—didn't want a bigger tank. "I could build a tank as big as the Pentagon if the generals in the field said they wanted one. But there is no evidence to date that they want or need tanks larger than we now employ. Those men know what they want—they're good judges of horseflesh."[22]

Campbell quoted General Eisenhower that "to date the Germans have lost two tanks to every one of ours. How could we have such a record if our tanks were inferior?"[23] This statement contradicts Eisenhower's own admission to Marshall (in early 1943) of US tanks being unable to stop Tigers, and, at the height of the Normandy tank losses, his July 1944 request to Marshall (through the Holly Mission) for better tanks. Like Patton's carefully chosen figures released to the press, Eisenhower's were misleading. For good measure, Gen. Campbell repeated Patton's boast that "Our tanks in combat with the German Tigers" had proven to be "the best in the world." As to the Tiger, Campbell dismissed it as "big and clumsy with a lack of maneuverability, plagued by a great deal of engine trouble and subject to being caught in the mud, where it's like a sitting duck."[24] He also ducked the heart of the scandal—how did the M4's firepower stack up to the Tiger and Panther?

Just a few weeks later, Under Secretary of War Robert Patterson told a press conference the long-obstructed T26 was now "America's answer to the German Tiger." A United Press story on March 5 was headlined "Patterson Reveals Secret Weapon—Huge New Tank—In Broadcast." Some versions of this article ended on a mildly mysterious note: "The War Department declined to add to the details disclosed by Patterson."[25]

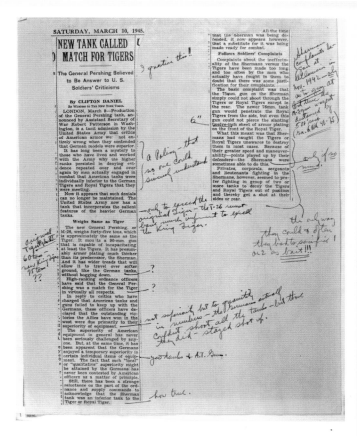

Added the Bellingham, Washington, *Herald* on March 6, quoting Under Secretary Patterson, "One of the strongest weapons of the war—a new tank—is being built in Detroit. That tank is America's answer to the German Tiger. It is the most powerful tank we have ever built…. it carries heavier firepower than any tanks we have built before."[26] The next day, headlines blazed with "Find Answer to German Tiger" another United Press article that called the T26 "the match for Nazi armor."[27]

As a confused American public (along with angry tankers serving overseas and their frightened replacements then in training stateside) might reasonably ask, if the M4 was the war winner that Army and administration bureaucrats had been claiming for years, and if the Tiger was so poor (according to Gens. Campbell, Patton, etc.), why was a replacement tank—an "answer" to the Tiger—now needed? And if heavy tanks were not wanted, as Gen. Campbell claimed, why were factories gearing up to build them in large numbers?

Observed the York, Pennsylvania, *Gazette and Daily*:

That our tanks…are greatly inferior to German tanks is quite a comedown from the generally accepted belief of most people of the United States that our soldiers are equipped in every instance with the very best there is.

It also indicates that somehow or other, somebody that should have known better "missed the boat" and failed to keep up with the development of the super tank used by the Germans and the Russians.

What we fear is that our command failed to understand the possibilities of the super tank and neglected to put it into production in time to have enough of them for the drive now being made on the Western European Front…one can only hope that the news item to which

Too little, too late: T26s of the Zebra Mission enter Germany.

A 1/35 scale T-26 model by the author. *Author photo*

we referred is not a correct picture of what is happening and that if it is, the defect will be remedied within the very near future.[28]

Another editorial, "They Need Those Tanks," had noted two days before:

For more than a year our tanks have been criticized as inferior to the German Tigers. Considerable space has been given recently to the front-line complaints about the disparity between our Shermans and the Nazi Tigers. The latest Tigers have eight-inch front armor. The Sherman's armor is four inches. The Tiger weighs seventy-five tons. The Sherman is a thirty-five tonner. The Tiger's 88-millimeter gun has a much greater range than the Sherman's 75.... Why the Army did not correct this disparity long ago is one of the question marks of the war. But apparently, with a major offensive already under way, a new tank is being built that will out match Hitler's best.... These new tanks ...may save thousands of American lives if they are put into the battle line.... That is, it will do the job if it gets there on time.[29]

For two years we have been asking for better tanks, especially better tank guns. Now, we are eagerly awaiting the new, big tanks...with the 90-millimeter guns—which we read about in the papers.[2]

—An American tank battalion commander, February 1945

In the *New York Times,* Clifton Daniel called Under Secretary Patterson's statement "a tacit admission by the United States Army that critics of American armor were not entirely wrong when they contended that German models were superior. There has been a strange reluctance on the part of the Ordnance and Supply commands to acknowledge that the Sherman tank was an inferior tank to the Tiger or Royal Tiger."[30]

Furthermore, "All the time that the Sherman was being defended, it now appears...that a substitute for it was being made ready for combat. Complaints about the ineffectuality of the Shermans versus the Tigers have been made too long and too often by the men who actually have fought in them to doubt that there was some justification for their complaints."[31]

But Secretary of War Stimson insisted at a March 8 press conference, "There is no actual conflict in [Campbell and Patterson's]...statements." The T26, he claimed, "is an answer to the German Royal Tiger in the sense that it is an improvement in line with the American concept of offensive warfare." Adding the mystery surrounding the new tank, he added, "When security permits, you will hear from them."[32]

Showing the Roosevelt administration to be as adept at damage control and spin as the generals, Stimson told reporters, "Statements that present tank destroyers, self-propelled artillery, and other weapons are capable of knocking out German tanks such as the Royal Tiger do not mean that we must stand still in the development of armored weapons. Fighting a war with weapons that have done, and are doing the job in hand does not place a prohibition on the use of something better."[33]

The T26, noted Stimson, was "as heavy as the sixty-ton tank we produced in limited quantity but abandoned back in 1941 [the M6]," and "heavier than the Sherman, which is about thirty-five tons."[34] Was this meant to appease critics calling for a heavier tank design, or to imply that more weight was better? As an extensive postwar history of the T26 noted, "The Pershing had the advantage of being almost four tons lighter than the Panther, and over 16 tons lighter than the Tiger I."[35] The weight of a tank does not necessarily dictate how well it handles; even the King Tiger, though a heavy tank, was more maneuverable than the lighter Sherman medium tank.

Weight was a factor so they could safely cross hastily repaired European bridges and travel on captured railroads, so Army Regulation AR 850-15 (revised in August 1943) limited US tanks to 35 tons. But Stimson avoided the crux of the Sherman tank problem. It was not weight, size, speed, mechanical reliability, or maneuverability; it was firepower.

Speculating on the new mystery tank in the March 9 *New York Times*, Clifton Daniels noted:

Although the War Department still has not prepared an official release about the Pershing, it is stated in authoritative quarters that its 90mm gun...firing high velocity armor-piercing shells is capable of penetrating at "battle range" some of the heaviest armor plate in existence. This fact has been proved in actual tests conducted in this country, according to the same sources. The armor referred to, incidentally, is much thicker than that of any tank in existence, German, Russian, or American. It is said that the Pershing's new gun will demolish formidable pillboxes at considerable range.[36]

Technicians had been designing the T26 since 1942. Marshall overruled McNair's objections in December 1943, ordering T26 production to proceed, but the damage had been done; while Eisenhower asked Marshall for better tanks to be shipped to the ETO in July 1944, T26 production did not begin until November 1944.[37] Some of the best US aircraft designs (such as the P-51 Mustang and F6F Hellcat) went from drawing board to flight testing in months, fielded in time to decisively impact the air war, but the T26 did not reach the battlefield until two and a half years later, in the last weeks of the war in Europe.

Roosevelt had spoken in January of "thousands" of Pershings. So where were they? At the time, although flawed American tanks were suffering embarrassing defeats in the Ardennes, some newspapers simply parroted the government line. "U.S. Develops Super Tank, FDR Reveals," the *New York Daily News* gushed: "WASHINGTON, Jan. 6 (UP). —The American Army now has developed a new tank with a gun more powerful than any yet mounted on a fast-moving vehicle, President Roosevelt revealed in his State of the Union message today." At Aberdeen Proving Ground, George Jarrett wrote next to this clipping in a firm hand, "This is horse collar—coming at this late date."[38]

"High-powered, heavily-armored tanks," the *Detroit Free Press* raved on March 7, "which War Department officials believe will be the answer to German strength, are rolling off Detroit's production lines. They are the new T26's. The Under Secretary for War, Robert P. Patterson, called the T26 'the most powerful tank we have ever built' and 'the answer to the German Tiger tank'… the T26 is sheathed with heavy armor and equipped with a 90mm gun."[39] Like the *Daily News,* the *Free Press* neglected to question the delay in producing the new tanks and getting them overseas.

Finally, Secretary of War Stimson sent some pre-production T26E3s to the ETO—a mere twenty—in what was code-named the "Zebra Mission." Arriving in Paris on February 9, 1945, this team was appropriately led by Gen. Barnes, who had championed

Another typical entry from Col. George Jarrett's "Little Green Book." As seen here, he also added his own pungent, handwritten comments. Jarrett's personal papers are preserved at the US Army Military History Institute, Carlisle Barracks, Pennsylvania. *Photo by Robert Coldwell Sr.*

In the last months of the war, the British fielded a new tank with improved firepower and armor protection. A restored Cruiser Tank A34 (Comet I) at the Tank Museum, Bovington, Dorset, UK. *Massimo Foti*

the new tank behind the scenes, and included Ike's armor expert Gen. Joseph Colby, another T26 supporter who had been warning of the dangers of the German "88" gun as far back as 1941, from North Africa.

To get the T26 to GIs overseas, Gen. Barnes had to overcome opposition from Army Ground Forces. Seemingly unaware of the Ardennes emergency, AGF continued to insist the long-overdue new tanks should be virtually perfected at home before being shipped to combat zones. In contrast, Gen. Barnes (like the Germans) appreciated that getting updated tanks, bugs and all, to the front was more important than seeking engineering perfection on stateside proving grounds. He got his wish, but only after threatening to appeal directly to Gen. Marshall.

In mid-February, twenty T26s arrived at the 559th Ordnance Battalion in Aachen, Germany, to be divided equally between the Third and Ninth Armored Divisions. Before being issued to combat units they needed final assembly and testing in rear areas, such as fitting machine guns and radios and sighting in and calibrating the main guns. New crews also had to be assembled and trained, and eager tankers received gunnery instruction from an Aberdeen Proving Ground civilian, L. R. "Slim" Price, an expert on the new 90mm main gun. Mr. Price "impressed some of Patton's tank crews," wrote armor historian Richard Hunnicutt, "by using German helmets as targets and picking them off with single shots from the 90mm gun, at a range of 625 yards. Such performance quickly overcame any objections that many tankers

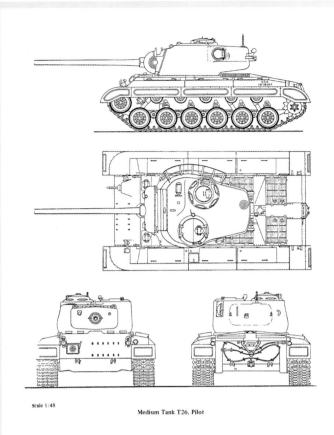

Profile view of a T26 pilot (prototype). *Photo by Robert Coldwell Sr.*

might have had to receiving gunnery instruction from a civilian. In fact, the veterans rapidly duplicated Price's marksmanship once they got the 'feel' of the weapon."[40]

In his diary for March 15, British Army Brigadier Ross repeated rumors the T26s, according to Col. L. V. Hightower, president of the Armored Board, were "in action on the north edge of the Bulge."[41] The precise number that made it to frontline units and engaged German tanks is unclear. Hunnicutt estimates that of roughly 310 to reach the European Theater, only 200 were delivered to frontline units, with few seeing action.[42] Other sources claim that by VE Day, just 200 (not 310) had arrived at the docks of Antwerp, Belgium, and other rear area supply depots, but were delayed due to the need for final assembly, maintenance, and inspection.

There were several comedies of errors. The improved 90mm ammunition for a tank that Roosevelt implied was given the highest priority was shipped to the wrong unit, only discovered when "The 635th Tank Destroyer Battalion telephoned to ask why the ammunition received was 12 1/2 inches too long for their gun."[43] When the modified T26E4 "Super Pershing" (a single prototype tank with an even more powerful gun and better armor than the standard T26E3) was readied for shipment to the ETO, stateside technicians had installed a custom made, painstakingly adjusted telescopic gun sight for the new gun that disappeared when the tank reached Germany. Capt. Elmer Gray then "checked back through all of the units handling the tank since its arrival in Europe," only to find that the one-of-a kind gun sight had been removed and a standard M71C sight installed in its place by "an overzealous depot crew when preparing the tank for shipment.... Since it proved impossible to obtain a new

special sight, [gunnery expert "Slim"] Price had to work out a range data sheet for use with the standard scope."[44] In contrast to Roosevelt's State of the Union implications, most T26s never reached the front.

The controversial memoir *Death Traps* describes testing one of the few T26s to arrive. The standard model was impressive enough, but GIs saw a rare, modified "Super Pershing." As excited tankers put it through its paces they watched it test fire against a disabled German *Jagdpanzer IV* assault gun similar to an American TD.

When M4s fired, they sometimes blew up dust clouds and smoke that revealed their positions and prevented American gunners from seeing if they had hit their target (tankers refer to this as "obscuration"). M4 projectiles were also visible in flight.

There was a different result when the T26 discharged its new high-velocity 90mm gun. "When we fired the first round, we could barely see the projectile. It appeared to rise slightly as it struck the target. This was an optical illusion, but the effect was awesome. When it hit the target, sparks shot about sixty feet into the air, as though a giant grinding wheel had hit a piece of metal."[45]

Examining the target up close, GIs were happily "dumbfounded."[46] Sherman rounds would likely have bounced off a *Jagdpanzer*, "probably the best tank destroyer of the war,"[47] with 80mm of sloped armor protection on its front.[48] But the Pershing's "90mm projectile penetrated four inches of armor; went through a five-inch final drive differential shaft, the fighting compartment and its rear partition; ...penetrated the four-and-a-half inch crankshaft of the Maybach engine, and the one-inch rear armor plate."

Completely exiting the enemy vehicle, the Pershing round "dug itself into the ground so deep, we could not locate it.... it was difficult to believe this awesome power. We all realized that we had a weapon that could blast the hell out of even the most powerful German Mark VI Tiger tank."[49]

Sgt. Nick Mashlonik was one of the few to fight a Tiger with the new tank; his T26 "Fireball" was part of Task Force Lovelady. "Since I was the oldest tank commander alive [in combat experience, not age] in Company E, 33rd Armored Regiment, I was given the opportunity of selecting a crew and attending school at Aachen, Germany on the new T26":

Up to this time I had lost, or been knocked out of, seven M4 Sherman tanks, but had also knocked out twelve various German tanks, and hundreds of other vehicles.

A rare, field-modified variant of the T-26 with enhanced firepower known as the "Super Pershing."

Crew of the Zebra Mission T26 "FIREBALL."

"FIREBALL," one of few T26s to reach the ETO, was assigned to the 33rd Armored Regiment. According to one of her gunners, "I decided that I could take this Tiger with my T26's 90mm gun."

Our first exposure to the enemy with the new T26 was very fruitful. We were hit hard by the Germans from Elsdorf. The enemy appeared to have much armor, as we received a lot of direct fire, and this kept us pinned down. Our casualties kept mounting and the C.O. of my company asked me if I thought I could knock out the Tiger that was almost destroying us. He and I did some investigating, crawling out to a position where we could

see from ground level a sight to behold: The Tiger was slightly dug in, and this meant it would be more difficult to destroy.

I decided that I could take this Tiger with my T26's 90mm gun.

Restored Jagdpanther at the Musée des Blindés, Saumur, France. Note the prominent, checkerboard-shaped Zimmerit anti-magnetic coating. *Massimo Foti*

Cologne, Germany, 1945: A T26 versus a Panther. Unusually, the duel was dramatically captured on film.

Just as we started our tank and moved very slowly forward, creeping, I noticed that the Tiger was moving out of his position, exposing his belly to us. I immediately fired, put a shell into its belly, and knocked it off.

The second shot was fired at his tracks and knocked his right track off. The third shot was fired at the Tiger's turret with High Explosive Point-Detonating [ammo], and destroyed the escaping crew.

At the time, three other German armored vehicles were leaving Elsdorf, and were on the road driving to my right flank. I waited until all of them were on the road with their rear ends exposed, and then I picked off each one with one shell each—getting the last one first, then the second one, and then the first one—just like shooting ducks. Then I came back to each vehicle with HE point detonating, and destroyed the crews as they were dismounting from the burning vehicles. It was our first day in combat with the Pershing, and it was both fruitful and exciting.[50]

Our T26 was in defilade position, more or less hidden, in a little valley. I detailed my driver T/5 Cade and my gunner Corporal Gormick to accompany me on this mission. I would be gunner, and have Gormick load. I instructed both of them that once we had fired three shots—two Armor Piercing, and one High Explosive, Point-Detonating—we would immediately back up, so as not to expose ourselves too long on the top of the hill.

Combat tankers' reaction to the T26 was not surprising: they wanted as many as they could get, immediately. Before returning to the States at the conclusion of the Zebra Mission, on March 5, Gen. Barnes requested Gen. Campbell send all available T26s and an adequate supply of improved HVAP 90mm ammunition to the ETO ASAP.[51]

Gen. Campbell responded by promising "everything humanly possible"[52] to fulfill the request, including giving the T26s highest priority. In an early March letter to Charles Wilson, president of General Motors (whose Fisher Body Division of Chrysler was building the T26), Campbell stated some "250" of them "went into action on the Western Front last month."[53] (This figure was not accurate, since most T26s were delayed in Antwerp

A restored M26 Pershing tank. *Author photo, courtesy of the National Armor and Cavalry Heritage Foundation*

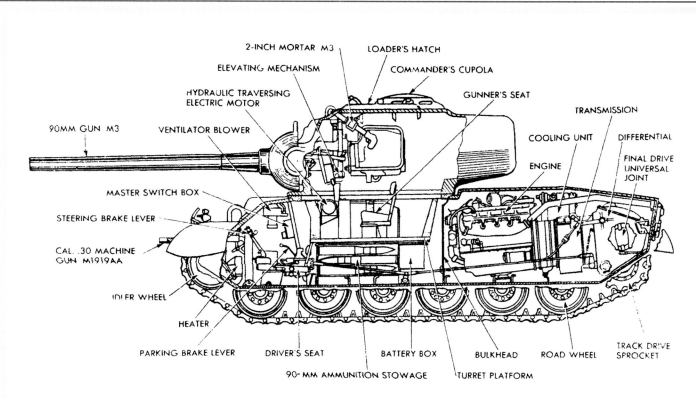

and other rear area docks and warehouses). The tankers, added Gen. Campbell, needed "the maximum number in the least possible time."[54]

This urgency was underscored on March 8, when a personal cablegram from Eisenhower to Gen. Brehon Somervell, who led the Army's Services of Supply, repeated the request.[55]

> Combat operations to date, while limited, convince me that the T-26 tank has what it takes. [Gen.] Barnes thinks you may have some 200 available for shipment now. Urge strongly that you get every tank this type to us as quick as possible displacing M-4s or other types as necessary to find requisite tonnage. Would appreciate immediate advice as to what you can do so we can arrange assignment and get maximum number into current action at earliest possible date.[56]

On March 10, the *Washington Post* ran "Output of U.S. Tanks Rushed," reporting T-26 production "is being rushed in at least six major war plants":

> The General Motors Corporation announced that five of its Fisher Body Division plants were in volume production, and Chrysler Corporation said its tank arsenal is at work on them.
>
> ...General Motors said the tanks, which mount 90-millimeter guns, are being "produced in quantity" at Fisher Body plants at Cleveland, Ohio, and Detroit, Grand Blanc, Grand Rapids, and Flint, Mich.[57]

But there were not enough T26s to go around. Col. Joseph Colby (in charge of development and engineering at Ordnance's Detroit Tank-Automotive Center) tried to placate "battalion commanders of the 3rd Armored Division," arguing that maybe their M4s weren't so bad. Instead, "He ran into a Hornet's nest. After the heavy casualties of the winter, they were beginning to regard the 75mm Shermans as deathtraps." In the 2nd Armored Division,

Brigadier Ross observed, "One tanker had six M4's shot out from under him."[58]

Here at last was a solution to the scandal that had reached to the White House and Pentagon. Predictably, agencies that had delayed adoption of the T26 now rushed to praise it; on March

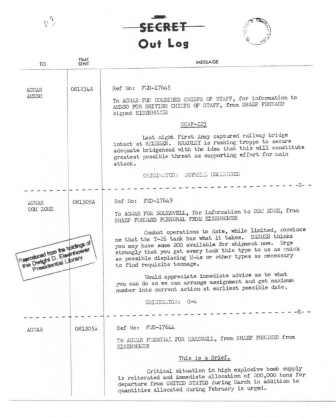

March 8, 1945, "Personal from Eisenhower": As GIs rush over the newly captured Remagen bridgehead into Germany, Ike calls for Army Ordnance to get "the maximum number" of T-26s "into current action at the earliest possible date." Even 200 would have helped, but it was not to be. *Courtesy Kevin Bailey, Dwight D. Eisenhower Presidential Library and Museum*

One of the T26 crews involved in the notorious duel in Cologne, 1945.

15, the *Bulletin of the Army Ordnance Department* echoed Secretary Stimson, calling it "America's answer to the German Tiger tank."[59]

But most T26s never made it to the ETO. According to Ordnance's official history, "On 02 April 1945, the first question General Eisenhower asked [War Department New Developments Director Gen. William Borden] was when the tanks with the super guns would arrive. The earliest date that Borden could give was June,"[60] a month after the guns would fall silent in Europe.

The *Washington Post* reported on March 22, 1945:

A Bronx Cheer comes out of Germany to greet the news that the Pershing tank has gone into mass production. It is the opinion of the men at the front...that they will get the new tank in numbers when it is no longer needed, i.e., when the war is over...an investigation is thoroughly in order. It should take up the reasons for the long delay in getting the Pershing into production. It should likewise find out why our tanks are inferior to the enemy's...whatever the cause of our deficiency, the facts should be revealed.

All that we know for sure is the oft-repeated claim of.... Army hierarchs that our equipment is the best in the world is not the verdict of the men who use that equipment. The myth has blown up in their faces. Griping, of course, is the special privilege of soldiers. But the griping about the American tank in particular has become so widespread, and is so fortified by such detail, that the criticism can no longer be ignored.[61]

But there was no investigation. For decades, authors have accepted simplistic myths, parroting the administration's version of the T26 story until it has hardened into "fact." Although most Pershings never arrived until after the war, today one reads of a happy ending little different from wartime propaganda: the T26 "solved" the Tiger/Panther problem and "arrived just in time to help the Allies invade Germany in 1945."[62]

While at least 49,234 Shermans were mass produced,[63] author Zaloga observes that from November 1944 to Victory in Europe Day, only 705 T26E3 tanks were completed at the Grand Blanc and Detroit tank arsenals.[64] Like Richard Hunnicutt, armor historian Michael Green estimates only 310 T26s reached ETO rear areas, with perhaps 200 issued to frontline combat units. Of those 200 tanks, Green estimates just 40 saw combat.[65]

Soviet T-34 tank at the Tank Museum, Bovington, Dorset, UK. Six decades after WWII, the author encountered T-34 tanks while serving in Bosnia with the US Army's 1/104th Cavalry. *Massimo Foti*

A GI contemplates a knocked-out Panther near Cologne Cathedral after the duel.

Yet in his "Report on the Winning of the War" to Congress and the public soon after the war's end, "special emphasis," Gen. Marshall stated, "was placed on the development of...heavy tanks...as well as expediting the production and shipment overseas of improved types of many of our new weapons.... As a result the T-26 tank began to reach the battle lines last winter [early 1945]."[66] In the national celebrations after VE and V-J Day, politicians and generals routinely cited Sherman tank production numbers as evidence of an American industrial miracle. In his highly publicized speech, Gen. Marshall neglected to mention how many of the new tanks "reached the battle lines," even with "special emphasis" and expedited "production and shipment overseas."

Seventy years after VE Day, a myth continues to be perpetuated. Roosevelt had hinted that "thousands" of T26s were on the way, but according to another estimate (lower than Michael Green's 40), barely twenty saw combat.[67] Few dueled with the King or Royal Tiger, so a decisive showdown never occurred. One author even claims that far from turning the tide of tank warfare as FDR implied, only *one* documented Pershing was able to "succeed in killing" a grand total of "one Tiger and two Panzer IVs during the 1945 advance into Germany."[68]

Far removed from wartime censorship, few have questioned the delays getting the T26 built and to the war zones. The Army had been developing the T26 since 1942, and proved the feasibility of fitting a more powerful 90mm main gun and improved turret to existing M4s, or into a new tank design. Yet in his 2015 biography of Gen. McNair, Calhoun assures us with little explanation that "by this time [after the Normandy invasion], the process of developing and fielding a heavy tank or even an upgraded Sherman would take a significant amount of time and overburden America's already stretched production and shipping capacity."

"One can only wonder," states Calhoun, "what effect development and fielding of such a tank before D-Day would have had on the logistical supportability of Allied operations in Western Europe."[69] So we are to believe that for a nation that designed and produced revolutionary new jet fighters, advanced, hemispheric long-range bombers such as the B-29 (the first B-29 combat mission was flown on June 5, 1944—before D-Day) and

atomic bombs, mass producing and shipping overseas a decent new tank by 1945 would overload Roosevelt's vaunted "Arsenal of Democracy."

What had gone wrong? Due to doctrinal confusion and inter-branch rivalries, combined with petty bureaucratic politics, there had been little demand or support for building heavy tanks when America entered the war. This sentiment was reinforced by the poor performance of the awkward M6 heavy tank of 1941, and the determination of Gen. McNair and others to stick with the M4, warts and all—to "Win the War with the M4."

This led to American complacency: T26 production was given a low priority, and tank assembly lines were slowed or shut down after the 1943 high level decision to reduce future tank production and tanker training. Meanwhile, the success of Russia's T-34 had forced Germany into a tank arms race. In response to Russia's excellent new medium tank Germany created the Tiger, Panther, and King Tiger.

Author Zaloga is charitable toward Gen. Eisenhower:

> The Army's complacency about the adequacy of the 76mm gun confused field commanders who might otherwise have supported Devers' request for the T26E1. In December 1943, Eisenhower refused to support the T26E1 request since he felt that its only advantage was the heavier armor. He did not feel that such a heavy tank was needed for the armor protection alone, and he failed to appreciate the substantial advantage that its 90mm gun offered. Eisenhower had been informed repeatedly that the 76mm gun would prove more than adequate against new German tanks, and after Normandy he would bitterly charge that he had been deceived on the tank gun issue.[70]

By the time the generals and politicians realized the extent of the Sherman's weaknesses, it was too late; closed assembly lines could not be restarted to build thousands of new Pershings overnight. As early as February 1942, Roosevelt had predicted to the American people a day when "our flow of supplies gives us clear superiority."[71] In contrast to propaganda showing innumerable tanks rolling out of factories, only ten Pershings were delivered in the first half of 1944, and just fifty by the close of the year.[72] In a repeat of the 1918 fiasco, when promised American-built tanks only arrived "Over There" after the guns fell silent on November 11 (and in negligible numbers), in 1945, instead of the "thousands" Roosevelt had mentioned on the radio, only a few T26s were delivered weeks before European guns also fell silent.

To Gens. Barnes and Colby, "the best American tank of the war" had been delayed by "bitter opposition by the using arms," the Armored Force and AGF.[73] To Col. Robert Icks:

> That they were late in arriving in the combat zone can be blamed on a few Ground Forces and Armored Board officers. Most such officers were dedicated, but a few had closed minds and lacked imagination. Unfortunately, those were the ones who were in positions of authority. Had it not been for concerned Ordnance officers,

A restored M26 Pershing tank. *Author photo courtesy of the National Armor and Cavalry Heritage Foundation*

who were determined to provide a better tank for the troops and went over the heads of the obstructionists to have them overruled, the development which led to the Pershing, and the shipment of the few which eventually got to combat zones, probably would not have taken place.[74]

Why was there such opposition to a better armed, better armored tank? Perhaps it was a matter of pride, a refusal to abandon pet theories and outdated anti-tank doctrine. Gen. McNair had argued for small towed guns and self-propelled tank destroyers since the blitzkrieg of 1940; when eyewitness reports from North Africa and Sicily showed they were not working he refused to recognize the need for reassessment. After all the praise heaped on the Sherman, in the face of all the propaganda, how could Ordnance Chief Campbell and Gen. Barnes—while privately supporting T26 development within the Army, as did Col. Colby—now contradict all that and publicly call for replacing a tank that had been sold to the civilian public as a war winner for years?

Though offered the T26, Gen. Patton refused it, partly on the grounds it contradicted Army establishment's prewar doctrine favoring light designs—an interesting attitude on the part of a tank pioneer who, in the 1920s and '30s, was willing to challenge the status quo and embrace progressive thinking about armor.

As early as 1918, Patton had written that in tank design, "mobility of strategic employment" and "speed and radius of action on the battlefield" should outweigh firepower (and presumably armor protection for the crew).[75] Over a quarter of a century later, the views of this alleged forward thinker on the use of tanks had changed little. The T26 was a leap forward, but not yet combat tested. The Sherman, though flawed and years behind German and Russian designs, was familiar, and available in large quantities. Now that this old challenger of the Army status quo wore four stars, approaching the highest levels of power, Patton chose the safer bet at the expense of thousands of American lives. According to one of his favorite maxims, the best was the enemy of the good.[76]

By the time of the Ardennes offensive, deficiencies with US armor moved Eisenhower (even while issuing public denials of the problem) to privately ask Gen. Marshall to expedite delivery of the new T26 to the European Theater. It was too little, too late. The T26 would not be "standardized" by the War Department (declared fit for mass production and distribution) until May 1945.

The Pershing was not a panacea; being a leap forward in tank design, it experienced engine, transmission, and suspension problems in its development. It also showed the danger of "The Ordnance engineers' failure to ask advice from tankers: stowage for ammunition was manifestly unsatisfactory":

Besides the fact that only forty-two rounds could be carried, the system for stowage, carried forward from the T23...[featured] ammunition stowed in metal satchels that each held two rounds. As the shells were used, the satchels had to be removed to expose more ammunition. These satchels soon filled the turret, but could not be discarded since they were needed when the tank was resupplied with more ammunition. Obvious defects such as this should have been identified at the mock-up stage, yet it was an inescapable fact that the problem persisted all the way into the prototypes. Reflecting a genuine concern for the users' point of view, the Armored Board objected vehemently to this feature. It is difficult to understand how this obviously defective ammunition stowage system remained unnoticed all the way into the prototypes, unless the tankers' point of view had been ignored during design. This flaw underlines the Ordnance Department's repeated failure to solicit the active and informed participation of the user early in the development process.[77]

"The Pershing story," armor historian Richard Hunnicutt concluded in an exhaustive study of the T26, "might well be summarized by the words of Captain Elmer Gray [of the Zebra Mission] replying to tank crews at Aachen, Germany, when they asked if the Pershing was equal to the King Tiger, or the Panther. His answer was, 'Hell no, but it's the best tank we have yet developed, and we should have had it a year earlier."[78]

The reasons for the Pershing's delay were many; among them, the Army Ground Forces' adherence to the "exploitation" role, emphasizing smaller tanks with lighter armor, and to doctrine that insisted tanks should not fight tanks. The latter view, supported by General McNair, retarded the development of adequately armed and armored American tanks for years, until experience with German heavyweights showed that such encounters could not be avoided.[79]

What might have been if the Pershing was fielded earlier in large numbers? After seeing what the new tank could do through the Zebra Mission, "All Commanders of Armored Divisions," reported an enthusiastic Gen. Barnes to Ordnance Chief Campbell in March 1945, "thought that the heavy tank T26E3 represented the ideal type of tank."[80] After the war, Gen. Joe Colby asserted, "if AGF had given the go-ahead early enough, the Pershing could have been available in quantities for the beachhead landings on D-Day." Even the Ordnance Department's official history agrees: "the record supports his belief."[81]

Hunnicutt found that "while the Pershing, Panther, and Tiger I were close enough in fighting power so that each could defeat the others under favorable circumstances," overall, the Pershing's gun had an edge on the Tiger's.[82] The Pershing, with similar ground pressure to the Panther (12.5 psi) and better than the Tiger's (13.9 psi), also enjoyed improved handling; GIs had marveled at the Panther's tight turning ability and skill at negotiating muddy fields while the lighter Sherman bogged down in the same terrain.

A 1/35 scale T-26 model by the author. *Author photo*

In frontal armor protection the three were similar. The Pershing and Tiger I were slightly better than the Panther at absorbing hits to the sides and rear. The T26 had a lower silhouette than both German tanks, reducing the risk of it being seen. Hunnicutt also noted that while a strike on the Pershing's frontal armor could bounce up and hit the mantlet (gun shield), possibly disabling the gun or turret, the Panther's turret was set back on the hull to avoid this.[83] He described the Panther's main gun as better able to penetrate armor plate than the other two tanks. The Panther also had a better power-to-weight ratio, "13.8 gross horsepower per short ton" versus "11 horsepower per ton for the Pershing and Tiger I."[84]

In concluding his technical comparison, when Hunnicutt rated the three tanks, "based on the criteria of firepower, mobility, and protection.... The Panther...ranked first, followed by the Pershing, and lastly the Tiger I."[85]

Hunnicutt had studied the standard model T26, not the "Super Pershing"; the war ended with only *one* of them being sent to Europe. Had the "Super Pershing" been mass produced the comparative results may have been even more impressive.

Sent to the ETO in large numbers just months earlier, the T26 might have helped tilt the tide of the tank war toward the Allies. Perhaps it could have helped reduce the number of soldiers' lives lost, used up like so many expendable, redundant components—literal "Tiger bait."

As the Wehrmacht collapsed internally for lack of fuel, trained crews, and spare parts, with Tigers and Panthers abandoned by roadsides or destroyed by fleeing crews, hundreds or thousands of powerful new American tanks rolling into Germany would have impacted not only tank-to-tank duels, but also Allied and German morale. But for exhausted American tankers there would be no much-needed, last-round shot in the arm to reinvigorate them, potentially saving tankers' lives and helping end the war in Europe sooner.

The T26 had been designed specifically to fight the Tiger I (the first production model), and Hunnicutt concluded it could do so, but he found the standard Pershing was outclassed by the King Tiger and the first-ranked Panther. Ordnance, tasked with keeping up to date on enemy weapons to help American tanks match or exceed Germany's, had been blindsided by the 88mm gun in the late 1930s; by the introduction of the Tiger, which it dismissed as impossible; and again by the advent of the excellent Panther.

Now, in the closing weeks of the war, Ordnance stumbled again. Although the Third Reich was in ruins and the Panzerwaffe that stunned the world in 1939–40 had ground to a halt for lack of gas or shot up by Allied fighter-bombers, German tank technicians had won the tank design war. In 1945, America's latest tank was a generational leap forward compared to the M4, but only on par with the Tiger, lagging behind the King Tiger and Panther.

The controversial book *Death Traps* notes the devastation a Tiger could wreak on a Sherman and its crew, and conversely what a "Super Pershing" could do to German armor. It includes an exercise in hyperbole, one acknowledged as "pure speculation": what might have been if the T26 had reached the ETO sooner:

> Few if any military historians have ever understood the importance of our not having the M26 Pershing heavy tank in time.... Many combat soldiers felt that the initial assault [into Germany] would have succeeded if we had the Pershing, with its better protection, and better mobility in muddy terrain...to capture the bridgeheads on the Rhine River. Major elements of the German army would have been annihilated on the west bank of the Rhine, and the Ardennes attack might have been preempted...we would have been behind the German Panzer units building up for the offensive.
>
> The Battle of the Bulge may never have taken place; some 182,000 German and American casualties might have been averted.... This, of course, is pure speculation, however, it is based on the tragic experiences of many armor and Infantry troops. After the tankers saw their buddies slaughtered in our M4 tanks when they tried to engage the heavier German tanks, they could not help but agree.[86]

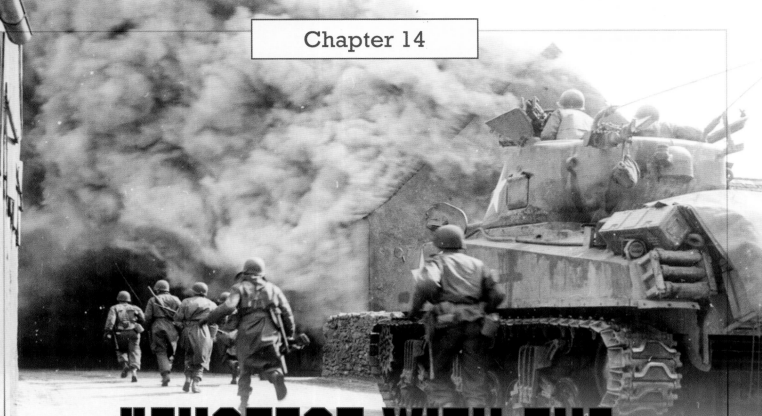

# "FUSTEST WITH THE MOSTEST"

## A Reckoning Denied: The Controversy That Wasn't

Even in the last weeks of the war, over *two years* since Gen. Eisenhower privately warned Gen. Marshall of the Tiger threat, the inadequacy of American tanks remained. On March 30, 1945, a Third Armored Division column (supported by the 703rd Tank Destroyer Battalion) of tanks, tank destroyers, and Infantry in open top half-tracks, trucks, and jeeps ran into four King Tigers near the Paderborn tank training facility—Germany's Fort Knox. The GIs had been assured the Tigers were ineffective, knocked out by fighter-bombers, but when "the column advanced, the very functional Tigers opened fire with their deadly 88s. Seven Shermans were soon burning. The TDs of the 703rd returned fire and knocked out two Royal Tigers, a job that required thirty-five rounds of AP and five of HE."[4]

Sir Max Hastings elaborated on this battle:

As the Americans approached a road junction, the Tigers cruised down the line in the opposite direction. "Ob-

> Our fellow citizens are entitled to know every fact about our weapons that does not jeopardize the winning of the war. For their peace of mind, the facts of our tank position should be stated by all concerned.[1]
> —The Army Ordnance Association, January 15, 1945

servers said it looked more like a naval engagement than a land battle." One Sherman hit a Tiger on the thin armour above its engine compartment, and another German crew bailed out when hit by a white phosphorous shell, convinced that its Tiger was on fire. But the Americans suffered appallingly: seventeen Shermans, seventeen half-tracks, three trucks, two jeeps and a tank destroyer were knocked out in a matter of minutes.[5]

The Allies had also failed to counter the German *Panzerfaust* and *Panzerschreck*, cheap, disposable anti-tank weapons fired by one man. To Maj. Al Irzyk, the Panzerfaust was "weird looking—an absolutely incongruous object, an oddity, if there ever was one—but extremely reliable. It had what looked like a small, round, iron pipe about two inches in diameter and about a meter long. At the end of this pipe was a large, bloated, bulbous object":

Not every German gun was a Tiger: At the Tank Museum, Bovington, Dorset, UK, a German anti-tank Hetzer tank destroyer, and a Jagdpanther assault gun. *Massimo Foti*

Eichstatt, Germany, April 25, 1945: Even in the last weeks of the war, Shermans of the 25th Tank Battalion, 14th Armored Division, are covered with sandbags in a crude attempt to increase the crews' odds of survival. The effectiveness of the sandbags may have been minimal, but the tankers' concerns were very real.

German Hetzer tank destroyer at the Musée des Blindés, Saumur, France.
*Massimo Foti*

Cologne, Germany, 1945: An M4 tank commander (standing in the turret) contemplates the ruins of Hitler's "thousand year Reich."

When the Panzerfaust was fired, and it had to be at close range, it blew off the bulbous object, which was really a shaped charge. It sort of wobbled off unhurriedly through the air. But once it hit, it hung in there and penetrated. When it hit the side of a tank, it clung to it, and forged a large hole. As the charge bored through the metal, the hole got progressively smaller, but metal fragments were pushed forward inside the tank, where they rattled around in all directions.

The Panzerfaust was amazingly reliable; all it took to damage or destroy an Allied tank was a fanatical,

**ABOVE:** The Panzershrek (tank terror), 1944: Easy and cheap to manufacture, man portable, and deadly to Allied tanks. *Courtesy German Federal Archives* **LEFT:** Boy soldier with a Panzerfaust (tank fist). *Courtesy German Federal Archives*

suicidal zealot firing it. He dug himself a trench, like an enlarged foxhole usually along a road, raised up when the tank got near, put the weapon to his shoulder, fired it, and he had himself a tank. Often, however, before he was able to settle back into his trench, he would be riddled with bullets from accompanying Allied vehicles.[6]

As the European war approached a violent climax, losses of tanks and tankers from these weapons increased, especially in last-ditch Germany. On April 17, fighting for Magdeburg, the 743rd Tank Battalion suffered their last "casualty" of the war: "A Pan-

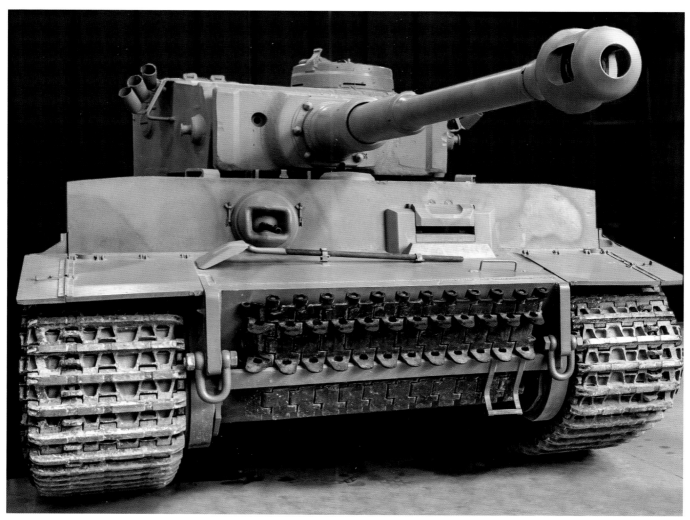

Rare Tiger I restored to running condition at the Tank Museum, Bovington, Dorset, UK. This tank was used in the film *Fury*. *Massimo Foti*

Entrance hole on a T26 turret from a German tank round. The resulting damage killed the tank's driver.

zerfaust hit a Sherman turret, killing the gunner and wounding the commander and loader. It was fired by a German woman."[7]

At home, papers like the Abilene, Kansas, *Reporter-News* (in Eisenhower's hometown) on March 27, 1945, featured effusive statements from Gen. Patton for civilian consumption: "Sherman Vs. Tiger - Patton Into Row With Loud Praise for Tanks." As instructed by Ike, Patton (in an open letter to Gen. Handy, Army Deputy Chief of Staff) publicly damned "misguided or perhaps deliberately mendacious individuals" raising concerns about American tanks, dismissing their concerns as "wholly incorrect."[8]

Across the country, articles reporting on Eisenhower's Paris press conference carried headlines like "Ike Says New Allied Tanks Equal To Best Nazi Models" in the March 28, Lincoln, Nebraska, *State Journal*. Reflecting wartime censorship, the paper noted "Eisenhower did not identify the new tanks but it has been announced previously that the new American T26 'Pershing' tank is in production." The numbers of T26s actually in the ETO were "not large, but will increase if the war lasts, the Supreme Commander of the western allies said at a press conference."[9] On March 26, Eisenhower forwarded the secret White-Rose Reports to Gen.

*Photo by Robert Coldwell Sr.*

Marshall with a personal cable, also commenting that "the German bazooka [the panzerfaust and panzershreck] and one other weapon may be considered superior to a similar item of ours."[10] The other American weapon that fell down, in Ike's candid opinion? Tanks:

Dear General: Enclosed are copies of the two letters relating to comparisons between our equipment and that of the German. You will note that [Gen. Maurice] Rose, one of our finest Division Commanders, as well as junior officers and enlisted men serving within his Division, are all dissatisfied with the performance of the present Sherman tank. Their criticisms, of course, relate primarily to direct duel between the Sherman and the Panther or Tiger.

We have always known that the Sherman, particularly with the 75mm gun, was very badly handicapped in this specific set of circumstances. As long ago as last June we had correspondence with the War Department on the matter and my own Armored Force officer [Gen. Joe Colby] was sent home to confer with the Ordnance Department about it.

There is general agreement that the new T26, particularly when it gets the newest high-velocity gun, will be a match for the Tiger and Panther even in single combat. Nevertheless you will note that one or two of the tank commanders would like to have even more armor, particularly in front.

The fact is that when a man is actually on the frontline

M3 Lee medium tank, 1/35 scale model by the author. *Photo by Robert Coldwell Sr.*

engaging a gun or a tank, he could not have, in his own estimation, a big enough gun or enough armor. While this would result in nothing but a steel pillbox, it is clear that the Ordnance Department should do everything it can to speed up production of the T26 with the very high-velocity gun.[11]

Eisenhower's private assessment of the M4 for Marshall was at odds with years of rosy press releases from official sources and later denials of problems with it. But to the brass at home all was well: April 13 was the fourth anniversary of the first M3 medium tank, and Ordnance Chief Campbell wired Chrysler's Detroit Tank Arsenal, "The more than 20,000 tanks you have turned out in four years have played a key part in shifting the tide of war. Today our armies are advancing along the road to victory, and that advance is spearheaded by your tanks. The assembly lines of Chrysler have been basically instrumental in breaking the battle lines of the Axis."[12]

Building 20,000 mediocre M3 mediums was impressive, but what would have been the result if they had faced large numbers of Panthers? Author and WWII Army officer Paul Fussell noted the irony that in "this highly modern war," instead of improving after years of experience, "the Allied ground army" and its weapons seemed to grow "worse as the war proceeded."[13]

What if the tank war had continued? "Data suggest," concluded historian and former Canadian Army tank officer Roman Jarymowycz, that the resulting "battles of attrition would have eventually reduced the Allied armor to near impotence…despite the aggregate attrition to the German armor. Notwithstanding overwhelming air and tank superiority, total Allied [armor] casualties were almost three times that of the Wehrmacht. Thus, the longer the ground war lasted in Europe, the greater the casualties to Allied armor."[14]

On March 26, Eisenhower conceded to the *New York Times*, "If the war lasted a number of weeks longer, the enemy might be met on the battlefield with something equal to the Tiger and Panther, but it is now idle to pretend that when the other fellow was met in a village street, he could be met on equal terms."[15]

While the 1970 film *Patton* portrayed the general as a victim of hostile civilian press, he benefited from his reputation as an armor expert in that same press to defuse criticism of the tank scandal. To historian Nicholas Molnar, Patton "directly manipulated the media correspondents who tagged along with the Third Army during its operations in Europe. During a press conference the same week in which he wrote the letter [to Gen. Handy, publicly denying problems with the M4], he forthrightly asked reporters for positive publicity for the Sherman…. His advocacy work seems to have paid off because a week later, he declared at another press conference with the same correspondents, 'I first want to thank all of you for helping me out with those remarks I asked you to make about weapons. I read several editorials from home and while I was not quoted, it was damn well said.'"[16]

Far from seeing himself as a victim of predatory reporters, "I permitted the newspaper correspondents to question me," Patton wrote in his diary for September 22, 1945, "I did this weekly during active operations and always had them on my side."[17] Concluded Molnar, "all of Patton's efforts to defend the Sherman proved wildly successful in stopping criticism of the tank in the media. Patton waged the propaganda war magnificently, using his personal influence to drastically change the direction of the debate."[18]

The Wehrmacht's collapse enabled American political and military leaders to evade reckoning after GIs and the public had been lied to for years. Committees like Missouri Senator Harry S. Truman's had exposed ineptitude in weapons procurement, but a congressional investigation into the tank scandal never took place. The guilty were protected, closing ranks around powerful culprits. In "Our Tanks Are Without Equal," *Army Ordnance* magazine insisted, "General Eisenhower…and General Patton… have put their respective approvals on our American ordnance in no uncertain terms—approvals which should go a long way toward reassuring the American people in their hour of trial."

A restored late model M3 Lee medium tank. *Author photo courtesy of the National Armor and Cavalry Heritage Foundation*

Ed Reep, *Tanks Ready to Roll*.

*Kamerad*, by Mitchell Jamieson.

But Col. George Jarrett was not buying it. In "Old Weapons and New," a similar article in the January-February issue of the magazine, Maj. Gen. C. T. Harris Jr. wrote, "Our present ordnance is superior to that of the enemy." To Col. Jarrett, "This always guessed assumption can be dangerous—Are we kidding ourselves to the point of national danger?"[19]

Many newspapers accepted the government line. "U.S. Tanks Fill Bill," editorialized the Evansville, Indiana, *Courier* on February 10, 1945. "One question which now seems to have been answered with reassuring finality concerns the quality of American tanks.... General Eisenhower reports that...'We have a general superiority in quality and quantity of our ordnance...'" Ordnance Gen. Campbell, the *Courier* noted, "Quoted field commanders such as Gen. George S. Patton, Jr. and Gen. Jacob L. Devers as saying they don't want any heavier tanks than they have now. The

Col. George Jarrett became Curator of the Ordnance Museum at Aberdeen Proving Ground, Maryland, until retiring in 1966. Many of the captured enemy tanks and armored fighting vehicles that Col. Jarrett helped preserve will be the centerpieces of the Army's future National Museum of Cavalry and Armor. *Courtesy US Army Military History Institute, Carlisle Barracks, Pennsylvania*

Sherman tank, they said, is entirely satisfactory.... American commanders in the field are in the best position to know what they want and what they have in the matter of equipment. If they are satisfied, comparison of American tanks with others on a purely technical basis loses most of its meaning."[20]

An honest reckoning would have implicated leaders at the highest levels of the Army and Roosevelt administration. A week before Eisenhower's public acknowledgment the M4 was less than a war winner, the March 19 *New York Times* quoted an anonymous but perceptive "lieutenant of Cavalry," who pointed out the tank scandal's political dimensions and career repercussions:

Generals can face the wrath of the enemy, but never that of the people. The only reason our foremost exponent of armor [Patton] does not champion the tanker's cause is, I suspect, because the blame belongs to a fraternity of which he is a member, and would result in professional suicide for an ambitious man to do so.[21]

*Photo enhancement by Robert Coldwell Sr.*

Three old pals: "Ike," "Georgie," and "Brad."

On March 17, after a personal visit from (and private talk with) Eisenhower, Patton scolded inquisitive reporters that same day. "We have the best tanks in the world," he insisted, "and there is no doubt about it, and it has a very bad effect on people back home when we say otherwise. Any talk that our Army is inferior to the German Army is not only a malignant lie, but it has a bad effect on the soldier."[22]

It does not seem to have occurred to Patton that publicly dismissing the concerns of tankers with years of hard experience was not conducive to improving their trust in leadership. To George Jarrett, the generals' attitude toward the tank scandal seemed to be "Never tell [the truth] about these things—the men need not know—[it's] bad for morale."[23]

On March 18, Eisenhower privately addressed the tank scandal in a letter to Marshall written from Reims, France:

Only receipt of recent letters and telegrams from you has warned me that criticism at home against our equipment is of a really serious nature. Yesterday I visited Patton and have asked him to make an appropriate statement on the matter, and then to interest a few good reporters in going further down to seek stories from officers and enlisted men who will make statements in favor of our equipment, to counteract adverse ones. A sergeant's statement seems to mean more to the average person than does one from a higher officer.

Very recently I ran into a sergeant in a tank who said something to this effect:

"These big old Panthers are poison when you run square into them. The big thing is to prevent them catching you by surprise. This platoon has learned how to handle them and we have knocked off a lot more than we have lost."

I looked at Third Army totals yesterday. Patton has lost about 800 tanks, and has knocked out about 820 German tanks. For myself, I am tentatively planning to have a large press conference shortly after we have cleared up the Saar Basin...in that conference I will take up the whole matter of equipment. I should guess that I could do it about the 26th or 27th.

I have likewise spoken to Bradley about the manner, and he will try to give us some help.

There are, of course, certain points in which honest complaints could be registered.[24]

While it would be unrealistic to expect top generals to reverse previous positions and concede the extent of the tank scandal, pleading ignorance was not an option, because it would show negligence. On March 9, Eisenhower received a cable from Director of the War Department's Bureau of Public Relations Gen. Alexander Surles. Surles was concerned about a story "prepared by a correspondent attached to the 3rd Armored Division" that "quoted some noncommissioned officers who made statements highly critical of U.S. tanks, the most damning of which read, 'Our tanks not worth a drop of water on a hot stove. We want tanks to fight with, not just to drive over the countryside.'" Gen. Surles then proposed attempting to "balance the unfavorable statements with those of other soldiers or Commanders pointing out the reasons a particular action may have resulted badly or the reasons our tanks were knocked out if they were."[25]

In response to this cable and that day's rocket from Marshall, Eisenhower cabled Secretary to the SHAEF General Staff Col. Carter L. Burgess. "I have spoken to Bradley and Patton on this," he wrote. "See if you could have some bright youngsters…write me up something I could use in a press conference—tanks, planes, artillery, trucks, DUKs, Jeeps, bazookas, machine guns, clothing, etc."[26]

The resulting March 27 Paris press conference was a model of equivocation, in which Eisenhower carefully avoided blame. It is worth quoting his comments on the tank controversy in full, courtesy of his aide, Navy Capt. Harry Butcher:

Incidentally, there is one point that has been discussed in the American press.... It involves comparisons of equipment. Some very broad statements have been made that seventy-five percent of the equipment used by the Allies is definitely inferior to the equipment used by the Germans. Of course, that is silly. But it's perfectly true that when the Tiger and the Panther tanks appeared on the battlefield there came against us a tank that, in

---

U. S. ☆    # MEDIUM TANK, M4A3  105-MM HOWITZER

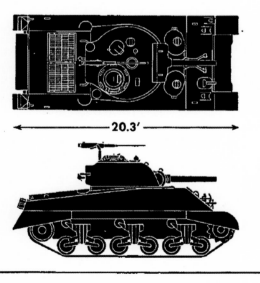

← 20.3' →

9.5'

← 8.6' →

**CHARACTERISTICS:**

Turret: Large, dome-shaped. Flat top, with cupola on right, second hatch on left. Radio bulge in rear. Set at center of hull.
Hull: Angular, but has streamlined appearance from the side. Slopes down gradually in rear, abruptly in front. High and square-cut as seen from the front because of steep forward plate and vertical sides.
Armament: One 105-mm howitzer in turret. One coaxial caliber .30 machine gun. One caliber .30 machine gun in bow. One caliber .50 AA machine gun on turret.
Traction: Full track. Six equally spaced bogie wheels suspended in pairs in prominent brackets. Three support rollers. Driving sprocket in front.

**INTEREST DATA:** This vehicle gives armored units a powerful assault gun in a dependable, heavily armored vehicle. The howitzer is very similar to the main armament of the M7 howitzer motor carriage, the "Priest." The tank has the new cupola, hatches, and steep front hull plate which are among the improvements on all late models of the M4 tank.

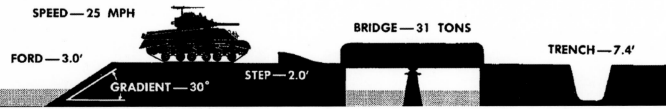

SPEED — 25 MPH

FORD — 3.0'

GRADIENT — 30°

STEP — 2.0'

BRIDGE — 31 TONS

TRENCH — 7.4'

*Photo by Robert Coldwell Sr.*

"The Panther Pup" Petit Tier, Belgium, February 1945: A new M24 Chaffee light tank of the 18th Cavalry Squadron, 14th Cavalry Group. As the original wartime caption notes, it had only "1¼" armor on the front, with "11/8" armor on the gun turret." The M24 may have been adequate for traditional Cavalry scouting and reconnaissance duties in rear areas, but (in spite of Eisenhower's assurances to the contrary at a Paris press conference the next month), if forced to fight a Panther or Tiger head-on, Allied tankers already frustrated with the undergunned, inadequately armored M4 medium tank were not likely to pick the little M24 as their weapon of choice. *US Signal Corps photo courtesy Ralph Riccio*

a tank-to-tank duel, was capable of knocking ours out, particularly at extreme ranges. Also there is one other item of equipment in which they have comparatively held the edge—their bazookas are more penetrating.

Remember this: when the British Eighth Army was fighting its way back across the desert, the Sherman tank was the greatest tank on the battlefield, by all odds. The German began to try to find something with which he could stop it. He developed a tank which, in many of its characteristics, is a defensive tank. Nevertheless, it's a very fine piece of mechanism. Then our people started to get something to beat that.

Our effort, of course, is not to fight our tanks with his tanks. If we possibly can, we fight his tanks with our anti-tank weapons, while our tanks go on to rip up his Infantry and try to encircle and defeat him. That can't always happen. If you make a penetration, the German will meet you with his most mobile weapons. New tanks have appeared on the battlefield, and so far both British

and Americans are handling themselves well; I should say definitely that if this war unfortunately lasts a number of weeks longer, there will be items of ours on the battlefield that will lick that fellow head-to-head in a duel.

You see, once we started to produce Sherman tanks—and with mass-production methods used in the United States and England, you couldn't stop production and start on a new one overnight—the question facing the armament people was, "Shall we go on and produce a pretty good tank in great numbers or stop and not have anything in an effort to get something that head-on could beat the Panther or Tiger?" It's my opinion that our people in the rear, [in] both producing countries, have pursued the very best policy, which was to produce a good tank in numbers. In that way we could always overwhelm the other fellow if necessary, while our home fronts went about the business of producing an even better tank individually than the best the Germans had.[27]

## U.S. ☆                         # LIGHT TANK, M24

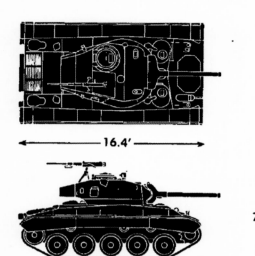

**CHARACTERISTICS:**

Turret: Irregular and angular, with inclined sides undercut sharply. Top slopes down front and rear from a flat center section. Prominent cupola set left of center. Large gun mantlet. Storage box in rear forms overhanging extension of tapered rear of turret.

Hull: Low, compact; slopes down gently at front and rear. Front formed by two flat, inclined plates

which meet in sharp V and form prominent horizontal line at forward end of tank.

Armament: One 75-mm gun (aircraft type) in turret. One coaxial caliber .30 machine gun. One caliber .30 machine gun in bow. One caliber .50 AA machine gun on turret.

Traction: Full track. Five large, closely set bogie wheels sprung independently. Driving sprocket in front, high-set idler in rear.

**INTEREST DATA:** This light tank differs greatly from any other American design. Its 75-mm gun makes it the most heavily armed light tank known. Performance is excellent, partly because of the torsion bar suspension which is similar to that of the M18 tank destroyer. The M24 is equipped with a vision cupola, an important piece of equipment now standard on all new American tanks.

← 16.4' →        ← 9.3' →        7.9'

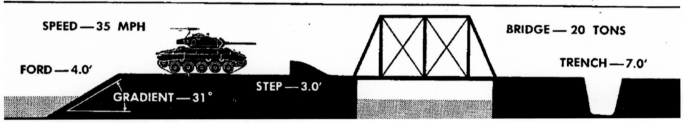

SPEED — 35 MPH        BRIDGE — 20 TONS

FORD — 4.0'        TRENCH — 7.0'

GRADIENT — 31°    STEP — 3.0'

*Photo by Robert Coldwell Sr.*

But the Tiger was designed to counter the impressive Soviet T-34 (itself influenced by American inventor J. Walter Christie), not the M4. It is difficult to know what Ike was referring to as "something to beat [the Tiger]"; perhaps the 76mm gun Sherman, which, while a mild improvement, could only penetrate the Tiger's armor an inch thicker? Perhaps the "new tanks appearing on the battlefield" also refers to the 76mm M4, or the small, light M24, a replacement for the obsolete M3 and M5 light tank series. But the odds of a poorly armored light tank being an improvement over the inadequate M4 medium tank were slim.

Notice Ike implies the only alternative to the Sherman was halting production of it, stopping assembly lines to design and build an entirely new tank, but several alternatives were available to up-gun the M4s already in service, such as installing an American 90mm gun (proven feasible as early as 1942), or adapting the British 17-pounder Firefly that the Americans rejected when it was offered to them. Eisenhower does state accurately that if it eventually reached the European front, the T26 would be an improvement, but it arrived too little, too late, and in small numbers. He also avoids the tank destroyer sideshow, by 1945 thoroughly discredited in the TD men's bitter joke that they needed not a "tank killer" but a "killer tank."

When a reporter asked, "In the tactical operation we are in now, isn't the Sherman quite good?" Eisenhower responded with a statement likely to anger combat tankers:

And so the propaganda continued. The American public was fooled, while the troops were betrayed. The tankers in Germany were saying, "Tell them our tanks are not worth a drop of water on a hot stove," and "In one field we lost half the… tanks assigned to our Company." Thus Sergeant Robert Early [Third Armored Division] of Fountain, Michigan, who commanded the first tank into Cologne.[3]
—Brigadier G. Macleod Ross, Chief British Technical Liaison to the US Army Ordnance Department, 1942–45, *The Business of Tanks*

**ANSWER:** Once you break through and are not meeting the other fellow's tank, I think every tank commander would rather have the Sherman. They would rather have our new light tank, the M-24, than anything else. The tank sergeant and the tank lieutenant, when he talks about the quality of tanks he means, "When I meet the fellow in a village street." In that circumstance we would be idle to say that the Sherman can meet the Panther or Tiger on equal terms.[28]

This was a hypothetical argument befitting necktie generals in starched uniforms and polished shoes. True, on paper the new M-24 light tank was good for certain conditions (for example, swiftly advancing in the face of light opposition) and the T26 better for others (tank vs. tank duels). But were GIs in the heat of battle supposed to ask the Germans to call a halt to switch tanks depending on the opposition—the M-24 to face only soft targets, while the T26 would confront Tigers and Panthers? Eisenhower's comment reflects the doctrinal confusion that, as late as 1945, plagued American armor after nearly thirty years—what, exactly, was the role of a tank?

Was the ideal tank a light, thinly-armored model stressing mobility such as the M-24, used to support Infantry, and attack mostly soft targets, somehow avoiding duels with the enemy's most powerful tanks? Or was it a heavy one like the T26, emphasizing firepower and armor protection, better able to slug it

## HYDRA-MATIC *Stands Up!*

### ... IN THE FIERCEST BATTLE ACTION!

The mechanism that drives a tank has got to be rugged. The strain of long hours of combat, in all types of weather, over all types of terrain, is a tough test for any vehicle. And Hydra-Matic Drive is proving that it can "take it," in these fast, Cadillac-built M-24 tanks that are seeing so much battle action.

*Pictured below: The M-24 tank, built by Cadillac, armed with Oldsmobile-built 75 mm. cannon.*

### ... IN THE TOUGHEST WARTIME DRIVING!

OLDSMOBILE introduced Hydra-Matic Drive to the motoring public in the fall of 1939 ... more than five years ago. By the time war broke out, Hydra-Matic had already proved its worth through millions of miles of driving by nearly two hundred thousand Oldsmobile owners. It wasn't surprising, then, that one of the tanks sent into action by the Army was the Cadillac-built M-24, *equipped with a Hydra-Matic transmission* ... Hydra-Matic for extra maneuverability! ... Hydra-Matic for ease of control! And, on battle fronts all over the world, these speedy tanks have shown that it's Hydra-Matic for *durability,* too!

On the home front, Hydra-Matic Drive has been establishing another impressive war record. In the hands of thousands of essential drivers, Hydra-Matic Oldsmobiles have been meeting all the toughest wartime tests of time and mileage ... saving gasoline ... saving energy for war-busy owners by eliminating clutch-pushing and gear-shifting ... providing dependable, economical transportation just when America needs it most!

Buy Bonds ... to Keep 'em Firing!

## OLDSMOBILE DIVISION OF GENERAL MOTORS

*Courtesy Henry Smith. Photo by Robert Coldwell Sr.*

In 1940, the Ordnance Department, though aware of Germany's notorious "88" gun since the late 1930s, had rejected military attaché reports of it as exaggerated, even while imagining hordes of phantom German "assault tanks." Later they erred to the other extreme, dismissing warnings of the very real Tiger. These failures of intelligence and evaluation continued throughout the war. Ordnance had technical intelligence teams in the ETO to evaluate German equipment and suggest countermeasures, but they were shorthanded and started late. By April 1945, weeks before the German surrender, one would hope the teams were operating smoothly. But to Ordnance Col. Holger Toftoy, head of the Enemy Equipment intelligence Branch (EEIB), his job was comparable to a "mouse trying to chew down a huge oak tree."[29]

Stateside bureaucrats not only persisted in their support for failed prewar doctrine, they opposed new tank designs and relatively straightforward improvements to the M4s already in use. Meanwhile, the Germans and Soviets got new generations of improved tanks to the front, working out bugs under real world conditions. Thus, a bitter irony: the dictatorships built and fielded some of the war's

out with Tigers and Panthers? Ike seemed to channel the late Gen. McNair in presuming textbook conditions would prevail—circumstances the enemy would not be likely to accommodate by only opposing our light tanks with their light tanks.

What would happen when a little M-24 (jokingly nicknamed the "Panther Pup") had to fight a King Tiger? Tanks could not be neatly divided into such specific, inflexible roles as "Infantry tank" or "Cavalry tank" because battlefield conditions are unpredictable; the enemy refuses to conform to desired ideal conditions. Rather than distinct types of tanks for rigid roles, such as light, medium, and heavy tanks and tank destroyers, what was needed was a flexible combination of firepower, armor protection, and mobility. But it would be decades until the Army developed the author's M1 Abrams Main Battle Tank, able to move quickly and support Infantry while also having the firepower and armor protection to duel the enemy's best.

best tanks, while the American democracy's celebrated industrial capacity was crippled by inter-agency bureaucratic rivalries, and disagreement over something as fundamental as the tank's role on the battlefield.

In vital areas, the Sherman was undoubtedly a good design. Unlike the Panzers, it was easy to mass produce and maintain. Instead of correcting its weaknesses on a large scale, the brass rejected expedient fixes and willfully delayed the adoption of a Sherman replacement. When battlefield reality showed otherwise, Gen. McNair and his followers continued to insist "The answer to heavy tanks is the tank destroyer."[30]

What Allied tankers needed was a machine that balanced the three unchanging principles of successful tank design: firepower, mobility, and crew protection. The Soviets came closest to reaching this ideal in the T-34, with Germany's Panther a distant second.

## TRACTION

I was that boy on the tractor.

I felt the Iowa sun on my bare back.

I felt the thrill of power beneath my feet.

In my heart was the glow of pride. I was anticipating the words "well done" from my father when he saw the clean straight furrows, the crumbled surface of the soil—to provide a seed bed for the season's grain.

I didn't appreciate then, the sturdiness of those giant tractor tires.

Today as I drive my tank destroyer through the churned earth of battle . . . meeting sterner tests, greater obstacles, I know well their qualities . . . their unfailing grip, their traction . . . their sturdy dependability—called *backbone!*

Tested by the demands of war, the tires like the boy, show that quality men call backbone . . . the ability to shoulder a job, to master it no matter what the obstacles.

That quality was developed long ago by men who first had faith in rubber. In tires they put it to work for the farmer, the logger, the road builder, the quarryman, and the miner.

With war these Peacetime skills were turned to new and stern demands. The tire builders who fashioned the tractor tire of '41 met the challenge for greater loads, greater stresses, greater speeds in the tank destroyers, Army trucks and tractors, Super Fortresses — Navy fighters that land on carrier decks—for every tire-borne vehicle of war.

In this *you* had an important hand. Because you liked our tires, we put more men to work building them. More scientists, engineers, textile experts and craftsmen pooled their skills in the common effort of building better tires to serve your needs. You helped us grow. You made us strong.

When war came we were ready. And the lessons gained from war will serve us in building better tires for the constructive days ahead.

*SERVING THROUGH SCIENCE*  Listen to "Science Looks Forward"—new series of talks by the great scientists of America—on the Philharmonic-Symphony program. CBS network, Sunday afternoon 5:00 to 4:30 E.W.T.

## UNITED STATES RUBBER COMPANY

1230 SIXTH AVENUE, ROCKEFELLER CENTER, NEW YORK 20, N. Y.  •  *In Canada:* DOMINION RUBBER CO., Ltd.

*Courtesy Henry Smith. Photo by Robert Coldwell Sr.*

One of the tank scandal's most frustrating aspects is that at different times, the M4's flaws *were* addressed, but in a disjointed fashion: a better suspension less likely to bog down in rough terrain; redesigned interior ammo storage bins to lessen the risk of secondary explosions and fires when hit; and improvised slabs of armor welded to the exterior's vulnerable sides by resourceful frontline mechanics. The greatest weakness, the main gun, was upgraded in relatively small numbers from 75mm to 76mm, 17-pounder, 90mm, and 105mm, and improved ammunition was developed and fielded, but not in adequate amounts.

But all of these fixes were small scale; had thousands or even hundreds of improved M4s been built earlier there might never have been a Sherman tank scandal. In hindsight, the possibilities are intriguing: a better tank fielded earlier might have accelerated the Allied pursuit across France. The Battle of the Bulge might not have been the Army's worst European defeat. GIs might have entered Germany sooner, with repercussions on the decades-long Cold War struggle for political influence over Europe.

Even before American tankers first met their German adversaries in Tunisia, Ordnance had considered arming the Sherman with a 90mm gun. On October 31, 1942, Aberdeen Proving Ground's Ballistics Research Laboratory reported this was feasible.[31] But inter-agency power struggles ensured little was done on a decisive scale. To historian John Mosier, the failure to up-gun the Sherman was an "appalling error… compounded by the refusal of the experts in the United States to pay any attention to the feedback from the men in the field."[32] British Army Brigadier Ross, observing the tank design and production process in Detroit and Washington, argued in his memoirs the solution "which so long eluded the staffs" was "the shotgun wedding of a British gun to American reliability—the Firefly"[33]

The United States overcame bureaucratic squabbles and red tape to build a complicated, world-changing weapon, the atomic bomb—yet dropped the ball on the Sherman tank. The American tanker was let down by bureaucrats unable to give him even a steady supply of decent tank ammunition; never mind an adequate tank to fire those rounds. As a biography of General Marshall— ironically celebrated as the "Organizer of Victory"—laments, "the Army planners miscalculated even America's capacity to produce the tools of modern war. They had, for example, estimated the number of armored divisions needed by U.S. forces at sixty-one. Instead, the Army could field only sixteen. In the end, the number of proposed armored divisions exceeded the capacity of American plants to produce the necessary tanks and other armored-force equipment."[34]

A leader at the highest levels to decisively address the tank scandal was needed, but never rose to the challenge. Five months before VE Day Roosevelt, in his 1945 State of the Union Address, spoke of the need for "thousands" of new T26s—tanks that his "Arsenal of Democracy" failed to deliver.

While the state of American tank technology advanced relatively slowly, in contrast, aircraft designs leaped forward by generations. By 1945, pilots who had trained on 1930s-era biplanes in 1941 were deploying jet fighters to Europe. In the Pacific, massive, long range "hemispheric" heavy bombers carried the first atomic weapons. While the Army Ground Forces had a stifling climate at its highest levels, the Army Air Forces, unbound to tradition, encouraged innovation. There, raved Gen. Marshall in his postwar *Report*, "Theoretical conceptions have been successfully demonstrated in action and modified or elaborated accordingly.... New conceptions are welcomed and quickly tested."[35]

So why was this not the case with the Army Ground Forces and the medium tank?

Like their 1917 predecessors, leaders of the Army's established branches saw the tank as an interloper, a competitor. Supporting tank development took funding and influence away from the Infantry and Artillery. This resentment led to a climate of opposition to tanks, as well as disagreement on how to use them that continued for decades.

Some authors have argued that it would have taken a long time to introduce a Sherman replacement, as if this was the only way to address the tank scandal. Yet the Army Air Forces fielded advanced new weapons with great success. While certainly one of the more complicated ground weapons, tanks were easier to design and build than a YP-80 Shooting Star or a giant B-29 Superfortress. As Dr. Richard Hallion—military historian, author, graduate history professor, and advisor to the Pentagon—expressed to the author, "The Army Air Forces had already made the transition from thinking about surface warfare, to war in the air, and 'just' had to go from the era of the biplane and piston engines to that of the streamlined monoplane and jet engine. I think the Army Ground Forces had a problem adjusting to mechanized warfare in general—leaping from horse Cavalry and horse-drawn Artillery to mechanized vehicles, especially tanks and self-propelled guns."[36]

The Sherman's flaws, according to *Death Traps*, were "by no means predestined; we enjoyed a great superiority in other weapons systems. After a twenty-year period of isolationism between the wars, in just four years the United States was able to produce superior weapons in vast quantities, including rifles, artillery, motor transports, and aircraft."[37]

As the war neared its climax, US pilots flying advanced fighters and bombers were bringing in the jet and atomic age, but on the ground, light tanks still mounted puny main guns not unlike those of the first tankers of 1917. The armor on American light tanks was even more inadequate than that on the Sherman. Fighting in Germany, Pvt. Don Evans was assigned to a reconnaissance company of the 66th Armored Regiment, still equipped with the obsolete M5 light tank, essentially an updated M3 Stuart of 1942 vintage. Early on the morning of March 31, 1945, Evans' tank was short one man after his bow gunner had been wounded. Hoping to escape the winter wind and cold, a well-meaning soldier volunteered to fill in as loader, the better to take shelter inside a tank turret:

Private Buren Mercer, known as "Shorty," was a very likable guy...everyone liked him and was always ready to give him a hand. Climbing into the tank that morning was to be the greatest mistake he would ever make—

it cost him his life. Our vehicle was about the fifth one in a column, and while standing in the turret and awaiting the order to proceed, the platoon leader came by, informed me that we would now be the point vehicle, and ordered us to the head of the column. No one but no one wants to ride point, and I tell you, this order shook me up. When you realize that the only people in front of you are the enemy, lying in wait, it puts a different perspective on your mission.

We had scarcely gone 30–45 seconds when I noticed a huge red flash on the right side of the road. I immediately dropped [down] into position to reach for the gun and turret switches, and in that instant, a ball of fire lit up the interior of the turret. What had probably been a Panzerfaust penetrated the steel on the right front, at about the position of the .30 caliber machine gun—directly into the face of "Shorty" Mercer. I was to learn later that this had taken off his head, and the ensuing fire burned most of his body. What a quirk of fate—I'm sure his body took a lot of punishment that I would have received, had he not volunteered to be my loader.[38]

Pvt. Evans, injured in the fire, was captured after his M5 was knocked out—a light tank that should have been retired years before being destroyed by a cheap, hand-held German weapon. But back home, the Roosevelt administration, generals, and some compliant press assured the public of the alleged superiority of American weapons and equipment.

The disparity was not due to any inability of US industry, but to the obstinacy of Army leaders and Roosevelt's choice of political expediency over soldiers' lives. While aviation advanced exponentially, tank design was stifled throughout the war, a blemish on the American war effort.

At the height of the tank controversy, an editorial cartoon[39] epitomized Army and administration leaders' attitudes. It showed Patton in a courtroom, not as a defendant, but as a defense attorney for the M4. Quoting the apocryphal worlds of Gen. Nathan Bedford Forrest, CSA, Patton submitted the Sherman had beaten the Tiger and Panther because it "got there fustist with the mostest."

From January 1945 to the German surrender in May, the US Army in the ETO lost some 2,977 tanks, including 2,238 M4s, 739 M5A1 light tanks, and 540 tank destroyers (276 M10s, 140 M18 Hellcats, and 124 M36 Jacksons).[40]

Back home, rather than a reckoning for the tank scandal, the canonization of the recently deceased President Roosevelt was the order of the day. The myth making continued for decades; in a popular 1976 work, instead of the shrewd, conniving politician he was, Roosevelt is depicted as a "Great White Father" who "worried constantly about winning the war as fast and as thoroughly as possible...to bring the boys home and keep them there." With typical patronizing, elitist condescension towards enlisted men ("the boys") noted by Sgt. James Jones, the author (a Yale history professor and former Navy officer with a Harvard

Cartoon by "Berryman," Washington, DC, *Evening Star*, March 25, 1945. *Photo by Robert Coldwell Sr.*

*Photo by Robert Coldwell Sr.*

background) refers to the GIs as "the soldier boys" and Roosevelt's "political children…. The soldier boys were always glad to see him. When, to their astonishment, he appeared, smiling his wonderful smile and waving his wonderful wave from a seat in an open car, they were delighted."[41]

It was easier to tout FDR's production figures than question tank and tanker losses. For decades this has been conventional historical wisdom: boasting of thousands of mediocre tanks produced while glossing over their inferior main gun and inadequate armor protection. Hiding behind boastful charts and statistics allowed culprits to avoid awkward issues, like the responsibility for thousands of dead and wounded tankers. As Sir Max Hastings observed after decades of historical research and writing, "written evidence" about matters of life and death, which all documentation about the WWII is, should be treated with at least as much caution and skepticism as interviews with witnesses. "Over the years, I have encountered extraordinary deceits in official war diaries and suchlike, often designed to achieve post-facto rationalization of what was, to those who took part, merely a 'cock-up' which cost lives."[42]

Army Ordnance made the tanks requested by stateside generals, but not the ones needed by the combat tanker overseas. With all its industrial potential, America could have produced tens of thousands of improved M4s, Fireflies, M36B2s, or T26s. But Army leaders—either not realizing the extent of the tank problem or willfully denying it and refusing to concede mistakes—never asked for them. Instead, Ordnance built over 88,000 mediocre tanks of all types,[43] often unwanted by the soldiers they were intended for.

The Sherman muddled through, "winning" by sheer weight of numbers and American casualties. Following the Normandy invasion Bradley conceded in his memoirs, "For the remainder of the war our tank superiority devolved primarily from a superiority in the number rather than the quality of tanks we sent in battle."[44] Or, as he put it more bluntly, "Our tanks were expendable."[45]

"It must not be forgotten," wrote Lt. Col. Al Irzyk in a 1946 article "Were German Armored Vehicles Better Than Ours?," that "though the cards were stacked against the American tank, it defeated the enemy and gained the desired ground. Though the Shermans were easily bested tank for tank, they could always bank on a numerical superiority, which fact was considered in our tactics and strategy."[46]

The report of a May 1945 Army general board on tank gunnery inadvertently revealed this willingness to sacrifice tanks and the soldiers inside them. The board found the gun tubes on US tanks outlasted those on Germany's, but this qualitative superiority was irrelevant: "Due to the short battle life of our tanks, the present accuracy of gun tubes greatly exceeds that of the tanks in which they are mounted."[47] In other words, so many US tanks were being destroyed so quickly that their quality or accuracy was irrelevant. American tanks and crews were expendable, redundant components.

Such a cold-blooded calculus might look good in a Pentagon briefing or in Roosevelt's boastful production figures, but it overlooks the suffering of the GIs, victims of bureaucratic rivalries and a decade of intelligence failures. Bankrupt of means to defeat the "Tiger Terror," the brass used men as decoys to distract them, in the hope that other Shermans (if they could close without being destroyed from long distance) might get in a lucky shot to the flanks or rear.

Historian John Ellis cited a German artillery officer's complaint that "though the Allies insisted on charging their Shermans right down the barrels of his battery of 88s, and were picked off one after another, he ran out of ammunition before they ran out of tanks."[48] If American industry could crank out mediocre tanks in huge numbers, Army and administration leaders reasoned, they could afford to lose perhaps four or five M4s to knock out each Tiger or Panther—and by extension to lose some of the four or five men inside them to death or wounds.

Italy, April 1945: A Fifth Army Sherman rolls forward near the Po River. Note the improvised armor (spare track lengths) on the turret. *US Signal Corps via Ralph Riccio*

Army boards, typically composed of career officers unwilling to rock the boat, rarely produce dramatic headlines. Yet just weeks after VE Day, with the Pacific War still ongoing, the Army Ground Forces Equipment Review Board recognized the repercussions of Gen. McNair's reorganization of the War Department, which not only put McNair's own Army Ground Forces, not tankers, in charge of tank training and doctrine, but also removed the end users from the tank development process.

Dated June 20, 1945, the board's report finally conceded a point that had led to the deaths of thousands of tankers and TD men:

> A weapon…must represent the best possible solution to the needs of the user…the user who is to fight the weapon in the combat zone must completely control the development of the weapon he is to employ. The complete and sole objective of the development agency must be to reflect the needs of the user…. Neither a development agency nor a using agency should at the same time, be a procurement agency.[49]

Decades removed from wartime propaganda and censorship, Gen. McNair is still praised as "the brains of the Army." But while their leadership not only failed to recognize the extent of the tank scandal and obstructed solutions, the sixteen US armor divisions in WWII suffered at least (Gen. Marshall's figures submitted to Congress were higher) 58,905 "casualties": 12,947 men killed in action or died of wounds and 45,958 wounded.[50] This is the equivalent of almost six entire Infantry divisions of roughly 10,000 men each. While the majority of losses were Infantry attached to the armored divisions, the figure includes many tank crewmen.

The GI's leadership failed him from 1939–1945 (or, in light of the decades-long failure to fully integrate tanks into the Army, since 1917), but his courage and perseverance shine through. Even as his leaders outdid each other with denials of the problem, he addressed it to the best of his ability. The GIs accomplished miracles, but they needed advocates at the top to take decisive action to correct the fatal flaws in their vehicles and doctrine.

Eisenhower made the attempt, but like the T26's long-anticipated debut just weeks before the guns fell silent in Europe, it was too little, too late.

# "WHO'S IN CHARGE HERE?"
## The Roles of FDR, Marshall, Eisenhower, and Patton

Even a cursory glance at the Sherman tank scandal invokes the question raised by author Charles Baily in his pioneering *Faint Praise*: "Who's in charge here?" One looks in vain for a leader to intervene in a bureaucratic nightmare. Why did not powerful leaders like Roosevelt, Marshall, and Eisenhower take decisive action?

### FDR: "The Lifeblood of our Sons"

President Franklin Roosevelt is glorified today as the "Arsenal of Democracy's" creator. While we recall dramatic newsreels of innumerable tanks rolling off assembly lines, some were obsolete before leaving the factories. Roosevelt endangered soldiers' lives to score political capital; after decades of American military unpreparedness and wanting to be seen making bold gestures in response to the blitzkrieg, he ordered the Army to build thousands of inferior tanks. The Army was ordered to "freeze" outdated designs and rush them into production so

> We cannot afford to fight the war of today or tomorrow with the weapons of yesterday.... we pay for our backwardness with the life's blood of our sons.[1]
> —President Franklin Roosevelt, 1945 State of the Union Address

Roosevelt could cite impressive sounding figures in his radio "fireside chats." His cynical manipulation of a national emergency to gain political points contributed to the deaths and injury of thousands of GIs.

Roosevelt's monumental ego led him to second guess and blindside Army leaders, and played a large part in the tank controversy. His comments at a February 1943 press conference are typical:

> You can't leave things to the military, otherwise nothing gets done. Now that's a dreadful thing to say, but the fact is that if you get almost all admirals and generals from different nations, or even one nation, talking over future plans, they spend a month or two in talking about why each plan or suggestion won't work—just get a series of "No's."
>
> On the other hand, if you get certain laymen to stick pins into them all the time—prod them, if you like—and say you have got to have an answer to this,

Photo enhancement by Robert Coldwell Sr.

Three old pals: "Ike," "Brad," and "Georgie" inspect stolen art hidden in a German salt mine, April 1945. *US Signal Corps photo*

that, and the other thing within so many days, you get an answer.[5]

Roosevelt, who never served, attempted to equate his civilian job as Assistant Secretary of the Navy with military experience. In conversation with his White House naval aide Capt. John McCrea he would refer to "when I was in the Navy."[6]

Reading his August 1936 "I have seen war" speech given at Chautauqua, New York, one might think he had frontline experience to rival Sgt. Alvin York, one of the most decorated American soldiers of WWI:

> I have seen war. I have seen war on land and sea. I have seen blood running from the wounded. I have seen men coughing out their gassed lungs. I have seen the dead in the mud. I have seen cities destroyed. I have seen two hundred limping exhausted men come out of line—the survivors of a regiment of one thousand that went forward forty-eight hours before. I have seen children starving. I have seen the agony of mothers and wives. I hate war.[7]

But he derived these dramatic lines from a short VIP visit made in 1918, to inspect Navy installations in England and France. On the voyage over in a destroyer, recounts biographer Jean Edward Smith, there was a mild submarine scare that "never materialized." Yet "as Roosevelt retold the story through the years, the German submarine came closer and closer, until he had almost seen it himself."[8]

"Shortly after the Great War," wrote historian Martin Gilbert, "Roosevelt wrote to a fellow alumnus who was preparing a WWI tablet for their school, "I believe that my name should go in the first division of those who were 'in service,' especially as I saw service on the other side and was missed by torpedoes and shells."[9] Although Roosevelt's time at the front amounted to mere

hours, it seems he felt no shame equating a stage-managed visit with the hardships endured by Doughboys in the trenches at places like Belleau Wood, St. Mihiel, and the Argonne Forest.

Roosevelt's predecessor, the less flamboyant Herbert Clark Hoover, had seen more of the horrors of war during his relief work for starving, homeless Belgian refugees, but Roosevelt exaggerated his own brief trip for political purposes. "I speak to you," he said in a November 7, 1942, radio address to the French during the Allied invasion of French North Africa, "as one who was with your Army and Navy in France in 1918...I know your soldiers."[10]

Not a humble man, Roosevelt obsessed over the title of Commander in Chief. At a White House dinner, when Secretary of State Cordell Hull rose to give a toast, Roosevelt ordered him to "...try to address me as Commander in Chief, not as President."[11]

A rare victory over FDR's monumental ego occurred when Chief of Naval Operations Adm. Ernest King—no shrinking violet himself—was visited by Chairman of the Joint Chiefs of Staff Adm. William Leahy. King was so mean, sailors joked that he shaved with a blowtorch. Leahy informed King that Roosevelt, on reflection, "wanted one of King's titles modified." Leahy said that "'Commander in Chief of the United States Fleets' seemed too expansive when Franklin Roosevelt, President of the United States, was the Navy's constitutional Commander in Chief":

*Photo by Robert Coldwell Sr.*

King looked at Leahy. "Is that an order?" he asked.

"No," said Leahy sheepishly, "but he'd like to have it done."

King gave Leahy a hard stare. "When I get the orders I will do exactly that. Otherwise not."

Unwilling to put that kind of order in writing, Roosevelt let the matter drop.[12]

Signing a United Nations declaration, Roosevelt sighed to his close advisor Harry Hopkins that he should have written "Commander in Chief," not "President." The laconically witty Hopkins responded, "'President' ought to do."[13]

This arrogance led Roosevelt—who also insisted on being photographed in a regulation Naval officer's cape, perhaps equating his boyhood sailing around Campobello Island to Adm. King's decades of experience—to overrule military advisors and experts throughout the war.

When Gen. Marshall proposed streamlining the chiefs of staff by placing one officer over all of them, FDR seemed perplexed; who could replace *him*? "I'm the Chief of Staff," he told Marshall, "I'm the Commander In Chief."[14] In Marshall's opinion, "With great frankness," it was "impossible to conceive of one man with all of his duties as President being also, in effect, the Chief of Staff of all the military services."

Confronted with such an enormous ego, even Marshall—a dour man not known for his sense of humor—was moved to inform Roosevelt, "You are not Superman."[15]

Roosevelt's arrogance also led him to conceal his ill health from the American public when he ran for a fourth term in 1944;

he would be dead less than six months after the election. One author noted his "stubbornness, his preoccupation with destiny, his consuming sense of indispensability, and the willingness of the Democratic party to allow its famous standard bearer to remain in harness."[16]

But for public consumption, Gen. Marshall wrote shortly after Roosevelt's death in April 1945, "The confidence he gave to the management of the Army was a tremendous source of assurance to the officers of the War Department."[17]

Roosevelt's haphazard methods—his tendency to improvise, and to make symbolic gestures to score political points—contributed to the tank scandal. When a dramatic response to the blitzkrieg was needed, he demanded large production of obsolete tanks. Later, when he guessed (incorrectly) the need for tanks had decreased, he was just as quick to slash the same production goals with further negative effects.

Were his decisions based on realistic assessments of the Army's needs, or a desire to score political capital through bold gestures? In September 1940, with the Army desperately short of aircraft, Roosevelt announced in a typically flippant remark that every other B-17 heavy bomber coming off the assembly lines would go to Britain, "even-Stephen."[18] Not only would this endanger American preparedness by delaying the training of US pilots waiting for new bombers, it was illegal, violating neutrality laws. Gen. Marshall called it "Wholly unconstitutional," but Roosevelt insisted on taking symbolic action.[19]

Two months later, Marshall told Roosevelt his decision to turn over half of all B-17 production to Britain appeared "to be based on a political speech."[20] Gen. Marshall also showed Roosevelt charts indicating a dangerous shortage of US aircraft—

"FIREBALL," a T26 of the Zebra mission. 1/35th scale model by the author. *Author photo*

less than one-third of the target goal for that month. Were the British to be given half of the aircraft actually built or half of the target numbers once production caught up? Roosevelt's response to Marshall's dose of reality was an angry "Don't let me see that chart again."[21] If this was his attitude toward the most powerful man in the Army, an officer almost universally esteemed, how could lesser ranked men get through to him? Who would dare challenge such a colossal ego?

Roosevelt made grave decisions on the fly and was notorious for telling different things to different people concerning the same issues: "It was very difficult to deal with the President under these conditions,"[22] concluded Marshall's biographer Forrest Pogue. Marshall recalled another troubling aspect of working with Roosevelt. "Mr. Roosevelt didn't want things on the record. He didn't want a recorder. I brought up an aide once to keep some notes. He had a big notebook, and the President blew up."[23]

Even in the midst of a world war, FDR was not above engaging in petty partisan politics. When a school of military government was set up to teach Army officers how to administer "liberated" territories, Roosevelt used a cabinet meeting to question why a Republican and rumored friend of former President Hoover had been accepted into the program. "The cherubs around the White House," Secretary of War Stimson vented to his diary, "scented danger...when they found that the school had enrolled a man by the name of Julius Klein...they thought the worst had happened and rushed to the President with the bad news. Apparently, he swallowed the story, and I found a rather sharp memo from him wanting to know what the Army was doing, and by what authority it was doing it, without going to him." Soon after, added Stimson, FDR's cabinet spent a second afternoon complaining about a Republican attending an Army school. "I had all the typical difficulties of a discussion in the Roosevelt cabinet," wrote Stimson. "The President was constantly interrupting me with

discursive stories which popped into his mind while we were talking, and it was very hard to keep a steady thread."[24]

Gen. Marshall also recalled the incident. "Mr. Stimson came back from a cabinet meeting that lasted almost all afternoon, and I discovered they had been discussing entirely this particular officer, whose name was the same as that of an intimate of [President] Hoover.... Mr. Roosevelt was very bitter about this matter, and Mr. Stimson was very much stirred up over it." As if the petty politics were not unseemly enough, Marshall and Stimson also learned that the man in question had never met President Hoover—it was all a case of mistaken identity. "I was shocked when I found out how long the cabinet spent—all afternoon—warring over this thing," remembered Marshall.[25]

Ignorance of the tank scandal cannot be pleaded in Roosevelt's case; in late November 1943, he personally saw the results of inadequate American tank design—with Eisenhower as his tour guide. En route to the Tehran conference with Churchill and Stalin, the two rode out of Tunis in a convoy toward Tunisian battlefields. The Presidential party saw "burned-out tanks, American and German," FDR's naval aide Lt. William Rigdon wrote, "and other vehicles, still on the battlefield where they were destroyed...a large salvage dump filled with burned-out tanks."[26]

Eisenhower, as a book on the Tehran conference notes, "gave Roosevelt a running commentary of the battles and described the bitter combat at Medjez el Bab, at Tebourba, at Bizerte...of the 70,000 Allied casualties, the Americans had more than 2,700 dead and another 14,000 wounded or missing.... Eisenhower stepped out of the car and walked out into the desert to inspect some...bullet-riddled tanks. Roosevelt watched his general deciphering the sequence of events, the exchange of shells, the twisted metal, the gaping holes."[27]

Although Roosevelt's ego and slapdash methods directly impacted the tank scandal, some biographers have not only overlooked them, but spun them into assets. James MacGregor

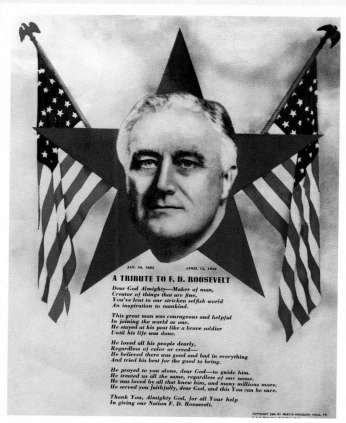

*Photo by Robert Coldwell Sr.*

Burns's *Roosevelt: The Soldier of Freedom* ignores the tank controversy, instead praising "the speed of weapons development" that "resulted from just those Rooseveltian habits that produced confusion elsewhere: division of authority, overlapping responsibilities, no unified program, changing agencies [and] improvisation in crisis."[28] "The improvisations of Roosevelt," insists Burns, "fitted the imperatives of war…productively."[29]

In author Ted Morgan's massive biography, there is no mention of a controversy that rated blazing headlines in the *New York Times* and the *Washington Post*, as well as calls for congressional investigations. The only discussion of the Sherman is this passage that stresses quantity over quality:

> The wartime production effort worked so well that in 1943 there was a glut. The United States had overproduced Sherman tanks, but after these splendid plants had been built and these thousands of men had been given jobs it was embarrassing politically for FDR to have to shut them down. The British had to be asked to cut down their own production so they could take more American tanks. The Russians did not want them, and there was no other way to unload them. FDR appealed to Churchill to accept 8,300 American tanks in 1943.[30]

Notice that Morgan ignores the tank, ammunition, and tanker shortages of 1944–1945. In early 1945, when public outrage forced Roosevelt to address the tank scandal, he spoke of the need for "thousands" of T26s to address a problem denied for years. "The American Army has now developed a new tank with a gun more powerful than any yet mounted on a fast-moving vehicle. The Army will need many thousands of these new tanks in 1945."[31] But like the Sherman tank scandal itself, the speech is missing from Morgan's biography.

As tentative production schedules for the T26 show, its bureaucratic opponents succeeded in de-emphasizing and stalling it as a Sherman replacement. In January 1944, Ordnance estimated 15 T26s a month could be built beginning in July, rising in September to a peak of 60 new tanks a month. Weeks later (February 1944), Ordnance downgraded these already unimpressive figures and put off the start date. If mass production began in October 1944, it was now predicted, six Pershings might be built that month. This output would rise to 25 tanks in November, and 40 in January 1945. The peak of production, it was hoped, would be attained in February and March 1945: a mere 50 tanks completed each month. And even this meager figure would taper off in April, down to just 29 tanks rolling off assembly lines.

So much for Roosevelt's State of the Union talk of "thousands" of T26s on the way to embattled tankers overseas.[32]

It is also sobering to compare these anemic production estimates to another set of figures that are sadly all too real: the Army's 1945 tank and tank destroyer losses in the ETO: in January, 944 tanks and TDs were lost (614 Shermans, 208 M5A1 light tanks, and 122 M10, M18, and M36 tank destroyers); in February, 615 total (382 Shermans, 93 M5A1s, and 140 TDs of all types); and in March 668 (463 Shermans, 135 M5A1s, and 69 TDs). April 1945, with last ditch fighting in Germany, would see the Army's ETO tank and TD losses reach a violent climax: 883 tanks and TDs lost (567 Shermans, 190 M5A1 light tanks, and 126 TDs of all types).[33]

In light of these losses, building a mere 29 T26s in April 1945 while losing 883 tanks and TDs in the ETO would have been a drop in the bucket. Even when one considers the technical challenges inherent in mass producing a new generation of American tank involving new transmissions, engines, suspensions, guns, etc., given that the Sherman's firepower and armor protection were years behind Germany's best, these numbers are embarrassing for a president that boasted of overwhelming dictators with allegedly superior (in quantity and quality) US weapons.

Jean Edward Smith's *FDR*, while acknowledging Roosevelt's tank production goals were far fetched, never mentions the tank scandal. Instead, Smith praises FDR's "staggering"[34] production figures, exulting that even "the Soviet Union was provided the materiel that it required."[35] What about the American GI, who lacked a tank with adequate firepower and armor protection until the war's last weeks? Were his needs met? While praising FDR's generosity towards the Soviets, Smith assures the reader that FDR "did not second-guess or micro-manage the military,"[36] which would be news to his cabinet, from Stimson to Marshall.

Did Roosevelt's own struggle with polio harden him to the suffering of others? Observed biographer Kenneth Davis, "There was at the core of him a curious icy coldness that, streaking the general warmth of his nature, enable him to turn off or on at will, seemingly, his remarkably empathic sensitivities, enabling him to bear with equanimity, if not wholly without guilt feelings, human suffering he might have prevented."[37]

For decades after the war, instead of honest critiques of Roosevelt's role in the tank scandal, authors piled on fawning adulation hardly distinguishable from wartime propaganda:

Franklin Delano Roosevelt died a soldier's death. He died, like the young men who were shot in caves on Okinawa or who were hit by shell fragments while crossing the Rhine, in combat. His form of combat was…leading the Allied coalition…the long and unrelenting effort had killed him as surely as a bullet.[38]

In May 1945, few generals, politicians, or reporters would publicly criticize the recently deceased president. The timing of his death precluded a reckoning for the tank scandal, ensuring for decades his culpability would remain largely unknown.

## General George Marshall: "The American soldier has a very active imagination"

Gen. Marshall was the one man in the Army hierarchy powerful enough to come between conflicting factions and bureaucracies and push through up-gunned M4s or mass production of the T26. Instead of being centralized, the tank design and building process was scattered among competing bureaucracies. Marshall's creation of the Armored Force and Tank Destroyers diffused some of the tank's best strengths, rather than concentrating them into one independent branch. Instead of direct responses to military necessity, these moves were political compromises, an attempt to sweep decades of doctrinal dissension and inter-agency power struggles under the rug.

As a recent biography notes, Marshall's imposing stature as America's "Organizer of Victory" has long shielded him from criticism. A January 3, 1944, *Time* magazine cover story feted him as "Man Of The Year," who turned a "worse-than-disarmed U.S. into the world's most effective military power…laid out a program of training and a schedule of equipment that are unmatched anywhere…avoided 'hastily planned-out or ill-advised military operations,'" and on it went until Marshall had become "the indispensible man."

"Many of these achievements," wrote biographers Unger and Unger, "were either mythical or half-truths."[39]

Marshall had seen the cost of America falling behind in tank development in 1918, as a First Infantry Division staff officer. In his memoirs of WWI he recalled the Meuse-Argonne offensive, in which "Everywhere on the battlefield individuals were paying the price of long years of national unpreparedness. They paid with their lives and their limbs."[40] He had also noted high casualties among Infantrymen lacking tank support: "Here was a commentary on the price of unpreparedness to be paid inevitably

A Tiger I heavy tank at Villers-Bocage, France, June 1944. *Courtesy German Federal Archive*

in human life. With America the master steel-maker of the world, American Infantrymen were denied the support and protection of these land battleships."[41]

When history repeated itself during WWII, Marshall—while not directly involved in the tank design and manufacturing process—had the power to make a difference. The Army's General Staff, he confessed after the war, was "a huge, bureaucratic, red-tape-ridden operating agency [that] slowed down everything."[42] But when American armor suffered embarrassing routs, Marshall had the influence to decisively intervene and order T26 mass production or up-gunned M4s after the early 1943 disasters in North Africa and Tunisia, when Eisenhower warned him that GIs had no answer to the new Tiger; after the July 1943 Allied invasion of Sicily was nearly thrown off the beaches and back into the sea by a handful of Tigers; and during the vast preparation for Operation Overlord, when exotic versions of the M4 were built in small numbers for obscure jobs. The inadequate firepower and armor protection of the standard model that would face German tanks and armored fighting vehicles went uncorrected.

*The American soldier has a very active imagination and…is inclined to endow the death-dealing weapons of the enemy with extraordinary qualities.*[2]
—Gen. George C. Marshall, Chief of Staff US Army

General Marshall's intervention was needed in late 1943, when Army leaders reduced tank production for 1944, and lowered the numbers of tank crewmen to be trained for 1944, as well as rejecting the new T26 *and* retrofitting a better gun to the M4s already in service.

In January 1944, Marshall had ordered a tired Eisenhower home to the States for a rare two-week furlough. Then, "in a series of talks at the Pentagon, they had discussed new weapons programs, including…the development of a heavy tank capable of standing up to the Germans' best."[43]

After hearing of the M4's shortcomings from his trusted subordinate, the soon-to-be Supreme Allied Commander in Europe, why had not Marshall taken decisive action to give production of the new T26 the highest priority, ordering large numbers—not small quantities for testing purposes—to be built, perhaps in time for the Normandy invasion?

General Marshall's authority was needed in the summer of 1944, as "Tiger Terror" swept Allied troops, along with a dire shortage of tanks, tankers, ammo, and parts, because Gen. McNair et al. had lowered the numbers for 1944. And during the Ardennes offensive, in which the problems with American armor were laid so bare in the stateside media the scandal could no longer be suppressed.

"What efforts did you make," Marshall's biographer Forrest Pogue asked him in 1957, "to keep yourself informed of soldier gripes, and to remove their discontentment?" The general answered, "I had trained men—civilians—travel all over the Army and see the individual soldiers":

> That had to be handled very carefully, because you don't want to begin encouraging the men to make criticisms, and yet we wanted to find what their reactions were. But they did it very well and they graphed it for me so that I could see the thing graphically when they came back and rendered their reports. In that way I kept fair contact. I did a tremendous amount of traveling myself,

and I had all the officers who went make these surveys for me in addition to what other duty they were performing…having an airplane, we did a great deal of traveling and covered vast territory in order to keep in touch with what the morale factors were.[44]

Even if one overlooks Eisenhower's early 1943 warnings of the Tiger, six months passed from the Bulge to VE Day. Army Chief of Staff Marshall could have ordered emergency mass production of a Sherman replacement, the T26. In October 1943, Marshall's theater commanders were polled on their needs for newer tanks. The ETO leaders expressed a preference for the new, experimental T20, T22, or T23 tanks, "if the Armored Command accepts [them] after performance and gunnery tests," and supported further development of the T25 and T26.[45]

Eisenhower, then commanding the North African theater, preferred the prototype "T23 medium tank…as the T25 and T26 are considered too heavy."[46] A response to Army Service Forces elaborated, "The T26 tank is not favored because it is not believed that the proposed increased armor protection over that of the present M4 series of medium tanks is justified by the corresponding increase in weight and decrease in maneuverability."[47] In Charles Baily's judgment, Ike, ever the diplomat, had responded with "an attempt to reconcile varied opinions about new tanks."[48]

In December 1943, Marshall approved building 250 prototype T26s for Gen. Devers, then commanding the ETO. According to a December 16 cable to Gen. Somervell at ASF, "It is directed that immediate steps be taken to effect the early production of 250 additional T26 tanks to fill the operational requirements of the Commanding General, ETO."[49] But the low emphasis placed on the job is indicated through Marshall's own comment in a December 21, 1943, cable to Gen. Devers that from that date forward, it would take nine months to get the T26 production lines rolling.

By January 1944, Eisenhower had taken over from Devers in the European Theater. Given that Ike had recently opposed building the T26, Marshall asked him to clarify his views. Marshall had supported production of 250 T26s for then-ETO commander Devers; did new Supreme Commander Eisenhower, who had considered them "too heavy," want them?

"Has any change in this requirement arisen to make advisable delay or cancellation of project [T26 production?]" Marshall cabled to Ike in January. In his November 14 letter, Eisenhower had forwarded comments from Second Armored Division Gen. Ernest Harmon, who advised "to procure large masses of this type [of tank] would be a mistake since they cannot be maneuvered or fought over the average type of terrain and in the average situation such as the Armored Division should be expected to be employed." But Harmon also wrote, "There may be opportunities in special situations for the employment of very heavy [sic] armed and armored tanks; therefore, a few battalions of this type should be procured."[50]

Eisenhower then withdrew his previous opposition to the T26 and supported the production order, but the Pershing's arrival was delayed until the war's last weeks. As an anonymous

staff officer in the ETO—where the T26 was desperately need-ed—scribbled in red ink on a copy of Marshall's "nine-month delay" cable to Devers, "We can forget about this one."[51]

In fairness to Marshall, his dealings with Roosevelt were made more difficult by FDR's haphazard methods, including his liking for dramatic gestures and favoritism towards the Navy. At one point Marshall had to ask Roosevelt to stop referring to the Navy as "us" and the Army as "them."[52]

Marshall recalled, "I found these difficulties in dealing with the President. All his advice was coming in from the Navy, which needed the steel and materials of that nature—and needed men, too—and he was personally, intimately, of course, familiar with the Navy, and naturally very responsive to its requests."[53]

In addition to Roosevelt's anti-Army bias, another hurdle that Marshall as Army Chief of Staff faced getting support to build tanks was the public's decades-long love affair with aviation. "The airplane is very photogenic," recalled Marshall after the war, "[but] it was not at all dramatic to ask for the force we needed in the ground Army, which was going to be compelling-ly needed once the real fighting started."[54]

Charles Lindbergh's 1927 Atlantic crossing had inspired Americans to follow the adventures of flyers like Jimmy Doolittle, Howard Hughes, and Amelia Earhart. Later, as WWII loomed, this aviation mania translated into public support for military aircraft, helping loosen congressional purse strings for aircraft design and production.

> The Army possesses no inherent right to conceal the history of the United States' affairs behind a cloak of secrecy…. The history of the Army in World War II must, without reservation, tell the complete story of the Army's participation.[3]
> —Gen. Dwight D. Eisenhower, Supreme Commander SHAEF

As Marshall described the period leading up to Pearl Harbor, the Army's "fight" for funding "was conducted without any real understanding of the question by the columnists, by the various writers, and by the public. They all played to the dramatics of the thing—which was the budding air force. Of course we had to have an air force. But if we didn't have an Army—and a ground Army—we didn't have anything."[55]

While the 1940s public knew of WWI aces like Capt. Eddie Rickenbacker and Lt. Frank Luke—"the Arizona Balloon Bust-er"—there was no tradition of tanker heroes to perpetuate. Fighter pilots like Richard Bong and Francis "Gabby" Gabreski, Tokyo Raid and Eighth Air Force leader Gen. Jimmy Doolittle, and *Enola Gay* pilot Col. Paul Tibbets became household names, but the idea of "tank aces" was unknown. Sherman tank command-er Staff Sgt. Lafayette Pool and his crewmen may have destroyed some 270 German armored vehicles (including 12 tanks), but few general readers recognize him today.

The public's love affair with airplanes and Roosevelt's pro-Navy bias had consequences for US armor. In January 1942, Roosevelt called for all out tank production in a dramatic State of the Union Address, and Ordnance's "Overall Requirements for War Munitions Program" as of February 11 listed a staggering goal of 169,000 tanks: 3,000 heavies, 61,000 light tanks, and crucially, 105,000 mediums like the M3 Lee and M4 Sherman.

But less than a year after Pearl Harbor, in spite of his calls for more tanks and insistence that "Let no man say that it cannot be done. It must be done,"[56] Roosevelt reversed himself in November 1942, ordering the Army to reduce production of all tanks for 1943—the better to build more glamorous airplanes and more of his beloved ships.

By November 12, 1942, the Army supply program listed reduced goals from the February figures: 99,230 tanks of all types, including 230 heavies and 37,000 lights. The most dra-matic cut was in the estimated requirements for medium tanks, the backbone of the Armored Force: the February goal of 105,000 was lowered to 62,000.[57]

George Marshall acknowledged the shortcomings of the American tank in his 1945 "Report on the Winning of the War," but his explanations were disingenuous, and his views reveal the vast gap between GIs and their leadership. "Credit to Nazis: General Marshall Compares the War Weapons…Foe's Tanks The Best," reported the *Kansas City Star* for October 10, 1945.[58] Publicly, the man who had promised in 1943 to "see that for once in the history of this country, [the GI] is given a fair break in the terrible business of making war"[59] seemed to show little empathy for the scandal's victims; Ike had the decency to hear his men out, but a patronizing Marshall not only dismissed the GIs' fears, he faulted their officers for not si-lencing those who raised concerns:

> The American soldier has a very active imagination…he covets anything new, and is inclined to endow the death-dealing weapons of the enemy with extraordinary qualities, since any weapon seems much more formidable to the man receiving its fire than to the man delivering it.

If given slight encouragement, this reaction can be fatal to the success of our forces. Commanders must always make every effort to show their men how to make better, more effective use of what they have. The technique of handling a weapon can often be made more devastating than the power of the weapon itself.[60]

Such views echo the Japanese *yamato damashi* (Japanese fighting spirit) the Empire of the Rising Sun's leaders offered their men in place of weapons in the war's last months: surely, if the Japanese soldier led by fanatical officers *believed* enough, he could stop Sherman tanks on the beaches of mainland Japan with bamboo spears, pikes, and samurai swords.

"This was best illustrated by the correct, the intended, tactical employment of the United States medium tank," wrote Marshall in another example of the doctrinal confusion over the use of armor.[61] Few would disagree that ideal hypothetical use of tanks would be to attack "soft" enemy targets like troops in the open, trucks, or machine gun positions—the classic "Infantry support" role—but what were tankers to do when the enemy, refusing to conform to textbook conditions, confronted tanks with tanks? Marshall's comments epitomize what Gen. Isaac White (who described himself as one "who pitted our out-gunned Shermans against German armor") called "the seeming insensitivity to the realities of the battlefield on the part of those responsible for the design and procurement of our fighting vehicles."[62]

Apologists may respond that leaders like Gen. Marshall were unaware of the problems of frontline tankers because they operated at such a high level, but Marshall was directly impacted by the Sherman tank scandal. He had two stepsons in the service,

> America, as a nation, has the greatest ability for the mass production of machines. It therefore behooves us to devise methods of war which exploit our inherent superiority… while we have ample manpower, it is too valuable to be thrown away.[4]
> —Gen. George S. Patton Jr.

and one, 2nd Lt. Allen Tupper Brown—a tank commander with the Thirteenth Armored Regiment, First Armored Division—was killed in his M4 in Italy on May 29, 1944. "War Hits Home in Marshall's Family," reported the Cleveland *Plain Dealer* for May 31. "No details of the action near Campoleone in Italy had been reported when the War Department issue a brief announcement today of Brown's death."[63]

Joining the Army as a buck private, Lt. Brown had worked his way up to a commission through Officers' Candidate School. "When Allen prepared to enlist in the Army in September 1942, his stepfather had recommended [that he become a tanker], and had, after his stepson graduated from the Armored Force School at Fort Knox, facilitated his transfer to North Africa."[64] There, Lt. Brown served as part of Gen. Mark Clark's Fifth Army. Perhaps reflecting on the cost of armored combat, Allen had written home to Katherine Marshall, "Mother, there are no American 'boys' in Italy. They may have been boys when they arrived here, but they are all men now."[65]

On May 29, Marshall's wife Katherine read him a letter in which Allen joked about a "lucky" horseshoe he had nailed to the door of a barn at Dodona Manor, their Leesburg home. "That horseshoe has held my luck. I shall take it down this Christmas and keep it for the rest of my life."[66]

Tankers had warned the M4's height and cupola design exposed crews to danger, but that same day on the road to Rome, as Lt. Brown pulled out his binoculars, seeking a clear view from the turret (which exposed tank commanders to enemy fire from the chest up), he was killed in action. "Stepson of Gen. Marshall Killed," read a June 2 Associated Press story datelined "With the Fifth Army South of Rome." It elaborated, "Lt. Brown was

Tiger I at the Musée des Blindés, Saumur, France. *Massimo Foti*

KILLED IN ITALY — The death of Lt. Allen Tupper Brown, son of Mrs. George C. Marshall, wife of the U.S. army chief of staff, has been announced by the War Department. Lt. Brown, killed in a tank action near Campoleone, Italy, on May 29, is survived by his wife, the former Madge Shedden of New York, and a 2½-year-old son.

A letter from Katherine Marshall to her tank officer son Allen marked "Return to Sender," after he was killed in action in an M4 Sherman on the road to Rome, June 1944.

commanding a …tank detachment…he was standing up in the turret of his tank—a necessary procedure for armored commanders," when he was killed by a sniper "in ambush."[67]

Sgt. Tony Glenister, also with the First Armored Division in Italy, recalled a gruesome sight the day after Allen's death, when "some 23 tanks and tank destroyers" were lost:

An 88mm round blew up the Sherman in front of us and we could hear the screaming inside. It was a tank man's worst nightmare, being burned alive…. We saw one of our non-coms [sergeants] run up to the side of the tank and let loose with his machine gun at the side, between the treads, until the screaming stopped. I doubt that his bullets penetrated the armor, but it was terrible to listen to men being burned to death and not be able to help.[68]

In a brief June 1944 trip to the Italian front, Marshall met fellow tank officers in his stepson's company and the members of Allen's tank crew who had been with him in their M4 when he was killed.[69] Even as Gen. Marshall struggled to meet diplomatic and logistic responsibilities on a global scale, personally he was painfully all too aware of the Sherman tank's shortcomings.

Though often stern in public, privately George Marshall was not an insensitive man; he recognized the war's tragic costs. Receiving an angry letter from a woman whose husband had been killed in action, he responded:

Your recent letter…expressing resentment over the death of your husband…has been brought to my attention. I much regret the bitterness you express toward the War Department and I wish to indicate to you something of the situation confronting the Army.

The tragedy of the war has struck homes all over America. It has reached my family, Mrs. Marshall's younger son having been killed in a tank battle in Italy.

Her other son and her son-in-law are fighting in Germany. The sons and husbands of many of our friends have been added to the casualty lists…. So I can well appreciate the depth of the blow that has struck at your happiness and your future, and I therefore regret all the more your present feeling of bitterness.

I witnessed the same tragic aftermath of the battles in the last war and because of my position, the daily casualty lists bring to me the full impact of the tragedy of war. I deplore the unfortunate policies this country has followed which have led us into unpreparedness and, I think, possibly have failed to avoid wars with their fearful cost to young Americans and to the progress and peaceful prosperity of the country.[70]

Marshall's wife Katherine wrote of his having to "steel himself to carry a burden so tremendous in magnitude, and so diverse in its demands, that it was difficult to comprehend how one man could carry it alone."[71]

His biographer Forrest Pogue recounts an inspection tour Marshall made of Fort Benning, Georgia. There, a first sergeant (the highest ranking sergeant in an Army unit) approached Marshall's orderly, Sgt. James Powder, for help: soldiers of the First Infantry Division were short of wool blankets and barracks stoves during winter and were unable to procure them through the usual slow channels. Would Gen. Marshall help?

As Pogue tells the story, although Marshall promised help, the blankets remained undelivered. "That was the first time I had ever seen anger in his face," Sgt. Powder recalled, as Marshall promised, "We'll find out why they weren't sent."[72]

When Marshall made inquiries in Washington, he found supply officers had dragged their feet, claimed petty errors in the requisition forms submitted, and falsified paperwork stating the problem had been "fixed up," so Marshall would hear no more of it. According to Pogue, "This combination of formal washing of hands and sweeping the dirt under the rug infuriated the General."[73]

Sgt. Powder described the Chief of Staff's response. "I am not worried about hearing any more about it, I want the matter arranged," yelled Marshall. "Get those blankets and stoves and any other damn thing that's needed out tonight, not tomorrow morning, and not two weeks from now. I don't care what regulations are upset or anything of that character. We are going to take care of the troops first, last, and all the time."[74]

A wonderful story, but why wasn't such decisive action taken to address the inadequacies of the Army's tanks? Knowing that cold Infantrymen at Fort Benning waited weeks for blankets in winter infuriated him, yet tankers were killed and wounded

overseas while waiting years for better tanks and tank ammunition.

Are we to believe that Gen. Marshall was unaware of the extent of the tank problem? "During General Marshall's visit," Eisenhower aide Capt. Harry Butcher wrote in his diary for June 3, 1943, from Algiers, "he told me of one important improvement in our tanks. We have one almost ready now to combat the Tiger. It is lower than the Sherman, weighs only thirty-two tons, and carries numerous improvements which would make it our most outstanding contribution in this line."[75] So what happened to *that* tank, or the one Butcher wrote of two months later, which he called a "new Sherman, of which General Marshall spoke so glowingly last spring?"[76]

According to historian Stanley Weintraub, General Marshall stayed keenly aware of what was going on throughout the Army. "Pentagon agents were constantly flying to various theaters to be Marshall's eyes and ears. He had noted early in December 1942 in a talk to the National Association of Manufacturers, 'In a single morning a few days ago I interviewed two General Staff officers just in from the Kokoda Pass and Milne Bay in New Guinea and from Guadalcanal; another from Chungking, China, and New Dehli in India; and still another from Moscow, Basra [Iraq], and way points.'" Marshall, noted Weintraub, "could separate photo-ops and phony communiqués from reality."[77]

In contrast to the GI blanket story, one searches for dramatic examples of Marshall taking firm action to get better tanks built and overseas in time. Yet he made a curious comment in 1957, during interviews with historian S. L. A. Marshall (no relation). Surely with an eye to posterity, Marshall claimed that after investigating problems with American tanks, "…it was comparatively easy to get the matter adjusted—doing it all behind the scenes."[78] His use of that phrase is a reminder that in the Army of his day, where official censorship reigned, problems were often concealed from the public, and admission of mistakes was rare.

Radio commentator H. R. Baukhage recalled a "conspiracy of silence," in which the press simply did not report bad war news, not only for patriotic reasons, but also in fear of government and military censors canceling their credentials. He called the conspiracy to conceal Roosevelt's declining health from American voters "the greatest conspiracy of silence in the history of journalism."[79]

Sgt. Ralph G. Martin reported for the Army's *Stars and Stripes* and *YANK* magazine. "The tendency was," he told Ernie Pyle biographer James Tobin, "to write what the people wanted to hear. [Editors] felt that nobody wanted to hear about the blood and death. Most people wanted to hear about the successes and the heroes. Most papers urged their correspondents to do just that…very few people [among the reporters] cared deeply about all the horror and terror…I don't think they thought about it much."[80]

As author Paul Fussell (a former WWII Army Infantry officer) cautions modern readers in his refreshingly caustic *The Boy's Crusade*:

> Readers should realize that all writing sent from the frontlines…had to pass rigorous censorship. To a soldier's homebound observations by V-mail or letter, the censorship was applied by one of his company officers wielding his little PASSED BY CENSOR rubber stamp, which, with ink pad, he carried everywhere. The writing and pictures by official, accredited reporters and photographers had to pass censorship in Paris or New York. The result was that during the war, nothing really nasty as the troops knew it could reach nonmilitary minds, and readers…should realize that even when writers describe gruesome experiences and sights, the most appalling details have probably been excised or softened. Things were worse than they were allowed to seem, and many were literally unspeakable.[81]

In recent years, online media has enabled the public to learn of scandals involving the Army in Iraq or Afghanistan within hours, but in the 1940s, it was easier for the Army to protect its image, and high-ranking officers, not surprisingly, were eager to do so. As far back as 1919, Marshall had experienced the Army's distasteful washing of its dirty linen in public, when General of the Armies John J. Pershing quarreled with Army Chief of Staff Gen. Peyton March over the Army's future. George Marshall vowed to avoid a repetition such as a thorough airing of the tank scandal. "The unpleasant publicity" over the Pershing-March quarrel, states a 2014 biography, "…would make a deep impression on Marshall. Ever after he would make it a point never to allow his personal judgment of generals and prominent civilians to become public knowledge."[82]

Forrest Pogue mentions a late 1944 cigarette shortage for troops in the ETO; they were being stolen from frontline GIs and resold on the black market by corrupt rear echelon supply troops. Hoping to minimize the outrage back home, Gen. Marshall applied careful damage control: "The first notice the press had of these activities was accompanied by the announcement that the guilty parties had been punished. If dirty linen had to be washed in public, Marshall and his commanders preferred that they report the crime and punishment at the same time."[83]

While he rarely mentioned it publicly, George Marshall felt the loss of his tanker stepson. Visiting Dodona Manor—his Leesburg, Virginia, home—one sees signed photos from kings, queens, prime ministers, and warlords hailing America's "architect of victory." Yet the images that leave a sad impression are of Marshall's tanker stepson Allen, killed in his Sherman tank in Italy. Each night, Marshall walked past pictures of kings and queens to climb upstairs to his bedroom. At the bottom of the staircase he would pass a large oil painting of Allen on the wall to his left. His wife Katharine had Allen's photo across the room from her bed, probably the first and last sight she would see every day and night.

Visiting Dodona, one senses the Marshalls were deeply hurt by the loss of their tanker son and stepson, but Gen. Marshall's job required him to expend tankers by the thousands if necessary to win the war. And when tankers became in short supply after excessively optimistic estimates of the Army's needs, untrained men such as mechanics, supply clerks, cooks, and bakers were thrown into tanks—men with no business being near weapons, let alone dropped into a combat tank crew. To Maj. Al Irzyk, 4th Armored Division, "Tank training was absolutely essential, for by now [December 1944], most arriving replacements were not armor trained. The majority had never seen a tank before."[84]

Sir Max Hastings lays the blame on poor decisions made in Washington, where Gen. Marshall was the Army's Chief of Staff:

> The U.S. had created a ground army far smaller than its population would have allowed because the War Department woefully underestimated the size of the force that would be needed to defeat Hitler. Millions of potential recruits were rejected by medical boards, which were encouraged to set high standards…it remains astonishing that only eighty-nine U.S. Army divisions were deployed for active service. It may be argued that, given the difficulties of supplying America's armies in Europe, the commitment of more ground soldiers would merely have compounded these.
>
> Yet, even among the five million men drafted to the U.S. Army, only two million served in combat roles, in the loosest interpretation of that phrase. Barely 300,000 men were available in north-west Europe even in 1945 to confront direct German fire, as members of rifle companies or armoured units…. The campaign could have been won more quickly, and Allied forces might have advanced much further East, if Eisenhower had been given more soldiers.[85]

"At times it was almost funny—well, perhaps *laughable* is a better term," recalled 4th Armored Division tank commander Sgt. Nat Frankel of the shortage of trained armor replacements:

> There was a mechanic [assigned to] my tank named Green, a likable fellow who wore these thick, horn-rimmed glasses. I had known him well enough to talk to him, since he was also from New York…after his arrival as a "combatant," we were standing some seven feet away from each other.
>
> "Hello, Mazursky," he said.

"Frankel," I corrected him, figuring he had forgotten my name.

He walked about three feet closer, craned his neck forward, and said, "Oh! Nat! I thought you were Mazursky."

All I could see was my own reflection in those opaque glasses of his. "Green, are you blind?"

"Just don't let me fire at any of our own boys," he said.[86]

When American civilians expressed outrage at eighteen-year-olds being sent into battle, Gen. Marshall's reaction was there was "no military reason for not doing so…it was a clear question of either relinquishing our momentum in the battles in Europe, or of using troops of this age…. The only reason for not using 18-year-olds in combat was the expressed preference of a great many Americans who felt there were moral reasons for not exposing men so young to the great risk of battle."

Eventually, "A new policy was then adopted to supersede the use of men under 19 in combat," along with Congress imposing "a formal requirement, that 18-year-olds have at least a total of six months of training before they were sent into battle," but these reforms did not begin until after Germany surrendered.[87] As Gen. Marshall described his duty as the leader of a worldwide war effort, "I cannot afford the luxury of sentiment; mine must be cold logic. Sentiment is for others."[88]

On February 6, 1944, reporter Cyrus Sulzberger of the *New York Times* cabled a prospective article home from the Italian theater. It had been inadvertently passed by censors overseas and sent home for final clearance, "prefixed unpublishable without consent of War Department."[89] Among other topics, the story referred to the growing shortage of replacement GIs, including tankers:

> Many fine Platoon and Company leaders lost…. When [a] tank is knocked out its crew is much harder to replace than the vehicle itself…. As soon as time permits many of these troops need replacements but correspondents talked over this subject with many officers including principal Commanders in Italy and they complain that fault does not lie in this theater but in the draft policy in the United States which does not produce enough units.[90]

Another subject mentioned in the article further infuriated Gen. Marshall; as he put it, the "references to inferiority American weapons and morale," including tanks. "Any American civilian," Sulzberger had written, "probably assumes from political speeches and advertisements that his army is fighting with finest weapons existent":[91]

> This is sheer baloney. Weakest portion of armor on German Tiger tanks equals strongest armor plating on Sherman. Either German Mark IV or Mark VI outguns Sherman. New German anti-tank gun has at least double muzzle velocity of best American weapon. There isn't a single American gun in this theater which can equal the range of the German 170 by thousands of yards. In other words our tanks and guns must close with the enemy before they are able to deal a blow.

Even if we are numerically superior that does not equalize the situation.

...Just yesterday night writer sat up in tent with 2 tank Colonels gloomily discussing their particular mission. "Send out the photographers" they said. "There will be plenty of flamers [i.e., Sherman tanks destroyed]. Germans have been able to make this sector regular trap and we haven't got guns to stand up to them. But we have got to get in action. As our General says "a tank doesn't make a very good mantelpiece."[92]

Marshall's response was a fiery "Secret - Personal for eyes of Devers only from Marshall" cable to the theater commander, Gen. Jacob Devers. "What is the purpose of [your] theater passing this on to the War Department? Does it partake of a form of alibi? If not why is it passed on here for us to censor, particularly at this time? Does the theater desire this to be published? Please reply to me immediately."[93]

A chastened General Devers cabled back on February 11 that his "theater had no purpose in passing the article...on to the War Department, it was done through sheer stupidity. Drastic action is being taken to see that articles of this type are handled here [i.e., censored] and not passed on to Washington. The theater does not desire the article to be published."[94]

Seven decades after the Second World War, a more objective view of Gen. Marshall might question his shared responsibility for the surprise at Pearl Harbor, or the tank and ammunition shortages, or the lack of replacement tankers after the Normandy invasion that led untrained clerks to be thrown into tanks as drivers and machine gunners.

Instead, Marshall is typically depicted as a virtual second George Washington. Visiting Dodona Manor in 1949, *New York Times* reporter William White did not claim Marshall refused to lie about chopping down a cherry tree as a boy, but he came close, calling him "a remote great gentleman...laconic and honorably strong and distant...the net impression is of a man to whom duty and honor are as real as the oak trees which stand with such sure strength about him here."[95]

A 2014 biography of Marshall speculates on why he has been mythologized, seemingly above criticism: "Americans' yearning for a platonic ideal of a triumphant military leader above politics, deceit, and selfish ambition—in a word, a George Washington.... In effect, the Olympic persona that Marshall himself created protected him, though imperfectly, from criticism, both in his prime and in his future historical reputation."[96]

While studies of Gen. Marshall that transcend the George Washington cliché are rare, Mark Calhoun's 2015 biography of Gen. McNair is unique in blaming the Tank Destroyer debacle on Marshall as the Army's final decision maker. Conducting a veritable "Nuremburg Defense" of Gen. McNair, Calhoun argues he was merely following Marshall's orders:

After a long and indecisive debate about anti-tank defense...Marshall finally took direct control, ordering development of the tank destroyer in a very specific manner to avoid any branch taking control of it, and morphing it into a vision that did not match the vision for the weapon that Marshall had in mind.

"Ironically, Marshall's tank destroyer concept has long served as a key target for criticism of McNair, who initially opposed the concept."[97]

To Charles Baily, "as the story of tank and tank destroyer development unfolds, it is difficult to see who was in charge"[98]:

There was a definite lack of a thorough grasp of tank or tank destroyer development at the highest levels in the US Army. General Marshall was aware of the serious controversy as a result of the dispute over production of the T26 in the fall of 1943. In retrospect, it may be surprising that he did not try to assemble all the interested parties and settle that important issue. But his consciousness of the need to meet the desires of the theater commanders in a global war may have made him reluctant to act on a problem in which the theater commanders had little interest (until it was too late). Eisenhower was surprised by the First Army tests in July 1944, though his own staff had enough information before D-Day to warn him that there might be a problem.[99]

Baily argues that Marshall's subordinates were not screaming for help until it was too late. "Given Gen. Marshall's willingness to answer demands from his theater commanders, there is no doubt that changes would have occurred if they had been requested."[100]

But this gentle treatment is a little too convenient—too much benefit of the doubt and deference to rank. Are we to believe that a man who became enraged when GIs lacked blankets in winter (and took immediate corrective action), who was well aware of the problems with American tanks since at least early 1943, when Eisenhower privately informed him, "We don't yet know exactly how to handle the Tiger tank," would refuse to use his authority to get 90mm guns into the existing Shermans, or to rush production of many T26s out of a "reluctance" to pull rank on his subordinates?

Marshall deserves full credit as the American "Organizer of Victory" in WWII, yet his towering accomplishments in building a tiny peacetime army into one that straddled the world in 1945, his worldwide military and diplomatic responsibilities, and his tanker son's death in action in a Sherman tank do not absolve him from exercising his prerogative and power as the Army's Chief of Staff to separate squabbling bureaucracies such as McNair's AGF, Campbell's Ordnance, Devers' Armored Force, Barnes' Ordnance Technical Division, etc., to decisively address the Sherman tank issue.

## General Dwight Eisenhower: "The Last To Hear About This Stuff?"

Although Supreme Commander Eisenhower rose to popular acclaim through a reputation for amiability, to historian Max Hastings, "Dwight Eisenhower was a steelier and less genial figure than his public persona allowed."[101] But as Ike wrote home to his wife Mamie in October 1943, "Our soldiers are wonderful.... No one knows how I like to roam around among them—I'm always cheered up by a day with the actual fighters."[102] In his best selling postwar

memoir *Crusade in Europe*, he mentions talking "to American soldiers both individually and in groups up to the size of a division":[103]

> Through constant talking to enlisted men, I gained accurate impressions of their state of mind...news of my visit would soon spread throughout the unit. This, I felt, would encourage men to talk to their superiors, and this habit, I believe, promotes efficiency. There is, among a mass of individuals who carry the rifles in war, a great amount of ingenuity and initiative. If men can naturally and without restraint talk to their officers, the products of their resourcefulness become available to all. Moreover, out of the habit grows mutual confidence, a feeling of partnership that is the essence of espirit de corps. An army fearful of its officers is never as good as one that trusts and confides in its leaders.[104]

Like Marshall, Eisenhower was in a difficult moral position with the tank scandal. The Supreme Commander may have been insulated by subordinates about the extent of the worsening problem for three years; more likely he was aware, but intentionally misled the public about it, issuing denials and ordering his subordinates Patton, Bradley, and Devers to do the same. If true, what does this willful obfuscation say about his leadership? On the other hand, if Eisenhower and others had "come clean" earlier in the war, publicly acknowledging the tank problem, how would this have affected the men required to climb back into those tanks day after day—especially in 1942–1943, when the Allies were on the defensive against a victorious Wehrmacht?

Perhaps it was a question of which path would be harder on GI morale. As the White-Rose Reports show, tankers resented their leaders' dishonesty. Certainly, morale would have been impacted had politicians and generals conceded the extent of the tank problem, but a large-scale, determined effort to improve or replace the M4, with firm backing from Marshall and/or Roosevelt, would have helped to restore it.

Instead, even after the embarrassing reverses in the Ardennes, Eisenhower still insisted to the press (as quoted in "Our Tanks Are Without Equal," a March 1945 *Army Ordnance* magazine editorial), "Battlefield reports from every front in the European Theater of Operations continue to tell of the splendid quality of our weapons."[105]

Patton's diary and Eisenhower's personal letters to Marshall, White, and Rose leave little room for doubt about their true opinions of the M4: Army leaders engaged in a whitewash, lying to GIs, the press, and to the stateside public. Worse, echoing Marshall's condescending views, they rejected the hard-won wisdom of those who knew best: the men Ike called "the actual fighters."

As *Time* magazine put it on April 2, 1945, "In the case of the Royal Tiger and its 88mm gun, front-line criticism was impressively dismissed by fighting commanders, including Eisenhower and Patton, as a gripe. It was not until recently that field commanders decided the front-line men might be right, and asked—but too late—for the T26."[106]

Rather than decisively confront the problem in time, field commanders saddled tankers with flawed weapons that led to thousands of Allied dead and wounded. For years, generals repeated boasts that contradicted what they knew to be true, but coming clean might require pointing fingers at Roosevelt or Marshall, and career officers had postwar careers to consider.

Eisenhower's stature made him one of few Army leaders able to decisively address the issue, and he attempted to do so several times through Gen. Marshall. Yet in Omar Bradley's postwar memoirs, Ike is depicted as surprised that 76mm Shermans could not stop Tigers and Panthers, insisting with righteous indignation that the Ordnance Department had misled him—that he was the "last to hear" of the tank gun problem. But his aide Capt. Harry Butcher (recruited to help Eisenhower with public relations) recorded a conversation with him in a July 11, 1944, diary entry from England. "Our own reporters," wrote Butcher, "relate that after two years, the Allies still do not have as a good a tank as the Germans":

> Ike told me yesterday that the problem of finding ammunition that will penetrate the Tiger and the Panther is complicated. Tests made by the Ordnance people in the United States show that our ammunition does not penetrate these tanks, except the Panther in front, which is practically impossible. Ike felt confident we would lick the problem.[107]

Author and Army ETO officer Paul Fussell observed, "Despite his occasional apparent lapses into Kansas naiveté, Eisenhower was a shrewd publicist, who at one time sent an urgent message to Washington requesting the immediate shipment to Europe of twelve more public-relations officers...on one visit to France during the Normandy battle, Eisenhower was met by fifty newsmen—cinema and still photographers as well as correspondents."[108]

For the Supreme Commander to be unaware, according to Gen. Bradley, of the severity of the tank problem after speaking to hundreds of GIs not only strains credibility, but were this true, he would be guilty of negligence as a leader. Biographer Jean Edward Smith notes in the 1944 buildup to the Normandy invasion, during the four-month period February 1 to June 1 alone, Eisenhower "visited twenty-six divisions, twenty-four airfields, and countless depots, hospitals, and installations, his grin always at the ready." "Soldiers like to see the men who are directing operations," wrote Eisenhower. "Diffidence or modesty must never blind the commander to his duty of showing himself to his men, of speaking to them, of mingling with them to the extent of physical limitations."[109]

Eisenhower prided himself on his closeness to the troops; soon after the war's end, he testified before a Senate committee questioning the slowness of the Army's demobilization process: why were the boys still stuck overseas? Biographer Geoffrey

Perret records Eisenhower's anger at grandstanding Senators attempting to second guess Army senior leadership:

> Eisenhower nearly lost his temper. "If there is anyone in this world who has an undying interest in the enlisted men, it is I," he said, teeth gritted, cheeks flaming crimson, reading glasses tightly clenched. "Those fellows are my friends. I have commanded more American soldiers than anyone else in history. You cannot possibly have a greater interest in them than me.[110]

Strong words for the Senate and the public, but was he angry over the GIs' homecomings being delayed or at his leadership being questioned? To his son John, "When it came to his military judgments, [Eisenhower] was vociferous in defending the validity of his decisions."[111]

Until just weeks before the end of the European war, Ike had colluded with fellow generals and Roosevelt administration leaders in sweeping the tank controversy under the rug. And his private words to Marshall in March 1945, after Senator Robert Taft criticized the War Department's throwing untrained eighteen-year-olds into combat, hardly sound like the caring Ike the public thought they knew. "Misery loves company," he wrote to Marshall. "Sometimes when I get tired of trying to arrange the blankets smoothly over several prima donnas in the same bed I think that no one person in the world can have so many illogical problems. I read about your struggles concerning eighteen year old men in combat, and about the criticism of our equipment, and went right back to work with a grin."[112]

Like Roosevelt, Eisenhower publicly addressed the tank scandal late in the game, when press scrutiny and calls for congressional investigations forced him to do so; for this one historian has rendered a harsh judgment on him. "During the Battle of the Bulge, when the qualitative disparity between American and German tanks...became patently obvious at the level of the tanker, it remained invisible to Eisenhower.... Only when the press paraded the irate comments of his soldiers before him did Eisenhower turn his attention to tanks."[113]

Acknowledging the problems openly would have led to embarrassing questions for the powerful political and military leaders who had issued boasts and denials about the M4 from 1941–1945, so Eisenhower and other leaders went along to get along, adding their own denials and misleading statistics on German tanks destroyed. "His amiable personality and avuncular enthusiasm," writes Jean Smith, "concealed a calculating political instinct that had been honed to perfection."[114]

Throughout his career, Eisenhower was willing to sanitize the historical record to duck criticism or obtain career or political advantages. To Smith, "few figures in public life have proved more adept at making a silk purse out of a sow's ear than Dwight Eisenhower."[115] In the early 1920s, Eisenhower told fellow officer Bradford Chynoweth that his success in the small peacetime Army would come through pleasing "the strongest and ablest man" above him. "I forget my ideas," Eisenhower said, "and do everything in my power to promote what he says is right."[116] In 1932, disregarding orders from President Herbert Hoover to avoid violence, Eisenhower's then-boss Army Chief of Staff Douglas MacArthur used Infantry with fixed bayonets and tear gas, mounted Cavalry, and tanks against desperate WWI veterans seeking benefits in Washington—the Bonus Army, or Bonus Expeditionary Force.

In the face of resulting public outrage, Eisenhower ghost-authored a self-serving justification for MacArthur's actions using what one historian calls "cover-up language."[117] Ironically, Eisenhower—who would have his own problems in the press concerning tanks a decade later—praised MacArthur's use of them "in quelling civil disorder," writing they gave "an impression of irresistible and inexorable power." Ike also excused the use of tear gas on unarmed, disabled veterans and civilian women and children because "this harmless instrument quickly saps the will to resist."[118]

Just weeks before the Normandy invasion, American soldiers and sailors were killed when Operation Tiger, a dry run exercise, was ambushed by German E-boats. More men died in the practice for Utah Beach than on actual Utah Beach. Yet while Churchill mentioned the tragedy in his memoirs, the Supreme Commander omitted it in his 1948 *Crusade in Europe*. Noted one author:

> If anyone possessed the knowledge, and the popular clout, to put the story of Convoy T-4 on the historical map, it was Eisenhower. His failure to do so should be set...against his "virtually sacred" relationship with the GI, and his postwar reverence for, and consistent honoring of, America's war dead...it still seems strange that a British leader should mention an American wartime disaster, and an American leader make no mention of it at all.[119]

His attempts to obscure his relationship with his driver and assistant Kay Summersby are also troublesome. After Eisenhower was named to command the Normandy invasion, Marshall (who had heard gossip about Eisenhower and Summersby) ordered him home for a private talk and a fast visit with his wife. When Eisenhower responded that he was too busy, Marshall explicitly cabled him on December 29, 1943, "Now come on home and see your wife." But when Eisenhower reprinted the message in his memoirs *Crusade In Europe*, that line had disappeared.[120] Later, when German Gen. Alfred Jodl surrendered to Eisenhower on May 7, 1945, ending the European war, a smiling Kay Summersby was there, standing behind Eisenhower. Yet "In some [official War Department] photos as published," she was carefully airbrushed out.[121]

This oddity is apparent in some color photos of the event showing Gen. Walter Bedell Smith standing close to Eisenhower. Smith's hair, which he wore slicked straight back, now has an odd halo of feminine curls around it; presumably, because Summersby is directly behind him. Army censors, not wanting to incite further gossip, may have airbrushed Summersby out, as Weintraub alleges. Or, though multiple images were available (showing a grinning Summersby standing close to Ike), they released for public consumption one of the few photos of the historic event in which Summersby is almost entirely obscured by Smith.

Concerning the Ardennes offensive, Stanley Weintraub has written that the shock of being blindsided by Germany "haunted" Eisenhower. To Max Hastings, "His nerve had been badly shak-

Photo by Robert Coldwell Sr.

en."[122] Added John Eisenhower, "I suspect he was frazzled from the strains of the Battle of the Bulge."[123] But while fighting it, he could count on Marshall's support. Author Joseph Hobbs has collected Eisenhower's private wartime letters to Marshall; from June 1942 to April 1945, he wrote about 108 of them. At times they helped him blow off steam; Eisenhower would complain about criticism in the civilian press, pass on GI gossip, or mention a Persian rug he was sending home as a present to Katherine Marshall. More typically, he would informally explain his latest command decisions to Marshall, speculate on the enemy's future actions, and bring his theater's equipment and logistical needs to the attention of the Army's Chief of Staff.

Yet during the Ardennes campaign—an embarrassment to the Supreme Commander—there is a near one-month halt in Ike's private letters to Marshall. On December 13, 1944, three days before the German surprise offensive began, he wrote to Marshall from London. Then, aside from a four-sentence Christmas message on December 23, his next letter is not until January 12, 1944.

On Marshall's end, to his credit, he refused to second guess Eisenhower or bother him during the Bulge by sending trivial messages (even giving his staff orders to this effect), allowing him to concentrate on reacting to the German assault. In fairness to Eisenhower, certainly most of his attention was focused on that task, but given the magnitude and obvious historic importance of the battle as it unfolded, why did he suspend his usual, habitual accounts to Marshall of his thoughts, actions, and decisions as they took place?

According to his son John, Eisenhower was "an avid reader of history, especially military history," and had been since boyhood.[124] As he commanded a huge Allied army in the US Army's largest European battle, surely he realized that future historians would be full of curiosity over his actions and decisions during this critical time.

Yet his frequent personal correspondence to Marshall—a reassuring, constant habit since 1942, which even facilitated the occasional healthy gripe session, general-to-general—conspicuously stops during the Ardennes campaign. Instead, he waits until the smoke clears to write a carefully reasoned "official" version for posterity.

As Eisenhower notes in a January 12, 1945, letter from Versailles—his first one in nearly a month—"within the past two weeks" he had sent Marshall, through formal channels and for the record, "telegraphic words that in their total would fill a good sized volume." But since December 13, 1944, he had not "recently written you a personal, confidential letter."[125] In other words, rather than explain his actions as the battle unfolded, Ike was careful to wait for the benefit of hindsight, preferring to compile a formal account of the battle for the record, after the fact, when the smoke and confusion had cleared away.

Ike's reticence towards detailing his conduct during the Bulge fighting is in interesting contrast to Patton, who enjoyed confiding his gripes, scathing opinions of his fellow officers (including jealous jabs at his old friend Eisenhower, whose first initials, Patton joked, stood for "Divine Destiny"), and boastful justifications for his actions to his diary, later sanitized and published after his death as the mildly scandalous *War As I Knew It*.

While Patton was a flamboyant showman (who compiled his thoughts on his wartime actions for posterity), when it came to publicity, Eisenhower was no amateur. A secret report to Secretary of War Henry Stimson after the Patton "slapping incidents" exploded in the stateside press is illuminating. Dated November 24, 1943, Ike's telegraphed report to Stimson notes he ordered his Chief of Staff Walter "Beedle" Smith to address the press, "because of reports of the publication in the United States of exaggerated versions of this story." Few people today realize that reporters in WWII served at the whim of the military and federal government, who could yank their credentials and banish them from the theater of war if they incurred a commander's displeasure.

In this report, Ike "commend[s] the great body of American newspapermen in this theater because all of them knew something of facts involved and some of them knew all.... These men chose to regard the matter as one in which the High Command acted for the best interests of the war effort and let the matter rest there. To them I am grateful."[126] In other words, Eisenhower preferred reporters who sat on a damaging story. To Ike, it would seem a "commendable" reporter should accept the Supreme Commander's word that all was well and ignore or downplay scandals that might embarrass powers-that-be.

One wants to give Eisenhower the benefit of the doubt as having been too busy during the Ardennes confusion to send personal reports and insights to Marshall, but coming from one with a lifelong respect for military history, given that he had previously written to Marshall of his desire to avoid negative press at home, his conspicuous neglect of what could be a gold mine for future historians and critics—his justifications of his actions while leading one of the Army's most significant battles, brought on by an embarrassing surprise attack—is questionable.

As the campaign was going on, newspapers large and small across the country asked "What Is The Cause?" as the Sayre, Pennsylvania, *Evening Times* asked on December 27, 1944:

It is to be presumed that General Eisenhower…has also moved to learn the true facts behind the apparent ease with which the Nazis broke through the American lines to nullify much of the hard-earned gains made by our forces, take a terrific toll of our men and materiel, and delay the end of the war appreciably…the fact that the enemy was able to make a penetration at one point is an indication that he may be able to repeat the performance somewhere else, if the conditions which permitted the advance are allowed to repeat themselves.

There has been considerable criticism of the Army's intelligence service voiced since the breakthrough…. The enemy was able to mass two, perhaps three, full armies on the front opposite our First Army, and to launch their attack against thinly-defended sectors. At one point a single regiment was spread out to cover a ten-mile stretch of front, and the fact that this regiment held against the initial push is no excuse for its having been given such an impossible task. The truth remains apparent—that some units were unable to hold. Were they spread too thinly?

We are disinclined to assess blame without being in possession of the full facts of the case, and it is unlikely that we will have the full story until General Eisenhower announces it. However, we feel that the American people are entitled to a detailed explanation of what happened, so that they can know whether someone has blundered, and if so, who.[127]

But Eisenhower was not inclined to air "the full story" of the Ardennes embarrassment. "I am unalterably opposed to making any effort to publicize at this time," he wrote in 1946 to Robert Patterson, President Truman's Secretary of War, "any story concerning the Ardennes Battle, or even allowing any written explanation to go outside the War Department." To Eisenhower, the Bulge—the largest battle fought in US Army history—was just "a mere incident to a large campaign." He would not explain or defend his actions, "something where no defense is necessary."[128]

Years later, he had his final break with the notoriously rude British Gen. Bernard Law Montgomery. To his son John, it was not because of Monty's lack of tact or diplomacy, but because in his 1959 memoirs Monty had criticized Ike's leadership and decisions. To John Eisenhower, "What meant most to [Ike] was approval, not of himself, but of his conduct of the European campaign. To the best of my knowledge, Ike and Monty never communicated again."[129]

Regarding the tank scandal, throughout the war Eisenhower had called for up-gunned tanks, at times from Gen. Marshall. At the 1945 height of the controversy he solicited the enlisted tankers' opinions from Gens. White and Rose. After seeing the results, he again called for action from Marshall, but in the last weeks of the war, when it was too late. The stateside public never read of the secret White-Rose Reports; the views expressed in them were so devastating, and soldiers of all ranks so unanimous in their condemnation of American tanks, that their views were suppressed.

Eisenhower was a fundamentally decent man; attending the 1948 Arlington National Cemetery funeral of General of the Armies John Pershing, which took place on a rainy day, he refused to take shelter by riding a car from the capitol to Arlington. Instead, he marched in the procession the whole way, later writing, "I was certainly not going to give an example of the brass running from a rainstorm when all the marching [enlisted] men in the long column had to take things as they came."[130]

Biographer Carlo D'Este recounts Eisenhower's reflections on the twentieth anniversary of the Normandy invasion. Given as he sat on a wall overlooking Omaha Beach, in "painful remembrance of those haunting days of June 1944," they could be an epitaph for his lost tankers: "Many thousands of men have died for freedom...but these young boys were cut off in their prime. I devoutly hope that we will never again have to see such scenes as these."[131]

Honorable words in 1964, but if Eisenhower and other leaders had taken decisive action in 1943 or 1944, "many thousands" would not have been "cut off in their prime." Instead, Eisenhower responded to years of warning signs with obfuscation, such as "We have knocked out twice as many tanks as we have lost."

The GIs who knew better, making up in candor what they lacked in eloquence, labeled Eisenhower's excuses "cock-and-bull stories."[132] It is unlikely the pent-up frustration they expressed in the White-Rose Reports of 1945 (percolating for three years) would have been much worse if their leaders had tackled the problem years earlier. Instead, the cover-up continued.

The Supreme Commander with the likable grin (and subsequent president) has been treated gently on this episode by historians; his culpability in the tank scandal (as well as his

disregarding intelligence warnings of the German surprise attack in the Ardennes) is rarely explored, or appears as little more than a footnote in large biographies. Pulitzer Prize finalist Jean Edward Smith's 2012 best seller *Eisenhower in War and Peace* tantalizes the reader with little clues, such as Gen. Lucius Clay lamenting, "We were never able to build a tank as good as the German tank. But we made so many of them it really didn't matter."[133]

Easy for a general to say, but tell it to the loved ones of tankers killed and wounded. While Smith's biography is a pleasure to read, at times it is too easy on Eisenhower, assuring us that Ike was "parsimonious with the lives of the troops entrusted to his command...ready to take responsibility for whatever occurred.... He did not dodge difficult decisions, he did not pass the buck."[134] But Smith also recognizes Eisenhower's willingness and "ability to reshape the record," to "spin the record," and to "rewrite history" to present his actions in a more flattering light, for example, "his rewriting of his wartime relationship with Kay Summersby."[135]

Why did the top American brass not take action to address the tank problem? One could argue that most were detached from the situation: Roosevelt was far from the battlefield; Marshall was running a global war from a Washington office; and Eisenhower, though in the ETO, did not judge the problem serious enough to address publicly until it exploded in the headlines of 1945.

## General George S. Patton: "Weapons are only weapons after all"

We turn to the role of General George S. Patton Jr., allegedly one of the Army's experts and innovators in the use of tanks, and of the leaders listed, the closest to the GIs' level. To say the least, Patton had a love-hate relationship with his men, who in the Fourth Armored Division identified themselves as "Georgie's boys" and never forgot him.

"I had actual personal contact with this man, and it lasted ten seconds, that's all," wrote tanker Sgt. Nat Frankel, "and yet the memory of those ten seconds continues to haunt my life, as if it had been a thousand years. I could have been married to the goddamn guy, that's how forceful the encounter was and that's how persistent its memory":

An angry Patton yells at a Sherman tank crew for daring to add sandbag "armor." Patton felt this would strain the tank's transmission and make the GIs feel they might be injured or killed.

We were on our way to Bastogne, having just gotten the order to beat it north and rescue the First Army…we were tired, shot-up, and our maintenance status was a God-awful mess. We had been rolling so fast that my tank had never been properly tended to. I bogged down in the mud, and, perplexed and frustrated, I stuck my head out the turret. I looked around and who did I see?

The first thing I saw was those two damn pistols of his. Ivory-handled—ivory, not pearl, for as he himself so famously said, only St. Louis pimps wear pearl—gripped pistols…. Then I saw his eyes, glowering like two jewels planted in a Polynesian idol…. His arms were waving, randomly but not frantically. He was the very picture of total energy combined with godlike self-control.

I knew it was Patton, but I didn't think, "That's George Patton, a man with a body and mind just like mine, a man who worries, loves, shits, and pisses just like me." For the duration of our encounter, for that unreal ten seconds, he was barely human. It was like my tank had run up against a mountain. And if that mountain there was a gorge, and out of that yawning abyss words came forth; there was a god in the mountain, and when he spoke, the whole valley trembled.

"What's wrong?" he bellowed.

I told him.

"Goddamn! This is no time to get stuck! Get this goddamn thing rolling!"

Now, I didn't take this lying down. I answered him loudly, intrepidly, clearly…I was man enough for the occasion. I said the only tough and intelligent and sensible thing that a man can say to George Patton at such a time.

I said, "YESSIR!"[136]

While Patton's popular image is of an aggressive rebel spoiling for a fight, the Sherman tank scandal shows him in a very different light. At times in his career he was a forward-think-ing, outspoken armor advocate, and had been since WWI. But

Carlo D'Este has written that Patton gave "mixed messages" during the bitter mechanization debate in the 1930s, showing "ambivalence" and "flip-flopping which appeased his superiors and enabled him to keep a foot in both camps."[137]

Patton's awkward position as a tank innovator and a rising career Army officer was "a classic conflict of interest which for Patton…meant an unhappy obligation to serve two masters."[138] By 1944, wearing four stars and nearing the pinnacle of the Army establishment, he was unwilling to challenge obsolete tank doctrine that he also believed in. The cost of his silence was the loss of men's lives.

Though Patton's adherence to outdated doctrine necessitat-ed the use of suicidal tactics, he wrote in his diary that Ameri-cans—"the foremost mechanics in the world"—should use weapons that preserved life, not wasted it needlessly:

American Ingenuity: America, as a nation, has the greatest ability for the mass production of machines. It therefore behooves us to devise methods of war which exploit our inherent superiority. We must fight the war by machines on the ground…to the maximum of our ability, particularly in view of the fact that the two races left which we may have to fight [presumably the Japanese and Russians] are both poor mechanics, but have ample manpower. While we have ample manpower, it is too valuable to be thrown away.[139]

Given his occasional callousness towards his men, from the notorious August 1943 "slapping incidents" in Sicily to his angry objections when desperate tankers attempted to reinforce the M4's vulnerable armor, Patton's shedding of crocodile tears over needless loss of life because of inferior weapons seems partic-ularly obscene. Instead of addressing a problem obvious to any private, he forbade them from supplementing their thin frontal armor after they saw what one or two shots from a distant Panther or Tiger could do to it.[140]

Yet the same emotionally complex man boasted in his diary of how "When they recognized me," some of the same men "stood up in their tanks and cheered."[141] At the height of the 1943 slapping scandals he had also written, "My men are crazy about me."[142]

Patton's opinions on tank design and armor doctrine are a far cry from the simplistic reputation he enjoys today. Books and television documentaries enjoy depicting him as a progressive supporter of tanks, taking on stodgy old generals with outdated ideas who impeded the tank's progress. But his true views are a bit more muddled than the depiction of Patton as an interwar martyr to the armor cause. Back in 1930 Patton—supposedly fighting to build a future for tanks—objected to a proposal to create six American armored divisions. "The expenditure of twenty seven million [dollars] on lightweight .50 caliber machine guns," he argued, "would probably do much more towards the winning of the next war than will the expenditure of two hundred and seventy million on tanks."[143]

Fifteen years later, under real world circumstances that made Fuller's "Plan 1919" fantasies seem modest, the views of this alleged forward thinker had not evolved very much. As late as January 1945, this supposed innovator in the use of armor re-vealed the backwardness of his views on it.

Since 1942, Patton had personally seen burned out Shermans littering the roadsides of North Africa, Tunisia, Sicily, and Europe, photographed wrecks with his own camera, and mentioned them in his diary. As far back as North Africa/Tunisia, Patton recognized the Sherman's weakness in two key measures of a tank's effectiveness: firepower and armor protection. His comments in a March 1943 letter to Armored Force Commander Gen. Jake Devers give the lie to his 1945 assurances that all was well with the M4. "If you get some 3-inch [i.e., 90mm] guns, place them in M4s and add another set of armor plate to the front silhouette, we will have a very powerful tank and tank destroyer."[144]

Almost two years later, and with more knowledge of the problem, Patton met with visiting Chief of Ordnance Gen. Campbell on January 15, 1945. Given a veritable blank check from Campbell, Patton did not insist that a more powerful 90mm main gun be installed in the existing M4s, as he had personally suggested to Devers in 1943, nor demand hundreds of new T26s that would impress tankers when the Zebra Mission finally arrived weeks later with just twenty of the new tank.

The recent shock of the German Ardennes offensive that began a month before was another reminder of the M4's inability to stop the most powerful German tanks due to its inadequate firepower. Patton could have asked Campbell for an up-gunned Sherman (whether 90mm or 76mm) that he had refused when offered before the Normandy invasion, albeit for understandable reasons.

Instead, when face-to-face with the Army's Chief of Ordnance, the powerful four-star general hailed as a tank expert for decades merely asked Campbell...to add a second .50 caliber machine gun to the existing Sherman's main gun mantlet.[145] Such thinking reflected prewar ideas, in which light tanks with multiple machine guns were considered the last word in tank design. It was as if to Patton, evaluating US tanks in January 1945, the disaster at Sidi-bou-Zid and the Bulge had never occurred.

As one biographer tactfully put it, "Patton was not involved in tank development or production before he left the United States for Operation Torch. [Thus], his technical awareness correspondingly atrophied."[146]

In words that would be little comfort to the average enlisted man, the long suffering American tanker, Patton once confided to his diary:

> New weapons are useful in that they add to the repertoire of killing, but be they tanks or tomahawks, weapons are only weapons after all. Wars are fought with weapons, but they are won by men.... It was the spirit of the Lord, courage, that came mightily upon Samson at Lehi which gained victory—not the jawbone of an ass.[147]

Combat had shown weaknesses in American armor and doctrine since North Africa and Tunisia. In December 1942, Patton toured the front at Eisenhower's request to learn "why the Germans were destroying so many American tanks."[148] Later, though he had seen the destruction wreaked by German models, he refused up-gunned M4s, and like Eisenhower, over two years after the African debacles denied problems with the Sherman to the press.

Like Gen. McNair, who had opposed air power prophet Gen. Billy Mitchell, Patton was stubborn, and not open to reevaluating old ideas. In one of the many ironies of the tank scandal, when the supposedly hard-charging Patton was offered a more powerful tank (T26) he refused it, arguing that to adopt it would contradict the existing textbook doctrine the Germans had rendered obsolete. This archetype of the offensive minded armor leader, like the late Gen. McNair, insisted tanks were not to fight other tanks, as per the rules in outdated manuals. Thus, giving GIs a more powerful tank was to be discouraged, because it might encourage them to violate field manuals.

Patton is often praised for his dash across France, yet some historians have argued he was able to go so far so fast because he encountered weak German opposition. As the late Russell Weigley (who taught the author) put it, "The speed of the Third Army's advance was accomplished in large part through the avoidance of fighting.... When it could not bypass opposition, its record was not nearly so impressive as its performance traveling on the open road."[149] British author John Ellis expressed a similar idea, but without Weigley's graceful tact; Patton, wrote Ellis, "should always be remembered as one of the best traffic policemen in the history of warfare."[150]

Patton expected American tanks to evade slugging matches with enemy tanks that were occasionally unavoidable. A horse Cavalryman to the bone, his preferred use of armor was pure Cavalry: breakouts, encirclements, and dramatic sweeping movements. In a perfect world, tanks would move quickly, cover much ground, and not get bogged down in duels where they would be stuck in the same place absorbing hits.

His diary abounds with orders to "attack...rupture the Siegfried Line...break through...advance ...prepare for exploitation...

*Tank Driver*, by Peter Hurd.

judgment, lost much of his ability in armored combat. These tanks are so heavy, and their road life so short, that the German is driven to use them as guns rather than as tanks."[154] But the "fleet-footed" M4's mobility was not its biggest flaw; it was the main gun's lack of stopping power when facing Germany's best armor.

Accepting Patton's ruse, a March 1945 editorial, "They Get There," attempted a journalistic shell game. Considering "claims… that our tanks compared unfavorably with those manned by Nazis," it conspicuously omitted GIs' complaints of the Sherman's firepower; the scandal was dismissed as "invidious distinctions." "If American tanks are inferior to the German Panthers and Tigers, how in the world do they 'go places' as they do?… Who better than Lieutenant General George S. Patton could straighten us out on this manner?… If the dashing Patton is satisfied with the quality of the tanks furnished him, what more is there to be said?"[155]

On closer examination, the seemingly impressive statistics Patton gave to reporters *weaken*, rather than bolster, his arguments. Though he boasted of an impressive-sounding 2,287 German tanks knocked out from August 1944 to March 1945, once the figures are broken down into Panthers and Tigers lost versus Shermans lost, it was another story. According to Patton, since his Third Army's activation in August 1944, it had "accounted for 808 German tanks…of the Tiger or Panther variety, and [lost] 851 on our side, [all of which] were M4s."[156] Hardly an impressive ratio, it validates the GIs' criticism of the M4, as well as their demand for the better tank Patton refused.

On other occasions, Patton claimed two German tanks were taken out for every American one lost. Even if correct, since Shermans had a four or five-man crew (sometimes carrying a second, assistant driver), potentially losing up to five men to stop every two German tanks was not very impressive, particularly to the tankers that would comprise such impersonal statistics and to their loved ones at home. That Patton thought such numbers worth boasting about to the press (or that they refuted GIs' concerns) exemplifies the callousness towards the human cost of sacrificial tactics adopted to compensate for under-gunned, poorly armored tanks.

The true figures may have been worse, and angry GIs saw through the cooked statistics. Patton's public hyperbole not only reflects poorly on him, it contradicts his own diary, where he described being driven to Bastogne on January 30, 1945:

> On the way we passed the scene of the tank battle
> during the initial German break-through. I counted over
> a hundred [wrecks of destroyed] American armored
> fighting vehicles along the road and as a result, issued
> an order, subsequently carried out, that every tank
> should be examined and the direction, caliber, and type
> of hit which put it out made of record, so that we would
> have data from which to construct a better tank. These
> data are now in the hands of the Ordnance Department.[157]

This entry shows the hypocrisy of Patton's public denials of the need for "a better tank." He was well aware of problems with the M4, yet he refused "a better tank" when it was offered by Army Ordnance. His rejection of the T26 (unmentioned in the

take the high ground…continue attacking…attack…drive…make a rush."[151] To a romantic like Patton, this was the preferred method: dashing, glorious, and upholding the horse Cavalry tradition of speed, mobility, and shock. But like the tank destroyer theorists' unrealistic assumptions that the Germans would behave in certain ways, battlefield reality refused to conform to the textbook ideal.

When given a choice between ambushing a defenseless column of "soft" enemy targets (like helpless Infantry or thin-skinned, lightly armed trucks) or dueling a King Tiger, naturally, most tankers preferred the safer option, but sometimes they had to slug it out with Germany's most powerful tanks. In this case, the optimal "school solutions" went out the window. When compiling his thoughts for posterity in 1945, Patton insisted, "The primary mission of armored units is the attacking of Infantry and artillery. The enemy's rear is the happy hunting ground for armor. Use every means to get it there."[152]

His adherence to obsolete doctrine meant tankers landed in Normandy with weapons inferior to Germany's. This contributed to a shortage of tanks, tankers, and spare parts, more deaths, and prolonged the war. At the scandal's height in 1945, instead of respecting the views of combat veterans (some with two or three invasions under their belts) who called for a better tank, Patton dismissed their criticism and damned them as "deliberately mendacious individuals."

He also presumed to speak for the men he disparaged, claiming they had "the finest tanks in the world" and "just loved to see the German King Tiger come up on the field."[153] As if such a statement was not ridiculous enough, he attempted to duck the gun issue. "The great mobility of our fleet-footed Sherman usually enables it to evade the slow and unwieldy Tiger. With their adoption of this cumbersome tank, the German, in my

Sgt. Bill Mauldin, 45th Infantry Division, in Italy.

Sgt. Bill Mauldin's popular "Willie and Joe" cartoons in *Stars and Stripes* captured the harsh world of the combat GI, but to Patton they were seditious, able to "incite a goddamn mutiny."[161] Mauldin's confrontation with Patton sheds light on the general's unsympathetic attitude towards the tank scandal and its human toll.

Patton is known for his distinctive, immaculately tailored uniforms: starched horse Cavalry officers' jodhpurs, a gleaming helmet liner, shiny leather officer's pistol belt and holster with ivory-handled weapon (sometimes two), and gleaming riding boots polished to perfection by his orderly, Sgt. George Meeks.

Not surprisingly, Patton took great offense at Mauldin's unromantic but accurate depiction of the frontline, enlisted GI: grimy, unshaven, and ripped, filthy uniforms looking as if they had been slept in, which they had. To the sartorially impeccable Patton, these "soldiers" looked like burned-out, hung over Great Depression hoboes; bindle stiffs—an affront to the romantic image of the chivalric warrior of old that persisted in Patton's romantic mind, the gleaming knight on horseback, the upper class cavalier.

To General Patton, Sgt. Mauldin's GIs not only *looked* disgraceful, but their bitingly sarcastic views of their leadership were near mutinous. Mauldin accurately showed them to be contemptuous of detached, uncaring, and hypocritical authority. The subjects of his cartoons—loved by the GIs—were quick to ridicule the pampered, sheltered brass in the rear.

And on top of his near-seditious cartoons, Mauldin had entered the Army through the Arizona National Guard in 1940. In an era where West Point graduates could barely conceal their contempt for National Guard "citizen soldiers"—considered by career Army officers to be too casual, independent, and slack in the discipline department—this did little to endear young Mauldin (with all of four years Army experience) to Patton, now involved in his second world war after decades of service.

Sgt. Mauldin was ordered to Gen. Patton's office for what Army slang calls a "butt chewing." In his plain, mussed field uniform, the sergeant faced the general, whose "collar and shoulders glittered with more stars than I could count...an incredible mass of ribbons started around desktop level and spread upward in a flood over his chest to the very top of his shoulder, as if preparing to march down his back, too."[162]

To Mauldin, Patton lived "in a world of his own, sort of a medieval world, where officers are knights, and soldiers are dumb peasants."[163] If true, might this shed light on why Patton would not only fail to use his considerable authority as a tank expert to save lives by speaking up about problems with American armor, but also forbid his frightened men to augment the weak armor on their tanks?

After lecturing Mauldin on the importance of soldier-like appearance and military discipline, Patton repeated his opinion that Willie and Joe looked like "Goddamn bums."[164] In the end, the sergeant got the last laugh on the general; he was awarded a 1945 Pulitzer Prize for his work.[165]

Like Franklin Roosevelt, Patton's death after a December 1945 car accident sanitized his image and spared him a reckoning for his role in the tank scandal. For decades after VE Day and Patton's death, the controversy surrounding the emotionally complex old Cavalryman was:

carefully edited version of his diary published in 1947, after his death) and insistence that M4s were to avoid fighting Panzers contradict his pugnacious image. Like many a general's memoirs (especially posthumous ones), his reflect an effort to sanitize his reputation for posterity.

Gen. Patton, like Eisenhower, was a decent man. His diary also records the loving care given to his beloved bull terrier after being "attacked by a large number of ferocious hornets. It took the Commanding General, the Chief of Staff, the Deputy Chief of Staff, several soldiers, and about 5 gallons of gasoline to burn out the hornets. Willie was very sorry for himself, and we put soda and water on his wounds."[158]

Stories abound of Patton giving his own sweater to a shivering jeep driver, or paying French tailors out of his own pocket to make white snow camouflage capes for his soldiers in the Ardennes. But unlike Eisenhower, this emotionally complex man from a privileged background had a paternalistic, feudal attitude towards his men. John Eisenhower (then a young Army lieutenant), who visited Patton shortly after VE Day, witnessed him going into a "rage" when one of his young officer aides picked up a suitcase, which Patton saw as "the job of an enlisted man."[159]

GIs sensed Patton's feudal attitude towards them; when Eisenhower and Patton walked onto the field at a soldiers' postwar intramural football game in Frankfurt, Germany, "The GI spectators cheered wildly [for Ike], but when they realized that Ike's companion, in tailored riding breeches and gleaming Cavalry boots, was Patton, the cheers changed abruptly to jeers. They were not his troops, and knew him only by clouded reputation."[160]

Sicily, 1943: "Blood and guts" Patton lords over his GIs in 1943, who responded, "Yeah, our blood—HIS guts!"

Patton, we are told:

insisted that the modern military commander become familiar with all the weapons systems at his disposition, including the newest and still-emerging ones. Patton was not only a master of tank doctrine and tactics, he thoroughly understood the mechanics of his tanks, their armor plating, endurance, fuel demand, speed, and capabilities over various terrain. The nuts and bolts of war were not to be left to non-commissioned technicians. Patton insisted that these details also be made the province of each and every commander.[167]

To *From Here To Eternity* author and Army Sgt. James Jones, postwar accounts of WWII reminded him of rough Navajo stones being polished and buffed up with the awkward, unsightly rough spots carefully smoothed out. This is an apt description of the Patton of modern legend, as well as of "The Good War" myth of America in WWII.

A less fawning look at Gen. Patton in the tank scandal reveals him unwilling to question the Army establishment's adherence to obsolete doctrine. In 1944, he rejected T26s and up-gunned Shermans; in 1945, he requested not T26s or a better main gun for the M4, but only more machine guns, an idea that had been on the cutting edge of tank design almost a decade previously. "Patton knew as little about tanks as anybody I knew," armor historian Steve Zaloga quoted Gen. Bruce Clarke, who was "one of the U.S. Army's best tank commanders in World War II... striking to the heart of the matter." Zaloga's judgment? Patton knew how to use tanks in combat, but did not know much about tank design.[168] Yet Patton's biographer Ladislas Farago hailed him as "the most up-to-the minute soldier...an amazingly broad-minded commander to whom...no new weapon was alien... he avidly adopted all the mechanical wonders that burst onto the battlefields."[169]

swept aside, if not forgotten, in a rush to depict Patton as a very great general, perhaps the greatest of World War II...the popular image of Patton as a heroically simple and direct man of action became most seductively appealing...upon his death, Patton was enshrined in the American mythic imagination.[166]

Today it is seldom recalled that Patton resisted the idea—now elementary to Army planning and operations—that tanks fight tanks. Or that, in spite of evidence of the M4's weaknesses in firepower and armor protection, he opposed both the up-gunned 76mm Sherman and the better armed and armored T26. Or that he failed to challenge the Army leadership's outdated, flawed anti-tank and armor doctrine.

Patton's refusal to use his authority and influence to champion the cause of the common GI—though his own diary entries confirmed their criticisms of the Sherman—echoed his actions decades earlier. In the 1920s, when he was chastised by superiors for advocating an independent armor branch, the soldier depicted today as a defiant rebel unafraid to buck authority appeased the powers-that-be. He took the safe route, shut his mouth, and transferred back to the more traditional and socially acceptable horse Cavalry.

Yet we rarely read of this; a 2006 biography praises him for his "technical proficiency" as "the ideal of the warrior leader... who wanted a modern army, equipped with the latest weapons."

In one of the many ironies of the Sherman tank scandal, a general who damned his soldiers as "wholly incorrect...misguided, or perhaps deliberately mendacious individuals" for warning that the M4 might "not be comparable with the German Mark VI"[170] is celebrated today as a challenger of authority; an aggressive, forward-thinking expert and innovator in the use of tanks.

# "GLORY WITHOUT BLOOD"

Soon after VE Day, career Army leaders closed ranks to insert the "official" explanations for the tank scandal into the historical record of the war. As bitter fighting in the Pacific continued, Gen. Marshall addressed the European tank controversy in his report to the Secretary of War later published as his "Report on the Winning of the War in Europe and the Pacific."[5]

His observations in a section titled "Our Weapons" could apply verbatim to the Tiger tank:

> The appearance of an unusually effective enemy weapon, or of a particularly attractive item of enemy equipment, usually provoked animated public discussion in this country, especially when stimulated by criticism of the Army's supposed failures to provide the best.... In some of the public discussion of such matters, criticism was leveled at the Ordnance Department for not producing better weapons.[6]

> I think we have kidded ourselves for the past 3 years, and Normandy and Germany have proven it.... I've seen this day by day, since 1 year before El Alamein—we never beat Jerry, but catch up to [his] last year's model, next year.... Even John Q. Public finally begins to wonder, too!!! Lincoln was right—you can't fool all the people all of the time.
> —Army Ordnance colonel and captured weapons expert George Jarrett in a private scrapbook he kept on the Sherman tank scandal.[4]

In a classic example of "shooting the messenger," the most powerful man in the Army pointed fingers not at generals and politicians whose negligence, shortsightedness, and arrogance contributed to the inadequacy of American tanks, but at the soldier victims who had warned of the problem. Virtually accusing them of sedition, Marshall almost equates them with Nazis: "The morale of the fighting man is a matter of primary importance. To destroy his confidence in his weapons or in the higher command is the constant and intense desire of the enemy."[7]

Apparently, for experienced combat tankers overseas to question ineffective weapons and doctrine coming from their desk-bound leadership was to strike a blow for Hitler. Marshall also criticized the GIs for bringing about

the advantage given to the enemy by informing him which of his weapons is hurting us most. And along with this goes the similar embarrassment of not wishing to disclose to the enemy

Ogden Pleissner, *Sherman Tanks Invade*

the state of the measures you are most certainly taking to correct any demonstrated weakness in a particular weapon...nor do you wish to sacrifice surprise by advising him in advance of the improved weapon to come or actually in the process of deployment.[8]

Marshall noted the head start the Germans had enjoyed by testing their tanks in the Spanish Civil War, "a matter of great importance, preliminary to decisions for quantity production of any weapon." But his account of the "Arsenal of Democracy" is questionable:

Since we had some time in which to mobilize our re- sources, the vastly superior industrial establishment of the United States eventually overcame the initial ad- vantage of the enemy.... During the past two years [1943–1945] the United States Army was well armed and well equipped.... Were it not for superiority...in mobility and in firepower we could not have achieved tactical superiority at points chosen for attack, nor have prevented the enemy from bringing greater forces to bear against us.[9]

This would be news to survivors of Sidi Bou Zid or the ill-fated "TD" men who confronted Tigers on the Sicilian beaches with toy-like 37mm towed guns in the summer of 1943. GIs who had run from King Tigers near Bastogne and St. Vith in 1944 would likely take exception, along with those who were still du- eling Panthers in 1945 Germany with a lackluster, circa-1941 75mm tank main gun, praying for the arrival of the "thousands" of T26s mentioned by President Roosevelt in his 1945 annual message to the country.

In condemning "the advantage given to the enemy by inform- ing him which of his weapons is hurting us most,"[10] Gen. Marshall also fell back on the old saw used to conceal and excuse military mistakes—security. But having examined burned out Sherman hulks from 1942 North Africa to 1945 Germany, the enemy was well aware of the effectiveness of his armor.

While Marshall made passing reference to a tanker shortage in the Sicilian and Italian campaigns, he did not elaborate on the shortage of trained tank crewmen that occurred from Normandy forward and worsened as the Allies entered Germany. He spoke of a "drain [on] our manpower" and "ground force attrition," but claimed:

Some of the forecasts [of losses] were accurate; others were not.... After the North African campaign, it seemed that we could reasonably expect heavy casualties in our armored units. So in preparation for the Sicilian operation, we built up a sizable backlog of tank drivers and crewmen, and at the same time geared the training program in the United States to this expectation.

But once ashore in Sicily our armor raced around the island against feeble opposition and received few casualties. Then we moved directly into the battle for Italy's jagged terrain, where armor was difficult to employ, and found ourselves with a surplus of armor personnel.[11]

Instead of addressing the post-Normandy shortage of tanker replacements, Marshall mentions "...after North Africa... too many men being trained for the Armored Forces," and a "surplus of armor personnel" in Italy, a "backlog"; yet he passes lightly over a deficit of trained men in Western Europe so des- perate, untrained soldiers were thrown into tanks as emergency replacements with tragic results.

While acknowledging a "final manpower crisis" and "short- age of replacements" occurring "during the prolonged and very heavy fighting in the fall of 1944 and the winter of 1944–45... in Europe," he attempted to deflect criticism by stating, "our own tribulations of this nature were much less serious, it is believed, than those of our Allies and certainly of the German enemy."[12]

"The War Department," General Marshall claimed, "took vigorous corrective action" to address the shortage, which would come as a surprise to stunned clerks, cooks, and bakers abrupt- ly assigned to tanks with zero training or experience. "All the while," recalled 4th Armored Division tank commander Sgt. Nat Frankel, "we had to teach these men how to fight. I spent long hours in the turret when I was literally showing men how to feed bullets into the gun. Could they shoot straight? They couldn't even hold the gun right! In the midst of the toughest fighting of the Third Army's campaign, I was teaching men what I had learned in basic training."[13]

General Marshall reported a figure of 62,417 combined armored division casualties (killed in action, wounded in action, died of wounds, self-inflicted wounds, etc.) in the ETO, but this number must be approached with caution in at-

*Time* makes Gen. Marshall "Man of the Year."

"Ike," "Georgie," and President Harry Truman watch a U.S. flag go up over Berlin, July 1945.

tempting to gauge losses of tank crewmen alone; by 1944, a typical American armored division, in addition to three battalions of tank crewmen, also had three battalions of self-propelled artillery and three battalions of armored Infantrymen. There would be a signal company, engineer battalion, ordnance maintenance battalion, and other support troops, further complicating the

July 1945: Gen. George Marshall (in half-track, right) inspects M4 tanks of the Second Armored Division.

historian's search for a precise figure of Sherman tank crew casualties. Oddly, Marshall's figure excluded casualties suffered in the Italian campaign.

Marshall's patronizing response to frontline tankers' warnings exemplifies the gap between stateside generals and enlisted combat GIs overseas:

The American soldier has a very active imagination and usually, at least for the time being, covets anything new, and is inclined to endow the death-dealing weapons of the enemy with extraordinary qualities, since any weapon seems more formidable to the man receiving its fire than to the man delivering it. If given slight encouragement, the reaction can be fatal to the success of our forces. Commanders must always make every effort to show their men how to make better, more effective use of what they have.[14]

He did acknowledge the "noteworthy example of German superiority, the heavy tank" over the M4. "From the summer of 1943 to the spring of 1945, the German Tiger and Panther heavy tanks [sic, the Panther was a medium] outmatched our Sherman tanks in direct combat."[15]

And why, in the Chief of Staff's opinion, was the M4 "outmatched?" One factor, he claimed, was American armor doctrine: "We designed our armor as a weapon of exploitation. In other words, we desired to use our tanks in long-range thrusts deep into the enemy's rear, where they could chew up his supply installations and communications. This required great endurance— low consumption of gasoline and ability to move great distances without break-down."[16] This was the "Cavalry tank" doctrine that had dominated thinking on tank design since WWI. One has to question the assumption that a decent main gun would drastically lower a tank's reliability or "endurance."

What happened when the hypothetical "desires" of powerful generals like Marshall, McNair, Eisenhower, and Patton failed to match battlefield reality? "While this [the "weapon of exploitation" armor doctrine] was the most profitable use of the tank," Marshall

admitted, "it became unavoidable…to escape tank-to-tank battles. In this combat, our [M4 Sherman] medium tank was at a disadvantage, when forced in a head-on engagement with the German heavies."[17] Marshall recognized far too late that unrealistic doctrine had led to thousands of American deaths, including that of his own Sherman tank commander stepson.

While popular culture plays up the dramatic image of mammoth Tiger vs. underdog Sherman, M4 crews faced a menagerie of German weapons: not just tanks, but also tank destroyers, self-propelled guns, towed guns, the Panzerfaust and Panzershreck, etc. Thankfully, Tigers and Panthers were not typically the M4's most numerous, day-to-day opponent.

Nevertheless, AGF doctrine inevitably meant US medium tanks were not optimized for tank fighting, and that most of the attention in the development of anti-tank guns was focused on the tank destroyer. No other major army in WWII accepted or practiced this type of armored doctrine, with the Germans, Soviets, and British relying primarily on their tanks to fight enemy tanks.[18]

General Marshall's version of the T26 story is notable for what it omits. "Early in 1944 it was decided that a heavy American tank, on which our Ordnance experts had been continuously experimenting since before the war [sic, the disappointing M6 heavy was different from the T26 series, which became the Pershing; design work did not begin on the T26 until late 1942] must be put into mass production. As a result the M-26 tank began to reach the battle lines last winter [March 1945]."[19] There, it was "equal in direct combat to any the Germans had and still enjoyed a great advantage in lighter weight [43 tons], speed, and endurance."[20]

But why the delay? Marshall's mention of the new tank reaching the front at the end of the war ignores the question of why this did not happen until weeks before V-E Day, and then only in piddling numbers. Not surprisingly, in the tradition of hiding a bureaucracy's dirty laundry from the public he neglected to mention the bitter internal feuding among Ordnance, the Armored Force, and McNair's Army Ground Forces—arguments that kept the T-26 from being produced and sent overseas in time for the Normandy invasion or earlier.

While tens of thousands of Shermans were built during the war, barely 200 T26s reached Europe. Army Chief of Staff Marshall—who also stated in his "report" to Congress and the public that "Excuses and explanations are not acceptable to the soldier, and would not be tolerated by the political leaders,"[21] did not say why.

*There can be no excuse for the abysmal ignorance of tank tactics generally, and tank operations in Europe in particular…the simple answer was to design a better gun, something infinitely easier than to design a new tank.[2]*
*—British Army Brigadier G. MacLeod Ross*

He ended his *Report* with a defiant blast, giving what he may have hoped was the last word on the tank scandal. The Ordnance Department, insisted Gen. Marshall, had "produced with rare efficiency what it was told to produce…these instructions came from the General Staff of which I am the responsible head, transmitting the resolved views of the officers with the combat troops…of the commanders in the field."[22]

Marshall's word choice is interesting; "what it was told to produce" by out of touch, stateside leaders was not the same as *what was needed* by GIs overseas. With hindsight, one can't help noticing that press releases boasting about the M4 and denying its flaws often came from desk-bound generals, not the men in the field actually using the Sherman in combat, whose opinions derived from years of battlefield experience were suppressed.

"The Army's efforts to encourage suggestions from soldiers," an Ordnance officer admitted to the *New York Times*' Hanson Baldwin in February 1945, "have been utterly ineffectual." Although Marshall boasted of his observers in the field, to this officer, "Higher officers are given a 'good show' close to the frontlines, but they have mighty sketchy contact with the enlisted men whose knowledge would help them the most."[23]

To this honest Ordnance officer, the observer was part of the problem: "Usually, he is a high-ranking officer chosen for the closeness of his connections with influential officers in his own branch of service…these administrative officers are asked to investigate the performance of materiel in combat, when in fact, they have only the foggiest notion of the technical problems involved."[24] And even when "junior officers who are technically proficient" were able to "ask the right questions, draw out the intimate knowledge of the men in the lower ranks, and finally bring home the data…they do not have the power or contacts to get needed action."

He elaborated on "the example of Ordnance":

In fulfilling his mission, the observer questions all sorts of military men, from privates to generals. Some enlisted men have seen their buddies killed in tank turrets by the defective recoil of their own guns, and these are the men who pull no punches in making reports to the observer. A modification to remedy the defect may come through in a year, or may never come through at all because the report was pigeonholed in Washington to avoid embarrassing questions.

While all this is going on, American tankers prove weak spots in German Tiger tanks, only to find that the Germans will have corrected their mistakes within one month—or nearly as soon as they discover them. As a bewildered first lieutenant who just came back to the States after two years of hard tank fighting puts it, "Who the hell buries all these reports? Two years ago I started screaming to anyone who would listen that our tanks didn't need speed. All they needed was armor and a little more firepower than the popgun 75. They needed wider tracks too, but for over a year our boys had to install our own wider tracks, rigged up as field expedients. A couple of observers listened to all this stuff, and wrote it down, but that's the last we ever heard. Now look what the German Tigers are doing to us.[25]

In June 1945, the Army Ground Forces equipment review board convened to assess the effectiveness of weapons and doctrine. Not surprisingly, AGF faulted its rival agency Ordnance for "not sufficiently consulting Army Ground Forces during the design stages of new equipment."[26]

Returning the venom, Ordnance claimed the AGF had "lacked foresight." For good measure, Gen. Barnes blamed the using services (such as the Armored Force) "for acting as a brake on the efforts of the Ordnance Department to arm the U.S. troops adequately." From the middle ground, Col. George Petersen in AGF's Ordnance Section lamented "The policy of our development has too often been a mere copying of revolutionary enemy equipment. Why can't we be the first with revolutionary development?"[27]

General Marshall's report to Congress and the American public was followed in 1946 by Eisenhower's grandly titled *Report by the Supreme Commander to the Combined Chiefs of Staff on the Operations in Europe of the Allied Expeditionary Force, 6 June 1944 to 9 May 1945*. While Marshall had acknowledged the tank scandal and responded somewhat to the critics, Eisenhower's detailed report contains glaring omissions; other than the exotic, rare DD Sherman "swimming tanks" floundering on the Norman beaches, there is little mention of problems with American tanks.

When faced with larger, more powerful German tanks, light models were ineffective, but high-level support for them contributed to the M4's weaknesses. Eisenhower's choice of language, like Patton's in *War As I Knew It*, shows the persistence of this obsolete "Cavalry tank" doctrine.

Describing the big picture goals of Allied generals, Eisenhower uses words like "sweeping," "thrust," "drive," and "extremely rapid advances." When imagining the hypothetical, optimal conditions for tank fighting, he, Patton, and other Army leaders had hoped to avoid costly slugging matches in which advances might be halted—stopped, for instance, by better German tanks. As noted, the optimal, "textbook" use of American tanks involved continuous movement that took ground rapidly. Patton had shown how effective this could be when faced with light enemy resistance, which could not be presumed. The best tank for this ideal situation was small and nimble, like an M3 Stuart.

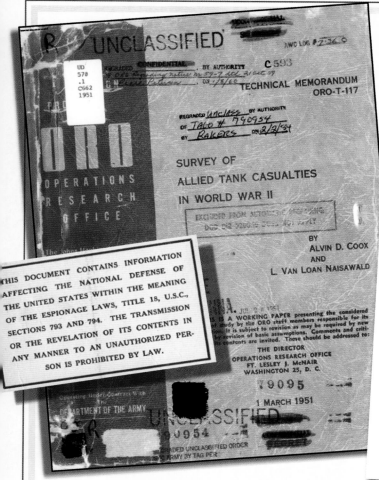

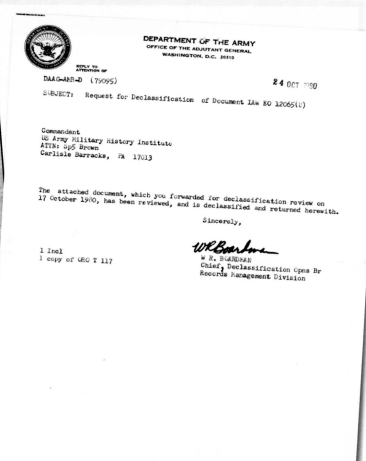

Courtesy US Army Military History Institute, Carlisle
Barracks, Pennsylvania. Photo by Robert Coldwell Sr.

Restricted for decades, this is the declassification letter for
the 1951 study of Allied tank casualties. *Courtesy US Army
Military History Institute, Carlisle Barracks, Pennsylvania.
Photo by Robert Coldwell Sr.*

What is often misunderstood today is Patton's drive across
Europe was so successful and covered so much ground because
it met light resistance from the disintegrating Wehrmacht. As
Eisenhower observed of fighting around Brittany, France, "The
opposition encountered by General Patton's flying columns in the
course of this sweep ...was negligible, for the enemy's flank had
collapsed so completely that there was hardly any resistance
offered by organized units above company strength."[28]

Such ideal conditions were an anomaly; the Germans could
also meet light Allied tanks with larger, more
powerful ones, refusing to conform to the desired
textbook conditions for the most advantageous
use of American armor. But generals continued to
resist heavier tanks, instead favoring out-of-date
doctrine that assumed "best case" scenarios and
battles of movement and maneuver.

Another cause of doctrinal confusion and poor
tank designs was the recently deceased Gen.
McNair's muddled pet tank destroyer project, which
delayed production and adoption of up-gunned tanks by using
tank substitutes—near-tanks. But General Eisenhower graciously avoided rendering judgment on the TDs in his report; instead,
he simply commented on the bombing that killed Gen. McNair,
"His death was a heavy blow to the United States Army and a
source of keen sorrow to me personally."[29]

So much for the TD debacle. Eisenhower was being polite,
but also had little to say about the difficult hedgerow tank fighting in Normandy or the paralyzing initial rout around Bastogne,
which he blandly described as "some penetrations of the American line...effected, with the enemy using tanks."[30] Declining to
address the shortcomings of specific weapons, he insisted, "No
army...was ever supported so generously or so well. Never, during
the entire campaign, were we forced to fight a major battle
without weapons that were needed."[31]

Thanks to the White-Rose Reports that Eisenhower personally initiated, he knew of the desperate tank ammo shortages that had plagued GIs;
the shortage, he had written home in October
1944, was "not merely one of port capacity and
distributional facilities; it likewise involves limitations
in production."[32] So unless Ike was splitting hairs
over what constitutes "support" or a "major battle,"
this is not an accurate statement.

Classified, high-level, internal Army reports
were not common knowledge in 1946, but decades later, obfuscation over the tank scandal continues. Instead of reading of the
human cost of technical inferiority, we often hear recitations of
production figures that echo FDR's wartime boasts, or the com-
forting myth that the T-26 arrived just in time.

American industry is celebrated for technological marvels
like atomic bombs, jets, and B-29 Superfortress heavy bombers,
but the public then and now never learned of the failure to
supply adequate numbers of something as simple as tank am-

> No single Allied failure had
> more important conse-
> quences on the European
> battlefield than the lack
> of tanks with adequate
> punch and protection.[3]
> —Sir Max Hastings, mili-
> tary historian

munition. The shortage was so severe, conceded Ordnance Chief Campbell in early February 1945, that measures to rectify it (begun in May 1944) would not even *begin* to correct the problem until August 1945, the month the Pacific war ended.[33]

The cheery, simplistic "Arsenal of Democracy" has been fed to the public for decades. "The production necessary to equip and maintain our vast forces of fighting men on global battlefronts is without parallel," Roosevelt stated shortly before his death. "I need not repeat the figures. The facts speak for themselves."[34] Added Donald Nelson, who led Roosevelt's War Production Board, "The American war production job was probably the greatest collective achievement of all time. It makes the 'seven wonders' of the ancient world look like the doodling of a small boy."[35] State-of-the-art B-29 bombers and YP-80 fighter jets made for better copy in administration press releases (and postwar sanitized Roosevelt biographies and accounts of the war effort) than the embarrassing truth that during the Ardennes fighting and beyond, outnumbered tankers were forced to confront King Tigers with only *four rounds* of tank ammunition.

Composer Frank Loesser, who wrote cheery songs for the home front at government request, later described the propaganda that has become the accepted historical "fact." "You give [civilians] hope without facts, glory without blood. You give them a legend, with the rough edges neatly trimmed."[36] As author and war correspondent John Steinbeck conceded, "We were all part of the war effort. We went along with it, and not only that, we abetted it…. I don't mean that the correspondents were liars… it is in the things not mentioned that the untruth lies."[37]

Thus, rather than explore why scared young GIs as late as 1945 were stacking sandbags on light tanks that had been obsolete back in 1942, the seminal 1970 biography *Roosevelt: Soldier of Freedom* omits mention of problems with American armor and Roosevelt's role in it. Instead, it brags, "the weapons rolling off American assembly lines startled even science fiction writers: radar-guided rockets, amphibious tanks, bazookas, proximity-fused shells, napalm-jellied gasoline flame throwers."[38]

Four decades later, even after Vietnam and Watergate eroded public trust in government, little has changed in the simplistic myths of Rooseveltian infallibility. A 2014 work, *The Arsenal of Democracy*, assures us that far from misjudging the types and numbers of tanks that would be needed, "Even before the war had started, Roosevelt had envisioned the future of modern combat."[39] A 2010 account celebrates him along the same lines, citing his December 29, 1940, speech calling for America to "…be the great Arsenal of Democracy…to put forth a mightier effort…to increase our production of all the implements of defense…the planes, the tanks, the guns…. Emphatically we must get these weapons to [Allied soldiers] in sufficient volume and quickly enough, so that we and our children will be saved the agony and suffering of war which others have had to endure."[40]

While acknowledging the obvious, that "as the end of the war approached, the fighting became more brutal,"[41] the author ignores the tank scandal that made front page headlines across the country, was grudgingly addressed in Roosevelt's 1945 State of the Union Address, and contributed to the death and wounding of thousands of GIs. The chapter on Roosevelt's wartime performance is even titled—seemingly with no irony intended—"How the Democrats Won World War II."

Author and WWII Army combat veteran Paul Fussell mocked the sunny postwar celebration of what he called "Bright Ideas":

The "D.D." [Dual Drive Sherman] tanks launched offshore on D-Day were equipped to float with impermeable canvas skirts, and were to propel themselves to the beach with an ad hoc propeller and to resume normal operation. Thirty-two were launched, their skirts deployed, but in high seas and, doubtless because of fear, too far from land. Twenty-seven sank with their complete crews, a tribute to stubborn hope, for tank after tank was launched seriatum, each sinking like a stone, observed by everyone on the launching ship. Yet in 1977, the Time-Life World War II series volume dealing with the invasion denotes a full-color page to the D.D. tank without in any way suggesting that something went fatally wrong. "A TANK THAT COULD SWIM" is the caption.[42]

Decades removed from censorship, books repeat cheery wartime propaganda while whitewashing the bumps. Instead of unsentimental candor, often we get production figures in a bragging tone similar to FDR's speeches that praised large numbers of obsolete tanks. For example, a book called *America Ascendant* tells us:

The amount and range of American production were truly astounding. Between 1940 and 1945 the United States produced 296,429 warplanes; 102,351 tanks; 872,431 pieces of artillery; 2,455,964 trucks; 87,620 warships; 5,425 cargo ships; 5,822,000 tons of aircraft bombs; 20,086,061 small arms, and 44 billion rounds of small arms ammunition.[43]

Instead of acknowledging and lamenting M4 tankers' avoidable deaths, books exult it "was built in greater numbers than any tank outside the Soviet Union. The total of 48,000 Shermans and its variants exceeds the total of all German tanks, tank destroyers, and assault guns produced during the war years."[44]

During the war, the Ordnance Department had a motto that reflected the grim mood of the times: "Let no soldier's ghost ever say, 'The Ordnance service let me down.'"[45] Today, the hypocrisy is obvious in hindsight. Yet in most "histories," we rarely learn of young men in their prime burned to death in seconds in a "Purple Heart Box" after a few shots from a Tiger or Panther.

Instead, we are spoon-fed paeans to sheer numbers. The lackluster Sherman has been transformed into "the Army's premier armored vehicle…. American industry would produce some forty thousand Shermans in a bewildering variety of versions—enough to equip every medium tank company in the Army, not to mention those supplied to the Marine Corps and Lend-Lease recipients."[46]

Certainly, the sheer quantity of Shermans produced is impressive; author Zaloga cites a figure of 49,234 of all variants produced,[47] while Germany (according to Max Hastings) built only 5,976 Panthers and 1,354 Tigers.[48] But if one can rise above the usual clichés of an aroused democracy supposedly at its technological best, an honest look shows they were flawed tanks

ELDORADO

March 1945, Bitche, France: Civilians greet an M4 of the 781st Tank Battalion, Seventh Army. Note the extensive, improvised sandbag "armor" that Patton would have forbidden had these GIs been under his command.

generations behind Germany's and Russia's. The Germans and Russian dictatorships continually upgraded their tanks as the war went on, but the M4 remained under-gunned and poorly armored until 1945.

Since Ordnance knew a 90mm gun could be fitted into a Sherman tank turret since 1942, even if one argues today the T26 could not have been built in decisive numbers and fielded in time to make a difference, the expedient M36B1 shows a remedy was at hand: a more powerful 90mm gun in a new turret added to a standard M4 hull on the assembly lines. It is ironic the British were innovative and flexible enough to devise the Firefly to counter the Tiger and Panther, while the US refused to field the Firefly in large quantities because an obstinate Gen. McNair rejected it as an "unbalanced design."[49]

Steve Zaloga has pointed out the danger of McNair's passive, reactive "battle need" doctrine (essentially, waiting for the GI in the field to call for better weapons in response to the enemy's, rather than anticipating what was needed presently and in the future):

> The problem with battle need was the tyranny of time. Modern weapons take months, if not years, to develop, so there could be no fast response to a sudden technological crisis in the theater of battle, such as the

Don't think you're going to conceal faults by concealing evidence that they ever existed.[1]
—President Dwight Eisenhower, 1953

appearance of a new anti-tank weapon or a new enemy tank. Battle need was a reactive philosophy; it presumed that action would not be taken until the enemy acted first…in the case of tanks, a new enemy tank impervious to the American tank's gun could unexpectedly appear. The development of a new tank gun to deal with the new enemy tank could not be designed overnight, and even if a bigger gun was already available, it would take months to modify tanks to accommodate it, months to ramp up ammunition production, and months more to ship the gun and ammunition overseas from the United States. The Army Ground Forces' reactive battle need doctrine, combined with Ordnance's weakness in the use of technical intelligence to predict likely German developments, lay at the root of the Sherman's shortcomings in 1944–45.[50]

Another aspect of the tank scandal that is little known today is the sad impact of Gen. McNair's late 1943 tank production decisions that led to raw replacements (or soldiers from other branches, like clerks and cooks) being thrown into tanks with no training.

In early 1945, Maj. Forrest Dixon's 712th Tank Battalion received 69 replacement troops to replace heavy losses of tank crewmen in the Ardennes battles. After one of the new men (attempting to clean his unfamiliar M3 submachine gun, a typical tanker weapon) accidentally shot another man in his tank crew, Maj. Dixon investigated:

> The soldier told Dixon that he had never seen the weapon before, or been trained on its safe use.
>
> I said, "Soldier, how long have you been in the Army?"
>
> He thought a minute and said, "Sir, I believe just six weeks."
>
> "You mean you've been over here in Europe six weeks?"
>
> "No Sir," he said, "Seven weeks ago I was a civilian."

Maj. Dixon and one of his non-commissioned officers scanned the replacements' records. Out of 69 men, *all* 69 had been civilians just weeks or months before. Yet on their arrival at the front, they were thrown into tanks with little or no instruction, to do the job of men with years of armor training and experience.

When Dixon passed this news to his battalion's commanding officer, Col. Kedrovsky responded, "Get hold of all the tank companies and get those men up to battalion headquarters [for training in basic tanker skills]. They are more dangerous than the Germans."[51]

Until the release of the film *Fury*, the use of raw, untrained American young men as cannon fodder—literal "Tiger bait"—was not well known. "Our most valued, our most costly asset," then-President Dwight Eisenhower proclaimed in 1954, "is our young men." Surely without any irony intended he continued, "Let's don't use them any more than we have to."[52]

"Our most valued, our most costly asset is our young men. Let's don't use them any more than we have to." – President Dwight D. Eisenhower, 1954. Bernard Ahrnest, *2 Soldiers*.

Trieste, 1948: The M4 rolls on; Shermans of the 15th Tank Company near an area disputed by Yugoslavia and Italy.

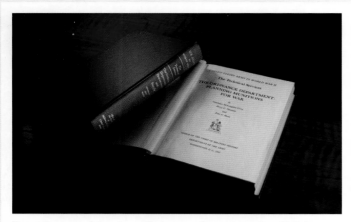

Two volumes of the Army Ordnance Department's official histories of its role in WWII. *Photo by Robert Coldwell Sr.*

The Ordnance Department's official histories of its role in WWII comprise three volumes: *Planning Munitions for War* (1955), *Procurement and Supply* (1960), and *On Beachhead and Battlefront* (1968). In a model of understatement they acknowledge "How well the Ordnance Department succeeded in matching the Germans in quality continues to be a matter of debate both within the Ordnance Department itself, and between the using arms and the Department."[53]

But reading them, one notes a litany of excuses. "For the sake of the morale of the general public in wartime," claims *Planning Munitions for War*, "there was reason to announce emphatically and repeatedly that American fighting equipment was the finest in the world."[54] So the years-long failure of the responsible agency to deliver adequate weapons to tankers overseas was...the home front *civilians'* fault?

Ordnance tops this by lamenting the "injustice" of the "unwarranted" criticism the department received. An array of buck-passing ensues, including the idea that "the inadequacies of materiel on the battlefields of World War II were the result of the 'dead hand' of the using arms, which blocked development of weapons badly needed before the war was over."[55]

Concerning tanks specifically, "The dreaded German 'Panthers,'" conceded Ordnance, "were more heavily armored and had more fire power than any American tanks that saw action."[56] But like Marshall and Patton, Ordnance attempted to explain away the tank scandal by blaming the victims. "Unflattering comparisons of some American weapons with those of the enemy, Ordnance officers were convinced, grew out of American soldiers' tendency to regard only the deadly effectiveness of an enemy arm without taking into consideration its weaknesses."[57]

Again echoing Gen. Marshall, Ordnance cites Germany's "head start" in tank design as a cause of the trouble: "We now know [1955] that ever since 1933 Nazi Germany had been applying most of her science and productive capacity to preparing for war [sic, Ordnance knew this from at least the mid-1930s, if not earlier]."[58]

Among the more novel arguments is that the agency merely designed and built what the using arms requested, regardless of whether the weapon was effective (the 37mm towed cannon comes to mind); that the Department was merely following orders. In an example of the supposed "restrictions" placed on Ordnance, Gen. Campbell is cited concerning the production of an experimental trackless tank:

As long as I am in the chair, the Ordnance Department is going to act as a servant of the [using arms] its public. If they want an 18-wheeled car that will run sidewise, we will do our best to give it to them. If we don't think it can be made, we will advise you to that effect. If you still want it, we will try our best to get it. That is our stand on this car right now.... It is up to the [using arms] to determine, with our advice, what they would like to have done with this car. As far as the Ordnance Department is concerned, it is your [the using arms'] decision.[59]

According to this defense, if Ordnance was guilty of anything, it was merely that it "...exposed itself to unwarranted criticism from other branches of the Army by not explaining the limitations imposed upon Ordnance Research and Development Service."[60]

To complete this impressive washing of hands, Ordnance concludes "In most cases, as General Marshall stated, shortcomings in American fighting equipment in World War II were attributable not to Ordnance Department slow-wittedness, but to War Department and Army Ground Forces instructions." Furthermore, we are assured, "Despite the late start, American ordnance had overtaken and outdistanced enemy ordnance by 1945."[61]

While one might hope that Ordnance's account of the scandal would be less hyperbolic than civilian publications, *Procurement and Supply* (the department's official history of tank production) repeats the usual boasts about quantity of production. It also has a defensive tone, an interesting contrast to Ordnance's wartime denials.

In a closing section, as if to settle the embarrassing tank scandal once and for all, the reader is presented "The Balance Sheet" and told, "the best way to take the quantitative measure of U.S. tank production in World War Two is" to brush "Qualitative considerations aside." Instead, we are to accept an impressive "Comparative Table of German, British, and American Tank Production, 1940–1945," which "clearly reveals the extent to which the United States out produced Germany."[62]

According to Ordnance, "these figures should serve to demolish some of the myths that have grown up around German tanks. They should demonstrate for all to see that German tank successes were due more to skilled tactical use, and the employment of heavy German tanks against Allied mediums, than to any failure of American industry to produce in quantity the tanks desired by the using arms."[63]

A perceptive author has noted that while impressive sounding on the radio, FDR's statistics came at a cost. "Nearly continuous combat in under-gunned, under-armored Shermans... exacted a terrific toll. In the long run, sheer numbers might provide an advantage, but the price for technical inferiority was tremendous...the ability to build numerous M4s and fill them with men is perhaps one of the least known and poorly understood tragedies of American military industry of the Second World War."[64] This candid assessment came decades after the war, but in 1945, who was going to criticize the allegedly martyred Commander in Chief? Or in 1955, with the Supreme Commander who was supposedly the "last to hear" of tank gun problems in the White House?

In *Procurement and Supply*, the Ordnance Department—which bears major responsibility for the tank scandal—treats it as an act of God or nature: no one to blame and beyond understanding:

Arguments about American tanks in World War II will no doubt continue as long as veterans of that conflict survive to continue the discussion. They will continue because the subject is so involved, with so much to be said on all sides, that no simple analysis can encompass the whole. To draw up a balance sheet fairly representing the views of all concerned and weighing every factor in due proportion is extremely difficult, if not impossible.[65]

As to *individual* culpability, after Gen. McNair was killed during the war by American bombers he became available as a convenient reason. His obstinate defense of the TD concept, overly optimistic pronouncements on the M4's effectiveness, crusty personality, and obstruction of the T26 made him an ideal villain. Charles Baily, who calls him "a perfect scapegoat," notes that while Gen. McNair's "success in keeping such tanks as the.... T26 off the battlefield and the acid disputes of 1944 confirmed the bitterness of the Ordnance Department,"[66] "The nine months that elapsed before the Ordnance Department managed to build the first T26 were not the result of AGF interference":

McNair's firm stand against producing extra T26s in the fall of 1943 had been overruled by Marshall only three months after the Ordnance Department first recommended production. Before the first prototype of a T26 had moved a track block, the Ordnance Department had orders for 300 of the tanks. These tanks did not begin arriving on the battlefield for fourteen months... furthermore, the original T26 had serious deficiencies that had to be corrected during the summer of 1944 before the tank was ready for combat.[67]

AGF, concluded Baily, "did not invent those deficiencies. McNair supported efforts to perfect the T26 and in fact, came to the rescue when Campbell wanted a large production order in 1944."[68]

Shortly before his death by friendly fire in July 1944, in words that could serve as an epitaph for the tank scandal, McNair recalled the frantic American response to the blitzkrieg in the early days of 1939–1940:

We didn't know how soon the war would come, but we knew it was coming. We didn't know when we'd have to fight, but we knew it might come at any time, and we had to get together something of an Army pretty darn fast.

We didn't dare stop for the progressive and logical building of a war machine. As a result, the machine was a little wobbly when it first got going. The men knew it. The officers knew it. Everyone knew it.[69]

The image of a fastidious Gen. McNair carrying a flyswatter everywhere to smash vermin and having a dictionary always at arm's length to critique his subordinates' grammar is a Hollywood script writer's dream of the neurotic bureaucrat. That he exhorted GIs overseas with bloodthirsty speeches to kill, but had never led men in combat (while residing in a palatial mansion) also invites ridicule today. But while Gen. McNair bears blame, the causes are too complicated to pin responsibility for the tank scandal on one man, and McNair's family (like George Marshall's) was not spared from sacrifice; on August 6, 1944, just two weeks after his father's accidental death in Normandy, Col. Douglas McNair of the 77th Infantry Division was killed by a Japanese sniper on Guam.

It is also tempting to view Gens. Barnes and Campbell as culprits, in light of their objections to up-gunning the M4 and the public statements they made at the height of the scandal (perhaps on the orders of higher ranking generals). Like McNair, at first glance they appear to be perfect villains, but fairness requires a closer look: Barnes, Campbell, and others were in a bitter power struggle with McNair, and with agencies like Army Ground Forces and the Armored Command. Barnes and Campbell resisted quick fixes to the M4 not because they considered the M4 a superior tank, but because they wanted another solution: mass production of the up-gunned, up-armored T26 heavy tank.

With Gen. Devers' support, they wanted to send T26s into combat as early as February 1944, but like Patton's refusal of the new 76mm M4 he was offered before the Normandy invasion, AGF rejected a Sherman replacement on the grounds it was unknown "whether [the T26s] are...fit for combat." While the best way to find this out was to field them, AGF responded haughtily, "This headquarters does not view with favor the idea of making any combat zone a testing agency."[70]

While Gens. Campbell and Barnes were well intentioned, their objections to expedient solutions had sad consequences. Like Gen. McNair, they obstructed improvements in favor of their own pet project. The T26 was one of the best *long-term* answers to the Sherman's weaknesses, but to object to upgrading the gun on existing M4s in the hope that a Sherman replacement would be fielded prolonged the problem.

Over a decade after his wartime "Report," in a series of 1956–57 interviews with his official biographer Forrest Pogue, Gen. Marshall spoke of the tank scandal. "As to mobility, speed, handling, and matters of that sort, the American tank was incomparable,"[71] he insisted. He had changed some of his wartime views; presumably referring to the Firefly, Marshall now conceded that in "fighting characteristics," Britain's tanks were better.

With more candor than he had shown during the war, Marshall expressed frustration that "we could be so far off center on the matter and not realize it at all.... Our tanks were easily the most mobile, the most perfectly controlled of all the tanks [a view a tanker bogged down in an Italian or Norman field because of the M4's high ground-to-weight ratio would contest].... But they were deficient, very decidedly, in their fighting qualities, in the arrangement of the tank so they could be fought with efficiency...the British had it right on the fighting part and we had it right on the mobility of the tank."[72]

"My effort [in tank design]," claimed Gen. Marshall, "was to bring about the settlement of the thing on the basis of what the Americans did best and what the British did best."[73]

In his 1945 "Report," Marshall had planted the seeds of an excuse that generations of historians continue to perpetuate:

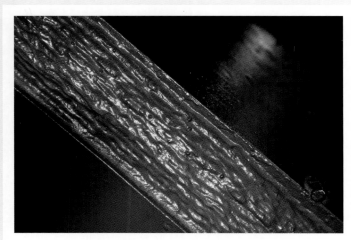

Close-up of the crude but effective extra armor plate on a "Jumbo" Sherman. *Author photo, courtesy of the National Armor and Cavalry Heritage Foundation*

the idea that American tanks were *intentionally* inferior. "Our tanks had to be shipped thousands of miles overseas and landed on hostile shores amphibiously. They had to cross innumerable rivers on temporary bridges, since when we attacked we sought to destroy the permanent bridges behind the enemy lines from the air. Those that our planes missed were destroyed by the enemy when he retreated. Therefore, our tanks could not well be of the heavy type."[75]

Gen. McNair laid the groundwork for Marshall in December 1943, when opposing adoption of the T26 in a memo to the Armored Command. Bigger, heavier tanks, McNair claimed, were "incompatible with the requirements of standard Army bridges, rail transportation, and unloading of ships. [Such tanks would have]...greatly reduced tactical and strategic mobility, and as such, are not capable of replacing the M4."[76]

True, the T26 was too wide to be transported by rail and exceeded the optimal weight and size standards in Army Regulation 850-15. Because they affect performance, weight and size need to be considered carefully in tank design; while the King Tiger's size had inspired awe and fear, its nearly 70-ton weight (compared to the average Sherman's 35 tons and the Pershing's roughly 45 tons) hampered its mobility. Apologists then and now may play up the "weight" or "bridge" aspect of the scandal, but the chief of engineers of SHAEF, after testing the T26 extensively in the field, concluded the new heavy tank could safely cross standard Allied pontoon, treadway, and Bailey bridges used all over the world.[77]

Marshall, McNair, and others never explained what the weight of a tank had to do with the effectiveness of the main gun. Upgrading the M4 in 1942 with a 90mm gun would not have affected its ability to fit into an LST, or to cross bridges. The heavier M4A3E2 ("assault tank") version of the Sherman had increased side and turret armor up to seven inches thick. While this raised its weight to 42 tons, slightly reducing its speed and range, it could still negotiate European roads and bridges, and survive hits that would take out a typical M4:

> The added armor made the "Jumbo" extremely resistant to German anti-tank guns and tanks. [Panzer IVs] had to use their heavily rationed APCR solid shot ammunition at all but point-blank range against it, and even Panthers

couldn't penetrate the [Jumbo's] frontal armor at long range. M4A3E2s became popular for leading armor columns, as they often absorbed hits that would have destroyed standard Shermans, and gave the other vehicles warning of German anti-tank guns.[78]

Up to the end of the war, frontline tankers would have rejoiced at an expedient, Sherman "of the heavy type," with thicker armor and firing improved, high-velocity, armor-piercing rounds from a better gun. Field technical orders from March 1945 show authorization was given—probably at local theater level—to install 76mm guns in the "Jumbos."[79] The number of "Jumbos" built (only 254 built by Fisher Automotive in June–July 1944) were too few to make a difference.

The "Jumbo" could have been upgraded with the British 17-pounder, one of the most effective Allied tank guns of the war, or the M36 Jackson's turret and 90mm gun. Instead, unheeded solutions cost lives, and Gen. Marshall's "landing craft" or "bridge" excuse that shipping requirements prohibited better tanks is now part of the historical mythology surrounding the tank scandal; few pause to ask how Germany, while conquering most of Europe, was able to negotiate roads and bridges with *their* heavier tanks, which had to be transported across supply lines stretching from Germany to Russia and North Africa.

When the guns fell silent wartime censorship was eased. Instead of an honest reckoning for the failure to design, build, and field in large numbers a tank able to take on Germany's best, the culprits obscured the issue by glorifying production numbers.

The fix was in long before VE Day. In April 1943, shortly before M4s were nearly thrown off the beaches of Sicily by Tiger tanks, Ordnance Chief Campbell wrote to the head of the Detroit Tank Arsenal, "Words, of course, are totally inadequate to describe how we in Ordnance feel about the accomplishments of the Chrysler Tank Arsenal.... Surely when the history of the war is written, this job will rank without a peer."[80]

Typical of the historical whitewash laid down soon after the war is a December 1945 newspaper article, "Tanks Pour Into Ogden Arsenal Storage Grounds," ostensibly about tanks being mothballed for a future war. Quoting Col. W. A. Capron, the arsenal's commanding officer, it is an impressive attempt at rewriting the facts of the tank scandal just three months after V-J Day. Missing are any references to the M4's fatal flaws, or to Ordnance's failure to deliver the T-26 to the European front until the last weeks of that war (and in the Pacific theater not until after the Japanese defeat on Okinawa). Instead, we are assured these "famed tanks...smashed through the vaunted Siegfried Line, met head-on the charging German Tiger and Panther tanks, and came off victorious."[81] The article's mention of the tank scandal employs a classic "straw man" argument, distorting the criticism into something that was never argued, then cavalierly dismissing it:

> There was a time during the war when well-meaning news commentators shook the confidence of the American people in our equipment by stating that the German tanks with their thick skins made it impossible for Americans armed with the M4 tank to punch through the German lines. They contended that American armor was outclassed.

While many citizens were worrying over the matter, General "Ike" was concentrating his troops and materiel for a great push against the Germans. When this push came, a great hole was torn in the enemy lines through which our troops poured out over France.

In one battle, a medium tank, M-4, moved forward against the Germans. It was confronted by three German Panther tanks. When the smoke of the conflict rolled away, the American M-4 Sherman marched triumphantly forward past three dead Panther tanks (incidents authenticated by War Department records).[82]

The reader will notice the obvious dishonesty of this contention: the focus of the Sherman tank scandal was GIs' valid criticism that the M4 Sherman, due to inadequate firepower and armor protection, was unable to duel Germany's best tanks one-on-one—not the respective mobility of German vs. Allied tanks. And while Eisenhower was certainly involved in "a great push" during which "a great hole was torn in the…lines" through which "troops poured," this would more aptly apply to the Ardennes disaster led by German heavy tanks. As to a Sherman knocking out three Panthers, there is no doubt that underdog GIs, through sheer guts alone, the use of sacrificial decoy tactics, a willingness to get dangerously close to the enemy, and an occasional "lucky shot" accomplished miracles of bravery, but this example is atypical—what about the other approximately 50,000 Shermans built?

Another attempt at an early rewrite of the tank scandal is Patton's posthumous 1947 memoir, *War As I Knew It*. His Deputy Chief of Staff Col. Paul Harkins was asked to organize and edit Patton's diaries. His comments on Patton's role in the scandal are illuminating, showing an "official version" taking shape, as well as the detachment of the staff officer, miles apart from the terrible reality that combat tankers faced.

Harkins glossed over the inferiority of the Sherman's main gun. Instead, he gushed about the M4's mobility, as if this compensated for the gun problem. Mobility was little comfort when the enemy could punch through the M4's sides from afar, knocking it out long before its crew could get close enough to attempt a lucky shot. Frontline soldiers from privates to generals (including Eisenhower) had warned of the growing Tiger threat since early 1943. After examining a captured Tiger from Tunisia, a British intelligence report that year had rated it with classic English understatement "a considerable advance on any Allied tank."[83]

"The Tiger," another secret British evaluation dated September 30, 1943, concluded, "is a formidable vehicle, the heavy armour of which gives it a very large degree of protection. The front of the tank is immune to 6-pdr gunfire except at normal and very short range; the sides at a rather longer range, are immune at angles over 30 degrees."[84] After the war, perhaps seeking to tone down the recently-deceased Patton's culpability in the scandal, Harkins claimed concern about the Tiger's superiority (and the M4's inferiority) originated not from Allied soldiers' battlefield experience with them, but instead in the United States, through false "rumors" spread by civilians—presumably the press?

The story that spread throughout America about our tanks being inferior to German tanks finally reached the soldiers on the frontlines and caused some apprehension among them. Taking two individual tanks and comparing them on a point-by-point basis—gun, muzzle velocity, armor protection, etc.—perhaps gives a shade to the German tank, if you compare their top heavies to ours at that time [sic, Americans had no heavy tanks in action until the last days of the war, and perhaps as few as twenty].

If the two tanks met on a village street and were to fight it out…the American tank probably would have suffered. However, this was not General Patton's idea of how tanks should be used in battle. His idea was never to use tanks in a tank-to-tank fight, but to break through the enemy lines and let them run amuck in the rear areas.

General Patton, knowing how such rumors were apt to affect adversely the morale of the troops, tried to explode the rumor before its unfortunate results took effect. Patton probably knew tanks as well as any other American soldier.… He pointed out the advantage of mobility, lack of mechanical failures, power turrets, gyrostabilizers, and total numbers, in all of which we held the upper hand over the enemy…

The results were self-evident, and General Patton's faith in the American soldier, coupled with the soldier's ingenuity, guts, and fighting ability when in an American tank, did a lot to spike the nasty rumor that was likely to affect not only American fighting morale at the front, but also the morale of the workers at home, who were striving hard to produce nothing but the best.[85]

Patton liked to say, "Wars are fought by weapons but won by men." In other words, fighting spirit could compensate for inferior weapons—an easy view to hold for a general not having to directly counter Tiger and Panther tanks, cushioned from the risks faced by the typical nineteen-year-old US Army draftee buck private. This view is not unlike the thinking of Japanese leaders in the Pacific War. Facing an imminent Allied invasion of mainland Japan, they insisted to children and women training to fight that "Japanese Fighting Spirit" (*yamato damashii*), *kamikazes*, and civilians with bamboo pikes could stop invading fleets disgorging Shermans onto the Japanese mainland.

Harkins' patronizing account virtually ignores the gun issue and Patton's obstruction of the T26. The idea that GIs were incapable of forming their own views about German tanks (based on real world experience of fighting them for years), but instead had them spoon fed by civilians at home, is particularly insulting. And for Patton to supposedly mention Army leaders' faith in their men is particularly obscene, because those leaders had betrayed what faith GIs had in them by avoiding the tank problem for years and willfully obstructing solutions. Later, the brass offered weak excuses to sweep their sins under the rug, the better to protect their careers, never mind the thousands of American dead and wounded.

In a similar postwar cleanup of the scandal, Patton's West Point classmate Gen. Jacob Devers (who had led the Armored Force) argued the M4 "did the job,"[86] while glossing over the cost. Tankers who had to wait until 1944 for such basic improvements as a second (loader's) escape hatch added to the M4's

turret—to say nothing of a better main gun—would dispute this. Since North Africa, they had been warning Ordnance that wounded loaders were being burned to death trying to exit the single hatch they shared with the tank commander and gunner.

A 1946 retrospective by Chrysler Corporation (one of eleven builders of Shermans and other tanks) also ducks the issue of tank gun effectiveness. Instead, the late FDR is channeled to bombard the reader with statistics. Detroit had spewed out "…25,059 medium and heavy tanks of twelve different types…. Of these, 22,234 were new, 2,825 were rebuilt. This was twice the number of all B-17 Flying Fortresses built…. The plant built tanks enough to equip more than 100 armored divisions, plus 3,126 [railroad] car loads of replacement parts." To drive home the point, readers were assured the Nazis "…were not whipped by quantities alone. Our tanks were better and we used them more intelligently…. No one was more outraged by the critics of the Sherman tank than was the late George Patton, and no one was better qualified to reply." The book then quotes Patton's public "deliberately mendacious individuals" letter to Gen. Handy.[87]

Gen. Gladeon Barnes, as head of Ordnance's Research and Design Service and an advocate for the T26, was a central figure in the tank scandal. He had privately damned the M4 in a 1944 diary entry as a "waste of government money"[88] and disagreed with Patton, who rejected mass production of the T26 to replace the M4. Yet in his 1947 book *Weapons of World War II* this was whitewashed; changing his tune, Barnes now insisted the Sherman had been "gradually developed into one of the most reliable track-laying tanks in the world's history…. Praise of the M4 medium tank was universal in all theaters, and it would take many pages to record adequately the performance of this important weapon of war." For good measure, Gen.Barnes jumped wholeheartedly on to the late Gen. Patton's bandwagon of excuses and attacks on the Sherman's critics by also reproducing Patton's "mendacious individuals" letter to Gen. Handy.[89]

Today production figures of US weapons are still celebrated, while the fundamental question of their quality is often glossed over or ignored. The boasting has become so pervasive it appears in works unrelated to military history. A cultural history of the American middle class exults over the "miracle" of "wartime production…this magnificent increase in production":

> In 1939 America manufactured 2,000 military planes; in 1944 it made about 100,000, including 16,000 heavy bombers. By 1944, the American work force turned out almost half of the total armament production of all other nations, allies and enemies combined. Productivity increased as well. The first standard freighter, the Liberty Ship, took eight months to build; before the end of the war, it was finished in seven weeks.[90]

Instead of questioning his involvement in the Sherman tank scandal, a 1990 biography of Gen. Marshall exults in the satisfaction he could take in "the torrents of tanks, more than 88,000 built since 1940; …the 2.5 million jeeps and trucks…of 12.6 million rifles and carbines, and a million machine guns."[91]

Occasionally, a rare account will poke at the outer edges, hinting at the truth behind the numbers. "The American decision to postpone development of the Sherman's successor," observes a 2005 work, "was nearly disastrous."[92] But it also falls prey to the big production myth; while claiming the US hoped to "depend upon vast numbers of improved Shermans,"[93] the author fails to mention they were never built.

Or we read, "The situation…was only partially redeemed when the British fitted the Sherman with their own good 17-pounder (76.2mm) gun in 1944."[94] While this statement is correct, the author neglects to elaborate that the Firefly was built in inadequate numbers, and that when the British offered one of the war's best expedient solutions to the tank scandal, a tank with a more effective gun, the American brass rejected them outright.

Some books written decades after the war, while acknowledging American technical inferiority in tanks, gloss over the cost in young men and the shortage of replacements. From 1994: "Fortunately for the Allies, the Wehrmacht lacked the numbers of tanks that might have proven decisive, and the superiority of German manufacture was in the end overcome by the plenitude of Shermans…"[95]

For decades, the accepted "history" of the Sherman tank scandal has also reflected a rank and class bias noted by Sgt. James Jones, in which the lowly enlisted GI is expendable; the human cost is often ignored or brushed aside. In 2015 work on Gen. McNair, author Mark Calhoun laments that "media attention" during the war and "many of the historical accounts of the war written in the intervening decades…remained focused on tanks." He condemns an alleged "disproportionate focus" on what he calls "relatively minor issues related to the U.S. Army's combat effectiveness."[96]

Recall Sgt. Jones' bitter but accurate observation:

> History is always written from the viewpoints of the leaders….and always filtered through the ideals system they and the other members of their class, the commanders, shared and adhered to. The Private remembers it from the viewpoint of his lower class ideals, or lack of them, while the historian has written it from the viewpoint of the upper class commanders and their totally different ideals. That is why there can be such a glaring discrepancy between the history of a battle, and the way it was played out in reality on the field.[97]

The loss of thousands of tankers killed and wounded in action is hardly a "minor issue" to their families, fellow soldiers, and loved ones. Calhoun is a retired Army field-grade officer who praises Gen. McNair for his "remarkably accurate concept of modern warfare."[98]

When it debuted in 1942, the M4 was a decent tank. The problems arose when the US failed to keep up with German and Russian advances that improved their equipment by leaps and bounds, even as American tank design stagnated, crippled by bureaucratic and doctrinal disputes among stateside brass. Notes one author, "The United States, while certainly not producing the war's finest tank, had a more sensible strategy [than Germany's]. It designed one tank, the M4 Sherman, stuck with it through a variety of upgrades and alterations, and produced it in incredible mass…. In sum, the Sherman was a versatile, sturdy, reliable design…. U.S. industry churned out nearly 50,00 of them during the war." However, like others, author Michael Citino lets the brass off the hook, indulging in the excuse that the end justified the means. "U.S. tank units sustained heavy casualties against their German adversaries, but superior numbers usually gave them victory anyway…. That [the M4] was never a 'supertank' like the Panther should not blind anyone to the fact that it did, after all, win the war."[99]

The 1970s was a time of great mistrust of government; media and historians exulted in exposing the sins of Watergate, the Pentagon Papers, the CIA, etc. Yet "The Good War" myths remained sacred, inviolate. *Total War* was published in 1973, a comprehensive history of WWII by historians Peter Calvocoressi, Guy Wint, and John Pritchard. Yet in this massive volume (later revised and updated several times) the authors tread lightly on the tank scandal.

Even in revised 1989 and 2001 editions, while it is acknowledged that "The Sherman did not give the western allies the superiority over German models which they were looking for," esteemed historians whose credentials include Oxford University and the London School of Economics assert the T26 "…which came into service in 1944 [sic—recall the T26 did not arrive in the ETO until early 1945, in the last weeks of the European war], proved a match for the latest German tanks, the Tiger and Panther."[100] There is also the usual exaltation over Sherman production numbers, but no mention of how few Pershings were actually built, or of the years of delay in getting even small numbers of them to the front.

In an extensively researched and documented 2002 biography of Eisenhower there is barely any mention of it. Author

Trieste, January 1948: A dependable M4 of the 15th Tank Company rolls on into the postwar era. Note the Yugoslavian communist slogan (red star) on the building in this disputed area between Italy and Yugoslavia. Decades later the author, an M1 Abrams tank crewman, served with the 1/104th Cavalry in Bosnia-Herzegovina. *US Army Signal Corps*

Carlo D'Este includes only two vague passing references describing Ike in North Africa in December 1942, sending "his old friend Patton...to inspect the front and report back why Allied tank losses were so high."[101] While noting M3 Lees were "helpless" against Mark IV tanks (without explaining why), and that "Patton's somber report to Eisenhower offered little encouragement," D'Este concludes incorrectly, "the eventual arrival of the new Sherman tank would even the playing field somewhat."[102] He then leaves the subject of American tank quality vs. German suspended in 1943, as if the next two years of worsening problems never happened.

The only other veiled reference to the tank scandal is an aside with no elaboration that in the late 1944–1945 battles to enter Germany, American tanks "functioned poorly."[103] The tankers' ordeal in Normandy and the Bulge, the scandal reaching the front pages of major national newspapers and the president's State of the Union Address by early 1945, and the calls for a congressional investigation all had Eisenhower as a central figure, yet they rate no mention.

This is not to imply that D'Este or others are intentionally perpetuating a cover-up; rather, it reflects wartime culprits' postwar success at obscuring the issues. The whitewash has been so thorough that even recent accounts like D'Este's ignore the scandal entirely, or overemphasize the "landing craft" or "bridge" argument. Perhaps D'Este unconsciously identified with the senior officer's lofty viewpoint and frame of mind of Eisenhower, rather than that of the lowly draftee private. "No man is a hero to his valet," as the saying goes; visiting his father at Camp Ord, California, John Eisenhower met his valet, a "handsome, slow-moving Southern boy who bore the contradictory name of [Pvt.] Blizzard.... He was probably straight off the farm, and also, like so many of the soldiers of that day, a fugitive from the Great Depression. I liked him." But in John's view, then-Col. Eisenhower barely noticed him. "None of us ever asked Blizzard's first name.... I doubt that Ike even saw him that evening.... Though Ike always respected every man and woman as an individual, some people attracted his notice and others did not. Blizzard fell into the second category—only a name, totally interchangeable with any other Army private."[104]

Perhaps Ike needed this detachment to send men to their deaths, but it is easy to see how such a callous attitude to one's subordinates can lead to, for example, Gen. Marshall virtually damning the GIs as cowards giving aid and comfort to the enemy, or Patton attacking his own men as ignorant, "deliberately mendacious" troublemakers for warning of problems with the Sherman tank.

Like novelist James Jones, British historian John Laffin has written that military history often overlooks the enlisted soldiers who *make* that history. Instead, one reads

> accounts of strategy and tactics and political and logistical considerations, and after reading them, a reader might well wonder why they rarely mention soldiers, except in terms of military units. Even regimental histories devote much more space to plans and concepts than to the men who were used to implement the plans.... Some generals talk about "the troops" in their memoirs, but rarely in any personal way; at best they are no more than patronizing.[105]

Historian Gerald Linderman has noted a gap in the history of WWII: "the absence from the literature of a corrective for a bias of social class." The experiences recorded in memoirs of prominent, high-ranking leaders like Eisenhower, Patton, Bradley, etc., were hardly that of the typical GI, but "Combat soldiers did not often issue from those sectors of society given to the habit of recording experience..."[106] Ironically, "Even in an American army enlisting significant numbers of middle-class privates, those who bore the most extended combat often did not write, and those who wrote seldom sustained prolonged combat. The reactions of visitors [i.e., civilian correspondents, or generals not long exposed to the frontlines] dominated the written record."[107]

Generals writing for posterity after the war showed a rank and class bias that obscured the real story as lived on the ground, reflecting a career officer's frame of reference. Historians writing decades later continue to perpetuate a rank and class bias in favor of the Army brass, further obscuring the true history of the tank scandal. Sgt. James Jones, who championed the WWII enlisted GI in *From Here to Eternity*, later wrote of this class bias:

> In my old age I have come to believe that the whole of written history is miscreated and flawed by the discrepancies in the two ideals systems: the one of how we would all like to believe humanity might be, but only the privileged can afford to believe it is; and the one of how we all really know humanity in fact is, but none of us wants to believe it.... So that one can perhaps honestly say that history is in fact written by the upper classes for the upper classes. And if that is so, then the whole history of my generation's World War II has been written, not wrongly so much, but in a way that gave precedence to the viewpoints of strategists, tacticians and theorists, but gave little more than lip service to the viewpoint of the hairy, swiftly aging, fighting lower class soldier.[108]

One notes this rank and class bias in a 2015 biography of Gen. Lesley McNair; in a veritable "Nuremberg defense," author

Mark Calhoun argues that McNair was not to blame for the TD debacle because he was merely following the orders of the ultimate authority: Gen. Marshall. The book cover's glowing reviews omit the opinions of the average enlisted or non-commissioned GI in WWII—the supposed beneficiaries of McNair's alleged genius. Instead, two current generals assure us that Gen. McNair was "the right man in the right place and the right time," deserving of "the position of honor as one of our top military thinkers of all time."[109]

One wishes throughout the book that he had included the views of the end users of McNair's failed Tank Destroyers, the enlisted tankers. While Calhoun describes his work environment at the Army's School of Advanced Military Studies (SAMS) and Combined Arms Command (CAC) Headquarters at Fort Leavenworth as one that encourages "intellectual curiosity and creative thinking,"[110] such an ivory tower atmosphere is far removed from that endured by a lowly TD man in 1942–43, for example: saddled with the disastrous M6 Fargo, a small pickup truck mounting only a puny 37mm gun to fight Tiger tanks in North Africa, Tunisia, and Sicily. This and other failed TDs were the result of McNair's arrogant refusal to reconsider obsolete doctrine that reflected the desired ideal conditions of 1940, rather than the battlefield reality of 1943. Yet Professor Calhoun insists McNair "deserves the nickname that Marshall gave him: the brains of the Army." McNair, he assures us, "... stands out as a key figure in moving American thinking about modern warfare forward."[111]

Surprisingly, historians from generations made cynical by Vietnam and Watergate, conditioned to instinctively question the actions of the government and military, have virtually ignored the Sherman tank scandal. Sir Max Hastings has noted the tendency to romanticize WWII, for example, in the popular books of Stephen Ambrose. "There is absolutely nothing wrong with the creation of romantic records of military experience, which bring a glow to the hearts of many readers—as long as their limitations as history are understood."[112]

Even while reading the vilest motives into President Nixon's actions in Cambodia or President Bush's actions in Iraq, historians who repeat FDR's recitations of production figures ignore or excuse away the lack of an American medium or heavy tank able to best Germany's. They also repeat the fairy tale that the T-26 arrived in the nick of time to save the day in the ETO; "The President," a typical entry in the canon of FDR worship assures us, "took care not to promise more than he could deliver,"[113] a claim that would come as a surprise to GIs whose only contact with FDR's promised "thousands" of T-26s was seeing them in newspaper photographs.

The Vietnam War, and more recent wars in Afghanistan and Iraq, saw fervent criticism of American leaders—yet the same critics continue to sanitize and mythologize WWII as "The Good War" led and fought by "The Greatest Generation." Ironically, those who protested the political and military "establishment" of the 1960s have become apologists for the "establishment" of the 1940s.

Recent accounts have taken a less fawning look at Roosevelt's loose relationship with the truth. "Duplicity was second nature to FDR," writes author Jonathan Jordan:

> His mind was not a windowless house, but a house with mirrors, prisms, and false doors, easy to enter but hard

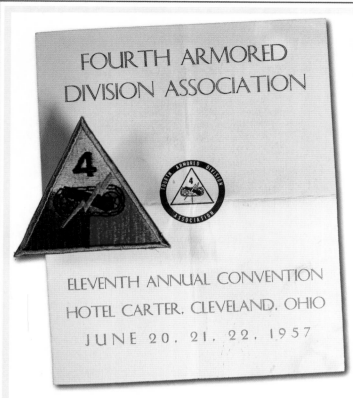

to navigate. Visitors on opposite sides of an issue left the White House convinced that Roosevelt was in their corner, and FDR's compulsion to tell visitors what they wanted to hear sometimes required him to affirm untruths. He rarely placed himself in the position of telling a bald-faced lie he'd have to ask forgiveness for it later, but he would go to extraordinary lengths to stretch facts and conceal the truth, when the truth become uncomfortable.[114]

But Jordan, while refreshingly unsentimental through most of his account, instinctively lapses into the conventional wartime hyperbole to describe the Normandy beachhead as "breathtaking… it was as if a titanic bin holding the jumbled product of the capitalist world had been upended onto Normandy's shingle… tanks, self-propelleds, ambulances, and bulldozers. Crates of medicines, grenades, bread ovens, spare tires…. The farms and factories of the New World had crashed into the Old with the fury of a democracy roused to anger."[115]

While Roosevelt's dishonesty is a factor in the complicated causes of the scandal, the stodgy climate of Army high command bears major blame as well. Author David Johnson has pointed out the temptation of Army leadership to blame the anti-military spirit of the 1930s (in which civilians and Congress were unwilling to finance large amounts of military spending on new tanks, for instance) for the scandal.

In 1941 General Marshall described the Army on September 1, 1939—the day the European war began and the day he was sworn in as Chief of Staff—as "ineffective," its equipment "in a large measure obsolescent." Marshall blamed this on "the continuing paring of appropriations" that "had reduced the Army virtually to the status of a third-rate power."[116]

Gen. John Wood, who led the 4th Armored Division, described the interwar climate in his 1979 memoir *Tiger Jack*:

Gen. John S. Wood, 4th Armored Division, nicknamed "P" for "Professor."

Back to normalcy was the post-war slogan, and back to normalcy the post-war Army went, struggling to keep alive a flickering flame and faltering spirit of national preparedness, struggling to maintain and modernize its arms and equipment, and struggling for its very life to obtain the funds necessary for its meager existence. Back it went to promotions few and far between, to small posts and small units, and to the apathy that follows periods of high endeavor.[117]

But as Johnson (a retired Army colonel and author of the acclaimed *Fast Tanks and Heavy Bombers: Innovation In The U.S. Army, 1917-1945*) observed, even when Army leaders had massive funding spurred by the emergency conditions of 1940, they maintained outdated ideas on the use of armor. As the war began and went on for years, generals failed to give US tanks and armor doctrine a hard, realistic reassessment in light of changing battlefield conditions. The scarcity of funding for tank development in the interwar years had certainly contributed to later problems, but Army leadership's intolerance for institutional self-criticism also bears major responsibility for the Sherman tank scandal. As David Johnson (a senior research staff member at RAND and former National Defense University professor) elaborated to the author, "the failure was before the war" in the Army's flawed organizational response to the blitzkrieg, including outdated, unrealistic armor doctrine to which the enemy refused to conform. To Johnson, Army senior leadership was "trapped inside their cultures, preferences, and ways of doing things":

As Generals Isaac White and Maurice Rose's reports to Eisenhower show, even senior Army officers were concerned about the mismatch with German armor. But to put it in context from a strategic perspective, the fact that our tanks were inferior to massed German armor was not blatantly apparent at high levels until after the Bulge.

My bigger concern is not what Eisenhower knew and when, but what did the Army as an institution know? We developed the tank in a way that made it a good Infantry support weapon, or an "iron horse" for traditional Cavalry missions. General McNair was in charge of developing organizational solutions for the Army Ground Forces, and he was convinced that tank destroyers were the answer to massed German armor; [instead of fighting enemy tanks], armored divisions were to support breakthrough operations.

Although General Jacob Devers, Chief of the Armored Force, had reported back from North Africa that Tiger Is were present there, I don't believe the tank problem was apparent to Eisenhower until after the Bulge. The

US Marine Cpl. Jim Diodato, the author's great-uncle, survived the ordeal of the 4th Marines, 6th Marine Division on Okinawa in 1945. Over five decades later, recalling images of burning Sherman tanks and tankers on "Okie," he warned the author of the dangers of becoming a tank crewman. He is pictured here as a raw but proud "Boot," Parris Island, May 1943. *Photo by Robert Coldwell Sr.*

initial problem in Normandy was fighting through the hedgerows, and once Patton broke out, our armored divisions were doing what McNair and others had designed them to do. There were difficulties, like bumping into a tank or a few tanks in defense, but a combination of [Allied] air, artillery, and tank fire prevailed. It wasn't until the Bulge that the Germans actually massed armor against U.S. formations [the ideal but rarely occurring "textbook" conditions for which US armor doctrine had been created to handle].

In the aftermath of the Bulge, and in the difficult fighting into Germany, tankers and others began talking to the press. [After receiving the White and Rose reports], Eisenhower immediately got on the problem and requested T-26s, but by then, the war was almost over; U.S. formations were driving into Germany, and only facing small numbers of German tanks at a time.

This is where the Army got it wrong: by not seeing what the Germans were doing. We were trapped inside our own cultures, preferences, and ways of doing things. This is not to excuse anybody, but to point out that once the war was on, there were so many looming catastrophes that in many cases, we had to make do with what we had.[118]

That in early 1945 Patton, visited by Ordnance officials from the States and asked to suggest improvements in tank design, only asked for more coaxial machine guns exemplifies this bu-

reaucratic inertia and resistance to change. After years of photographing burned out hulks of American tanks from North Africa to Bastogne, and witnessing the success of better armed and armored German tanks; after all he had seen of tank warfare in North Africa, Tunisia, Sicily, and Western Europe, Patton's views on tank design in 1945 remained vintage 1938. This alludes to a larger, institutional problem, a lack of flexibility at the Army's highest levels.

Few military historians (never mind the general public) realize there was a second T26 tank scandal after VE Day—in the Pacific Theater. The largest battle of the Pacific War—the Okinawa Campaign—began on April 1, 1945, during which the author's great-Uncle, Cpl. James Diodato, made the initial Easter Sunday assault landings with the 4th Marine Regiment, Sixth Marine Division and fought throughout the campaign as a machine gunner and occasional flame thrower operator.

When the fighting on Okinawa continued for months against steep Japanese resistance and inadequately armored M4s took losses from potent Japanese anti-tank guns, artillery, and mines, it was planned to ship a mere 12 Pershings (which had missed the initial Easter Sunday assault landing in April, when they might have been most effective) to Okinawa. As a 4th Marine Tank Battalion report from April 1945 described the need, based on problems during the Iwo Jima campaign alone, the M4 "should be replaced" by the T26:

M4 series tanks are extremely vulnerable to 47mm AT fire, magnetic mines, shaped charges, and field artillery. This is especially true in operations against a well-manned, heavily fortified position or in a situation over difficult terrain, where the M4 loses its maneuverability. The 75mm M3 Tank [main gun], the primary armament of the M4 series tank, is not effective against well-constructed, reinforced concrete positions.... The M26 presents the following advantages over the M4. It is shorter, wider, and lower, presenting a lower silhouette; it weighs forty-four tons, the additional weight being caused by increased armor.[119]

Eventually T26s were delivered to "Okie," but in a sad repeat of the 1918 fiasco—and of the recent Zebra Mission in the ETO—the Pershings were still on the loading docks when the Japanese on Okinawa surrendered; the mere dozen that were sorely needed never reached the front during the fighting.

There was no reckoning for the Sherman tank scandal in the Pacific, and it barely made the papers and radio shows back home. Perhaps civilians were exhausted after the long war. Roosevelt had conveniently died just in time to avoid questions about why a mere twelve Pershings arrived too late for the biggest, bloodiest battle of the Pacific War, missed the entire campaign (82 days long), and never left the docks before the Japanese surrender on Okinawa in mid-June.

While Japan's artillery, anti-tank guns, and mines took a toll of M4s, Hirohito's army lacked large numbers of heavy tanks. No Japanese tank design matched the infamy of the King Tiger, Tiger, and Panther in the European Theater, which may explain why the failure to get the T26 to the Pacific is virtually unknown to most historians today.

*Tank - Infantry Team on Cape Gloucester* by Marine Sgt. Vick Donahue.

Okinawa was the war's largest battle and the greatest amphibious invasion, involving more men, ships, planes, landing craft, etc., than the more publicized Normandy landings. Considering how many thousands of ships, men, planes, and tanks were delivered halfway around the world to Japan's doorstep, why the failure to send a mere dozen Pershings in time for the initial April 1, 1945, assaults? Most popular and specialized accounts of the war ignore this debacle, sanctifying the fruits of the "Arsenal of Democracy" in the European Theater.

The Japanese may not have had a Tiger tank equivalent, but tank fighting on "Okie" was no picnic; the US lost an estimated 225 tanks. Sherman crews encountered Japanese "special attack" troops willing to charge them with dynamite on bamboo poles and wired up with satchel charges to blow themselves up against the Sherman's thin belly. I vividly remember my uncle's reaction when announcing I was joining the US Army to become a new generation of tanker; in addition to his congratulations and best wishes, my salty WWII Marine uncle, Cpl. Jim Diodato, vividly recalled to me a still-clear memory from Okinawa in 1945: seeing the body of an American tanker sitting in the burned-out hulk of a knocked out Sherman.

The Pershing was needed for the biggest battle of the Pacific War, in which some 62,000 Americans were killed, wounded, or missing in action. Once again, Army and political leaders failed to deliver better tanks—just as they had in the European theater and in 1918. But today, this Pacific War tank scandal remains a footnote to the problems in the ETO.

Soon after the final Japanese surrender in September 1945, the US Army General Board convened to distil the lessons of the European campaign. It put the last nail in the coffin of the Tank Destroyer fiasco, deciding that with the trend toward "tanks with high velocity weapons capable of destroying other tanks," the once-hyped TD, a poor substitute for a true tank, was now superfluous: "If a tank is given to the Infantry with a proper anti-tank gun, the division commanders favor the replacement of a tank destroyer with a tank."[120]

Even before the German surrender, Eisenhower had written the Army's Adjutant General Gen. James Ulio on April 5, with his thoughts on "Post-Hostilities Planning" and "the Post-War Military Establishment." As well as calling for "...a separate branch for the mechanized forces...called the Armored Branch," he wrote, "I personally believe that the armored anti-tank or tank destroyer weapon is an anomaly. In this type of weapon we should seek merely to have a better tank in armor and in gun then we expect to encounter."[121]

The seemingly obvious conclusion that tanks fight tanks, and that beating an enemy tank requires a better American tank, was finally conceded. The September general board agreed that future designs (even light tanks) should not mount a puny 37mm gun. Instead, the armored divisions should adopt as the "minimum standard for future development" tanks with "a gun capable of penetrating the sides and rear of any enemy armored vehicle and the front of any but the heaviest assault tank, at normal fighting ranges."[122]

Addressing the M4's inadequate armor and tendency to catch fire when hit, the board called for "frontal armor and armor over the ammunition stowage...capable of withstanding all foreign tank and anti-tank weapons at normal combat ranges."[123] Recall an Austrian tank expert had recommended this for German tanks as well in 1935.

The "radical" ideas of tank pioneers, debated and opposed since 1918, were vindicated at last, but at a terrible cost. After decades of acrimony, the reality that tanks fight tanks was not only conceded, it became official US Army tank doctrine. Today the cause of so much bitter controversy from 1918–1945 that led to thousands of American deaths is accepted without a murmur. This doctrine is epitomized by the present M1 Abrams main battle tank, designed to not only shoot up "soft" targets in the enemy's rear, but also to take on and beat their best heavy tanks.

The General Board's conclusions and acceptance of these hard-fought ideas gave tankers a measure of vindication, but the human price of the failure to keep up with German armor remains.

About the closest to an apology and confession to the victims of the tank scandal and their survivors came from Gen. Marshall

An M4 Sherman on "Okie" (Okinawa). Note the improvised enhanced armor to deflect the growing threat of Japanese anti-tank guns.

Fort Benning, Georgia: Two views of an M1A1 Abrams tank in desert paint scheme. *Author photo, courtesy of the National Armor & Cavalry Heritage Foundation*

in October 1945. "Some German Weapons Topped Ours, Marshall Admits," read headlines:

> Now that there is no longer need for secrecy, the Army can and does admit there was some truth in the frequent wartime reports that American weapons did not always measure up to German ones. In his biennial report as Chief of Staff, made to the Secretary of War, Gen. George

C. Marshall frankly says the Sherman tanks were never able to stand up to the heavier Nazi Tigers and Panthers...

He made what amounted to an apology for the failure of the Army to admit these things during the war. Indeed, high-ranking military chiefs, while the fighting was still going on, answered critics of American equipment by praising it to the skies and never admitting there was anything wrong with it.[124]

*Photo by Robert Coldwell Sr.*

Motivated, confident German tankers had boasted *Wir werden sieger—durch unsren Tiger* ("We will be victorious—thanks to our Tiger"). In the end, the "victory" went to the plain, utilitarian M4, but the cost was high. As a tanker sergeant opined in the secret White-Rose Report to Ike, "We've got a good tank—for parades and training purposes—but for combat, they are just potential coffins."[125]

GIs with firsthand experience had warned their leaders for years of the need for a better tank, but they went largely unheeded until it was too late. Yet in May 1945, Patton, who preferred "spirit" to the better weapons his men were begging for, admonished them in his General Orders 9 (to all "soldiers of the Third Army, past and present"): "let us never forget our heroic dead whose graves mark the course of our victorious advances, nor our wounded whose sacrifice aided so much in our success."[126]

Distinguished British historian Sir Max Hastings' 1984 *Overlord: D-Day and the Battle for Normandy* was a standout in a sea of upbeat, jingoistic fortieth anniversary works, because Hastings poked at the edges of some sacred myths: he questioned "the greatest failure...that of the tank. How could American and British industries produce a host of superb aircraft, an astonishing variety of radar equipment, the proximity fuse, the DUKW, the jeep—yet still ask their armies to join battle against the *Wehrmacht* equipped with a range of tanks utterly inferior in armour and killing power?" After an unsentimental look, Hastings suggested "Hitler's army was the outstanding fighting force of the Second World War."

For questioning the established "Good War" propaganda, Hastings was hit with "a revisionist movement against such a view. Several writers, notably in the United States, have written books arguing that authors such as myself overrate the German performance."[127] The cherished, simplistic, John Wayne version of Normandy from *The Longest Day* died hard.

Some recognized and resented the dishonesty in popular culture's depictions of the war; in oral historian Studs Terkel's seminal *"The Good War"* (1984), a civilian woman's anger was still perceptible decades later:

As the war dragged on and on and on, we read of the selfish actions of men in power.... You can only feed 'em so much bullshit.... I was lied to. I was cheated. I was made a fool of. If they had said to me, "Look, this has to be done and we'll all go out and do the job... we'll all get our arms and legs blown off, but it has to be done," I'd understand. If they didn't hand me all this shit with the uniforms and the girls in their pompadours dancing at the USO and all those songs—"There'll Be Bluebirds Over The White Cliffs of Dover"—bullshit... we were sold a bill of goods.[128]

Former Army Infantry officer Paul Fussell laconically judges this "A fairly accurate characterization...of the whole fictive world created by wartime Public Relations."[129] A perceptive cultural and literary critic as well as a WWII Infantry officer, Fussell described Eisenhower's intelligence failures in the Ardennes in words that could be an epitaph for the tank scandal. "The problem was not really one of paucity of evidence and data. It was, as so often, complacency and the lust for intellectual comfort overriding the meaning of evidence.... Given the numerous failures of the mind to detect what afterward seems almost obvious, one must conclude that the mind is not so capable as it pretends of producing trustworthy knowledge, so easily is it threatened by fatigue, pride, laziness, and selfish inattention."[130]

Most American civilians never heard the full story of the Sherman tank scandal, and families of tankers killed in action never learned the complicated reasons why.

Trying to cushion the blows, Lt. Jim Gifford gave a mother a sanitized account of her tanker son's gruesome death:

I was from Gloversville, New York, There was a fellow from Albany in my outfit, Fred Putnam. He was killed at Mairy, France. He was a [tank] bow gunner...an armor-piercing shell came in and went through him, killed him instantly.... Then the tank burned, so they didn't bury Putnam. There was nothing to bury.

After the war, I went to see his mother. She asked me how he died. I told her some of the details, but I didn't have the heart to tell her how he was cremated.

I said there was a church nearby, and there was a cemetery in the churchyard, a walled yard with a cemetery in it, and that he and some other soldiers that were unknown were buried there, and the people in that church tended to the graves.

She said to me, "Oh, I'm so glad. I wondered what happened to him."

I didn't have the heart to tell her. It gave her something to live with, you know?

I don't know if I was right or I was wrong, but I think I was right.[131]

Today, instead of the complicated truth—that the American war effort in WWII featured not only heroism, but also folly, tragedy, pride, arrogance, and incompetence at the highest levels of government and military—we are often provided with a heroic Roosevelt, the martyr and "soldier of freedom" who fell leading the "Arsenal of Democracy." Stern, dignified Gen. Marshall, a second George Washington. Lovable, grinning Ike. And bold, dashing, and rebellious Patton.

In Leesburg, Virginia, I have walked up Gen. George Marshall's stairs leading to his and Mrs. Marshall's bedrooms and felt the sadness that permeates Dodona Manor, a home in which, beside signed pictures of kings and prime ministers hailing the Allies' "Organizer of Victory" also hang a prominent oil painting and bedside photos of Lt. Brown, killed in his Sherman tank on the road to Rome.

In my native Pennsylvania, I have walked the grounds of Camp Colt, Gettysburg, where toy-like, two-man FT-17 Renaults rolled in 1918 as a young "Captain Ike," one of America's first tankers, began to make a name for himself. As an old soldier, I would have been honored to be led by an Army officer whose innate decency inspired even the notoriously rude and aloof Charles de Gaulle to tell his widow at his 1969 funeral, *Vous savez, que le general etait pres de mon Coeur* ("You know that the general was close to my heart").[132]

The United States was blessed with leaders like Marshall, Eisenhower, and Patton, who accomplished miracles of improvisation, organization, and diplomacy, and injected the rookie US Army with an aggressive fighting spirit. But their impressive accomplishments under very difficult circumstances should not blind us to the fact that these men were all too human, as much subject to arrogance, pride, and short-sightedness as anyone. The true story of American leadership in WWII should acknowledge this. Instead, George Marshall, who grieved for the loss of his tanker stepson, is depicted as a cold, infallible "Marble Man." Ike is served up as a genial back-slapper, a babe in the political wilderness instead of a tough-minded leader as willing and able to exploit public relations to smooth out the rough spots in the historical record as any disingenuous Roosevelt appointee. By depicting them today in cartoonish, shallow terms we diminish them.

This book was not written in a spirit of malice, nor to "tear down" great American heroes; instead, it attempts to humanize them, in rejection of the one-dimensional "good war." My research took me to places like Ft. Benning, Georgia, where I have walked through one of Gen. George Patton's original 1942 maintenance sheds full of rare, restored WWII tanks. There, I felt the excitement his live-wire personality—in the finest US Cavalry tradition of boldness, élan, dash, and daring that I was privileged to inherit as a member of the First Troop Philadelphia City Cavalry—brought to a new generation of American tankers about to take on Hitler's best.

At Fort Knox, Kentucky, I have seen the car in which Patton suffered the traffic accident wounds that would kill him in 1945, a bitter irony for an old soldier who wanted to fall from the last bullet in the last battle. On Campobello Island, New Brunswick, Canada, I stood in Franklin Roosevelt's bedroom, on the very wooden floor that he crawled across one frightening night in 1921, crying out for help when stricken with polio.

But as a wartime photographer recalled his carefully stage-managed coverage of the Normandy landings to Studs Terkel, "You were told which was their good side and which was their bad side, and you only photographed them from their good side."[133]

After it was followed by controversial wars like Korea, Vietnam, and Iraq, WWII is still portrayed as a model of the alleged efficiency and effectiveness of America's political and military leadership: Why could not wartime leaders Johnson, Nixon, or George W. Bush be more like FDR, the martyred, sanctified Commander in Chief?

Author and soldier James Jones observed that over time, the rough edges of America's role in WWII were carefully smoothed out, polished until they gleamed.

Much of the folly of American leadership in WWII is typically smoothed over, and it is revered as "The Good War." A 2014 book sounds little different than wartime propaganda in exulting that by 1945, "Chrysler's Detroit Tank Arsenal—a factory that didn't exist three years earlier—had now succeeded in building roughly as many tanks as all the factories in Nazi Germany combined."[134] Quantity was achieved, no doubt, but were they *quality* tanks?

A History Channel series called "Man, Moment, Machine"— about the impact of decisive technology throughout history—included an episode on Patton and the Sherman tank in 2006. A one-minute snippet from the documentary was airing in 2012. In the short feature, the young narrator is shown inside a restored Sherman's turret, at the loader's position and next to the breech of the main gun that was the cause of so much controversy and tragedy decades earlier.

Combat surgeon Brendan Phibbs, who treated 12th Armored Division tankers for wounds seen and unseen, wrote of an angry

GI damning the Sherman tank as "a ridiculous thin-walled, under-gunned piece of shit."[135] Yet for new generations unfamiliar with the passions and nuances of American participation in WWII, the smooth-cheeked documentary host confidently assures audiences born long after 1945 that the M4 was "one of the key pieces of technology that allowed Patton to be so successful in World War Two."

Some may argue, decades removed from the GIs' bitterness, "What does it matter—we won in the end, right?" As Charles Baily wrote, "after all, the US Army never suffered a major tactical reverse because of the quality of its tanks or tank destroyers.... Gen. Devers was right—the Sherman did the job. We won the war with the M4. But in northwest Europe in 1944 and 1945, particularly in the snow-clad forests of the Ardennes, the American citizens who manned the Army had to pay in blood for the US Army's failure to provide them with better weapons."[136]

Even in the second decade of the twenty-first century, uncomfortable reminders remain that behind FDR's massive production figures was a terrible human cost. In September 2015, the author spoke with 92-year-old Cpl. Jack Myers, a gunner with the 692nd Tank Destroyer Battalion in the later days of WWII. The setting, ironically enough, was Gen. and President Eisenhower's farm on the Gettysburg battlefield, close to the long-vanished site of Camp Colt.

Cpl. Myers addressed an appreciative audience in a tent within sight of Eisenhower's personal putting green in the backyard of the general's restored farmhouse. From a hole in the immaculately manicured lawn, a gentle wind blew Ike's red general of the Army flag, with its circle of five white stars, as Myers recalled his time as a "TD man" seven decades before.

Jack Myers was drafted at nineteen from Maryland, and left for training three months after marriage. At Fort Hood, Texas, home of the "TDs," he became a gunner on the M10 self-propelled TD, and on the towed three-inch gun known as "McNair's Folly" pulled around by a half-track. Disembarking at Cherbourg, France, in September 1944, he fought around Antwerp, Belgium, into the Siegfried Line, and in the Ardennes campaign, crossing the Ruhr River into Germany.

His combat experience reflects the confusion at the Army's highest levels over the role of TDs and tanks; in January 1945, Myers' unit was disrupted, reorganized. He went from fighting with the towed 3-inch guns, which were unceremoniously dumped after years of training on them (and after Gen. McNair's stubborn insistence that towed guns, not better tanks, were the answer to stopping Panzers) to the new M36 Jackson TD with a more powerful 90mm gun—which he liked. About half the 692nd transitioned to the new vehicle, while the unlucky half were packed off to the Infantry.

## SECRET

Battalion, and the third platoon Company "B", vicinity of LUCHER-BERG, Germany, supporting the 929 Field Artillery Battalion. Two platoons and extra sections were in Anti-Tank positions and/or in support of Field Artillery Battalions, as follows:

| Platoon | Location | Supporting | Mission |
|---|---|---|---|
| 1A | 036471 | 386 FA & 413 CT | Indirect |
| 2A | 057466 | 413 CT | Direct |
| 3A | 085454 | 413 CT | Direct |
| Extra Section | 013484 | 413 CT | Direct |
| 1B | 073504 | 415 CT | Direct |
| 2B (atch'd "A") | 070483 | 413 CT | Direct |
| 3B | 044506 | 929 FA & 415 CT | Indirect |
| Extra Section | 015512 | 413 CT | Direct |
| Extra Section | 016497 | 413 CT | Direct |
| 1C - 1st Sec | 085439 | 413 CT | Direct |
| 2nd Sec | 092452 | 414 CT | Direct |
| 2C | 102409 | 414 CT | Direct |
| 3C - 1st Sec | 061432 | 414 CT | Direct |
| 2nd Sec | 084409 | 414 CT | Direct |
| Extra Section | 075405 | 414 CT | Direct |
| Extra Section | 084407 | 414 CT | Direct |

Map: Area "K", 1/25,000, Germany

The reconnaissance platoons operated under Battalion control. Two OP's in the vicinities of LENDERSDORF-KRAUTHAUSEN, Germany, and GURZENICH, Germany were established and maintained by the first reconnaissance platoon during this period. The second reconnaissance platoon remained in Battalion Reserve in the vicinity of ESCHWEILER, Germany.

During this period, the Battalion suffered one (1) battle casualty (killed), resulting from enemy mines. One (1) EM was given a thirty (30) day furlough in the United States as authorized by rotation plan in effect in ETO.

Since the situation was stabilized, the Battalion made a concerted drive to salvage all abandoned equipment and ammunition, both friendly and enemy. The Battalion S-4 section made organized tours within the Division Area to recover equipment and supplies of all types. As of the end of this period, the drive has been successful as large quantities of equipment have been recovered.

### Period 11 January 1945 to 20 January 1945

There was no change in disposition or support throughout the Battalion during this period.

During the period, the Battalion continued to strengthen and improve positions occupied, prepared additional "Dummy Positions", and

**SECRET**    4

## SECRET

continued in preparation of supplementary and alternate positions in accordance with FO No. 16, 104th Infantry Division, dated 29 December 1944.

The reconnaissance for positions was completed and coordinated under Plan "A", FO No. 17, 104th Infantry Division, dated 10 January 1945. These positions were prepared, which preparation was expedited by the use of bulldozers and dynamite. Plans for withdrawal, strategic or tactical, to these positions were completed in coordination with Division Plan. The preparation of these positions gave considerably more depth to the Anti-Tank defenses within the Division Sector.

Reconnaissance for sectors of responsibility and for gun positions under Plan "B", 104th Infantry Division, was completed. Selection of such positions was in conjunction with a furtherance of Division's Plan for defense in depth.

The first reconnaissance platoon continued operation of OP's at positions previously mentioned. The second reconnaissance platoon established a daylight OP in the vicinity of HOVEN, Germany, for the purpose of registering the first platoon, Company "A", and the third platoon, Company "B", and to be forward observer for targets of opportunity.

During this period the Battalion suffered two (2) Non-Battle casualties (One death resulting). Three (3) EM received the Purple Heart Award for injuries received by the result of enemy action.

The Battalion continued the salvage drive. Companies organized "Salvage-Teams" to supplement S-4 personnel in recovery of equipment and supplies. Excellent results were obtained.

Officers and EM were given "Rest Periods" under various Division Allocations.

The Battalion made preparation for instruction in weapons, tactics, etc. to be held daily within each Company.

### Period 21 January 1945 to 31 January 1945

Effective 1800 hours, 28 January 1945, first and second platoons, Company "A", inter-changed positions. Second platoon now in indirect fire position in support of 386 Field Artillery Battalion. There were no other changes in disposition throughout entire Battalion.

The Second Platoon, Company "B" relieved from attachment to Company "A", effective 2400 hours, 26 January 1945, reverted to Company "B" control. Company "C" received three (3) additional 3" guns, replacing three (3) German 75mm PAK's. As of 31 January 1945, the disposition of guns were as follows:

**SECRET**    5

## SECRET

| | 3" | 75mm | 88mm | Total |
|---|---|---|---|---|
| Company "A" | 14 | 1 | 0 | 15 |
| Company "B" | 14 | 2 | 0 | 16 |
| Company "C" | 15 | 0 | 1 | 16 |
| | 43 | 3 | 1 | 47 |

During this period the Battalion conducted training in camouflage, weapons, and tactical employment. Also, the orientation program was intensified.

The Battalion began preparation for possible conversion to Self-Propelled Tank Destroyers. A program of training was coordinated with the 692nd Tank Destroyer Battalion (SP) in assembly position in vicinity of LINCE, Belgium. Selected personnel from this Battalion attended classes being held on maintenance, employment of M-36, Self-Propelled Tank Destroyers, and observed range practice of Self-Propelled Tank Destroyers. As of 31 January 1945, this Battalion had sent four (4) Officers and forty-two (42) EM to such classes.

On 31 January 1945, meeting with Company Commanders was held at Battalion Headquarters, discussing probable conversion to Self-Propelled.

The following awards were approved during this period:

```
1 - Silver Star
9 - Bronze Stars
6 - Purple Hearts
26 - Certificates of Merit
```

The Battalion suffered two (2) Battle casualties during the period.

SAMUEL S. MORSE
Lt Col - FA
Commanding

OFFICIAL:

*George V. Carracio*
GEORGE V. CARRACIO
Maj - Cav
S-3

**SECRET**    6

## SECRET

HEADQUARTERS
692D TANK DESTROYER BATTALION
APO 230    US ARMY

ESCHWEILER, GERMANY
31 January 1945

### PART II

#### Period 1 January 1945 to 10 January 1945

The 692D Tank Destroyer Battalion, attached to 104th Infantry Division, continued to support the Infantry Regiments and to deliver reinforcing Artillery Fire in support of organic Field Artillery Battalions, as follows:

| | Infantry | Artillery |
|---|---|---|
| Company "A" | 413 | 386 |
| Company "B" | 415 | 929 |
| Company "C" | 414 | --- |

The Battalion continued to organize and deepen the Anti-Tank defense in the Division Sector, and continued the preparation of supplementary and alternate positions in accordance with FO No. 16, 104th Infantry Division, dated 29 December 1944. The Battalion prepared "Dummy Positions" in forward position areas for purposes of deception.

In accordance with FO No. 17, 104th Infantry Division, dated 10 January 1945, the Battalion initiated reconnaissance for positions for Division Plan "A".

At the beginning of this period, the Battalion had forty (40) 3" guns operational. During the period, the Battalion received five (5) additional German 75mm PAK guns; recovered and emplaced one (1) German 88mm gun and one (1) German 75mm PAK. All enemy guns were test fired prior to emplacing in position. At the end of this period, the Battalion had forty (40) 3" guns, six (6) German 75mm PAK's, and one (1) German 88mm Gun, distributed within the Battalion as follows:

| | 3" | 75mm | 88mm | Total |
|---|---|---|---|---|
| Company "A" | 14 | 1 | 0 | 15 |
| Company "B" | 14 | 2 | 0 | 16 |
| Company "C" | 12 | 3 | 1 | 16 |
| | 40 | 6 | 1 | 47 |

During this period, the Battalion had two (2) platoons in indirect fire positions, in support of the artillery. The first platoon, Company "A", vicinity of LANGERWEHE, Germany, supporting the 386 Field Artillery

**SECRET**    3

Cpl. Jack Myers, tank destroyer gunner, with his crew and an M10. On the right is his driver, Pvt. Albert Haschke, who died of combat wounds just weeks before the end of the war in Europe.

Myers was lucky, chosen to fight with the Army's newest, most powerful self-propelled "TD." Decades later, he still reflected the cockiness and pride of a motivated young tank destroyer gunner in 1945. With the M36, he bragged, "Now I could match the Germans, buddy-up to 300 yards—if I could put the crosshairs on a target, I HAD it!"[137]

Army leaders at home had information going back to the mid-1930s on the state of German tank designs—including the steadily increasing firepower of their tank guns—yet only in the last months of the war could they accept the idea that the solution to stopping powerful German tanks was a better tank. Meanwhile, GIs were saddled with thinly armored, under-gunned substitutes for real tanks. "The M10 and the M36 were vulnerable to shrapnel, with thin armor and open top turrets," remembered Myers. "We'd be shelled by German artillery, and it was like a thunderstorm. In towns, their shells would explode on the second story of a building and come down on us. We wore our steel pots [helmets] in that open turret, but we still got hit."[138]

Cpl. Myers showed me a large, rough piece of German shrapnel that struck him in 1945, denting his helmet but leaving him unscathed. He had traveled to Europe with a small group of fellow WWII veterans. In France, he got to examine a restored Tiger tank close up. "I was amazed to see how thick the armor is. When I was fighting them back in 1944–45," he joked with a grim smile, "I didn't have time to admire them up close!"[139]

When he dueled Tigers and Panthers, "Our shells bounced off of them," Myers remembered, "…they just ricocheted off. We tried to outnumber and outmaneuver them; we had to. We went around the back, or tried to knock their tracks off." Lamenting the weak firepower of most TDs, Myers damned "that 76mm main gun" as "just a peashooter compared to the German 88."[140]

Considering what he endured, Myers is cheerful, seemingly at peace, yet the human cost of being saddled with "McNair's Folly" still lingers with him seventy years later. In old sepia photos, a young, handsome Myers and his crew pose around an M-10 tank destroyer during training in Tennessee: "That's Sam Fena, Chester Bartoszek, Joe Kelley, me, Jack Myers, and Albert Haschke." Most of the crew is smiling, as if they have been interrupted during the typical Army horseplay, pranks, and ribbing that characterizes a close knit tank crew. One man stands up in the turret; three of the crew, smiling, stand close together, while off to the right, slightly apart, is an older, more mature and pensive looking soldier: "Albert was our driver, part American Indian, a farmer from Nebraska, or maybe Kansas," ironically enough Gen. Eisenhower's home state.[141]

"We lost Albert in combat in Germany," Myers laments. Records show that Technician 5 Albert T. Haschke, Army Serial Number (ASN) 37256450, succumbed to his combat wounds on March 3, 1945, barely nine weeks before the Nazi surrender. "I think about him all the time, especially around Memorial Day," Myers says.[142]

Myers has attended reunions of the 692d TD Battalion, but the years have thinned out the old muster roll. "At first, we'd have 100 men. Now we're down to only four of us left. I hope to make the next one in Hagerstown, Maryland, in 2016, probably our last reunion." After receiving another invitation to return to Europe with a select few aging WWII veterans, he jokes, "There aren't that many of us old TD men still living, so I guess they have to take me."[143]

As British tanker veteran Peter Beale wrote, "It is all too late for those tank soldiers who lie buried in a foreign field, and it is a long time ago anyway; but a nation must always be prepared to defend itself, and it should take all reasonable steps to ensure that those entrusted with its defence are properly prepared to do so."[144]

While the high and mighty fair poorly in the tank scandal, the young American enlisted and non-commissioned tanker accomplished miracles of endurance and improvisation in spite of their leaders' obstinacy. The lowly GI adapted, improvised, and overcame, doing the best he could to improve his tanks—sometimes against orders—to increase his chances of survival and victory.

Cpl. Jack Myers, M-36 Jackson gunner, 692nd Tank Destroyer Battalion, at Gettysburg, Pennsylvania, September 2015. *Photo enhancement by Robert Coldwell Sr.*

Though knowing they were inferior, day after day, he continued to climb back into tanks called "Ronsons," after a lighter guaranteed to light up the first time, every time. Eventually the Allies won a bitter victory, but today, the cost in blood remains largely unknown to the general public. We hear proud boasts of the approximately 49,234 Shermans built,[145] but rarely of the more than 60,000 killed, wounded, and deformed tankers.

As Cpl. Thomas McLane noted in comparing the Panther's superiority to the Sherman, "Our successes in Europe are a result of superiority in numbers and superiority in good, cold guts—not a result of superior tanks."[146]

Of the losses required to gain such "successes," combat surgeon Maj. Brendan Phibbs, 12th Armored Division, wrote of the GI victims, "They grasped slowly and in fragments what had been the truth of their lives all along: they were the ultimate sacrifice of the whole war."[147]

The Hollywood epic *Fury* debuted in 2014, a refreshingly unsentimental look at American tankers in WWII. A few cranky and politically correct reviewers complained WWII is ancient history, why another film honoring long dead men, even if it peels back decades of entrenched government propaganda?

In the twenty-first century, some may question what relevance the Sherman tank scandal of the 1940s has to contemporary Americans. Quite a lot: witness the ongoing Department of Veterans Affairs scandal and cover up. FDR's breezy assurances that all is well and the generals' fervent denials of the scandal have a familiar ring.

Furthermore, with the active-duty US Army in 2016 reduced to its smallest size since 1940, the issue of military preparedness for potential future conflicts in the face of foreign threats is as relevant as ever.

Fourth Armored Division tanker Sgt. Nate Frankel recalled fragmentary images of his combat in the ETO. "An American tank blows up and a man jumps out of the turret. He runs along the ground towards the nearest friendly tank, his head down, his arms dangling. A dead American Infantryman lies in his way. A German tank advances from his rear. He picks up the dead man's gun and fires at the advancing enemy, even as he runs backward towards his own. That man, whose name I can't recall," embodied to Frankel the US tanker in WWII.[148]

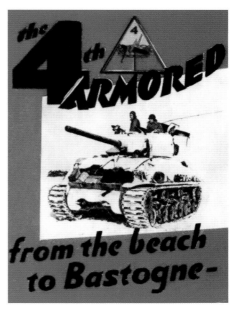

*Photo by Robert Coldwell Sr.*

History reveals the American tanker to be a lion led by goats: not only the victim, but also the hero of one of the greatest unknown, and unreckoned, scandals of WWII.

**ABOVE:** The human cost of the Sherman tank scandal: while popular culture continues to spout impressive numbers of tanks produced by FDR's "Arsenal of Democracy," the price in men has been commemorated in an accidental, little-known paper monument: the wartime Army morning reports detailing casualties in armor units. These daily lists show the grim toll of tankers killed, wounded, and died of wounds in just one unit, on just one day of a long war. *Photo by Robert Coldwell Sr., courtesy US Army Military History Institute, Carlisle Barracks, Pennsylvania*

In memory of the thousands of
American tankers killed, wounded,
and missing in action 1941–1945.

# Acknowledgments

In stepping outside the comfortable, entrenched "Good War" and "Greatest Generation" mythology to present a less sentimental view of WWII, this book stirred up heated opposition and highly personalized attacks well before its release. One author called my ideas "disruptive and antagonistic," which—considering they dare to reexamine long-accepted platitudes—they just might be. Long before the publication date I was vilified for daring to reassess the old Allied propaganda with a more detached eye, and for being open to the idea that the M4 might not have been the flawless war winner depicted in the censored, government-controlled Allied wartime press.

One website attacking this book sight unseen and unread nine months before its release called me "Pro-Fatherland," and featured a painting of a uniformed Nazi as Christ. I come from a family with dozens of WWII veterans who sacrificed to end the Nazi scourge, including an uncle buried in Arlington Cemetery who served at the Nuremburg war crimes trials that brought those criminals to justice. Having also served with the US Army in Bosnia myself to prevent political extremism I will leave it to the reader to decide on that point.

One comfortably established tank author damned me for what he presumed was going to be an attack on Col. George Jarrett, one of the heroes of the tank scandal to whom the book is dedicated. Strangely, while not a veteran himself, he also assumed that my intention was to attack my fellow Army veterans of the "Greatest Generation," belittling them as (in his phrase) "whiny cry-babies." Again, as a disabled Army veteran and proud American Legion and VFW life member, I'll let the reader decide if this book is an attack on my fellow veterans.

Ironically, for a book that is critical of WWII US Army leadership and questions the conventional wisdom on long-established Army heroes, it is remarkable how much steady support along the way came from present and former soldiers, spanning from the Pentagon, to Fort Benning, to Carlisle Barracks, and to many other locations. This support often took the form of a simple "That story needs to be told—long overdue."

Having served on four continents beside some admirable officers, there was no intent to be "anti-officer." One of my literary role models is Sgt. James Jones, an old soldier who exposed some of the Army's worst traits in novels like *From Here To Eternity* and *Whistle*, yet clearly loved the Army, warts and all, and his fellow soldiers. His generation of veterans, including the enlisted GI victims of the Sherman tank scandal, needed to read the sometimes angry truth that Jones' writing has preserved, some of the best ever written on the US Army. His books are as relevant to soldiers and concerned civilians today as in the WWII era that Sgt. Jones, who witnessed Pearl Harbor and Guadalcanal, captured so well.

From present and former soldiers, my requests for information, access, and support never met with "That's too controversial," or "Why does it matter—in the end, we won?" but usually, "Great idea—how can I help you?" or "I'd read that book!"

During my own service as an M1 Abrams tank gunner with the historic First Troop Philadelphia City Cavalry and Apache Troop, 1/104th Cavalry, 28th Infantry Division, I was taught tanks from the ground up, as well as Army and Cavalry pride, spirit, and integrity, from exemplary non-commissioned officers like SFC Logan Fenstermacher, who taught me to drive and gun the Abrams tank, as well as many other things about gruff but caring leadership; and SFC Christopher J. Heyman, now serving as Readiness NCO of A Troop. SFC Heyman, who denies (but not with much conviction) that Brad Pitt's "Wardaddy" character in *Fury* is based on him, personifies the dashing spirit and élan of the US Cavalry tanker and non-commissioned officer—"On The Way!"

The late SFC Steve Allseits, Marine, First City Trooper, tank commander, and exemplary Army NCO, also taught and inspired me much by his example and constant good cheer. RIP and Semper Fi Sarge—save us a few bar stools in Fiddler's Green.

To the officers and gentlemen of the First Troop Philadelphia City Cavalry, since November 10, 1774, "For These We Strive!"

To fellow Troopers of Apache Troop, 1/104th Cavalry, "Over, Under, or Through!"

Through years of dogged research and writing many soldiers, NCOs, and officers named and unnamed here—ranking literally from Private, to Command Sergeant Major, to General—offered steady support and encouragement. Serving in places like Bosnia, Germany, Egypt, and South Korea, sometimes working in or around tanks, I would overhear "DeJohn is writing a book on WWII tanks" typically greeted with "When is it coming out? I want to read that story." Many was the time I would be driving, loading, or gunning an M1A1 Abrams tank in places like Ft. Knox, Kentucky; Ft. Stewart, Georgia; or Fort Drum, New York, when Logan Fenstermacher, my platoon Sergeant in the 1/104th Cavalry, would gruffly ask, "DeJohn, when are you going to finish that book? You have to tell that story." Here it is—hope you like it, Sergeant.

While this book has harsh things to say about Army officers, I was blessed to serve alongside a few good ones in the 1/104th Cavalry who embodied the US Cavalry spirit. 1/104th CAV Squadron Commanders Col. William "Wild Bill" Spaulding, Col. Tyrone Twyman, and Capts. David Thayer and David Calhoun all made me proud to be a Trooper.

Army Vietnam veterans like Gen. William Matz and Maj. Ralph Riccio, who know a little bit about dishonest politicians and Army leaders with "credibility gaps," offered support, networking, and encouragement that moved the project along beyond my wildest dreams. Gen. Matz has been outspoken in the cause of VA reform, as well as encouraging me to tell this story and facilitating that by graciously opening doors within the Army.

Retired Army Command Sgt. Maj. Rick Young, now Executive Director of the National Armor and Cavalry Heritage Foundation, could not be more cheerfully supportive. You have to be an old soldier to appreciate the humor in driving up to the front gate at Ft. Benning, Georgia, in civilian clothes and receiving a rather slack reception from the soldiers on duty until telling them, "Son, we're running late for an appointment with COMMAND SERGEANT MAJOR YOUNG!"

Maj. Len Dyer, USMC (Ret.), Director of the National Museum of Cavalry and Armor, also offered blunt but helpful criticism and shared his extensive knowledge of not only the history and scholarship behind armor, but also his hands-on restoration of some of the world's rarest tanks. Please support the National

Armor and Cavalry Heritage Foundation—it is a noble cause, even though its name commits the sin of listing "Armor" before "Cavalry"—fighting words to an old Trooper!

Meeting with Cpl. Jack Myers of the 692nd Tank Destroyer Battalion drove home to me my intent of this book: to show the enlisted tanker and Tank Destroyer man's worm's-eye view. I have been around a few cocky tank gunners in my time, but when a smiling, 93-year-old Cpl. Myers boasted to me of his 1945 gunnery skills in the M-36 Tank Destroyer decades vanished. Any present day Army tanker would be honored and inspired to hear his stories. It is one thing to dig through dusty archives, but to personally hear the anger in the voice of one of the GIs that paid the consequences of the tank scandal as he discussed fighting Tigers and Panthers (at the Eisenhower Farm no less) validated my decision to expose the Sherman tank scandal.

Dr. Russell F. Weigley, eminent historian, professor, and author, was a wonderful mentor. He encouraged me as early as 2002 to tell this story in a book. My being called to active duty in Bosnia-Herzegovina after the September 11, 2001, attacks with other officers and gentlemen of the First City Troop and "A Troopers" (Apache Troop, 1/104th Cavalry) delayed it, but here we are. Dr. Weigley has passed on, but these pages have bene-fited greatly from the example he set for me in his courses. What a privilege to have been one of his graduate pupils in military history and to be gently encouraged to "argue" with him in class, to promote independent student thinking, rather than the intel-lectual complacency he despised.

Dr. Weigley's example of grace and class in an age where political correctness and slavish devotion to political agendas has trumped "scholarship" and academic inquiry is an example that sadly few professors choose to emulate. Fittingly, this book about a controversy led to a new controversy over the First Amendment and academic freedom. In that fight, I was sustained and encouraged by men of honor who came forward to stand up for the First Amendment and campus free speech.

At the Alliance Defending Freedom David French, David Hacker, Len Brown, and Travis Barham were pillars of integrity, dedication, and justice. Dramatically illustrating the timeless link between GIs past and present, in the middle of our fight Maj. French received deployment orders to Iraq. In the finest US Cavalry tradition reinforcements arrived in the nick of time: Nate Kellum stepped up and into the First Amendment breech, suc-cessfully continuing our fight for academic freedom. At the Foundation for Individual Rights in Education in Philadelphia Will Creeley, Samantha Harris, Robert Shibley, and Greg Lukianoff were fonts of faithful, steady support and wisdom.

You can see the results of these good men and women in the historic *DeJohn vs. Temple University* decisions (at state and federal court levels) that are helping to protect student campus free speech across the country.

My Bosnia service taught me the importance of standing up for the underdog; how appropriate somehow that an underdog Bosnia veteran—with incredible support from many—would resolve to stand up to academic bullies. While I heartily endorse the American myth (?) that "one good man can make a difference," many good men (and a few good women!) fought beside me to do it.

Tankers are not very fond of entrenching tools (shovels—they're an Infantry thing), but at Ridgway Hall, the US Army Military History Institute's research facility at the Army War College, Carlisle Barracks, Pennsylvania, dedicated experts like Rich Baker, Tom Buffenbarger, Steve Bye, and Jack Giblin made digging through mountains of archival documents a pleasure. For the assistance and support through years of research a snappy CAV salute to them—and when Steve and Tom get up a petition to add a cigar lounge to the research library I will be the first to sign it.

At the Dwight Eisenhower Presidential Library reference archivist Kevin Bailey helped me untangle some of the mysteries of US tanker casualties in WWII. While I would have liked to unearth a "one size fits all" set of casualty statistics that would please all the critics and armchair experts, as Kevin put it, "I am afraid that the only way to try and ascertain casualty reports among [all US M4 tank crewmen in the ETO] would be a laborious, unit-by-unit survey of all after action reports. As the quantity and quality of records varies widely from unit to unit, even this approach would probably wind up with fragmentary and incomplete results."

Beyond the tank scandal's cold production and casualty figures we must recall there was flesh and blood. At the George C. Marshall International Center in Leesburg, Virginia, Dr. Laurie Van Hook graciously assisted me in clarifying some details about Dodona Manor, the Marshalls' home. A visit there today reminds us that the scandal, beyond cold statistics and figures, involved human loss and tragedy. Every day they spent in the house, alongside many signed photos of kings and prime ministers, the Marshalls walked past an oil painting (to the left of the ground floor stairway) and a photo (in Katherine Marshall's bedroom—perhaps her first and last sight every day) of their beloved Lt. Brown, who was killed in a Sherman tank in Italy.

In the production of the book, Pete Schiffer's support and encouragement at Schiffer Publishing has been a pleasure. Editor Ian Robertson pulled this thing together into its final production with patience, dedication, and welcome sarcasm, while Jamie Elfrank cheerfully applied her marketing skills.

Henry Jones contributed wonderful wartime advertisements, and in Italy, Massimo Foti was generous in offering his wonderful photographs of rare tanks across Europe—Avanti, Italia!

My friend Bob Coldwell, photographer extraordinaire, created a monster when he told me, "You should meet Ralph Riccio—maybe he can help you get your tank book rolling!" Many enjoyable hours were spent in Bob's studio posing everything from original 1943 tanker helmets to GI gas cans, and his enthusiasm was infectious. It was a dramatic outdoor photo session with a pre-served M4 Sherman in which we were subjected to thunder, lightning, hail, and tornadoes, but it led to Bob capturing some stunning photo effects that showed us we were on to something very special here.

Historian, professor, and author Dr. Richard Hallion is a godsend, an inspiration to a young writer. While his resume awes, it is one thing to be a good, established historian, but to turn around and offer help to a then-stranger to help him finish this journey and get started down the path leading to this book shows Dr. Hallion as a class act. I was reading and inspired by his books as a student at Philadelphia's LaSalle College High School in the 1980s, so how appropriate that we should connect.

Dr. David Johnson, historian, retired Army Colonel, author, and RAND senior staffer greatly inspired me with his book *Fast Tanks and Heavy Bombers*, especially the questions he posed about Eisenhower and the tank scandal. While deployed to Bosnia in 2002–2003, I kept a copy of his seminal book close at hand, which got me thinking, "Someone needs to tell the full extent of this story!"

Col. Johnson could not have been more encouraging to an old Trooper, methodically reviewing many topics with me and playing devil's advocate—good to know there are a few decent Army officers out there (joking!).

Coworkers at the Department of Veterans Affairs in Philadelphia have offered support and encouragement for years. In the ongoing VA scandal I have been encouraged and inspired by the example of great writers like David Boyer, White House correspondent for the *Washington Times*, and Pete Kasperowicz, editor and reporter at the *Washington Examiner*, who have brought the truth on this sad state of affairs to the American public.

At the House Veterans Affairs Committee "former" Marine (no such animal) Eric Hannel has fought to get a square deal for a new generation of underdog GIs, and responded to my messages about "Congress and the taxpayers should know about XXX..." with patience and grace. As I joked with him, the last time the Army and Marines fought together side-by-side in such a just cause they ended up accepting the enemy's surrender in Tokyo Bay.

For an author exploring the challenges of reform at a dysfunctional bureaucracy (in this book Army agencies) led by an arrogant elite out of touch with their "customers," working at the US Department of Veterans Affairs in Philadelphia has given me daily, real-world examples of the challenge of reforming same, and of the heated opposition this stirs up. Beyond the corrupt leadership making headlines there are many decent employees at the VA (often disabled veterans themselves) that the American taxpayer can be proud of and get behind in the fight for reform— our Veterans, widows, and orphans deserve better.

Closer to home, my parents Emil and Bette Anne, sister Leisa DeJohn Nappi, and brother-in-law Paul Nappi have always encouraged and supported my literary endeavors, not only saying "Go for it," but teaching me things like perseverance, standards, and attention to detail. That this thing went from a controversial MA thesis at Temple University to the final product you hold in your hands is a testament to their steady belief in it.

I was blessed to grow up around many larger-than-life WWII veterans who would later inspire me during my own Army service in places like Bosnia-Herzegovina. I was also privileged to know Army, Navy, Army Air Corps, and Marine veterans, and further honored to follow in their footsteps in a very small way by serving myself overseas after September 11. Col. Harry Cruver, who led the 100th Bomb Group, Eighth Air Force in WWII, was a hero to me, and Lt. Bob Beatson, B-24 Liberator navigator with the 577th Bomb Squadron, 392nd Bomb Group, made me an honorary member of the Eighth Air Force Historical Society and encouraged me to sit down and write these stories of his era and to pass them on to younger generations after his had passed. Staff Sgt. Byron Schlag, tail gunner on the 711 Bomb Squadron, 447th Bomb Group's *Ol Scrap Iron* and former guest of the Luftwaffe and SS as a POW, was another wonderful example and inspiration to me of the good humor and scrappy bulldog courage of the men of that generation. He also encouraged me to write a book.

I am always humbled to visit the grave of my great-uncle, Col. Benjamin Norcia, US Army and US Force (WWII, Korea, and Vietnam) in Arlington Cemetery, who went from a 1939 Army Private to a 1960s Air Force Lieutenant Colonel. Other relatives and friends that personally inspired me to tell this story are: Lt. Col. Angelo Aquaro, a B-26 Marauder pilot with the 455th Bomb Squadron, 323rd Bomb Group, 9th Air Force ("That B-17 was overrated!"); and US Marine Corps Okinawa combat and Tokyo Bay surrender veteran Cpl. Jim Diodato, 4th Marines, 6th Marine Division, who into his '90s proudly wore a scarlet jacket with yellow letters proclaiming "Class of 1943—University of Parris Island."

Old friends who have stayed with me for the long haul include Sam Hillanbrand, who will always remain my class president at LaSalle College High School; American University rugby hero J. Edward McGrath; and fellow curmudgeon and syndicated columnist Christopher Friend, who embodies Kingsley Amis' advice that "If you can't annoy somebody, there's little point in writing!"

Closest to home, Lindsay Fraschilla has been an angel in so many ways, not only in her steady personal and professional support, understanding, and encouragement, but in helping to organize and prioritize the assembly of a manuscript, and in her diplomatic way of resolving bumps in the road along the way to publication, both personal and professional. For bringing this book to the finish line she will always have my gratitude and love.

## NOTES

### Front Matter

1. Stanley Wells and Gary Taylor (eds.), *William Shakespeare: The Complete Works* (Oxford, England: Clarendon Press, 1991), 585.
2. James Jones and Art Weithas, *WWII: A Chronicle of Soldiering* (New York: Grosset and Dunlap Publishers, 1975), 11.
3. Ladislas Farago, *Patton: Ordeal and Triumph* (New York: Ivan Obolensky, 1963), 513.
4. Lawrence Stallings, *The Doughboys: The Story of the AEF, 1917-1918* (New York: Harper and Row, 1963), 1.
5. Jean Edward Smith, *Eisenhower in War and Peace* (New York: Random House, 2012), 265.
6. Albyn Irzyk, *He Rode Up Front For Patton* (Raleigh, North Carolina: Pentland Press, 1996), 97.
7. George Campbell Macaulay (ed.), *Complete Works of John Gower, Volume III* (Oxford, 1901): *Confessio Amantis*, verses 4785-4787.
8. Steven J. Zaloga, *Armored Thunderbolt: The U.S. Army Sherman in World War II.* (Mechanicsburg, Pennsylvania: Stackpole Books, 2008), 336.
9. General George C. Marshall, *General Marshall's Report: The Winning of the War In Europe and the Pacific—Biennial Report of the Chief of Staff of the United States Army, July 1, 1943 to June 30, 1945, to the Secretary of War* (New York: Simon and Schuster, 1945), 108.

### Introduction

1. Fred L. Israel (ed.), *The State of the Union Messages of the Presidents, 1790-1966* (New York: Chelsea House, 1966), 2888-2889, 2882.
2. Major General Isaac D. White, *United States Versus German Equipment*. Annotated reprint of the 1945 original edition titled *United States Versus German Equipment: As Prepared for the Supreme Commander, Allied Expeditionary Force* (Bennington, Vermont: Merriam Press, 2011), 66.
3. Ibid, 89.
4. Hanson Baldwin, "The American Tanks, Part II: Men In Field Weigh Merits of Armored Vehicles And Declare Much Is Wanting." *New York Times*, March 19, 1945.
5. Paul Fussell, *The Boy's Crusade: The American Infantry in Northwestern Europe, 1944-1945* (New York: The Modern Library, 2003), xii.
6. Paul Fussell, *Wartime: Understanding and Behavior in the Second World War* (New York: Oxford University Press, 1989), 290.
7. Thomas Childers, *Soldier From the War Returning: The Greatest Generation's Troubled Homecoming From World War II* (Boston: Houghton Mifflin Harcourt, 2009), 4, 5, 2.
8. Ibid, 5.
9. Max Hastings, *Armageddon: The Battle for Germany, 1944-1945* (New York: Alfred A. Knopf, 2004), xii.
10. William S. Triplett, *A Colonel in the Armored Divisions: A Memoir, 1944-1945* (Columbia, Missouri: University of Missouri Press, 2001), dust jacket commentary by Russell Weigley.

11. A. Hoehling, *Home Front, U.S.A.* (New York: Thomas Crowell Company, 1966), xi.
12. Ibid, 61-62.
13. Gerald Linderman, *The World Within War: America's Combat Experience in World War II* (New York: The Free Press, 1997), 334.
14. Maury Klein, *A Call To Arms: Mobilizing America for World War II* (New York: Bloomsbury Press, 2013), 117.
15. Ibid, 764-765.
16. Ibid, 516.
17. Zaloga, *Armored Thunderbolt*, vi.
18. Lloyd Clark, *Anzio: Italy and the Battle for Rome-1944* (New York: Atlantic Monthly Press, 2006), 310.
19. Ibid, 301.
20. Triplett, *A Colonel*, 42.
21. Max Hastings, *Inferno: The World At War, 1939-1945* (New York: Vintage Books, 2012), 522.
22. Linderman, *World Within War*, 25.
23. Hastings, *Armageddon*, 377.
24. Linderman, *World Within War*, 26.
25. Marshall, *Report*, 5.
26. Harry Thomson and Lida Mayo, *The Ordnance Department: Procurement and Supply* (Washington, DC: Office of the Center of Military History, US Army, 1960), 222-223.
27. Linderman, *World Within War*, 24.
28. Larry Bland (ed.), *George C. Marshall: Reminiscences for Forrest Pogue* (Lexington, VA: George C. Marshall Research Foundation, 1991), 361.
29. Marshall, *Report*, 112.
30. Katherine Tupper Marshall, *Together* (London: Blandford, 1947), 147.
31. Fussell, *Boy's Crusade*, 174.
32. Nat Frankel and Larry Smith, *Patton's Best: An Informal History of the 4th Armored Division* (New York: Hawthorn Books Inc., 1978), 86.
33. Belton Y. Cooper, *Death Traps: The Survival of an American Armored Division in World War Two* (New York: Ballantine Books, 1998), vii.
34. Russell F. Weigley, *History of the United States Army* (New York: Macmillan Company, 1967), 472, 411.
35. Max Hastings, *Overlord: D-Day and the Battle for Normandy* (New York: Simon and Schuster, 1984), 193.
36. John Ellis, *Brute Force: Allied Strategy and Tactics in the Second World War* (New York: Viking Penguin, 1990), 334-335.
37. John C. McManus, *The Deadly Brotherhood: The American Combat Soldier in World War II* (New York: Presidio Press, 2003), 42.
38. Roman J. Jarymowycz, *Tank Tactics from Normandy to Lorraine* (Mechanicsburg, Pennsylvania: Stackpole, Books, 2009), 255.
39. David E. Johnson, *Fast Tanks and Heavy Bombers: Innovation in the U.S. Army, 1917-1945* (Ithaca, New York: Cornell University Press, 1998), 193.
40. "U.S. Ordnance is Defended: Eisenhower Quoted in Answer to Criticism of Weapons." The *Baltimore Sun*, February 3, 1945.

**41.** Sidney Shalett, "Ordnance Head Backs U.S. Tank; Calls Heavier Types Not Wanted." *New York Times*, February 3, 1945.

**42.** Ernest Leiger, "Shells 'Bounce Off' Tigers, Veteran U.S. Tankmen Say." *Stars and Stripes*, February 23, 1945.

**43.** White, *US vs. German Equipment*, 16.

**44.** James Tobin, *Ernie Pyle's War: America's Eyewitness to World War II* (Lawrence, Kansas: University Press of Kansas, 1997), 141, 139–140.

**45.** Marshall, *Report*, 114.

**46.** Joseph P. Hobbs, *Dear General: Eisenhower's Wartime Letters to Marshall* (Baltimore: The Johns Hopkins University Press, 1999), 85.

**47.** Smith, *Eisenhower*, 469.

**48.** A. J. Baime, *Arsenal of Democracy: FDR, Detroit, and an Epic Quest to Arm an America at War* (New York: Houghton Mifflin Harcourt, 2014), 276.

**49.** Hanson Baldwin, "American Tanks - II: Men In Field Weigh Merits of Armored Vehicles and Declare Much is Wanting." *New York Times*, March 19, 1945.

**50.** Jones and Weithas, *WWII*, 70–71.

**51.** Richard P. Hunnicutt, *Pershing: A History of the Medium Tank T20 Series* (Berkeley, CA: Feist Publications, 1971), 6.

**52.** Carlo D'Este, *Patton: A Genius for War* (New York: Harper Perennial Books, 1996), 618.

**53.** Ibid, 622; also see D'Este, *Eisenhower*, 561.

**54.** Harry Thomson and Lida Mayo, *The Ordnance Department: Procurement and Supply*; Constance Green, Harry Thompson, and Peter Roots, *The Ordnance Department: Planning Munitions for War*; and Lida Mayo, *The Ordnance Department: On Beachhead and* Battlefront. All: US Army in World War Two series (Washington, DC: Office of the Center of Military History, US Army, 1960, 1955, and 1991, respectively).

**55.** Cooper, Belton Y. *Death Traps: The Survival of an American Armored Division in World War Two.* New York: Ballantine Books, 1998; Irwin, John P. *Another River, Another Town: A Teenage Tank Gunner Comes of Age in Combat, 1945.* New York: Random House, 2002.; Jensen, Marvin. *Strike Swiftly! The 70th Tank Battalion From North Africa to Normandy to Germany.* Novato, CA: Presidio Press, 1997.; and Frankel, Nat, and Smith, Larry. *Patton's Best: An Informal History of the 4th Armored Division.* New York: Hawthorn Books Inc., 1978.

**56.** Arthur Schlesinger, *A Life in the 20th Century: Innocent Beginnings, 1917–1950* (New York: Houghton Mifflin Harcourt, 2000), 353.

**57.** Israel, *State of the Union Messages*, 2882.

**58.** Thomas Parrish, *Roosevelt and Marshall, Partners in Politics and War* (New York: William Morrow and Company, Inc.), 452.

**59.** D'Este, *A Genius for War*, 609.

**60.** Klein, *A Call To Arms*, 365.

**61.** Fussell, *Wartime*, 142.

**62.** Linderman, *World Within War*, 197.

**63.** Jones and Weithas, *WWII*, 70.

**64.** Fussell, *Wartime*, 131.

**65.** Fussell, *Boy's Crusade*, 174, 165.

**66.** David Nichols, *Ernie's War: The Best of Ernie Pyle's WWII Dispatches* (New York: Random House, 1986), 33, xii.

**67.** Marshall, *General Marshall's Report*, 108.

**68.** "Omissions in the Record." Kansas City *Star*, October 21, 1945.

## Chapter 1: "TREAT 'EM ROUGH . . ."

**1.** Dale Wilson, *Treat 'Em Rough: The Birth of American Armor* (Novato, California: Presidio Press, 1989), 223.

**2.** Ibid, 226.

**3.** Patrick Wright, *Tank: The Progress of a Monstrous War Machine* (New York: Penguin Books, 2003), 146.

**4.** Ibid, 104.

**5.** Smith, *Eisenhower*, 41.

**6.** Ibid, 43.

**7.** Mildred Gillie, *Forging the Thunderbolt* (Harrisburg, Pennsylvania: The Military Publishing Service, 1947), 8.

**8.** Wilson, *Treat 'Em Rough, 86.*

**9.** Ibid, 86.

**10.** Dale Wilson, "World War I: The Birth of American Armor." In George Hofmann and Donn Starry, *Camp Colt to Desert Storm: The History of U.S. Armored Forces* (Lexington, Kentucky: The University Press of Kentucky, 1999), 9.

**11.** Ibid, 1.

**12.** Ibid, 24.

**13.** Roger Nye, *The Patton Mind: The Professional Development of an Extraordinary Leader* (New York: Avery Publishing Group, 1993), 41.

**14.** Ibid, 43.

**15.** Farago, *Patton*, 73.

**16.** Smith, *Eisenhower*, 55.

**17.** Martin Blumenson, *The Patton Papers, Volume One: 1885–1940* (New York: Houghton Mifflin Harcourt, 1972), 784.

**18.** Nye, *The Patton Mind*, 52.

**19.** D'Este, *Patton*, 300.

**20.** Farago, *Patton*, 101.

**21.** *The Infantry Journal,* Volume XX, No. 5, May 1922 (Washington, DC: The United States Infantry Association), 560.

**22.** John S. D. Eisenhower, *General Ike: A Personal Reminiscence* (New York: The Free Press, 2003), 4.

**23.** Wilson, *Treat 'Em Rough*, 224.

**24.** D'Este, *Patton*, 299.

**25.** Jonathan Jordan, *Brothers, Rivals, Victors: Eisenhower, Patton, Bradley, and the Partnership that Drove The Allied Conquest In Europe* (New York: NAL/ Caliber-Penguin Group, 2011), 24.

**26.** Johnson, *Fast Tanks*, 68.

**27.** Michael Keane, *Patton: Blood, Guts, and Prayer* (Washington, DC: Regnery Publishing Inc., 2012), 97.

**28.** Farago, *Patton*, 102.

**29.** Keane, *Patton*, 102.

**30.** Gillie, *Forging the Thunderbolt*, 193.

**31.** Ibid, 15.

**32.** Ibid.

**33.** Ibid, 22.

**34.** Johnson, *Fast Tanks*, 98.

**35.** John B. Wilson, *Maneuver and Firepower: The Evolution of Divisions and Separate Brigades* (Washington, DC: United States Army Center of Military History, 1998), 123.

36. Ibid.
37. Gillie, *Forging the Thunderbolt*, 67.
38. Wilson, *Maneuver and Firepower*, 123.
39. George Forty, *United States Tanks of WWII* (Dorset, England: Blandford Press, 1983), 13.
40. Weigley, *History of the U.S. Army*, 411.
41. Robert Slayton, *Arms of Destruction: Ranking the World's Best Land Weapons of WWII* (New York: Citadel Press, 2004), 119.
42. Johnson, *Fast Tanks*, 140.
43. Ibid; see also John Clemens, "Waking Up from the Dream: The Crisis of the Cavalry in the 1930s." *ARMOR*, May–June 1990.
44. Gillie, *Forging the Thunderbolt*, 43.
45. Gillie, *Forging the Thunderbolt*, 14.
46. "Gaps in US Preparedness." *Newsweek*, August 28, 1939, 11.
47. Weigley, *History of the U.S. Army*, 411, 414; see also the *Annual Report of the Chief of Staff of the U.S. Army, 1934. Hearings before the House Committee on Appropriations* (Washington, DC: 72nd Congress, 2nd Session, 1933.)
48. Gillie, *Forging the Thunderbolt*, 74.
49. Johnson, *Fast Tanks*, 114.
50. Bland, *Marshall Reminiscences*, 261.
51. Johnson, *Fast Tanks*, 115.
52. Hoehling, *Home Front, U.S.A.*, 48.
53. Jonathan W. Jordan, *American Warlords: How Roosevelt's High Command Led America To Victory in World War Two* (New York: NAL/ Caliber-Penguin Group, 2015), 16.
54. George Hofmann and Donn Starry, *Camp Colt to Desert Storm: The History of U.S. Armored Forces* (Lexington, Kentucky: The University Press of Kentucky, 1999), 114.
55. Gillie, *Forging the Thunderbolt*, 61.
56. Weigley, *History of the U.S. Army*, 410.
57. Gillie, *Forging the Thunderbolt*, 58-59.
58. Fussell, *Wartime*, 4-5.
59. General John Herr and Edward Wallace, *The Story of the U.S. Cavalry* (Boston: Little, Brown, 1953), 250.
60. Christopher R. Gabel, *The U.S. Army GHQ Maneuvers of 1941.* (Washington: US Army Center of Military History, 1991), 30.
61. Johnson, *Fast Tanks*, 135.
62. Gillie, *Forging the Thunderbolt*, 118.
63. "Army Is Not Ready," Lawrence, KS, *Journal-World*, December 28, 1939.
64. Ibid.
65. Ronald Powaski, *Lightning War: Blitzkrieg in the West, 1940* (Hoboken, New Jersey: J. Wiley and Sons, 2003), 47.
66. Janusz Piekalkiewicz, *Tank War, 1939-1945,* trans. Jan van Heurck (Dorset, England: Blandford Press, 1986), 12.
67. Col. George Jarrett, "A British Tommy's Grave In Libya." Unpublished manuscript in his personal papers at the U.S. Army Military History Institute, Carlisle Barracks, Pennsylvania.
68. Ibid.
69. Jarrett "A British Tommy's Grave," 12.
70. Parrish, *Roosevelt and Marshall*, 259.
71. Ibid, 260.

72. Mark Perry, *Partners In Command: George Marshall and Dwight Eisenhower in War and Peace* (New York: The Penguin Press, 2007), 250.
73. Jarrett, "A British Tommy's Grave," 11–12.
74. Gillie, *Forging The Thunderbolt*, 98.
75. Parrish, *Roosevelt and Marshall*, 121.
76. Ibid, 120.
77. Ibid, 121.
78. Cooper, *Death Traps*, 295.

## Chapter 2: "TWENTY YEARS OF NEGLECT"

1. Basil Rauch, *The Roosevelt Reader: Selected Speeches, Messages, Press Conferences, & Letters of Franklin D. Roosevelt* (New York: Holt, Rinehart, & Winston, 1957), 312–315.
2. Krock, Editorial Page, *New York Times*, October 1, 1940.
3. Thomson and Mayo, *Procurement and Supply*, 223.
4. Hugh Sebag-Montefiore, *Dunkirk: Fight To The Last Man* (Cambridge, Massachusetts: Harvard University Press, 2006), 7.
5. Ibid, 70.
6. Ibid, 97.
7. Ibid, 96.
8. Quoted in Robert Citino, *Armored Forces: History and Sourcebook* (Westport, Connecticut: Greenwood Press, 1994), 58.
9. Charles Williams, *The Last Great Frenchman: A Life of General DeGaulle* (New York: John Wiley and Sons, Inc., 1993), 76.
10. Ibid, 81.
11. Ellis, *Brute Force*, 10.
12. Piekalkiewicz, *Tank War*, 56.
13. Ibid, 26.
14. Ibid, 27.
15. Slayton, *Arms of Destruction*, 98.
16. Steve Zaloga, *Panzer IV vs. Char B1 Bis: France, 1940* (Oxford, England: Osprey Publishing, 2011), 20–21.
17. Eric Grove, *German Armour: Poland and France, 1939–1940* (London: Almark Publishing Company Ltd., 1976), 25, 71.
18. Ted Morgan, *FDR: A Biography* (New York: Simon and Schuster, 1985), 522.
19. Ibid.
20. Thomson and Mayo, *Procurement and Supply,* 7.
21. Piekalkiewicz, *Tank War*, 57.
22. "Artillery and the Tank" *Field Artillery Journal*, July–August 1940.
23. Johnson, *Fast Tanks*, 119.
24. Charles M. Baily, *Faint Praise: American Tanks and Tank Destroyers During World War II* (Hamden, Connecticut: Archon/ Shoe String Press, 1983), 128.
25. "Ideal Tank?" *Time*, December 15, 1941.
26. Baily, *Faint Praise*, 128.
27. Piekalkiewicz, *Tank War*, 98.
28. Hoehling, *Home Front, U.S.A* , 47.
29. Forrest Pogue, *George C. Marshall: Ordeal and Hope, 1939–1942* (New York: Viking Press, 1966.), 17.
30. Hoehling, *Home Front, U.S.A* , 48.
31. Thomson and Mayo, *Procurement and Supply*, 2.

**32.** *Time*, "Billions for Defense" May 27, 1940, 18–19.

**33.** Smith, *Eisenhower*, 154, 156.

**34.** Clemens, "Waking Up from the Dream," 22.

**35.** Israel, *State of the Union Messages*, 2857–2858.

**36.** Nye, *The Patton Mind*, 119.

**37.** Thomson and Mayo, *Procurement and Supply*, 225.

**38.** Ibid, 226.

**39.** Farago, *Patton,* 150.

**40.** Richard Hunnicutt, *Sherman: A History of the American Medium Tank* (Belmont, California: Taurus Enterprises, 1978), 96

**41.** C. R. Kutz, "Break-Through Tanks: Will They Bring Freedom of Action to Armored Divisions?" (*Army Ordnance*, November–December 1940), 242.

**42.** Ibid.

**43.** Ibid, 243.

**44.** Ibid, 245.

**45.** Johnson, *Fast Tanks*, 192.

**46.** Ibid, 147.

**47.** Michael Green, *American Tanks & AFVS of World War II* (Oxford, England: Osprey Publishing 2014), 27.

**48.** Forty, *US Tanks*, 88.

**49.** Cooper, *Death Traps*, 296.

**50.** Geoffrey Perret, *There's A War to Be Won: The United States Army in World War II* (New York: Ballantine Books, 1992), 104.

**51.** Thomson and Mayo, *Procurement and Supply*, 3.

**52.** Ibid, 226.

**53.** Ibid, 4.

**54.** US Department of State, *Peace and War 1931–1941*, 633.

**55.** Jordan, *Warlords,* 27–28.

**56.** Ibid, 80.

**57.** Ibid, 82.

**58.** Klein, *A Call to Arms*, 265.

**59.** Johnson, *Fast Tanks*, 58.

**60.** Thomson and Mayo, *Procurement and Supply*, 23.

**61.** Ibid, 235.

**62.** Johnson, *Fast Tanks*, 151.

**63.** Pogue, *Ordeal*, 289.

**64.** Ibid, 290.

**65.** Klein, *Call to Arms*, 251.

**66.** Pogue, *Ordeal*, 293.

**67.** Constance Green, Harry Thomson, and Peter Roots, *The Ordnance Department: Planning Munitions for War* (Washington, DC: Office of the Center of Military History, US Army, 1955), 93.

**68.** Ibid, 91.

**69.** Thomson and Mayo, *Procurement and Supply*, 224.

**70.** Ibid, 224.

**71.** Ibid, 225.

**72.** Piekalkiewicz, *Tank War*, 88.

**73.** Blumenson, quoted in Hastings, *Inferno*, 182.

**74.** Jarrett, "A British Tommy's Grave in Libya," 12.

**75.** Thomson and Mayo, *Procurement and Supply*, 34–35.

**76.** Ibid, 34.

**77.** Ibid.

**78.** Jarrett, "A British Tommy's Grave In Libya," 7.

**79.** Ibid, 9.

**80.** G. MacLeod Ross, *The Business of Tanks, 1933 to 1945* (Elms Court, United Kingdom: Stockwell Ltd., 1976), 213.

**81.** Jordan, *Warlords*, 26.

**82.** Stanley Weintraub, *15 Stars: Eisenhower, MacArthur, Marshall - Three Generals Who Saved The American Country* (New York: The Free Press, 2007), 60.

**83.** Perret, *A War To Be Won, 30.*

**84.** Thomson and Mayo, *Procurement and Supply*, 231-232.

**85.** Ibid, 232.

**86.** Ross, *The Business of Tanks, 207.*

**87.** Thomson and Mayo, *Procurement and Supply*, 232.

**88.** Israel, State of the Union Messages, 2864.

**89.** Baime, *Arsenal of Democracy, 132.*

**90.** Jordan, *Warlords*, 236.

**91.** Ibid, 139.

**92.** Jean Edward Smith, *FDR* (New York: Random House, 2007), 548.

**93.** Thomson and Mayo, *Procurement and Supply*, 60.

**94.** Ibid, 234.

**95.** Jordan, *Warlords*, 139.

**96.** *Thomson and Mayo*, Procurement and Supply, 60.

**97.** *Jordan*, Warlords, 27.

**98.** Johnson, *Fast Tanks*, 115.

**99.** Baily, *Faint Praise*, 47.

**100.**   Thomson and Mayo, *Procurement and Supply*, 238.

**101.**   Ibid, 237.

**102.**   Baime, *Arsenal of Democracy*, 141.

**103.**   Ross, *The Business of Tanks*, 213.

**104.**   *Time*, Dec. 15, 1941, 43.

**105.**   Hoehling, *Home Front, U.S.A.*, 61.

**106.**   Ibid.

**107.**   Jarrett, "A British Tommy's Grave In Libya," p. ?

## Chapter 3: "AVOIDING ACTION . . ."

**1.** Cooper, *Death Traps*, 139.

**2.** Johnson, *Fast Tanks*, 191.

**3.** Ibid, 152.

**4.** Ibid,149.

**5.** Ibid.

**6.** Ibid.

**7.** Ibid.

**8.** Ibid, 150.

**9.** Eli J. Kahn, *McNair: Educator Of An Army* (Washington, DC: The Infantry Journal Press, 1945), 42.

**10.** Ibid, 10.

**11.** Ibid, 52.

**12.** Ibid, 11.

**13.** Ibid, 57.

**14.** Ibid, 19.

**15.** Ibid, 10, 58, 40.

**16.** Ibid, 28.

**17.** Ibid, 21.

**18.** Mark Calhoun, *General Lesley J. McNair: Unsung Architect of the U.S. Army* (Lawrence, Kansas: University Press of Kansas, 2015), 234.

**19.** Gabel, *GHQ Maneuvers*, 49.

**20.** Ibid.

21. Irzyk, *He Rode Up Front*, 12.
22. Farago, *Patton,* 161–162.
23. Gabel, *GHQ Maneuvers,* 171.
24. Johnson, *Fast Tanks*, 149.
25. Gabel, *GHQ Maneuvers,* 149.
26. Ibid, 48–49.
27. Ibid, 125.
28. Ibid.
29. Ibid, 110.
30. Ibid, 175.
31. Ibid, 45.
32. Calhoun, *General Lesley J. McNair*, 234.
33. Johnson, *Fast Tanks*, 192.
34. Jim Mesko, *US Tank Destroyers In Action* (Carrollton, Texas: Squadron/Signal Publications, 1998), 28.
35. Johnson, *Fast Tanks*, 152.
36. Army Service Forces. "Summary Report of Acceptances-Tank-Automotive Materiel, 1940–1945," December 1945.
37. Citino, *Armored Forces*, 89.
38. G-2 Section, *Tank Destroyer Combat Reports from Theaters of Operations* (Fort Hood, Texas: Tank Destroyer School, February, 1944).
39. Harry Dunnagan, *A War To Win: Company B, 813th Tank Destroyers* (Myrtle Beach, South Carolina: Royal Dutton Books, 1992), 79.
40. Mesko, *U.S. Tank Destroyers*, 28.
41. Baily, *Faint Praise*, 61.
42. Mesko, *U.S. Tank Destroyers*, 8, 28.
43. Dunnagan, *A War To Win*, 81.
44. Johnson, *Fast Tanks*, 226.
45. Ibid.
46. Kahn, *McNair*, 54.
47. Army Service Forces. "Summary Report of Acceptances—Tank-Automotive Materiel, 1940–1945," December 1945.

## Chapter 4: "A BETTER TANK THAN . . ."

1. Hobbs, *Dear General*, 102.
2. Baily, *Faint Praise*, 53.
3. Klein, *A Call to Arms*, 400.
4. Lida Mayo, *The Ordnance Department: On Beachhead and Battlefront* (Washington, DC: Office of the Center of Military History, US Army, 1991), 27.
5. Jordan, *Warlords*, 181.
6. Forty, *US Tanks*, 98.
7. Ibid, 100.
8. Ibid, 101.
9. Ibid.
10. Aaron Elson, *They Were All Young Kids* (Hackensack, New Jersey: Chi Chi Press, 1994), 123.
11. Ibid.
12. Jim Mesko, *M3 Lee in Action* (Carrollton, Texas: Squadron/Signal Publications, 1995), 40.
13. John Latimer, *Alamein* (Cambridge, Massachusetts: Harvard University Press, 2002), 221.
14. Ibid, 222.
15. Triplett, *A Colonel*, 18.
16. Mayo, *Beachhead*, 25.
17. Ibid, 23.
18. Baily, *Faint Praise*, 53.
19. Johnson, *Fast Tanks*, 190.
20. Mayo, *Beachhead*, 29.
21. Johnson, *Fast Tanks*, 190.
22. "American Tank Called Best on Battlefield," Del Rio, TX, *News Herald*, February 26, 1943.
23. Frank Carey, "Most Of America's Weapons Better Than Those of the Enemy," Danville, VA, *Bee*, April 29, 1943.
24. Ibid.
25. Johnson, *Fast Tanks*, 189.
26. Steven J. Zaloga, *M3 and M5 Stuart Light Tank, 1940–1945*. Oxford, England: Osprey Publishing, 2009, 21, 23.
27. Forty, *US Tanks*, 90.
28. Ibid, 92–94.
29. Mayo, *Beachhead*, 140.
30. Harry C. Butcher, *My Three Years With Eisenhower* (New York: Simon and Schuster, 1946), 286–287.
31. Hunnicutt, *Sherman*, 89–90.
32. Christopher R. Gabel, "World War Two Armor Operations in Europe," in *Camp Colt to Desert Storm: The History of U.S. Armored Forces,* ed. George F. Hofmann and Donn A. Starry (Lexington, Kentucky: University Press of Kentucky, 1999), 149.
33. Forty, *US Tanks*, 92, 90.
34. Steven Zaloga, *Sherman Medium Tank, 1942–45.* (Oxford, England: Osprey Publishing, 2003), 21.
35. Rick Atkinson, *An Army At Dawn* (New York: Henry Holt, 2002), 322.
36. Gabel, "World War Two Armor Operations," in Hoffman and Starry, *Camp Colt to Desert Storm*, 152.
37. Gillie, *Forging The Thunderbolt*, 225–226.
38. Smith, *Eisenhower*, 261.
39. Orr Kelly, *Meeting the Fox: The Allied Invasion of Africa, from Operation Torch to Kasserine Pass to Victory in Tunisia* (New York: John Wiley and Sons, 2002), 219.
40. Ibid, 206.
41. Nichols, *Ernie's War*, 88–89.
42. Franklyn A. Johnson, *One More Hill* (New York: Bantam Books, 1983), 40.
43. Nichols, *Ernie's War*, 96.
44. Zaloga, *Sherman Medium Tank*, 21.
45. James Hagan, Comments in World War Two Veterans' Survey Files: First Armored Division, First Armored Regiment, Box 1 of 2. US Army Military History Institute, Carlisle Barracks, PA.
46. Kelly, *Meeting The Fox*, 220.
47. Ibid, 221.
48. Smith, *Eisenhower,* 264.
49. D. A. Lande, *I Was With Patton: First Person Accounts of WWII In George S. Patton's Command* (Saint Paul, Minnesota: MBI Publishing, 2002), 48.
50. Ibid, 48-49.
51. Baily, *Faint Praise*, 56-57
52. Nichols, *Ernie's War*, 96.
53. Dunnagan, *A War To Win*, 179.
54. Steven J. Zaloga, *U. S. Anti-Tank Artillery*. (Oxford, England: Osprey Publishing, 2005), 11-12.

55. Triplett, *A Colonel*, 19.
56. Kelly, *Meeting The Fox*, 282, 283.
57. Nichols, *Ernie's War*, 105.
58. Omar Bradley, *A Soldier's Story* (New York: Henry Holt and Company, 1951), 40.
59. Hunnicutt, *Sherman*, 142.
60. Hobbs, *Dear General*, 102, 103.
61. Ibid, 102.
62. Ibid, 104.
63. Ibid, 102 – 103.
64. Debi and Irwin Unger, *George Marshall: A Biography* (New York Harper Collins, 2014), 201.
65. Hobbs, *Dear General*, 108.
66. Nichols, *Ernie's War*, 87.
67. Johnson, *Fast Tanks*, 192.
68. Gabel, "World War Two Armor Operations," in Hofmann and Starry, *Camp Colt to Desert Storm*, 150.
69. Lawrence Robertson, *Comments in World War Two Veterans' Survey Files, First Armored Division, First Armored Regiment.* US Army Military History Institute, Carlisle Barracks, PA.
70. Piekalkiewicz, *Tank War*, 205.
71. Ibid.
72. Baily, *Faint Praise*, 53.
73. Mayo, *Beachhead*, 33.
74. Kahn, *McNair*, 50.
75. Ibid.
76. Ibid, 1.
77. Gillie, *Forging The Thunderbolt*, 232.
78. Ibid.
79. Ibid.
80. Baime, *Arsenal of Democracy*, 207.
81. Israel, *State of the Union Messages*, 2870-2872.
82. Slayton, *Arms of Destruction*, 123-124.
83. Ibid.
84. David Fletcher, (editor). *Tiger! The Tiger Tank: A British View.* (London: Her Majesty's Stationary Office, 1986), 6.
85. Ibid.
86. Ibid, 7.
87. Ibid, 9.
88. Ibid, 3.
89. Ibid, 4.
90. "Decision to the Tiger: Doubt on Caliber of U.S. Arms Raised by New German Weapons," *Newsweek, January 15, 1945.*
91. Johnson, *Fast Tanks*, 200.
92. Fletcher, *Tiger!*, 12.
93. Mayo, *Beachhead*, 149.
94. Fletcher, *Tiger!*, 11.
95. "Will Russia Seize The Summer Offensive?" Uniontown, PA, *Morning Herald*, June 19, 1943.
96. Captain George Drury, "Panzer VI Tiger Model B Design Study, Technical Analysis and Tests." Undated memo from "Ordnance Technical Intelligence Team No. 1, APO 230," in George B. Jarrett personal papers, US Army Military History Institute, Carlisle Barracks, PA.
97. Mayo, *Beachhead*, 150.
98. Jarymowycz, *Tank Tactics*, 262.
99. Hobbs, *Dear General*, 102–103.
100. Weintraub, *15 Stars*, 171–172.
101. John Thompson, "Sicilian Orchard Quiet After Yank 'Chutists' Battle Through Eyeties." Amarillo, TX, *Daily News*, July 16, 1943.
102. Harold V. Boyle, "American Colonel Single Handed Slays Giant 52-Ton Tiger Tank in Sicily." Paris, TX, *News*, July 21, 1943 .
103. Ibid.
104. Gabel, "World War Two Armor Operations," in Hofmann and Starry, *Camp Colt to Desert Storm*, 159.
105. Baily, *Faint Praise*, 53.
106. Lande, *I Was With Patton*, 70–71.
107. Marshall, *Report*, 14.
108. Alfred Chandler Jr. (ed.). *The Papers of Dwight David Eisenhower: The War Years*, Volume II (Baltimore: Johns Hopkins University Press, 1970), 1275.
109. Lande, *I Was With Patton*, 67.
110. Gabel, "World War Two Armor Operations," in Hofmann and Starry, *Camp Colt to Desert Storm*, 159.
111. George S. Patton, Jr.,*War As I Knew It*. (New York: Houghton Mifflin, 1994), 43.
112. Zaloga, *US Anti-Tank*, 22.
113. Ibid.
114. Baily, *Faint Praise*, 59.
115. Ibid, 60; also, Zaloga, *US Anti-Tank*, 10.
116. Mesko, *US Tank Destroyers*, 28.
117. Jack Myers, Presentation at Eisenhower Farm, September 2015.
118. Zaloga, *US Anti-Tank*, 18.
119. Ibid; see also Mesko, *US Tank Destroyers*, 28.
120. Zaloga, *US Anti-Tank*, 18.
121. The Armored School. *The Second Armored Division in the Sicilian Campaign: A Research Report* (Fort Knox, Kentucky, 1950), 69.
122. Ibid.
123. Baily, *Faint Praise*, 85.
124. Ibid, 86–87.
125. Butcher, *My Three Years With Eisenhower*, 397.
126. Steven J. Zaloga, *Sherman Medium Tank, 1942–45*. (Oxford, England: Osprey Publishing, 2003), 23.
127. Clark, *Anzio*, 298.
128. Zaloga, *US Anti-Tank*, 23.
129. Gillie, *Forging The Thunderbolt*, 197.

## Chapter 5: "NO FACTUAL DEVELOPMENTS . . ."

1. Cooper, *Death Traps*, 28.
2. Johnson, *Fast Tanks*, 193. Thomson and Mayo, *Procurement and Supply*, 264. Smith, *Eisenhower*, 404. Ross, *The Business of Tanks*, 270.
3. Capt. A. Robert Moore, "Suggested Improvements, Design of Medium Tank," memorandum to the Chief of Ordnance, Washington, DC, dated October 30, 1943; In World War Two Veterans Survey Files: First Armored Division. US Army Military History Institute, Carlisle Barracks, Pennsylvania.
4. Smith, *Eisenhower*, 404.

5. Ross, *The Business of Tanks*, 270.
6. Capt. A. Robert Moore, "Suggested Improvements."
7. Ibid.
8. Ibid.
9. Ibid.
10. Ibid.
11. Ibid.
12. Ibid.
13. Ibid.
14. Ross, *The Business of Tanks*, 263.
15. Quoted in Lt. Col. Kenneth Steadman, "The Evolution of the Tank in the U.S. Army." Study prepared for the Commander, Combined Arms Center, US Army Command and General Staff College, 1982.
16. Johnson, *Fast Tanks*, 193.
17. Kahn, *McNair*, 24.
18. Ibid, 28.
19. Ibid, 31.
20. Ibid, 8.
21. Ibid, 60.
22. Ibid, 63.
23. Ibid, 16.
24. Kahn, *McNair*, 18.
25. Ibid, 4.
26. John Whitaker, "These Are The Generals: Lt. Gen. Lesley McNair," quoted in Calhoun, *General Lesley J. McNair*, 221.
27. Harry Yeide, *The Tank Killers: A History Of America's World War II Tank Destroyer Force* (Havertown, Pennsylvania: Casemate, 2004), 188.
28. Jarymowycz, *Tank Tactics*, 260.
29. Zaloga, *Sherman Medium Tank 1942-45*, 4.
30. Hobbs, *Dear General*, 102–103.
31. Baily, *Faint Praise*, 97.
32. Zaloga, *Armored Thunderbolt*, 124.
33. Baily, *Faint Praise*, 87.
34. Steven J. Zaloga, *M26/M46 Pershing Tank, 1943–1953.* Oxford, England: Osprey Publishing, 2008, 13–14.
35. "U.S. Officers Inspect Russian Trophies." The Pottstown, PA, *Mercury*, July 1, 1943.
36. Zaloga, *M26/ M46*, 13–14.
37. "British Gun Answer To Nazi Tiger Tank," Abilene, TX, *Reporter-News*, October 11, 1943
38. Baily, *Faint Praise*, 87–88.
39. Mesko, *U.S. Tank Destroyers*, 19.
40. Thomson and Mayo, *Procurement*, 65
41. Hastings, *Armageddon*, 85–86.
42. Israel, *State of the Union Messages*, 2878.
43. Frankel, *Patton's Best, 86.*
44. Marshall, *Report*, 104.
45. "Two General Sherman Tanks Route 14 Nazi Tigers In Italy." Neosho, Missouri, *Daily News*, November 2, 1943.
46. William B. Folkestad, *The View From the Turret: The 743rd Tank Battalion During World War II* (Shippensburg, Pennsylvania: Burd Street Press, 2000), 32.
47. Baily, *Faint Praise*, 101.
48. Tankers in England Impress Eisenhower" *Armored News*, March 6, 1944.
49. "Royalty, Military Visit Invasion Armor," *The Armored News*, March 27, 1944.
50. Marshall, *Report* (1996 edition, Washington, DC: US GPO, 1996), 133.
51. Baily, *Faint Praise*, 102–103.
52. "Tankmen Stage Firepower Show for Visitors," *Armored News*, March 27, 1944.
53. Baily, *Faint Praise*, 126.
54. Blair Bolles, "American Weapons Called World's Best."
55. Zaloga, *Armored Thunderbolt*, 128.
56. Bolles, "American Weapons."
57. William White, "M4 Tank Reassuring, Says Writer," *Armored News*, March 6, 1944.
58. Baily, *Faint Praise*, 99.
59. Ibid, 100–101.
60. Mayo, *Beachhead*, 238.
61. White, "M4 Tank."
62. Nichols, *Ernie's War*, 257.
63. Martha Kearney. "U.S. War Equipment Superior To Others." The Bristol, PA, *Daily*, May 4, 1944.

## Chapter 6: "HYSTERICAL FEAR"

1. John P. Irwin, *Another River, Another Town: A Teenage Tank Gunner Comes Of Age in Combat, 1945* (New York: Random House, 2002), 137–138.
2. John Buckley, *British Armour In The Normandy Campaign 1944* (London: Frank Cass, 2004), 109.
3. Bertrand Close, World War Two Veterans Survey Files: 32nd Armored Regiment, Third Armored Division (US Army Military History Institute, Carlisle Barracks, PA), 13.
4. Jarymowycz, *Tank Tactics*, 110.
5. Ibid.
6. Ibid, 255.
7. Close, WWII Vet Survey File, 13.
8. Cooper, *Death Traps*, viii.
9. Gabel, "World War Two Armor Operations," in Hoffman and Starry, *Camp Colt To Desert Storm*, 161.
10. Smith, *Eisenhower*, 38.
11. Close, WWII Vet Survey File, 13.
12. Ibid, 14.
13. Ibid, 12.
14. Irzyk, *He Rode Up Front*, 171.
15. Mayo, *Beachhead*, 255.
16. Ibid.
17. Jarymowycz, *Tank Tactics*, 110.
18. Baily, *Faint Praise*, 106, and Hunnicutt, *Sherman*, 213.
19. Weintraub, *15 Stars*, 257.
20. "From My Own Men," *Time*, August 14, 1944.
21. Zaloga, *US Anti-Tank*, 33.
22. Zaloga, *M3 & M5 Stuart*, 38–39.
23. Ellis, *Brute Force*, 358.
24. Chandler, *Papers of Dwight D. Eisenhower - The War Years, Volume III*, 1973.
25. Butcher, *My Three Years With Eisenhower*, 605.
26. Gen. George C. Marshall, Cable WDCSA/473 to Gen. Dwight Eisenhower, dated July 13, 1944 (on responses to Tiger and

Panther tanks). George C. Marshall Research Library, Lexington, Virginia.

27. Ibid.

28. Headquarters, First U.S. Army. "Action Against the Enemy After Action Report, 31 August 1944." Record Group 338, ETO AFV and Weapons Section. National Archives and Records Administration, Suitland, Maryland.

29. Russell Hart, *A Clash of Arms: How The Allies Won In Normandy* (Boulder, Colorado: Lynne Rienner Publishers, 2001), 309.

30. Marshall, *Report*, 38.

31. Zaloga, *Armored Thunderbolt*, 180–181.

32. Folkestad, *The View From The Turret*, 47–48.

33. Aaron Elson, *Tanks for the Memories: An Oral History of the 712th Tank Battalion in World War II* (Hackensack, New Jersey: Chi Chi Press, 1997), 141.

34. Hastings, *Inferno*, 522.

35. Wright, 302.

36. Hart, *Clash of Arms*, 309.

37. Irzyk, *He Rode Up Front*, 129.

38. John Buckley, *Monty's Men: The British Army and the Liberation of Europe* (New Haven, Connecticut: Yale University Press, 2013), 138.

39. Ibid.

40. Ibid.

41. Hastings, *Inferno*, 522–523.

42. Ellis, *Brute Force*, 378.

43. Triplett, *A Colonel*, 128.

44. Hart, *Clash of Arms*, 331.

45. Hunnicutt, *Sherman*, 312.

46. Hastings, *Inferno*, 523.

47. Ellis, *Brute Force*, 536.

48. Buckley, *Monty's Men*, 127.

49. Hastings, *Overlord*, 186–187.

50. Butcher, *My Three Years With Eisenhower*, 602.

51. Handwritten note (undated) in the George B. Jarrett personal papers, Army Military History Institute, Carlisle Barracks, PA.

52. Jarrett comment from "My Little Green Book," George B. Jarrett personal papers, Army Military History Institute, Carlisle Barracks, PA.

53. Buckley, *Monty's Men*, 105.

54. Ibid, 136–137.

55. Ibid, 128.

56. Nichols, *Ernie's War*, 310–311.

57. L. S. B. Shapiro, "Frontline Tankers Prefer Sherman Tank to Mark V Panther of Germans." Lincoln, NE, *State Journal*, August 5, 1944.

58. Baltimore *Evening Sun*, August 14, 1944. Jarrett's comment is from "My Little Green Book," George B. Jarrett personal papers, Army Military History Institute.

59. Kahn, *McNair*, 6.

60. Jarymowycz, *Tank Tactics*, 263.

61. Russell Weigley, *Eisenhower's Lieutenants: The Campaigns of France and Germany 1944–45* (London: Sidgwick and Jackson, 1981), 21; see also Zaloga, *Sherman Medium Tank 1942-1945*, 35.

62. Bradley, *A Soldier's Story*, 322

63. Ellis, *Brute Force*, 384.

64. Michael Collins and Martin King, *Voices of the Bulge: Untold Stories from Veterans of the Battle of the Bulge*. Minneapolis, Minnesota: Zenith Press: 2011, 269–270.

65. Irzyk, *He Rode Up Front*, 305.

66. Aaron Elson, *They Were*, 38–41.

67. Patton, *War As I Knew It*, 215.

68. Forty, *US Tanks*, 6.

69. *United States vs. German Equipment*, 2011 edition, 96–97.

70. Buckley, *Monty's Men*, 125.

71. Ibid, 174–175.

72. Peter S. Kindsvatter, *American Soldiers: Ground Combat in the World Wars, Korea, and Vietnam*. (Lawrence, Kansas: University Press of Kansas, 2003), 87.

73. Close, WWII Vet Survey File, 21.

74. Ibid.

75. Frankel, *Patton's Best*, 20.

76. Ellis, *Brute Force*, 384.

77. Marshall, *Report*, 38.

78. Elson, *Tanks*, 289.

79. Mayo, *Beachhead*, 322.

80. Folkestad, *The View From The Turret*, 53.

81. Marshall, *Report*, 105.

82. Elson, *Tanks*, 196.

83. Elson, *They Were*, 47, 54.

84. Irzyk, *He Rode Up Front*, 136.

85. Harry Yeide, *Steel Victory: The Untold Story of America's Independent Tank Battalions at War in Europe* (New York: Presidio Press/ Ballantine Books, 2003.) 121–122.

86. Elson, *They Were*, 46, 49–50.

87. Ibid, 50.

88. Marshall, *Report*, 110.

89. Thomson and Mayo, *Procurement and Supply*, 300.

90. Hastings, *Armageddon*, 23–24.

91. Elson, *Tanks*, 336.

92. Cooper, *Death Traps*, 33.

93. Hastings, *Armageddon*, 146.

94. Thomson and Mayo, *Procurement and Supply*, 257.

95. Ibid, 257.

96. Ross, *The Business of Tanks*, 280.

97. Ibid.

98. Ike, *Letters to Mamie*, 219.

## Chapter 7: "WIN THE WAR WITH THE M4"

1. Thomas Berndt, *American Tanks of World War II*. (Osceola, Wisconsin: Motorbooks International, 1994), 10.

2. Captain Addison F. McGhee Jr., *He's In The Armored Force Now* (New York: Robert M. McBride & Company), 11, 113.

3. Zaloga, *Sherman Medium Tank*, 35.

4. Elizabeth M. Conger, *American Tanks and Tank Destroyers* (New York: Henry Holt and Company, 1944), 7.

5. Ibid, 142.

6. Ibid, 11.

7. McGhee, *Armored Force*, 163.

8. Irzyk, *He Rode Up Front*, 59–60.

9. Berndt, *American Tanks*, 1.

10. The Infantry Journal, *The Armored Forces of the United States Army*, 22.

11. Ibid.
12. McGhee, *Armored Force*, 180.
13. Ibid, 136.
14. Conger, *American Tanks*, 27.
15. Ibid, 36.
16. Ibid.
17. Ibid, 35.
18. Ibid, 41.
19. Ibid, 145.
20. Wesley Stout, *Tanks Are Mighty Fine Things* (Detroit: Chrysler Corporation, 1946), v, 2.
21. Berndt, *American Tanks*, 10.
22. Jarrett comment from "My Little Green Book," George B. Jarrett personal papers, Army Military History Institute, Carlisle Barracks, PA.
23. "M-36 'Sluggers' Favored By 10 to 1 in Combat," the *Baltimore Sun*, April 26, 1945.
24. Yeide, *Tank Killers*, 175.
25. Conger, *American Tanks*, 41.
26. Ibid, 40
27. Ibid, 41.
28. Ibid, 125.
29. Infantry Journal, *The Armored Forces*, 5.
30. McGhee, *Armored Force*, 180.
31. Ibid, 180.
32. Ibid, 184–186.

## Chapter 8: "BUT YOU ALWAYS HAVE ELEVEN"

1. White, *US vs. German Equipment*, 27.
2. Close, WWII Vet Survey File, 13.
3. Jarymowycz, *Tank Tactics*, 255.
4. Fletcher, *Tiger!*, 3.
5. Ibid, 209.
6. Quoted in Citino, *Armored Forces*, 87.
7. Linderman, *World Within War*, 32.
8. Irwin, *Another River, Another Town*, 14.
9. Elson, *They Were*, 125.
10. Frankel, *Patton's Best*, 65.
11. Elson, *Tanks*, 296.
12. Jarrett, "A British Tommy's Grave In Libya," 16.
13. Ibid.
14. Citino, *Armored Forces*, 87.
15. "Plan No Changes In Sherman Tank," Lincoln, Nebraska, *State Journal*, December 6, 1944.
16. War Department Technical Manual, Volume 30, Issue 451, 80.
17. Mayo, *Beachhead*, 215.
18. Citino, *Armored Forces*, 87.
19. Triplett, *A Colonel*, 128.
20. Irzyk, *He Rode Up Front*, 127.
21. Col. George B. Jarrett, *Achtung Panzer — The Story of German Tanks* (unpublished manuscript; Aberdeen, Maryland 1948), 3; also quoted in Jarymowycz, *Tank Tactics*, 271.
22. Linderman, *World Within War*, 25.
23. Jarymowycz, *Tank Tactics*, 265.
24. Linderman, *World Within War*, 25.
25. White, *US vs. German Equipment*, 53.
26. Jarrett, "A British Tommy's Grave In Libya," 13.
27. Charles Whiting, *The Battle of Hurtgen Forest: The Untold Story of a Disastrous Campaign*. (New York: Orion Books, 1989), 220.
28. Hastings, *Overlord*, 186.
29. Otto Carius, *Tigers in the Mud*, 117.
30. Elson, *They Were*, 116.
31. Hunnicutt, *Sherman*, 255.
22. Elson, *Tanks*, 147.
33. Green, *Planning Munitions*, 253, 256.
34. Ibid, 253.
35. Ibid, 25.
36. War Department Technical Manual TM-E 30-451: *Handbook on German Military Forces*. (Washington: US Government Printing Office, March 1945), 390.
37. Ellis, *Brute Force*, 356.
38. Ibid, 395.
39. Frankel, *Patton's Best*, 137.
40. Ibid, 138.
41. Hastings, *Armageddon*, 227.
42. Jarrett, "A British Tommy's Grave in Libya," 8
43. Irzyk, *He Rode Up Front*, 357.
44. Ibid, 86.
45. Ibid, 191-192.
46. Piekalkiewicz, *Tank War*, 199–200.
47. Jarrett, *"A British Tommy's Grave In Libya,"* 10
48. Fredric Smoler, "Overrated/Underrated: [Sherman] Tank." *American Heritage*, October 2003.
49. Jarrett, "A British Tommy's Grave In Libya," 7
50. Irzyk, *He Rode Up Front*, 49.
51. Ibid, 62.
52. Nichols, *Ernie's War*, 254–255.
53. Yeide, *Steel Victory*, 223–224.
54. Frankel, *Patton's Best*, 27.
55. Jarrett, "A British Tommy's Grave In Libya," 7
56. Major J. B. McDivitt, 4th Tank Battalion, First Armored Division. Memorandum on "Combat Data" to the Office of the Ordnance Officer, First Armored Division, 09 April 1945. In World War Two Veterans Survey Files - First Armored Division. US Army Military History Institute, Carlisle Barracks, PA.
57. Buckley, *British Armour*, 127.
58. Frankel, *Patton's Best*, 136–137.
59. Irzyk, *He Rode Up Front*, 128.
60. Buckley, *Monty's Men*, 138.
61. Jarrett, "A British Tommy's Grave In Libya," 2
62. Gerald Astor, *A Blood-Dimmed Tide: The Battle of the Bulge by the Men Who Fought It*. (New York: Dell Publishing/ Random House, 1992), 159.
63. Irwin, *Another River, Another Town*, 138.
64. Irzyk, *He Rode Up Front*, 127–128.
65. Green, *The M4 Sherman*, 28.
66. Yeide, *Steel Victory*, 14.
67. Green, *M4 Sherman*, 28.
68. Nichols, *Ernie's War*, 349.
69. Cooper, *Death Traps*, 20.

**70.** Elson, *They Were,* 133.

**71.** Ibid, 147–153.

**72.** John Keegan, *The Second World War* (New York: Viking Press, 1990), 401.

**73.** Alvin D. Coox and L. Van Loan Naisawald, *Survey of Allied Tank Casualties in World War II.* Fort Lesley J. McNair, Washington, DC: Operations Research Office, Johns Hopkins University, 1951, 33.

**74.** Ibid.


## Chapter 9: "FOR WANT OF A GUN"

**1.** White, *US vs. German Equipment*, 13.

**2.** Moore, "Suggested Improvements, Design of Medium Tank," 1.

**3.** Hastings, *Overlord*, 192.

**4.** Jarrett, "A British Tommy's Grave In Libya," 4

**5.** Jarymowycz, *Tank Tactics*, 266–267.

**6.** Bradley, *A Soldier's Story*, 41.

**7.** Baily, *Faint Praise*, 87.

**8.** Ibid, 88.

**9.** White, *US vs. German Equipment*, 89.

**10.** Jarymowycz, *Tank Tactics*, 283.

**11.** White, *US vs. German Equipment*, 88–89.

**12.** Jarymowycz, *Tank Tactics*, 261.

**13.** Ibid, 283.

**14.** Baily, *Faint Praise*, 69.

**15.** George Jarrett "Personal Notes - Written March 1945." George B. Jarrett personal papers, Army Military History Institute, Carlisle Barracks, PA.

**16.** Zaloga, *Armored Thunderbolt*, 116.

**17.** Mayo, *Beachhead*, 322.

**18.** Bradley, *A Soldier's Story*, 322.

**19.** Hunnicutt, *Sherman*, 206.

**20.** Ross, *The Business of Tanks*, 284.

**21.** Ibid, 291.

**22.** "Plan No Changes In Sherman Tank," The Lincoln, Nebraska, *State Journal*, December 6, 1944

**23.** Buckley, *Monty's Men*, 40.

**24.** Jarymowycz, *Tank Tactics*, 263.

**25.** Baily, *Faint Praise*, 89.

**26.** Letter dated April 9, 1945, from Brigadier G. M. Ross to Lt. Col. George B. Jarrett, in George B. Jarrett personal papers, U.S. Army Military History Institute, Carlisle Barracks, Pennsylvania.

**27.** Hunnicutt, *Sherman*, 213.

**28.** Mesko, *US Tank Destroyers*, 17.

**29.** Baily, *Faint Praise*, 109–110.

**30.** Mesko, *US Tank Destroyers*, 17.

**31.** Baily, *Faint Praise*, 110.

**32.** Jarymowycz, *Tank Tactics*, 261.

**33.** Ibid, 257.

**34.** Ed Cray, *General of the Army: George C. Marshall, Soldier And Statesman* (New York: W.W. Norton, 1990), 485.

**35.** Yeide, *Steel Victory*, 131.

**36.** Called to active duty after the September 11, 2001, attacks, the author, as a member of the historic First Troop Philadelphia City Cavalry, served in Bosnia-Herzegovina in 2002–2003 with Apache Troop (Forward), 1/104th Cavalry, 28th Infantry Division, part of NATO's Multi-National Division North, Stabilization Force 12 (SFOR 12).

**37.** Yeide, *Steel Victory*, 134–135.

**38.** Bradley, *A Soldier's Story*, 428–429

**39.** Cray, *General of the Army*, 484.

**40.** Ibid, 485.

**41.** Gordon A. Blaker, *Iron Knights: The United States 66th Armored Regiment* (Shippensburg, PA: Burd Street Press, 1999), 287–288.

**42.** Blaker, *Iron Knights*, 321.

**43.** Ibid, 303.

**44.** Ibid, 304.

**45.** Marshall, *Report*, 97.


## Chapter 10: "HYSTERICAL DESPAIR"

**1.** Jack Bell, "Shermans Defeat Nazi Tigers." Baltimore *Evening Sun*, December 16, 1944.

**2.** New York *Sun*, December 28, 1944. Editorial – "Not Explanation Enough"

**3.** Rudyard Kipling, *Rudyard Kipling's Verse, Inclusive Edition 1885–1919* (Garden City, New York: Doubleday, Page and Company, 1922), 443.

**4.** Collie Small, "Bastogne: American Epic." Cited in Henry Steele Commager, *The Story of the Second World War* (Washington, DC: Potomac Books, 2004), 354.

**5.** Triplett, *A Colonel*, 129.

**6.** Hastings, *Armageddon*, 211.

**7.** Weintraub, *15 Stars*, 287.

**8.** Ibid, 288.

**9.** Ibid, 280.

**10.** AFV and Weapons Section, Headquarters, European Theater of Operations, United States Army. "Final Historical Report." Record Group 338, US National Archives, Washington, D.C.

**11.** Yeide, *Steel Victory*, 217.

**12.** Ibid, 217–218.

**13.** Kenneth L. Dixon, "They Found A Moral In German Pictures." Santa Cruz, California, *Sentinel*, January 9, 1945.

**14.** Henry Paynter and Roland Gask, "Must We Defeat Germany With Inferior Weapons?" *Newsweek*, February 26, 1945, 28.

**15.** Paynter and Gask

**16.** Hastings, *Armageddon*, 217.

**17.** Ibid, 234.

**18.** "Post-Mortem on the Ardennes," *Time* magazine, January 15, 1945. Jarrett comment from "My Little Green Book," George B. Jarrett personal papers, US Army Military History Institute, Carlisle Barracks, PA.

**19.** Barry Turner, *Countdown to Victory: The Final European Campaigns of World War Two.* (London: Hodder and Stoughton Ltd., 2004), 25–26.

**20.** Parrish, *Roosevelt and Marshall*, 465.

**21.** Yeide, *Steel Victory*, 220–221.

**22.** "German Tanks Have Edge: Superior Maneuverability is Revealed in Bad Weather." New York *Times*, January 18, 1945.

**23.** Lt. Col. Albin Irzyk, "Were German Armored Vehicles Better Than Ours?" *Army Ordnance*, March–April 1946, 240.

**24.** Irzyk, *He Rode Up Front*, 292.

**25.** Yeide, *Tank Killers*, 175.

**26.** Bell, "Shermans Defeat Nazi Tigers."

**27.** Ibid.

**28.** Ibid.

**29.** Ibid.

**30.** Frankel, *Patton's Best*, 83.

**31.** Marshall, *Report*, 38–39.

**32.** Johnson, *Fast Tanks*, 197.

**33.** "Superior Tanks Get Credit for Nazi Advances: U.S. Ordnance Experts Call Army Far Behind Enemy in Armored Equipment." New York *Herald-Tribune*, December 27, 1944.

**34.** Ibid.

**35.** New York *Sun*, December 28, 1944.

**36.** Zaloga, *US Anti-Tank*, 40.

**37.** Morse, "Combat Report, 692nd TD BTN, January 1945," 3.

**38.** Ibid, 4.

**39.** Ibid.

**40.** Collie Small, "Bastogne: American Epic." The *Saturday Evening Post*, February 17, 1945.

**41.** Forty, *US Tanks*, 149.

**42.** Ibid.

**43.** Zaloga, *Armored Thunderbolt*, 126.

**44.** Jack Myers, Presentation at Eisenhower Farm, 2015.

**45.** Forty, *US Tanks*, 151.

**46.** Baily, *Faint Praise*, 118.

# Chapter 11:
## "SUCH DETAILS CAN NO LONGER . . ."

**1.** Ann Stringer, "Our Tanks Worthless, Say Yanks." Washington *Post*, March 10, 1945.

**2.** "U.S. Ordnance Is Defended: Eisenhower Quoted In Answer To Criticism Of Weapons." The *Baltimore Sun*, February 3, 1945.

**3.** Baldwin, "American Tanks, Part II."

**4.** Hoehling, *Home Front, U.S.A*, 144.

**5.** Jarrett comment from "My Little Green Book," George B. Jarrett personal papers, US Army Military History Institute, Carlisle Barracks, PA.

**6.** Hanson Baldwin, "The German Blow III: New German Tank Proves Superior To Ours - Inquiry By Congress Urged." *New York Times*, January 5, 1945.

**7.** Jarrett comment from "My Little Green Book," George B. Jarrett personal papers, US Army Military History Institute, Carlisle Barracks, PA.

**8.** Israel, *State of the Union Messages*, 2889, 2887.

**9.** Ibid, 2887.

**10.** Ibid, 2888.

**11.** Jordan, *Warlords*, 59.

**12.** Israel, *State of the Union Messages*, 2889.

**13.** "U.S. Develops Super Tank, FDR Reveals." New York *Daily News*, January 7, 1945.

**14.** Elson, *Tanks*, 147.

**15.** Ibid, 257.

**16.** Ibid, 268.

**17.** Ibid, 258.

**18.** Ibid, 265–268.

**19.** "Decision to the Tiger." *Newsweek*, January 15, 1945.

**20.** Ibid.

**21.** Victor Jones, "Why Don't We Have Big Tanks To Combat Nazis'?" The Canton, Ohio, *Repository*, January 28, 1945.

**22.** "The Nation's Press: Warsaw To Berlin." Pampa, Texas, *Daily News*, via the New York *Daily News*, February 5, 1945.

**23.** "The Tanks are O.K." *Time*, February 12, 1945.

**24.** Ibid.

**25.** Smith, *Eisenhower*, 418–420, 829.

**26.** Tobin, *Ernie's War*, 164.

**27.** "U.S. Weapons Superior, Says Eisenhower." Wilkes-Barre, Pennsylvania, *Record*, February 3, 1945.

**28.** Hobbs, *Dear General*, 22.

**29.** "The Tanks are O.K."

**30.** "Patton Corrects a Canard, That M4s Are Too Light." Washington *Daily News*, March 27,1945.

**31.** Ibid.

**32.** Johnson, *Fast Tanks*, 196.

**33.** Keane, *Patton*, 219.

**34.** Calhoun, *General Lesley J. McNair*, 290.

**35.** Ibid, 289–290.

**36.** "Bradley Defends Sherman Tanks," Portland *Oregonian*, March 26, 1945, 9.

**37.** Hunnicutt, *Sherman*, 213.

**38.** Leiger, "Shells 'Bounce Off' Tigers."

**39.** Paynter and Gask, "Must We Defeat Germany With Inferior Weapons?," 28.

**40.** "German Tanks Tops—Yanks: Said to Be Superior Both in Guns, Armor." *Baltimore Sun*, February 25, 1945.

**41.** Ann Stringer, "Our Tanks Worthless, Say Yanks." Washington *Post*, March 10, 1945.

**42.** Pogue, *Organizer*, 552.

**43.** Ibid., 553.

**44.** Clifton Daniel, "New Tank Called Match for Tigers: The General Pershing Believed to be Answer to U.S. Soldier's Criticisms." New York *Times*, March 10, 1945.

**45.** Wes Gallagher, "Better Tanks, Less Talking Asked By Army." The Eugene, Oregon, *Guard*, March 17, 1945.

**46.** Daniel, "New Tank Called Match for Tigers."

**47.** Patton, *War As I Knew It*, 177.

**48.** Ibid.

**49.** Ibid, 177–180.

**50.** Letter dated March 30, 1945, from Gen. Levin Campbell to Gen. George S. Patton; Box 34, George S. Patton Papers. Manuscript Division, Library of Congress, Washington, DC.

**51.** Mayo, *Beachhead*, 337.

**52.** Wes Gallagher, "U.S. Tankmen to Washington: Give Us Tanks Instead of Talk." Philadelphia *Record*, March 17, 1945.

**53.** Ibid.

**54.** Ibid.

**55.** Ibid.

**56.** Ibid.

**57.** Ibid.

**58.** Ibid.

**59.** Fussell, *Wartime*, 287.

**60.** Baldwin, "American Tanks, Part II."

## Chapter 12: "COCK AND BULL STORIES"

1. Johnson, *Fast Tanks*, 199.
2. Leiger, "Shells Bounce Off Tigers."
3. White, *US vs. German Equipment*, 103.
4. Ibid, 7.
5. Ibid.
6. Ibid.
7. Ibid.
8. Jordan, *Warlords*, 140.
9. White, *US vs. German Equipment*, 7.
10. Ibid.
11. Ibid.
12. Johnson, *Fast Tanks*, 199.
13. White, *US vs. German Equipment*, 103.
14. Ibid, 78–79.
15. Ibid, 55.
16. Ibid, 27.
17. Ibid, 27–28.
18. Ibid, 30.
19. Ibid, 17–18.
20. Ibid, 17.
21. Ibid, 16.
22. Ibid, 15.
23. Ibid, 9–10.
24. Ibid, 13.
25. Ibid, 12.
26. Johnson, *Fast Tanks*, 199.
27. "U.S. General Was Murdered By Nazi Tankmen Captors," *Sacramento Bee*, Tuesday, April 3, 1945.
28. Hastings, *Armageddon*, 418–419.
29. Johnson, *Fast Tanks*, 199.
30. Ibid.
31. Ibid.
32. White, *US vs. German Equipment*, 66–67.
33. Ibid, 101.
34. Ibid, 83.
35. Ibid, 97–98.
36. Ibid, 105.
37. Ibid, 50.
38. Ibid, 75–76.
39. Ibid, 108.
40. Johnson, *Fast Tanks*, 199.
41. Weintraub, *15 Stars*, 172.
42. Ibid.
43. Johnson, *Fast Tanks*, 200.
44. Weintraub, *15 Stars*, 369.
45. Johnson, *Fast Tanks*, 200.
46. Ibid.
47. White, *US vs. German Equipment*, 65, 68, 70, 82.

## Chapter 13: "TOO LITTLE AND TOO LATE"

1. "Decision to the Tiger: Doubt on Caliber of U.S. Arms Raised by New German Weapons." *Newsweek*, January 15, 1945.
2. Paynter and Gask, "Must We Defeat Germany With Inferior Weapons?"
3. Hanson Baldwin, *New York Times*, January 1945.
4. The author served as an M1A1 Abrams tank gunner with the 104th Cavalry, 28th Infantry Division, Pennsylvania Army National Guard.
5. "New Tank." *Time*, March 19, 1945.
6. Mayo, *Beachhead*, 329.
7. Ibid, 330.
8. Hunnicutt, *Pershing*, 5.
9. Irzyk, *He Rode Up Front*, 70–71.
10. Michael Green and James Brown, *M4 Sherman at War* (St. Paul, Minnesota: Zenith Press, 2007), 56; Zaloga, *M26/M46 Pershing Tank*, 28.
11. Irwin, *Another River, Another Town*, 147.
12. Baily, *Faint Praise*, 138.
13. Blaker, *Iron Knights*, 323.
14. Ibid, 321.
15. Baily, *Faint Praise*, 128.
16. Forty, *US Tanks*, 136.
17. Mayo, *Beachhead*, 327–328.
18. Ibid, 328.
19. Thomson and Mayo, *Procurement and Supply*, 257.
20. Ibid, 259.
21. "U.S. Weapons Tops, Reports General." *Stars and Stripes*, February 6, 1945.
22. Ibid.
23. Ibid.
24. Ibid.
25. "Patterson Reveals Secret Weapon - Huge New Tank - In Broadcast." Monongahela, Pennsylvania, *Daily Republican*, March 5, 1945.
26. "They Need Those Tanks," The Bellingham, Washington, *Herald*, March 6, 1945, 4.
27. "Find Answer to German Tiger," Piqua, Ohio, *Daily Call, March 7, 1945.*
28. "German Tanks Better?" York, Pennsylvania, *Gazette and Daily*, March 8, 1945.
29. "They Need Those Tanks," 4.
30. Clifton Daniel, "New Tank Called Match for Tigers: The General Pershing Believed to be Answer to U.S. Solders' Criticisms." *New York Times*, March 10, 1945.
31. Ibid.
32. "New U.S. Tank To Take Field Soon," Belvidere, Illinois, *Daily Republican*, March 9, 1945.
33. Daniel, "New Tank."
34. Ibid.
35. Hunnicutt, *Pershing*, 200.
36. "New Heavy Tank Made for Offense: Stimson Asserts There is No Conflict With Army's Demand for Present Mobile Models." *New York Times*, March 9, 1945.
37. Baily, *Faint Praise*, 136.
38. "U.S. Develops Super Tank, FDR Reveals" New York *Daily News*, January 7, 1945. Jarrett comment from "My Little Green Book," George B. Jarrett personal papers, US Army Military History Institute, Carlisle Barracks, PA.
39. Ross, *The Business of Tanks*, 275.
40. Hunnicutt, *Pershing*, 17.
41. Ross, *The Business of Tanks*, 273.
42. Hunnicutt, *Pershing*, 38.
43. Ibid, 16.

44. Ibid, 28.
45. Cooper, *Death Traps*, 233–234.
46. Ibid, 234.
47. George Forty, *World War Two AFVs* (London: Osprey Publishing, 1996), 100.
48. Slayton, *Arms of Destruction*, 191.
49. Cooper, *Death Traps*, 234.
50. Forty, *US Tanks,* 138–139.
51. Mayo, *Beachhead*, 335.
52. Ibid.
53. "T26 Tanks Already In Western Front Action," Mason City, Iowa, *Globe-Gazette*, March 12, 1945.
54. Ibid.
55. Mayo, *Beachhead*, 335.
56. Chandler, *Papers of Dwight D. Eisenhower - The War Years, Volume IV*, 2511.
57. "Output of New U.S. Tanks Rushed." *Washington Post*, March 10, 1945.
58. Ross, *The Business of Tanks*, 273.
59. "Our Tanks are Without Equal: An Editorial." *Army Ordnance*, March–April 1945.
60. Mayo, *Beachhead*, 336.
61. "Death of a Myth." *Washington Post*, March 22, 1945.
62. Kenneth Macksey, *Tank Versus Tank*. London: Grub Street/Barnes and Noble Books, 1999, 146.
63. Zaloga, *Armored Thunderbolt*, 336.
64. Zaloga, *M26/M46*, 18.
65. Green, *American Tanks and AFVs*, 191.
66. Marshall, *Report*, 96.
67. Green, *American Tanks and AFVs*, 192.
68. David Miller, *The Great Book of Tanks*. (London: Salamander Books, 2002), 321.
69. Calhoun, *General Lesley J. McNair*, 286.
70. Zaloga, *M26/M46*, 11.
71. Jordan, *Warlords,* 142.
72. Thomson and Mayo, *Procurement and Supply*, 262.
73. Mayo, *Beachhead*, 338.
74. Hunnicutt, *Pershing*, 5.
75. Nye, *The Patton Mind*, 44.
76. Keane, *Patton*, 204.
77. Baily, *Faint Praise*, 122.
78. Hunnicutt, *Pershing*, 194.
79. Ibid.
80. Baily, *Faint Praise*, 138.
81. Mayo, *Beachhead*, 338.
82. Hunnicutt, *Pershing*, 199.
83. Ibid, 200.
84. Ibid.
85. Ibid.
86. Cooper, *Death Traps*, 155.

## Chapter 14: "FUSTEST WITH THE MOSTEST"

1. Army Ordnance Association, *Bulletin 51* (January, 1945).
2. Baldwin, "American Tanks, Part II."
3. Ross, *The Business of Tanks*, 293.
4. Yeide, *Tank Killers*, 242.
5. Hastings, *Armageddon*, 377.
6. Irzyk, *He Rode Up Front*, 343.
7. Hastings, *Armageddon*, 434.
8. "Sherman vs. Tiger - Patton Into Row With Loud Praise For Tanks." Abilene, Texas, *Reporter-News*, March 27, 1945, 6.
9. "Ike Says New Allied Tanks Equal To Best Nazi Models," Lincoln, Nebraska, *State Journal*, March 28, 1945.
10. Mayo, *Beachhead*, 476.
11. Hobbs, *Dear General*, 219.
12. Wesley Stout, *Tanks Are Mighty Fine Things* (reprint of the 1946 original; Middletown, DE: Periscope Film LLC, 2013), 64.
13. Fussell, *Boy's Crusade*, 100.
14. Jarymowycz, *Tank Tactics*, 267.
15. Ross, *The Business of Tanks*, 293.
16. Nicholas D. Molnar, "General George S. Patton and the War-Winning Sherman Tank Myth." In G. Kurt Piehler and Sidney Pash, *The United States and the Second World War: New Perspectives on Diplomacy, War, and the Home Front*. New York: Fordham University Press, 2010, 140.
17. Ibid.
18. Ibid, 140–141.
19. "Our Tanks Are Without Equal." *Army Ordnance Magazine*, March–April 1945; Gen. C.T. Harris, "Old Weapons and New." *Army Ordnance Magazine*, January–February 1945. Jarrett comment from "My Little Green Book," George B. Jarrett personal papers, US Army Military History Institute, Carlisle Barracks, PA.
20. "U.S. Tanks Fill Bill," Evansville, Indiana, *Courier*, February 10, 1945, 4.
21. Baldwin, "American Tanks, Part II."
22. Molnar, "Patton And The War Winning Sherman Tank Myth," 141.
23. Jarrett comment from "My Little Green Book," George B. Jarrett personal papers, US Army Military History Institute, Carlisle Barracks, PA.
24. Hobbs, *Dear General,* 218.
25. Chandler, *Papers of Dwight D. Eisenhower - The War Years, Volume IV*, 2534.
26. Ibid, 2533.
27. Butcher, *My Three Years With Eisenhower*, 785–786.
28. Ibid, 786.
29. Mayo, *Beachhead*, 349.
30. Jarymowycz, *Tank Tactics*, 91.
31. Hunnicutt, *Sherman*, 212.
32. John Mosier, *The blitzkrieg Myth: How Hitler and the Allies Misread the Strategic Realities of World War II* (New York: HarperCollins, 2003), 183.
33. Ross, *The Business of Tanks*, 324.
34. Unger and Unger, *George Marshall*, 115.
35. Marshall, *Report*, 113.
36. Dr. Richard Hallion, e-mail message to author January 28, 2016.
37. Cooper, *Death Traps*, 308.
38. Blaker, *Iron Knights*, 326–327.
39. "Berryman." Cartoon on US tank scandal, Washington *Evening Star*, 25 March 1945.

40. AFV and Weapons Section, Headquarters, European Theater of Operations, United States Army. "Final Historical Report." Record Group 338, US National Archives, Washington, DC.
41. John Morton Blum, *V Was For Victory* (New York: Harvest/HBJ, 1976), 5.
42. Hastings, *Armageddon*, 521.
43. Thomson and Mayo, *Procurement and Supply*, 263.
44. Bradley, *A Soldier's Story*, 323.
45. Ibid, 305.
46. Irzyk, "German Armored Vehicles," 236–240.
47. Army General Board, *Tank Gunnery*, 26.
48. Ellis, *Brute Force*, xvii.
49. Calhoun, *General Lesley J. McNair*, 288.
50. Gabel, "World War Two Armor Operations," in Hofmann and Starry, *Camp Colt to Desert Storm*, 178–179.

## Chapter 15: "WHO'S IN CHARGE HERE"

1. Israel, *State of the Union Messages,* 2888–2889.
2. N. T. Kenney, "Some German Weapons Topped Ours, Marshall Admits." Baltimore *Evening Sun*, October 10, 1945.
3. Hart, *Clash of Arms*, 1.
4. Patton, *War As I Knew It*, 248.
5. Jordan, *Warlords*, 256.
6. Parrish, *Roosevelt and Marshall*, 239.
7. Ibid.
8. Smith, *FDR*, 158.
9. Martin Gilbert, *The First World War: A Complete History*. (New York: Henry Holt and Company, 1994), 448.
10. James MacGregor Burns, *Roosevelt: The Soldier of Freedom* (New York: Harcourt Brace Jovanovich, 1979), 292.
11. Parrish, *Roosevelt and Marshall*, 239.
12. Jordan, *Warlords*, 379.
13. Parrish, *Roosevelt and Marshall*, 239.
14. Pogue, *Ordeal*, 299.
15. Parrish, *Roosevelt and Marshall*, 250.
16. Hoehling, *Home Front, U.S.A*, 151.
17. Marshall, *Report*, 115.
18. Pogue, *Ordeal*, 65.
19. Ibid, 66.
20. Ibid, 67.
21. Ibid.
22. Pogue, *Organizer*, 69.
23. Ibid, 70.
24. Jordan, *Warlords,* 208–209
25. Ibid.
26. L. Douglas Keeney, *The Eleventh Hour: How Great Britain, The Soviet Union, and The U.S. Brokered the Unlikely Deal That Won The War* (New York: Turner Publishing Company, 2015), 112.
27. Ibid.
28. Burns, *Roosevelt*, 343.
29. Ibid.
30. Morgan, *FDR*, 667.
31. Israel, *State of the Union Messages,* 2888.
32. Baily, *Faint Praise*, 120.
33. AFV and Weapons Section, "Final Historical Report."
34. Smith, *FDR*, 572.
35. Ibid, xv.
36. Ibid, 598.
37. Klein, *A Call to Arms*, 347.
38. Morgan, *FDR*, 764.
39. Unger and Unger, *George Marshall*, 300–301.
40. Cray, *General of the Army*, 77.
41. Ibid, 79–80.
42. Pogue, *Ordeal and Hope*, 289.
43. Cray, *General of the Army*, 443.
44. Bland, *Marshall Reminiscences*, 488.
45. Baily, *Faint Praise*, 92.
46. Ibid.
47. Baily, *Faint Praise*, 93.
48. Ibid.
49. Baily, *Faint Praise*, 96–97.
50. Ibid, 97.
51. Baily, *Faint Praise*, 98.
52. Pogue, *Ordeal*, 22.
53. Ibid, 78.
54. Ibid, 77.
55. Ibid.
56. Thomson and Mayo, *Procurement and Supply*, 84.
57. Ibid, 64.
58. "Credit to the Nazis." Kansas City *Star*, October 10, 1945, 5.
59. Cray, *General of the Army*, 403.
60. Kenney, "Some German Weapons Topped Ours."
61. Marshall, *Report*, 98.
62. Hunnicutt, *Sherman*, 5.
63. "War Hits Home In Marshall's Family," Cleveland, Ohio, *Plain Dealer*, May 31, 1944, 9.
64. Unger and Unger, *George Marshall*, 286.
65. Cray, *General of the Army*, 450.
66. Jordan, *Warlords*, 340.
67. "Stepson of Gen. Marshall Killed by Hand Grenade," Muscatine, Iowa, *Journal* and *News Tribune*, June 2, 1944, 6.
68. Clark, *Anzio*, 306.
69. Cray, *General of the Army*, 465–466.
70. Pogue, *Organizer*, 103.
71. Parrish, *Roosevelt and Marshall*, 243.
72. Pogue, *Ordeal*, 109.
73. Ibid.
74. Ibid.
75. Butcher, *My Three Years With Eisenhower*, 325.
76. Ibid, 397.
77. Weintraub, *15 Stars*, 147.
78. Pogue, *Ordeal*, 67.
79. Hoehling, *Home Front, U.S.A*, 144.
80. Tobin, *Ernie's War*, 141–142.
81. Fussell, *Boy's Crusade*, 176.
82. Unger and Unger, *George Marshall*, 49.
83. Pogue, *Organizer*, 77.
84. Irzyk, *He Rode Up Front*, 226.
85. Hastings, *Armageddon*, 187.
86. Frankel, *Patton's Best*, 85.
87. Marshall, *Report*, 106.

88. Parrish, *Roosevelt and Marshall*, 243.
89. Larry Bland (ed.), *The Papers of George Catlett Marshall, Volume 4* (Baltimore: The Johns Hopkins University Press, 1996), 290–291.
90. Ibid.
91. Ibid.
92. Ibid.
93. Ibid.
94. Ibid.
95. Unger and Unger, *George Marshall*, 453–454.
96. Ibid, 490.
97. Calhoun, *General Lesley J. McNair*, 279.
98. Baily, *Faint Praise*, 145.
99. Ibid.
100. Baily, *Faint Praise*, 142.
101. Hastings, *Armageddon*, 232.
102. Dwight Eisenhower, *Letters to Mamie* (New York: Doubleday and Company 1978), 150.
103. Dwight Eisenhower, *Crusade in Europe* (New York: Doubleday and Company, 1948), 422.
104. Ibid, 314.
105. "Our Tanks Are Without Equal: An Editorial." *Army Ordnance*, March–April 1945.
106. "The Arms of the U.S." *Time*, April 2, 1945.
107. Butcher, *My Three Years With Eisenhower*, 611.
108. Fussell, *Wartime*, 160–161.
109. Smith, *Eisenhower*, 343.
110. Geoffrey Perrett, *Eisenhower* (New York: Random House, 1999), 362.
111. John Eisenhower, *General Ike*, xii.
112. Jordan, *Warlords*, 429.
113. Johnson, *Fast Tanks*, 200.
114. Smith, *Eisenhower*, 393.
115. Ibid, 266.
116. Weintraub, *15 Stars*, 89.
117. Ibid, 84.
118. Ibid, 83.
119. Nigel Lewis, *Exercise Tiger* (New York: Prentice Hall Press, 1990), 169–170.
120. Ibid, 221.
121. Ibid, 335.
122. Hastings, *Armageddon*, 236.
123. John Eisenhower, *General Ike*, 167.
124. Ibid, 146.
125. Hobbs, *Dear General*, 212.
126. Farago, *Patton,* 354.
127. "What Is The Cause?" Sayre, Pennsylvania, *Evening Times*, December 27, 1944.
128. Weintraub, *15 Stars*, 305.
129. John Eisenhower, *General Ike*, 140.
130. Dwight Eisenhower, *At Ease: Stories I Tell To Friends* (Garden City, New York: Doubleday, 1967), 210.
131. D'Este, *Eisenhower: A Soldier's Life* (New York: Henry Holt and Company LLC, 2002), 705.
132. Hanson Baldwin, "American Tanks, Part I: New General Pershing Tank Awaits Test on the Battlefields of Europe." *New York Times*, March 18, 1945.
133. Smith, *Eisenhower*, 265.
134. Ibid, xii.
135. Ibid, 301, 367, 670.
136. Frankel, *Patton's Best*, 41, 55.
137. D'Este, *Patton*, 346.
138. Ibid, 347.
139. Patton, *War as I Knew It*, 248.
140. Ibid, 215.
141. Ibid, 83.
142. Nye, *The Patton Mind*, 146.
143. Ibid, 87.
144. Gen. George S. Patton Jr.; letter dated March 26, 1943, to Gen. Jacob Devers. Patton Papers, Box 34, US Library of Congress, Washington, DC.
145. Patton, *War As I Knew It*, 151.
146. Dennis Showalter, *Patton And Rommel: Men Of War In The Twentieth Century* (New York: Berkeley Caliber, 2006), 380.
147. Martin Blumenson, *The Patton Papers, Volume One: 1885–1940* (New York: Houghton Mifflin, 1974), 17.
148. Martin Blumenson, *Patton: The Man Behind the Legend, 1885–1945* (New York: Berkley Books, 1987), 176.
149. Weigley, *Eisenhower's Lieutenants*, 244.
150. Ellis, *Brute Force*, 386.
151. Patton, *War As I Knew It*, 107, 120, 155, 162, 164, 167.
152. Ibid, 279.
153. "The Tanks are OK." *Time*, February 12, 1945, 17.
154. Stout, *Tanks Are Mighty Fine Things*, 84.
155. "They Get There." The Charleston, South Carolina, *Evening Post*, March 28, 1945.
156. "The Tanks are OK," 17.
157. Patton, *War As I Knew It*, 158.
158. Ibid, 79.
159. John Eisenhower, *General Ike*, 70.
160. Weintraub, *15 Stars*, 381.
161. Linderman, *World Within War*, 201.
162. Bill Mauldin, *The Brass Ring* (New York: W.W. Norton and Company, Inc., 1971), 259.
163. Ibid, 247.
164. Ibid, 259.
165. D'Este, *A Genius for War*, 694.
166. Alan Axelrod, *Patton: A Biography* (New York: Palgrave Macmillan Ltd., 2006), 174.
167. Ibid, 175–177.
168. Zaloga, *Armored Thunderbolt*, 131.
169. Farago, *Patton,* 686–687.
170. "Patton Corrects a Canard, That M4s Are Too Light." Washington *Daily News*, March 27, 1945.

## Conclusion: "GLORY WITHOUT BLOOD"

1. Smith, *Eisenhower*, 588.
2. Ross, *The Business of Tanks*, 275.
3. Hastings, *Overlord*, 193.
4. Comments from Col. George Jarrett's "My Little Green Book." George B. Jarrett personal papers, US Army Military History Institute, Carlisle Barracks, PA.
5. Ibid, 98.
6. Ibid.

7. Ibid.

8. Ibid.

9. Ibid, 95.

10. Ibid, 98.

11. Ibid, 103–104.

12. Ibid, 103–105.

13. Frankel, *Patton's Best*, 85.

14. Marshall, *Report*, 98.

15. Ibid, 95.

16. Ibid, 95–96.

17. Ibid.

18. Zaloga, *M26/M46*, 4.

19. Marshall, *Report*, 96.

20. Ibid.

21. Ibid, 114.

22. Ibid, 99.

23. Hanson Baldwin, "Our Weapons, Part I: Time Lag From Blueprint to Battlefield and Vice Versa Termed Soldier's Loss." *New York Times*, February 28, 1945.

24. Ibid.

25. Ibid.

26. Mayo, *Beachhead*, 477.

27. Ibid.

28. Eisenhower, *Report*, 40.

29. Ibid, 37.

30. Ibid, 75.

31. Ibid, 122.

32. Weintraub, *15 Stars*, 271.

33. Sidney Shallett, "Ordnance Head Backs U.S. Tank; Calls Heavier Types Not Wanted." *New York Times*, February 3, 1945.

34. Baime, *Arsenal of Democracy*, 286.

35. Ibid, 285.

36. Fussell, *Wartime*, 185.

37. Ibid, 285.

38. Burns, *Roosevelt*, 343.

39. Baime, *Arsenal of Democracy*, 69.

40. Julian E. Zelezer, *Arsenal of Democracy: The Politics of National Security - From World War II To The War On Terrorism* (New York: Basic Books, 2010), 4, 49.

41. Ibid, 58.

42. Fussell, *Wartime*, 24.

43. Sean D. Cashman, *America Ascendant: From Theodore Roosevelt to FDR in the Century of American Power, 1901–1945* (New York: New York University Press, 1998), 426; see also Cashman, *America, Roosevelt, and World War Two* (New York: New York University Press, 1989), 199.

44. Jim Winchester, *Tanks and Armored Fighting Vehicles of World War Two.* (New York: Barnes and Noble Books, 2004), 10.

45. Mayo, *Beachhead*, 339.

46. Gabel, "World War Two Armor Operations," in Hoffman and Starry, *Camp Colt to Desert Storm*, 156.

47. Zaloga, *Armored Thunderbolt*, 336.

48. Hastings, *Inferno*, 369.

49. Baily, *Faint Praise*, 87.

50. Zaloga, *Armored Thunderbolt*, 47–48.

51. Elson, *Tanks*, 247.

52. Smith, *Eisenhower*, 634.

53. Constance Green, Harry Thomson, and Peter Roots, *The Ordnance Department: Planning Munitions for War* (Washington, DC: Office of the Center of Military History, US Army, 1955), vii.

54. Ibid, 259

55. Ibid, 259, xi

56. Ibid, 13

57. Ibid.

58. Ibid.

59. Ibid, 258.

60. Ibid, 259.

61. Ibid, 259, 13.

62. Thomson and Mayo, *Procurement and Supply*, 263–264.

63. Ibid, 264.

64. William B. Folkestad, *The View from the Turret: The 743rd Tank Battalion During World War II.* (Shippensburg, PA: Burd Street Press, 2000), 127.

65. Thomson and Mayo, *Procurement and Supply*, 262.

66. Baily, *Faint Praise*, 140.

67. Ibid.

68. Ibid.

69. Kahn, *McNair*, 24.

70. Baily, *Faint Praise*, 131.

71. Bland, *Marshall Reminiscences*, 263.

72. Pogue, *Ordeal*, 67.

73. Parrish, *Roosevelt and Marshall*, 451.

74. Pogue, *Ordeal*, 67.

75. Baily, *Faint Praise*, 127. The Bailey Bridge (no relation to author Charles Baily) was a portable, pre-fabricated, temporary bridge invented in 1939. Made of interchangeable parts, it could be carried by Allied vehicles and set up quickly without heavy equipment, such as cranes. It played a major role in helping the Allies cross to Western Europe and enter Germany. Its British inventor, Donald Bailey, was knighted for his work in 1946.

76. Bailey, *Faint Praise*, 82.

77. Ibid.

78. Bruce Culver, *Sherman in Action* (Carrollton, Texas: Squadron/ Signal, 1977), 39.

79. Ibid, 41.

80. Stout, *Tanks are Mighty Fine Things*, 48, 49.

81. "Tanks Pour Into Ogden Arsenal Storage Grounds." Ogden, Utah, *Standard-Examiner*, December 20, 1945.

82. Ibid.

83. Fletcher, *Tiger!*, 141.

84. Fletcher, *Tiger!*, 48.

85. Col. Paul Harkins in Patton, *War As I Knew It*, 180.

86. Baily, *Faint Praise*, 33.

87. Stout, *Tanks are Mighty Fine Things*, 2, 71, 82.

88. Gen. Gladeon M. Barnes, diary entry for February 28, 1944, in Medium Tank Series T20 - Box Number A744, Record Group 156, US National Archives, Washington, DC.

89. Gen. Gladeon M. Barnes, *Weapons of World War II.* New York: D. Van Nostrand Company, 1947.

90. Baritz, *The Good Life*, 177

91. Cray, *General of the Army*, 554.

**92.** I. C. B. Dear and M. R. D Foot (eds.), *The Oxford Companion to World War II* (New York: Oxford University Press, 2005), 861.

**93.** Ibid.

**94.** Ibid.

**95.** Linderman, *World Within War*, 26.

**96.** Calhoun, *General Lesley J. McNair*, 285.

**97.** Jones and Weithas, *WWII*, 13, 70–71.

**98.** Calhoun, *General Lesley J. McNair*, 329.

**99.** Citino, *Armored Forces*, 90, 100.

**100.** Peter Calvocoressi, Guy Wint, and John Pritchard, *The Penguin History of the Second World War* (originally published as *Total War*). London: Penguin Books, 2001, 584.

**101.** D'Este, *Eisenhower*, 370.

**102.** Ibid.

**103.** Ibid, 673.

**104.** John Eisenhower, *General Ike*, 36–37.

**105.** John Laffin, *On The Western Front: Soldiers' Stories from France to Flanders, 1914–1918*. Gloucester, England: Alan Sutton Publishing Ltd., 1986, 1–2.

**106.** Linderman, *World Within War*, 247.

**107.** Ibid.

**108.** Jones and Weithas, *WWII*, 71.

**109.** Calhoun, *General Lesley J. McNair*, dust jacket reviews.

**110.** Ibid, xvi.

**111.** Ibid, 22.

**112.** Hastings, *Armageddon*, xii.

**113.** Blum, *V Was For Victory*, 10.

**114.** Jordan, *Warlords*, 266.

**115.** Ibid, 361.

**116.** Johnson, *Fast Tanks*, 176.

**117.** Ibid, 219–220.

**118.** Dr. David Johnson, e-mail message to author March 25, 2016.

**119.** Green, *American Tanks and AFVs*, 195.

**120.** Johnson, *Fast Tanks*, 227.

**121.** Chandler, *Papers of Dwight D. Eisenhower - The War Years, Volume IV*, 2585–2586.

**122.** Johnson, *Fast Tanks*, 227.

**123.** Ibid.

**124.** Kenney, "Some German Weapons Topped Ours."

**125.** Green, *M4 Sherman*, 34.

**126.** Keane, *Patton*, 234.

**127.** Hastings, *Overlord*, 190; *Armageddon*, xii.

**128.** Studs Terkel, *"The Good War": An Oral History of World War Two*. (New York: Pantheon Books, 1984), 120–122.

**129.** Fussell, *Wartime*, 163.

**130.** Fussell, *Crusade*, 126.

**131.** Elson, *Tanks*, 291.

**132.** John Eisenhower, *General Ike*, 175.

**133.** Terkel, *"The Good War,"* 384.

**134.** Baime, *Arsenal of Democracy*, 209.

**135.** Brendan Phibbs, *The Other Side of Time: A Combat Surgeon in World War II* (Boston: Little Brown, 1987), 75.

**136.** Baily, *Faint Praise*, 146.

**137.** Jack Myers, Presentation at Eisenhower Farm, 2015.

**138.** Ibid.

**139.** Ibid.

**140.** Ibid.

**141.** Ibid.

**142.** Ibid.

**143.** Ibid.

**144.** Peter Beale, *Death by Design: The Fate of British Tank Crews in the Second World War*. Gloucestershire, England, UK: Sutton Publishing, 1998, ix.

**145.** Zaloga, *Armored Thunderbolt*, 336.

**146.** White, *US vs. German Equipment*, 76.

**147.** Linderman, *World Within War*, 334.

**148.** Frankel, *Patton's Best*, 14.

# Bibliography

## Archival materials: unpublished wartime and postwar documents, letters, memos, reports, diaries, oral histories, veteran surveys, etc.

AFV and Weapons Section, Headquarters, European Theater of Operations, United States Army. "Final Historical Report." Record Group 338, US National Archives, Washington, DC.

"Armor-Piercing Ammunition for Gun, 90mm, M3." Washington, DC: Office of the Chief of Ordnance, January 1945.

Army Service Forces. "Summary Report of Acceptances- Tank-Automotive Materiel, 1940–1945," December 1945.

Barnes, Gen. Gladeon M. Diary entry for February 28, 1944, in Medium Tank Series T20 - Box Number A744, Record Group 156, US National Archives, Washington, DC.

Campbell, Gen. Levin. Letter dated March 30, 1945, to Gen. George S. Patton; Box 34, George S. Patton Papers. Manuscript Division, Library of Congress, Washington, DC.

Close, Bertrand. World War Two Veterans Survey Files: 32nd Armored Regiment, Third Armored Division. US Army Military History Institute, Carlisle Barracks, PA.

Drury, Capt. George D. "Panzer VI Tiger Model B Design Study, Technical Analysis and Tests." Undated memo from "Ordnance Technical Intelligence Team No. 1, APO 230," in George B. Jarrett personal papers, US Army Military History Institute, Carlisle Barracks, PA.

General Board, United States Forces, European Theater of Operations. *Study No. 53: Tank Gunnery*. May 1945.

Grow, Robert W. *The Ten Lean Years: From the Mechanized Force (1930) to the Armored Force (1940)*. Unpublished manuscript in his personal papers, US Army Military History Institute, Carlisle Barracks, Pennsylvania.

Headquarters, First US Army. "Action Against the Enemy After Action Report, 31 August 1944." Record Group 338, ETO AFV and Weapons Section. National Archives and Records Administration, Suitland, Maryland.

Historical Section, Army Ground Forces. Study No. 27: "History of the Armored Force, Command, and Center," 1946.

"How to Kill A Panther." First United States Army Ordnance Service pamphlet, n.d., US Army Military History Institute, Carlisle Barracks, Pennsylvania.

Jarrett, Col. George B. "A British Tommy's Grave in Libya." Unpublished manuscript in his personal papers, US Army Military History Institute, Carlisle Barracks, Pennsylvania.

———. "Middle East 1942." Unpublished manuscript in his personal papers, US Army Military History Institute, Carlisle Barracks, Pennsylvania.

———. "My Little Green Book." Scrapbook of wartime newspaper clippings on the Sherman tank scandal, with Col. Jarrett's handwritten marginalia. George B. Jarrett personal papers, US Army Military History Institute, Carlisle Barracks, PA.

———. "Personal Notes - GBJ - Written March 1945." George B. Jarrett personal papers, US Army Military History Institute, Carlisle Barracks, PA.

Marshall, Gen. George C. Cable WDCSA/473 to Gen. Dwight Eisenhower, dated July 13, 1944 (on responses to Tiger and Panther tanks). George C. Marshall Research Library, Lexington, Virginia.

McDivitt, Major J. B. (4th Tank Battalion, First Armored Division). Memorandum on "Combat Data" to the Office of the Ordnance Officer, First Armored Division, 09 April 1945. In World War Two Veterans Survey Files: First Armored Division. US Army Military History Institute, Carlisle Barracks, PA.

Moore, Capt. A. Robert (1st Armored Regiment, First Armored Division). Memorandum to Chief of Ordnance, Washington, DC, on "Suggested Improvements, Design of Medium Tank," dated 30 October 1943. In World War Two Veterans Survey Files: First Armored Division. US Army Military History Institute, Carlisle Barracks, PA.

———. (Ibid). "Memoirs - World War II" (personal recollections from 1993). World War Two Veterans Survey files - First Armored Division. US Army Military History Institute, Carlisle Barracks, PA.

Morse, Lt. Col. Samuel S. "Combat Report - 692nd Tank Destroyer Battalion." Eschweiler, Germany, January 31, 1945.

Myers, Jack. Presentation on his WW Two service with the 692nd Tank Destroyer (TD) Battalion. Eisenhower Farm National Site, Gettysburg, PA, September 20, 2015.

Patton, General George S. Jr.; letter dated March 26, 1943, to Gen. Jacob Devers. Patton Papers, Box 34, US Library of Congress, Washington, DC.

Ross, Brigadier G. MacLeod. Letter dated April 9, 1945m to Lt. Col. George B. Jarrett, Aberdeen Proving Ground. In Col. George B. Jarrett personal papers, US Army Military History Institute, Carlisle Barracks, PA.

Statistical and Accounting Branch, Office of the Adjutant General, Department of the Army. *Army Battle Casualties And Nonbattle Deaths in World War II: Final Report, 7 December 1941–31 December 1946*. Washington, DC: Department of the Army, 1953.

Steadman, Lt. Col. Kenneth A. "The Evolution of the Tank In The U.S. Army." Study No. 1, prepared for the Commander, Combined Arms Center, Combat Studies Institute, US Army Command and General Staff College, 1982.

US Department of State Publication 1983: *Peace and War: United States Foreign Policy, 1931–1941*. Washington, DC: US Government Printing Office, 1943.

White, Maj. Gen. Isaac D. *United States Versus German Armor: As Prepared for the Supreme Commander, Allied Expeditionary Force*. 1945.

———. *United States Versus German Equipment*. Annotated reprint of the above original edition. Bennington, Vermont: Merriam Press, 2011.

Wright, Major B., (British) Royal Army Medical Corps (RAMC). *Military Operational Research Report - Battle Study No. 82: A Survey of Tank Casualties*. Department of the Scientific Advisor to the Army Council, March 1947.

## Wartime and Postwar US Army Publications: Books, Reports

Allied Forces Headquarters. *Training Memorandum No. 50: Lessons from the Sicilian Campaign*, November 20, 1943.

The Armored School. *The Second Armored Division in the Sicilian Campaign: A Research Report*. Fort Knox, Kentucky, 1950.

Cameron, Robert. *Mobility, Shock, and Firepower: The Emergence of the U.S. Army's Armor Branch, 1917–1945*. Washington, DC: US Army Center of Military History, 2008.

Camp, Brig. Gen. T. J. *Tankers in Tunisia*. Headquarters, Armored Replacement Training Center, Fort Knox, Kentucky, July 31, 1943.

Cole, H. M. *United States Army in World War II: The European Theater of Operations: The Lorraine Campaign*. Washington, DC: Historical Division, Department of the Army, 1950.

Coox, Alvin D., and Naisawald, L. Van Loan, *Survey of Allied Tank Casualties in World War II*. Fort Lesley J. McNair, Washington, DC: Operations Research Office, Johns Hopkins University, 1951.

Eisenhower, General Dwight D. *Report by The Supreme Commander to the Combined Chiefs of Staff on the Operations in Europe of the Allied Expeditionary Force, 6 June 1944 to 8 May 1945*. Washington, DC: US Government Printing Office, 1946.

G-2 Section, Tank Destroyer School. *Tank Destroyer Combat Reports from Theaters of Operations* (Fort Hood, Texas, February 1944).

Gabel, Christopher. *Seek, Strike, and Destroy: U.S. Army Tank Destroyer Doctrine in World War II*. Fort Leavenworth, Kansas: Combat Studies Institute, 1985.

———. *The U.S. Army GHQ Maneuvers of 1941*. Washington: US Army Center of Military History, 1991.

Green, Constance, Harry Thomson, and Peter Roots. *The Ordnance Department: Planning Munitions for War*. (US Army in World War Two Series). Washington: Office of the Center of Military History, 1955.

Marshall, Gen. George C. *General Marshall's Report: The Winning of the War in Europe and the Pacific - Biennial Report of the Chief of Staff of the United States Army, July 1, 1943 to June 30, 1945, to the Secretary of War*. New York: Simon and Schuster, 1945.

Marshall, Gen. George C. *Report on the Army, July 1, 1939 to June 30, 1943: Biennial Reports of Gen, George C. Marshall, Chief of Staff of the United States Army, to the Secretary of War*. Washington: *Infantry Journal*, 1943.

Mayo, Lida. *The Ordnance Department: On Beachhead and Battlefront*. (US Army in World War Two Series). Washington: Office of the Center of Military History, 1968.

Stubbs, Mary L., and Connor, Stanley R. *Army Lineage Series: Armor-Cavalry Part I: Regular Army and Army Reserve*. Washington: US Army Center of Military History, 1969.

Tank Destroyer School, Fort Hood, Texas. *Tank Destroyer Combat in Tunisia*. January 1944.

Thomson, Harry, and Mayo, Lida. *The Ordnance Department: Procurement and Supply* (US Army in World War Two Series). Washington: Office of the Center of Military History, 1960.

United States War Department Technical Manual TM-E 30-451: *Handbook on German Military Forces*. Washington: US Government Printing Office, March 1945.

United States War Department. *Lessons From the Tunisian Campaign*. Washington: US Government Printing Office, October 15, 1943.

Wilson, John B. *Maneuver and Firepower: The Evolution of Divisions and Separate Brigades*. Washington: United States Army Center of Military History, 1998.

## US Army and Affiliated Wartime and Postwar Periodicals - Magazines, Journals, Newsletters, etc.

"Artillery and the Tank." *Field Artillery Journal*, July–August 1940.

Barnes, Brig. Gen. Gladeon M. "Supertanks." *Army Ordnance*, Volume XXII, No. 131 (March–April 1942).

Cameron, Robert. "Armor Combat Development, 1917–1945." *ARMOR*, January–February 1997.

Carruthers, Bob (ed.). *Panzer Combat Reports*. Barnsley, England: Pen and Sword Books Ltd., 2013.

Christmas, Lt. Col. John. "Tanks: The Ideal Combination of Fire Power, Mobility, and Protection." *Army Ordnance*, January–February 1941.

———. "Our New Medium Tank." *Army Ordnance*, Volume XXII, No, 127 (July–August 1941).

Clemens, John. "Waking Up from the Dream: The Crisis of the Cavalry in the 1930s." *ARMOR*, May–June 1990.

Colby, Col. Joseph M. "From Designer to Fighter." *Armor*, January–February 1950.

Cranston, John. "1940 Louisiana Maneuvers Lead to Birth of Armored Force." *ARMOR*, May–June 1990.

"Editors Approve President's Defense Plan; Score 'Fireside Talk.'" *Army and Navy Journal*, June 1, 1940.

Grow, Robert W. "Mounted Combat: Lessons From the European Theater." *Cavalry Journal*, November– December 1945.

Harris, Maj. Gen. C.T. "Old Weapons and New." *Army Ordnance Magazine*, January–February 1945.

Irzyk, Brig. Gen. Albin F. "Were German Armored Vehicles Better Than Ours?" *Army Ordnance*, March–April 1946, 236–240.

Kutz, C. R. "Break-Through Tanks: Will They Bring Freedom of Action to Armored Divisions?" *Army Ordnance*, November–December 1940, 242–245.

Leiger, Ernest. "Shells "Bounce Off" Tigers, Veteran U.S. Tankmen Say." *Stars and Stripes*, 23 February 1945.

Miller, H. W. "After the Tank, What? The Armored Vehicle May Have Reached Its Limit of Development." *Army Ordnance*, January–February 1944.

Nenninger, Timothy K. "The Development of American Armor, 1917–1940." Part One: "The World War One Experience." *ARMOR*, January–February 1969.

———. "Part Two: The Tank Corps Reorganized." *ARMOR*, March–April 1969.

———. "Part Three: The Experimental Mechanized Forces." *ARMOR*, May–June 1969.

———. "Part Four: A Revised Mechanization Policy." *ARMOR*, September–October 1969.

"New Army Tank." *Army and Navy Journal*, March 10, 1945.

"N.Y. Times Expert Asks Why German Tanks are Better." *Stars and Stripes*, January 23, 1945.

"Our Tanks Are Without Equal: An Editorial." *Army Ordnance*, March–April 1945.

"Patton Defends U.S. Tanks." *Army and Navy Journal*, March 31, 1945.

Reilly, Henry J. "Proving Ground in Spain: Armament Trends as Revealed by the Spanish War." *Army Ordnance*, May–June 1939.

Schreier, Konrad Jr. "U.S. Army Tank Development, 1925–1940," *ARMOR*, May–June 1990.

"Tankmen Stage Firepower Show for Visitors." *Armored News*, March 27, 1944.

"Tanks and the Ardennes Reverses." Bulletin 51, Army Ordnance Association, January 15, 1945.

"Troops Overseas: Royalty, Military Visit Invasion Armor." *Armored News*, March 27, 1944.

"Troops Overseas: Tankers in England Impress Eisenhower." *Armored News*, March 6, 1944.

"U.S. Weapons Tops, Reports General." *Stars and Stripes*, February 6, 1945.

Wedemeyer, Maj. Albert C. "Anti-Tank Defense." *Field Artillery Journal*, May 1941.

White, William. "M-4 Tank Reassuring, Says Writer." *Armored News*, March 6, 1944.

Woolner, Sgt. Frank. "The Texas Tanker." *YANK - The Army Weekly*. n.d., 1945.

### Wartime/ Early Postwar Books, Civilian Publications

Barnes, Gen. Gladeon M. *Weapons of World War II*. New York: D. Van Nostrand Company, 1947.

Conger, Elizabeth Mallett. *American Tanks and Tank Destroyers*. New York: Henry Holt and Company, 1944.

Gillie, Mildred H. *Forging the Thunderbolt*. Harrisburg, Pennsylvania: The Military Publishing Service, 1947.

Infantry Journal. *The Armored Forces of the United States Army*. Chicago: Rand McNally and Company, 1944.

Johnson, Franklyn A. *One More Hill* (reprint of 1949 original). New York: Bantam Books, 1983.

Kahn, Eli J. *McNair: Educator of an Army*. Washington, DC: The Infantry Journal Press, 1945.

McGhee, Capt. Addison F., Jr. *He's In The Armored Force Now*. New York: Robert M. McBride & Company, 1944.

Nelson, Donald. *Arsenal of Democracy: The Story of America's War Production*. New York: Harcourt Brace and Company, 1946.

Patton Jr., George S. *War As I Knew It*. New York: Houghton Mifflin, 1994 edition of 1947 original.

Pyle, Ernie. *Here Is Your War*. New York: Henry Holt & Company, 1943.

Stout, Wesley W. *Tanks Are Mighty Fine Things*. Detroit: Chrysler Corporation, 1946.

Whitaker, John T. "Lieutenant General Lesley McNair," in *These Are The Generals*. New York: Knopf, 1943.

### Wartime Newspaper Articles - Civilian:

"Army Denies Tanks are Second Rate," *New York Times,* November 22, 1936.

"Army Is Not Ready." Lawrence, Kansas, *Journal-World*, December 28, 1939.

Baldwin, Hanson W. "The German Blow III: New German Tank Proves Superior to Ours - Inquiry by Congress Urged." *New York Times*, January 5, 1945.

———. "American Tanks, Part I: New General Pershing Tank Awaits Test on the Battlefields of Europe." *New York Times*, March 18, 1945.

———. "American Tanks, Part II: Men in Field Weigh Merits of Armored Vehicles and Declare Much is Wanting." *New York Times*, March 19, 1945.

———. "American Tanks, Part III." *New York Times*, March 20, 1945.

———. "Our Policy on Weapons: Ordnance Expert Suggests Special Authority to Study Improvement Ideas of Men in Field." *New York Times*, February 21, 1945.

———. "Our Weapons: Time Lag From Blueprint to Battlefield and Vice Versa termed Soldier's Loss." *New York Times*, February 28, 1945.

———. "Tanks and Weapons II: Observers Sound Warning Against Underestimating the Still High Quality of German Army's Equipment." *New York Times,* n.d. on original, 1945.

Berryman, Clifford K. Cartoon on US tank scandal, Washington *Evening Star*, March 25, 1945.

Bolles, Blair. "American Weapons Called World's Best." *Baltimore Sun*, April 3, 1944.

"Bradley Defends Sherman Tanks." Portland, Oregon, *Oregonian*, March 26, 1945

Carey, Frank. "Most of America's Weapons Better Than Those of Enemy: 'Box Score' Comparisons Are Given By Tester; Nazi Equipment Rated High." Danville, Virginia, *Bee*, April 29, 1943.

"Credit to the Nazis." Kansas City *Star*, October 10, 1945.

Daniel, Clifton. "New Tank Called Match for Tigers: The General Pershing Believed To Be Answer to U.S. Soldier's Criticisms." *New York Times,* March 10, 1945.

"Death of a Myth." Washington *Post*, March 22, 1945.

Dixon, Kenneth L. "They Found A Moral In German Pictures." Santa Cruz, California, *Sentinel*, January 9, 1945.

"Ex-Farmer and Milkman Halt Attack: 2 Yank Tanks Repel Panzer Drive, Bag 3." Washington *Daily News*, October 29, 1943.

Gallagher, Wes. "Fighters Ask Better Tanks, Less Washington Boasting." Chicago *Tribune*, March 17, 1945.

———. "New Nazi Tank is Best in World, Yanks Declare." New York *Daily News*, December 4, 1944.

———. "U.S. Tankmen to Washington: Give Us Tanks Instead of Talk." Philadelphia *Record*, March 17, 1945.

"German Expert Finds U.S. Tanks Would Not Stand Test of War," *New York Times*, November 22, 1936.

"German Tanks Have Edge: Superior Maneuverability is Revealed in Bad Weather." *New York Times*, January 18, 1945.

"German Tanks Tops—Yanks: Said to be Superior Both in Guns, Armor." *Baltimore Sun*, February 25, 1945.

Kenney, N. T. "Some German Weapons Topped Ours, Marshall Admits." *Baltimore Evening Sun*, 10 October 1945.

"M-36 "'Sluggers' Favored By 10 to 1 in Combat." *Baltimore Sun*, 26 April 1945.

"New Heavy Tank Made for Offense: Stimson Asserts There is No Conflict With Army's Demand for Present Mobile Models." *New York Times*, March 9, 1945.

"Omissions in the Record." Kansas City *Star*, October 21, 1945.

"Out-Armed In Tanks." Rhinelander, Wisconsin, *Daily News*, January 4, 1945.

"Patton Corrects a Canard, That M4s Are Too Light." Washington *Daily News*, March 27, 1945.

"Patton Supports American Tanks." Atchison, Kansas, *Daily Globe*, March 27, 1945.

Pinkley, Virgil. "'Give Us Bigger Guns,' Plea of American Tank Crews." March 12, 1945. Periodical not specified; in George B. Jarrett personal papers, US Army Military History Institute, Carlisle Barracks, PA.

Shallett, Sidney. "Ordnance Head Backs U.S. Tank; Calls Heavier Types Not Wanted." *New York Times*, February 3, 1945.

"Sherman Vs. Tiger - Patton Into Row With Loud Praise For Tanks." Abilene, Kansas, *Reporter-News*, March 27, 1945.

"Stepson of Gen. Marshall Killed by Hand Grenade," Muscatine, Iowa, *Journal* and *News Tribune*, June 2, 1944, 6.

Stringer, Ann. "Our Tanks Worthless, Say Yanks." Washington *Post*, March 10, 1945.

"Tankmen Want Better U.S. Tanks." *Baltimore Sun*, n.d. on original, 1945. In George B. Jarrett personal papers, US Army Military History Institute, Carlisle Barracks, PA.

"Tanks at Aberdeen Speedy, Powerful." Baltimore *Evening Sun*, September 5, 1944.

"They Need Those Tanks," Bellingham, Washington, *Herald*, March 6, 1945.

Thompson, John. "Sicilian Orchard Quiet After Yank 'Chutists Battle Through Eyties." Amarillo, Texas, *Daily News*, July 16, 1943.

"2 Yank Tanks Repel Panzer Drive, Bag 3: Ex-Farmer and Milkman Halt Attack." Washington *Daily News*, October 29, 1943.

"U.S. Develops Super Tank, FDR Reveals." New York *Daily News*, January 7, 1945.

"U.S. Ordnance is Defended: Eisenhower Quoted in Answer to Criticism of Weapons." *Baltimore Sun*, February 3, 1945.

"U.S. Tanks Fill Bill." Editorial, Evansville, Indiana, *Courier*, February 10, 1945.

"U.S. Weapons Superior, Says Eisenhower." Wilkes-Barre, Pennsylvania, *Record*, February 3, 1945.

"War Hits Home In Marshall's Family," Cleveland, Ohio, *Plain Dealer*, May 31, 1944.

"Weapons of War." Baltimore *Evening Sun*, July 13, 1944.

"What Is The Cause?" Sayre, Pennsylvania, *Evening Times*, December 27, 1944.

"Yank Tanks Defended by Gen. Patton: The Man Who Ought to Know Says They're OK." *PM New York*, March 27, 1945.

## Wartime Era Magazine Articles - Civilian:

"The Arms of the U.S." *Time*, April 2, 1945.

"The Battle of the Tanks." *Life*, March 26, 1945.

"Big Jim Leaps Swinging." *Time*, August 17, 1942.

"Chasing the Tiger." *Newsweek*, March 19, 1945.

"Decision to the Tiger: Doubt on Caliber of U.S. Arms Raised by New German Weapons." *Newsweek*, January 15, 1945.

"Doubt on Caliber of U.S. Arms Raised by New German Weapons," *Newsweek*, January 15, 1945.

Embed, Staff Sgt. Charles. "Yank in a Tank." *American Magazine*, September 1943.

"From My Own Men." *Time*, August 14, 1944.

Gallagher, Wes. "Driblets of Tanks." *Newsweek*, March 26, 1945.

"Gaps in U.S. Preparedness." *Newsweek*, August 28, 1939.

Grahame, Arthur. "Why America's Tanks Are The World's Best." *Popular Science*, March 1943.

Hemingway, Ernest. "Battle for Paris." *Collier's Magazine*, September 30, 1944.

———. "The G.I. and the General." *Collier's Magazine*, November 14, 1944.

"Ideal Tank?" National Defense News - Army. *Time*, December 15, 1941.

"Is it Good Enough?" *Time*, June 16, 1941.

"New Tank." *Time*, March 19, 1945.

Nichols, Herbert B. "Prepare for Action." *Christian Science Monitor*, September 28, 1940.

Paynter, Henry, and Roland Gask. "Must We Defeat Germany with Inferior Weapons?" *Newsweek*, February 26, 1945.

"Post-Mortem on the Ardennes." *Time*, January 15, 1945.

Ratcliff, John D. "Better Men in Better Tanks." *Collier's Magazine*, November 28, 1942.

"Rehearsal." *Time*, September 2, 1940.

Small, Collie. "Bastogne: American Epic." *Saturday Evening Post*, February 17, 1945.

"Tanks Pour Into Ogden Arsenal Storage Grounds." Ogden, Utah, *Standard-Examiner*, December 20, 1945.

"The Tanks are OK." *Time*, February 12, 1945.

"They Get There." Charleston, South Carolina, *Evening Post*, March 28, 1945.

"Tiger to Tame." *Time*, January 8, 1945.

"Two General Sherman Tanks Route 14 Nazi Tigers In Italy." Neosho, Missouri, *Daily News, November 2, 1943.*

## Postwar Civilian Journal Articles, Theses, etc.

Davis, Cecil G. *Tarnished Armor: The Development of Armor Doctrine in the United States.* MA thesis submitted to Central Missouri State University. Ann Arbor, Michigan: Dissertation Services, 1997.

Hofmann, George. "The Tactical and Strategic Use of Attaché Intelligence: The Spanish Civil War and the U.S. Army's Misguided Quest for a Modern Tank Doctrine," *Journal of Military History*, January 1998.

Smith, Kevin D. "War-Winner: A Re-Appraisal Of The M4 Sherman Tank In World War Two." Masters' degree thesis submitted to Middle Tennessee State University, 2013.

Smoler, Fredric. "Overrated/Underrated: [the Sherman] Tank." *American Heritage*, October 2003.

## Books

Ambrose, Stephen. *Citizen Soldiers: The U.S. Army From The Normandy Beaches to the Bulge, to the Surrender of Germany*. New York: Simon and Schuster Paperbacks, 1997.

Astor, Gerald. *A Blood-Dimmed Tide: The Battle of the Bulge by the Men Who Fought It*. New York: Dell Publishing/ Random House, 1992.

Atkinson, Rick. *An Army At Dawn*. New York: Henry Holt, 2002.

———. *The Day of Battle*. New York: Henry Holt, 2007.

———. *The Guns At Last Light*. New York: Henry Holt, 2013.

Axelrod, Alan. *Patton: A Biography* (Great Generals series). New York: Palgrave Macmillan Ltd., 2006.

Baily, Charles M. *Faint Praise: American Tanks and Tank Destroyers during World War II*. Hamden, Connecticut: Archon Books/ Shoe String Press, 1983.

Baime, A.J. *The Arsenal of Democracy: FDR, Detroit, And An Epic Quest to Arm An America at War*. New York: Houghton Mifflin Harcourt, 2014.

Baldwin, Hanson. *Tiger Jack* (Fort Carlson, Kentucky: Old Army Press, 1979).

Baritz, Loren. *The Good Life: The Meaning of Success for the American Middle Class*. New York: Harper and Row, 1990.

Beale, Peter. *Death by Design: The Fate of British Tank Crews in the Second World War*. Gloucestershire, England, UK: Sutton Publishing, 1998.

Berndt, Thomas. *American Tanks of World War II*. Osceola, Wisconsin: Motorbooks International, 1994.

Blaker, Gordon A. *Iron Knights: The United States 66th Armored Regiment*. Shippensburg, PA: Burd Street Press, 1999.

Bland, Larry (ed.). *George C. Marshall: Reminiscences for Forrest Pogue*. Lexington, VA: George C. Marshall Research Foundation, 1991.

———. *The Papers of George Catlett Marshall, Volume 4: "Aggressive and Determined Leadership-" June 1, 1943, December 31, 1944*. Baltimore, Maryland: Johns Hopkins University Press, 1996.

Blum, John Morton. *V Was For Victory: Politics And American Culture During World War II*. New York: Harvest/ HBJ, 1976.

Blumenson, Martin. *Patton: The Man Behind the Legend, 1885-1945*. New York: Berkley Books, 1987.

Botham, Noel, and Montague, Bruce. *Catch That Tiger: Churchill's Secret Order That Launched the Most Astonishing and Dangerous Mission of World War II*. London. John Blake Publishing Ltd., 2012.

Bradford, George. *Great Tank Battles of WWII: A Combat Diary of the Second World War*. New York: Arco Publishing, 1970.

Bradley, General Omar N. *A Soldier's Story*. New York: Henry Holt and Company, 1951.

Bradley, Omar, and Blair, Clay. *A General's Life*. New York: Simon and Schuster, 1983.

Buckley, John. *British Armour in the Normandy Campaign 1944*. London: Frank Cass, 2004.

———. *Monty's Men: The British Army and the Liberation of Europe*. New Haven, Connecticut: Yale University Press, 2013.

Burns, James MacGregor. *Roosevelt: The Soldier of Freedom*. New York: Harcourt Brace Jovanovich, 1979.

Butcher, Harry C. *My Three Years With Eisenhower*. New York: Simon and Schuster, 1946.

Butler, William, and Strode, William (eds.). *Chariots of Iron: Fifty Years of American Armor*. Louisville, Kentucky: Harmony House Publishers, 1990.

Caidin, Martin. *The Tigers Are Burning*. New York: Hawthorn Books, 1974.

Calhoun, Mark T. *General Lesley J. McNair: Unsung Architect of The U.S. Army*. Lawrence, Kansas: University Press of Kansas, 2015.

Calvocoressi, Peter, Guy Wint, and John Pritchard. *The Penguin History of the Second World War* (originally published as *Total War*) Revised edition; London: Penguin Books, 2001.

Calvocoressi, Peter, Guy Wint, and John Pritchard. *Total War: The Causes and Consequences of the Second World War. Volume 1: The Western Hemisphere*. Revised second edition; New York: Viking Penguin, 1989.

Carius, Otto. *Tigers in the Mud: The Combat Career of German Panzer Commander Otto Carius*. Mechanicsburg, PA: Stackpole Books, 2003.

Cashman, Sean D. *America Ascendant: From Theodore Roosevelt to FDR in the Century of American Power, 1901-1945*. New York: New York University Press, 1998.

———. *America, Roosevelt, and World War Two*. New York: New York University Press, 1989.

Childers, Thomas. *Soldier From The War Returning: The Greatest Generation's Troubled Homecoming From World War II*. Boston: Houghton Mifflin Harcourt, 2009.

Churchill, Winston S. *The Second World War*, Vol. II: *Their Finest Hour*. Boston: Houghton Mifflin Company, 1949.

Citino, Robert M. *Armored Forces: History and Sourcebook*. Westport, Connecticut: Greenwood Press, 1994.

Clark, Lloyd. *Anzio: Italy and the Battle for Rome—1944*. New York: Atlantic Monthly Press, 2006.

Cole, H. M. *United States Army in World War II: The European Theater of Operations: The Lorraine Campaign*. Washington, DC: Historical Division, Department of the Army, 1950.

Collins, Michael, and Martin King. *Voices of the Bulge: Untold Stories from Veterans of the Battle of the Bulge*. Minneapolis, MN: Zenith Press: 2011.

Cooper, Belton Y. *Death Traps: The Survival of an American Armored Division in World War Two*. New York: Ballantine Books, 1998.

Cooper, Bryan. *Tank Battles of World War I*. Yorkshire, England: Pen and Sword Books LTD, 2014.

Cray, Ed. *General of the Army: George C. Marshall, Soldier and Statesman*. New York: W. W. Norton, 1990.

Culver, Bruce. *Sherman in Action*. Carrollton, Texas: Squadron/ Signal Publications, 1977.

Davis, Kenneth S. *FDR: The War President, 1940–1943: A History*. New York: Random House, 2000.

Dear, I. C. B., and M. R. D Foot (eds.). *The Oxford Companion to World War II*. New York: Oxford University Press, 2005.

D'Este, Carlo. *Eisenhower: A Soldier's Life*. New York: Henry Holt and Company LLC, 2002.

———. *Patton: A Genius for War*. New York: HarperPerennial Books, 1996.

Donnelly, Thomas, and Sean Naylor. *Clash of Chariots: The Great Tank Battles*. New York: Berkley Books, 1996.

Doubler, Michael D. *Closing With the Enemy: How GIs Fought the War in Europe, 1944–1945*. Lawrence, Kansas: University Press of Kansas, 1994.

Dunnagan, Harry. *A War to Win: Company B, 813th Tank Destroyers*. Myrtle Beach, SC: Royal Dutton Books, 1992.

Edwards, Roger. *Panzer: A Revolution in Warfare, 1939–1945*. London: Arms and Armour Press, 1993.

Eisenhower, Dwight D. *At Ease: Stories I Tell To Friends*. Garden City, New York: Doubleday, 1967.

———. *Crusade in Europe*. New York: Doubleday and Company, 1948.

Eisenhower, Dwight D., edited by Robert H. Ferrell. *The Eisenhower Diaries*. New York: Norton, 1981.

Eisenhower, Dwight D., edited by Alfred Chandler Jr. *The Papers of Dwight David Eisenhower: The War Years, Volume IV*. Baltimore, Maryland: The Johns Hopkins University Press, 1970.

Eisenhower, Dwight D, edited by Daniel Holt and James Leyerzapf. *Eisenhower: The Prewar Diaries and Selected Papers, 1905–1941*. Baltimore: Johns Hopkins University Press, 1998.

Eisenhower, John S. D. *General Ike: A Personal Reminiscence*. New York: Free Press, 2003.

Eisenhower, John S. D. (ed.). *Letters to Mamie, by Dwight D. Eisenhower*. Garden City, New York: Doubleday & Company, Inc., 1978.

Ellis, John. *Brute Force: Allied Strategy and Tactics in the Second World War*. New York: Viking Penguin, 1990.

Elson, Aaron. *Tanks for the Memories: An Oral History of the 712th Tank Battalion in World War II*. Hackensack, New Jersey: Chi Chi Press, 1997.

———. *They Were All Young Kids*. Hackensack, New Jersey: Chi Chi Press, 1994.

Failmezger, Victor. *American Knights: The Untold Story of the Men of the Legendary 601st Tank Destroyer Battalion*. Oxford, England: Osprey Publishing, 2015.

Fletcher, David (ed.). *Tiger! The Tiger Tank: A British View*. London: Her Majesty's Stationary Office, 1986.

Folkestad, William B. *The View from the Turret: The 743rd Tank Battalion During World War II*. Shippensburg, PA: Burd Street Press, 2000.

Forty, George. *Tank Aces: From blitzkrieg to the Gulf War*. Gloucestershire, Great Britain: Sutton Publishing, 1997.

———. *Tank Action: From the Great War to the Gulf*. London: Allan Sutton, 1995.

———. *Tank Warfare in the Second World War: an Oral History*. London: Constable, 1998.

———. *United States Tanks of World War II*. Dorset, England: Blandford Press, 1983.

———. *World War Two AFVs*. London: Osprey Publishing, 1996.

Frankel, Nat, and Larry Smith. *Patton's Best: An Informal History of the 4th Armored Division*. New York: Hawthorn Books Inc., 1978.

Fussell, Paul. *The Boy's Crusade: The American Infantry in Northwestern Europe, 1944–1945*. New York: The Modern Library, 2003.

———. *Wartime*. New York: Oxford University Press, 1989.

Gabel, Christopher. "World War Two Armor Operations in Europe." In *Camp Colt to Desert Storm: The History of U.S. Armored Forces*, edited by George F. Hofmann and Donn A. Starry, 144–184. Lexington, Kentucky: The University Press of Kentucky, 1999.

Gilbert, Martin. *The First World War: A Complete History*. New York: Henry Holt and Company, 1994.

Green, Michael. *M4 Sherman*, Osceola, Wisconsin: Motorbooks International, 1993.

———. *Patton's Tank Drive*. Osceola, Wisconsin: Motorbooks International, 1995.

———. *American Tanks and AFVs of World War II*. Oxford, England: Osprey Publishing, 2014.

Green, Michael, and James D. Brown. *M4 Sherman at War*. St. Paul, Minnesota: Zenith Press, 2007.

Green, Michael, and Gladys Green. *Panzers at War*. St. Paul, Minnesota: Zenith Press, 2005.

Grove, Eric. *German Armour: Poland and France, 1939–1940*. London: Almark Publishing Company Ltd., 1976.

Guderian, Heinz. *Panzer Leader*. New York: Ballantine Books, 1957.

Hart, Russell A. *Clash of Arms: How the Allies Won in Normandy*. Boulder, Colorado: Lynne Rienner Publishers, 2001.

Hastings, Max. *Armageddon: The Battle For Germany, 1944–1945*. New York: Alfred A. Knopf, 2004.

———. *Inferno: The World At War, 1939–1945*. New York: Vintage Books, 2012.

———. *Overlord: D-Day & The Battle for Normandy*. New York: Simon and Schuster, 1984.

Herr, General John K, and Edward S. Wallace. *The Story of the U.S. Cavalry*. Boston: Little, Brown, 1953.

Hobbs, Joseph P. *Dear General: Eisenhower's Wartime Letters to Marshall*. Baltimore: The Johns Hopkins University Press, 1999.

Hoehling, A.A. *Home Front, U.S.A*. New York: Thomas Crowell Company, 1966.

Hofmann, George, and Donn Starry. *Camp Colt to Desert Storm: The History of U.S. Armored Forces*. Lexington, Kentucky: The University Press of Kentucky, 1999.

Holt, Daniel, and James Leyerzapf. *Eisenhower: The Prewar Diaries and Selected Papers, 1905–1941*. Baltimore: Johns Hopkins University Press, 1998.

Houston, Donald. *Hell on Wheels: The 2nd Armored Division*. Novato, California: Presidio Press, 1977.

Howe, George. *"Old Ironsides": The Battle History of the 1st Armored Division*. Washington: Combat Forces Press, 1954.

Hunnicutt, Richard P. *Pershing: A History of the Medium Tank T20 Series*. Berkeley, California: Feist Publications, 1971.

———. *Sherman: A History of the American Medium Tank*. Belmont, California: Taurus Enterprises, 1978.

Hymel, Kevin M. *Patton's Photographs: War As He Saw It*. Washington, DC: Potomac Books, 2006.

Icks, Robert. *Famous Tank Battles: From World War I to Vietnam*. Garden City, New York: Doubleday: 1972.

Irwin, John P. *Another River, Another Town: A Teenage Tank Gunner Comes of Age in Combat, 1945*. New York: Random House, 2002.

Irzyk, Brig. Gen. Albin F. *He Rode Up Front for Patton*. Raleigh, North Carolina: Pentland Press Inc., 1996.

Israel, L. (ed.). *The State of the Union Messages, 1790–1966*. New York: Chelsea House, 1966.

Jarymowycz, Roman J. *Cavalry From Hoof to Track*. Mechanicsburg, PA: Stackpole Books, 2009.

———. *Tank Tactics from Normandy to Lorraine*. Mechanicsburg, PA: Stackpole Books, 2009.

Jensen, Marvin. *Strike Swiftly! The 70th Tank Battalion From North Africa to Normandy to Germany*. Novato, CA: Presidio Press, 1997.

Jentz, Thomas, and Hilary Doyle. *Tiger I Heavy Tank, 1942–45*. Oxford, England: Osprey Publishing, 2004.

Johnson, David E. *Fast Tanks and Heavy Bombers: Innovation in the U.S. Army, 1917–1945*. Ithaca, New York: Cornell University Press, 1998.

Jones, James, and Art Weithas. *WWII: A Chronicle of Soldiering*. New York: Grosset and Dunlap Publishers, 1975.

Jordan, Jonathan W. *American Warlords: How Roosevelt's High Command Led America To Victory in World War Two*. New York: NAL/Caliber-Penguin Group, 2015.

———. *Brothers, Rivals, Victors: Eisenhower, Patton, Bradley, and The Partnership that Drove the Allied Conquest In Europe*. New York: NAL/ Caliber, 2011.

Keane, Michael. *Patton: Blood, Guts, and Prayer*. Washington: Regnery Publishing, Inc, 2012.

Keegan, John. *The Second World War*. New York: Viking Press, 1990.

———. *Six Armies in Normandy: From D-Day to the Liberation of Paris*. New York: Penguin Books, 1994.

Keeney, L. Douglas. *The Eleventh Hour: How Great Britain, The Soviet Union, and The U.S. Brokered the Unlikely Deal That Won the War*. New York: Turner Publishing Company, 2015.

Kelly, Orr. *Meeting the Fox: The Allied Invasion of Africa, from Operation Torch to Kasserine Pass to Victory in Tunisia*. New York: John Wiley and Sons, 2002.

Kershaw, Andrew. *Tanks at War, 1939–1945*. London: Phoebus Publishing Company, 1975.

Kindsvatter, Peter S. *American Soldiers: Ground Combat in the World Wars, Korea, and Vietnam*. Lawrence, Kansas: University Press of Kansas, 2003.

Kipling, Rudyard. *Rudyard Kipling's Verse, Inclusive Edition, 1885–1918* (Garden City, New York: Doubleday, Page and Company, 1922).

Klein, Maury. *A Call to Arms: Mobilizing America For World War II*. New York: Bloomsbury Press, 2013.

Laffin, John. *On The Western Front: Soldiers' Stories from France and Flanders, 1914–1918.*Gloucester, England: Alan Sutton Publishing Ltd., 1986.

Lande, D.A. *I Was With Patton: First-Person Accounts of WWII in George S. Patton's Command*. Saint Paul, Minnesota: MBI Publishing, 2002.

Latimer, John. *Alamein*. Cambridge. Massachusetts: Harvard University Press, 2002.

Lewis, Adrian. *Omaha Beach: A Flawed Victory*. Chapel Hill, North Carolina: University of North Carolina Press, 2001.

Lewis, Nigel. *Operation Tiger*. New York: Prentice Hall Press, 1990.

Linderman, Gerald. *The World Within War: America's Combat Experience in World War II*. New York: The Free Press, 1997.

Macaulay, G.C. (ed.). *Works of John Gower* (4 volumes). Oxford, 1901.

MacDonald, Charles. *A Time for Trumpets: The Untold Story of the Battle of the Bulge*. New York: Morrow, 1985.

Macksey, Kenneth. *Tank Versus Tank*. London: Grub Street/ Barnes and Noble Books, 1999.

Marshall, Katharine Tupper. *Together*. London: Blandford, 1947.

Mauldin, Bill. *The Brass Ring*. New York: W. W. Norton and Company, Inc., 1971.

McCarthy, Peter, and Mike Syron. *Panzerkrieg: The Rise and Fall of Hitler's Tank Divisions*. New York: Carol and Graf Publishers, 2002.

McManus, John C. *The Deadly Brotherhood: The American Combat Soldier in World War II*. New York, Presidio Press, 2003 (reprint of the 1998 edition).

Mesko, Jim. *M3 Lee/Grant in Action*. Carrollton, Texas: Squadron/ Signal Publications, 1995.

———. *U.S. Tank Destroyers in Action*. Carrollton, Texas: Squadron/ Signal Publications, 1998.

Miller, David. *Tanks of the World: From World War I to the Present Day*. St. Paul, Minnesota: Salamander Books, 2003.

———. *The Great Book of Tanks*. London: Salamander Books, 2002.

Molnar, Nicholas D. "General George S. Patton and the War-Winning Sherman Tank Myth." In G. Kurt Piehler and Sidney Pash, *The United States and the Second World War: New Perspectives on Diplomacy, War, and the Home Front*. New York: Fordham University Press, 2010.

Morgan, Ted. *FDR: A Biography*. New York: Simon and Schuster, 1985.

Mosier, John. *The blitzkrieg Myth: How Hitler and the Allies Misread the Strategic Realties of World War II*. New York: HarperCollins, 2003.

Nichols, David. *Ernie's War: The Best of Ernie Pyle's WWII Dispatches*. New York: Random House, 1986.

Nowarra, Heinz, Uwe Feist, and Edward Maloney. *The Tiger Tanks*. Fallbrook, California: Aero Publishers, Inc., 1966.

Nye, Roger H. *The Patton Mind: The Professional Development of an Extraordinary Leader*. New York: Avery Publishing Group, 1993.

Odom, William. *After the Trenches: The Transformation of U.S. Army Doctrine, 1918–1939*. College Station, Texas: Texas A & M University Press, 1999.

Parrish, Thomas. *Roosevelt and Marshall: Partners in Politics and War*. New York: William Morrow and Company, Inc., 1989.

Perret, Geoffrey. *Eisenhower*. New York: Random House, 1999.

———. *There's A War to be Won: The United States Army in World War II*. New York: Ballantine Books, 1992.

Perry, Mark. *Partners in Command: George Marshall and Dwight Eisenhower in War and Peace*. New York: The Penguin Press, 2007.

Phibbs, Brendan, *The Other Side of Time: A Combat Surgeon in World War II*. Boston: Little, Brown, 1987.

Piekalkiewicz, Janusz. *Tank War, 1939–1945*. Translated from the German by Jan van Heurck. Dorset Poole: Blandford Press, Harrisburg, PA: distributed in the United States by Sterling Publishing, 1986.

Pogue, Forrest. *George C. Marshall: Education of a Soldier, 1880–1939*. New York: Viking Press, 1963.

———. *George C. Marshall: Ordeal and Hope, 1939–1942*. New York: Viking Press, 1966.

———. *George C. Marshall: Organizer of Victory, 1943–1945*. New York: Viking Press, 1973.

Powaski, Ronald E. *Lightning War: blitzkrieg in the West, 1940*. Hoboken, NJ: J. Wiley and Sons, 2003.

Rauch, Basil. *The Roosevelt Reader: Selected Speeches, Messages, Press Conferences, and Letters of Franklin D. Roosevelt*. New York: Holt, Rinehart, and Winston, 1957.

Reynolds, David. *In Command of History: Churchill Fighting and Writing the Second World War*. New York: Random House, 2005.

Robinson, Wayne. *Barbara: A Novel of Death and Survival in Tank Combat*. Garden City, New York: Doubleday & Company, Inc., 1962.

Ross, G. MacLeod. *The Business of Tanks, 1933 to 1945*. Elms Court, UK: Stockwell Ltd., 1976.

Rottman, Gordon L. *M3 Medium Tank vs. Panzer III: Kasserine Pass 1943*. Oxford, England: Osprey Publishing, 2008.

Schreier, Konrad, Jr. *The Classic Sherman*. Canoga Park, California: Grenadier Books, 1969.

Sebag-Montefiore, Hugh. *Dunkirk: Fight to the Last Man*. Cambridge, Massachusetts: Harvard University Press, 2006.

Senger und Etterlin, Dr. F. M. *German Tanks of World War II*. Translated by J. Lucas. New York: Galahad Books, 1969.

Showalter, Dennis. *Patton and Rommel: Men of War in the Twentieth Century*. New York: Berkeley Caliber, 2006.

Slayton, Robert A. *Arms of Destruction: Ranking the World's Best Land Weapons of WWII*. New York: Citadel Press, 2004.

Smith, Jean Edward. *Eisenhower In War and Peace*. New York: Random House, 2012.

———. *FDR*. New York: Random House, 2007.

Sorley, Lewis. *Thunderbolt: General Creighton Abrams and the Army of His Times*. New York: Simon and Schuster, 1992.

Spielburger, Walter J. and Uwe Feist. *Panzerkampfwagen V Panther*. Buena Park, California: Feist Publishing, 1968.

Terkel, Studs, *"The Good War": An Oral History of World War Two*. New York: Pantheon Books, 1984.

Tobin, James. *Ernie Pyle's War: America's Eyewitness to World War II*. Lawrence, Kansas: University Press of Kansas, 1998.

Trewhitt, Philip. *Armored Fighting Vehicles*. London: Brown Packaging Books Ltd., 1999.

Triplett, William S. *A Colonel in the Armored Divisions: A Memoir, 1944–1945*. Columbia, Missouri: University of Missouri Press, 2001.

Turner, Barry. *Countdown to Victory: The Final European Campaigns of World War Two*. London: Hodder and Stoughton Ltd., 2004.

Unger, Debi and Irwin. *George Marshall: A Biography*. New York: Harper Collins, 2014.

Weigley, Russell F. *Eisenhower's Lieutenants: The Campaigns of France and Germany 1944–45*. Sidgwick and Jackson, 1981.

———. *History of the United States Army*. New York: Macmillan Company, 1967.

———. *The American Way of War: A History of United States Military Strategy and Policy*. New York: Macmillan, 1973.

Weintraub, Stanley. *15 Stars: Eisenhower, MacArthur, Marshall - Three Generals Who Saved The American Country*. New York: Free Press, 2007.

Wells, Stanley, and Gary Taylor (eds.). *William Shakespeare: The Complete Works*. Oxford, England: Clarendon Press, 1991.

Whiting, Charles. *The Battle of Hurtgen Forest: The Untold Story of a Disastrous Campaign*. New York: Orion Books, 1989.

Wilbeck, Christopher. *Sledgehammers: Strengths and Flaws of Tiger Tank Battalions in World War Two*. Bedford, PA: The Aberjona Press, 2004.

Williams, Charles. *The Last Great Frenchman: A Life of General DeGaulle*. New York: John Wiley and Sons Inc., 1993.

Wilson, Dale E. *Treat 'Em Rough: The Birth of American Armor, 1917–1920*. Novato, California: Presidio Press, 1989.

———. *"World War I: The Birth of American Armor."* In Hofmann, George, and Donn Starry. *Camp Colt to Desert Storm: The History of U.S. Armored Forces*. Lexington, Kentucky: The University Press of Kentucky, 1999.

Winchester, Jim. *Tanks and Armored Fighting Vehicles of World War Two*. New York: Barnes and Noble Books, 2004.

Wright, Patrick. *Tank: The Progress of a Monstrous War Machine*. New York: Penguin Books, 2003.

Yeide, Harry. *Steel Victory: The Untold Story of America's Independent Tank Battalions at War in Europe*. New York: Presidio Press/ Ballantine Books, 2003.

———. *The Tank Killers: A History of America's World War II Tank Destroyer Force*. Havertown, PA: Casemate, 2004.

———. *Weapons of the Tankers: American Armor in World War II*. St. Paul, MN: Zenith Press, 2006.

Zaloga, Steven J. ———. *Armored Thunderbolt: The U.S. Army Sherman in World War II*. Mechanicsburg, Pennsylvania: Stackpole Books, 2008.

———. *M3 and M5 Stuart Light Tank, 1940–1945*. Oxford, England: Osprey Publishing, 2009.

———. *M26/M46 Pershing Tank, 1943–1953*. Oxford, England: Osprey Publishing, 2008.

———. *Panzer IV vs. Char B1 Bis: France, 1940*. Oxford, England: Osprey Publishing, 2011.

———. *Sherman Medium Tank, 1942–45*. Oxford, England: Osprey Publishing, 2003.

———. *U.S. Anti-Tank Artillery*. Oxford, England: Osprey Publishing, 2005.

Zelezer, Julian E. *Arsenal Of Democracy: The Politics of National Security - From World War II To The War on Terrorism*. New York: Basic Books, 2010.

# Index

# ABOUT THE PHOTOGRAPHER

**Robert Coldwell Sr.** is a freelance commercial photographer specializing in people and corporate photography. After forty-five years in photography Bob feels blessed to get up every day to do something he loves for "work." Bob makes remarkable and compelling images calmly and quickly whether in the studio or on location. His resourceful approach to photography is complemented by his attention to detail and the ability to listen to clients. Experienced at working in every camera format, whether digital or film, Bob is skilled, capable, and inventive, without needing to rely on heavy retouching or a single stylized look. While known for his elegant lighting constructs, Bob can be easily as effective behind the camera shooting with natural light. Bob also has a strong interest in American military history, tracing his family genealogy, traveling, and spending time with family and friends. He resides in Chester County, Pennsylvania.